Principles and Practices of Teaching Reading

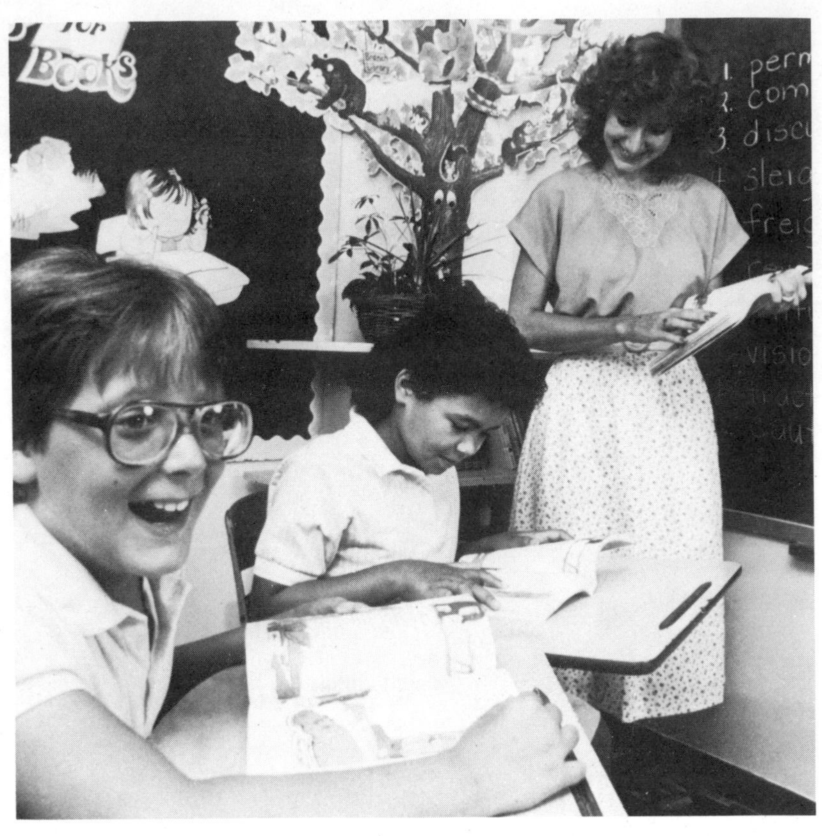

Arthur W. Heilman
The Pennsylvania State University
Professor Emeritus

Timothy R. Blair
Texas A&M University

William H. Rupley
Texas A&M University

Principles and Practices of Teaching Reading

SIXTH EDITION

CHARLES E. MERRILL PUBLISHING COMPANY
A Bell & Howell Company
Columbus Toronto London Sydney

Photo Credits

Mark Antman, The Image Works, pp. 87, 287, 334; Billy E. Barnes, p. 111 (bottom left); Janice Beaty, p. 17; Rich Bucurel/CEM, p. 104; Alan Carey, The Image Works, pp. 7, 28, 45, 84, 153, 187 (left), 297 (top left and right, bottom left), 334 (bottom right), 376, 380, 485, 521; CMACCO, p. 554; Paul Conklin, pp. 182, 196, 205, 480, 566; Jim Cronk, Photographic Illustrations, pp. 187 (right), 476; Jean Greenwald/CEM, pp. 10, 294, 465, 534; Vivienne della Grotta, pp. 98, 308, 514; Larry Hamill, p. 441; Bruce Johnson, p. 42; Richard Khanlian, p. 2; David Mansell, p. 435; Jim Pickerell, p. 22; Charles J. Quinlan, pp. 20, 111 (bottom right), 226, 394, 432, 450; Strix Pix, pp. 32, 51, 55, 66, 78, 111 (top left and right), 118, 137, 198, 214, 268, 283, 297 (bottom right), 314, 325, 334 (top left and right, bottom left), 386, 399, 500, 504, 546; Dan Unkefer/CEM, p. 89.

Other credits appear on pages v and vi, which constitute a continuation of the copyright page.

Published by
Charles E. Merrill Publishing Co.
A Bell & Howell Company
Columbus, Ohio 43216

This book was set in Trump Mediaeval and Helvetica
Production Editor: Linda Hillis Bayma
Cover Design Coordination: Cathy Watterson
Text Designer: Amato Prudente
Cover Photo: Mary Hagler

Library of Congress Catalog Card Number: 85-71976
International Standard Book Number: 0-675-20357-0
Printed in the United States of America
1 2 3 4 5 6 7 8 9—91 90 89 88 87 86

Credits

Chapter 1

p. 5 Woodcut by Thomas Bewick from *1800 Woodcuts by Thomas Bewick and His School* edited by Blanche Cirker courtesy Dover Publications, Inc., 180 Varick Street, New York, N.Y. 10014.

p. 12 From *Abraham Lincoln: The Boy. The Man* by Lloyd Ostendorf. Springfield, IL: Hamann The Printer, Inc., 1962. Copyright © 1962 by Lloyd Ostendorf.

p. 18 Library of Congress. Research courtesy of James R. Murray, Director, and Elio Gasperetti, Graphic Artist, Educational Media Center, D.C. Public Schools, Washington, D.C. 20022.

Chapter 2

p. 30 Drawing by James H. Hubbard.

p. 44 Photo courtesy of The Horn Book, Inc.

Chapter 3

p. 53 *The Country School* by Winslow Homer, the St. Louis Art Museum.

p. 56 Arthur I. Gates photo courtesy of Teachers College, Columbia University.

Chapter 4

p. 82 Photo by UPI/The Bettmann Archive.

p. 86 Drawing by James H. Hubbard.

pp. 92–93 Reproduced from the *Clymer-Barrett Readiness Test* courtesy of Chapman, Brook & Kent. Copyright © 1983 by the Institute for Reading Research.

p. 101 Drawing by James H. Hubbard.

Chapter 5

p. 123 Library of Congress. Research courtesy of James R. Murray, Director, and Elio Gasperetti, Graphic Artist, Educational Media Center, D.C. Public Schools, Washington, D.C.

p. 135 "Bob and His Pony" from *Real Life Readers* courtesy of Charles Scribner's Sons, 597 Fifth Avenue, New York, N.Y. 10017.

p. 172 Reprinted courtesy of Steck-Vaughn Company from *Sounds, Words, & Meanings, Book C,* by Barbara York et al. Copyright © 1981 by Steck-Vaughn Company.

p. 176 From Teacher's Edition, *Level 13 Skillpack* of the GINN READING PROGRAM by Theodore Clymer and others, © Copyright, 1985, 1982, by Ginn and Company (Xerox Corporation). Used with permission.

Chapter 6

p. 188 Edward L. Thorndike photo courtesy of Teachers College, Columbia University.

Chapter 7

p. 232 Reprinted from *Old Textbooks* by John Nietz by permission of the University of Pittsburgh Press. © 1961 by University of Pittsburgh Press.

p. 242 From Level 13 Skillpack, Teacher's Edition, *Flights of Color* of the GINN READING PROGRAM by Theodore Clymer and others, © Copyright, 1985, 1982 by Ginn and Company (Xerox Corporation). Used with permission.

Chapter 8

p. 274 From *McGuffey's First Eclectic Reader,* Revised Edition. New York: American Book Company, 1896.

pp. 275–282 From Teacher's Edition, Level 9, *Mystery Sneaker* of the GINN READING PROGRAM by Theodore Clymer and others, © Copyright, 1985, 1982 by Ginn and Company (Xerox Corporation). Used with permission.

p. 282 "Bursting" by Dorothy Aldis reprinted by permission of G. P. Putnam's Sons from ALL TOGETHER by Dorothy Aldis, copyright 1952 by Dorothy Aldis, copyright renewed © 1980 by Roy E. Porter.

p. 290 From *Fun With Our Family* by Helen M. Robinson et al. Copyright © 1962 by Scott, Foresman and Company. Reprinted by permission.

p. 303 Excerpt from *The Three Lost Friends* used with permission of Becca King.

Chapter 9

p. 320 Special permission granted by *Weekly Reader,* published by Xerox Education Publications, © 1928, Xerox Corp.

p. 322 From a poster of Caldecott Medal winners. Used by permission of Library Binding Service, Inc., 2134 East Grand Ave., Des Moines, Iowa 50305.

p. 371 Nancy Larrick photo courtesy of the International Reading Association.
p. 372 Excerpt from *Ulysses Fights the Zerc* used with permission of Ian King.
p. 373 First stanza of poem #436 beginning "Shall I take thee? . . " to "Till I have further tried.", p. 228 from BOLTS OF MELODY: New Poems of Emily Dickinson edited by Mabel Loomis Todd and Millicent Todd Bingham. Copyright, 1945 by The Trustees of Amherst College. Reprinted by permission of Harper & Row, Publishers, Inc.
p. 375 From Teacher's Edition, Level 3 Studybook, *Fish and Not Fish* of the GINN READING PROGRAM by Theodore Clymer and others, © Copyright, 1985, 1982, by Ginn and Company (Xerox Corporation). Used with permission.

Chapter 10
p. 391 Drawing by James H. Hubbard.
p. 396 From a poster of Newbery Award Medal winners. Used by permission of Library Binding Service, Inc., 2134 East Grand Ave., Des Moines, Iowa 50305.
p. 408 *Word Theater* E 100, SKIT E 140/SKIT E 141, by Richard A. Boning. Copyright 1978, Burnell Loft, Ltd, 958 Church Street, Baldwin, New York 11510.

Chapter 11
p. 438 From *Curriculum Referenced Tests of Mastery,* Grade 4, Level H, courtesy of Charles E. Merrill Publishing Co. Copyright © 1983 by Bell & Howell Company.
p. 455 Emmett A. Betts photo courtesy of the International Reading Association.

Chapter 12
pp. 484–85 Excerpt from David W. Johnson and Roger T. Johnson, "Many teachers wonder . . . will the special needs child ever really belong?" Adapted from INSTRUCTOR, February 1978. Copyright © 1978 by The Instructor Publications, Inc. Used by permission.
p. 487 Photo courtesy of the Milwaukee Public Schools.
p. 501 Willard C. Olson photo courtesy of Mrs. Willard C. Olson.
p. 507 From Aaron Lipton and Elaine Kaplan, "The Pupil-Teacher Reading Conference," The Reading Teacher 31 (Jan. 1978): 377. Reprinted with permission of Aaron Lipton and the International Reading Association.
p. 510 Code of Ethics courtesy of the Professional Standards and Ethics Committee of the International Reading Association.

Chapter 13
p. 517 Courtesy of International Business Machine Corporation.
p. 518 Cartoon courtesy of Walter X. Urban.
p. 520 Cartoon used with permission of Glen Dines.
p. 525 Photo by Strix Pix.
p. 532 Cartoon used with permission of Dave Gerard.

Chapter 14
p. 545 Reprinted from *Spanish Reading Keys Teacher's Manual,* Level One, by Dolores Rose Amato and Rogelio López del Bosque courtesy of The Economy Company. Copyright © 1977 by The Economy Company.
p. 556 Maria Montessori photo courtesy of the American Montessori Society.

Color Inserts
insert 1, p. 1 Courtesy of Addison-Wesley Publishing Co. from *Happily Ever After,* Teacher's Guide, Unit 7 by Jane R. Dyer. © 1982 by Addison Wesley.
insert 1, p. 2 From Level 13 Studybook, Teacher's Edition, *Flights of Color* of the GINN READING PROGRAM by Theodore Clymer and others, © Copyright, 1985, 1982, by Ginn and Company (Xerox Corporation). Used with permission.
insert 1, p. 3 Courtesy of Addison-Wesley Publishing Co. from *POINT,* Teacher's Edition, Reading Skills Book by Pleasant T. Rowland. © 1982 by Addison-Wesley.
insert 1, pp. 4–7 Courtesy of Charles E. Merrill Publishing Co. from *Accent on Science 4,* Teacher's Annotated Edition, by Robert Sund et al. © 1985 by Bell & Howell Company.
insert 1, p. 8 From Student Text, *Flights of Color* of the GINN READING PROGRAM by Theodore Clymer and others, © Copyright, 1985, 1982, by Ginn and Company (Xerox Corporation). Used with permission.
insert 1, p. 8 Poem "The Road Not Taken" from THE POETRY OF ROBERT FROST edited by Edward Connery Lathem. Copyright 1916, © 1969 by Holt, Rinehart and Winston. Copyright 1944 by Robert Frost. Reprinted by permission of Holt, Rinehart and Winston, Publishers and Jonathan Cape Ltd.
insert 2, pp. 1–7 From Level 9 Teacher's Edition, *Mystery Sneaker* of the GINN READING PROGRAM by Theodore Clymer and others, © Copyright 1985, 1982 by Ginn and Company (Xerox Corporation). Used with permission.
insert 2, pp. 1–5 Text adapted from MY FRIEND CHARLIE, copyright © 1964 by James Flora. Reprinted by permission of Harcourt Brace Jovanovich, Inc.
insert 2, pp. 6–7 Text adapted from WHAT EVERY KID SHOULD KNOW by Jonah Kalb and David Viscott, M.D. Copyright © 1974, 1976 by Sensitivity Games, Inc. Reprinted by permission of Houghton Mifflin Company.
insert 2, p. 8 From Level 9 Studybook, Teacher's Edition, *Mystery Sneaker* of the GINN READING PROGRAM by Theodore Clymer and others, © Copyright, 1985, 1982, by Ginn and Company (Xerox Corporation). Used with permission.

Contents

Preface

The sixth edition of *Principles and Practices of Teaching Reading* retains as its major premise that children will develop into mature, critical readers if provided appropriate instruction by caring and knowledgeable teachers. This edition has been updated to reflect the numerous changes in the teaching of reading in our schools. New and revised content appears in all chapters, a different organizational framework to enhance readability has been developed, and a new chapter on computers and reading has been added. Of particular importance is the continued emphasis on the quality of instruction afforded to children. Individual classroom teachers are responsible for excellence in their reading programs. All teachers of reading, both inservice and preservice, need to be aware of the classroom practices associated with successful student learning. Throughout the book, the important teacher behaviors leading to students' success are highlighted.

Unit 1 presents the foundations for effective instruction. Individual chapters focus on principles for teaching reading at any grade level, a discussion of language and the teaching of reading as a language process, a review of teacher effectiveness investigations in reading and specific implications for classroom teachers, and a discussion of reading readiness with practical ideas for teaching. Unit 2 covers all the essential reading skills and abilities taught in a developmental program. Separate chapters focus on word identification, comprehension and vocabulary, and study skills. In addition to a concise review of related research, each chapter contains practical lesson plans and activities to explain how these essential skills are taught to children. Unit 3 emphasizes popular reading approaches and the teaching of reading at different grade levels. First, a chapter is devoted to reading approaches, emphasizing the language experience and basal reader approaches. Next, separate chapters discuss reading in the primary grades and in the intermediate grades. For each grade level taught, teachers need to focus their time and effort in crucial areas. These areas are highlighted within the framework of Jeanne Chall's new work on "Stages of Reading Development." The final unit brings together essential and current topics in the organization and management of reading instruction. First, an expanded discussion is devoted to diagnosis of students' strengths and weaknesses, including a comprehensive treatment of the informal reading inventory. Second, there is a chapter on classroom organization and management, with several suggestions to maximize pupil learning in the classroom. Third, a new chapter is devoted entirely to computers and reading instruction. This chapter provides an essential discussion of the role of computers in the classroom and the teacher's role in utilizing the computer as an aid to effective instruction. Last, a detailed discussion of culturally and language-different, handicapped, and gifted children is given. Specific instructional recommendations are provided along with sample Individualized Education Plans (IEPs).

Throughout this book, practical examples, lesson plans, sample test results, and classroom activities are presented to heighten the reader's involvement and provide concrete ideas for instruction. Also provided are samples of commercial materials, reproduced within chapters and in the color inserts. Especially noteworthy in the text is the framing of classroom activities that provide the reader with practical ideas for immediate classroom use. The activities are labeled "introductory," "application," and "practice." These three terms mirror the components of a sound teaching lesson. Those activities marked introductory suggest ways to introduce a particular skill or ability to children for the first time. Application activities can be used to provide practice of a skill in varied reading situations under teacher supervision. Finally, the activities labeled practice are intended for children to complete on their own. While many of the activities could conceivably fit more than one category, it is important to provide activities that parallel pupil learning. The "Flashbacks" feature has been retained, with new flashbacks added to various chapters. We feel they serve as both a motivator and a learning tool for readers of this text. Readers will gain information and insight about significant writers in the field and about historical moments in reading education.

We wish to express our appreciation to Nancy Bertrand, Middle Tennessee University, Howard E. Blake, Temple University, Weldon G. Bradtmueller, Northern Illinois University, Bonnie Chambers, Bowling Green State University, Edna P. DeHaven, University of Oregon, Lana Low, Clinch Valley College of the University of Virginia, Fred MacLaren, Eastern Illinois University, Lonnie D. McIntyre, Michigan State University, Glennellen Pace, University of Wisconsin, J. R. Pope, Southwest Missouri State University, Edward C. Turner, University of Florida, Barbara Walker, Eastern Montana College, and Edna Warncke, Ball State University for their thoughtful and constructive suggestions.

We would like to thank Norma Hinojosa and Sherry Ealoms for typing several manuscript drafts. Our gratitude is also extended to the Merrill staff, especially Beverly Kolz, Tracey Dils, and Linda Bayma for their efforts, humor, and expertise. Most importantly, we would like to thank our wives and children, Dorothy, Jeanné, Agnes, Tim, and Billy, for their support and understanding.

UNIT 1 Foundations of Instruction

Chapters

1. **Principles of Reading Instruction**
2. **Language**
3. **Teacher Effectiveness and Reading**
4. **Reading Readiness**

Preparing to teach children reading in today's schools is a big responsibility. The task of using certain materials, of covering material, of meeting individual needs, of ensuring all children are literate, and of fostering independent learning is certainly not one for timid souls. Rather, teachers must be knowledgeable, sensitive people to whom parents entrust their children for many hours each day of the school year.

Before discussions of what to teach, how to teach, how to structure the classroom, and how to determine pupil strengths and weaknesses, teachers must have a firm foundation upon which to base their actions in the classroom. Unit 1 provides you with the base. Chapter 1 concerns itself with the reading process and principles of teaching reading at any grade level in any school. As you read this text, recall these principles. We would also hope that you would apply these principles to your teaching of reading. Chapter 2 deals with language—the core from which effective reading instruction follows. Your effectiveness as a teacher will have a direct relationship to your knowledge of the English language and its development. Chapter 3 highlights what we know an effective teacher of reading does in a classroom. Such information is critical before plunging into specific instructional strategies. Chapter 4 discusses reading readiness, an essential element in assuring that children get off to a successful start in beginning reading and an important consideration at all levels of reading instruction.

1

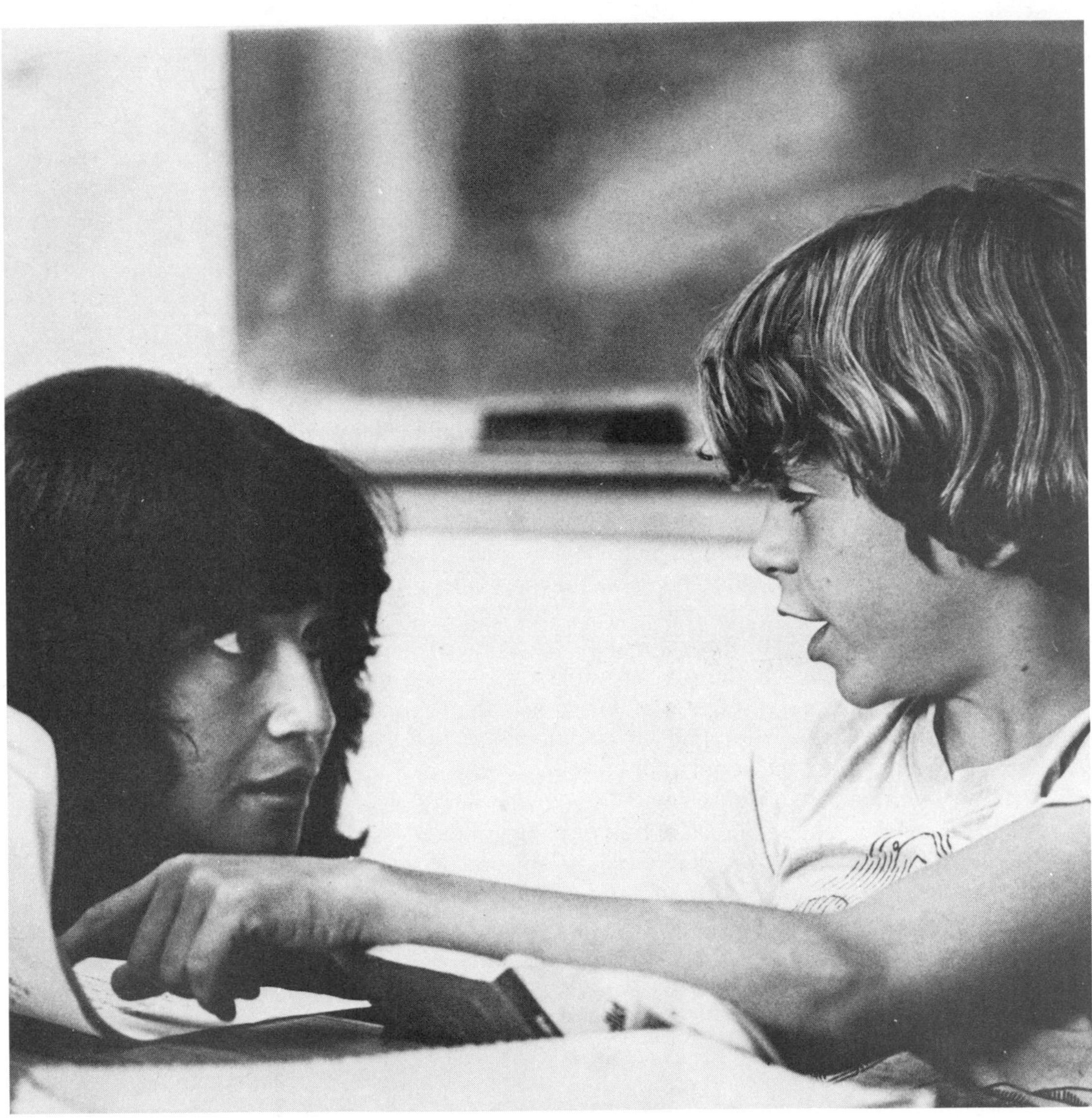

Principles of Reading Instruction

For the Reader

Imagine yourself, if you will, as a physical education teacher in charge of a course on tennis techniques for beginners. Even though there are several different approaches to follow, we are quite confident that you would be able to define the term *tennis* to your class and proceed to teach basic tennis techniques. Let's switch your role to that of a teacher of a course on "thinking." How would you define the term *thinking,* and how would you go about teaching it? We would venture that you, like anyone, would have more difficulty with that assignment. Very little is known about thinking, and its definition is imprecise.

Now we come to a teacher of reading. How would you define *reading?* (Can one read without thinking?) Reading is one of the basic communicative skills, but it is a very complex process. It is difficult to arrive at a precise definition of the reading process. Even though researchers have not resolved this problem of definition, this chapter will present some basic aspects of the reading process and set forth principles to help guide you at all grade levels of reading instruction.

One basic premise of effective reading instruction is that students be taught skills that will enable them to learn on their own. One such skill is the ability to read a content chapter as efficiently as possible. We would like to recommend that you employ a study skills approach to the reading of the chapters in this text. This approach will aid you both in retaining what you read and in increasing your reading rate.

Preview

- Read over the Key Ideas that will be presented in the chapter. These Key Ideas are intended to help you know (before reading each chapter) on what you should focus your attention.
- Read each heading throughout the chapter. These headings form the chapter outline. Each identifies a major topic or subtopic that is presented. As you read the headings, try to put them into questions that you will answer as you read. These questions become your purposes for reading.
- Read the chapter summary. It will give you an overview of the major topics in each chapter and their importance in effective reading instruction.
- Return to the beginning of each chapter and read it in its entirety. Read to answer your questions and to understand the chapter content. Writing marginal

notes, paraphrasing the text, and underlining major points are ways of highlighting parts of the text that relate to your questions.

Key Ideas

Reading is interacting with language that has been coded into print.
Reading is a language process.
The end result of reading instruction is comprehension.
There is no one best method of teaching reading.
Diagnosis is the nucleus of effective instruction.
Instruction must be differentiated to meet the needs of all students.

WHAT IS READING?

Most people read without giving much thought to how they do it. To them, "What is reading?" is a question of little concern. One's concept of what reading is, however, should be a major concern to the person whose primary task is to teach reading.

Many different models and theories of reading have been suggested by reading theorists in an attempt to better understand reading (7). Geyer (4) noted in 1972 that more than eighty models of reading had been suggested. Since the early seventies many additional models and theories of reading have been proposed, yet reading authorities are still not in agreement about a singular model or theory that completely describes the reading process (7, 13).

Recently, three conceptualizations for what reading is have received considerable attention by reading authorities (13). These views of reading are called *top-down, bottom-up,* and *interactive.* All three models have two basic similarities: a reader and written text to read. The differences between the three, however, are based on how readers process the text when they read. As can be seen in the following discussion, the name for each view is a good way to remember its basic characteristics and what features of the reading process are considered to be most important.

Those who consider reading to be a *top-down* process focus their attention on the reader. Readers do not begin reading with their minds totally blank, but bring information based on past experiences with language and their world to the act of reading. Fluent readers bring more information to the written text than the text itself provides. Because of this, readers do not give close attention to the words and word parts, but use their past experiences to predict meaning as they read. This

FLASHBACK

The Old Deluder Satan Act passed in Massachusetts in 1647 made reference to Satan's intention to keep men from knowledge of the Scriptures. It required every town of fifty householders to appoint a teacher of reading and writing and every town of 100 householders to provide a grammar school.

The preamble read: "It being the object of that old deluder, Satan, to keep men from the knowledge of the Scriptures, as in former times be keeping them in an unknown tongue, so in these later time be persuading them from the use of tongues, that so at least the true sense and meaning of the original might be clouded and corrupted with false glosses of deceivers: to the end that learning might not be buried in the graves of our forefathers, in church, and commonwealth the Lord assisting our endeavors."

predicting is also referred to as hypothesis testing, that is, readers have to only sample the written text to test their hypotheses. For example, if a reader is reading a magazine article about gardening and is very knowledgeable about this topic, he does not attend closely to words and word parts. Because he is knowledgeable about the words and the topic of the gardening article, the reader relies more on the information in his head (the top-down part) to predict information, and he samples parts of the written text to test his predictions.

Another explanation of what happens during reading is referred to as a *bottom-up* concept of the reading process. The essential element in reading is the written text, rather than what the reader brings to the text. That is, the text is processed by the reader without much prior information about the meaning or content of what he is reading. Close attention is given to words and word parts, and these are processed in order and meaning is gleaned from this processing. In the earlier example of reading about gardening, a *bottom-up* process would suggest that each word is given attention, the words synthesized, and meaning is revealed from this "putting the words together."

The third conceptualization of the reading process is that it is an *interactive* process. The concept is really a combination of the top-down and bottom-up views of reading. Fluent readers use both text features and what they bring to the written page (experiential/conceptual background about language and their world) in order to learn, understand, and remember printed language (8). A major distinction between the interactive theory of reading and the top-down and bottom-up theories is that the interactive view is based on the idea that both the reader's hypotheses and the written text are used by the reader as he attempts to get meaning. For example, if some of the information in the gardening article is familiar and some of it unfamiliar, a reader may be *top-down* when reading familiar information and *bottom-up* when reading unfamiliar information. Thus, these two concepts of reading are interacting with each other; the reader is not relying solely on one or the other.

Although no singular, agreed-upon model of reading is currently available to help you plan for reading instruction, there are some basic features of reading with which most authorities are in agreement.

- Reading is interacting with language that has been coded into print.
- The product of interacting with the printed language should be comprehension.
- Reading ability is closely related to oral language ability.
- Reading is an active and ongoing process that is affected directly by an individual's interaction with his environment (12).

It is not only important for teachers of reading to form a concept of the reading process, but also extremely critical that they distinguish between the reading process and reading instruction. Weaver and Shonkoff spoke to this very point as they summarized and interpreted current research on the nature of reading. They stated:

> What actually is the nature of reading? . . . The research findings currently available do not provide conclusive information, and it may take a long time for these issues to be resolved and supported by the results of research. Reading educators do not have time to wait. Whatever view of reading is accurate, an equally pertinent question for educators as we see it is, How should reading be viewed so that its acquisition and development are facilitated? We think it is helpful to make the distinction between the reading process and effective teaching of reading. (14, p. 6)

If teachers of reading accept the idea that a major aspect of the reading process is comprehension, then there are two facets of reading

Reading and oral language are closely related.

instruction that must be put into proper perspective: (1) decoding print into sound and (2) decoding a graphic representative of language into meaning.

The following examples deal with these two important perspectives and also illustrate the four basic aspects of reading presented earlier.

Ab se bo sem fleebat represents a series of speech sounds frequently heard in English. Anyone familiar with the sounds represented by these letter combinations could probably say the correct sounds with several intonation patterns. Correctly saying these sounds, however, would not meet the requirement of reading. One of the major aspects of reading is missing. There has been no agreement as to the meaning of those speech sounds in the order found here; therefore, comprehension of written language is missing.

If *ab se bo sem fleebat* happened to be a meaningful written representation found in the English language, you could not "read" it unless you knew or could discover what spoken words were represented by the written symbols. You might:

- Know each printed word symbol as a sight word.
- Recognize some words at sight and analyze letter sounds in others

until you "hit" upon the pronunciation of each of the printed word symbols.

- Assign intonation patterns that at least approximate those which would be acceptable in oral English usage.

Would you also, in order to qualify as a reader, have to assign particular meanings to each word symbol as well as to the "total word combination"? The following examples consider this question.

A third grader has just been asked to read silently the sentence, " 'I will sample your wares,' said the traveler." Following the child's reading, the teacher asked the child to interpret what the traveler was doing. After the child responded, the teacher said in a kindly voice, "John, you read that wrong—the traveler was going to buy something from the peddler, not sell him something." The point of this illustration is that the teacher had not heard John read the sentence in question yet she said, "You read it wrong."

A further insight might be gained by reference to another sentence in English. "As face answereth face in water, so the heart of man speaketh to man." Many primary-level readers could pronounce each word in this passage, but many of these children could not arrive at an understanding of its meaning. A school curriculum committee examining a science or social studies text that contained many concepts at the difficulty level of this example would agree that "This book is too difficult for third graders to read." Few, if any, critics of this position would counter with "Most third graders can recognize the words in this book. I recommend it be adopted."

The following are English sentences. Anyone who reads English will have no trouble with word recognition or intonation:

> Some squares do not have four sides.
> Thomas Jefferson was a friend of tyranny.

These sentences, like all reading situations, demand reader interaction. The person reading "Some squares do not have four sides" might react in any of a number of ways. "This is a misprint—it should say, 'All squares have four sides.' No, maybe that's not the kind of square it means; Michael Philbutt is a square, and he doesn't have four sides. No, that's not what it means. Now a square is a plane figure, but it has a front and back, or does it have a back side? That's either five or six sides. What is the author talking about? Well, no matter what he means, I don't see how he can say that some squares do not have four sides. Maybe this is one of those trick statements. I better read another paragraph or two. If that doesn't help, I'll ask someone."

In the second sentence, a reader with no background knowledge about Jefferson might reason, "Well, it's good to be apprised of this man's character. I'll be suspicious of everything he says or writes, particularly about government and people's rights." With any degree of historical background, however, you immediately say, "How ridiculous! Who is writing this stuff? Where was this book published? I better read a little more; this might be a misprint. Didn't Jefferson say, 'I have sworn eternal hostility to every form of tyranny over the mind of man'? This statement is weird."

Although the above discussion has not provided a specific definition of reading, it has attempted to put the two essentials—decoding and arriving at meaning—in proper perspective. Recognizing or detecting the differences among printed word symbols is a necessary prerequisite for reading. But the mere pronunciation of words is not reading until this act of recognition evokes meaning(s) that the written words in combination carry in oral language usage. The meaning(s) that you acquire from reading is highly related to your experiential/conceptual background. As we indicated earlier, as you interact with the environment your experiential/conceptual background broadens, thus enhancing your comprehension capabilities.

Teaching reading is undoubtedly as complex as defining it. Today, there is general agreement that reading programs never rise above the quality of the instruction found in them. Teaching must be based on an understanding of children as learners, and learning to read must be viewed as a long-term developmental process. These concepts lead logically into a discussion of principles of reading instruction.

PRINCIPLES OF READING INSTRUCTION

The following principles can be thought of as guidelines that should govern teacher behavior. Principles do not spell out instructional practices that are to be followed, but they can provide the criteria for evaluating practices. Sound principles of instruction tend to be learner oriented; therefore, they do not vary from grade level to grade level. They can be applied quite consistently to children who are noticeably different in regard to learning capacity, interest, and experience.

Principles of teaching reading should evolve from the best knowledge available from psychology, educational psychology, and curriculum planning; from studies in child growth and development; and from child guidance and psychological clinics. In formulating these principles, it is necessary to consider all facets of human growth and development, including intellectual, physiological, psychological, and emotional.

Some of you will undoubtedly feel that one (or more) of the following principles is not absolutely valid. Such questioning is healthy, especially if it stimulates the formulation of rational alternatives. If the following principles are a sound basis for teaching reading at all levels of instruction, there are many practices in our schools that need to be reexamined.

Here are some guidelines, or principles, of reading instruction that merit a teacher's attention.

1. *Reading is a language process. Children being taught to read must understand the relationship between reading and their language.* Much has been written about "what the child brings to school" and that the school must build on the skills children have acquired. A major capability that children bring to school that transfers directly to reading is their language background.

   Many children begin school with a variety of experiences and understandings about language that should help them get off to a good start in a formal reading program. For example, many of them can recognize letters of the alphabet, write their names, identify brand names of products, use a book properly, retell all or parts of their favorite books, and so forth (2). Children may also exhibit knowledge of written language and its purpose to communicate when they scribble (write) letters and stories and read their com-

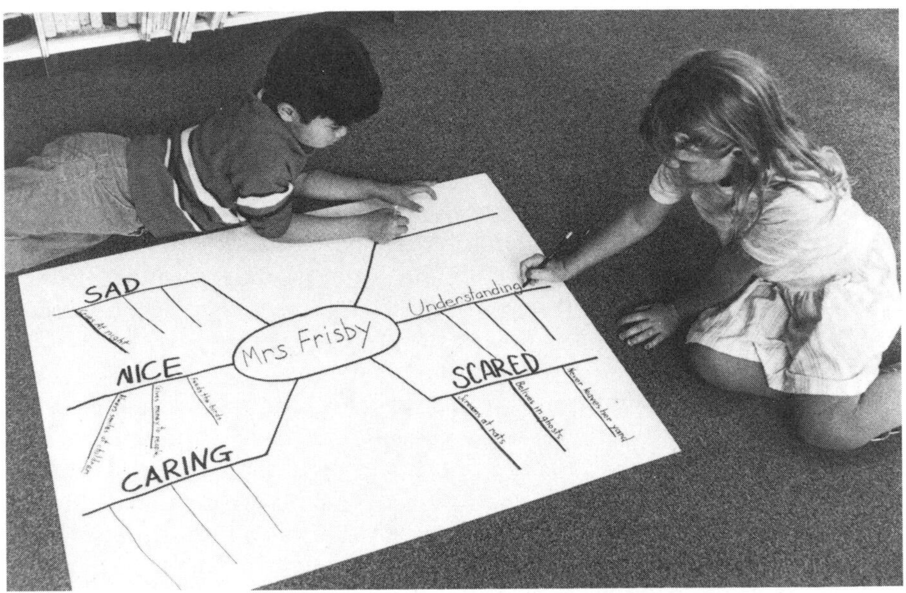

The meanings acquired from reading are closely related to our experiential/conceptual background.

positions to others, make up spellings, and create letterlike forms (15). Unfortunately, many of these early understandings and capabilities with language are ignored, and children's early experiences in beginning reading mask the fact that they are engaged in a language process (see chapter 2). They are often asked in beginning reading programs to focus on single letters and words. Instruction in word identification is not reading; it is only one tool for getting at meaning and understanding.

Children's language background has direct implications for where and when to begin reading instruction. Children who come from homes full of rich literary experiences will most likely bring language experiences with them. They may already be reading with understanding and have strategies to help identify words. For such children, the starting point for reading instruction is probably beyond basic decoding instruction. However, for children who have had little or no experience with written language before entering school, the starting point should be a focus on the concept that print conveys meaning. Teaching word identification without helping children understand that reading is comprehension will often result in developing incompetent readers. Beginning with word identification for either type of child would not be an appropriate point upon which to build reading instruction.

2. *Instruction should lead children to understand that reading must result in meaning.* This principle applies to all stages of reading instruction. It means that reading is more than a mechanical process. It rejects the thesis that beginning reading deals only with mechanics and that meaning is an additive to be inserted at some later point on the learning continuum.

   If this principle is followed from the beginning, it lessens the possibility that children will develop a set that reading is saying or sounding out words. For some reason, this particular set resists extinction, and unless children are reading for meaning, they cannot translate print into the language patterns that it represents. This principle is enhanced by giving major consideration to point number 3.

3. *During every reading instruction period, students should read or be read something that grabs their minds.* This can be a brief passage through which children experience the power and beauty of language. Many children are turned away from reading because of what they are asked to read. The curriculum and curricular material are often fact oriented. Teachers should make sure that, each day, students have an opportunity to apply their reading skills for the purpose of enjoyment. Kindergarten and first-grade children

FLASHBACK

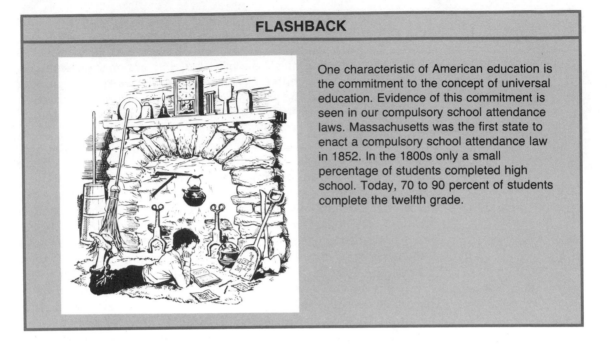

One characteristic of American education is the commitment to the concept of universal education. Evidence of this commitment is seen in our compulsory school attendance laws. Massachusetts was the first state to enact a compulsory school attendance law in 1852. In the 1800s only a small percentage of students completed high school. Today, 70 to 90 percent of students complete the twelfth grade.

who cannot yet read should be provided with opportunities to become familiar with picture books and to listen to stories.

4. *Pupil differences must be a primary consideration in reading instruction.* This implies that instruction cannot be dominated by the grade-level system, promotion practices, or *graded instructional materials.* It is hypothesized that any classroom will house pupils whose present achievement and instructional needs vary greatly. Identical educational experiences, particularly the reading of the same material, cannot be equally effective for all. Differentiation of both instruction and free-choice reading will inevitably result in greater pupil differences, which in turn will call for more differentiation.

5. *Proper reading instruction depends on the ongoing diagnosis of each child's reading strengths, weaknesses, and needs.* This principle is applicable to ordinary classroom teaching as well as to remedial reading. Individual diagnosis in reading has somehow become associated more with pupils who are experiencing severe reading problems and those with a clinical history of nonlearning than with ordinary classroom procedures. Effective reading instruction is based on meeting pupils' needs, and proper diagnosis is essential for identifying all pupils' reading strengths and weaknesses if they are to progress in reading at a level equal to their abilities.

6. *The best diagnosis is useless unless it is used as a blueprint for instruction.* Diagnosis itself has no beneficial effect on the performance of the child tested. If it did, it would be possible to raise a child's level of performance indefinitely by more and more diagnosis. It may be noted that extensive testing and metal filing cabinets full of individual folders do not necessarily make a better school. Testing in many American schools has become an end in itself. When reading diagnosis information is not used for instructional purposes, the educational objectives of the diagnosis are defeated.

7. *Any given technique, practice, or procedure is likely to work better with some children than with others.* The teacher of reading must have a variety of approaches. Virtually every method and procedure described in the vast literature on reading are reported to have been successful with some children and unsuccessful with others.

   Authorities in the field of reading are in general agreement that there is no one best method of teaching (5, 9, 10).

   The evidence indicates that one method is not necessarily superior to another. Regardless of the efficiency of a given method of teaching reading, it will produce its share of problem cases and impaired readers if used exclusively. Because there are significant individual differences in the way children learn to read, it follows that different approaches are advisable.

   When a teacher uses only one method to the exclusion of others, she shuts out the possibility of changing her instructional approach to meet an individual's needs. Although such a teacher may be highly successful in teaching some of her pupils, she will overlook the needs of others who cannot meet her demands. If she is authoritarian and presses hard, some of these pupils will develop behavior which results in such labels as *bad, dull, dreamer, lazy,* and *antisocial.* This behavior, instead of being interpreted as the logical psychological outcome of failure, frustration, and tension evolving from the reading situation, becomes the explanation of why the child failed in reading.

8. *Early in the learning process the child must acquire ways of gaining independence in identifying words whose meanings are known to him but which are unknown to him as sight words.* Pronouncing words is not reading, but identifying words not known as sight words is essential in independent reading. The more widely a child reads, the less likely it is that he will know as a sight word every word he meets. Hence, developing independence in reading depends on acquiring methods of identifying words to get at meanings. The clues used in identifying words, discussed in later chap-

ters, include sight recognition, structural analysis, context clues, language patterns, and phonic analysis.

The principle just described is not in conflict with our previous statement that the child must see reading as a meaning-making process. To read for meaning, one must be able to identify printed word forms.

9. *Learning to read is a long-term developmental process extending over a period of years.* This principle rests on two premises. First, every aspect of the instructional program is related to the ultimate goal of producing efficient readers. What is done during this period influences the child's concept of what it means to read.

The second premise is that the child's early attitude toward reading is important from an educational standpoint. It can influence a student's reading habits for life (10). Nothing should be permitted to happen in beginning instruction that impairs later development of efficient reading.

There are several approaches to beginning reading that may result in a "fast start" or relatively high achievement at the end of a year of intensive instruction. The materials used stress analysis of letter sounds and, in the opinion of some observers, fail to achieve a balanced program. The overemphasis on analysis permits rapid initial growth, but carries with it the potential of producing readers who overlearn this specific technique. Some pupils will tend to rely too heavily on analysis to the detriment of reading for meaning.

The question that teachers must answer is, Do higher reading achievement scores at the end of first grade establish the procedures and materials used as the best approach to beginning reading instruction? If this ninth principle is accepted as valid, the question cannot be answered on the basis of short-term achievement.

10. *The concept of readiness should be extended upward to all grades.* In the area of reading, there seems to be a preference for associating readiness with beginning or first-grade reading. This is the level at which we have "readiness tests," and much of the literature on readiness is concerned with the beginning reader. Even though readiness has been achieved at one level of experience, it does not necessarily follow that readiness is retained at a higher level of experience. There should be as much concern with readiness at the third-, fourth-, and sixth-grade levels as there is at the first-grade level.

11. *Emphasis should be on prevention rather than cure. Reading problems should be detected early and corrected before they deterio-*

rate into failure-frustration-reaction cases. However excellent the instruction in our schools, some children will not profit as much as others. The early detection of reading problems and immediate attention to them are cornerstones of effective reading instruction. Although this may be obvious, the emphasis in our schools is still on cure, not prevention.

12. *No child should be expected or forced to attempt to read material that he is incapable of reading.* Although applied here specifically to reading, this principle has a much wider application in our schools. All curriculum study and the placing of learning tasks at different points on the educational continuum are related to this principle. It should be followed in all areas of child growth and development—physical, social, emotional, intellectual. The principle amounts to a rejection of the myth that the child is a miniature adult. We know that he is not. Today, informed teachers and parents expect the average six year old to have developed social and emotional responses only to a level of maturity equal to his experience.

    This principle is also related to the fact that different children develop at different rates; the growth pattern of each child is different. The data from which we derive norms or averages of physical, emotional, social, and intellectual growth warn us that there are differences in rates of development. The principle does not imply that children should avoid difficult tasks or that a child should be able to read a passage perfectly before he attempts to read it. It does imply that we cannot expect a child to perform up to a given standard when at the moment he is incapable of such performance. To do this is to expect the impossible.

13. *Provisions for the needs of exceptional children must be incorporated into regular classroom reading instruction.* This principle warns against instruction becoming a prisoner of graded materials. Exceptional children range in ability from those with mild to severe learning difficulties to those with considerably advanced learning abilities. Demands placed on teachers to modify their reading instruction to meet these pupils' needs are increasing. Many children with learning difficulties are no longer being placed in special classrooms. As a result of Public Law 94-142, a large number of these children are now being mainstreamed into regular classroom programs.

    Children who have learning problems often need reading instruction that contains additional or different features from that which is typically found in most classrooms. This is especially important if these children are experiencing language processing problems (6).

Intellectually gifted children may be able to move through graded materials at a much faster pace than average readers. They may also have less need for and less interest in these materials. Gifted children often benefit most from teacher-directed instruction that alllows them to move at their own pace. They should also be allowed greater flexibility in selecting their own materials.

14. *Learning to read is a complicated process, one sensitive to a variety of pressures.* Too much pressure or the wrong kind of pressure may result in nonlearning. A fact that attests to the complexity of the reading process is that authorities have never agreed on one definition of reading. There are, however, many statements about the complexity of reading on which experts would agree: reading is a language function, and it is the manipulation of symbolic materials. Psychologists and other observers of human behavior tell us that the symbolic process is sensitive to many pressures. Language is a sensitive indicator of personal or emotional maladjustment. Yet, in no area of learning in our schools is greater pressure brought to bear on the pupil than in the area of reading. This is partly due to the high value that our society places on education and to the recognition that education is based on reading skill.

Reading is the first school task in which the child is deliberately or inadvertently compared with others in her peer group. It is the first task in which she must compete. How she fares in this competition has a tremendous impact on her ego, her concept of herself, and the attitudes of her peers toward her. But, most important, this is the first school activity in which her performance has a direct impact on her parents' egos. Parents may sense that their anxiety is not an intelligent or mature response. Insofar as the average parents can be coldly analytical of their motivation and involvement in their child's nonsuccess in reading, they know their feelings are never far below the surface. These feelings of disappointment are often perceived by the child as a judgment that she does not measure up to her parents' expectations.

15. *Culturally and language-different children should be accommodated in the reading program rather than forced to meet the demands of the curriculum.* Culturally and language-different children are more likely to experience success in learning to read if teachers accept and capitalize upon their differences. Reading instruction is generally more effective when teachers understand culturally and/or language-different children and accommodate these differences rather than forcing the children to adjust to the cultural and language values of the school.

16. *Reading instruction should be thought of as an organized, systematic, growth-producing activity.* If any combination of strictly environmental factors will, in the absence of systematic instruction, produce optimum growth in reading, then instruction by itself is meaningless. Sound instruction will start from the premise that the classroom environment is an integral part of instruction. The presence of adequate reading materials and the development of good classroom organization are prerequisites for good instruction. The absence of these precludes effective instruction, but their presence does not assure it.

17. *The adoption of certain instructional materials inevitably has an impact and influence on a school's instructional philosophy.* How reading should be taught has for many decades been the most widely debated topic in American education. Always, the major emphasis has been on beginning reading instruction. In recent years this debate has intensified.

    It is interesting to note that for years our schools used basal reader materials almost exclusively. All such materials provided an instructional program covering the entire elementary school pe-

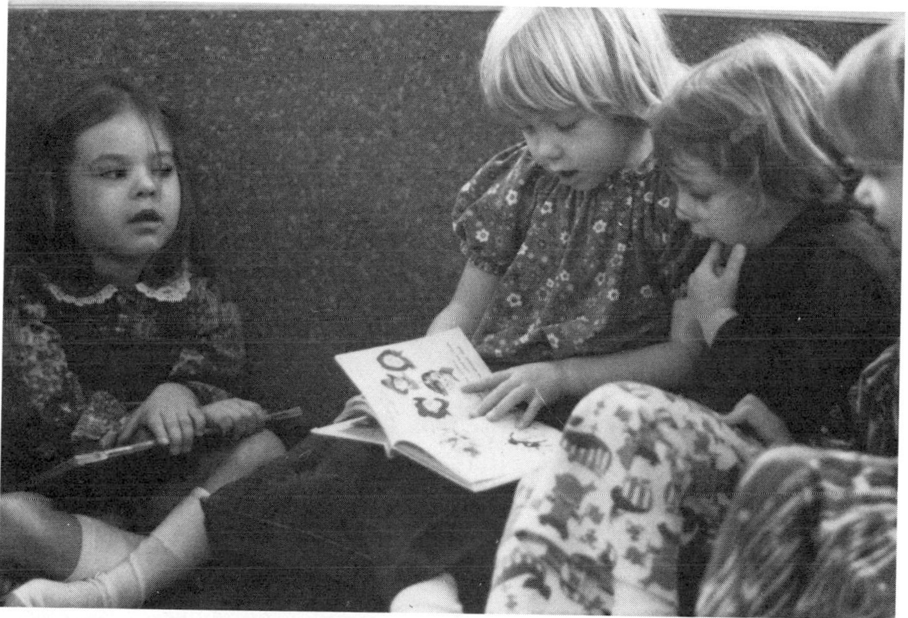

Reading is one of the first school tasks in which children are compared with peers.

FLASHBACK

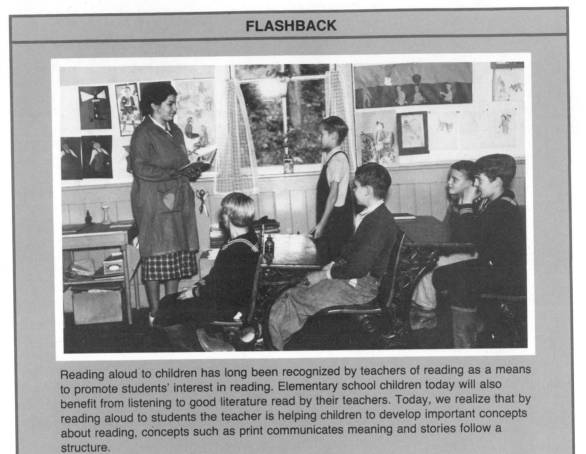

Reading aloud to children has long been recognized by teachers of reading as a means to promote students' interest in reading. Elementary school children today will also benefit from listening to good literature read by their teachers. Today, we realize that by reading aloud to students the teacher is helping children to develop important concepts about reading, concepts such as print communicates meaning and stories follow a structure.

riod. In contrast, the past several years have seen many materials and methodologies (linguistic and intensive phonic materials, for example) that focus only on beginning reading.

The majority of materials available for beginning reading instruction reflect different philosophies that in large measure determine initial instructional strategies (5). The major difference in materials can be traced to how the following pedagogical issues are treated:

a. The way initial reading vocabulary is controlled.
b. The amount of phonics (letter-sound relationships) taught.
c. The emphasis on *meaning* in beginning instruction.
d. The degree to which various facets of the total language arts program are integrated, specifically the emphasis on children's writing.

e. "Content" of materials is determined by prior decisions made in regard to items *a, b, c* above.

18. *The key to successful reading instruction is the teacher.* As some of the earlier principles indicated, a lack of supporting evidence exists by which to recommend any one particular reading method, material, or approach as best for all children. The role of the teacher has been established as one of the major variables that determines the effectiveness of reading instruction (1, 3, 9, 10).

Specific instructional practices that effective reading teachers use in their instruction have been pinpointed by the results of a large number of investigations. Specifically, effective reading teachers employ ongoing diagnosis of pupils' reading development, structure and direct pupils' learning, provide opportunities for pupiles to practice and apply skills in meaningful context, and attend to maintaining a high level of pupil involvement in learning. Each of these four areas of effective reading instruction is discussed fully in the following chapter.

SUMMARY

Principles and practices should be compatible. It is logical that a book on teaching reading should open with a statement of the principles upon which good teaching is based. Principles should evolve ahead of practices so that teacher and school practices can be evaluated in light of these principles. The view accepted here is that the principles mentioned in this chapter are sound and that those who agree should follow them in teaching reading.

In recent times, reading instruction has been subject to considerable criticism. One response to this has been the emergence of many new (or modified) instructional materials, hailed by their producers as instructional breakthroughs. Another response—made by many schools—was to accept any new material at its advertised face value and hope that a panacea had been found. Reading instruction seems particularly susceptible to overenthusiasm for whatever bears the "new" label. Soon, interest wanes and approaches heralded as breakthroughs are deserted for some other new approach in which interest builds to a peak and then recedes (5, 11).

During periods of change and uncertainty, it is easy to lose sight of fundamental principles of instruction. Much time and energy can be spent in climbing on and off so-called instructional bandwagons. Occasionally, a "new emphasis" in instruction emerges that has some excellent features but which may neglect certain essentials while overem-

The key to successful reading instruction is the teacher.

phasizing others. Sound principles of instruction apply with equal validity to any instructional approach and to all levels of instruction.

YOUR POINT OF VIEW

Discussion Questions

1. Review the four basic aspects of reading presented on page 6. Attempt to apply each of them to specific features of the examples presented on pages 7 and 9.
2. In your opinion, which one of the principles discussed in this chapter is the most important for improving reading instruction? Provide a rationale for your choice.
3. Assume that you are assigned the task of improving the teaching of reading in a school and that you want each teacher to realize that all reading instruction should lead to improved comprehension. How would you illustrate this to teachers? What examples would you use to show them that reading is a communication skill?

Take a Stand For or Against

1. A person's definition of reading would, in the final analysis, have little impact on practices followed in teaching the reading process.
2. A child's problems in learning to read can usually be attributed to one factor.
3. Handicapped children can be mainstreamed effectively in a reading class.

BIBLIOGRAPHY

1. Bond, Guy L., and Dykstra, Robert. "The Cooperative Research Program in First-Grade Reading Instruction." *Reading Research Quarterly* 2 (Summer 1967): 5–142.
2. Chall, Jeanne S. "The Great Debate: Ten Years Later, With a Modest Proposal for Reading Stages." In *Theory and Practice of Early Reading,* edited by L. Resnick and P. Weaver. Hillsdale, N.J.: Lawrence Erlbaum Associates, 1979.
3. Gates A. I. "The Necessary Age for Beginning Reading." *Elementary School Journal* 37 (1937): 497–508.
4. Geyer, John J. "Comprehensive and Partial Models Related to the Reading Process." *Reading Research Quarterly* 7 (1972): 541–87.
5. Harris, Albert J. "Practical Applications of Reading Research." *The Reading Teacher* 29 (1976): 559–65.
6. Johnson, Stanley W., and Morasky, Robert L. *Learning Disabilities.* Boston, Mass.: Allyn & Bacon, 1977.
7. Lueers, Nancy M. "The Short Circuit Model of Reading: A Synthesis of Reading Theories." *Reading Psychology* 4 (1983): 79–94.
8. Mason, Jana M. "A Schema-Theoretic View of the Reading Process as a Basis for Comprehension Instruction." In *Comprehension Instruction: Perspective and Suggestions,* edited by G. Duffy, L. Roehler, and J. Mason. New York: Longman, 1984.
9. McDonald, F. I. *Beginning Teacher Evaluation Study, Phase II Summary.* Princeton, N.J.: Educational Testing Service, 1976.
10. Rupley, William H., and Blair, Timothy R. *Reading Diagnosis and Remediation: Classroom and Clinic.* 2d ed. Boston, Mass.: Houghton-Mifflin Publishing Co., 1983.
11. Rutherford, William L. "Five Steps to Effective Reading Instruction." *The Reading Teacher* 24 (1971): 416–21.
12. Smith, Frank. *Understanding Reading.* 2d ed. New York: Holt, Rinehart & Winston, 1978.
13. Stanovich, Keith E. "Toward an Interactive-Compensatory Model of Individual Differences in the Development of Reading Fluency." *Reading Research Quarterly* 15 (1980): 32–71.
14. Weaver, Phyllis, and Shonkoff, Fredi. *Research Within Reach.* St. Louis, Mo.: Research and Development Interpretation Service, CEMREL, 1978.
15. Wiseman, Donna L. "Helping Children Take Early Steps Toward Reading and Writing." *The Reading Teacher* 37 (1984): 340–44.

2

Language

For the Reader

Language continually shapes our view of the world and ourselves. The ability to read is language based, as are the language abilities of listening, speaking, and writing. All language activities have as their central purpose the communication of meaning. It is the school's task to take advantage of the listening and speaking abilities of pupils and to foster the understanding of written language. This can be achieved by integrating all language abilities. The teaching of reading must not be isolated from other language activities but should draw on the children's rich language background. Your ability to devise and carry out an integrated, language-based reading program hinges upon your understanding of our present knowledge of language. A final message urging your careful study of this chapter is presented on the next page:

> Language is the only magic available to the school; all the rest is routine, ritual and rote. The magic of language must come through loud and clear in the teaching of reading. If this does not occur, we produce children who may learn the mechanisms but whose later behavior gives use to the question, "How do you motivate children to read?" (12, p. 3)

Preview

- Read the Key Ideas that follow.
- Read each heading and subheading.
- Read the summary.
- Read the questions and statements at the end of the chapter.
- Return to the chapter text that follows the Key Ideas and begin reading.

Key Ideas

All of the following communication abilities are language based:

speaking
listening
reading
writing

The purpose of reading is to communicate.
Linguistic and psycholinguistic contributions have aided in understanding the reading process and reading instruction.
The major functions of schools are to help children develop and expand concepts and foster language development.

A COMMUNICATION PROCESS

Proficiency in using language to communicate is an ongoing, developmental process. Much of the responsibility for developing and refining children's language occurs in the classroom. No longer is the idea widely accepted that children come to school as mature and competent language users. Admittedly, young children possess considerable language capabilities upon entry into school; however, the development of their communication skills is enhanced, expanded, and refined as they explore ideas, interact with others, and grow intellectually in an educational environment. Language allows children to learn in school and also aids in their socialization and individual development (15).

The communication skills that children are taught in school—speaking, listening, reading, and writing—are all language based. Realizing that reading is language based is extremely important for teachers of reading. Part of the process of learning to read involves children using what they have learned about language by school age to learn that print represents most forms of that language (17). Significant similarities between oral language and reading center around an individual's language competencies and experiential/conceptual background. Both speaking and reading involve an interaction between either a speaker and a listener or an author and a reader. Normal individuals are dependent upon their language capabilities to both produce and receive meaningful information (16). Such abilities relate directly to children's experiences with language in their environment and to meaningful instructional experiences (15).

Even though the school curriculum is almost totally language dependent, educators may be underestimating the potential for learning that most preschool children have developed.

Upon entering school, children

- Have well-developed control of their oral language system and can communicate efficiently with peers and adults.
- Have an amazing understanding of the language heard in their environment.
- Have a partial mastery of the *supra-segmental phonemes* (pitch, stress, and pause), which account for intonation patterns found in their language.

- Have the ability to make fine auditory discrimination among words which sound very much alike *(bath–path, drink–drank, feed–feet).*
- Have mastered the meanings of words and the ability to string words into meaningful sentences and larger language units.

All of these skills and abilities are developmental in nature, as is reading (2). Each must be expanded and refined if normal growth in reading is to be achieved.

Social, emotional, and intellectual growth reflect and interact with language growth (15). Individuals learn and use language in social-emotional settings, and their language use is a key to needs, frustrations, and self-concepts. It is important that teachers *read* these clues if they hope to teach all children to read. Learning, and particularly learning to read, is a process related to and controlled by other facets of growth.

LANGUAGE AND SOCIALIZATION

A major responsibility of a public school is the socialization of its pupils. Without concern for socializing pupils, instruction and learning in the classroom would be virtually impossible or, at best, extremely difficult. Children must learn how to behave appropriately in the classroom if they are to actively participate in instruction and to learn. Up to the time children reach school age, spoken language is their chief means of communication. One of the better tools for gauging the social needs and the social maturity of children is their language facility. Social growth is among one of the first experiences provided in the school's curriculum. Many children have had little or no experience in a group as large as that in which they will find themselves upon beginning school. There will be many learning situations that call for large-group cooperation, small-group cooperation, and independent functioning. Each child will have to follow certain social patterns in order not to disrupt the learning situation for others in the classroom.

Gradually, the teacher moves in the direction of establishing social control within the class so that learning can take place. Various types of instruction call for children to understand different kinds of social interactions. Some activities in the classroom demand cooperation and sharing among pupils in group settings. Other classroom activities require pupils to work individually or in small-group settings. Language is an important basis for developing both pupil cooperation and independence. Cooperating, sharing, and working independently help the child develop and adjust to the different conditions of a classroom environment (11). If the classroom socialization process breaks down, and the individual, for any reason, does not learn the social rules (or does not follow them within certain limits) his behavior sets him apart from the group. When his teacher or the group reacts to this behavior, he and the group are often out of adjustment.

The failure among some children to adjust to the social demands of school is almost inevitable because some have further to go in order to meet classroom standards, some learn slowly, and some have learned to use antisocial responses when attempting to satisfy needs. A teacher who does not perceive the symptoms of social adjustment problems fairly early may soon have pupils who feel that they do not belong. These can develop rapidly into isolates, or children rejected by the group. The teacher may be the best teacher of reading in the school district, but if she lets the security of some children become seriously threatened in the school situation, the odds are that she will not teach them reading.

LANGUAGE AND EMOTIONAL ADJUSTMENT

Clinicians state that language is a sensitive indicator of maladjustment and psychological needs. Both as adults and as teachers, we sometimes learn very little about children from children. This happens when we consciously or unconsciously feel that what children say is not important. The truth of the matter is that their language mirrors their needs, feelings, aspirations, and fears; if one's job is to help children grow, sensitivity to these aspects is essential.

A child's need for ego satisfaction seems to increase in the face of frustration. That is, a little denial of love, attention, and acceptance or a small threat to self-worth and integrity is reacted to by an increased drive for these goals. If rebuffed, the children seem to increase their efforts to maintain prestige and selfworth. It is apparent that when children are trying to fulfill ego needs, they invariably use behavior which by adult logic seems ill-conceived and not likely to achieve the child's goal. The child who wants and needs friendship and is rebuffed may resort to the use of aggressive, hostile behavior and abusive language. Such children perhaps feel that they can force acceptance or that their language will reduce the stature of those persons to whom it is addressed. Other children, after each failure, may withdraw more and more and make very few language overtures to others in their peer group. This nonuse of language is itself a clue that should have major diagnostic value for the teacher. Children who have elected to withdraw from participation will continue to seek satisfaction within themselves. This absence of overt language behavior is more likely a sign of emotional distress than of cognitive or linguistic deficiency. These children,

FLASHBACK

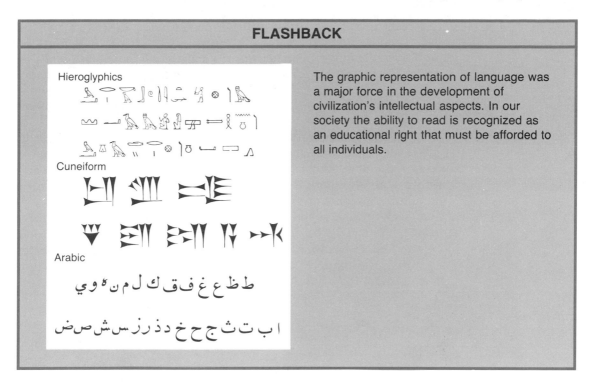

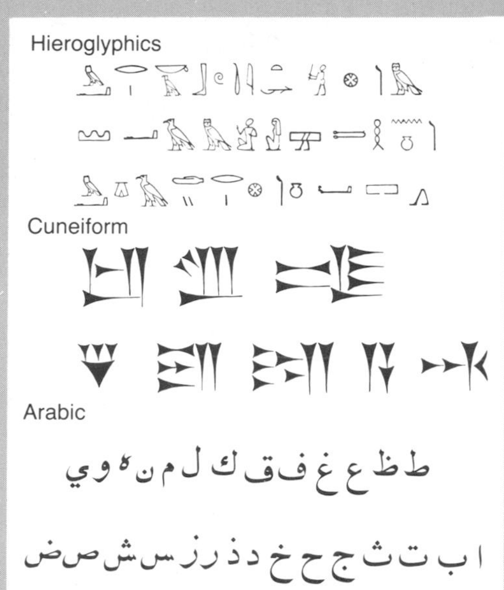

The graphic representation of language was a major force in the development of civilization's intellectual aspects. In our society the ability to read is recognized as an educational right that must be afforded to all individuals.

at the moment, pose no problem to the teacher or society, but their response is potentially more dangerous than overt aggression.

LANGUAGE AND MENTAL GROWTH

Psychologists agree that valuable insights into a child's mental growth are gained from a study of the development of language facility. A brief though acceptable definition of intelligence is that it is the ability to manipulate in a meaningful manner symbolic materials, of which language is the best example. Intelligence itself cannot be measured but is inferred from behavior that can be measured. We measure certain behavior that by agreement is said to be representative of intelligence. One kind of behavior most universally measured on intelligence tests is language behavior. Our society puts a high value on the ability to use and understand language. The degree of the child's mastery of communication skills determines to a large extent her readiness to do school tasks and to profit from instruction. Although many children cannot read, spell, or write when they start school, they have had years of experience with language. Their language proficiency is used as an index of mental growth, just as it provides data for appraisal of social and emotional growth and adjustment. Furthermore, when we wish to assess what pupils have learned at any grade level, we rely on language usage. Language is a valid indicator of the number and breadth of concepts individuals have acquired. All concepts exist within the framework of some symbolic process, and all are arrived at and refined through thought processes. Language is used to construct models of our world and where we fit in it (3). Therefore, acquisition of concepts and understanding or making sense of these concepts are dependent upon the manipulation of language symbols. In other words, a change in language behavior is often a major criterion of learning.

A society such as we have today could not have evolved without language. It is equally obvious that education would not have developed along the lines it has without language. Language is the bridge that permits ideas, information, and data to pass between parent and child, teacher and pupil, and child and peer. As individuals master new forms

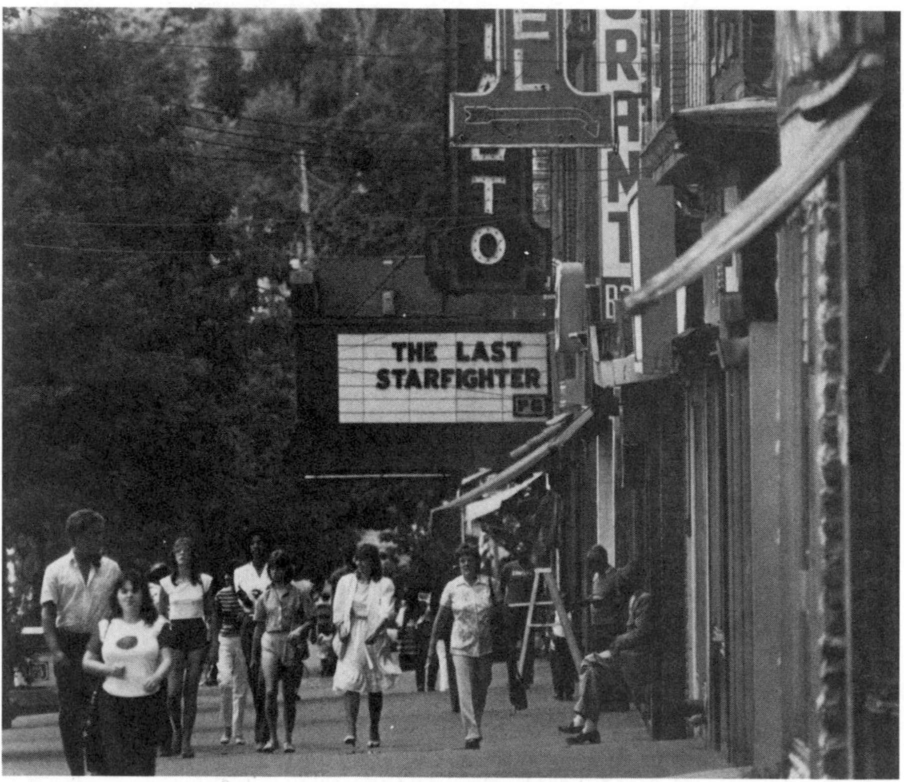

Our society could not have evolved without language.

of language usage, they are developing "mind tools" that they can use from that time forward in the pursuit of knowledge. Reading is the best example of such a tool.

LANGUAGE AND READING

Although language usage provides a teacher with information about a child's development and is a means for socialization, previous experience with language is probably most important as it relates to the specific task called reading. Reading is a language process requiring the understanding of written language. The teaching of reading has a unique relationship to and with language. Since most of our concepts are either acquired or refined through the use of language, reading enables us to go beyond that which we can only see or manipulate. In a broad sense, reading frees both language and thinking from immediate experiences (22).

Reading instruction involves the learner in solving two codes. One is the relationship between letters seen in print and the speech sounds these letters represent. Knowing the letter-sound code permits the reader to "say," "pronounce," "recognize," "decode," "solve," or "approximate" the pronunciation of words not recognized as sight words. The second code focuses on meaning, or decoding the "message." For instance, by the end of the third grade many students can correctly say the speech sounds, that is, pronounce all the words in the following passage:

> The louder he talked of his honor, the faster we counted our spoons.

However, many high school students and some college students are even at a loss to solve or approximate the meaning codes.[1]

Reading for meaning is in many ways closer to children's previous experiences with language than is associating visual symbols (letters) with the sounds they typically represent. Prior to reading instruction, they have spent several years listening to and speaking meaningful language. However, this language usage usually occurs within the context

---

1. A few interpretations of college students: "It simply doesn't make any sense"; "The after-dinner speaker was giving a boring speech, so we counted the spoons at our place setting"; "The more this guy boasted of his great feats at the banquet the more we ignored him by eating our soup"; The last two interpretations are indications that the readers have in fact arrived at meaning, but their experiential/conceptual background docs not allow the *expected* meaning to arise; i.e., they're not familar with the expression "count our spoons" as a figurative way of saying we were suspicious.

FLASHBACK

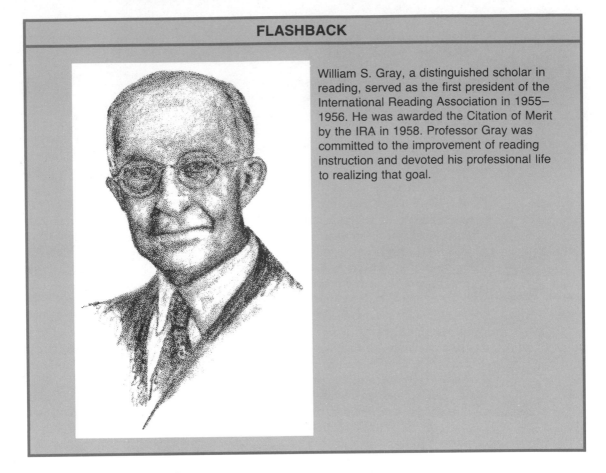

William S. Gray, a distinguished scholar in reading, served as the first president of the International Reading Association in 1955–1956. He was awarded the Citation of Merit by the IRA in 1958. Professor Gray was committed to the improvement of reading instruction and devoted his professional life to realizing that goal.

of familiar settings, such as in the home, with friends, on the playground, and so forth. The process of learning to read in school often takes place under circumstances that mask the relationship between their past language experiences and printed language. The child who is learning to read may fail to see that he is really involved in a language process. This failure can be because what he is asked to read is not in a familiar contextual setting, either socially or physically, and he must reason about it primarily through words alone (13).

Another reason for a child's failure to see that reading is a form of language is due to many of the ways that have been developed to teach reading. Oftentimes the materials and methods used for reading instruction thoroughly divorce the act of reading from language involvement. This outcome is traceable to the fact that reading instruction overemphasizes letter-sound relationships and fails to stress the language-meaning features of print. Lack of balanced reading instruction may or may not be deliberate. Our concern is how the learner perceives what is going on.

Cracking the letter-sound code can provide its own motivation for only a limited time—it is not a self-sustaining activity. Teaching the variety of reading skills must be accompanied by a sense of involvement with language. Through this direct involvement children can then "gradually become capable of transforming an experience into language, oral or written, and of decontextualizing it. That is, they can think about that verbalized (written) experience, analyze it, compare it to previous experiences, and, perhaps, reinterpret it" (3, p. 753).

The Reading Curriculum as a Potential Enemy

The school has two major functions, which are to help children:

- Develop and expand concepts.
- Develop the language tools that will permit them to continue this process in or out of school.

The importance of these goals has been recognized since the early 1900s. William S. Gray, a scholar in the field of reading, stated in 1933 that an enriched program of activities during reading should

> possess features to provide numerous purposeful reading activities that are highly charged with interests; to extend and enrich the experience of children through wide reading; to stimulate habits of good thinking and clear interpretation while reading; to lay the foundation of reading and study habits that are common to various school activities; to arouse strong motives for, and permanent interests in, independent reading. . . . (10, p. 45)

These functions appear to be totally compatible, yet in actual practice the school has not been successful in providing the ideal mix or maintaining the proper balance between teaching concepts and developing language facility. In the professional literature it is often stated that reading is a tool. It might be better to go back one step and establish the fact that language is the *tool* and that reading is the manipulation of or a specific use of that tool.

Over the years, the curriculum materials that are widely used in the schools have focused primarily on teaching concepts that can be characterized as facts. This practice has been prevalent in the various content areas such as social studies, science, and health. Teachers and

In a language-rich classroom, teachers encourage children to talk with them.

other observers of the educational scene are aware that "fact-oriented" reading materials do not always grab students' minds or hold their interest. One of the most frequently heard questions among reading teachers is, How do you motivate children to read?

Part of the answer lies in achieving a proper balance between teaching facts and helping students develop and sharpen language usage and facility. Language facility is developed and enriched as students use language for a variety of real purposes. Negotiating meaning with children (6), which means that teachers talk with children and encourage children to talk with them and others in the classroom, enables students to expand and refine both their experiences and language. Children must experience and be guided to appreciate the power and beauty of language.

Elementary schools are filled with the two essentials needed for language growth—people to talk to and things to talk about (12). Utilizing these resources to refine and expand children's capabilities in reading becomes more a matter of changing viewpoints than of changing methods. Children should be provided with opportunities to experience involvement with written language through jokes, riddles, proverbs, books, magazines, writing activities, and other types of both brief and lengthy language samples.

LINGUISTICS AND READING

Various facets of linguistics are discussed throughout this book. For example, both the phonology and syntax of nonstandard dialect speakers are treated in chapter 14. This discussion will explore some of the areas in which linguistics appears to be related to reading instruction. In order to understand what linguists have proposed, why they disagree about reading intruction, and what contributions they have made to reading instruction, we must have some understanding of the terms *linguist* and *linguistics.*

Linguists are trained individuals who make a scientific study of human language. Such study implies accurate observation and recording of data. The linguist studies and identifies the building blocks of language—speech sounds or phonemes. He discerns how these are combined into words (semantics) and word parts that have assigned meanings (morphemes). This is the groundwork for further study of language; namely, the patterns in which words may occur (syntax) and those patterns that cannot occur in a particular language. When these discoveries are made, one has the key to the structure, or the grammar, of a language.

The linguist discovers facts unique to each language and others that are common to various languages. The average person can verbalize some of these findings without grasping their full significance. For instance, the linguist states that language is arbitrary. This applies to all facets of language. The normal child growing up in an English-speaking environment learns to make many speech sounds that will have to be discarded if he restricts his language usage to English. The sounds he will use are not a matter of individual choice. This matter has been arbitrarily established along with the patterns or sequences in which sounds may be combined.

The order in which words may be combined into utterances has also been established. Language has a definite structure. The linguist notes that this structure permits a sentence like, "I runned all the way home," yet English structure cannot accommodate "I all the ran home way." Although six year olds have mastered a tremendously large portion of English grammar, they project certain characteristics into word meanings that do not exist. When asked Piaget's question, "Can the sun be called the moon?" they answer: "No, because the moon comes up at night" or "No, because the sun is brighter." This reaction implies that they perceive word meaning residing in the word itself.

Linguistics is a broad term which can cover many orientations to language study. One linguist may be primarily interested in comparing different languages, another in the sound patterns of a language, another in the structural (grammatical word order) features of one or more languages, and another in the changes (phonological and structural) that occur in any living language. Also, linguists are interested in the rule systems underlying language use, that is, what the language user knows (22).

Linguistic science has moved rapidly in the past fifty years because linguists were able to agree on the precise meaning of many crucial terms. Linguists were the first and possibly the only group who thus far agree on the definition of language. They define language as a rule-governed code. To reading specialists and psychologists, this definition may seem to be somewhat narrow, but the mark of a science is that its basic terms are unequivocal.

On the other hand, the field of reading provides many examples of frequently used terms for which there is no universal agreement as to meaning. Examples include *reading, phonics method, individualized reading, critical reading, sight word method, reading disability, traditional method, remedial reading,* and *phonics instruction.* All of these represent concepts, but none has a fixed meaning for all people who use it. Obviously, confusion often results. The problem is accentuated when terms are used by persons in different disciplines. An illustration is provided in the use of the term *language* at a national reading conference.

A linguist, speaking to teachers of reading, remarked that he had little patience for the educators who made such absurd statements as, "English is not a phonetic language," or "English is not phonetically lawful." He stated that "English is perfectly phonetic—100 percent phonetic." He was followed on the same platform by a teacher of reading who, probably not having heard her predecessor, stated: "One of the major problems of teaching children to read is the fact that English is not phonetic. The language contains a large number of phonetically irregular words."

Each of the speakers started from different premises based on different connotations for the words used. The linguist worked from the linguistic definition of language that "language is oral—language is speech." Thus, all English language (speech) is 100 percent phonetically regular. Such words as *freight, light, come* and all other words can be transcribed within the framework of English phonemes.

The teacher of reading used language to mean written English. The linguist, of course, would refer to this as "a graphic representation of language." The teacher of reading meant that many English spellings were irregular, that is, there was not a one-to-one relationship between printed letters seen and speech sounds heard when one is reading English. With this the linguist would agree, but he would convey this information by using the term *phoneme-grapheme relationship.*

Communication between reading teachers and linguists depends on each group making an effort to understand the other. In recent years terminology from the science of linguistics has been used frequently in material addressed to the reading teacher. These terms have fixed meanings, and there is little point in not adopting them for use in discussion of reading instruction. Some of the more often used linguistic terms related to reading follow.

Linguistic Terminology

Phoneme. This is the smallest unit of sound within a language. When the word *man* is pronounced, three phonemes are utilized: /m/, /ae/, /n/.

Morpheme. This is the smallest meaningful unit of language. There are two types of morphemes: free and bound. A *free morpheme* is one that functions independently in larger language units. For example, *son* is a free morpheme composed of three phonemes. *Bound morphemes* must be used with another morpheme. This class includes affixes and inflectional endings. If *s* is added to *son* to form a plural, the final *s* in *sons* is a bound morpheme.

Alphabetic Principle. English is one of the many languages for which an alphabet has been devised for writing. We use twenty-six letters to represent graphically the sounds of English. Thus, English is an alphabetic language. English writing follows an alphabetical principle, that is, certain graphic symbols represent speech sounds. However, English spellings that are used in writing of words do not follow a one-to-one relationship of letter seen, phoneme heard. Exceptions are discussed in relation to phonics instruction (see chapter 5).

The irregular spellings of English words can create problems for the person attempting to learn to write or read English. The fact that a large majority of English words follow regular grapheme-phoneme patterns leads some individuals to minimize the effect of irregular spellings on learning how to write or read English. Establishing what percentage of the 10,000 most frequently used words happens to be regular in grapheme-phoneme relationships and then generalizing from the data to the reading process ignores the *frequency of the use* of irregularly spelled words. This point becomes clearer as we examine structure words.

Structure Words. This term is used to cover some 300 or more frequently used words which have no concrete referent. Various other descriptive terms have been used to describe these words, such as *signal words, glue words,* and *service words.* Structure words do signal the listener, or more importantly, the reader, that a particular syntactical pattern is coming.

- Noun markers: *my* house, *any* house, *this* house, *a* house, *some* houses, *the* house.
- Verb markers: *am* coming, *are* coming, *is* coming, *was* coming.
- Clause markers: *now, like, until, if, although, since, before, however.*
- Question indicators: *when, where, who, which, why.*

It is easy to see why structure words have been called "the glue words of the English language" or *service words.* Both of these concepts are consistent with the way these words function in sentences. They both introduce and bind together utterances, while not conveying meaning in and of themselves. Many structure words have irregular spellings and are often designated as being *sight words.* Both their irregular spellings and their high frequency of usage make it mandatory that they be instantly recognized in context.

The frequency with which particular words are used will of course vary with the material under consideration. The previous sentence used eight different structure words for a total of ten words *(the, with, which, are, will, of, course, with, the, under).* Whether one is talking about reading material specifically designed for the primary grades or the professional writing of historians and linguists, these words will comprise 25 to 50 percent of all words.

Structure words pose no problem for mature readers. Seriously impaired readers, however, have been unable to learn or recognize these words, even after hundreds of experiences of seeing them in print and various types of drills designed to facilitate their becoming sight words.

Syntax. This term is used to describe the meaning patterns found within any language, in essence, the *grammar* of that language. Syntax includes the various order patterns in which words can be strung together. The following word orders represent, respectively, a standard English sentence, regional-dialect expression, and a non-English pattern:

> I go up the steps.
> I go the steps up.
> Up the go I steps.

Syntax includes the ways in which words may function in different patterns. The same word may function as a verb, noun, or adverb:

> *Light* the fire.
> She saw the *light.*
> He danced *lightly* across the ring and threw a *lightning* punch.

English syntax rules out "He danced *lightning* across the ring and threw a *lighted* punch." By carefully studying the syntax of a language, you can describe the basic sentence patterns that occur in that language as well as the ways in which these patterns may be varied by means of expansion, substitution, or inversion.

Since linguistic science has not been concerned with *how children learn to read,* there is little research data upon which to base conclusions. For this reason, it has been difficult for linguists to apply the same scientific rigor to reading instruction that they have applied to the study of language. Nevertheless, linguistics provides a number of important concepts that focus on and hold promise for improving reading instruction. The following are illustrated.

- Despite irregularities in English spelling, important phoneme-grapheme *patterns* do exist. These should be stressed to a larger degree in reading instruction.
- Reading instruction can overemphasize dealing with words as units. Graphic symbols must be read to parallel normal oral language patterns. The reader must "put together meaning-bearing patterns."
- The printed page represents oral language. The child beginning to read generally knows much about the grammar or syntax of oral language. However, the printed pages do not contain all the language clues found in speech. The "graphic representation" of language does not indicate various levels of pitch and stress. Punctuation (which indicates junctures) is the only graphic intonational help that is provided, and it too is somewhat imperfect. Intonations (juncture, stress, and pitch) are part of the language, not optional additives.
- The purpose and function of structure words need to be better understood for the mastery of the reading process. These words (approximately 300), sometimes referred to as *glue* or *service words,* have little or no meaning in and of themselves, but they provide significant clues as to the types of patterns (questions, noun markers, verb markers, parallel constructions) they introduce.
- Language has a definite structure, and this structure plays an important role in conveying meaning. Structure is revealed in sentence patterns, not in word units.
- Linguists describe language *as it is used,* not as they or others think it should be used. Thus, a given dialect is not incorrect, nor is standard English superior to other dialects.
- Although linguists have and will continue to provide accurate descriptions of the phonology and syntax of various nonstandard dialects, the problem of how best to teach reading to dialect speakers is still unresolved.
- Linguistic findings can and should be translated into meaningful curricular changes in the school. Teachers of reading should place more emphasis on how reading reflects language.

PSYCHOLINGUISTICS

A body of literature is rapidly accumulating on the general topic of psycholinguistics and, more specifically, on psycholinguistics and reading. In defining the term, Smith writes: "Psycholinguistics, as its name suggests, is a field of study that lies at the intersection of two broader disciplines, psychology and linguistics" (18).

Psycholinguists have made several major contributions that can help reading teachers gain insights into the reading process (7,8). Many of these contributions have direct implications for classroom reading instruction. First, as we emphasize throughout this text, reading is viewed as a communication process, and as such its goal is comprehension of information by the reader. Second, psycholinguists have pointed out that there is "a trade-off between visual and nonvisual information in reading" (19). The more familiar a reader is with a given topic, the less she needs to rely solely on the printed text. The reader's knowledge of the topic and her language competence allow her to predict information and rely less on print. Third, readers who overly depend on visual information when reading generally cannot process the information in a meaningful fashion. They are often dealing with isolated word identification, which interferes with reading for meaning.

Results of psycholinguistic research and the opinions of authorities have encouraged more of an eclectic view of what reading is. Kenneth Goodman, a pioneer in reading miscue analysis (chapter 11 discusses the use of miscue analysis in reading diagnosis), has identified three cueing systems used by readers (7). Using *graphophonic* cues involves relating visual patterns to the corresponding sound sequences. Using the *syntactic* cue system involves the reader's use of word order, inflectional endings, and function words to predict structure as she reads. *Semantic* cue system use refers not only to the reader's knowledge of word meanings but also to her conceptual and experiential background that aids her in getting meaning from what she reads.

Psycholinguists have essentially helped put reading instruction in proper perspective in relation to the product of that instruction. Getting meaning from what is read not only depends on pronouncing words, but on understanding them as well (1). Meaning comes from the reader's experiences with language and the topic being read. Words by themselves, as we mentioned earlier, have no specific meaning; it is the association of words that provides the meaning for the reader.

Although many insights can be gained from the information rapidly accumulating in the area of psycholinguistics, teachers have been cautioned about viewing psycholinguistics as the solution to teaching reading. Fortunately, these cautions are frequently found in books and articles whose titles are (or include) *Psycholinguistics and Reading.*

Smith, after expressing the opinion that the field has something to offer teachers of reading, warns: "But I must admit that I feel a growing anxiety about the word 'psycholinguistics' itself. Already there are signs that 'psycholinguistic' is becoming one of those faddish labels that suffer a brief career of indiscriminate application in education in order to deceive, dissemble, or convey an image of totally false authority" (18). Smith's opinion is important to consider because findings of psycholinguistic research do not, in themselves, clearly specify a "best" methodology for teaching reading. Recent research (4) suggests that reading methods employing word identification strategies (phonics, context clues, structural analysis, etc.) combined with application in meaningful contexts are more successful than strict adherence to only one method of instruction.

IMPORTANT CONSIDERATIONS FOR LANGUAGE-BASED INSTRUCTION

The process of learning to read is not dependent upon moving through a particular body of content. Children can learn needed reading skills through the use of any of a number of printed passages. These materials may be children's books, stories dictated by the child himself, basal texts, experience charts, myths, biographies, riddles, children's newspapers, or subject-matter content in any area. The important criterion that any material would have to meet is that of appropriateness to the reader's present level of language and experiential/conceptual development.

The major question in reading instruction is not what printed material to teach from, but what skills to teach and when and how to teach them (see chapter 3). There are many ways in which teachers can involve students in exciting and growth-producing language-based experiences. Individual differences among students make it mandatory that approaches be adapted to fit each student's abilities. Activities can be structured so that they hold the student's interest and lead to the expansion of reading skills and language facility.

The following are important areas related to language-based reading instruction and focus on developing reading skills in relation to concepts represented by language.

Different Meanings (Concepts)

Native speakers of English are frequently unaware that so many different words we use have five, ten, or twenty or more different meanings. This does not imply that we do not use or understand many meanings of a given word. The point is that we seldom think about how this feature of our language operates. Thus, working with different meanings is an excellent way for children to learn about language while developing and expanding concepts about their world (5, 14).

The fact that many words have a large number of connotations adds to the problem of developing a precise order of difficulty of words, or the order in which words should be introduced and taught. For example, the word *rhinoceros*, while very concrete in meaning, might be considered more difficult than the word *heavy*, but only if you are discussing a particular and limited connotation for *heavy*.

A child may acquire one meaning for *heavy* (opposite of light in weight) before he acquires a concept for (or even the ability to pronounce) *rhinoceros*. But once he has had the experience of seeing a rhinoceros, or even a picture of one, he will have established a workable concept. He can expand his knowledge of this animal, such as its average weight, height, habitat, feeding habits, degree of aggressiveness, and economic value. However, he will not have to develop a series of different meanings for this word.

The word *heavy* has dozens of connotations that range from fairly concrete to highly abstract. However, it is only when *heavy* appears in context that it has specific meaning associated with it.

They had a *heavy* load on the wagon.
The voters registered a *heavy* vote.
The guide led them through a *heavy* fog.
Time hung *heavy* on his hands.
Their eyes became *heavy* with sleep.
The actor complained, "I am always cast as the *heavy*."

A large number of words that children encounter in reading also have varying connotations in terms of how they are used in context. Such words can be categorized in terms of actions, places, feelings, states of being, and so forth to help children understand the varying concepts such words represent. Instruction aimed at helping pupils understand these concepts should provide for meeting their needs, allowing for practice, and maximizing application in meaningful, familiar context (see chapter 3).

Figurative Language

Many groups of words have special meanings, and it is the concept represented by the words that is essential in comprehending language, rather than the literal meanings associated with the words. For example, if someone writes "raining cats and dogs" or "tall as a mountain" she does not want her readers to take her words literally. Expressions such as these are examples of figurative speech, which can interfere with children's language comprehension if interpreted literally (see chapter 6).

Instruction that helps pupils understand that figurative language is intended to make picturesque comparisons, show exaggeration, or convey meaning by stating the opposite of what is meant is essential to both oral language and reading development. The focus here is not on teaching children a wide variety of figurative language expressions, but rather expanding their experiential/conceptual background about figurative language so they can make sense of what they read. A few of the more common types of figurative language are:

- *Hyperbole:* An exaggeration—an obvious overstatement. "So hungry I could eat a bear."
- *Simile:* An actual comparison between things that are basically different. Usually these comparisons include the words *like* or *as.* "Hearing this, he turned white as a sheet." "He drifted about town like a ship without a rudder."
- *Irony:* Humorous light sarcasm. If you hand in a rough copy of a theme that contains misspellings, marked out passages, improper punctuation, and no evidence of organization, your professor may say, "This is a fine piece of work," but your grade on the theme should provide a clue as to what he meant.
- *Metaphor:* An implied comparison between two different things. "The ship plowed the ocean." "Tom remained rooted to the spot." "The king had a heart of stone."

Word Analogies

An excellent way to develop children's abilities in seeing relationships, associating or contrasting word meanings, and applying analytical processes is through working with analogies. Analogical reasoning helps children to expand their understandings of their world and develop broader, more refined concepts. Analogies involve a relationship or similarity between concepts. That is, one thing can be related to another thing in terms of a shared relationship. Examples of more common relationships include:

Part to Whole:	finger–hand; toe–foot
Whole to Part:	hand–finger; foot–toe
Sequence:	six–seven; f–g
Origin:	paper–tree; wheat–bread
Class:	orange–fruit; carrot–vegetable
Function:	shoe–foot; glove–hand
Opposite:	weak–strong; cold–hot
Synonym:	hate–depise; expand–enlarge

Reading Aloud to Children

Reading aloud books, poems, newspaper articles, magazine articles, and other appropriate types of written materials can serve several important learning purposes. First, it can help children develop the understanding that the purpose of reading is to communicate meaning. The value of reading aloud to students becomes readily apparent when children laugh, cry, or express other emotions when they listen to stories read to them. Such reactions indicate that they are comprehending what they hear through another person's reading to them. Second, reading aloud to students can foster a desire to want to read and help students associate value with reading. Children in many of the classrooms we visit look forward to the teacher reading aloud to them daily. Many of the books and magazines from which the teacher reads are often read later by the children. Third, reading aloud to students can enable the teacher to take advantage of "teaching moments." Teaching moments are those situations that arise during a school day where the teacher can reinforce, reintroduce, or illustrate something that had been taught previously. For example, if a lesson about different meanings of words had preceded reading aloud to children and what was being read aloud had some examples of multiple-meaning words, the teacher could point this out and illustrate it with examples from the selection being read.

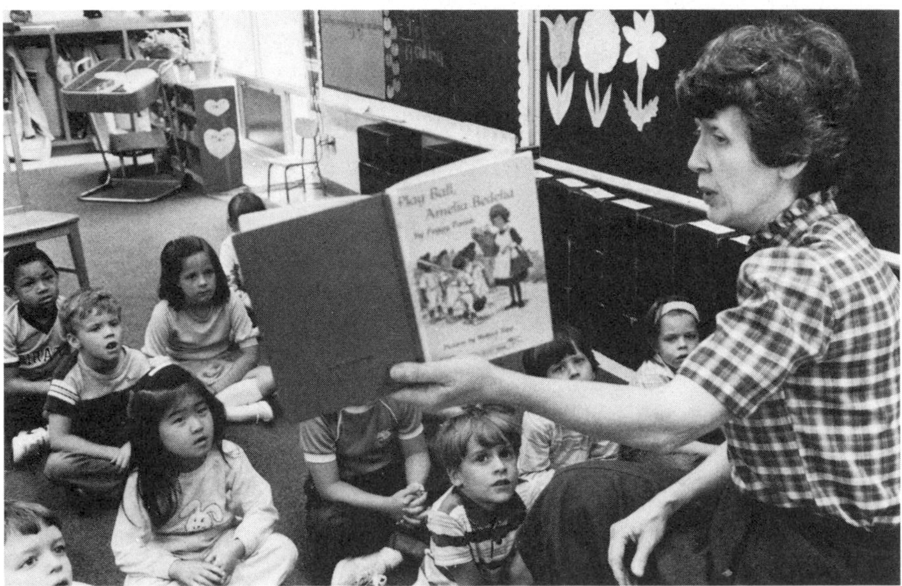

Reading aloud to students helps them understand that reading is a communication process.

Reading aloud to children gives them the opportunity to see the relationships between reading, writing, speaking, and listening. It is one way to expose children to experiences that will enable them to connect, through the use of language, old learnings with new learnings. Encouraging students to discuss and ask questions about what is read aloud to them is an effective way to engage them in the reading and language relationship. Questions, however, should not focus on just literal content, but should be aimed at broadening experiences and the concept that reading is a communication process. Therefore, questions that encourage children to express their feelings about favorite parts, the author's language, characters, and so forth will be more beneficial than questions about literal information. Reading written materials aloud to students will add to children's language acquisition and development as well as create an enjoyable period of the day for both teacher and students. (See chapter 4 for more on reading aloud to students.)

READING/WRITING CONNECTION

The connection between reading and writing should seem to be apparent, although each is treated differently by many teachers. As with listening, speaking, and reading, the purpose of writing is to communicate meaning. Children who understand that others read their writing and that they read the writing of others will better realize the communication concept of reading and are more likely to understand that reading is getting meaning, not just sounding out words.

It is generally accepted that reading and writing are interrelated. Tierney and Pearson (20) indicate that reading and writing are multiple types of processes, both of them being acts of composing. Writers are composing meaning as they record their thoughts on paper; readers are composing meaning as they process the written text. The experiential/conceptual background of both writer and reader plays a major role in this composing process. Students can write best about those things for which they have background experiences. Likewise, students can read with comprehension about those things that are in their experiential/conceptual background.

Opportunities for building the connection between reading and writing should be developed around the range of personal uses of written language. Kenneth and Yetta Goodman (9) have identified several activities that focus on the practical functions of reading and writing. Several of these activities are briefly described below:

- List-making writing activities, such as shopping lists, birthdays, attendance taking, library books, and so forth can engage children in

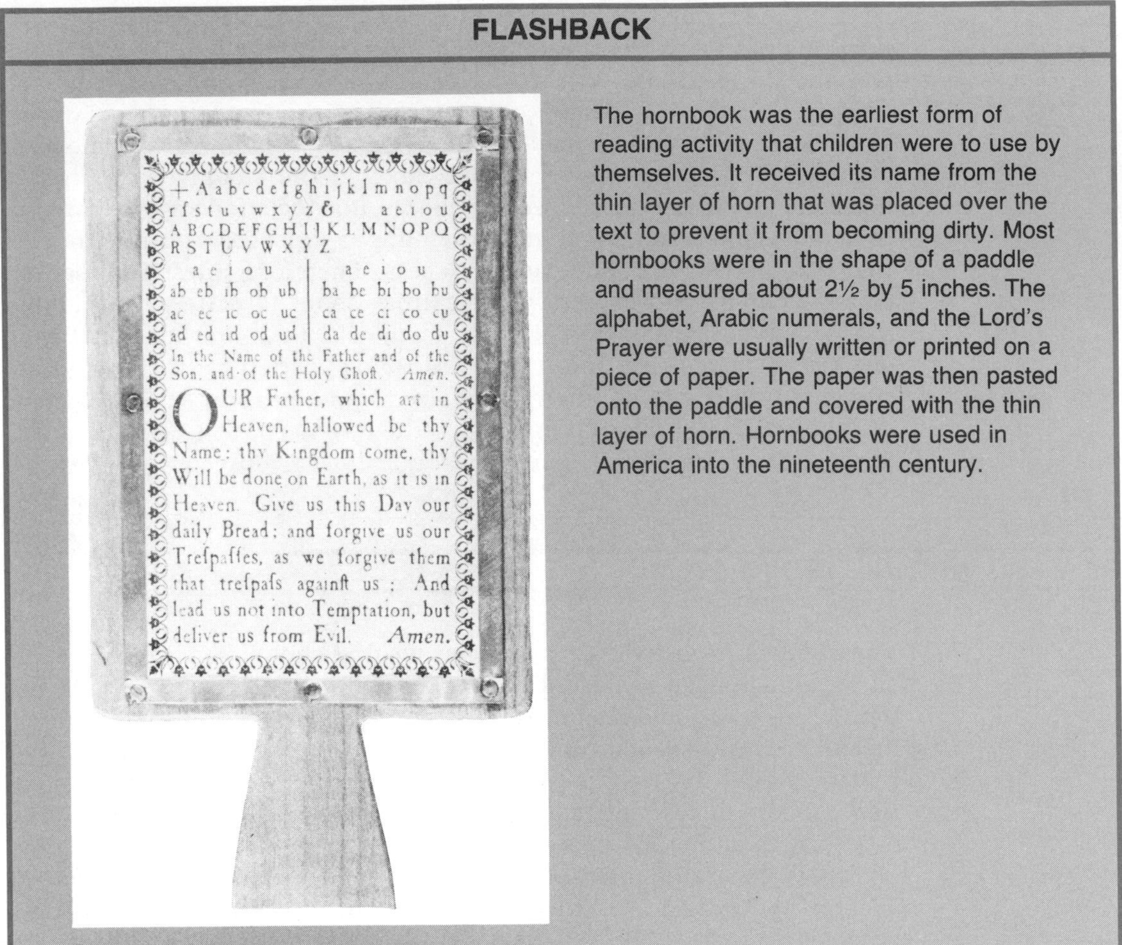

FLASHBACK

The hornbook was the earliest form of reading activity that children were to use by themselves. It received its name from the thin layer of horn that was placed over the text to prevent it from becoming dirty. Most hornbooks were in the shape of a paddle and measured about 2½ by 5 inches. The alphabet, Arabic numerals, and the Lord's Prayer were usually written or printed on a piece of paper. The paper was then pasted onto the paddle and covered with the thin layer of horn. Hornbooks were used in America into the nineteenth century.

both reading and writing. Children can either compose the lists or read lists composed by classmates and the teacher. List making is a frequent type of writing that many children are aware of because they see it used by parents and teachers and in fast-food restaurants. Such list-making activities can help students understand organizing, categorizing, and alphabetizing.

- Diary writing is personal writing that children can read because it is based on their own experiences. Teachers can use a classroom diary to record classroom events; help students record what they learned; and record special events, such as a birthday party, field trips, and so forth. Such classroom diaries could be either dictated by the students and recorded by the teacher, or they could be written by the students and shared with the class.

- Journal writing focuses on students sharing their feelings, making requests, noting important events in their lives, or making complaints. Their writing is intended for the teacher to read and, therefore, attention is given to communicating to a reader. Response journal writing requires that the teacher read and respond to the children's journals. The teacher responds in writing, and this serves to reinforce the connection between reading and writing for the students.
- Function writing is intended to make the classroom a literate place that emphasizes to the children that they are involved in reading and writing. Students can write labels for work areas of the room, write uses for work areas, write instructions for the care of plants and animals, and so forth. The communicative functions of writing can be emphasized by having children personalize their belongings and areas of control, such as labeling their desks "Johnny sits here," job responsibilities "Mary is the librarian," and group work areas "Bill, Tim, and Sally are building this Indian village."
- Note and letter writing is another familiar type of writing for most children and involves a writer with one or more readers. Classroom pen pals, teachers, parents, brothers and sisters, and other familiar

Writing letters to friends helps students develop writing skills and learn that reading and writing are interconnected.

individuals can be the audience to whom notes and letters are written. Readers such as these share many common experiences with the writer, thus less attention has to be given by the writer to communicating with the reader. Since the writer and reader share experiences, the writer does not need to be as complete in his communication because the reader can infer meaning. Writing notes and letters to people less familiar offers children the opportunity to communicate with new audiences. Children can write notes and letters to their favorite authors, to request free materials and information, to national and community leaders, or to pen pals. The responses that the students receive from their letters provide an opportunity to further understand the communicative features of reading and writing.

The above recommendations for connecting reading and writing will help students to better understand that the function of language is communication with others.

SUMMARY

Language serves several crucial purposes for children's social, emotional, and intellectual growth. Socially, language is the key means for both teachers and children to establish and allow for cooperation and sharing in the classroom. It is a means through which children become learners in the range of instructional settings that occur in classrooms. Language is an important indicator of children's feelings, aspirations, and fears. Furthermore, language is the bridge that permits the exchange and sharing of ideas. As children's language capabilities are refined and enhanced, their world knowledge is expanded and becomes more diversified—they can move from dealing with only the concrete to understanding the abstract. Attention to enhancing and developing students' language development in speaking, listening, and writing will aid them in their reading growth. Language enables them to grow intellectually and develop "mind tools" that they can use throughout their lives.

Reading is a language process that (as do all language processes) focuses on the communication and understanding of information. The process of learning to read should take place under circumstances that maximize a child's awareness that she is involved in a language process. Reading instruction should enable children to readily grasp the relationships between spoken and written language by helping them experience the power and beauty of language. We must find ways to include meaningful language in the teaching of reading.

YOUR POINT OF VIEW

Discussion Questions

1. How does children's speaking, listening, and writing language growth affect their reading development?
2. Why is it important for teachers to plan language activities that are meaningful and highly related to students' existing language capabilities?
3. What are the major benefits in fostering children's language by reading aloud to them and providing them with varied writing opportunities?

Take a Stand For or Against

1. The processes of learning to speak and learning to write are basically the same as learning to read.
2. Formal language instruction is not necessary in today's schools.

BIBLIOGRAPHY

1. Artley, A. Sterl. "Words, Words, Words." *Language Arts* 52 (1975): 1067–72.
2. Chall, Jeanne S. *Stages of Reading.* New York: McGraw-Hill Book Co., 1983.
3. Dyson, Anne H., and Genishi, Celia. "Children's Language for Learning." *Language Arts* 60 (1983): 751–57.
4. Federal Reserve Bank of Philadelphia and the Philadelphia Public Schools. *What Works in Reading.* Philadelphia: Office of Research and Evaluation, 1979.
5. Floriana, Bernard P. "Word Expansions for Sight Vocabulary." *The Reading Teacher* 33 (1978): 155–57.
6. Fox, Sharon E. "Oral Language Development, Past Studies and Current Directions." *Language Arts* 60 (1983): 234–43.
7. Goodman, Kenneth S. *Miscue Analysis: Application to Reading Instruction.* Urbana, Ill.: National Council of Teachers of English, 1973.
8. Goodman, Kenneth S. "Psycholinguistic Universals in the Reading Process." In *Psycholinguistics and Reading,* edited by Frank Smith, pp. 21–27. New York: Holt, Rinehart & Winston, 1973.
9. Goodman, Kenneth S., and Goodman, Yetta. "Reading and Writing Relationships: Pragmatic Functions." *Language Arts* 60 (1983): 590–99.

10. Gray, William S. *Improving Instruction in Reading: An Experimental Study*. Chicago, Ill.: University of Chicago, 1933.
11. Hamilton, Stephen F. "Socializing for Learning: Insights from Ecological Research in Classrooms." *The Reading Teacher* 37 (1983): 150–56.
12. Heilman, Arthur W., and Holmes, Elizabeth A. *Smuggling Language into the Teaching of Reading.* 2d ed. Columbus, Oh.: Charles E. Merrill Publishing Co., 1978.
13. Olson, D., and Torrance, N. "Learning to Meet the Requirements of Written Text: Language Development in the School Years." In *Writing: The Nature, Development, and Teaching of Written Communication,* edited by C. Frederiksen and J. Dominic. Hillsdale, N.J.: Lawrence Erlbaum Associates, 1981.
14. Ribovich, Jerilyn K. A Methodology for Teaching Concepts." *The Reading Teacher* 33 (1979): 285–89.
15. Rupley, William H., and Russell, Mary T. "The Interaction of Cognitive, Social, and Language Development." *Language Arts* 56 (1979): 697–99.
16. Rupley, William H.; Stansell, John C.; and Thomas, Jacqueline. "Relationship Between Reading and Writing." *English in Texas* 11 (Winter 1979): 41–43.
17. Shuy, Roger W. "What the Teacher Knows Is More Important Than Text or Test." *Language Arts* 58 (1981): 919–29.
18. Smith, Frank. *Psycholinguistics and Reading.* New York: Holt, Rinehart & Winston, 1978.
19. Smith, Frank. *Understanding Reading: A Psycholinguistic Analysis of Reading and Learning to Read.* 2d ed. New York: Holt, Rinehart & Winston, 1978.
20. Tierney, Robert J., and Pearson, P. David. "Toward a Composing Model of Reading." *Language Arts* 60 (1983): 568–80.
21. Weaver, Constance. *Psycholinguistics and Reading: From Process to Practice.* Cambridge, Mass.: Winthrop Publishers, 1980.
22. Wells, Gordon. *Learning through Interaction: The Study of Language Development.* London: Cambridge University Press, 1981.

3

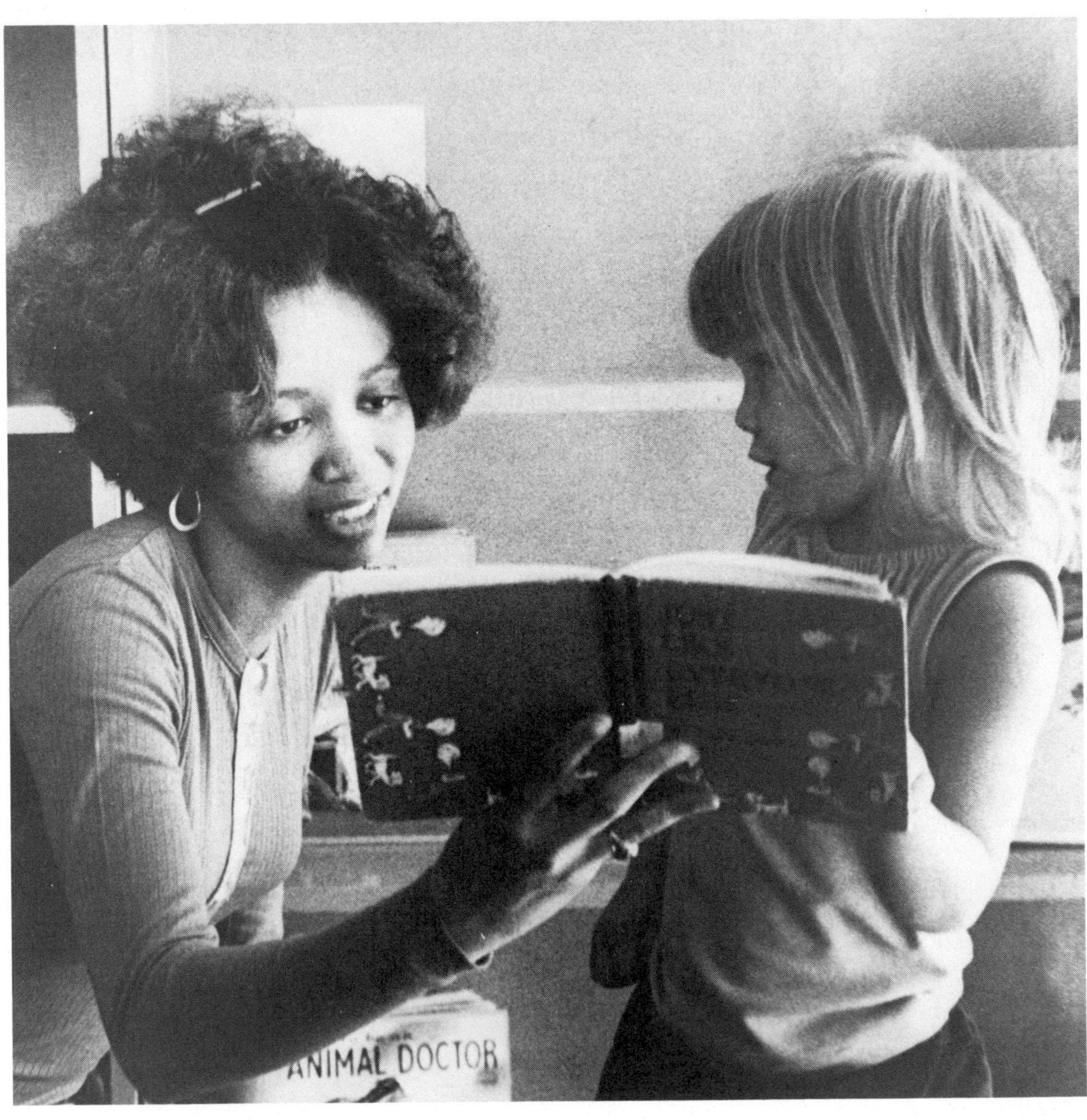

Teacher Effectiveness and Reading

For the Reader

The tremendous influence of teachers upon pupils' learning has been documented and emphasized for years. What has not been a large issue until relatively recently is what specific instructional behaviors teachers in various areas should use in order to have the greatest impact on pupils' learning. General qualities such as being mentally healthy and enthusiastic are certainly important, but what specifically sets apart effective teachers of reading from those who are not as effective? If you have had experience teaching reading, you realize the tremendous responsibilities you have in the classroom. If you are preparing to become a teacher, the realities and complexities of working with twenty-five to thirty-five students in a teaching situation might justifiably seem mind boggling to you. Every day you will be responsible for covering certain material, for ensuring your students' learning, for keeping discipline problems to a minimum, and for maintaining a pleasant atmosphere for learning. Appropriate questions at this stage would be, What exactly does an effective teacher of reading do? Where should I place my efforts so that the classroom experience is rewarding and profitable for both me and my students?

The text has as its overall objective that of providing you with the essential knowledge, concepts, skills, and abilities of an effective teacher of reading. Reading educators do not have all the answers to the above questions, but they do know some of the specific characteristics of an effective teacher of reading. The following chapter will synthesize for you those teacher characteristics that make a difference in teaching reading.

Preview

- Read over the Key Ideas that follow.
- Read each heading and subheading.
- Read the summary.
- Read the questions and statements at the end of the chapter.
- Return to the chapter text that follows the Key Ideas and begin reading.

Key Ideas

Major categories of research findings are
- universal traits
- process-product studies

student variables
experimental research
effective school characteristics

The four areas of importance in regard to competent reading instruction are
ongoing diagnosis
direct instruction and structure
opportunity to learn and apply reading abilities
pupil attention to and engagement in learning

A pattern of teaching practices is more likely to be related to learning than to a single practice.

Teaching patterns of effective teachers will differ by subject matter and grade level.

THE IMPORTANCE OF THE TEACHER

It is a generally accepted fact that the teacher plays a major role in determining the effectiveness of a reading program. Recognition of the major role that teachers have in effective reading instruction is not an idea unique to present-day reading instruction. Over the past fifty years, several major research efforts have pointed out just how important the teacher is. In the 1930s, Gates (22) found that not only was mental age correlated with beginning reading success, but also the type of teaching and the teacher's expertise and effectiveness were of equal importance. In her three-year study conducted during the mid 1960s, Jeanne Chall (15) concluded that it was the teacher who generally determined children's attitudes toward learning to read rather than the methods or materials used for instruction. The importance of the teacher is apparent in a major investigation that compared different reading instruction methods at the second-grade level (20). Wide differences in reading achievement were noted among classes and school systems even though they were using similar instructional methods. The differences call attention to the importance of the teacher's role in reading instruction.

Although these research projects were not the only ones conducted prior to the 1970s, they represent some of the major efforts that led to a strong belief that teacher quality determines the effectiveness of reading instruction. Some of these early investigations have implications for identifying effective teaching practices for today's reading instruction. However, more recent studies in this area hold considerable promise for improving the effectiveness of reading teachers. This chapter addresses both early and recent process-product research findings in teacher effectiveness that have been identified as being associated with effective reading instruction.

FLASHBACK

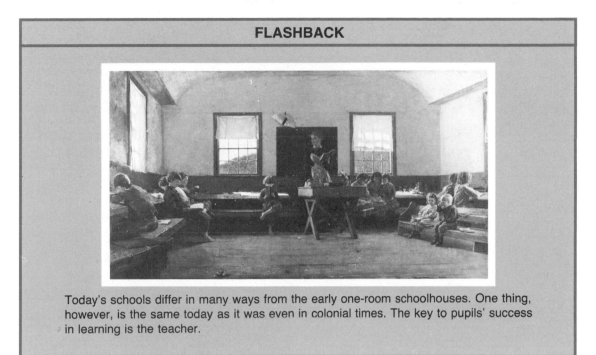

Today's schools differ in many ways from the early one-room schoolhouses. One thing, however, is the same today as it was even in colonial times. The key to pupils' success in learning is the teacher.

EARLY THINKING

From the mid 1950s into the late 1960s, the majority of investigations in reading teacher effectiveness looked at instructional materials and methods, teacher characteristics, and universal traits. In the early portion of this time span, the focus was on identifying the best methods or best materials to teach reading. Investigators were, in a sense, trying to identify teacher-proof methods and materials (15, 20). The implication of these earlier studies was that if a general method or material could be identified as successful for teaching all children to read, then the role of the teacher would simply be to serve the demands of the method or material. The results of such investigations were not very promising, and neither a best method nor a best set of materials was identified across various classroom settings.

Teacher characteristics such as personality, sex, education, years of experience, race, and so forth were also early areas of interest in terms of their effect on pupils' reading achievement. However, the information gained from such studies was not helpful in improving reading instruction. For example, information on personality supported the notion that effective reading teachers and teachers in general were good, decent individuals. They possessed characteristics associated with most well-adjusted people regardless of their occupation. However, educators are keenly aware that "Just being a 'nice' person doesn't a teacher of reading make, but a nice person doing some important things in terms of the reading process results in good teaching and good learning."[1]

In general, the early information gained from investigations of effectiveness did not produce many clear-cut guidelines for improving classroom reading instruction. They did, however, contribute significantly to the direction that later researchers took. A major contribution of these early studies was that they highlighted time and time again the importance of the teacher in effective reading instruction. They confirmed that the role of the teacher is extremely important and turned the focus toward process-product dimensions of effective teaching of reading (2, 25).

PROCESS-PRODUCT RESEARCH

During the late 1960s and into the 1970s researchers began to attend more to teachers' instructional activities and how these affected pupils' achievement. Actual teaching activities were referred to as *process variables.* These variables included behaviors that could be observed or reported on in classroom settings, such as teacher-initiated talk, pupil-initiated talk, and time spent on an instructional task (18). Another way of conceptualizing process variables is to look at how a teacher behaves when actually teaching (31).

The product dimension in process-product investigations in teacher effectiveness most often refers to pupils' achievement gain. Achievement gain focuses specifically on an important feature of any instruction, that is, how much pupils learned from the teacher's instruction. In terms of the major investigators who are interested in identifying teaching behaviors related to pupil achievement, the focus has been on either achievement gain or actual achievement versus expected or predicted achievement. Although this product is not the only outcome measure that teachers should be concerned with in teaching, it is a major thrust of public education and clearly within the domain of educators' primary responsibilities.

Most of the process-product research in teacher effectiveness has included reading achievement as a variable of interest. One reason that reading is a variable of interest is that pupils' reading gains can be mea-

1. John D. Pescosolido, 1980: personal communication.

sured. As a result, identification of effective process variables can often be related to effective reading instruction practices.

EMPHASIS ON THE STUDENT

Recently, a new focus has begun to develop in the area of teacher effectiveness research. Researchers are beginning to investigate not only teacher behavior but also student variables. Although many of the student variables that are investigated fall within the domain of direct teacher influence and control, the trend is not to specify specific teacher behaviors (35). For example, two variables of interest that pertain to stu-

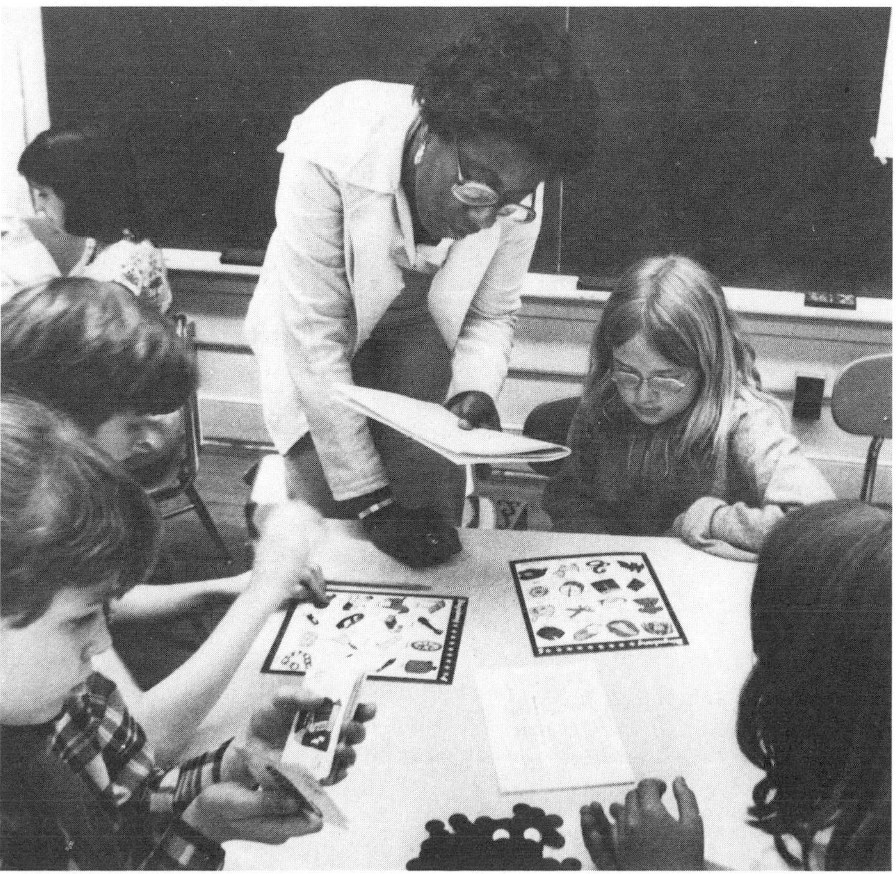

Knowing the characteristics of effective teaching improves the quality of reading instruction.

FLASHBACK

Arthur I. Gates was one of the most influential scholars in reading. His research and writing in areas of vocabulary control, reading interests, spelling, diagnosis, remediation, reading readiness, and handicapped children have influenced reading instruction and materials since the 1920s. Arthur I. Gates was truly a "man ahead of his time." He pointed out in the 1930s that a key factor in determining pupils' success in beginning reading was the teacher. Professor Gates' contribution to reading was recognized by the International Reading Association in 1961 when he received the Citation of Merit and again in 1968 with the International Award.

dents are *content covered* and *academic engaged time. Content covered* refers to whether or not pupils had an opportunity to learn the information or skills that were measured to determine their level of achievement. Academic engaged time is the time that students interact with pertinent academic materials at a moderate level of difficulty (5).

In addition to these two student variables, there are several others that appear to be related to achievement gain, particularly in the areas of reading. Several student variables that warrant teacher attention in reading instruction are discussed in the following sections.

The basic areas of interest and developmental characteristics of teacher effectiveness in reading instruction presented above identified some of the major areas of research over the last forty or fifty years. Essentially, the focus has shifted from broad, difficult-to-define variables to those that deal specifically with the process of teaching as it relates to pupils' achievement. Although there is still much to learn about what makes an effective teacher of reading, there exists a core of information that can stimulate concern for maximizing the effectiveness of classroom reading instruction.

Even though we cannot say for sure what makes an effective teacher of reading, we can identify some implications for practice. These instructional implications for practice become more credible when they are based on several investigations and viewed from a broader perspective than a single study. The following section discusses research findings that support a variety of instructional practices that have the potential to improve reading instruction.

IMPORTANT CONSIDERATIONS

It must be emphasized that research in reading teacher effectiveness cannot yet specify exact instructional guidelines that cause pupil learning. The results of this research are, perhaps, best viewed as having a positive effect on pupils' reading achievement. Yet, studies of teacher effectiveness have agreed to a remarkable degree on a number of characteristics related to student learning of basic skills (7). Teacher effectiveness in these studies is equated with increased student achievement on standardized reading tests. Thus, researchers have studied teachers as well as children to identify characteristics associated with significant achievement gain. To avoid simplistic explanations of teacher effectiveness, it must be acknowledged that the majority of studies have been nonexperimental, prohibiting the declaration that specific teacher behaviors actually cause student achievement. Too, the research has focused predominantly on mastery of word identification skills and literal comprehension skills as measured by standardized tests. The acquisition of critical and creative reading skills, essential goals of education, has not received much attention. Thus, it is entirely possible that teacher behaviors associated with positive growth of basic reading skills could be detrimental to the development of other types of outcomes such as the ability to evaluate and to synthesize information. Therefore, the following discussion should be regarded as providing tentative guidelines. As Medley (31) indicated in his extensive review of 289 teacher effectiveness research investigations:

> Suppose then, that we forget about the cause-and-effect inferences the researchers worry about and examine their findings for information about competent teacher performance. Suppose we examine them to see what they tell us about how the day-to-day practices of competent teachers differ from the day-to-day practices of less competent teachers. Does it not seem reasonable to expect that a novice teacher can benefit from learning the best current practices of competent teachers? What techniques and strategies are more likely to work for the novice on the job than those techniques and strategies that work best for other teachers? (p. 6)

We feel strongly that it is reasonable to expect that a reading teacher can benefit from knowing about practices of competent teachers. Results of process-product research can aid reading teachers in pinpointing some characteristics associated with effective teaching of reading.

Before proceeding to the discussion of reading teacher effectiveness studies, another cautionary note is needed. You must keep in mind that there is no teaching strategy or method that works best for all pupils all the time. Pupil factors such as socioeconomic status, experiential background, language capabilities, grade level, learning style, and so forth are important to consider as you sort out and analyze characteristics associated with competent reading teachers.

The major areas that appear to be of primary importance in competent reading instruction include:

- Diagnosing pupils' reading strengths and weaknesses.
- Structuring reading activities around a direct instructional format.
- Providing pupils with opportunities to learn and apply skills in actual reading tasks.
- Assuring that pupils attend to the learning tasks.

Diagnosing Pupil Reading

Teachers' use of reading diagnosis and its effect on pupils' reading achievement has been a part of many research investigations. In the early 1960s, Pescosolido (33) focused on identifying and appraising the effect that a variety of teacher factors had on pupils' achievement. One of the major factors associated with pupils' level of reading achievement was the teacher's ability to accurately judge pupils' attitudes toward reading.

Wade (50) included several measures of teacher diagnostic skills used in reading instruction in the second through the fifth grades. Skill areas that related directly to diagnosis included placement of students into groups, determination of reading growth following instruction, diagnosis of reading deficiencies, and categorization of word recognition errors. Interpretations of the results indicated that teachers in the schools who scored in the upper quartile on the skill measures had students who achieved at a higher level in reading than did teachers who scored at the bottom quartile.

An important diagnostic variable was identified by Weber (51) as being associated with successful teachers teaching in four inner-city schools. Among the instructional process variables that these successful teachers used that were not exhibited by less successful teachers was attention to reading diagnosis. Specifically, the successful reading teachers employed more ongoing evaluation of pupils' progress than did the less successful teachers.

A major research effort undertaken by the American Institute for Research (11) was to identify effective reading programs from across the country and develop dissemination packages about these effective programs. Over 1,500 program candidates were reviewed, of which 728 were evaluated for their effectiveness. One of the ten criteria used to evaluate these reading programs was that program evaluation data must focus on cognitive and academic achievement. Based on this criterion, only 9 of the 728 elementary programs were deemed effective. Several similar teacher process variables that related directly to reading diagnosis were evident in the 9 programs (37).

Teachers in the effective programs utilized procedures for closely monitoring their pupils' reading progress. These included using pre- and post-test achievement data in instructional decision making, employing instructional strategies based on diagnostic information, and specifying educational goals and objectives related to observable outcomes.

An attempt to determine whether or not a positive relationship exists between teacher effort in selected areas in the teaching of reading and student achievement was the focus of an investigation conducted by Blair (6). Elementary teachers were rated on the "Teacher Effort Scale in Reading." The scale compares teachers who manifested a great deal of effort in their work to those who did not. It has four subscales, including efforts to secure and use supplementary materials, provide differentiated instruction, keep records of student progress, and arrange conferences dealing with student progress. Results indicated significant differences in class achievement scores for teachers who exerted a greater amount of effort on the job in reading than for teachers who exerted a lesser amount of effort.

An ongoing longitudinal investigation over a two-year period on process variables associated with effective teachers of reading at third- and sixth-grade levels indicated that effective teachers of reading employ different diagnostic procedures than do less effective teachers (39). Effective teachers of reading used more ongoing diagnosis than did less effective teachers of reading. One ongoing diagnostic procedure that the effective teachers employed was a test-teach-test cycle to determine instructional causes for pupil difficulties in word recognition and comprehension skill areas.

Implications for Reading Instruction. Several instructional implications can be gleaned from the finding that diagnosis is an integral part of most effective instruction. First, effective reading teachers generally employed informal, ongoing diagnosis rather than infrequent administration of standardized achievement tests. Second, procedures were related to desired instructional outcomes rather than simply to a determination of pupils' grade level placement. Third, ongoing diagnosis combined with formal diagnosis allowed effective teachers to evaluate pupil outcomes more regularly than a diagnostic schedule occurring only a few times during the school year. Effective reading teachers seem to use diagnostic data to frequently adjust instruction in terms of its impact on pupils' learning in order to increase pupils' chances of success in instructional tasks.

The fact that effective teachers diagnosed pupils' reading more frequently than less effective teachers needs to be carefully analyzed. Diagnosis, as mentioned in chapter 1, has by itself no beneficial effects. Therefore, you could not expect that by increasing the frequency of diagnosis pupils' reading achievement would improve.

Effective reading teachers appear to expend considerable effort in developing and using ongoing types of diagnosis; however, it is how they incorporated this information into their process of reading instruction that probably led to higher reading achievement. Another plausible explanation is that the teachers were able to select instructional strategies appropriate to the desired pupil outcomes in relation to pupils' existing reading capabilities.

Reading instructional tasks that are too difficult for pupils limit their chances of being successful while learning. Teachers who pace their reading instruction by progressing from one reading objective to the next in small, closely related steps and maximize pupils' success rates in answering questions and completing independent assignments increase pupils' chances of being successful (13). Ongoing reading diagnosis that focuses on both pupils' reading strengths and weaknesses should enable the teacher to identify instructional procedures that increase the pupils' chances of success. A balance of high- and medium-success reading tasks, with greater emphasis given to high-success tasks, results in pupils who achieve more at the end of the school year, retain more over the summer, and have a positive attitude toward school (45). Rather than responding to each pupil's individual needs, the effective teachers appear to have used diagnostic information to select teaching strategies that maximized the likelihood of success so the majority of pupils could achieve the goals of reading instruction.

Effective teachers of reading employ of ongoing, informal diagnosis combined with standardized diagnosis to:

- Adjust instruction in terms of its impact on pupils' learning.
- Identify instructional activities and tasks that ensure maximum pupil success.
- Select instructional strategies appropriate to desired reading outcomes in relation to pupils' existing reading capabilities.
- Pace reading instruction by progressing in small, related steps to maximize pupils' success rate.

Classroom Structure and Direct Instruction

Important features of diagnosis employed by effective reading teachers appear to be frequency of occurrence and how data are used to identify appropriate instructional strategies at an appropriate level of difficulty for the pupils. Although many of these investigations did not specify what process variables teachers employed, it seems logical that many of the teachers used information about their pupils to plan instruction that was structured and based on a direct format. This idea becomes more credible because some of the researchers who looked at teachers' use of diagnosis also investigated instructional practices. For example, Wade (50), Pescosolido (33), Bowers et al. (11), and Rupley (39) reported that effective teachers either taught or perceived that reading should be taught in a structured, teacher-directed fashion.

Teachers who employ a direct instruction format in teaching reading are being identified across several recent research investigations as effective. Direct instruction is conceptualized clearly by Barak Rosenshine (35), a recognized authority in teacher effectiveness research, as:

> teaching activities focused on academic matters where goals are clear to students; time allocated for instruction is sufficient and continuous; content coverage is extensive; student performance is monitored; questions are at a low cognitive level and produce many correct responses; and feedback to students is immediate and academically oriented . . . teacher *controls* instructional goals, *chooses* materials appropriate for student's level, and paces the instructional episode. Interaction is characterized as structured but not authoritarian; rather, learning takes place in a convivial academic atmosphere. (p. 9a)

The major characteristics of direct instruction identified by King (28) are "objectives projected into experiences, emphasis on intellectual development, analysis of necessary knowledge and skills, sequence of specific learning experiences, formal scheduling with definite time allocations, specific skills activities and objective evaluation" (p. 505).

Direct instruction is defined by Good (23) as "active teaching." He perceives it as an instructional program where a teacher identifies and specifies learning outcomes, uses ongoing diagnosis to assess pupils' progress, and makes frequent, clear presentations that illustrate and set purposes for doing assigned tasks.

The importance of structure and direct instruction and their effects on pupils' acheivement were a major finding in a review of teacher effectiveness research conducted by Medley (31). He evaluated 289 process-product studies to determine whether or not reported relationships should be included in his review. Only 14 of the studies met the rigor-ous criteria established for inclusion. These investigations were conducted in the first through third grades with children from primarily low socioeconomic status (SES) homes. All fourteen studies employed measures of gains in reading, which have direct bearing on identifying effective reading instructional practices.

Medley's extensive review identified some important features of classroom structure and direct instruction associated with competent reading teachers of low SES primary grade pupils.

Effective teachers of low SES primary level pupils devoted more time to task-related activities or "academic" activities than did less effective teachers. They spent less time discussing things that were not related to lesson content, and the major part of each day was devoted to structured activities, which left less time for pupils to be unoccupied.

Organization of the environment was also highly structured in effective teachers' classrooms. Results from five studies (4, 13, 17, 29, 46) offered evidence that competent teachers' classrooms are characterized by less deviant or disruptive pupil behavior. Generally, classrooms were controlled with little use of criticism, and pupil behavior was directed by the use of task-related comments. This does not mean that classrooms were always quiet and regimented, but that pupils were busy with instructional tasks rather than disruptive behavior. Effective teachers' classrooms were teacher centered in the sense that the teacher monitored pupils' learning and guided the direction of that learning. Less competent teachers permitted more independent learning, gave pupils choices, and allowed pupils to participate in activities without the teacher present.

The effect of direct instruction on low SES pupils' reading achievement is another prominent finding of Medley's review. One of the notable findings dealt with the effect of teachers' questioning on pupils' level of achievement.

Results from three of the studies (14, 32, 46) indicated that effective teachers do not generally amplify, discuss, or use pupil answers when reacting to pupil responses. This was interpreted to be consistent with effective teacher preference for low-level questions that are primarily fact oriented. It seems that the competent teachers of low SES pupils keep the level of interaction low in terms of complexity and pupil initiative. They ask and encourage pupils to respond to low-level, narrow questions. Further evidence to support the conclusion that competent teachers keep the level of questions asked at low levels was found in studies conducted by Soar and Soar (47), Coker et al. (17), and Stallings and Kaskowitz (48).

The pattern of questioning was that the teacher asked a low-level factual question, pupil responded, and feedback that addressed pupil's response was given. In low SES classrooms, teacher feedback was usually an attempt to aid the pupil in giving the correct answer often by rewording the question or by asking an easier question. This type of questioning strategy seems to maximize the probability that pupils will experience success.

It should not be inferred from these findings on questioning techniques that teacher expectations for low SES students are lower than for other students. This research evidence only deals with the difficulty level of the questions presented and with maximizing student success. Also, the research described is predominantly concerned with basic skill mastery. Effective teachers certainly encourage all children at various times of the day to sharpen their higher cognitive processing, that is, analysis, synthesis, and evaluation and to practice reasoning and problem solving abilities.

Structure and direct teaching appear to be important features associated with effective teaching of reading. Reviews of recent process-product investigations (23, 36) generally conclude that these features are associated with higher achievement gains; however, the degree of structure and direct teaching vary according to SES, subject matter, and grade level. For this reason they should be addressed in relation to different educational settings and adjusted accordingly. The importance of this can be seen in the following discussion.

An important concern of the research conducted by McDonald (29) was to determine the influence of a variety of factors on both pupil learning and teacher performance in reading and mathematics. Two important implications for effective teaching were identified. First, a *pattern* of teaching practices is more likely to be related to learning than a single practice. This means that a group of teaching strategies in concert with each other, not a single strategy, is related to pupil mastery of reading skills. Second, teaching patterns of effective teachers will differ by subject matter and grade level.

In second grade, a pattern of reading instruction that allowed teachers to be accessible to pupils for instruction, to work in small groups, and to use a variety of materials was most effective. Question strategies related to reading skill processes were most effective when they included specific prompts and required locating the answer in the text.

In the fifth grade, different reading instructional process variables were associated with effective teachers. The use of a wide variety of materials did not correlate with effective reading programs. Also, teacher practices that encouraged and sustained interaction about ideas were most effective. Questioning used by competent fifth-grade teachers was thought provoking and dealt with stimulating pupils to think about and react to what they read.

A difference in effective instructional practices in terms of pupils' grade level is noted in Brophy's (13) review of teacher effectiveness research. In the early grades, effective teachers elicited responses and provided feedback to each child in small-group settings. In the middle and upper grades, large groups, more discussion at higher cognitive levels, less teacher direction, increased pace through content, and more pupil freedom are associated with effective teaching.

The critical need to analyze carefully the appropriate level of structure and direct teaching for a given classroom is pointed out by Soar and Soar (47). They found that effective teachers used a balance of "good" behaviors. Both pupil self-directed and teacher-controlled instructional activities were included. Variations in the type of activity appeared to be related directly to the learning task. Highly structured and task-focused learning was most effective for low-level types of learning, such as memorization. Pupil-directed, less-structured instruction was most effective for complex or abstract learning tasks. Even with higher-level learning tasks, however, it appeared that some structure and direction were needed.

An important consideration in whether or not to vary the level of structure and direct instruction in teaching reading is the educational objectives that pupils are to attain (34). If the desired reading outcome focuses on creative or inquiry skills, then structure and direct instruction should be minimized. If, however, the desired reading outcomes focus on basic reading skills such as word identification, context clues, and dictionary usage, then greater degrees of structure and direct instruction would be necessary. In both instances, some structure is needed. In the lower elementary levels, for low ability pupils and for pupils who are dependent on external control over instructional events, structure and direct instruction appear to be necessary (13, 34).

Implications for Reading Instruction. Two possible reasons why direct instruction works are offered by Good (23). First, direct instruction emphasizes the importance of the individual teacher. It may give teachers the motivation needed to plan their days fully, take their responsibilities seriously, and meet their expectations successfully. Second, teachers are charged with fulfilling and improving a variety of pupils' needs and abilities, ranging from personal hygiene and civic awareness to academic achievement. Direct instruction provides a clear focus on achievement and may help teachers conceptualize and emphasize achievement goals with greater specificity and enthusiasm.

The importance of reading teachers' giving analytical consideration to classroom structure and direct teaching as a means for improving their teaching effectiveness seems eminently clear. Structure in the reading program is not necessarily regimented and inflexible. Structure and direct instruction vary in relation to desired reading outcomes and grade level. Attending to these variables in teaching reading by analyzing how they influence pupils' reading and making changes when necessary could enhance teacher effectiveness.

Structure and a direct instruction model should not be viewed as universal traits that will result in effective teaching regardless of the setting. If they are viewed as promising variables and are evaluated critically in relation to an individual's teaching setting, then they can aid teachers in making informed choices and hold considerable promise for improving the effectiveness of reading instruction.

Effective teachers of reading attend to classroom structure and direct instruction to:

- Maximize pupils' involvement in tasks or academic activities related specifically to lesson content and desired outcomes.
- Control pupil behavior by the use of task-related comments rather than criticizing or scolding pupils for not focusing on learning tasks.
- Monitor and guide the direction of pupils' learning.
- Ask lower-level questions of low SES pupils that maximize their chances of responding successfully.
- Vary the degree of structure in relation to desired reading behavioral objectives. Less structure and less direct instruction are employed for inquiry or creative outcomes.
- Utilize a pattern of instruction at the primary level that allows them to be accessible to pupils, work in small groups, and use a variety of materials.
- Utilize a pattern of instruction at the intermediate level that allows for larger instructional groups, more discussion at higher cognitive levels, less teacher direction, and greater pupil-initiated learning.

Opportunity to Learn

Opportunity to learn refers to whether or not pupils have been taught the skills relevant to reading areas for which they are assessed. Teachers who specify outcome reading behaviors prior to teaching and teach content relevant to these outcomes often have pupils who achieve at a higher reading level than those teachers who do not specify pupil outcome behaviors prior to instruction (38).

Opportunity to learn is a variable associated with the direct instruction model. Although teachers could employ a structured and direct instruction teaching model, if the focus of instruction does not relate to an assessed learning task or a valued outcome, then pupils have not had an opportunity to learn the product. For example, if pupils do well in learning isolated reading skills as a result of intensive instruction, but do poorly in actual reading, it may be due to lack of opportunity to learn how to apply such skills in actual reading tasks.

The importance of providing pupils with opportunities to apply their reading skills in actual reading tasks was a major finding of a study

Effective teachers provide pupils with opportunities to apply reading skills to meaningful reading tasks.

of 1,828 Philadelphia fourth graders (49). When pupils were not in their daily whole-class or small-group reading instruction group, they spent a large portion of class time reading silently, which resulted in more growth in reading.

Does mastery of basic skills necessarily enhance independent learning? Results of a status study of middle school students by Blair and Turner (9,10) indicated basic skill mastery does not automatically equate with increased independent or recreational reading ability. Highlighting the teacher's role in this development, the authors concluded, "The ultimate success or failure of a developmental reading program has to be judged on the degree to which students can apply their abilities and skills in varied reading situations" (9).

The importance of providing opportunities for pupils to apply their reading skills in actual reading tasks is apparent in a reading program developed by the Irwin School in Charlotte, North Carolina (16). In addition to increasing the amount of pupils' engaged time, using ongoing diagnosis to plan instruction, and maintaining appropriate levels of structure and direct instruction, teachers also focus on applying reading skills to comprehension tasks and literature appreciation acitivites. Preliminary results indicate that the third, fourth, and fifth graders involved in the program are progressing at a rate of three months' growth for every two months of instruction.

Providing pupils with opportunities to apply their reading skills in silent reading appears to be extremely important. However, teachers need to be sure to use materials in which students can experience a high degree of success. The more time pupils spend in actual reading with which they can be highly successful, the more they will probably achieve. The more they are involved in actual reading tasks that limit success, the less likely they are to enhance their reading achievement (45).

Rosenshine noted in two reviews of teacher effectiveness research (35,36) that opportunity to learn has been studied in many ways. In the majority of these studies significant relationships were found between opportunity to learn and pupil achievement gain.

Implications for Reading Instruction. The effect of opportunity to learn is a commonsense factor associated with reading achievement. Pupils cannot be expected to do well in a reading area in which they have not had an opportunity to learn. When reading achievement is measured by the pupil's performance on a task or skill that has not been taught, then that pupil will not do well. Conversely, achievement should be higher when tested tasks and skills have been emphasized (41).

A distinction needs to be made between opportunity to learn and "coverage" of materials and topics. Opportunity to learn, ongoing diagnosis, structure, and direct instruction are interrelated. The reading instruction that is offered must relate to diagnostic data, desired outcomes, instructional format, and application in actual reading tasks. Opportunity to learn should be determined by the desired learning outcomes, not a compulsion to simply cover the content.

Effective teachers of reading attend to pupils' opportunity to learn and apply skills in actual reading situations to:

- Assure that instruction focuses on desired and valued reading outcomes.
- Guard against isolated reading skills becoming an end in themselves rather than a means to effective reading comprehension.
- Provide for application of reading skills in silent reading tasks that ensure maximum pupil success.
- Assure that pupils understand how to apply their reading skills for the purpose of reading enjoyment.

Attention to the Learning Tasks

Pupil attention to learning tasks and engagement in pertinent learning materials are logically under the direct supervision of the teacher. In the area of reading instruction, several investigations (3,6, 39) have found that teachers who employ ongoing diagnosis of pupils' reading development coupled with instruction based on diagnostic data had higher achieving pupils in reading. Again, the importance of ongoing diagnosis is pointed out. However, in these investigations, diagnostic data were used to identify appropriate levels of difficulty for instruction. You could speculate that pupil engagement and attention to learning tasks are enhanced when instruction is at a moderate level of difficulty rather than being too easy or too difficult.

The results of McDonald's Beginning Teacher Evaluation Study, Phase II (30) provide support for the critical importance of maintaining a reasonably high level of pupil involvement. Appropriate reading materials alone are not sufficient to maximize achievement. Effective reading teachers not only used appropriate materials, but also attended to actively engaging pupils in learning from the materials. Simply requiring that all pupils complete a similar learning task does not assure maximum attention to the task. Pupils approach various learning tasks with varying degrees of interest, capabilities, and understanding. It would seem that effective reading teachers take these into account as they attempt to engage pupils in meaningful reading instruction.

Rosenshine (35) presents a very clear example of the importance of the total daily engaged minutes. Two elementary teachers' classrooms were observed over ten weeks as they taught reading. Both teachers used the same materials for reading instruction and both had similar pupils. One teacher allotted thirty minutes per day to reading instruction and ran a highly structured classroom. Pupils were recorded as engaged in instruction 80 percent of the time. The second teacher allotted sixty minutes to reading instruction, but ran a less structured classroom and required less engagement in instruction. Pupils were engaged an average of 65 percent of the time.

The teacher who allotted thirty minutes daily to reading engaged the pupils in instruction twenty-four minutes daily. The second teacher engaged pupils in reading instruction an average of thirty-nine minutes per day. Over the ten-week period, the second teacher's pupils proportionately completed more reading materials than did the first teacher's pupils. Rosenshine notes: "A teacher is not obligated to maintain high student engagement at all times; what is more critical is the total number of academically engaged *minutes* and the amount of content covered" (p. 9).

Directly related to student engagement is the teacher's classroom management ability. Very simply, effective teachers are effective classroom managers. Although the previously discussed characteristics are components of good classroom management, the emphasis on techniques for managing students is not only popular today but necessary. It is necessary because how classroom time is spent has a direct influence on student learning. In addition to the instructional components of classroom management, chapter 12 is devoted to this topic; an excellent guide on organization and management techniques can be found in *Classroom Management for Elementary Teachers* by Evertson et al. (21).

Implications for Reading Instruction. Attention to learning and engagement in materials appear to be important features for pupils' learning in both directed and individual instruction. Pupils who do not attend to teacher instruction or to information presented in instructional materials cannot be expected to learn what is presented. The key here seems to be active engagement in reading instruction, not necessarily the total time allocated. Pupils could be passive or indifferent to reading instruction even though a large amount of instructional time is given to teaching reading. The number of minutes allocated for instruction has not been shown to have an effect on pupils' level of reading achievement (23, 43). However, with all other things being equal, the greater the amount of time spent on instruction, the higher the achievement will be (45).

Effective teachers of reading attend to maximizing pupils' attention to and engagement in learning tasks to:

- Allocate more time to reading instruction and to keep pupils actively engaged in learning during the instructional period.
- Utilize instruction at the primary level that allows for pupils' spending at least 50 percent of their time engaged in tasks with which they will be successful.
- Provide academic feedback to pupils about their work to increase attention to tasks and amount of engaged time.
- Utilize instruction at the intermediate level that provides for interaction with the teacher and other pupils and also allows intermediate level pupils to work cooperatively in achieving specified goals.
- Incorporate positive reward systems to reinforce specific attending behaviors, such as materialistic awards, sincere teacher praise, tokens, and so forth. Specific rewards are intended to reward pupils' thinking and effort rather than just correct answers.
- Set purposes for learning and present an overview of what is to be learned. Examples and illustrations are used to relate new learning to what has been presented previously and to help pupils understand how to apply what they are learning.

Experimental Research

The majority of studies on teacher effectiveness have been nonexperimental in nature. Although results of many studies identified the same characteristics of effective instruction, results of correlational research prohibit the declaration of cause and effect relationships between specific characteristics and student achievement (27). The next logical step in the evolution of teacher effectiveness research was the design of experimental studies utilizing the results of previous research. An example of an experimental study would be to train one group of teachers in specific teaching strategies and not train another group. Following an adequate amount of time, students of both groups of teachers would be tested to determine the effects of the specific training. One influential study of this type was carried out by Anderson, Evertson, and Brophy (1) in first grade reading instruction. Teachers were trained in techniques and procedures gleaned from process-product studies on teacher effectiveness. This study supported previous process-product results, including the importance of a high percentage of academic engaged time and the direct instruction format for teaching (12).

Effective Schools

Paralleling investigations of desirable teacher characteristics in the teaching of reading have been studies delineating the variables associated with effective schools (with respect to student achievement in reading and math). The plural "variables" is important to note because a major finding spanning a multitude of investigations on school effectiveness is that there are many factors, not just one or two, accounting for an effective school (44).

Although the teacher characteristics identified in effective school research match the qualities previously discussed, the effective school is influenced by the interaction of a host of variables—student, teacher, classroom, program, school administration, and home background (8, 19).

Hersh (26) reviewed the literature on effective schools and listed two sets of attributes associated with most effective schools (see Figure 3.1). While the discussion in this chapter has centered on the instructional and curriculum attributes, the social attributes highlight "that schools which are most effective create a distinctive sense of community within the school building, a community derived from conditions that profoundly affect how and why educators and students treat each other, how much that precious commodity time is valued, and how well academic and social learning skills are integrated" (26, p. 3). Effective schools communicate a heavy emphasis on basic skills and a student conduct code necessary for learning, hold high expectations for their students, retain teachers who possess a strong sense of efficacy (a belief

Social Organization	Instruction and Curriculum
Clear Academic and Social Behavior Goals Order and Discipline High Expectations Teacher Efficacy Pervasive Caring Public Rewards and Incentives Administrative Leadership Community Support	High Academic Learning Time (ALT) Frequent and Monitored Homework Frequent Monitoring of Student Progress Tightly Coupled Curriculum Variety of Teaching Strategies Opportunities for Student Responsibility

FIGURE 3.1 Attributes of effective schools. (Source: Richard M. Hersh, "What Makes Some Schools and Teachers More Effective," in *The Future of Teacher Education: Needed Research and Practice,* edited by D. Corrigan, D. Palmer, and P. Alexander. College Station, Tex.: Dean's Grant Project, Texas A&M Unversity, 1982.)

that all my students will learn and be successful), create an atmosphere of caring for students, reward student achievement, have supportive principals who create and promote reading excellence, and promote active parent and community involvement.

SUMMARY

Time and time again the importance of the teacher in effective reading instruction has been pointed out by many reading research studies. Although the number of research investigations focusing on the importance of the teacher in reading instruction is small in comparison with the total number of reading investigations conducted, the results are promising. Admittedly, there is much yet to learn about what makes an effective reading teacher. However, much information is available about quality reading instruction that warrants careful consideration by teachers. Teachers who include provisions for ongoing diagnosis, structure, and direct instruction and attention to and engagement in learning are being identified as being more effective than teachers who do not include these practices.

It seems reasonable that all reading teachers can benefit from knowing about practices of competent teachers. Results of teacher effectiveness research can aid in pinpointing some characteristics associated with effective teaching of reading. Teachers of reading can then sort out and analyze competent teacher characteristics in terms of their own capabilities and classrooms.

DIAGNOSIS

Focus: Pupils' reading strengths and weaknesses and instruction.

Features: Ongoing—combining both informal and standardized measures that focus on measurable reading outcomes related directly to instructional goals. Data are used to plan appropriate classroom structure and direct instruction.

Guiding Questions: Are your students placed on their instructional level in reading materials (i.e., not too difficult, not too easy, the "just right" level)?

Are you continually using informal observational techniques and diagnostic tests to detect your students' strengths and weaknesses in the various areas of word identification and comprehension?

Is the instruction your students are receiving based on a diagnosis of their needs?

Are you adjusting your instruction according to students' progress?

STRUCTURE AND DIRECT INSTRUCTION

Focus: Instructional organization and process.

Features: Stated pupil purposes for learning that focus on academic tasks. Emphasizes the importance of the teacher in learning and provides a focus on the product for identifying and conceptualizing instructional processes. Differentiated by grade level and type of task.

Guiding Questions: Do you vary the amount of structure in your class depending on student characteristics, grade level of students, and objectives of instruction?

Do you allow for less structure when teaching more complex tasks such as soliciting emotional responses to a story or judging the desirability on acceptability of a character's behaviors?

Do you devise more structured direct instruction lessons when teaching the basic reading skills of word identification and comprehension?

Do you give your students appropriate feedback?

OPPORTUNITY TO LEARN AND APPLY SKILLS

Focus: Instruction aimed at measurable and desired reading outcomes. Application of skills in actual reading tasks.

Features: Matching the instruction to desired outcomes and teaching content relevant to these. Providing opportunities to maximize pupils' understanding of the purposes for learning skills and applying these skills to actual reading situations.

Guiding Questions: Do you allow for sufficient instructional time to teach what your students need to know?

Do you allow time for your students to practice their reading skills in actual reading situations?

Do you plan ways to monitor student practice of targeted reading skills?

Are students practicing their reading skills in materials that will ensure a high degree of success?

ATTENTION TO AND ENGAGEMENT IN LEARNING TASKS

Focus: Maintaining a high level of pupil involvement in learning.

Features: Maximizing pupils' involvement and attention to learning by focusing on pupils' needs based on diagnostic data, involving pupils in instruction at a moderate level of difficulty, and monitoring engagement in and maximizing attention to learning by focusing on tasks related directly to desired outcomes.

Guiding Questions: Do you clearly communicate the specific purpose of each lesson to your students?

Do you plan your instruction to ensure a high percentage of academic engaged time?

Do you design seatwork assignments to ensure student involvement?

Do you use a reward system with students to reinforce specific positive behaviors?

FIGURE 3.2 Teacher process variables associated with effective reading instruction.

Keep in mind that there is no teaching strategy, method, or material that works all of the time. What seems to be reflective of quality reading instruction is presented in Figure 3.2. Attention to these four areas should enable teachers to better determine and improve the effectiveness of their reading instruction.

YOUR POINT OF VIEW

Discussion Questions

1. What possible reasons account for the different characteristics of effective primary grade teachers versus effective intermediate grade teachers?
2. What are the implications of the direct instruction model to "open education" advocates?

Take a Stand For or Against

1. Good teachers are born, not made.
2. The concept of "opportunity to learn" is the most powerful variable in education.
3. Small-group direct instruction is more beneficial than large-group direct instruction.

BIBLIOGRAPHY

1. Anderson, Linda; Evertson, Carolyn; and Brophy, Jere E. "An Experimental Study of Effective Teaching in First-Grade Reading Groups." *Elementary School Journal* 79: 193–223.
2. Artley, A. Sterl. "The Teacher Variables in the Teaching of Reading." *The Reading Teacher* 23 (1969): 239–48.
3. Averch, Harvey A., et al. *How Effective Is Schooling? A Critical Review and Synthesis of Research Findings.* Santa Monica, Calif.: Rand Corporation, 1971.
4. Bemis, K. A., and Luft, Max. "Relationships Between Teacher Behavior, Pupil Behavior, and Pupil Achievement." In *Mirrors for Behavior: An Anthology of Observation Instruments Continued,* Supplement, vol. A, edited by Anita Simon and E. Gill Boyer. Philadelphia: Research for Better Schools, 1970.
5. Berliner, David C.; Fisher, C. W.; Filby, N.; and Marliene, R. *Proposal for*

Phase III of Beginning Teacher Evaluation Study. San Francisco: Far West Laboratory for Educational Research and Development, 1976.

6. Blair, Timothy R. "Relationship of Teacher Effort and Student Achievement in Reading." Ph.D. diss., University of Illinois, 1975.
7. Blair, Timothy R. "Teacher Effectiveness: The Know-How To Improve Student Learning." *The Reading Teacher* 38 (1984): 138–42.
8. Blair, Timothy R. "What Makes An Effective Reading Program Effective?" in *Reading Research Review,* edited by Richard Thompson. Afton, Minn.: Burgess Publishing Co., 1984.
9. Blair, Timothy R., and Turner, Edward C. "Basic Skill Emphasis: Its Effect On Independent Reading Development." *Resources in Education* (1983) (ERIC Document Reproduction Service No. ED 226 324)
10. Blair, Timothy R., and Turner, Edward C. "Ideal and Real World of Recreational Reading." *Journal of Reading Education* 10 (1985): 15–21.
11. Bowers, John E.; Campeau, Peggy L.; and Roberts, A. Oscar. *Identifying, Validating and Multi-Media Packaging of Effective Reading Programs, Final Report.* Palo Alto, Calif.: American Institute for Research, 1974.
12. Brophy, Jere E. "Principles For Conducting First Grade Reading Group Instruction." In *The Effective Teacher of Reading: Research into Practice,* edited by James Hoffman. Newark, Del.: International Reading Association, 1986.
13. Brophy, Jere E. "Teacher Behavior and Student Learning." *Educational Leadership* 37 (1979): 33–38.
14. Brophy, Jere E., and Evertson, Carolyn M. *Process and Product Correlations in the Texas Teacher Effectiveness Study: Final Report.* Austin: University of Texas, 1974.
15. Chall, Jeanne S. *Learning to Read: The Great Debate.* New York: McGraw-Hill, 1967.
16. Cohen, Ruth G., and Irons, Bruce R. "Doubling Up in Reading." *The Allyn and Bacon Reading Newsletter* 7 (Nov. 1979): 4.
17. Coker, Homer; Lorentz, Jeffrey L.; and Coker, Joan. *Interim Report on Carroll County CBTC Project, Fall, 1976.* Atlanta: Georgia State Department of Education, 1976.
18. Cruickshank, Donald R. "Syntheses of Selected, Recent Research on Teacher Effects." *Journal of Teacher Education* 27 (Spring 1976): 57–60.
19. Duffy, Gerald G. "Fighting Off The Alligators: What Research in Real Classrooms Has to Say About Reading Instruction." *Journal of Reading Behavior* 14 (1982): 357–74.
20. Dykstra, Robert. *Continuation of the Coordinating Center for First-Grade Reading Instruction Programs, Final Report.* Washington, D.C.: U.S. Department of Health, Education, and Welfare, Office of Education, Bureau of Research, 1967.
21. Evertson, Carolyn M; Emmer, Edmund T.; Clements, Barbara S.; Sanford, Julie R.; and Worsham, Murray E. *Classroom Management for Elementary Teachers.* Englewood Cliffs, N.J.: Prentice-Hall, 1984.
22. Gates, Arthur I. "The Necessary Age for Beginning Reading." *Elementary School Journal* 37 (1937): 497–508.
23. Good, Thomas L. "Teacher Effectiveness in the Elementary School." *Journal of Teacher Education* 30 (1979): 52–64.

24. Guthrie, John T.; Martuza, V.; and Seifert, M. *Impacts of Instructional Time in Reading.* Newark, Del.: International Reading Association, 1976.
25. Hamachek, D. "Characteristics of Good Teachers and Implications for Teacher Education." *Phi Delta Kappan* 50 (1969): 341–45.
26. Hersh, Richard M. "What Makes Some Schools and Teachers More Effective." In *The Future of Teacher Education: Needed Research and Practice,* edited by D. Corrigan, D. Palmer, and P. Alexander. College Station, Tex.: Dean's Grant Project, Texas A&M University, 1982.
27. Hoffman, James, ed. *The Effective Teacher of Reading: Research into Practice.* Newark, Del.: International Reading Association, 1986.
28. King, Ethel M. "Prereading Programs: Direct Versus Incidental Teacher." *The Reading Teacher* 31 (1978): 504–9.
29. McDonald, Frederick J. *Summary Report: Beginning Teacher Evaluation Study: Phase II, 1973–74.* Princeton, N.J.: Educational Testing Service, 1976.
30. McDonald, Frederick J., and Elias, Patricia. *The Effects of Teaching Performance on Pupil Learning. Beginning Teacher Evaluation Study. Phase II, 1973–74.* Final Report: vol. 1. Princeton, N.J.: Educational Testing Service, 1976.
31. Medley, Donald M. *Teacher Competence and Teacher Effectiveness: A Review of Process-Product Research.* Washington, D. C.: American Association of Colleges for Teacher Education, 1977.
32. Perham, B. H. "A Study of Multiple Relationships Among Teacher Characteristics, Teaching Behaviors, and Criterion-Referenced Student Performances in Mathematics." Ph.D. diss., Northwestern University, 1973.
33. Pescosolido, John D. "The Identification and Appraisal of Certain Major Factors in the Teaching of Reading." Ph.D. diss., University of Connecticut, 1962.
34. Peterson, Penelope L. "Direct Instruction: Effective for What and for Whom?" *Educational Leadership* 37 (1979): 46–48.
35. Rosenshine, Barak V. "Academic Engaged Time, Content Covered, and Direct Instruction." Paper presented at the American Education Research Association Annual Meeting. New York, 1977.
36. Rosenshine, Barak V. "Recent Research on Teaching Behaviors and Student Achievement." *Journal of Teacher Education* 27 (Spring 1976): 61–64.
37. Rupley, William H. "Effective Reading Programs." *The Reading Teacher* 29 (1976): 612–23.
38. Rupley, William H. "Reading Instructional Practices of Third and Sixth Grade Teachers: An Exploratory Investigation." Paper presented at the Annual Meeting of the College Reading Association. Boston, 1979.
39. Rupley, William H. "Stability of Teacher Effect on Pupils' Reading Achievement Gain Over a Two Year Period and Its Relation to Instructional Emphases." In *Reading: Theory, Research and Practice,* edited by P. David Pearson, pp. 69–72. Clemson, S.C.: National Reading Conference, 1977.
40. Rupley, William H. "Teacher Instructional Emphases and Pupil Achievement in Reading." *Peabody Journal of Education* 54 (1977): 286–91.
41. Rupley, William H., and Blair, Timothy R. "Characteristics of Effective Reading Instruction." *Educational Leadership* 36 (1978): 171–73.

42. Rupley, William H., and Blair, Timothy R. *Reading Diagnosis and Remediation: Classroom and Clinic.* 2d ed. Boston: Houghton Mifflin Publishing Co., 1983.
43. Rupley, William H., and McNamara, James F. "Longitudinal Investigation of the Effects of Teachers' Reading Instructional Emphasis and Pupil Engaged Time in Reading on Pupils' Reading Achievement." Paper presented at the Annual Meeting of the National Reading Conference. St. Petersburg, Fla., 1978.
44. Samuels, S. Jay. "Characteristics of Exemplary Reading Programs." In *Comprehension and Teaching: Research Reviews,* edited by J. T. Guthrie, 255–273. Newark, Del.: International Reading Association, 1981.
45. Schneider, E. Joseph. "Researchers Discover Formula of Success In Student Learning." *Educational R & D Report* 2 (Fall 1979): 1–6.
46. Soar, Robert S. *Follow Through Classroom Process Measurement and Pupil Growth (1970–71). Final Report.* Gainesville, Fla.: Institute for Development of Human Resources, College of Education, University of Florida, 1973.
47. Soar, Robert S., and Soar, Ruth M. "An Empirical Analysis of Selected Follow Through Programs: An Example of a Process Approach to Evaluation." In *Early Childhood Education, Part II,* edited by Ira J. Gordon. Chicago: National Society for the Study of Education, 1972.
48. Stallings, Jane, and Kaskowitz, D. *Follow Through Classroom Observation Evaluation, 1972–73, A Study of Implementation.* Menlo Park, Calif.: Stanford Research Institute, 1974.
49. Vicino, Frank L., ed. "Philadelphia Study Pinpoints Factors in Improving Reading Achievement." *Pre Post Press* 5 (1979): 1.
50. Wade, Eugene W. "The Construction and Validation of a Test of Ten Teacher Skills Used in Reading Instruction, Grade 2–5." Ph.D. diss., Indiana University, 1960.
51. Weber, G. "Inner-City Children Can Be Taught to Read: Four Successful Schools." Washington, D.C.: Council for Basic Education, Occasional Paper No. 18, 1971.

4

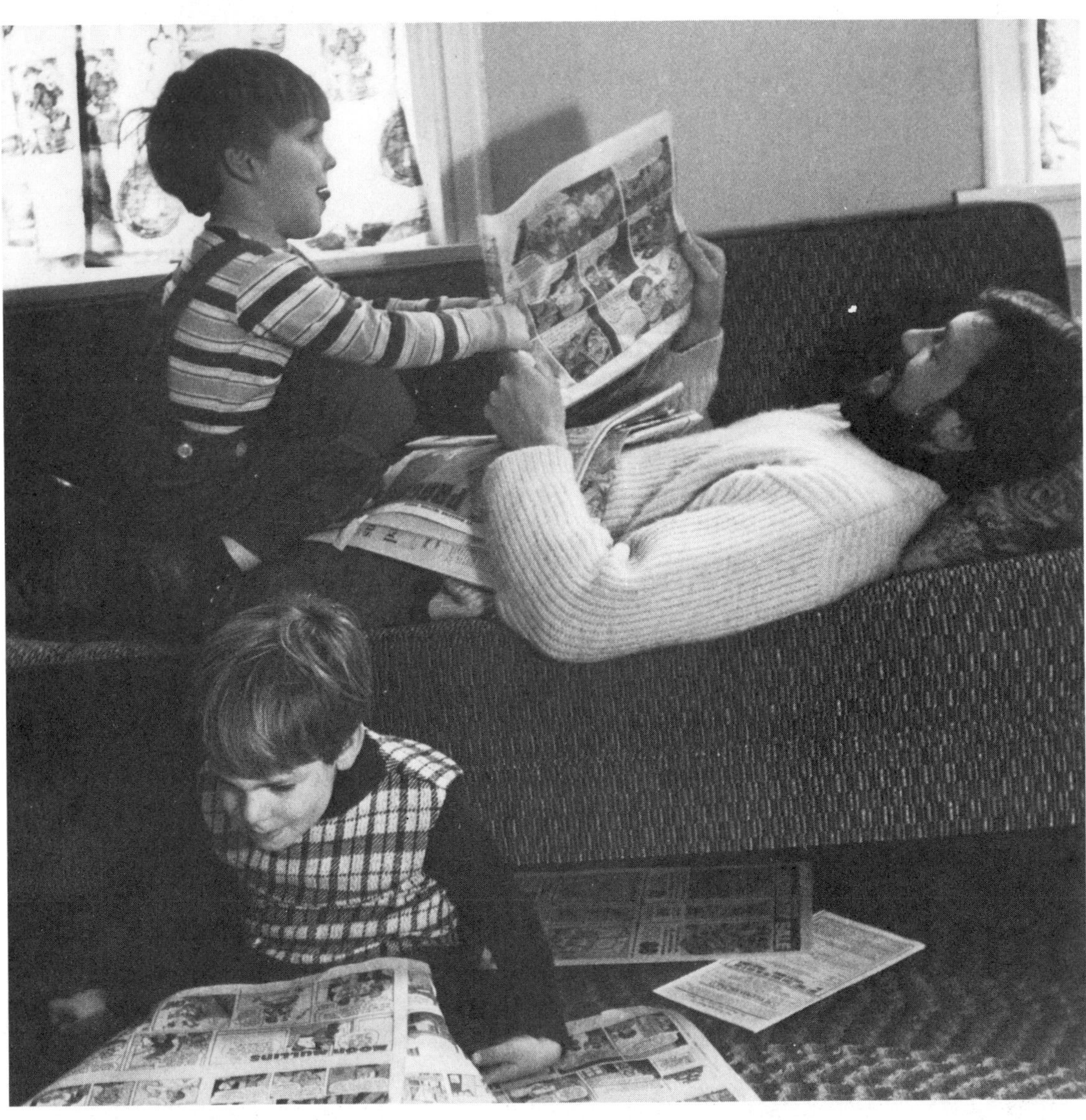

Reading Readiness

For the Reader

Can you recall your first experiences in learning to read? Chances are slim that you would remember unless perhaps you learned to read before entering school or if you "weren't ready" and experienced difficulty. A long-standing issue in reading is when children should learn to read and how exactly this should be accomplished. Imagine the kindergarten teacher's job of preparing twenty to thirty or more children from diverse backgrounds to read. Pressure is immense from a variety of sources, such as parents, school boards, and state education agencies, that these children be adequately prepared to read or that they read by the end of the school year. In this chapter we will attempt to review the concept and issue of readiness, the factors associated with successful reading, and instructional implications for teachers.

Preview

- Read over the Key Ideas that follow.
- Read each heading and subheading.
- Read the summary.
- Read the questions and statements at the end of the chapter.
- Return to the chapter text that follows the Key Ideas and begin reading.

Key Ideas

A variety of factors affect a child's readiness to read:

- verbal comprehension
- concepts about print
- demands of instruction
- understanding the language of instruction
- visual attention to print
- experiential/conceptual background
- phonological awareness
- methods and materials for instruction
- decoding speed
- language background

A child does not have to possess all of the readiness abilities in order to learn how to read; learning to read is being ready for one step after another.

A child's being "ready" to read depends upon the type and quality of instruction afforded the child.
There is no dichotomy between reading readiness instruction and reading instruction.
Reading readiness tests alone lack precision in predicting reading achievement.
A good readiness program provides for a high degree of flexibility.

THE CORRECT MATCH

Readiness for learning at all educational levels was highlighted in chapter 1 under Principle 10. Our concern in this chapter is readiness as it relates to beginning reading instruction. Many states have recently legislated that formal reading instruction begin in kindergarten. For example, the Texas State Board of Education (32) identified essential elements in kindergarten reading programs to include: (1) discriminating sounds for each letter of the alphabet; (2) discriminating visual shapes, forms, and letters; (3) understanding the direction of formal print; (4) following oral directions; (5) telling what a story is about; (6) appreciating repetition, rhyme, rhythm, and alliteration; (7) following simple story line in stories read aloud; (8) supplying missing words in oral context; and (9) recognizing the ordinal and spatial features of print. This list does not include all of the essential elements that are required in reading instruction at the kindergarten level in Texas; however, it is representative of the fact that many of the reading skills which were typically taught at the first-grade level are now expected to be taught in kindergarten.

Although the efforts of state boards of education are intended to enhance the quality of public education, they cannot legislate that all children will equally benefit from formal reading instruction in kindergarten. It is unrealistic to think that each child will profit equally from what is presented in the classroom. Most educators agree that children entering kindergarten and first grade vary in terms of learning style, learning rate, and experiential/conceptual and language backgrounds. A good readiness program is not aimed at removing individual differences among pupils, but at seeing that each child has experiences that will remove any hindrances to learning. Thus, it would be difficult to defend a readiness program that involved all children doing the same things for equal periods of time. Such a program would ignore the known facts about individual differences and the instructional cues that might be disclosed by readiness tests, teacher observations, parent comments, and informal evaluation.

CONCEPT OF READINESS

For several decades the term *reading readiness* has been used as if it had some universally accepted meaning. MacGinitie (25) points out that the question "Is the child ready to read?" is poorly phrased on at least two counts. First, it ignores that learning to read is a long-term developmental process, not a fixed point on a continuum. "Reading is a process that takes some time for any person at any age. Part way through the process, children become ready to profit from experience they would have found meaningless at the beginning" (p. 398). If reading is viewed as a developmental process, then readers must understand the essential features of the process, such as how it is used, how it functions, and what are its important elements at various stages of children's reading development (4, 7). Understandings such as these do not occur at a fixed point but are developed, enhanced, modified, rejected, or discovered as children synthesize past experiences/concepts with new experiences/concepts. Second, MacGinitie questions the idea that a child's readiness for reading can be determined through readiness scores, when actual reading methodology and instruction have not been specified. The reading readiness period can be viewed as an attempt to synthesize and augment new experiences with previous experiences children have had. Children's previous experiences with language and their experiential/conceptual backgrounds are extremely important because they determine, to a large degree, the kind and amount of experience that is needed, which must be provided by the school. How accurately the teacher identifies children's previous experiences, that is, their readiness in terms of reading, determines to a large extent their later success or failure in reading. This point is well illustrated by Durkin's (9) application of Ausubel's definition of "readiness" to reading. Ausubel (1) defined readiness as the "adequacy of existing capacity in relation to the demands of a given learning task" (p. 246). Considering this definition in relation to reading instruction in kindergarten and first grade leads to the following implications: (1) If learning tasks are fixed, that is, they cannot be modified to consider children's entering capabilities (existing capacities), then some children will be ready to read and some will not be ready. (2) If learning tasks are flexible, that is, they can be modified to appropriately meet the range of children's entering capabilities (existing capacities), then all children are ready for reading. The second implication would, therefore, encourage teachers to base their decisions about readiness on each child's learning needs. Reading readiness, then, is viewed as quality reading instruction that is aimed at helping children develop and enhance their reading capabil-

FLASHBACK

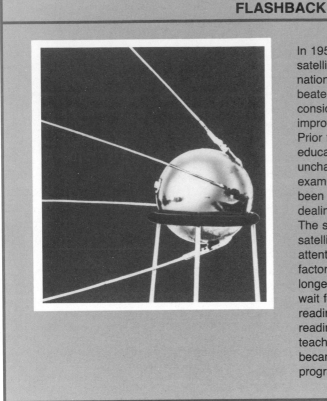

In 1957 the Russians launched the first satellite to circle the earth. There was much national concern that the Russians had beaten us into space, and, as a result, considerable attention was given to improving the quality of American education. Prior to the launching of Sputnik, American education had remained basically unchanged for a lengthy period of time. For example, reading readiness programs had been developed around hereditary factors dealing with maturation since the 1920s. The successful launching of a Russian satellite caused educators to give increased attention to the effects of environmental factors on young children's learning. No longer would teachers be encouraged to wait for a child to develop readiness for reading; they were now to begin developing reading readiness. Assessment and the teaching of reading readiness rapidly became a part of many kindergarten programs throughout the country.

ities: for some this may be an emerging understanding of rhyming words; for others it may be the use of context to identify words. The point is that readiness activities are not necessarily different from beginning reading instruction activities.

VARIABILITY IN LEARNING RATES

Prior to focusing on specific readiness factors and diagnostic measures, teachers should be aware of the differences that exist among children in regard to their rate of learning to read. One topic that has received considerable attention is sex differences in learning to read. Even though all aspects of these two areas may not be clearly understood at the moment, awareness of the data may provide insights for teachers who want to understand children as learners.

Sex Differences

Research data compiled over the past several decades have shown that girls as a group usually experience less difficulty in learning how to read than do boys as a group (23). A number of explanations have been offered for why girls are generally more successful than boys in early reading achievement. Among the major explanations are maturation differences, the school curriculum and environment, the content of reading materials, and cultural environments.

Maturation Differences. Boys and girls mature at different rates, and some phases of growth have been assumed to be closely related to reading. Since the data are conclusive that girls develop more rapidly than boys, this hypothesis is sometimes seen as the key to the problem under discussion. However, the likelihood of this factor alone being the key to sex differences in early reading achievement is questionable. If maturation were a primary factor in explaining sex differences in reading, you would expect to find such differences in the reading performance of children in other countries. Cross-cultural studies have not found major sex differences in pupils' reading achievement (8, 14, 21, 29, 33). Based on these cross-cultural comparisons, it appears very unlikely that maturation explains the differences between male and female early reading achievement.

School Curriculum and Environment. The school curriculum and environment at the primary level have also been considered as major reasons for sex differences in reading achievement. Two important variables related to both the school curriculum and the environment are the teacher and her behavior patterns. The effect of female teachers on the achievement of boys has been considered as a possible reason for explaining sex differences in reading development (3, 22). In a recent review of the effect of female teachers on boys' reading achievement, Johnson and Greenbaum (20) categorized their findings into four curriculum and environment areas with the following conclusions:

- *Negative treatment*—Boys appear to have more types of interaction with both male and female teachers. Female teachers do not exhibit a greater amount of negative treatment to boys.
- *Grades*—There is little evidence to suggest that female teachers are biased toward giving higher grades to girls.
- *Higher achievement*—No support was found for the idea that boys' achievement is higher when taught by males.
- *Alienation*—It does not appear, based on the research evidence, that female teachers structure their classrooms in ways that alienate boys.

Presently, there is lack of sufficient evidence to conclude that female teachers have a negative effect on boys' reading growth. In some instances, there may be boys who would profit by having male teachers, but at this time the sex of the teacher does not appear to explain the differences between boys' and girls' early reading achievement (20).

Content of Reading Materials. Another feature of beginning reading instruction that supposedly contributes to the early reading problems of boys is the content of what they are required to read. This hypothesis was based on the basal readers of the 1960s, which were rather sterile, repetitious, and centered on topics considerably less challenging to boys than to girls. However, you would think that this dull, uninspiring content should be equally unattractive to both boys and girls.

Some investigations (2, 20) have found that the content of reading materials has a similar appeal to both boys and girls. Furthermore, story content did not often reflect those things that would appeal only to girls.

Cultural Environments. Several recent studies have suggested that cultural factors may play a significant role in producing sex differences in

Boys may perceive reading as a female activity, which can negatively influence their motivation.

early reading performance. A number of these studies suggest that boys perceive reading as a female activity (7, 12, 15). This perception could result in a conflict between their role as a student and role as a male. In school, boys are encouraged to be passive and conforming, whereas socially they are encouraged to be active, aggressive, and achieving (20).

Cultural factors may be the most credible factors affecting sex differences in reading. A boy's perception of reading as a female activity could have a negative influence on his motivation to read and engagement in reading instruction. The important implication here is that there are variables within the learning environment that, when taken into consideration, could enhance the reading performance of boys. A major concern would be enhancing the appeal of reading to boys rather than reinforcing their conception that reading is for girls only.

READING READINESS FACTORS

Numerous factors have been studied in relation to their impact on learning to read. Since reading is a complicated process, it is difficult to establish precise relationships or to completely rule out certain factors as being of no importance. The following discussion will be limited to a few factors that have been either widely studied or accepted, but may not be necessarily valid.

Mental Age and Intelligence Factors

During the 1930s and 1940s, the importance of mental age for success in beginning reading appeared to be settled once and for all. A most interesting phenomenon of this period was the almost universal acceptance that children should have reached a mental age (MA) of six and one-half years before they were instructed in reading. This concept was based on the report and conclusions of one study published in 1931 by Morphett and Washburne (27).

During the 1950s and into the 1960s, the mental age concept of readiness for beginning reading instruction was one of the most prominent findings in reading research. This concept persisted despite the fact that the study suggesting it was never replicated. Another interesting event that occurred in the 1930s was that Gates (13) published a study containing data that contradicted those of Morphett and Washburne.

Gates challenged the idea that there was a critical mental age below which reading cannot be mastered. He stated, "The fact remains . . . that it has by no means been proved as yet that a mental age of six and a half is a proper minimum to prescribe for learning to read by all

FLASHBACK

The research conducted by Mabel V. Morphett and Carleton Washburne in the thirties and forties led to the almost universally accepted idea that children must attain a mental age of six and a half years before they are taught to read. The results of their investigation have been referred to as research that made a difference, but should not have. A child's readiness for reading is dependent on more than his mental age. The quality and demands of reading instruction determine, to a large degree, a child's success in beginning reading.

school methods or organizations or all types of teaching skills and procedures" (p. 497). In a study of four different first-grade classes, Gates maintained that much of a child's success in beginning reading is accounted for by the instructional procedures found in classrooms.

Even today there is a tendency to explain success in beginning reading as being due to high intelligence. One reason could be because some children master reading at an early age without the benefit of formal instruction. In our society these early readers are often viewed with fascination. There are many case studies that report on individual children as early readers. The biographies of a number of famous individuals noted for high achievement in science, art, and literature also report early reading. These data, along with certain other case studies of early readers, have tended to associate early reading with genius or very high intellectual ability.

Data from several inquiries have suggested that high intelligence is not an absolute for early reading. Durkin (10) found in her studies of early readers many youngsters who fell within an average range of intelligence (IQs in the range of 90–120). Recent research by Stanovich, Cunningham and Feeman (30) pointed out that general intelligence shares a moderate relationship with early reading; however, they noted three relatively independent abilities that are important in predicting early reading progress. These abilities were (1) verbal comprehension ability, (2) phonological awareness (knowledge of spelling-to-sound correspondence), and (3) decoding speed (rapidly recognizing words). They stated, "It appears that our understanding of early reading progress will not be enhanced by substituting notions of general intelligence for a process analysis of individual differences in reading ability" (p. 296). This does not mean that general intelligence is not important in early reading, it is simply not the sole explanation for success in beginning reading.

Culturally and Language Different Children

Both school and society have focused attention on the preschool experiences of children who are economically deprived or whose cultural background and language patterns differ significantly from those of middle-class children. The reason for this concern stems from the fact that many children who come from culturally different backgrounds exhibit difficulty in adjusting to a curriculum that was developed without regard for their previous experiences.

In theory, our educational philosophy is that the school will adjust to the child's needs and meet those needs with regard to what to teach.

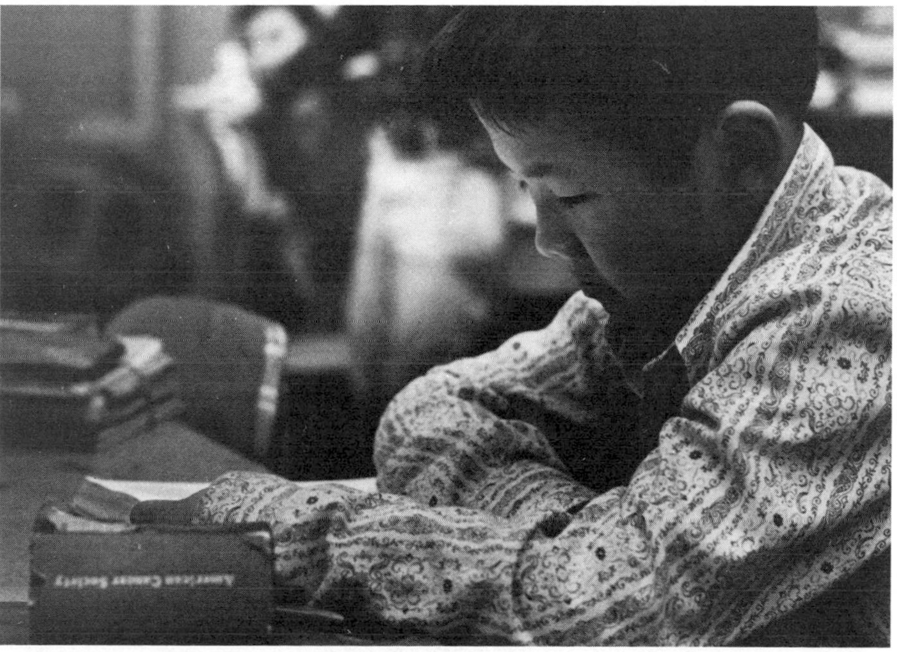

Children from different cultural backgrounds need a curriculum that reflects their previous experiences.

However, in actual practice, schools frequently expect children to "adjust" to a curriculum that is quite different from their present needs and past experiences. As children fail to learn under these circumstances, the school often places the blame on the learner, instead of making the necessary adjustments in instruction and content. The importance of meeting the needs of culturally and language different children is discussed in detail in chapter 14.

Language

The relationship of reading to language was discussed in chapter 2. Bridging the gap between a five- or six-year-old child's wealth of oral language facility and the child's ability to process written language depends upon a combination of factors and skills. A central factor associated with readiness is the child's understanding of the concepts of written language.

Adults often take for granted that young children are aware of what reading is all about, the concept of left-to-right progression of print, and the meanings of basic language terms used in teaching reading. For example, the term *word* is an essential one in most beginning reading instruction. The teacher may tell the children that they will look at words, learn how to figure out words, write words, and so forth (16). Before beginning school few children have been asked to think about words in their oral language usage and even fewer children have been asked to think about written words. Researchers have pointed out that for children between the ages of three and six there is a major gap between their understanding of language and their understanding of metalinguistics (26). Metalinguistics is an understanding of the language used to talk about language and how different features of language function. Downing (8) refers to the specialized terminology that teachers use in reading instruction (phrase, sentence, letter, and sound) as the reading register. He states that some children may have no idea what we are talking about when we use these terms in our reading instruction.

Children's understanding of the concepts represented by the reading register is not brought about by merely defining these terms, but through a rich, language-based reading program emphasizing oral and written activities. Such activities would focus on more exposure to print in the form of oral reading, the incorporation of various art forms (music, art, creative dramatics) with reading, and opportunities to experience language through writing (18). A sample lesson in a reading readiness program is illustrated on page 1 of the first color insert, located at the conclusion of chapter 4.

There is sufficient evidence in the research literature that integrating reading and writing may enhance reading achievement and chil-

Learning how to integrate reading and writing skills enhances the student's understanding of language.

dren's understanding of the function of print (31, 34). Through writing children begin to develop a better understanding of the language concepts of reading, the terminology used to talk about print (letters, words, sentences, etc.), and that both reading and writing require the "composition of meaning" (34). Two major language concepts that appear to be essential for success in both writing and reading are that print represents a message and that this message must be as sensible as spoken language (5).

In addition to helping children develop an understanding that print represents language, there are other important linguistic understandings that facilitate a successful start in learning to read. Important linguistic concepts include understanding that print is read left to right, a word is set off by spaces, and that a word and a letter are not the same (25).

READINESS AND READING: NOT A DICHOTOMY

Readiness activities are not necessarily different from activities used in beginning reading instruction. An effective first-grade teacher may honestly believe that she doesn't use a readiness program or teach readiness activities. The odds are, however, that she will also state that she moves along with reading at a pace the children can follow. If she were observed by individuals who strongly believe in readiness activities, they might well agree that her readiness program is the best in the district.

For example, assume you see a film clip of a group being taught the concept of a word by matching a sentence strip to a sentence on a chart and then cutting the sentence into words. Could you say with assurance that you are observing a readiness activity or reading instruction? Some teachers use this technique early in the school year and again (or a variation of it) in December and February. Teachers in higher grades may also use it with any child who has not mastered this important language-reading concept.

Some instructional materials have designated certain tasks as prereading activities, and this term is widely accepted as a synonym for readiness activities. Providing practice in discriminating rhyming elements in words is one excellent and widely used prereading activity. However, the use of rhyming elements goes beyond the prereading level. Work with rhyming words in context will often be presented in later reading instruction.

ASSESSING READINESS FOR READING

Assessing children's readiness for reading is an important feature of an effective reading program. Assessment techniques should focus on the experiential/conceptual areas associated with success in beginning reading. Many of these areas were presented earlier, such as language, concept of print, language of reading instruction, and phonological awareness. Several recent investigations dealing with success in beginning reading offer support for the importance of these areas. Clay (6) identified four cueing systems that children must attend to if they are to become readers: (1) visual attention to print, (2) directional rules about position and movement, (3) talking like a book, and (4) hearing sounds in words (4, 26). Chall (4) in her presentation of reading stages notes that for children to move into stage one, the initial reading or decoding stage, they must acquire knowledge and skill in (1) knowing that books are for reading; (2) understanding that certain words begin with certain sounds; (3) hearing rhyming in words; (4) recognizing some common signs and labels; (5) pretending to read by retelling stories while looking at the pages; (6) playing with and knowing uses of books, pencils, and paper; and (7) possibly engaging in early writing (invented spellings). The research of Stanovich, Cunningham, and Feeman (30) mentioned earlier supports the developmental view of reading offered by Chall (4). They identified verbal comprehension, phonological awareness, and decoding speed as skills and abilities that contribute to reading progress in the first grade. These skills and abilities become more interrelated as the age of children increases.

Major differences between above average and below average first-grade readers' understanding of print-related concepts were pointed out in a study by Johns (19). He found that above average readers possessed better understandings about print-related concepts for the areas of print direction, letter-word concepts, and advanced print (punctuation marks and reversible words) than did less capable readers. These findings add further support to the idea that success in beginning reading may be related to children's acquisition of basic skills and abilities similar to those noted by Clay (6) and Chall (4).

Many types of assessment techniques and strategies are available to determine children's readiness for beginning reading that focus on the skills and abilities noted above. Included among these assessment procedures are reading readiness tests, informal teacher observations and assessments, and information from parents. Those assessment procedures that are used in most elementary reading programs are discussed in the following section. They are not extremely time consuming nor do they require extensive training for a teacher to use them. However, when assessing students' reading readiness, keep in mind that readiness should be determined in terms of students' existing capabilities in relation to the demands of instruction.

Reading Readiness Tests

A large number of reading readiness tests are available, and they vary in terms of content, format, and purpose (35). These tests are often used to predict future performance in reading and to diagnose specific strengths and weaknesses. Readiness tests are, as a rule, administered as group tests, though some may contain one or more subtests that must be given individually. Representative test items include:

- *Associating pictured objects with the spoken word for that object.* The child is given a page with four or five different pictures in a line. One picture might be of a frog, another a boat, another a shoe, etc. He is asked to "underline (or circle) the shoe."
- *Visual discrimination.* Four or five similar objects are shown. One is already circled or checked. One other picture in the row is exactly like this one. The child is to mark the identical picture. Variations of this test include the recognition of one or more digits or letters that are identical to the stimulus at the beginning of the line.
- *Sentence comprehension.* The child must grasp the meaning of an entire sentence. Before the child are pictures of a calendar, clock,

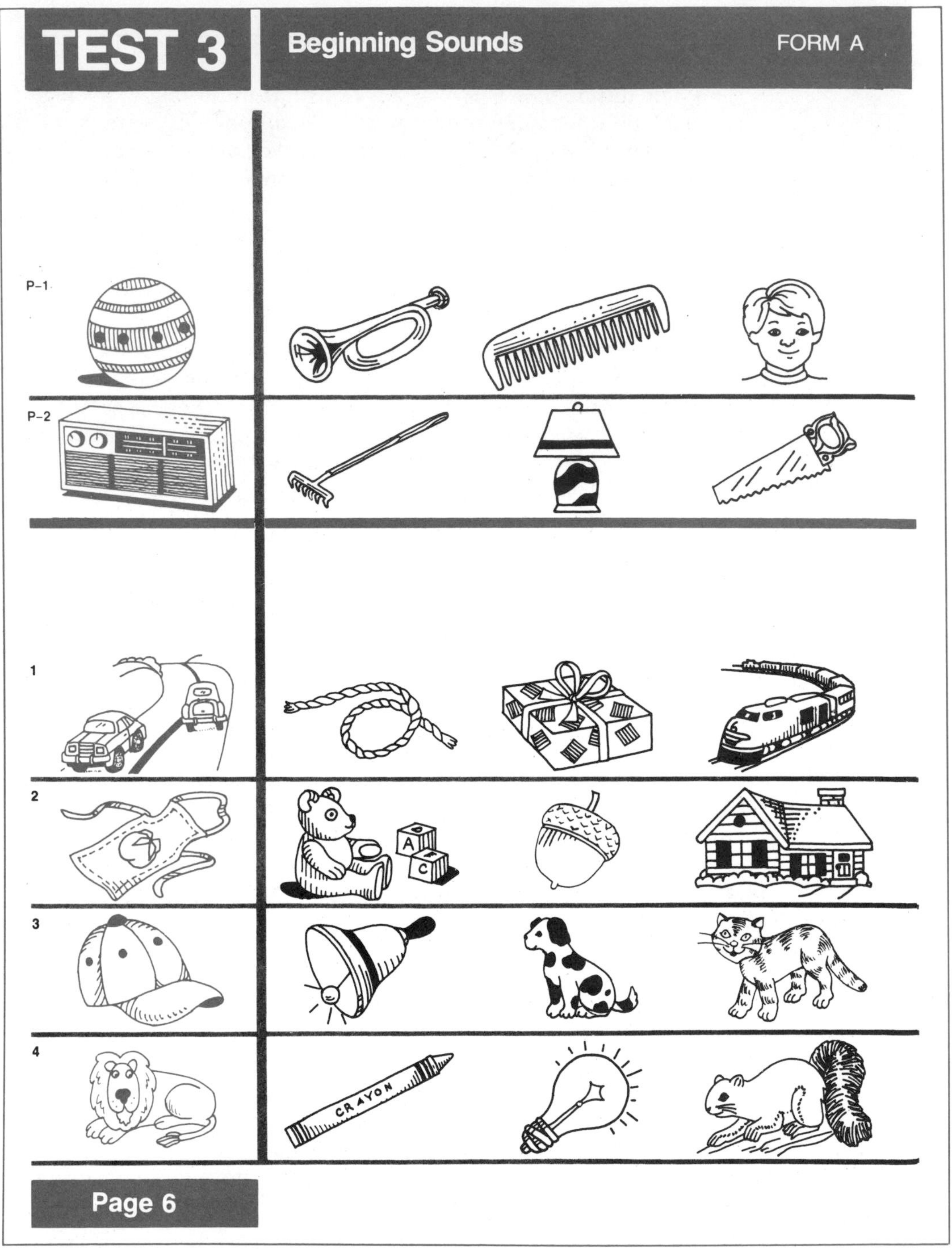

Above, ***An example of items found on a readiness test;*** **right,** ***a summary sheet to record a pupil's performance.***

a

Clymer-Barrett Readiness Test
Summary Page

FORM A

Name ____ Boy ____ Girl ____ Age (Years/Months) ____

Teacher ____ Grade ____ School ____

City ____ State ____ Testing Date ____

Full Form

Test	Score	Combined Scores	Stanine
Visual Discrimination			
1 Recognizing Letters	____	____	☐
2 Matching Words	____		
Auditory Discrimination			
3 Beginning Sounds	____	____	☐
4 Ending Sounds	____		
Visual-Motor Coordination			
5 Completing Shapes	____	____	☐
6 Copy-A-Sentence	____		

Total Score ☐ Percentile Rank ☐

Stanine ☐

Short Form

Test	Score
1 Recognizing Letters	____
3 Beginning Sounds	____

Total Score ☐ Percentile Rank ☐

Stanine ☐

Name

Percentile Rank

Comments

Readiness Survey Overall Rating

Low

Average

High

lawnmower, and thermometer. "Mark the one which tells us the time."

- *Drawing a human figure.* In a space provided in the test booklet, the child is asked to draw a person.
- *Ability to count and to write numbers.* A series of identical objects is shown, and the child is asked to mark the second, fourth, or fifth object from the left.
- *Ability to recognize digits.* The child is asked to underline or put an "x" on a certain digit in a series.
- *Word recognition.* A common object (doll, house, barn, cow, baby, etc.) is pictured. Three or four words, including the symbol for the picture, are shown, and the child is to mark the word represented by the picture.
- *Copying a model.* A series of geometric figures and capital letters serve as models. The child is to duplicate the stimulus.
- *Auditory discrimination.* On a group test this might consist of a series of pictures placed horizontally across the page. At the left of each series is a stimulus picture. The child marks each object in the series whose name begins with the same initial sound as the name of the stimulus. If the first picture is that of a dog, for example, it might be followed by illustrations of a doll, a cow, a door, and a ball. Another test situation would be marking each picture whose name rhymes with the name of the stimulus picture.

Readiness tests vary as to the types of skills tested. Some of the older tests lack provision for measuring auditory discrimination, but most of the more recently published ones include such a subtest. In general, norms are based on total scores that determine pupil placement in categories, such as superior, above average, average, or poor. Since a chief objective of readiness tests is prediction of success in learning to read, it is hoped that the test will separate the ready from the unready and that, when first-grade pupils are thus identified, the school will adjust the curriculum accordingly. This brings us to the question of just how accurately reading readiness tests predict success in beginning reading.

Predictive Value of Readiness Tests. Over the past fifty years, hundreds of studies involving the use of readiness tests have been reported. Any attempt to distill and interpret this large amount of data is complicated by a number of factors. Few studies are actually comparable since different studies used different population samples, measured the impact of different variables, controlled some variables and ignored others, and used different tests, statistical treatments, and limits of significance.

In addition, test items on readiness tests may purport to measure a particular skill that is generally viewed as an absolute necessity for learning to read. However, even though test items focus on a particular skill, they may call for responses that do not parallel the actual tasks children perform in reading. As a result, readiness tests are rather imperfect in predicting children's success in beginning reading because the methods and materials used for teaching vary considerably between programs and teachers.

Experimental data indicated that readiness tests and teacher evaluations appear to be equally effective in predicting success in beginning reading (35). This does not imply that readiness tests have little value for teachers, but it does suggest that educators should not project into these tests a degree of predictive infallibility that they do not possess. It is possible that readiness tests may "overrate" children in regard to their reading readiness because some of the tasks are more related to the child's previous experiences than to what he will encounter in beginning reading. Rather than using overall readiness test results to determine if a child is "ready" or "not ready," closer attention should be given to determining the child's strengths and weaknesses as they relate to the demands of instruction (see chapter 11 for a discussion of qualitative analysis in reading diagnosis).

It must be kept in mind that readiness tests measure only selected factors that are believed to be related to reading. There are many other factors that affect learning to read, such as the instruction the children receive, attitude toward the teacher and toward reading, children's reaction to varying degrees of success and failure, home stability, and so forth. The purpose of administering such tests is not to get a score for each child or to rank or compare children in the group, but rather to secure data for planning experiences that will promote successful learning.

In fact, unless the teacher is alert, actual scores may divert attention from the child's behavior meriting closer scrutiny. This tendency is particularly marked when the administration of tests has become an end in itself. If teachers would analyze readiness test results, and if they would adjust their teaching to each child's needs, many reading problems might be averted.

Informal Teacher Assessment and Observation

Two powerful assessment tools are available to the teacher as he gathers information about children's readiness: informal assessment procedures and observation. Pikulski (28) offers a rather straightforward approach for determining children's readiness for reading. He suggests, "children should be exposed to regular and frequent opportunities to read. . . . The question of ready or not ready becomes irrelevant when children are repeatedly offered the opportunity to read" (p. 194).

Implied in this statement is that by providing pupils the opportunity to read, teachers must evaluate carefully the appropriateness of their instruction in relation to pupils' progress. Therefore, each teaching situation is also a diagnostic situation where the teacher is diagnosing pupils' progress in relation to what is taught. Rather than assuming that those children who are not progressing are unready, the appropriateness of instruction can be evaluated and necessary changes made.

To facilitate the observation of pupils' reading readiness, checklists can be constructed by the teacher. Such checklists can focus on major instructional areas and be developed in relation to the goals of the instructional program. Four major areas that should be found on such checklists have been recommended by McDonell and Osburn (24).

- *Attends to visual cues*—left-to-right progression, concept of word boundaries and letters, and some word identification in context.
- *Uses intuitive knowledge of language*—makes up stories to accompany pictures, begins to use book talk, sees that pictures and print are related, and begins to read the words of memorized text, such as nursery rhymes.
- *Integrates visual and language cues*—begins to read sentences word by word, attempts to use all cues available (e.g., syntax, beginning sound, context, language predictability) when reading.
- *Expects meaning from print*—demonstrates that reading is a meaning-getting process.

In addition to using checklists to assess children's reading readiness in these major areas, there are several techniques that we have found to be successful.

- Give the children a book and ask them to point out or tell you where it begins; how to hold it; how to turn the pages; where to begin reading on a page; what are words, letters, and sentences.
- Present the children with a situation where a new student who doesn't know anything about reading is coming into your classroom and direct the children to explain to you what they would tell this student that reading is.
- Give the children short oral stories that are meaningless and ask them to tell you what is wrong with the stories. If they understand the concept that oral language must make sense, they will usually respond by indicating that they don't understand it or it is a silly story.

- Provide the children with a sentence strip and ask them to cut off a word, a letter, two words, the beginning word, and so forth.
- Engage the children in oral language discussions where the focus is on negotiating meaning (see chapter 2), getting them to expand and refine their use of language.
- Provide the children with writing opportunities and note their attempts to communicate meaning and invented spellings. The focus is on attempts to communicate meaning rather than sentence structure, spelling, grammar, and word usage.
- Tell the children short, unfinished stories within their experiential/conceptual background and direct them to orally complete the story. Evaluate whether their endings relate to the beginning part of the story and if children are attempting to provide endings that make sense.

Information from Parents

Children's home environments play a significant role in relation to their readiness for reading. Several home variables related to a child's readiness for reading have been identified, including educational television recognition, availability of reading materials in the home, specified parental criteria for television program selection, and preparatory questions prior to a parent/child reading episode (11). A major home variable that relates to boys' readiness for reading appears to be whether or not their fathers read to them. Henry (17) found that boys about to enter the first grade who were read to by their fathers were better prepared for reading than boys read to by their mothers.

The need for teachers to obtain information from parents about children's home background is extremely important. Teachers can better accommodate pupils' needs in beginning reading by compiling as much information as possible about children's home environments as one indicator of their level of readiness for reading. One procedure that many teachers use to gather such information is a questionnaire that parents are asked to complete about their child. Although each teacher may wish to develop her own questionnaire that parallels her instructional program, there are some important questions to consider. Some examples of these questions are listed below along with their potential value in assessing reading readiness and in planning reading instruction.

- Names and ages of other children in the family and whether or not the children ever "play" school or read to each other. Knowing the names of other children will enable the teacher to engage the child in oral language by talking about things that are extremely familiar

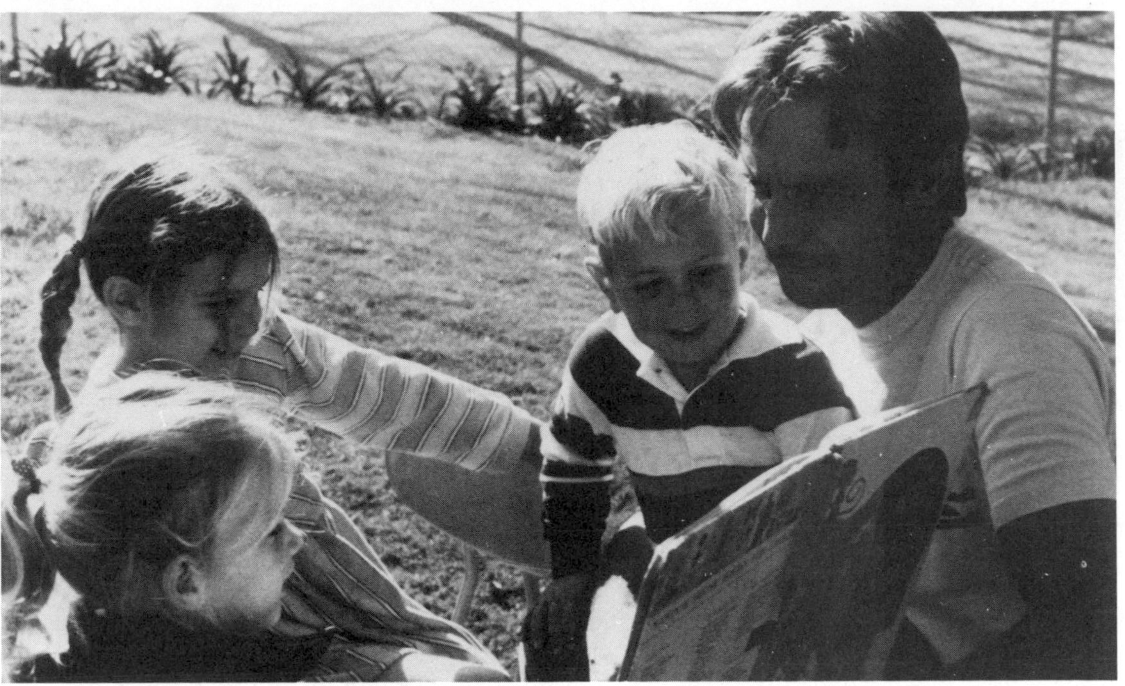

A good teacher understands that the students' readiness to read depends on their home environment.

to him. A child who has older brothers and sisters will often learn much about the concepts of reading through playing school.

- What are your child's special abilities and interests? Again, this will provide the teacher with background information for engaging the child in oral language situations that are based on familiar settings and information.
- Does your child enjoy being read to? Does he/she have a favorite book? Does he/she ever pretend to read this favorite book(s) to you or others? Does he/she ever (check the items that apply) 1. turn the pages ( ) 2. point to where you or he/she is reading ( ) 3. read along with you or others when they read aloud to him/her ( ) 4. show you where to begin reading ( ) 5. tell you what he/she thinks will happen in stories read to him/her ( ) 6. name the characters that are pictured in books read to him/her ( ) 7. know how to recognize some words in stories read to him/her (8) know how to recognize words, such as brand names, store names, his/her name (9) read books, magazines, and other printed materials ( ).

  Please list the names of your child's favorite books:

  Please list some of the words that he/she can read:

If your child is already reading please list some of the books, magazines, and other materials he/she reads:

The value of this information should be apparent as it relates to concepts associated with print and the function of printed language. Additional questions can be identified that will provide valuable insights into children's readiness for reading and their conceptualizations of the function of language. Parent questionnaires can also help the teacher plan for parent conferences and identify specific areas for which additional information would be warranted.

INSTRUCTIONAL FEATURES

In planning a reading readiness program, teachers should capitalize upon what is already known about effective teaching (see chapter 3), children, learning, and language (see chapter 2). To maximize the probability that children will be successful in learning to read, instructional consideration should be given to the following:

- Design activities around a language arts base (listening, speaking, reading, and writing) that takes advantage of and extends the rich language background of children.
- Develop in children the concept that reading is communication and that meaning is essential.
- Arrange a planned program to teach word meanings through the use of both oral and written context.
- Allow children varied opportunities to read and to be involved with meaningful reading activities.
- Use reading readiness tests only as a guide, followed by your own professional evaluation regarding pupil progress or lack of progress.
- Teach children in an integrated fashion essential reading terminology and concepts such as *word, letter, sound, sentence, left-to-right progression,* and *letter names.*
- Stimulate interest in reading by reading a variety of stories aloud to children.
- Incorporate the arts (music, art, drama) into your program to increase motivation and to foster language growth.
- Prepare systematic activities to teach good listening skills.
- Set short-term goals that children can readily achieve.
- Do not give children tasks that they do not understand or cannot do.
- Give responsibility to all children and not just to those who are already confident and at ease.

- Select goals for your program in relation to what children need—not in relation to what a commercially prepared reading readiness program states.

The following instructional activities are representative of those that can enhance pupils' success in beginning reading. The order that we have chosen to present these activities does not imply a fixed sequence of skills, because the child's needs would determine the appropriateness of any instruction. However, those activities that deal more specifically with the idea that reading is a language comprehension process are presented first. The reason for placing these activities first is that they can help children better realize what reading is and maximize their interaction with meaningful print.

Developing a Concept and Recognition of Words

The child beginning to read must very rapidly develop a concept for a word and the ability to distinguish between hundreds of written word symbols. Prior to the use of early level readers and long after their introduction, most teachers will provide classroom activities aimed at helping children learn to recognize words. Teachers will employ different methods, but most prefer to teach words related to the child's actual experiences. We discuss the language experience method and the use of experience charts in chapter 8.

Suggested Instructional Activities. Examples of readiness activities to help children in word recognition are described briefly here.

- *Child's name.* Probably the easiest word to teach a child is his own name. The child sees his name on his books and on pictures and drawings that the teacher displays. In addition, there will be many occasions when the teacher will write pupils' names on the board for birthdays, committees, special assignments, and the like. The child will notice similarities between his own name and other pupils' names and will learn a few words in this manner. To enhance the meaning-getting features of reading, the child's name should be written in a short phrase or sentence—Mike drew a picture, Today is Mary's birthday, Bill sits here. These phrases can be printed on strips of paper and matched to sentences written on the board. The concept of a word can be developed by cutting the sentence strips into words. Left-to-right progression can be pointed out as these sentences or phrases are read. Also, emphasis can be given to making sense of what is read by having the children reassemble the cut-apart sentence into the original sentence and focusing on whether or not it makes sense.

FLASHBACK

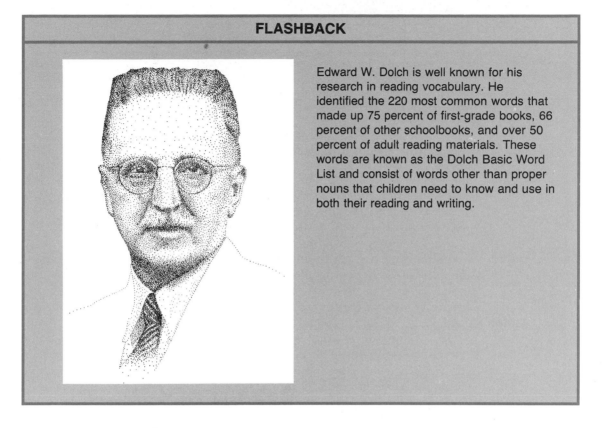

Edward W. Dolch is well known for his research in reading vocabulary. He identified the 220 most common words that made up 75 percent of first-grade books, 66 percent of other schoolbooks, and over 50 percent of adult reading materials. These words are known as the Dolch Basic Word List and consist of words other than proper nouns that children need to know and use in both their reading and writing.

- *Color names.* To teach color names, large circles cut from colored construction paper can be placed on the chalkboard or table. Names of colors are printed in short sentences—*This color is blue, This color is red,* etc.—on white cards. The pupil selects a card, says the word phrase, and places the color sentence on the properly colored circle.
- *Matching words with pictures.* All children in the readiness group are capable of identifying a great number of objects and pictures of objects. Familiar pictures are found, and word phrases are printed on separate cards: *a car, a swing, the duck, a cow, my house.* Each child selects a word phrase and places it beneath the proper picture.
- *Objects in the classroom.* A word-card sentence is made for familiar objects in the classroom, such as *This is a door, This is the table, This is a window, This is a book, This is a chair.* A child selects a word-card sentence, reads it, shows it to the group, and touches the object.
- *Following directions.* Words previously studied can be used in "direction sentences" printed on heavy paper or oaktag. A child selects a sentence, reads it aloud, and does what it suggests. Some examples: Walk to the door, Clap your hands, Ask John to stand.

In any exercise that uses word phrases as stimuli, the teacher can ask that the word be used in a different sentence or phrase. As she writes it on the board, she pronounces each word and then reads the entire sentence. Emphasis can be placed on visual clues found in words, on the sentence as a meaning unit, and on left-to-right progression in reading.

Developing Listening Skills

In developing listening skills, one deals with a much broader area than auditory discrimination of speech sounds. Listening is involved in every facet of the curriculum, and the school is programmed in such a way that children's listening skills must be effective if learning is to take place. Listening is required for following directions, developing and expanding concepts, maintaining discipline, planning curricular activities, and the like. Listening is closely related to many reading behaviors, such as utilizing intonation patterns in reading, developing auditory memory, and processing language presented orally in stories or discussion.

Children differ noticeably in listening ability. Some children come to school with poor listening habits, and others develop inadequate habits early in their school careers. This naturally has an impact on classroom activities and results in impaired learning.

Listening involves more than being physically present while the teacher or a pupil is speaking. It is just as important to provide experience in listening as it is to provide experience in reading, if we want learning to take place.

Suggested Instructional Activities. There will be a great number of learning activities in the school that depend on listening. These include listening to recordings of stories, poetry, and songs; listening to music and acting out what the music suggests; listening to the teacher read stories; and participating in speaking-listening situations. A few activities suggested for use in prereading as well as at higher levels are briefly described below. These activities involve the child in listening to and interpreting language units ranging from single sentences through paragraphs and stories. The learner is called upon to attend, process, retain, and respond to language stimuli.

- *Critical listening.* Here the teacher reads short, descriptive passages, and the children are asked to identify or draw a picture of what is described. This technique focuses on the meaning feature of reading. In addition to reading the short description aloud, we also recommend that it be written for the children to see. As the teacher reads aloud, she should make sure all pupils are focusing on the written description.

I grow outdoors.
I grow tall.
In the summer I am
full of leaves. Birds sit
on my branches and sing.
What am I?
Draw a picture of me.

People live in me.
I have windows and doors.
I come in many different
colors and sizes.
Draw a picture of me.

The descriptions the teacher reads can vary in length and complexity, depending on the maturity or age level of the group. These types of exercises can help teachers discover which children can listen effectively (and which cannot) and which children are self-sufficient (and which are dependent on others). Also, any unusual responses given may alert the teacher to other problems needing attention.

- *Story periods.* Practically all children can be held spellbound by a good story well told. When the teacher tells or reads stories, she plants the ideas in the children's minds that good listening is the key to enjoyment of the story and that print is meaningful. Equally important is the fact that she can stress a purpose for listening, whether for enjoyment, for information, for answers to specific questions, or for practice in social living.

- *Following directions.* This can be used either as a class exercise with small groups or with individual pupils. Several short commands are stated, and the child, or the group, is to execute them in the order given. The performance will reveal the ability to attend to oral directions and the ability to hold these in memory.

- *Finishing the story.* This provides practice in developing language skills in listening, in using imagination, in using language, and in expecting logic and meaning from the reading. The teacher, while reading a story, interrupts it at a point of high interest and asks the children, "What happens next?" Each pupil's response can be written on the chalkboard and discussed after that portion of the story is read.

Once upon a time Tim went to visit his grandfather and grandmother. They lived on a farm. He went with his father and mother

Children can begin to understand the relationships between speaking, reading, and writing by creating stories from pictures.

in their car. When they drove up his grandparents' house, a big dog rushed out to the car and barked and barked. The boy and his parents had never seen this dog before. Father said "________." (Child finishes story.)

Kate and Bill were tired of running and playing. They sat down on the porch to rest and talk. Kate said, "Bill, let's ask your mother to make us some lemonade." "Good," said Bill, "Cold lemonade; I'm so thirsty I could drink three glasses." They started into the house and Kate said, "Bill, do you think your mother would make enough lemonade so we could have a lemonade stand and sell lemonade in paper cups?" Bill said, "________."

- *Completing the sentence.* This is a variation of the above in which the child supplies a word which has been omitted.

  A big dog came up to the car and ________ at them.
  Bob was tired of running. He sat down to ________.

  This exercise gives practice in listening and in getting meanings from context.

- *What word disagrees with the picture?* While looking at a picture, pupils listen to the teacher as she says a series of four words, one of which could not be logically associated with the picture. Children are then asked to identify the word that does not belong. This can be a challenging game, because children must observe closely, listen carefully, and remember the word while other stimuli are presented.

- *Retelling a story.* The teacher reads a story or passage to one group who then tells the story to children who have not heard it. This experience motivates children to be good listeners since they must pay attention and comprehend if they are to retell the story successfully. Also, the emphasis on communicating meaning is highlighted.

- *Emphasizing expression.* The teacher reads a sentence or short passage word by word, without inflection, then reads it with good expression. Pupils are led to see that how a passage is read affects its interpretation.

- *Silly sayings.* Read the following or similar sentences one at a time. After each sentence, call on a volunteer to explain what is wrong with the sentence and how it might be changed to make sense.

  Mother cooked the corn in the old shoe.
  The boys played baseball in the sandbox.
  John turned on the radio to watch a program.

The elephant drank water through his ear.
Mary read the book from back to front.
The man went in the jewelry store and ordered breakfast.

- *Listen and do.* Prepare a series of commands or tasks. Explain that you will describe a task and will then call on a volunteer to carry it out. Children must listen carefully since they do not know ahead of time who will be called upon.

  Repeat this sentence: George Washington was our first president.
  Come to the front of the room and roar like a lion.
  Stand up, turn around completely, sit down.
  Move like an elephant (rabbit, snake, turtle, etc.).
  Go the chalkboard, make two marks, then erase one of them.

- *Whisper a sentence.* Whisper a sentence to a child who in turn whispers it to another child, continuing until four or five children have participated. The last child says the sentence aloud. Then determine what changes were made in the message. A number of groups or teams may participate at the same time using the same message.

Developing Visual Discrimination

By the time a child comes to a school, she has had thousands of experiences in seeing and noting likenesses and differences. The child has developed the ability to make fairly high-order visual discriminations, in many cases based on relatively small clues. At the age of three years she was able to identify and claim her tricycle from a group of three wheelers, even though she was not able to tell you exactly how she made this identification. All we do know is that it was a visual discrimination. Later, two coins much the same size but bearing different symbols will not confuse the child. The head of a man or woman no larger than a postage stamp will contain enough visual clues for correct identification. Common trademarks are correctly identified on the basis of size, color, and configuration. A pack of playing cards can be sorted by suit on the basis of visual perception.

The child's need to make fine visual discriminations is self-evident since the symbols that must be read are visual stimuli. Even a quick examination of words is sufficient to establish that many of them look very much alike. A child who cannot differentiate among the various words in a passage cannot possibly get meaning from that passage. The widely accepted definition that "reading is getting meaning from printed symbols" does, to some degree, slight the sensory skills that are essential to "getting the meaning."

Suggested Instructional Activities. After a few letter forms have been taught at the chalkboard or with flashcards, children may be provided with two or more letter cards. One letter such as *a, e,* or *b* is printed on both sides of a card. The group is then invited to hold up the letter *e,* then *a, b,* etc. As the children's responses are observed, the teacher notes diagnostic clues which become the basis for smaller group or individual practice. Other letter-word recognition activities that can be used for both teacher-directed instruction and practice follow.

Underline the letter or word that is exactly like the one at the left.

M	H	W	M	Z	U
WHO	HOW	WON	MAN	WHO	WAH

Match uppercase and lowercase letters. Connect uppercase and lowercase letter forms with a line.

E	e m a	M	h f m	R	s r n	D	c b d
H	n h a	A	m s a	G	g h f	P	p q r

Underline the beginning of each word that is exactly like the one at the left.

shall	Sally is	a ship	the hall	I shut
from	a frog	a flag	I fell	for it

Underline the ending of each word that is exactly like the one at the left.

hat	I hit	is hot	a cat	he has
hill	a bell	a mill	a bill	I can
ball	I fall	a pill	I call	some salt

Developing Auditory Discrimination

The major objective of auditory discrimination activities is to help the child become conscious of speech sounds within words. Specifically, the child should become able to recognize rhyming elements, the same sound at the beginning or end of words, blended sounds, and so forth.

Suggested Instructional Activities for Teaching Rhyming Elements in Words. Prior to each exercise, review the concept of rhyming words and explain and illustrate the importance of the activity as it relates to getting meaning, concept of words, and left-to-right progression.

- *Number rhymes.* Review the number words from one to ten. Then say, "I will read a sentence that is written on the board." (Make sure each child is looking at each sentence as it is read. Point to each word and move your hand across the sentence to emphasize left-to-right progression.) "Give me a number word that rhymes with these two words." (Pronounce the two words while pointing to each. Do a few examples to make sure each child understands the task. Call on children to give a number that rhymes with the two words and write the number name in the space. Discuss with the students why the sentences *make sense.*)

  Late and *gate* rhyme with ________. (eight)
  Sun and *fun* rhyme with ________. (one)
  Hen and *pen* rhyme with ________. (ten)
  Do and *shoe* rhyme with ________. (two)
  Free and *bee* rhyme with ________. (three)
  Sticks and *mix* rhyme with ________. (six)

- *Color-name rhymes.* "Name a color that rhymes with ________."

  Said and *Fred* ________ (red)
  Flew and *chew* ________ (blue)
  Mean and *seen* ________ (green)
  Down and *frown* ________ (brown)
  Night and *sight* ________ (white)

- *Animal-name rhymes.* "Name an animal that rhymes with ________." now (cow); cantaloupe (antelope); trunk (skunk); box (fox); sat (cat/rat); deep (sheep); coat (goat); fog (dog/frog); hair (bear).

- *Jingles and rhyming lines.* Intonation and rhyming elements may be stressed in jingles and rhyming lines. These usually involve longer language units that also provide experiences for developing auditory memory. The example that follows uses number words and calls for children to discriminate the word that is stressed and complete the statement with a number word that rhymes with that word. The same procedures as those used for number and color activities should be followed.

I saw a number on the door.
The number that I saw was ________.
The snakes I counted in the den
were more than six—I counted ________.
Words like bee and tree and see
rhyme with good old number ________.
To keep this rhyming game alive
we have to say the number ________.

Suggested Instructional Activities for Teaching Initial Sounds in Words. The following suggested exercises should help the child recognize the importance of speech sounds within words.

- *Use of children's names.* Listen to the sound that begins Mike's name. Mike. Can you think of any other children's first names which begin with this sound? (Mary, Mark, Marcia) The beginning sound should be emphasized but not distorted. The names of different children in the class may be used as stimulus words. Several names beginning with the same letter sound may be written in a column on the board to provide the child with the visual pattern (letter form) that represents the initial sound.

Sue	Cathy	John	Pat	Herman
Sam	Carl	James	Paul	Helen
Sally	Carol	Jerry	Peggy	Harry

- *Use of pictures.* Secure a number of pictures from workbooks, magazines, or catalogs. Select pictures whose naming words illustrate the sound that is to be taught. Label each picture with its name in a short phrase.

  Place several labeled pictures on the chalktray: *a red bird, a color television, a big house.* Call on pupils to tell which picture name begins with the same sound as stimulus words pronounced orally.

  Select four or five pictures, all of whose naming words except one begin with the same sound: *a red bird, a big bat, a little bug, a white cat.* Call on students to identify the picture names that begin with the same sound and group these together. Ask children to give you sentences for the pictures and write these on sentence strips. These sentence strips can be matched to the pictures, cut apart to be reassembled into the original sentences, and discussed in terms of meaning.

Place in random order on the chalkboard pictures that have been selected so that several of their naming words (written beneath picture in a short phrase) begin with the same sound: *a ceiling fan, a white fence, a big hen, a black tire, a big horn.* Children arrange the pictures into groups according to the initial sound heard in the picture names. Sentences can be provided by the children, and activities similar to the above can be developed.

Suggested Instructional Activities for Teaching Final Sounds in Words. The same procedures used for working with initial sounds can be used for teaching discrimination of final sounds in words.

- Children match or group pictures whose naming words end with the same sound: a cat–a bat; a man–a fan.
- Pronounce three words, two of which end with the same sound: the door, the house, the car. Pupils repeat the words that end with the same sound.
- After letter–sound relationships have been taught, children name or write the letter that represents the final sound heard in picture names or stimulus words spoken orally.

Developing a Concept of Reading and Reading Instruction Terms

Earlier, we discussed the fact that many beginning readers lack an understanding that reading is a communication process, and they are confused by the terminology (words, letters, sounds, sentence, etc.) used in teaching reading. We also noted in chapter 2 that when and where to begin reading instruction varies with individual children. Those children who have been exposed to print and print-related concepts before entering school will obviously have more understanding about what it means to read than those who have not had such previous experiences with printed language. Because children do enter school at many places on the continuum of learning to read, reading readiness instruction must be structured to meet their varying reading capabilities.

Suggested Instructional Activities. The following basic instructional activities can be used to enhance children's concepts of reading and reading instruction language; the complexity of the activities can be modified to meet varying needs.

- Reading to children. The importance of the relationship between language and reading was highlighted in chapter 2. Children need to un-

Children's readiness to read is based on the relationship between their existing capabilities and the demands of new tasks.

derstand early in their reading development that the purpose of reading is communication. Reading to youngsters stories and other written materials that will "grab their minds" and stimulate interest in reading helps them to conceptualize what written language is and the basic features of written text. Specifically, the daily oral sharing of books is tremendously important for children learning to read. Some of the basic concepts children learn from this practice are story language; expectations for story characters; and to tell their own stories, thus learning to talk like books. Also, their vocabularies are expanded, and they often want to read the books that the teacher reads to them.

- Storytelling is another important instructional practice that can help children to understand the relationship between oral language and reading. There are several variations of storytelling.

  The teacher tells the children a story and at appropriate places in the storytelling stops and asks the children to predict what they think will happen next. After telling a short story, the children can be dirccted to illustrate the story that was told, relating directly to comprehension of language. The teacher can then ask the children to talk about their pictures and write their comments at the bottom of each picture page. The pictures can also be used to illustrate story sequence by using the children's drawings to discuss when different events occurred. A story can be started by the teacher and the students directed to add to it. As each student makes a contribution to the story his response is written on a flip chart for all the children to see. This reinforces the relationship between oral and written language and illustrates for the children that print represents a communication process. The written features of storytelling can be used as concrete examples to illustrate the concepts associated with reading instruction language, such as words, letters, sentences, and punctuation marks.
- Combining writing and reading is a valuable procedure for helping children begin to conceptualize that both are composing processes (34) and provide concrete examples to illustrate the language of reading instruction. See chapters 2 and 8 for information about the value of writing in the reading program and for instructional activities that combine writing and reading.
- Read along books, where the children listen to an audiotape recording of a book while they follow along in the actual book, can help them begin to understand story language and structure, to learn how to talk like a book, and to expand their vocabularies. Read along books are available commercially, or teachers can tape record books appropriate to the reading capabilities and interests of their students (see chapter 9).

SUMMARY

Learning to read is an extension of language skills that the child has already developed. Yet reading calls for several skills and concepts that are different from those previously learned, such as the importance of meaning in reading; reading left to right; understanding the concepts of word, letter, etc.; visual discrimination of letters and word forms; and auditory discrimination of speech sounds within words. Failure to make adequate progress in these areas can slow or disrupt the entire developmental process of reading. Despite the importance of these factors, preparing for reading involves many other skills and capacities. Growing into reading is part of the child's total growth pattern. Certain, social-emotional factors are the key to success or failure in beginning reading for some children. These factors are not measured on reading readiness tests, and possibly this may be one reason why the predictive value of these tests is not higher.

The readiness period should not be thought of as ending with a calendar date or dealing with a limited number of specific skills measured by readiness tests. The length of the readiness period will vary for different children, since no predetermined school schedule could possibly fit all children's developmental patterns. The readiness program does not attempt to remove individual differences among pupils. No part of the readiness period should be thought of as a waiting period. Preparing for reading implies activity on the part of the child and a deliberate structuring of experiences on the part of the teacher and the school.

Concern for a child's readiness to read is highly justifiable. Expecting a child to read before she is ready violates an important principle of teaching reading. The chief aim of the readiness period is to assure that children get off to a good start in learning to read. Experiencing failure in the early stages of learning to read can lead to attitudes that have far-reaching influence on later development.

YOUR POINT OF VIEW

Discussion Questions

1. Assume you have worked closely with a group of six year olds who learned to read before entering school. Describe these children, touching on the behavioral characteristics you think they would display.
2. Many schools use reading readiness tests for determining children's specific skill deficiencies. What are the strengths and weaknesses of such an approach?

Take a Stand For or Against

1. Reading readiness tests could also be defined as intelligence tests.
2. The teacher is not a causal factor in the disproportionate number of reading failures among boys as compared to girls.

BIBLIOGRAPHY

1. Ausubel, David P. "Viewpoints from Related Disciplines: Human Growth and Development." *Teachers College Record* 60 (1959): 245–54.
2. Blom, Gaston E.,; Waite, Richard R,; and Zimet, Sara G. "Motivational Content Analysis of Children's Primers." In *Basic Studies of Reading,* edited by H. Levin and J. Williams. New York: Basic Books, 1970.
3. Brophy, Jere E., and Good, Thomas L. "Of Course the Schools are Feminine, But Let's Stop Blaming Women For It." *Phi Delta Kappan* 55 (1973): 73–75.
4. Chall, Jeanne S. *Stages of Reading Development.* New York: McGraw-Hill Book Co., 1983.
5. Clay, Marie M. *The Early Detection of Reading Difficulties: A Diagnostic Survey.* Auckland, New Zealand: Heinemann Educational Books, 1972.
6. Clay, Marie M. *The Patterning of Complex Behaviour.* Auckland, New Zealand: Heinemann Educational Books, 1979.
7. Downing, John. "The Reading Instruction Register." *Language Arts* 53 (1979): 762–66.
8. Downing, John, and Thomason, Doug. "Sex Role Stereotyping in Learning to Read." *Research in the Teaching of English* 11 (Fall 1977): 149–55.
9. Durkin, Dolores. *Teaching Young Children to Read.* 3rd ed. Boston: Allyn & Bacon, 1980.
10. Durkin, Dolores. "What Does Research Say about the Time to Begin Reading Instruction?" *Journal of Educational Research* 64 (1970): 51–56.
11. Flood, James. "Predictors of Reading Achievement: An Investigation of Antecedents to Reading." Ph. D. diss., Stanford University, 1975.
12. Gallimore, Ronald; Tharp, Roland; and Speidel, Gisela. "The Relationship of Sibling Caretaking and Attentiveness to a Peer Tutor." *American Educational Research Journal* 15 (Spring 1978): 267–73.
13. Gates, Arthur I. "The Necessary Mental Age for Beginning Reading." *Elementary School Journal* 37 (1937): 497–508.
14. Gross, Alice. "Sex-Role Standards and Reading Achievement: A Study of Israeli Kibbutz System." *The Reading Teacher* 32 (1978): 149–56.
15. Halperin, Marcia S. "Sex Differences in Children's Responses to Adult Pressure for Achievement." *Journal of Educational Psychology* 69 (1977): 69–100.
16. Hare, Chou Victoria. "What's in a Word? A Review of Young Children's Difficulties with the Construct 'Word'." *The Reading Teacher* 37 (1984): 360–64.
17. Henry, Bertraum. *Father to Son Reading: Its Effect on Boys' Reading Achievement.* Ph.D. diss., Syracuse University, 1974.
18. Hoskisson, Kenneth, and Krohm, Bernadette. "Reading by Immersion: Assisted Reading." *Elementary English* 51 (1974): 832–36.
19. Johns, Jerry L. "Does Our Language of Instruction Confuse Beginning Readers?" *Reading Psychology* 1 (1982): 37–41.
20. Johnson, Carole S., and Greenbaum, Gloria R. "Are Boys Disabled Readers Due to Sex-Role Stereotyping?" *Educational Leadership* 37 (1980): 492–96.

21. Johnson, Dale. "Sex Differences in Reading Across Cultures." *Reading Research Quarterly* 9 (1973–74): 67–86.
22. Lee, Patrick C. "Male and Female Teachers in Elementary School: An Ecological Analysis." *Teachers College Record* 75 (1973): 79–98.
23. Lehr, Fran. "Cultural Influences and Sex Differences in Reading." *The Reading Teacher* 35 (1982): 744–46.
24. McDonell, Gloria M., and Osburn, E. Bess. "New Thoughts about Reading Readiness." *Language Arts* 55 (1978): 79–98.
25. MacGinitie, Walter H. "Evaluating Readiness for Learning to Read: A Critical Review and Evaluation of Research." *Reading Research Quarterly* 55 (Spring 1969): 396–410.
26. Mass, Leslie Noyes. "Developing Concepts of Literacy in Young Children." *The Reading Teacher* (Mar. 1982): 670–75.
27. Morphett, Mabel V., and Washburne, Carleton. "When Should Children Begin to Read?" *Elementary School Journal* 31 (1931): 496–503.
28. Pikulski, John. "Readiness for Reading: A Practical Approach." *Language Arts* 55 (1978): 192–97.
29. Sheridan, E. Marcia. *Early Reading in Japan.* South Bend, Ind.: Indiana University at South Bend, 1981.
30. Stanovich, Keith E.; Cunningham, Anne E.; and Feeman, Dorothy J. "Intelligence, Cognitive Skills, and Early Reading Progress." *Reading Research Quarterly* 3 (Spring 1984): 278–303.
31. Stotsky, Sandra. "Research on Reading/Writing Relationships: A Synthesis and Suggested Directions." *Language Arts* 5 (May 1983): 627–42.
32. Texas Educational Agency. *State Board of Education Rules for Curriculum: Principles, Standards, and Procedures for Accreditation of School Districts.* Austin, Tex.: Texas Education Agency, 1984.
33. Thorndike, Robert L. *Reading Comprehension in Fifteen Countries.* New York: John Wiley & Sons, 1973.
34. Tierney, Robert J., and Pearson, P. David. "Toward a Composing Model of Reading." *Language Arts* 60 (May 1983): 568–80.
35. Weaver, Phyllis. *Research Within Reach.* St. Louis: CEMREL, 1978.

Lesson 10

Materials: Activity Board, scissors

ACTIVITY BOARD CARDS

ACTIVITY BOARD PUZZLES

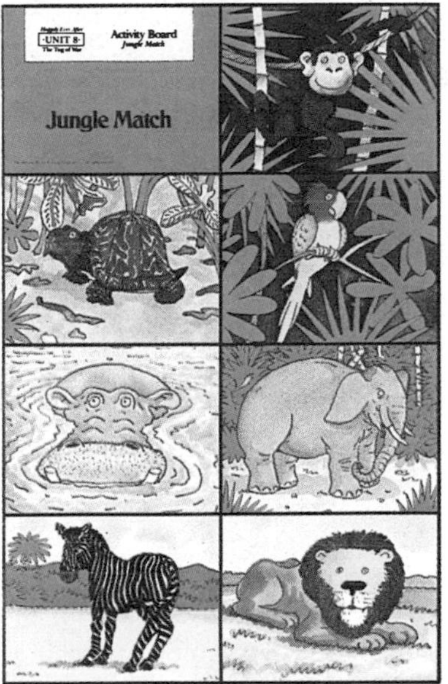

STEP 1

Play Guessing Games

Materials: Activity Board, scissors

to discuss pictures; to answer riddles; to recall an item removed from a group

Display Activity Board. Discuss pictures. Display the side of the Activity Board with the seven large pictures of jungle animals. Have the children name each animal as you point to it. Then turn the board over and point out that there are four smaller pictures of each animal on the reverse side of each large picture.

Cut apart Activity Board. Cut apart the Activity Board along the cutting lines to make twenty-eight animal cards. These cards may be used in a number of ways.

Play riddle game. Give one small Activity Board card to each child. Make sure that at least one picture of each animal has been distributed. Tell the children that you are going to ask them some riddles about the animals. Tell them to listen to each riddle and then hold up their cards if they think they have the animal that answers the riddle. Ask riddles similar to those which follow.

I swing on vines,
And I hang from trees.
I eat bananas.
Can you guess me? (monkey)

I'm king of the jungle.
I wear a mane.
I like to roar.
Can you guess my name? (lion)

Black and white stripes
Give me away.
What animal am I?
Can you say? (zebra)

I'm small, but clever.
I wear a shell.
What animal am I?
Can you tell? (turtle)

I'm a bird
Who sits in a tree.
I can guess you.
Can you guess me? (parrot)

I have a long trunk.
I'm big and wide.
Which animal am I?
Can you decide? (elephant)

I like muddy water.
I'm also big and wide.
What animal am I?
Can you decide? (hippopotamus)

Play guessing game. Place seven different cards face up. Have the children close their eyes while you remove one card. Then have them guess which animal is missing. Repeat with the other cards.

STEP 2

Complete Puzzles

Materials: Activity Board animal cards

to sort into categories; to complete a puzzle

Sort the cards. Do puzzles. Distribute all of the small animal cards to the children. Then have the children put the cards for each animal in separate piles. When the cards have all been sorted, divide the children into groups. Assign one or two piles of cards to each group. Turn over all the cards in each pile so that the small animal cards are face down. Have the children fit together the four pieces in each pile to complete the puzzles.

NOTE: When the children have completed Unit 8, have them take home their Activity pages, their storybooks, and any other work they have completed. Include Duplicating Master 31, the Take-Home letter. Parents will appreciate being informed about their children's work.

An example of materials for developing reading readiness.

Two Points of View

Life hasn't been easy around the Blakely house. It seems something is always going wrong. Look at the picture above. The arrows with letters in them point to five places where something has gone wrong. Each of these events was not only caused by something but had its own effect as well. Write what you think each event might have been, stating its cause and effect. Three answers have been provided to help you.

Possible answers:

A. Event: There is no hot water.

Cause: The boiler is broken. Effect: He can't take a shower.

B. Event: He can't start a fire.

Cause: There are no matches. Effect: The room will be cold.

C. Event: The oven doesn't work.

Cause: Something in it is broken. Effect: Dinner will not be ready.

D. Event: The telephone is not working.

Cause: A line is down. Effect: No one can make or receive calls.

E. Event: She can't find something.

Cause: She misplaced it. Effect: She will be late for school.

An example of a comprehension workbook activity.

Kenya Find Your Way from Here to Zaire?

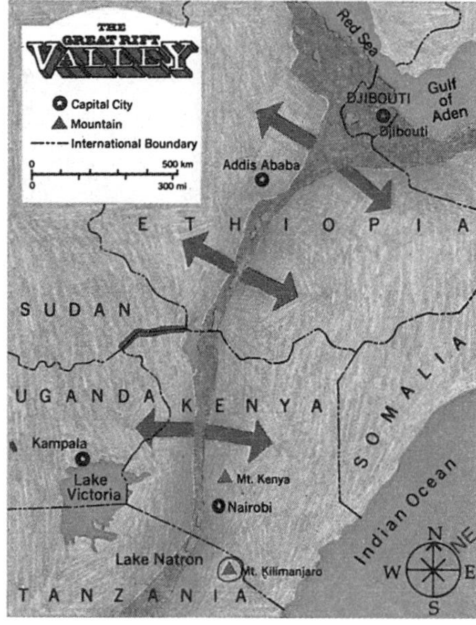

Use the map to answer the questions.

1. List four capital cities.

   Djibouti

   Addis Ababa

   Nairobi

   Kampala

2. Name two lakes.

   Lake Victoria

   Lake Natron

3. In what direction would you travel to get from Kampala to Nairobi? (Hint: Use the compass rose.) southeast

4. On your map, trace over the border between Sudan and Kenya with a crayon or colored pencil.

5. On your map, circle Mt. Kilimanjaro.

6. On the compass rose, label the direction between *N* and *E*.

7. Use string or a ruler and the scale of kilometers. Find out how far the rift runs north to south in Kenya. Write the distance here:

   about 700 kilometers

8. As the ocean forms, the land that Addis Ababa sits on will move. In what direction will it move?

   northwest

9. Use string or a ruler and the scale of kilometers. Find out how long the border is between Kenya and Somalia. Write the distance here:

   about 650 kilometers

10. What is the largest body of water shown on the map?

    Indian Ocean

EXTRA! Write a sentence or two telling how far and in what direction one should travel to get from Nairobi to Addis Ababa. Then tell how to get from Addis Ababa to the city of Djibouti.

Use after "Birth of an Ocean," pages 61–69
Study Skills: To use maps, TG page 149

Application activities must be provided to assure that pupils' study skills transfer to meaningful reading situations.

The application of the directed reading activity in a content area.

Chapter Two
Light and Color

Time Allotment: Allow four to five days to complete this chapter.

Objectives

Students should be able to:

Lesson 1

1. **describe** sunlight as being white light.
2. **name** the colors in the spectrum.
3. **operationally define** a prism.
4. **explain** how a prism separates the colors of the spectrum.

Lesson 2

5. **state** that white is a mixture of all colors and black is the absence of color.
6. **use** colored glass or cellophane to demonstrate that some transparent objects allow only certain colors of light to pass through.
7. **produce** colors other than the spectrum colors by mixing two or more spectrum colors.
8. **explain** why objects appear to have color.

Lesson 3

9. **recognize** that colors are useful and important.
10. **classify** objects by color.
11. **give examples** of uses of color in everyday life.

Key Science Words

white light prism
spectrum absorbed

Materials List

See page T34.

Introducing the Chapter

Use the chapter opening photograph to discuss color. Ask students to point out places in the photo where the colors are brightest. Students will probably say that colors are brighter in the sunlight and duller in the shade. Ask them why this is so. Ask what you think the dark circular area is in the lower right of the photograph. Why is it dark?

READINESS MASTER: You may wish to use the Readiness master on page 20 before students begin this chapter.

Chapter Two
Light and Color

1. The world would be drab shades of gray. 2. Colors are attractive, help us identify objects, and warn us of danger. 3. Accept all reasonable answers.

[1]What do you think the world would be like without color? [2]What are some ways color affects your life? [3]How do you use color?

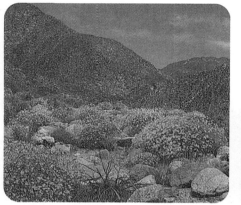

The Earth is made of objects with many different colors. Imagine flowers, fall leaves, and circus clowns without color. [2]What would our homes and schools look like without color?

Color Everywhere

We see color in books, paintings, and photographs. Ads and posters of all kinds attract our attention with bright colors.

Color can be used to tell us much about our environment. Color can be used to make our environment pleasant looking. [3]What is your favorite color?
3 What is the most popular color among your classmates?

Lesson 1 The Spectrum of Color

pages 51-53

This lesson explains the concept of color.

Science Background

A rainbow is an arch of colors that appears in the sky when the sun shines during or after a rain shower. The rainbow appears in the part of the sky opposite the sun. You can see the rainbow when you turn your back to the sun.

Sunlight is separated into colors when it is refracted by raindrops. Each drop of rain acts like a tiny prism and mirror to break up sunlight into colors and send colored light back to our eyes. A light ray is refracted as it enters a raindrop. As it strikes the inner surface of the drop, the light ray is reflected. On leaving the drop, the light ray is further refracted.

Colors that you see compose the visible portion of the electromagnetic spectrum. The electromagnetic spectrum contains other electromagnetic waves such as electric waves, radio waves, microwaves, infrared waves, ultraviolet waves, and X rays. Visible light is only a very small part of this spectrum.

The visible spectrum consists of six different wavelengths and frequencies. Therefore each color is bent at a slightly different angle as it passes through the raindrop. The six colors are red, orange, yellow, green, blue, and violet. Red has the longest wavelength and the lowest frequency and therefore is bent the least. It will always be found on the top of the arch. Violet has the shortest wavelength and the highest frequency, which causes it to be bent more sharply, placing it on the underside of the arch.

Teaching the Lesson

1. Refer to the pictures of the flowers and clown and ask students to name some of the colors in these pictures. Have students find pictures which show how colors make things more beautiful. Make a bulletin board display of these pictures.
2. Have students begin a list of how people use color. Ask the text question. What would our homes and schools look like without color? *Our surroundings would be drab shades of gray.*
3. To reinforce interest, have students conduct a survey among classmates regarding favorite colors. You may wish to review graphing skills by having students prepare histograms to portray their results. Answer the text questions. What is your favorite color? *Answers will vary.* What is the most popular color among your classmates? *Answers will vary.*

4. Refer to the photograph of the prism on this page. Ask students what effect the prism has on the white light. If possible, obtain several prisms to demonstrate the separation of white light into the spectrum.
5. Explain that light is refracted as it passes from the air through the prism. Each color of the spectrum is refracted differently. This causes the colors of the spectrum to be separated by the prism.
6. Ask students to recall when they have observed rainbows. Some students may notice that the colors in a rainbow (and the spectrum formed by a prism) are always in the same order. Answer the text questions. What colors do you see in the pictures? *The spectrum colors: red, orange, yellow, green, blue, and violet.* How were these rainbows made? *The top left photo shows a spectrum formed with prisms. The bottom photo shows a rainbow formed with water droplets.*

Reinforcement

- A rainbow can be formed by standing with your back to the sun and spraying a fine mist of water into the air with a garden hose.

Enrichment

- A spectrum can often be seen as light refracted as it passes through soap bubbles. Some students may wish to investigate.

SCIENCE SKILLS MASTER: The Science Skills master on page 21 may be used here.

Colors in Sunlight

Sunlight is white light. **White light** is a mixture of many colors. The colors can be separated. The separated colors that make up white light are called the **spectrum** (SPEK trum). The colors of the spectrum are red, orange, yellow, green, blue, and violet.

White light separates into the spectrum when it is refracted. As you know, light is refracted when it passes through different kinds of matter. Light is refracted when it passes from air through a prism (PRIHZ um). A **prism** is a transparent object that refracts light. We can see the separate colors because each spectrum color refracts or bends at a different angle. Blue light refracts more than red light. Green light refracts more than red light but less than blue light.

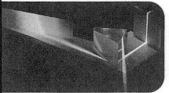

We see the spectrum in a rainbow. Tiny drops of water in the air act as prisms which refract sunlight.[6] What colors do you see in the pictures?
[6] How were these rainbows made?

Rainbows are often observed in the spray of a garden hose or lawn sprinkler.

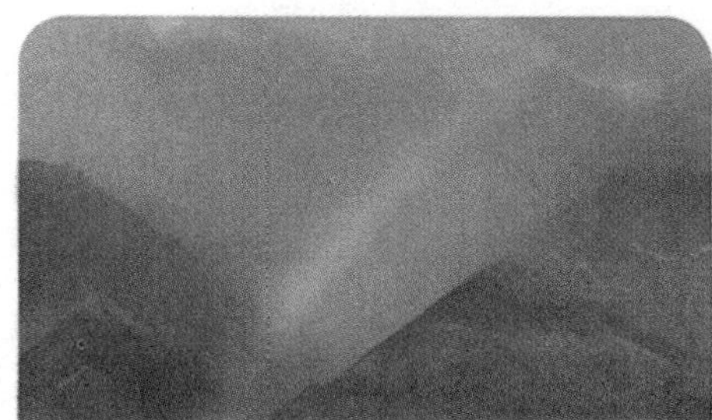

Activity

How Can You Make the Spectrum?

What to use: quantities needed for students working individually

prism 1
crayons 1 box
white paper 30 sheets
pencil and paper

What to do:

1. Make the room dark except for one window. Leave a small opening for sunlight to pass through.

2. Place the prism in the sunlight.

3. Adjust the prism and paper until you see the spectrum.

4. Use crayons to draw what you see.

What did you learn?

1. What colors did you see?
2. Through what kinds of matter did the sunlight pass to become refracted?

Using what you learned:

1. What caused the sunlight to form a spectrum?
2. What would have happened if you would have used a colored light for this activity?

This activity gives students an opportunity to make their own spectrum.

Activity
How Can You Make the Spectrum?

Time Allotment: Allow one 20-minute science period to complete this activity.

Objectives

Students should be able to:

1. **observe** the colors of the spectrum.
2. **use** a prism to separate white light into its spectrum.

Preparation Suggestions

- This activity works best using a relatively thin slit of light.
- If it is difficult to obtain a beam of light from a window, a projector could be substituted. Caution students not to look directly at the sun or any other bright light source.

Teaching Suggestions

- You may wish to review the concept of light refraction at this time. (See Chapter One of this unit.)
- Assist students in focusing the spectrum on the white paper.
- Encourage students to observe the colors and the order of the colors in the spectrum they observe.

What did you learn?

1. Students should report seeing red, orange, yellow, green, blue, and violet.
2. The sunlight was refracted as it passed through the air to the glass prism, and then again when it passed from the glass prism to the air.

Using what you learned:

1. The sunlight formed a spectrum when it was refracted by the prism.
2. Students should infer that colored light would not be broken down into a spectrum. White light is the mixture of all the colors of the spectrum. The students may be able to investigate this question by using two prisms.

Integrating Skills

- **Art:** Ask students to do an art project to show how color is important to them. This project could be a collage of pictures from magazines, catalogs, or other sources, an abstract or realistic drawing, a pattern made of fabric or paint samples, a combination collage and drawing, and so on.

The Road Not Taken

Two roads diverged in a yellow wood,
And sorry I could not travel both
And be one traveler, long I stood
And looked down one as far as I could
To where it bent in the undergrowth;

Then took the other, as just as fair,
And having perhaps the better claim,
Because it was grassy and wanted wear;
Though as for that, the passing there
Had worn them really about the same,

And both that morning equally lay
In leaves no step had trodden black.
Oh, I kept the first for another day!
Yet knowing how way leads on to way,
I doubted if I should ever come back.

I shall be telling this with a sigh
Somewhere ages and ages hence:
Two roads diverged in a wood, and I—
I took the one less traveled by,
And that has made all the difference.

ROBERT FROST

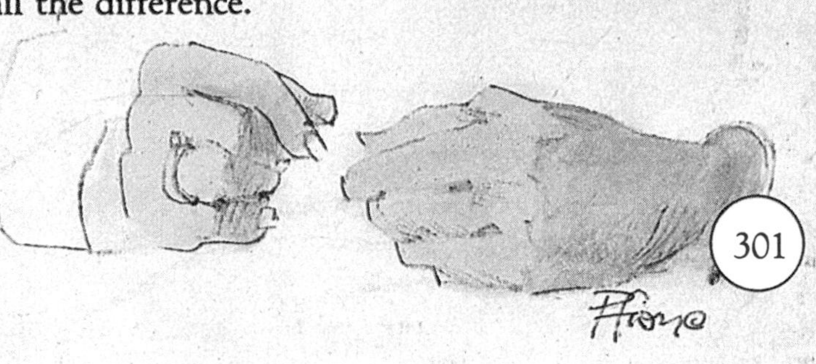

301

Poetry provides teachers and children with opportunities for meaningful oral reading.

UNIT 2 Essential Reading Abilities

Chapters

The core of an effective reading program centers on the instruction and application of those essential skills and abilities that produce good readers. This assertion applies equally at all grade levels, with specific instruction dependent upon student learning needs. Regardless of the reading method or materials utilized, research suggests good reading programs include emphasis on word identification strategies, comprehension abilities, and study skill techniques. Highlighted in chapter 1 as a principle of reading instruction was that learning to read is a long-term, developmental process. Building a solid foundation in the essential reading abilities should be a goal of every education program. Although these abilities need to be nurtured in a variety of independent ways to be fully usable, meaningful direct instruction that aids learners in recognizing, interpreting, and interacting with written language is mandatory.

5

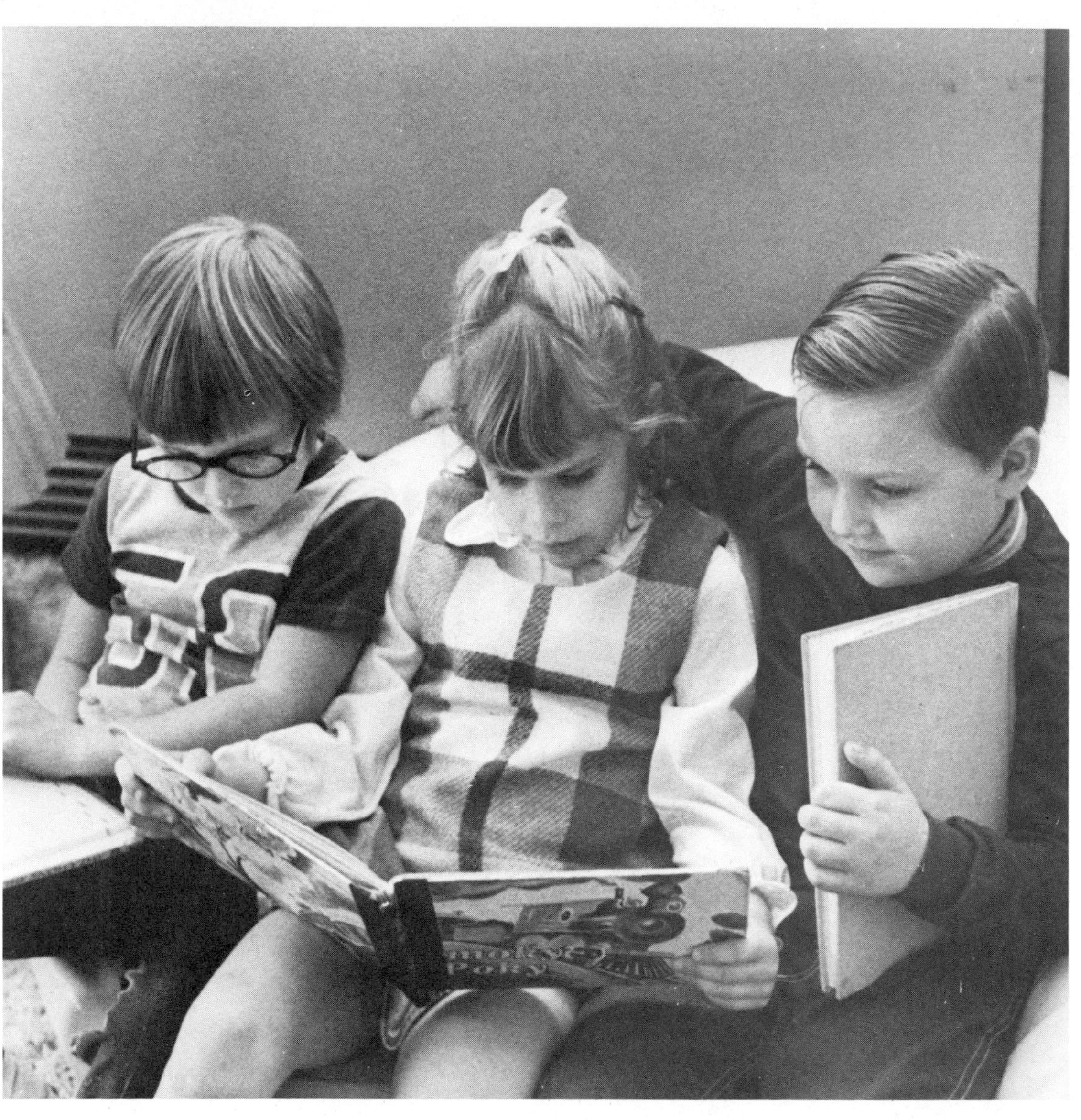

Word Identification

For the Reader

Many critics of public education often focus their attacks on the schools' reading programs. These critics often argue that children are not learning to read because the schools do not teach reading using a single method or a specific set of materials. As we have emphasized throughout this book, neither methods nor materials teach; it is the *teacher* who is the most important factor related to pupils' reading success.

In a position statement adopted by the Board of Directors of the International Reading Association (IRA), November 3, 1979, it was emphasized that "learning to read is a complex process requiring not only the ability to recognize words, but also the ability to comprehend and evaluate the meaning of written materials." It is extremely important that all teachers of reading understand the implications of this statement.

1. No one best method or set of materials is available to assure that all pupils become successful readers.
2. Reading is not pronouncing words or dividing words into syllables. These are tools that a reader may use to comprehend what is read.
3. The outcome of all word identification instruction should be application of skills in context, where the focus is on comprehension.

These implications should be foremost in your mind as you read and learn from this chapter.

Preview

- Read the Key Ideas that follow.
- Read each heading and subheading.
- Read the summary.
- Read the questions and statements at the end of the chapter.
- Return to the chapter text that follows the Key Ideas and begin reading.

Key Ideas

Children need to have a variety of word recognition skills to get at the meaning of what they read.

Each child needs to develop and continually expand a basic sight vocabulary.

Phonics, structural analysis, contextual analysis, and basic sight vocabulary are the four word identification skills that children should be taught so that they can comprehend written language.

Opportunities must be provided for the children to apply their word identification skills in meaningful context.

The major purpose of teaching word identification skills is to provide children with tools for getting meaning from what they read.

Children need to develop flexibility in identifying words so that they can use all available cue systems to get at meaning.

Instructional activities should possess the features associated with effective reading instruction that were presented in chapter 3.

WORD IDENTIFICATION STRATEGIES

Learning to read is an activity that involves the mastery of a wide variety of cues. Beginning readers need to develop and continually expand their sight vocabulary. A sight vocabulary is made up of words that are not spelled the way they sound (e.g., *to, know, they*) and that are recognized instantly by the child. These irregular words are taught using the whole word, look-say, or sight approach. Phonic instruction consists of teaching letter-sound relationships to provide an approximate pronunciation, whereby the sound elicits a meaningful association of the word meaning in the sentence. Structural analysis instruction focuses on visual patterns and meanings that are changed as a result of adding inflectional endings (*s, ed, ing, ly*), prefixes and suffixes *(ex, pre, ment, ous),* and root word to root word to form compounds *(sidewalk, farmyard, playground).* Contextual analysis instruction is aimed at helping children figure out meanings of a word by how it is used in the context of a sentence or passage. Applying letter-sound relationships, recognizing word parts, knowing words on sight, and using context clues are all important parts of the learning-to-read process (11, 13, 15, 26, 32). Equally important is an understanding of how all available word identification cues can be used simultaneously to comprehend written information. There is strong support for the idea that proficiency in using these cues for word identification is developmental (2, 13, 24, 31). Children who are in the learning-to-read stage rely predominantly on letter-sound relationships to identify words. More skilled and mature readers focus on larger units (word parts, whole words) and attend primarily to meaning because it is believed that their word identification strategies are operating at an automatic level (19, 28, 29).

Several language cue systems are available to children simply from their learning to communicate with oral language. Children's awareness of the communicative function of spoken and written language is one cue system that is highly related to their success in learning to read and write (9, 10). Reading and writing also involve the child's awareness that words are strung together in meaningful units governed by structure and syntax. These features of language apply to both spoken and written English. The learner can transfer these features from her knowledge of spoken language to the mastery of the reading process.

Two areas of concern that teachers of reading must keep in mind when teaching word identification skills are the following:

- Word identification instruction is not reading; it is providing children with tools to help them get at the meaning of written language. Opportunities for children to apply their word identification skills in meaningful reading situations must be a major part of instruction.
- Children need to develop flexibility in identifying words so that they can use all available cue systems to get at meaning. They need to develop independent and fluent mastery in the areas of phonics, structural analysis, contextual analysis, and sight words (12, 15, 18, 23, 24) so that these can be used to focus on the meaning of what they read rather than just word pronunciation.

Four Major Instructional Tasks

Insofar as mastering the reading process is concerned, there are four instructional tasks that represent the major thrust of beginning reading instruction. These instructional tasks are to help the child:

- Understand that reading is a language process.
- Develop and expand sight vocabulary.
- Learn to associate visual symbols with speech sounds.
- Realize that reading is always a meaning-making process and that printed word symbols represent language.

Some instructional materials and activities tend to overlook or give undue emphasis to one or two tasks. Children can learn much of what is taught in such an instructional approach, but in so doing they run the risk of developing attitudes and habits that are harmful to their concept of the reading process. When beginning reading instruction overemphasizes the mechanics and slights comprehension, children are not involved in meaningful reading instruction.

Too much emphasis on word identification skills can be detrimental to a pupil as she may develop a "set" that neglects one or more aspects of the reading process. This may result in habits that handicap the reader in her later development. For instance, a child may develop a set to sound out every word she meets. This means she will be sounding out the same word the tenth, twentieth, or even the fiftieth time it is met in reading situations. She has learned that reading is "sounding out words," and this becomes her goal in all reading situations.

On the other hand, overemphasis on learning sight words in the absence of word identification techniques overburdens the child with the task of making fine visual discriminations, where minimal sounding techniques would have made her task much easier. Sight words, plus context, plus the use of the minimal sounding clues necessary to solve unknown printed words are more efficient than relying on one technique alone.

The premise underlying this discussion is that the major instructional tasks identified earlier are inseparable parts of one total instructional process. Children should become skilled in maximizing the use of all the cue systems in written language—sight vocabulary, letter-sound relationships, context—in learning to read. Thus, the major task of reading instruction is to arrive at the proper blending of these instructional components.

What makes reading instruction complicated is that there is no blueprint that spells out precisely where and how much instructional time and effort should be devoted to each of these cue systems. And second, there is no blueprint that tells us what particular instructional techniques work the best with particular learners. Understanding individual differences among learners becomes the key to these questions.

DEVELOPING SIGHT VOCABULARY

The normal child's experience with reading will result in his acquiring a constantly enlarging stock of sight words. He will have established automatic stimulus-response patterns for dozens of frequently used words such as *that, with, be, are, and, was, it, the, in, to, than, you, they, said, when, can,* and the like. A number of these structure words and other frequently used words must be "overlearned" to the point where recognizing them is automatic (29).

There is a difference between overlearning certain frequently used words and learning to rely extensively on one approach to beginning reading, whether that approach be whole words, letter analysis, or context. The normal pattern of learning dictates that the child develop a sight vocabulary or learn some words "as wholes." A few of the many approaches that may help facilitate the learning of sight words are now discussed.

FLASHBACK

Horace Mann was responsible for the first educational reform related to reading in the nineteenth century. Mann was the secretary of the Massachusetts Board of Education in the mid 1830s. He was extremely critical of the prevailing ABC method of teaching reading. In a report to the board, Mann argued that using the alphabetic method to teach reading was presenting information to children that was totally unfamiliar to them. Mann's criticism had a major impact on the reading instruction practices used nationwide at this time. By the 1880s the alphabetic method had been abandoned in most of the progressive schools and replaced with the word method for teaching reading.

Learning to Read Names

Probably the first printed word a child learns is his or her name. The practice of learning names in printed form provides the basis for teaching letter-sound analysis, discussed later. Children also can begin to recognize names of common objects in the classroom if they are labeled.

INTRODUCTORY ACTIVITY

Reading Children's Names. Tape each child's first name on the front of his or her desk. Use other words with it so that each name is within a meaningful context. Doing this will more likely result in the processing of print as it is related to comprehension (1).

Mary sits here.	Mike sits here.
Sarah sits here.	Sandy sits here.

Children learn the names of other children in meaningful context, as well as the words in the sentence. Children will also learn very quickly to recognize a number of names in printed form.

You can also use chalkboard announcements involving pupils' names.

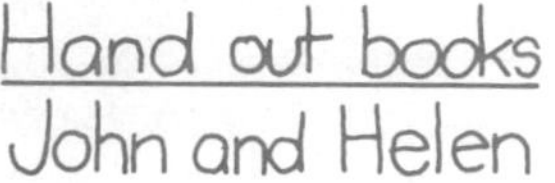

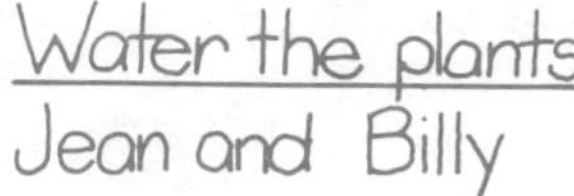

Labeling Objects. Printing a naming word in a short phrase on separate oak tag cards and label objects in the room:

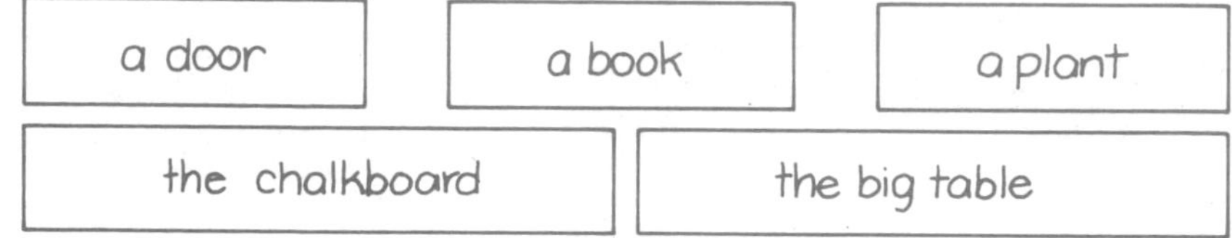

Secure a number of pictures that depict objects or animals within the children's range of experiential and conceptual background. Paste the pictures on cardboard and print the naming words in short phrases beneath them.

a cat

a cow

a horse

a house

To add the kinesthetic mode to the words, duplicate a page of drawings and leave space for the children to write (copy) the names from models displayed on the chalktray. In the first experience, the printed words may be outlined with dots. The child then marks over the dots and "writes" the words.

A later exercise may be one which omits the dotted outlines. The child copies from the printed models on the chalktray, chalkboard or bulletin board.

APPLICATION ACTIVITY

As children begin to recognize many words on sight, many opportunities can be provided for application of this skill in context.

Short, meaningful sentences can be written that relate directly to the names of children and objects in the classroom. The likelihood that children will be successful is enhanced because the concepts represented are meaningful to them. These sentences can be combined to construct a short story.

Our Class

John and Helen hand out books.
Jean and Billy water the plants.
Mary, Mike, and Sarah sit at the big table.
A plant, a book, and a door are in the room.

Similar application activities can be developed for objects and animal names. Read the short phrase and direct the pupils to select from a list of words those that make sense in the sentence. Write the words in the spaces and call on pupils to read the sentence. Several choices make sense; you should ask the child the meaning of each word selected.

On his farm there is ____ ________.
In the woods lives ____ ________.
Sandy went to the farm in ____ ________.
At the farm she saw ____ ________.

a cat a cow a bear a horse a car

Language experience stories are an excellent means for enhancing pupils' sight vocabulary in meaningful context (16). Pupils can be stimulated to dictate group experience stories by your posing questions that encourage pupils to use those words that have been introduced in teacher-directed instruction. What do we do at school? What is in our classroom? What do we know about a cat, a cow, and a horse? are examples of questions that can stimulate pupils to compose stories that allow for meaningful application of sight-word instruction.

Building a Picture-Naming Dictionary

A picture-naming dictionary is an excellent device to use for developing word meanings as well as a multitude of other skills, such as letter sounds and letter names.

INTRODUCTORY ACTIVITY

Secure a number of small pictures from workbooks, magazines, and the like. Have one page devoted to each letter of the alphabet. The pupils paste pictures and the teacher prints a *picture-naming word* beneath each picture. (Note the use of *a* or *some* with the words to maximize attention to them.) A partial **M-m** page is shown below.

APPLICATION ACTIVITY

The pupils' picture dictionaries can be used with the application activities for objects and names in determining other words not given by the teacher that also make sense in the sentences and stories. For example, ask pupils to find two words in their picture dictionaries that have the "long *a*" sound. Also pupils should be shown (with examples and illustrations) how to use their dictionaries to identify words for use in their writing activities.

How, What, When, Where, and Why Words

Instruction and practice on the various "reporter questions" (How? What? When? Where? Why?) help children learn some very important terms used in reading instructions and in following directions.

INTRODUCTORY ACTIVITY

Write the words *how, what, when, where,* and *why* on the chalkboard; say the words (making sure each child is focusing on the word as it is pronounced), and point to each word as you say it. Use the chalkboard, overhead projector, or duplicated materials to present materials similar to the following:

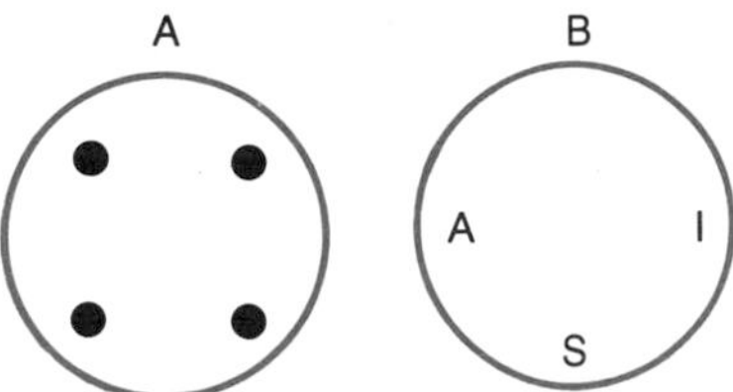

Direct pupils' attention to the written sentences for each of the materials. Call on pupils and write their responses next to the question.

Circle A

How many dots?	There are four dots.
How did you learn this?	We counted them.
When did you count them?	Just now!
What color are the dots?	They are black.
Where is the circle?	Around the dots!
Why is the circle around the dots?	So we could ask how, what, when, where, and why questions.

Circle B

Where are the letters?
How many letters are there?
What are the letters?
What is around the letters?
Why is it around the letters?

Each experience with these important words helps children learn them as sight words.

In, On, Above, Below, Over, Under . . .

The importance of teaching young children the meanings of certain crucial terms used in reading instruction will help avoid unnecessary instructional problems. The "position" words *in, on, above, below, over, under,* and the like need to be understood by children.

INTRODUCTORY ACTIVITY

Use a format similar to the circle-square-table shown below (prepared on oak tag and put on the chalktray or taped on the chalkboard so all can see). Provide each participating child with three or four word cards. Each card has the same "position word" printed on both sides. (As children hold up the card requested, you can check for accuracy.)

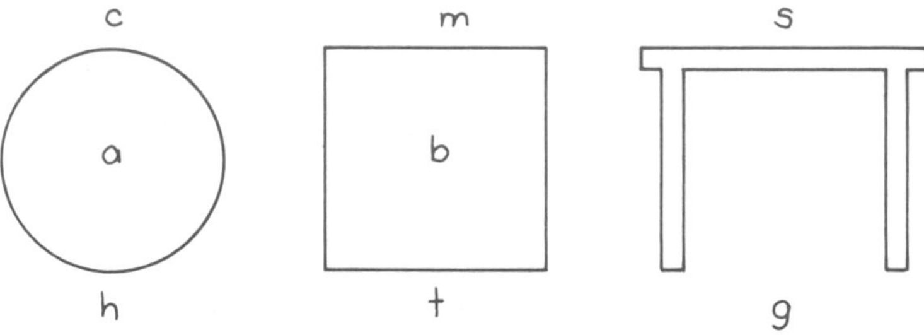

Read the following directions:
Hold up the word *in* (pause) What letter is *in* the circle?
Hold up the word *over* . . . What letter is *over* the square?
Hold up the word *on* . . . What letter is *on* the table?

Continue using all of the word cards issued to the children. Each can be used more than once if desired, for example, *in* the circle, *in* the square; *under* the circle, square, table.

High-Frequency Words Often Confused

Children need a great deal of varied and interesting practice on confusing words that are commonly found in their reading materials. This practice should result in the children knowing the words on sight.

INTRODUCTORY ACTIVITY

Use the chalkboard, overhead projector, or duplicated materials consisting of words frequently confused in early reading. Present these words in pairs and direct pupils' attention to the letter-combination differences.

their	every	when	four	which
there	very	where	for	with

Present the words in sentences and focus on meaning features of the words. Teacher and class (or group) read these sentences in unison, paying heed to the underlined words.

Their house is over there.
Every one said it was very cold.
When were they taken there?
These sell four for a dollar.
Which boy will go with you?

APPLICATION ACTIVITY

Prepare sentences that contain two blank spaces. In front of each sentence write the two words that will complete the sense of the sentence. Students are to write the correct word in each blank space. You may have to read the sentences aloud for many of the pupils.

to
two — 1. The ________ boys were going ________ the store.

for
four — 2. These boxes sell ________ ________ a dollar.

think
thank — 3. I ________ you should ________ him for it.

very
every — 4. ________ teacher was ________ busy.

you
your — 5. Have ________ had ________ dinner?

Reading Teacher-Printed Sentences

Opportunities are in abundance for teachers to enhance the oral vocabularies of children. After new words are learned by children, the words can be used in other areas of reading instruction.

Today is Tuesday.
Today we have our music lesson.
Miss Rogers comes to our room at 10 o'clock.

INTRODUCTORY ACTIVITY

Daily activities can be printed for pupils' information. The teacher reads each sentence, then asks the class to read with him. Following this, he may ask pupils to write (or copy) the sentences and to underline particular words such as *have, our, today, room.* Pupils can also be directed to write phrases pronounced by the teacher, for example, *our room, today we have,* and *today is.*

Assembling Scrambled Sentences

The ability to understand basic sentence structure is a factor related to successful comprehension. Besides helping to understand sentence structure, practice in assembling scrambled sentences aids in acquiring a basic sight vocabulary and a knowledge of terms used in reading instruction (e.g., *period, question mark*).

PRACTICE ACTIVITY

Individual words, from sentences used previously on the chalkboard, are printed on separate cards. These are presented in scrambled order, and pupils arrange the words in proper order, followed by a card bearing the proper punctuation.

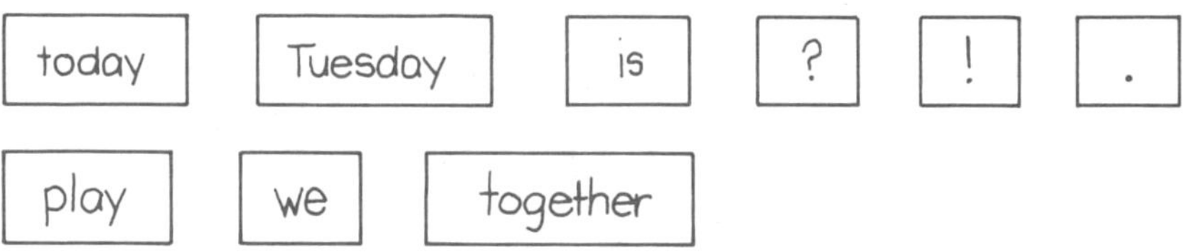

This is one of the many ways to provide repetition with frequently used words.

Classification

The ability to classify words is a beginning step toward successful comprehension. Interesting and concrete terms can be used to motivate children to be successful.

INTRODUCTORY ACTIVITY

Place the underlined classification words on the board. Point to and read each word. Pupils repeat each word after you pronounce it. Each of the other words to be used in the exercise is printed on oak tag or cardboard. Hold up one card at a time and call on a pupil to pronounce the word and to tell under which heading the word belongs.

animals	clothing	food	school
a dog	a hat	my milk	a book
a cat	the shoes	my cookies	a desk
a cow	a dress	my pie	the paper

PRACTICE ACTIVITY

Variations include duplicated seatwork pages with headings such as *toys, plants, months, days.* A number of appropriate words are placed in a box at the bottom of the page, and pupils copy the words under the correct heading.

Further categories can be developed, and pupils complete short sentences by selecting the words that make sense in context.

animals	animal sounds	animal homes
a dog	it moos	the farm
a cow	it barks	the house
a cat	it oinks	the woods
a bear	it meows	

__________ __________ barks.
__________ __________ is the home of a cow.
A dog __________.
On __________ __________ a cow moos.
A cat meows in __________ __________.

Sight words are learned from television, road signs, bulletin boards, label on cartons, and the like. Obviously, the most important source of learning is from meaningful reading situations such as those provided by charts, teacher-written stories, and easy-to-read trade books.

Thus far, the rationale for reading sight words has stressed only that reading development is enhanced as children acquire an ever-increasing stock of "instant recognition words." A skill of such significance to the total reading process should be taught effectively. A number of justifications for learning words as wholes are briefly summarized.

- If a child knows a number of words as sight words (instant recognition), she can be taught to see and to hear similarities between these known words and the new words she meets. Having a sight vocabulary is an invaluable tool in helping her identify other words.
- When words are recognized instantly, analysis is not necessary. The reader can put known words together in phrases, thus focusing on reading for meaning.
- There are numerous high-frequency words that should be learned as units simply because they are met over and over in any reading situation and contribute significantly to using syntax as a means of getting meaning from what is read.

PHONICS

Some knowledge of the history of phonics teaching in American education should be helpful in understanding the problems, attitudes, and misconceptions observable in education today. The following discussion is a brief summary of phonics practices advocated in the past.

Beginning around 1890 and continuing for a period of years, the cornerstone of reading instruction in American schools was a synthetic phonics method. Prior to this era, much time was spent on the rote learning of the ABCs. Apparently, it was believed that unknown words could be identified by saying the names of the letters that comprised these words.

The Synthetic Method

Rebecca Pollard's "synthetic method," introduced about 1890 (23), advocated reducing reading to a number of mechanical procedures, each of which focused on a unit smaller than a word. Reading became very mechanistic and, when mastered, often produced individuals who were adept at working their way through a given word. The result among both teachers and pupils was that reading became equated with "facility in calling words." A few of the teaching procedures recommended during this period are discussed below.

Isolation of Sounds. Drills in articulation were to precede any attempts at reading. The child was to drill on the "sounds of letters." Then, it was reasoned, she would be able to attack whole words. This was a form of phonics drill unrelated to meaning and in some instances unrelated to words in English. Children drilled on isolated sounds as illustrated below:

da	ha	la	ma	pa	ra
be	se	te	ne	le	re
pi	mi	ti	si	li	ri

This drill was not connected with actual reading, since the drills preceded the child's learning of words. It is easy to see that this type of introduction placed little, if any, emphasis on reading *as a process of discovering meaning.*

Single consonants were "sounded." Each consonant was given a sound equivalent to a syllable. Thus *b, c, d, p, h,* and *t* were sounded *buh, cuh, duh, puh, huh,* and *tuh.*

Use of Diacritical Marks. Diacritical markings were widely used in beginning instructional materials. Children used sentences from their reading materials and practiced "marking sentences" by inserting diacritical marks. For example:

> The gh̸ōst wăs ā cŏmmŏn sīg̸h̸t near the w̸rĕc̸k. He k̸new the īs̸lănd was ĕmpty.

Different diacritical marking systems varied as to the number of signs employed. Undoubtedly a few such "helpers" would be more effective than adding a great number of these signals, since they do drastically change the orthography. In the sentences marked above, a slant line indicates a letter that is not sounded; the macron (¯) signals a long vowel sound; the breve (˘) a short vowel sound. Other markings might be underlining digraphs that represent one sound (c̲h̲urch) and underlining single consonants that represent an irregular sound such as his̲ *(s = z)*; c̲ity *(c = s)* or g̲ym *(g = j).*

Word Family Drills. Drills on word families were stressed. These drills were not related to meaning. Sometimes children memorized lists of words ending in such common family phonograms as *ill, am, ick, ate, old, ack.*

A number of widely used reading texts adopted the suggestions of Pollard and, in many cases, extended them. For instance, if the objective of a unit was to teach the phonogram or "family" *ick,* a story might be built primarily from words in that family, without regard to meaning in the passage. The following example is illustrative and, it is hoped, exaggerated.

> Nick flick the tick from the chick with a stick. Prick the tick from the chick with a thick stick. Nick, do not kick the brick, kick the stick.

We do not mean to imply that instruction in word families should never be given. Drill on a column of words entirely unrelated to meaningful reading is a poor learning technique. On the other hand, when children recognize the words *make* and *take* on sight, and they meet the new word *lake* in reading, it would not be poor instruction to point out that this word, and certain others whose meanings are known, contain the common letters *ake* which in every case represent the same speech sound (*cake, bake, wake, snake, rake, shake).* By doing such, the teacher is increasing pupils' chance of success because new learnings are highly related to what pupils already know. Furthermore, it allows pupils an opportunity to apply existing word identification skills to a meaningful reading situation.

There is little point in opposing the teaching of "family groups" on the basis that a relatively small number of English words contain these families. This is not a sound argument because so many small, often used words *are* formed from some thirty such families, and these words are among those most frequently occurring in beginning reading materials (specifically such families as *an, at, it, am, in, as, ate, ask, et, ick, eat, arm, en, ing, ot, est, un, all, ell,* and *ame*). There are enough common or service words which are *not* phonetic to be learned as sight words that any clue, such as word families, that a child can pick up early in learning to read can be useful.

Wylie and Durrell (35) report that "whole phonograms are more easily identified by first-grade children than the separate vowels contained in the phonograms, suggesting that the recognition unit is the phonogram rather than the separate vowel" (p. 790). They report that approximately fifteen-hundred primary grade words include ending phonograms that contain a stable vowel sound.

Finding Little Words in Big Words. Since some of the regular word families are also words *(am, is and, ate, an, all, old, it, at, eat),* the practice of "looking for small words in large words" was advocated. The justification for this practice was that the little words were familiar to the child, and she could pronounce them. If she found little words she

FLASHBACK

Bob and His Pony

Bob has a pony.
He rides his pony.
Clippety-clap!
Clippety-clap!

2

In the early 1900s, materials for teaching reading became more widely available. Many readers included color pictures and related story content. However, the stories did not accurately reflect pupils' language and did not provide for meaningful application of word identification skills.

knew in larger unknown words, she had a start toward mastering the unknown larger word.

The procedure of looking for small words in large words fails for two reasons. First, there is little logic in having the child see the word *ill* in the monosyllabic words *will, Bill, fill, mill, kill,* and *pill,* unless it is the association of *ill* with *pill,* which leaves much to be desired. In teaching reading today, the clue will not be the word *ill* but the sound represented by *ill* in conjunction with the sounds represented by various initial letters: *w, b, f, m, g, k,* and *p.*

The second charge against finding little words appears to be so serious as to remove the practice from the list of justifiable procedures. Many of the little words which retain some degree of pronounceable autonomy in single-syllable words lose this characteristic in words of more than one syllable. In *pan, can, man, fan, tan, ran,* or in *ham, jam, Sam,* noting the little words *an* and *am* would not destroy the pronunciation of the words. However, seeing or pronouncing the *am* in *am*ong, *am*end, *am*en, *am*use, *am*ass would prevent a correct analysis. Likewise, seeing or saying the word *as* in *as*hore, *As*ia, *as*ide, *as*leep; *it* in *it*em; *at* in *at*omic and *at*hlete; or *all* in *all*ow or *all*ege would hinder attempts at word analysis.

The total emphasis on phonics brought the method into disrepute during the 1920s. Reform was not advocated, but rather the elimination of phonics instruction. It was commonly alleged that the abuses of phonics teaching were responsible for the reading problems found at that time.

The Phonics Controversy Today

No other aspect of the reading curriculum has received so much critical attention as phonics instruction. Each generation of reading teachers is faced with both old and new controversies that focus on phonics instruction. Even today, unfortunately, many people believe that phonics is the natural enemy of reading for meaning. Individuals who oppose phonics argue that teaching children to read by focusing on letter-sound relationships interferes with their comprehension. We, too, oppose phonics if a child is required to sound out every word with the correct pronunciation of words becoming the primary goal of reading instruction.

The first objective in sounding out an unknown word is to establish its identity, but this is not the end of the process. The word is identified so that its contribution to the meaning of the sentence can be utilized. If a child sounds out a word without pursuing the meaning of the sentence, she is either a casualty of poor instruction or not quite enough instruction. The objective in using letter-sound relationships is

The teacher should work closely with students who are learning phonics.

to identify unknown words so that the passage can be read for meaning, not to identify words simply because they are there (33).

As mentioned earlier, several studies have found that children progress in a developmental fashion in their word identification skills. In the learning-to-read stage, the learner depends primarily on knowledge of letter-sound relationships to identify words. There is also a strong belief that children who come to school knowing how to read possess basic phonics skills. Donald D. Durrell and Helen A. Murphy (10), who have devoted more than fifty years of work to beginning reading instruction, state:

> The [letter names, writing letters, letter name sounds, and syntax matching] appear to be early stages of reading which all children acquire before they become successful readers. Children who learn to read before coming to school invariably have these phonic skills; occasionally a child cannot write the letters, but the other abilities are always present. (p. 389)

Not only is the need for some phonics instruction supported by research findings and expert opinion (20, 30, 34), but strong support of such instruction has been voiced by the International Reading Association's Board of Directors. The statement that "word analysis skills, including phonics, are critical in learning to read" was adopted for legislative use in 1977 (25).

Rather than taking extreme positions for or against phonics instruction, teachers need to analyze how they will teach children to read. The optimum amount of phonics instruction for each child who is learning to read cannot be determined in terms of the number of hours of instruction. As in the case of all instruction, the teacher holds the key to the success of pupils' reading. You should keep in mind that letter-sound analysis is most effective when used in combination with other skills. The optimum amount of phonics instruction for any learner is the minimum needed to become an independent reader.

Purposes of Phonics Instruction

Phonics instruction consists of teaching letter-sound relationships. These techniques are taught so that the learner will be able to identify words that he does not recognize in print. Beginning readers inevitably meet many words that are not recognized. They cannot solve these unknown print jumbles by staring at them, and sometimes they cannot solve them by using available context clues. By applying their knowledge of letter-sound relationships in combination with available context clues, and understanding that printed language must make sense, children are better equipped to comprehend what they read.

Most likely, the written word that puzzles the child is a word he has spoken or heard many times. So the purpose of phonics instruction *is not* to teach learners "how to pronounce words." Applying letter-sound relationships simply reveals the pronunciation, or yields an approximate pronunciation, of the unknown word symbol. The purposes of phonics instruction are to:

- Teach the beginning reader that printed letters and letter combinations represent speech sounds heard in words. The speech sounds heard in words are quite different from those sounds heard in isolation. To identify the word *cat* in the sentence "the *cat* ran after the mice," three phonemes are blended just as they are in saying the word *cat*. Beginning readers should not be taught to produce three syllables *kuh-ah-tuh* = *cat*.
- Teach the learner to blend the sounds represented by the printed letters when he meets a word he does not recognize. Blending the sounds represented by letter patterns into meaningful words is an es-

sential part of phonics instruction (4,5,11,14). Blending permits the child to determine whether or not the word is in his speaking or listening vocabulary and whether it makes sense in context.

- Teach the learner to use all available cue systems in combination with letter-sound relationships to identify words and comprehend written text. Word meanings and comprehension should be given primary attention in teaching phonics (7,10,12,16). Too much emphasis on using letter-sound relationships to identify isolated words will develop a *set* within the learner that this is reading. The only way a child can miss the fact that reading is a meaning-making process is if he receives initial instruction that masks this fact.

Tasks Involved in Phonics Instruction

There is a series of instructional tasks which, taken together, constitute the phonics program. Different phonics teaching materials will include a number of techniques that are common to all approaches. They may differ as to the sequence in which skills are introduced, the emphasis on children's learning rules, the number of different steps taught, and how much phonics instruction is included in beginning reading. The major phonics instruction tasks cover:

- Auditory discrimination of speech sounds in words.
- Written letters that are used to represent these speech sounds.
- The sound represented by a letter or letters in a known word that can be used to unlock the pronunciation of unknown words in which these particular letters occur.
- Sounds of consonants in initial and final positions.
- Blended consonants.
- Special consonant digraphs *(th, ch, sh, wh).*
- Short and long vowel sounds.
- Double vowels, vowel digraphs, and diphthongs.
- Vowels followed by *r.*
- Effect of final *e.*
- Sounds of *y.*

It should not be inferred that each of the above steps is of equal importance in learning to read or that each should receive the same amount of instructional time. The steps listed are simply the framework, since some steps include many specific tasks.

The actual learning of phonics as it relates to reading usually begins quite early in the preschool years. The child learns the sound of a word like *mommy* and can easily differentiate it from similar-sounding words. He may have a pet kitty and a playmate Kathy and will differentiate if asked "Where is Kathy?" even though the kitty is also present. Phonics instruction begins when an adult talks with an infant, thus providing the child with a model.

When a child associates sounds with objects and does not confuse words that are very similar such as *mommy, money, monkey,* and *maybe,* he is mastering auditory discrimination, which is important for phonic analysis in the reading process. None of the later "steps" in learning phonics can take place in the absence of mastery of this basic language function. Beginning reading instruction in the school builds on the child's previous language experiences. In reading, the child will have to make visual discriminations among written word symbols and learn that the written symbols represent the speech sounds of words he speaks and understands.

Phonics Instruction

Why Begin with Consonant Sounds? Most instructional materials used in beginning reading advocate that the teaching of letter sounds begin with consonants. This position is supported by the following factors:

- A number of consonants *(b, f, d, h, j, k, p, m, l, r, t,* etc.*)* have only one sound. Once the child masters these letter-sound associations, this skill can be transferred when identifying other words in which these letters occur. On the other hand, vowels in written words are often inconsistent in the sounds they represent.
- Children must learn to read from left to right. Since most English words begin with consonants, the first letter or letters a child must sound out in an unknown word will be consonants.
- If a reader uses context along with sounding, the initial sound in the word helps eliminate most alternative possibilities. To illustrate, each of the following blank lines represents an unknown word.
  (a) ________
  (b) n________
  The blank space in (a) can represent any word in English, while in (b) *all* words which do not begin with the letter *n* are eliminated. Below, each sentence contains a different unknown word. It is likely that the one-sentence context and the initial consonant will permit you to solve the unknown word. Larger contexts would make the task even easier.
  (a) "Pull that n________ out of the board," said Grandfather.
  (b) "What's the n________ of that song?" asked Mary. "It's on the n________record I bought yesterday."
  (c) "The big right-hander struck out in the last of the n________."

Neither consonants nor vowels should be sounded in isolation *(cat = kuh-ah-tuh)*. Since no instructional materials advocate sounding letters in isolation, the statement has little relevancy as an argument for teaching vowels first. It should be kept in mind that one of the most important clues to the sounds of vowels is provided by consonants that follow vowels. A consonant-vowel-consonant pattern usually results in a short vowel sound—*cat, den, can.* The same is true if the vowel is followed by two consonants *(cattle, dentist, canvas).*

Teaching Initial Consonant Sounds

Starting from the premise that the child has learned to recognize a few words on sight, which for illustrative purposes we will assume includes the words *be, back,* or *ball,* she is now ready to associate the sound of *b* in these words with the written symbol *b.*

INTRODUCTORY ACTIVITY

Print an uppercase *B* on the chalkboard and say, "Today we will learn all about the letter *B*. Next to the uppercase *B* I will print a lowercase *b*. This uppercase *B* is also called a capital *B*. Now I am going to write some words which begin with lowercase *b*." Write *be, back,* and *ball* on the chalkboard. Point to each word and pronounce it. Stress the initial sound of *b* without distorting it. Direct pupils to look at each word as it is pronounced. "Who can give us another word that begins with the sound heard in the words? *Yes, bear, boat, big.* We write Bobby with a capital *B* because it is somebody's name."

Bb
be
back
ball
boat
Bobby

When a number of examples have been given, ask, "What sound do we hear at the beginning of each of these words? That's right, they all begin with the sound of *b*—*bear, ball, boat, bat, big, bomb.*" (Point to each word as it is pronounced.) As the words are called out by the children, add them to the list on the board. You should ask, "What do we *see* that is the same in all of these words? That's right, they all begin with the letter *b*." It should be noted that in no instance were the children asked to sound the letter *b* in isolation, although it was emphasized without distortion.

APPLICATION ACTIVITY

To provide for immediate meaningful application of the sound represented by the letter *b* and how initial consonants combined with context can provide clues to word identification, sentences such as the following should be written on the board.

B______ put the b______ in the water.
We will b_____ coming b____ to class after lunch.

"You all have done well telling me words that begin with the *b* sound. Look carefully at each word on the board as I say it. Each word begins with the letter *b* and the sound of *b*. I am going to read a sentence for you two times that has two words missing. The missing words begin with the letter *b* and the *b* sound. (Point to blanks and letter *b*.) Listen and watch carefully as I read this sentence one time. (Point to first sentence and move hand left to right under the words as sentence is read to the children.) Now, I want each of you to listen and watch carefully as I read the sentence again and tell me which of the words from our list makes sense in the sentence." Point to list and read aloud each word as it is pointed to. Read each sentence, asking a pupil for a word from the list that makes sense in each blank. Write each response in the appropriate blank. Engage all pupils in instruction by asking them if the word choices sound like something they would say. Ask if they could draw a picture of what is happening and so forth. Tell pupils why their choices are either correct (make sense) or incorrect.

Both of the activities described above for teaching letter-sound association possess features of effective reading instruction presented in chapter 3. Specifically these features include:

- Relating new learnings (letter-sound association) to past learnings (sight words).
- Asking literal-level questions (Who can give other words beginning with the sound represented by *b*?) Does the sentence make sense?
- Using direct instruction and structure (moving in small, highly related instructional steps).
- Providing for immediate application of skills in meaningful reading situations.
- Rewarding pupils' effort and thinking and not just the correctness of responses.

In addition to the group work just described, there can be workbook or teacher-made exercises that give each child an opportunity to practice the concept taught. The application activity would best be done in the group setting by giving children a worksheet that has two or three sentences similar to the earlier examples. Read each sentence several times as pupils follow along and have them print the correct word in each blank. Monitor their perfomance closely to assure that they are successful. Other exercises to provide for practice can be done as seatwork. Be sure to establish a purpose for these tasks and do a few practice exercises so pupils understand what they are to do and increase their chance of success. Be readily available to assist any child who experiences difficulty.

INTRODUCTORY ACTIVITY

In the row of pictures below, the child is to mark those objects whose names begin with the same sound as the name of the object in the picture on the extreme left.

A picture of a familiar object is shown along with the word represented by the object in the picture. The example shown here is a bell. The child can see the letter *b* and hear the sound *b* represents. She is then to mark all the other words in a supplied list which begin with the same sound.

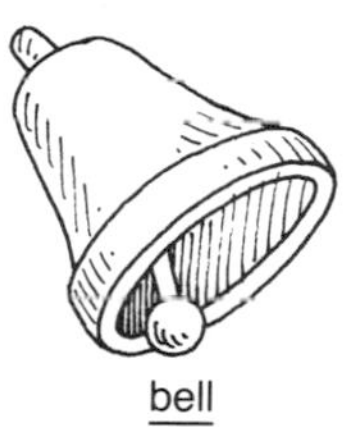

be play
lake boat
book

Words in columns are presented, some of which begin with the same sound and the same letter. The child is to draw a line from the word in column A to the word in column B which begins with the same sound.

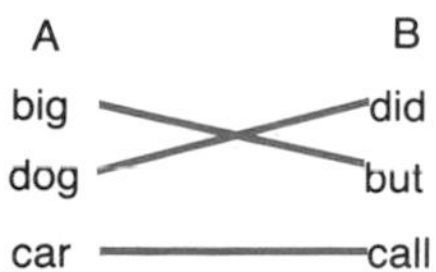

A pictured object is shown, followed by four words, none of which names the picture, but one or more of which begin with the same sound as the name of the pictured object. The child is to draw a circle around the boxes (or around the words) that begin with the same sound.

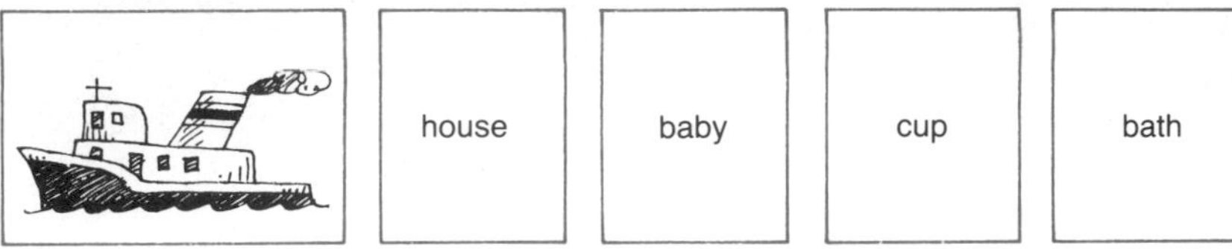

A series of boxes is shown, each containing three words. The teacher pronounces one of the words and the pupil underlines the word pronounced. She need not know all of the words as sight words, provided she is familiar with the initial sound of each. In the following example, the teacher could pronounce the italicized words. There are many other types of exercises and many variations of those illustrated.

1	2	3	4	5
call *bank* play	*tell* sell fell	hill fill *bill*	*may* pay say	hat show *bat*

A word of caution needs to be interjected here to point out that activities such as the above should be evaluated carefully in terms of whether or not they actually provide auditory practice. Children may simply complete some auditory discrimination activities by merely matching the initial letter shapes. The activities become visual discrimination exercises, and as a result the children do not have the opportunity to practice letter-sound associations. The teacher needs to closely monitor pupils to see that each of them actually *sounds out* the word symbols that are given as stimuli.

Furthermore, the majority of such activities provide no opportunity to apply auditory discrimination skills in meaningful context. Application is extremely important and will need to be provided by the teacher. One way to allow for continued application, direct instruction, structure, and highly related learning steps that maximize pupils' chance of success and engagement in learning is to utilize an application procedure similar to the earlier example. Workbook practice activities can be reviewed and discussed in group settings and the words found in these activities presented in meaningful context.

Substitution of Initial Sounds

The next important skill to be learned is to substitute known letter sounds in attacking unknown words. Assume the child knows the words *take* and *make* and meets the unknown word *rake.* She should be able to combine the *r* sound that she knows in words like *run, rain,* or *ride* with the sound of *ake* in *take.* By this process she should unlock the new word (21). If the reader has mastered the steps in phonics previously introduced, this step also starts from that which is known, that is, sight words and the sounds initial consonants contribute to words.

In beginning reading it is a common practice to teach a number of monosyllabic words containing frequently used phonograms. Practically all workbooks use these "word families" as a means of teaching new words. Work on the substitution of initial consonants parallels early levels of most basal series. Moving through early levels, the child meets such words as *came, fame, same, name, game* and words containing other common phonograms. Each of these words contains a familiar and often recurring phonogram. Children should not receive drill on these word endings in isolation. Nevertheless, a number of important words can be solved independently when the child knows some sight words containing commonly used letter combinations and can substitute initial letter sounds.

PRACTICE ACTIVITY

Pictures may be used in teaching letter-sound substitutions. It is important that the pictures present words that are in the child's experiential-conceptual background. In the example presented below, the picture of the hen could be a poor example for some children because they could perceive it as a chicken. Direct the children to name the picture, listen to the first sound in the picture name, and write the letter that represents this sound in the blank. Do the first two with the children to make sure they understand what they are to do.

APPLICATION ACTIVITY

Opportunities for the children to apply letter-sound substitution skills in meaningful sentence context must be provided by the teacher. By applying such skills in context, pupils begin to understand that phonics is a tool for getting meaning. The sentences below are examples of those that can be used in a group setting that allow for pupils' application of skills. Also, such instruction builds on past learnings to enhance pupils' chances of success. (Note that many of the words used for learning the sound represented by *b* are found in these sentences.)

Bobby has a ________ pet ________.

fat	cat
bat	hat
hat	mat

The ________ will be back at ________ o'clock.

pen	ten
men	hen
ten	pen

Bill took his ________, ________, and ________ to the baseball game.

hat	ball	cat
rat	fall	bat
fat	call	sat

Final Consonant Substitution

Some teachers prefer to teach consonant sounds at the ends of words at the same time that they deal with a particular initial consonant sound. Other teachers work through the initial sounds and then work on single consonant sounds at the ends of words. Regardless of which procedure is followed, the child is taught to notice visually and aurally the final consonants in short words. He knows words such as *men, log, pen, bold, leg* and the sounds of letters, including *t.* He is now asked to substitute the sound presented by *t* at the end of the words given above to get *met, lot, pet, bolt,* and *let.*

Initial Blends

To avoid confusion in dealing with many words that the child will meet early in the process of learning to read, attention must be focused on more than the initial consonant. These words fall into two classes: simple consonant blends and a smaller group of two-consonant combinations (consonant digraphs) representing special speech sounds in English *(th, sh, ch, wh).*

The twenty-four two- and three-letter blends may be divided into three major groups on the basis of a common letter:

Those which begin with *s: sc, sk, sm, sn, sp, st, sw, str*
Those which conclude with *l: bl, cl, fl, gl, pl, sl, spl*
Those which conclude with *r: br, cr, dr, fr, gr, pr, tr, scr, spr, str*

The above arrangement is not intended to suggest a particular order in which blends should be taught. A logical sequence would probably be determined by the vocabulary found in the instructional materials actually used in beginning reading.

There is a great deal of variance among teachers as well as among basal readers as to when blends are dealt with, which are taught first, and how rapidly the blends are covered. Most materials suggest teaching initial blends first and later stressing blends and special consonant sounds at the ends of words *(rest, nest, best, bark, mark).* Although there are numerous approaches for teaching consonant blends, the objectives of all methods are to lead the child to:

- See the printed letters involved.
- Understand that in every instance the letter sounds combine into a blended sound.
- Discriminate auditorily among the sounds of individual letters and blends—*d*ug, *r*ug, *dr*ug; *s*old, *c*old, *sc*old.

Any procedure for teaching initial consonant sounds can be utilized for teaching each of the different consonant blends. A few techniques are illustrated next.

INTRODUCTORY ACTIVITY

Secure a number of pictures of concrete objects with which children are familiar and whose names begin with a blend. Show the pictures one at a time and have the children write or say the blended letters. (They are not to simply name the picture.) Examples: *sk*ate, *tr*ain, *br*idge, *pl*ate, *gr*apes, *sl*ed, *fr*og, *cl*ock, *st*ar, *bl*anket, *sn*ake, *st*ore, *pl*ow, *cl*own, *sw*ing, *sch*ool.

Prepare and duplicate sentences containing a number of blends. Have pupils underline each blend.

The black crow flew away from the tree.
Pretty bright flowers grew near the bridge.
What is the price of the green dress in the store window?
We will rest when we reach the coast about dusk.

Add one of the letters *c, g, p, t* in front of each of the letter groups to produce a consonant blend. Underline the letters which blend.

__reat	__roud	__rain	__rop
__reek	__rail	__rice	__ruly
__rint	__reen	__row	__rize
__rip	__rack	__ree	__rand

Step 1. Place on the chalkboard a list of words that begin with *p* and to which *s* can be added as a first letter to form the blend *sp*. Pronounce these words with the children.

Step 2. Write the *sp* blend word to the right of each word. Have the children note the *visual* pattern *sp* at the beginning of each word. Guide the children in pronouncing the two words in each pair in rapid succession and in noting the blended sound in the second word in each pair (*p*ot-*sp*ot, *p*in-*sp*in; etc.)

Step1	Step 2
pot	spot
pin	spin
pill	spill
peak	speak
pool	spool
poke	spoke
park	spark

Most of the other initial blends can be handled in much the same manner. Illustrative word pairs with *tr:* *r*ace-*tr*ace; *r*ain-*tr*ain; *r*ip-*tr*ip; *r*ust-*tr*ust; *r*ap-*tr*ap; *r*ail-*tr*ail; *r*ay-*tr*ay; etc. In teaching *sl:* *l*id-*sl*id; *l*ap-*sl*ap; *l*ip-*sl*ip; *l*ed-*sl*ed; *l*ow-*sl*ow; *l*ack-*sl*ack; *l*ick-*sl*ick.

APPLICATION ACTIVITY

Use "reading clues" in teaching initial blends. Write the blend that spells the word that fits the clue. Examples:

We use our __ __ain to think.
Apples and pears are __ __uits we eat.
We put our nose on a rose to __ __ell it.
A __ __amp is needed to mail a letter.

Teaching Consonant Digraphs

A digraph is a combination of two letters which when pronounced results in one speech sound. This sound is not a blend of the two letters. Some digraphs have more than one sound *(ch* = *k* in *character; sh* in *chiffon; ch* in *church).* Techniques used in teaching consonants and blends and the illustrations of teaching *ch* and *sh* that follow will apply in teaching other digraphs.

INTRODUCTORY ACTIVITY

Place words beginning with *ch* on the board and direct children's attention to these initial letters. Pronounce each word, making sure pupils *listen* to the sound of *ch* in each word and look at the word at the same time you pronounce it. When pronouncing each word, emphasize, but do not distort the *ch* sound. Have pupils pronounce each word as it is pointed out. Point to words in a random fashion to encourage maximum attention. Ask pupils to provide other words which begin with a *ch* sound heard in *chair, child,* etc. Write these on the board beneath the original words.

chair
child
chance
chick
chill
chose

Contrast single initial consonant sounds and initial digraph sounds in words. Place words shown in column A on the chalkboard and pronounce these words with the children. Next, write the words in column B, pointing out the visual pattern *sh* at the beginning of each word. Have the children pronounce each pair of words (*h*ip-*sh*ip) to contrast the different initial sounds. The procedure outlined above may be used with words that begin with *s* or *sh*. As the children contrast the initial sound in each pair of words, they note the visual pattern *(s-sh)* and hear the initial sounds represented by these letters.

A	B
hip	ship
hop	shop
hot	shot
hark	shark
hare	share
harp	sharp
sell	shell
sort	short
sip	ship
save	shave
self	shelf
sock	shock

APPLICATION ACTIVITY

Provide for application in context by writing sentences such as the following on the board. Ask children to listen carefully as each sentence is read aloud and tell you which word should be written in the blank so the sentence makes sense.

Bill found a ________ to ________ to Bobby.
shell sell shell sell

Daddy has to __________ every morning.
save shave

A __________ was seen swimming next to the __________.
hark shark shop ship

Use "reading clues" in teaching initial digraphs. Read the clue—spell the word by adding a digraph. Examples:

Part of leg—rhymes with *ch*in: ___ ___in
Doesn't cost much: ___ ___eap

Use "reading clues" in another way to teach initial digraphs. Read the clue—spell the word by using one of the digraphs provided in parentheses.

Clue	Clue
Used in bread ___ ___eat (wh, ch)	not open ___ ___ut (th, sh)
find on seashore ___ ___ell (sh, th)	largest in ocean ___ ___ale (th, wh)
can sit on it ___ ___air (sh, ch)	not fat ___ ___in (wh, th)
never do it! ___ ___eat (th,ch)	sun can do it ___ ___ine (wh, sh)
use your head ___ ___ink (sh,th)	must be round ___ ___eel (wh, th)

At a later time children will be taught that *ch* = *k,* as in *chorus, chemistry, chrome, character* and *ch* = *sh,* as in *chauffeur, chamois, chef, Chicago.* Other frequently met digraphs include *sh, wh, th, gh, ng,* and *ph.* The sounds of these letter combinations are as follows:

sh—sound heard in *sh*oe, *sh*op, *sh*ell, *sh*ort, wi*sh*, fi*sh.*
wh sounds like *hw: wh*en-*hw*en, *wh*eel-*hw*eel, *wh*ich-*hw*ich. When *wh* is followed by *o,* the *w* is silent: *wh*ole-*h*ole, *wh*ose-*h*ooz, *wh*om-*h*oom.
th—two sounds. Voiced: *th*em, *th*ere, *th*ey, wi*th;* voiceless: *th*in, *th*ree, *th*row, wid*th.*
gh—sound of *f* in lau*gh,* tou*gh,* cou*gh*, etc. Silent in ni*gh*t, bou*gh,* ei*gh*t, thou*gh*t, etc.
ng—sounded as in sa*ng,* wi*ng*, so*ng,* ru*ng*.
ph—usually sounded as *f: ph*one, ne*ph*ew, gra*ph.*

Teaching Vowel-Letter Sounds

Vowels are the worst offenders in any examination of grapheme-phoneme irregularities. Regardless of these irregularities, mastering letter-sound relationships is absolutely essential. The function of the teacher and school is to provide guidance, and most children gain proficiency in phonic analysis more quickly with guidance that leads to insights. Requiring rote memorization of a great number of rules will hinder some children in understanding the relationship between the rules and their reading. They may become so involved with learning the rules that they miss the application. On the other hand, having a generalization verbalized is often a help to learning.

Short Vowel Sounds

Techniques for teaching letter-sound relationships are unlimited. Each illustration presented will deal with only one vowel-letter sound since all of the other vowel sounds can be taught in the same manner simply by changing stimulus words. Practically any lesson can be presented via the chalkboard, overhead projector, or on duplicated pages for seatwork. Paramount consideration, however, must be given to the use of ongoing diagnosis, structure and direct instruction, opportunity to apply skills, and pupils' attention to learning tasks (see chapter 3).

INTRODUCTORY ACTIVITY

Visual-Auditory Association (illustrated using short *e*). Select a few easy words which have been used previously and which contain the vowel pattern being taught. Write these words in a column and pronounce each word with the children. Have children note the vowel letter in the middle of the word and emphasize the sound it represents in *met, set, pet,* and so forth.

The material below might constitute three different presentations on different days. Column A contains one pattern of CVC words, column B mixed patterns, and column C longer words. Words having the CVC pattern should initially contain the short *e* and short *u.* The sounds represented by these vowels in CVC words are highly regular (21). This allows for structuring pupils' learning around tasks where they can experience success. Once pupils have mastered such CVC pattern words, this skill can be used to introduce the other CVC patterns that are less regular.

As pupils experience a high level of success with the one pattern of CVC words, this should enable them to experience success with mixed patterns. After high levels of success with the mixed patterns, instruction can focus on longer words. Thus, all instruction builds in small, highly related steps.

A	B	C
met	leg	desk
set	men	bell
pet	bed	dress
bet	pep	sled
let	wet	best
jet	hen	help

APPLICATION ACTIVITY

Application of the skill in context should be provided for each area of instruction before moving to the next area. Examples of meaningful application follow. Note that each group of sentences builds on and reinforces previous learning.

Write a word from the right-hand column in the blank that makes sense in each sentence.

I like to ________ a cat. Bobby ________ me that he could ring the bell. Bill ________ me sail the ship.	met set let bet pet
The ________ let me play in the big boat. The cat fell off of the boat and got ________. Bob took a nap in ________.	leg men pep bed hen wet
Bill had to ________ Bobby pull the ________ up the hill. They are ________ pals and like to play in the snow. Mary put her book on her ________ at school.	desk bell sled best help

INTRODUCTORY ACTIVITY

Contrasting Short Vowel Sounds in Words. Write a column of identical initial and final consonants, leaving a blank space for adding a vowel letter (step 1). Insert a vowel letter to complete the first word (step 2); call on a child to name the word (step 3). Continue using a different vowel letter for each blank space. When the column is complete, have the children read the words in rapid succession to contrast the vowel sounds (step 4). Present words in meaningful context, omitting the vowel letter. Call on each student to provide a vowel for the word that makes sense in the sentence (step 5).

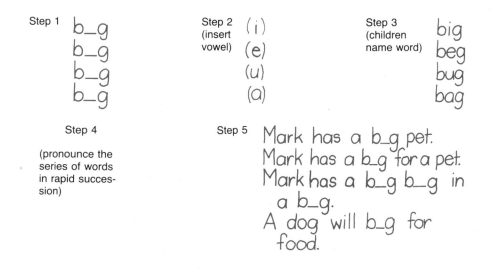

Step 1		Step 2 (insert vowel)		Step 3 (children name word)	
	b_g		(i)		big
	b_g		(e)		beg
	b_g		(u)		bug
	b_g		(a)		bag

Step 4

(pronounce the series of words in rapid succession)

Step 5

Mark has a b_g pet.
Mark has a b_g for a pet.
Mark has a b_g b_g in a b_g.
A dog will b_g for food.

Students practice word identification skills reading inside a reading tent.

Other stimulus patterns: b*u*d, b*a*d, b*e*d; p*a*n, p*u*n, p*i*n, p*e*n; p*a*t, p*e*t, p*i*t, p*o*t; h*u*t, h*i*t, h*o*t, h*a*t.

Working with Final Phonograms. Have children name the picture, then blend the initial letter (shown beneath the picture) with each of the phonograms at the right of the picture. Pupils' attention should be focused first on naming the picture and then selecting the final phonogram. Finally, they write the correct letter pattern in the blank spaces to complete the word. If they experience difficulties, have them say each phonogram /at/, /ot/, /ut/ and then blend the /c/ with each. Again, be sure that pupils can recognize each picture and name it. The pictures of the *well* and the *cot* might not be in all pupils' experiential-conceptual background. Using pictures that are familiar to the children is important in order to maximize their attention to learning and chance of success.

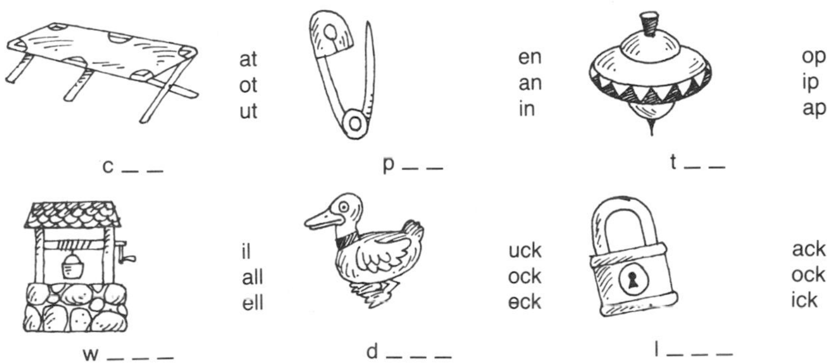

APPLICATION ACTIVITY

Prepare simple sentences, each of which contains a blank space. Each sentence is followed by two words which differ only as to vowel letter. One of these words makes sense in the sentence. If done orally via the chalkboard, a child *names* the correct word, and it is then written in the blank space to complete the sentence. (If the exercise is done as seatwork, the child reads both words and then writes the correct word in the blank space.)

The cat drank milk from the ________.	(cap, cup)
Tom hit the ball with the ________.	(bat, bit)
The ________ was in the pen.	(peg, pig)
We have ________ fingers.	(tin, ten)
John had a ________ of candy.	(bag, bug)

The various activities that have been presented illustrate the importance of teaching pupils to blend sounds represented by letters and letter combinations without distortion. Blending is an extremely important, yet often neglected area in many basal programs (4, 7, 11, 14).

Long Vowel Sounds

Generalizations covering vowel letter-sound relationships are quite numerous. However, many of these do not apply to a large number of letter patterns (3,6). Illustrative teaching procedures will be cited for two adjacent vowels (*ea, ai, ee, oa* patterns), final *e* words, and long vowel sounds at the end of short words.

Adjacent Vowels (same syllable). When two adjacent vowels represent a single sound they are referred to as vowel digraphs (f*ee*t, b*oa*t, s*ai*l, m*ea*n). One of the more widely quoted generalizations relates to vowel digraphs. "When two vowels come together they usually represent the long vowel sound of the first vowel" or "The first vowel represents a long sound and the second is not sounded," "When two vowels come together, the first vowel does the talking, the second goes walking." When this rule is applied to all two-vowel situations, there are about as many exceptions as instances where it applies. This rule has been found to apply less than half the time in word samples tested (3,6). For the specific vowel combinations of *ee, oa, ea,* and *ai,* it holds much more frequently.

INTRODUCTORY ACTIVITY

Contrast Single-Double Vowel Patterns. Prepare lists of words selected so that the first has a single vowel (met), and the second is identical except for an added vowel (m*e*at).

Children read the first word under column A and listen for the short vowel sound. Then they read the first word under column B, note the two-vowel pattern, and listen for the long vowel sound. As a final step, have the children read each pair in rapid succession to note the contrasting vowel sound (met-m*e*at; led-l*e*ad, etc.).

A	B	A	B	A	B
e	*ea*	*a*	*ai*	*e*	*ee*
met	meat	man	main	fed	feed
led	lead	lad	laid	met	meet
men	mean	pal	pail	pep	peep
bed	bead	ran	rain	bet	beet
stem	steam	bat	bait	wed	weed
set	seat	plan	plain	step	steep

Similar word lists can be prepared using the *o-oa, e-ea,* and *a-ai* patterns.

APPLICATION ACTIVITY

Provide opportunity for application by using sentences such as the following. Focus on selecting words that make sense in the sentence.

The __________ ate __________ for dinner.
(man, main) (meat, met)

Bobby put the ________ in the ________.
(bait, bat) (pal, pail)

The __________ had to __________ on the __________.
(men, mean) (step, steep) (weed, wed)

INTRODUCTORY ACTIVITY

Different Visual Patterns Represent the Same Sound. Prepare lists of homonyms in which one word in each pair contains either the *ai* or *a e* pattern. Other pairs contain either the *ea* or *ee* pattern.

The following exercise may be used for group work at the chalkboard or duplicated for independent seatwork. Provide practice with two or three examples, and specify clearly to the pupils what they are to do. Check often to make sure each child is successfully completing the task.

Two words may sound alike but not be spelled alike

Are these words		spelled alike? (yes/no)	pronounced alike? (yes/no)	vowel sound you hear
A	B			
the sail	the sale	________	________	________
I'm weak	the week	________	________	________
my heel	will heal	________	________	________
he made	a maid	________	________	________

APPLICATION ACTIVITY

Application in meaningful context is extremely important because children must understand that it is the context in which the word(s) appears that determines its meaning (not the correct pronunciation). Sentences such as the following can be introduced and the meaning of each sentence, in terms of the homonyms, pointed out and discussed.

Mark wants to learn how to ________.
(sale, sail)
Mark went to buy a new boat at the ________.
(sale, sail)
Mary was ________ because she did not eat.
(weak, week)
Mary did not eat for a ________.
(weak, week)

PRACTICE ACTIVITY

Association of Long Vowel Sounds with Letter Patterns. Line A shows a picture and three words which differ only as to vowel pattern. The child pronounces

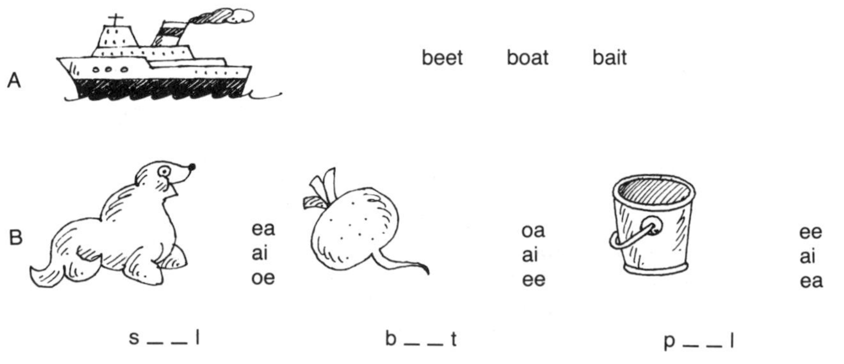

the words and circles the naming word. Line B shows a series of pictures and vowel patterns. The child names each picture, then blends each set of vowels (shown at right of picture) with letters shown below it. The correct vowel pattern is then written on the blank spaces to complete the naming word.

Final e Pattern. In order to better decode syllables, children should focus on the spelling pattern of consonant, vowel, consonant, vowel *e*. The "final *e*" does not represent a sound, and the other vowel letter represents the long sound.

INTRODUCTORY ACTIVITY

The Effect of Final e. Write a column of CVC words on the chalkboard, each of which contains the medial vowel *a* (step 1). As these words are pronounced have the children tell which vowel sound they hear in the word (ă). Explain that you will change each word by adding the letter *e* at the end of each word. (Print the words shown in step 2.) As these words are pronounced, have the children note the *a*__*e* pattern and tell the vowel sound they hear in each of the words (ā).

Step 1	Step 2
can	cane
hat	hate
mad	made
pal	pale
rat	rate
plan	plane

Have the children explain what vowel sound they hear in words with two vowels when one is a final *e*. Their explanations may then be restated: "In many short words showing two vowels, a final *e* is not sounded while the first vowel has its long sound."

Word pairs for other final *e* series: *bit-bite, pin-pine, hid-hide, kit-kite, rid-ride, slid-slide, not-note, hop-hope, rod-rode, rob-robe.*

PRACTICE ACTIVITY

Prepare an exercise for either chalkboard presentation or independent seatwork. Supply a list of CVC words, some of which can be changed to another word by adding a final *e*.

Children read the stimulus word and determine if adding the letter *e* will make a known word. Make sure they focus on asking themselves if the word they are making sounds like a word they have heard before. Make sure each child understands what she is to do by completing some examples in a group. The word is named (if an oral exercise) or the child writes the word in the space provided.

If the word can be changed into another word by adding a final *e*, write the new word on the line provided. If adding an *e* does not make a word, leave the line blank.

can	______	hid	______
rat	______	sob	___*___
top	___*___	mad	______
plan	______	bit	______
kit	______	not	______
hop	______	tap	______
cat	___*___	rob	______
cut	______	big	___*___

*spaces left blank

INTRODUCTORY ACTIVITY

Exceptions to Final e Rule. A number of high-frequency final *e* words do not follow the rule, and these irregularities should be pointed out to children. The following material focuses on these exceptions.

According to the rule, words under columns A and B should have a long vowel sound. Each pair of words should rhyme since they end with the same letters. One of the words is an outlaw and will not follow the rule. Write the outlaw word in the box.

A	B	Do they rhyme?	Outlaws
some	home	______	some
brave	have	______	______
move	stove	______	______
bone	done	______	______
wove	love	______	______
give	hive	______	______
come	dome	______	______
cone	gone	______	______
none	tone	______	______

APPLICATION ACTIVITY

The following connected set of sentences allows for application in a story setting. Continually encourage the students to ask themselves if the word sounds like a word they know, to ask themselves if it makes sense in the sentence, and to use context to help identify the best word choice.

Select a word from the list that makes sense in each of the blanks.

Bill has a ball and a bat.	give
The bat and ball c_________ in a set.	home
Dad will paint Bill's n_________ on the bat and ball in green paint.	came
When Bill got h_________ Dad g_________ him the bat and ball.	come
On the bat and ball was Bill's n_________ in green paint.	name
	none
	cone
	gave

Note that this application example is building on what the children have already learned about identifying words to get meaning. All of the words used should be from previously introduced phonics instruction. This feature allows for maximum success, purposeful learning, and meaningful application, as discussed in chapter 3. Furthermore, providing the initial consonant letter for the missing word helps children to attend to the task of using context clues along with minimal visual cues to get at meaning.

Long Vowel Sounds at the End of Short Words. There are two generalizations that cover single vowels at the end of words: "If a word has only one vowel which ends the word, the vowel sound usually is long" and "If a word has no other vowel and ends with *y*, the letter *y* serves as a vowel and is pronounced as long *i*." These generalizations apply in a limited number of high frequency words and can be taught at the chalkboard, using columns of words. Application activities similar to those discussed throughout the earlier sections should also be utilized.

be	by	try	go
me	my	sky	no
he	cry	fly	so
we	why	fry	ho
she	dry	shy	yo-yo

Vowels Affected by Particular Consonants

The long and short vowel sounds are by far the most important vowel clues in helping children unlock the pronunciation of words. In addition, there are other vowel patterns which should be explained, even though they may be of lesser importance in phonic analysis. When a vowel is followed by *r*, the sound of that vowel is affected by the *r*.

Usually a blend results, which is neither the long nor the short sound of the vowel *(car, curl, fir, for, park)*. When the vowel *a* is followed by *l* or *w*, the resulting sound is a blend *(yawn, tall, awful, talcum, awning, ball)*.

Although a number of words contain a vowel followed by *r*, it is debatable whether this particular letter-sound combination causes beginning readers much trouble. That is, if children master the long and short vowel relationships they are not likely to experience serious trouble with vowels followed by *r*. Undoubtedly, there are many successful readers who are unaware of the difference between the vowel sounds in the words *can* and *car*.

Diphthongs

Diphthongs are two adjacent vowels, each of which is sounded, such as the *ou* in *house*, *oi* in *oil*, *oy* in *boy*, *ow* in *how* (but not the *ow* in *blow*, *grow*, or *throw*, where the sound is long *o*). It is doubtful that teaching diphthongs is of major importance in the total phonics program. These sounds are met in a number of words that are learned as sight words, and certain words can serve as keys to help the pupil hear the sounds *(house, oil, boy, how)*.

INTRODUCTORY ACTIVITY

To teach that the visual pattern *ow* has two sounds, place two columns of words on the board. In column B the *ow* represents long *o;* in column A the *ow* is a diphthong. Have children note that words in a column rhyme, but that words under A do not rhyme with those under B.

A	B
now	low
how	snow
cow	grow
plow	blow

Write some three-word series and have the children identify the two words that rhyme.

1. plow	cow	slow		4. grown	clown	brown
2. snow	now	grow		5. crow	cow	low
3. how	now	low		6. clown	own	down

Write several columns of words selected so that each word contains the same diphthong and represents the same sound. Have the children read the words in unison, noting the visual pattern and sound represented.

oil	out	saw	boy
boil	mouth	jaw	joy
soil	south	law	Roy
toil	shout	paw	toy
spoil	found	raw	

APPLICATION ACTIVITY

Ask the children to give you sentences using some of these words. Provide them with some written examples to illustrate what they are to do. Write each sentence on the board and underline the word with the vowel pattern *(oi, ou, aw, oy)*. By asking questions of pupils, sentences focusing on a few of the words can be generated. Such questions as What do we do with oil? How do we buy oil for cars? Where does oil for cars come from? can elicit the following sentences.

1. Oil comes from oil wells.
2. Texas is a state in the south that has a lot of oil wells.
3. We put oil in cars.
4. Oil for cars comes in a can.
5. A spout is stuck in the top of the can.

These sentences can then be used to construct a short, meaningful passage, such as the one shown here.

Oil comes from oil wells. Many oil wells are in the south. Oil for cars comes in cans. The man at the gas station put a spout in the top of the can.

Once children have developed an understanding of these visual patterns, provide them with many varied opportunities to apply this skill in meaningful context. Two examples of meaningful application are presented below.

Either read sentences to the children or have them read the sentences themselves and select the word that makes sense in the sentence.

1. The ________ (cow, boy) broke out of the pen. He ate the green grass in the yard. A ____ (boy, oil) saw the cow and took him home. The boy's name is ________ (Roy, How). His ______ (house, mouse) is next door to the pen.

Have children read the sentences and write the words that make sense in each blank. Illustrate the importance of reading beyond the blank to help select a meaningful word. Questions can be asked that focus on meaningful comprehension after the children have completed the activity.

2. A cl____ came to t___ with a pet crow. The crow was white and his name was Sn___. Snow was white, with a br____ beak and yellow feet.

town
Snow
clown
brown
told
snap

Summary of Rules Related to Vowel Sounds

- A single vowel followed by a consonant in a word or syllable usually has the short sound: *can* or *cancel.*
- A single vowel which concludes a word or syllable usually has the long sound *(me, ti-ger, lo-co-mo-tive).*
- In the vowel digraphs *oa, ea, ee, ai, ay,* the first vowel is usually long and the second is silent *(coat, reap, bead, wait, play).* The digraphs *oo, au,* and *ew* form a single sound which is not the long sound of the first vowel *(food, good, haul, few).*
- In words containing two vowels, one of which is final *e,* the final *e* is usually silent and the preceding vowel is long.
- Single vowels followed by *r* usually result in a blend sound *(fir, car, burn, fur).* The vowel *a* followed by *l* or *w* usually results in a blend sound *(yawn, tall, claw, awful).*
- The letter *y* at the end of words containing no other vowel has the letter sound of *i (my, try, sky, shy).*
- Diphthongs are two-vowel combinations in which both vowels contribute to the speech sound *(house, boy, cow).*

Syllabication

A syllable is a vowel, or group of letters containing a vowel, that is pronounced as a unit. Children usually learn a number of one-syllable root words prior to meeting polysyllabic words. As they meet longer words, they learn that most prefixes and sufixes and some inflectional endings constitute syllables. During the child's early experience with high-frequency affixes, he breaks the word into parts and then combines the parts into the whole: *re*-read-*ing, pre*-heat-*ed, bi*-week-*ly, dis*-appear-*ance.* After many experiences, he reduces his reliance on this type of analysis, and the blending of the parts into the whole becomes smoother.

Understanding Syllables. A series of pictures may be used to help children develop the ability to distinguish syllables in words. Pictures can be presented that are familiar to the children. They either listen to the teacher's pronunciation of the picture's name or pronounce it themselves and indicate the number of syllables heard. Pupils can also clap out the number of syllables in words pronounced by the teacher.

A knowledge of vowel behavior within words is the second major aid in breaking words into syllables. The sounds of vowels and letter combinations are not as consistent as prefixes and suffixes. Nevertheless, many generalizations are useful. Although the following examples are not words, the letter combinations can be broken into syllables: *comration, ragmotex, obsebong, fasnotel.* The likely syllabication is: *com·ra·tion, rag·mo·tex, ob·se·bong, fas·no·tel.* Most fluent readers would pronounce these nonsense words in substantially the same way. These readers probably would not recite rules to themselves before attempting to pronounce the above words, but they would probably be subconsciously influenced by rules they had learned.

INTRODUCTORY ACTIVITY

When generalizations applicable to syllabication are taught, children should be provided with a number of examples and then led to see for themselves what happens. Out of this experience, rules can develop. Starting with the question, what usually happens when two consonants come between vowels, the teacher can place a number of words on the board:

af ter	win dow	rab bit	let ter
gar den	can dy	din ner	sum mer
fas ter	pen cil	lit tle	cot ton

The generalization will then emerge that "When two consonants come between vowels, the syllable division comes between the consonants" or "One consonant goes with each vowel." It should be pointed out that this rule will not always hold, but that it is the best guess to make when trying to pronounce an unknown word. In the case of double consonants, there are few exceptions to the rule.

To teach what happens when one consonant comes between two vowels, a list of known sight words may be placed on the board:

be gin	fe ver	to tal	de cide
o ver	di rect	ti ger	me ter
fa tal	mo ment	pu pil	ho tel

From these examples, children will both see and hear that "The single consonant goes with the following syllable." They will also note that when "The syllable is a vowel or ends with a vowel, it usually has the long sound." These two generalizations should be taught together because they work together. In cases where the first of two vowels separated by a single consonant has its short sound, the single intervening consonant closes the first syllable *(cam-el, mag-a-zine).*

A few generalizations about common word endings as they relate to syllabication might be taught. Children have had experience with prefixes and suffixes and may already follow these rules even though they are not able to verbalize them.

- Common endings which begin with a vowel such as *ing, est,* or *er* are usually sounded as syllables *(look-ing, long-er, long-est).* This is not true of *ed* except when preceded by *t* or *d (want-ed, need-ed).*
- Most one-syllable words remain intact as syllables when endings are added. In many instances, this violates the "divide between consonants" rule stated earlier. This is not a problem to children if they have learned to see prefixes and suffixes as units. Examples might include *spell-ing, want-ed, tell-ing* (not *spel-ling, wan-ted, tel-ling*).
- Certain letter combinations, when found at the ends of words, are rarely divided and thus stand as the final syllable.

un cle	fa ble	bu gle	sad dle
cir cle	tum ble	sin gle	can dle
sam ple	gen tle	puz zle	an kle
tem ple	rat tle	daz zle	spar kle

The generalizations are (1) the letter combinations *cle, ble, gle, dle, zle, kle, ple,* and *tle* at the ends of words usually stand as the final syllable; (2) the final *e* is silent, and the sound contains the *l* blend; and (3) this final syllable is not accented.

STRUCTURAL ANALYSIS

As discussed at the beginning of the chapter, structural analysis instruction is aimed at helping children identify words whose visual patterns are changed as a result of adding

- Inflectional endings *(s, ed, ing, ly)*
- Prefixes and suffixes *(pre, ex, un; tent, ment, ous,* etc.)
- Root to root to form compounds *(sidewalk, farmyard, playground, basketball)*

Application of structural analysis skills allows children to focus on larger units of letter patterns within known words (27). Obviously, the use of some of these techniques is predicated on previous learning. For instance, for a child to use structural analysis in unlocking words with inflectional endings, she must recognize the root word *(help)* as a familiar unit or be able to sound out the root word. Then she solves the ending *(ing)* and blends the two *(helping).* A bit later this type of analysis should be uncalled for since she perceives the word *helping* as one familiar unit.

In applying structural analysis skills to solve unknown words, the child is aided if she recognizes parts of words that she may already have studied. This is extremely important to assure that instruction is building on what the children have already mastered in reading. By building on pupils' prior learning, you can increase their attention to new learning, increase their chance of success with new learning, and use ongoing diagnosis that focuses on their progress from one learning outcome to the next.

Familiar parts that children know may be roots, inflectional endings, affixes, and the combining elements in compounds. They must also understand that a number of identical letter units are added either to the front or end of many different words to form new words *(pre, un, re, dis; s, ed, ing, ment, tive, able, ness,* etc.). Exercises illustrating these frequently met structural changes are often helpful to the learner. A few teaching examples follow.

PRACTICE ACTIVITY

Adding *s, ed, ing* to Words. In the space provided, add *s, ed,* or *ing* to the known word. Write each new word in the column, then read the words. (Note: Word endings are important features of syntax. By using one or two words with the new word being formed, pupils' attention to syntax can be heightened.)

Known Word	s	ed	ing
play	He ______	I ______	I am ______
look	He ______	I ______	She is ______
call	She ______	She ______	He is ______
flap	She ______	It ______	It is ______
wait	He ______	He ______	I am ______
rain	It ______	It ______	It is ______
work	She ______	I ______	They are ______

Adding *er, est, ly* to Words. In the space provided, add *er, est,* or *ly* to the stimulus word. Then read each word.

Known Word	er	est	ly
warm	______	______	______
great	______	______	______

high	________	________	________
soft	________	________	________
kind	________	________	________

In each blank space, add a prefix or suffix to make a word. Use: *in, dis, re;* and *ment, able, ness.*

______agree	disagree______	______agree______
______direct	indirect______	______direct______
______fill	refill______	______fill______

APPLICATION ACTIVITY

Present the known words *look, call, clap,* and *play,* and review them when *s* is added to the end. Do this on the chalkboard and direct pupils' attention to written words.

A	B
I look	He looks
I call	He calls
I clap	She claps
I play	She plays

Direct pupils to look at the following sentences as each one is read aloud, pausing briefly when coming to a blank space, then reading the rest of the sentence. Then, using words from list B above, have the pupils either write the sentences or orally give you a word that makes sense for each sentence. If a written exercise, several sentences should be completed together to make sure each child understands what she is to do.

Bobby ________ in the yard.
The robin ________ his wings to fly.
The dog by the door ________ mean.
Bill ________ his dog to come in at night.

Sentences can then be prepared for children to do as seatwork.

Further application can be provided by using the following activities. Students are to select the word that makes sense in each sentence.

play	1. He ________ ball with us.
plays	2. I ________ ball with him.
	3. They will ________ ball with us after school.
	4. She ________ a game with a bat and a ball.

work	1. Dad ________ at home on Saturday.
works	2. Mother ________ at school on Monday.
	3. Jane has to ________ at the game.
	4. The horse ________ on the farm.

Sentences such as the following can be used to provide further application of suffixes in meaningful context. Activities should build on what pupils have learned, as noted in the examples. Encourage children to think about whether or not their choice makes sense in the sentence.

1. I like to __________ in the yard on ____________________ days.
   (play, plays) (warmer, warm, warmest)
2. Today is the ____________________ day of the year.
   (warmer, warm, warmest)
3. This doll __________ like the ________________ one in the store.
   (look, looks) (soft, softest, softly)

Additional activities can pont out how inflectional endings deal with degrees of comparison.

1. Mark is __________________ than John. He is at the __________________
   (high, higher, highest) (high, higher, highest)
   point on the ladder.
2. This fur is the ________________ fur of all.
   (soft, softer, softest)
3. Jane is a _________________ person. She is _________________ than Fred,
   (kind, kinder, kindest) (kind, kinder, kindest)
   Bill and Bob. She is the _________________ person I know.
   (kind, kinder, kindest)

For application activities to help children apply their knowledge of prefixes and suffixes, the following can be used. Pupils are to select the prefix or suffix to complete the word so that the sentence makes sense.

1. I *agree* with Dan that we should buy a dog.
2. I __________agree with Dan that we should name the dog Spike.
   (in, dis, re)
3. Dan and I are in disagree__________ about the name for our dog.
   (ment, able, ness)
4. I guess I am a disagree__________ person.
   (able, ment, ness)

1. Joe drank all of the water in the bottle.
2. He will __________fill the bottle with water.
   (re, in, dis)
3. The bottle is ________ fill ______________.
   (re, in, dis) (ment, able, ness)

PRACTICE ACTIVITY

Working with Compounds (different levels of difficulty). Each line below contains one compound word. Underline the compound word and write it in the blank space at the end of the line.

1. children	dancing	firefighter	________
2. someone	beaches	crawling	________
3. alike	mousetrap	puzzle	________
4. downpour	happily	permitted	________
5. autumn	mistake	handbag	________

Illustrating How the Same Word May Be Used in a Number of Compound Words. Write three compound words for each group of words. To maximize success, begin with two words to combine, then as pupils experience success increase the number of combinations.

1. air	plane	________	
2. book	case	________	
3. door	way	________	
4. air	plane	craft	port
	________	________	________
5. book	case	keeper	worm
	________	________	________
6. door	way	bell	mat
	________	________	________

Lists of words that can be combined to form compound words are presented, and the pupil is to combine them to form meaningful compound words.

A	B
shoe ________	ball
sun ________	light
basket ________	maker

Similar activities can be used for inflectional endings, prefixes, and suffixes.

APPLICATION ACTIVITY

Complete each sentence by writing a compound word in the blank space. Provide practice in a group setting to make sure each child understands the task.

1. A player can hit a home run in the game of ________.
2. The teacher wrote on the ________ with a piece of chalk.
3. The front window in a car is called the ________.
4. The mail carrier puts mail in our ________.

In addition to the previous sentences, encourage students to suggest their own sentences that include compound words. If they have difficulty, provide them with a written list of compound words to use in a sentence. Either write the students' sentences on the chalkboard or have them write them on a sheet of paper. Discuss each sentence and its meaning. This activity could also be used to write group-composed stories.

Read the clue and add a suffix to the underlined word. The new word must fit the clue.

Examples:

Clue
a. full of *fear* = fearful
b. has no *fear* = fearless

or less ful est

	Clue	
1.	one who *visits*	__________
2.	*sweeter* than all others	__________
3.	to be of *help*	__________
4.	no *end* in sight	__________
5.	one who *invents*	__________
6.	*taller* than others	__________
7.	has no *hope*	__________
8.	that which can *harm*	__________
9.	one who *sails*	__________
10.	not *use*ful	__________

able er ly ness ish

	Clue	
11.	to be *alike*	__________
12.	can be *wash*ed	__________
13.	one who *paints*	__________
14.	has a *fever*	__________
15.	*swift* action	__________
16.	to *agree*	__________
17.	one who plays *golf*	__________
18.	thinks only of *self*	__________
19.	to be *idle*	__________
20.	can be *adjust*ed	__________

Upon successful completion of clue activities, have pupils use words formed from the clues in their own sentences or stories. Some of these can be written on the chalkboard and used for class discussion. Discuss as a group the meaning of the stories or sentences. Some example sentences for clues 1 through 4 are as follows:

Uncle Frank was a visitor at our house.
The apple is the sweetest of all the apples we picked.
Our teacher is very helpful.
The road was endless.

CONTEXT CLUES

A child can use context clues only when she has the ability to recognize or sound out most of the words in a sentence that contains perhaps one unknown word. It should be emphasized that phonics is only one of many skills that can aid reading for meaning. For instance, when a child does not know the meaning of a word, arriving at its *exact* pronunciation through phonic analysis will not help her. In the following sentence there is an unknown symbol:

The man was attacked by a marbohem.

Everyone reading this page can sound out *mar-bo-hem,* but no one knows what attacked the man since saying *marbohem* does not convey meaning to the reader. Words can be substituted for *marbohem,* and some readers would still have trouble with the meaning even though they successfully analyze the speech sounds in the words. For example:

The man was attacked by a peccary.
The man was attacked by a freebooter.
The man was attacked by an iconoclast.
The man was attacked by a fusilier.
The man was attacked by a hypochondriac.

Context clues can be useful aids in solving unknown words if the reader demands meaning from what she reads. Using context plus a minimal amount of letter analysis focused on the beginning of the words is far better than context alone. This combination of clues is also better than intensively analyzing each word while ignoring the contextual setting of the unknown word.

In the following illustration, a blank line is used to represent an unknown word:

The boy waved good-bye as the train left the __________.

Even when the sentence has a blank line substituted for the word, most readers have no problem in supplying the correct word. You would really have to strain in order to miscall the unknown word if you heeded the first letter supplied below:

The boy waved good-bye as the train left the s__________.

Other reading situations will present more difficult problems, for example:

The girl waved good-bye to her ________.

Here, quite a number of possible word choices would make sense: friend, mother, sister, teacher, brother, parents, family, playmate, aunt, cousin, uncle, and so forth. Select *any* word that makes sense and insert only its first letter in the blank space. Note how many of the words that were possibilities are now eliminated when the reader pays attention to the sound associated with that initial letter.

The importance of combining skills is often more dramatically illustrated in larger contexts. In the first version of a story provided below, it is possible to get the sense of the story even if one is not sure of the identity of a number of the missing words. The second version provides only the initial letter of each missing word.

> John and his cousin ________ started on their fishing trip. John said, "I have my trusty ________ pole, a ________ full of lunch, and a can of ________." After walking a long time, John said, "Not far from here there is a ________ across the stream. We can sit on the ________ and fish." When they started fishing, John said, "I'm not going to ________ from this ________ until I catch a ________ ________." Finally ________ said, "I am tired of sitting on the ________. I am going to take a walk along the ________." ________ had walked only a short way when he lost his ________ and fell into the stream. The water was not very deep, and he waded out. "Hey," said John, "You're lucky. You won't have to take a ________ when we get home."

This next version inserts the initial letter in each unknown word, which in all cases happens to be the letter *b*.

> John and his cousin B________ started out on their fishing trip. John said, "I have my trusty b________ pole, a b________ full of lunch, and a can of b________." After walking a long time, John said, "Not far from here there is a b________ across the stream. We can sit on the b________ and fish." When they started fishing, John said, "I'm not going to b________ from this b________ until I catch a b________ b________." Finally B________ said, "I am tired of sitting on the b________. I am going to take a walk along the b________." B________ had walked only a short way when he lost his b________ and fell into the stream. The water was not very deep, and he waded out. "Hey," said John, "You're lucky. You won't have to take a b________ when we get home."
>
> (Words in order of their omission are Bob, bamboo, bag, bait, bridge, bridge, budge, bridge, big bass, Bob, bridge, bank, Bob, balance, bath.)

To figure out words, think of the sounds letters stand for.
And think what the other words in the sentence are saying.

Read each sentence. What does the word in color mean?
Circle the best answer below the sentence.

1. Boyd wants to put his house on a plain
   very big hill   flat place   bunch of trees

2. You can broil some kinds of food.
   way to cook   way to eat

3. The animal had to crouch to hide behind the rock.
   stand tall   bend low   run

4. I can tell Lan is mad, because she has a scowl on her face.
   frown   smile   grin

5. The ship has just left for a voyage around the world.
   trip across the street   long trip   kind of drink

6. The face of that clock will glow in the dark.
   light up   tick   laugh

7. Leave the clothes on the line if they are still moist
   a little wet   dry   dirty

8. Joe fell and hurt his shoulder
   arm between elbow and wrist   body between neck and arm

9. The family rode up to the palace in the royal coach.
   owned by a king or queen   owned by your brother or sister

10. The cat made its bed in the straw
   barn   house   hay

88 Using Context and Letter-Sound Associations for Vowel Digraphs and Diphthongs To Decode Words

Many materials are available to provide practice with language in meaningful context.

The preceding discussion emphasized the importance of using word identification skills in combination. Learning to read is a very complicated task. From the very beginning, the learner attempting to identify unfamiliar words should look for and accept help from all available clues. This simultaneous usage of all options helps simplify beginning reading. Occasionally, phonics will be the only key to meaning that a child can utilize. More often than not, all of the word identification skills—basic sight vocabulary, phonics, structural analysis, context—can be used together. Phonics should be used only when needed.

The importance of context has been illustrated throughout this chapter. The application activities focused specifically on applying various word identification skills in meaningful contexts. These application suggestions allow for maximum use of all available options to get at the meaning of what is read. Rather than providing direct instruction in using different types of contextual analysis, we recommend ongoing attention to developing in pupils the concept that what they read *must make sense to them.*

Essentially, there are two basic types of contextual analysis that transfer to a wide variety of reading situations. The way that words are ordered in a sentence is referred to as syntax (see chapter 3). Using our example presented earlier, knowledge of language allows you to determine that a person, place, or thing fits in the blank.

> The girl waved good-bye to her ________.

This knowledge allows a reader to eliminate all possibilities that would not make sense in this sentence. If several related sentences either precede or follow this sentence, the reader has additional contextual information available to get at the meaning of what she is reading. For example, if the next sentence read "He waved back and wiped tears from his eyes as the train began to move," the reader has additional contextual information to solve the unknown word and comprehend the text.

"He" in this sentence is helpful to the reader who understands that the unknown word is a male referent. If the reader makes the connection between the referent and the initial letter pattern or patterns of the unknown word and the sounds represented, then she can better determine meaning. This is illustrated in the following sentences.

> The girl waved good-bye to her f________. He wiped tears from his eyes as the train began to move.

Contextual clues, such as making the connection between the male referent and the unknown word in the above example, are related to the use of semantic clues (see chapters 2 and 6). Semantics refers to both the reader's knowledge of word meanings and her conceptual-experiential background in relation to comprehending what is read.

Syntactic Clues

Syntactic clues, when used in combination with phonics and structural analysis, enable children to figure out the meaning of unknown words.

- *Structure words.* Noun markers (*my, this, any,* etc.), verb markers (*am, are, is,* etc.), clause markers (*now, if, before,* etc.), and question indicators (*why, who, which,* etc.)—signal what is coming next.
  He took *my* brother to the game.
  He *is* going to the game.
  My brother will go to the game, *if* he is home.
  Who is he taking to the game?
- *Phrases.* A group of words that describes or refines the word.
  Mike, *who is my younger brother,* is going to the game.
  The game, *which is a heated rivalry,* is sold out.
  Language grammar. Meaning patterns in language that indicate where certain words fit.
  He took my *brother* to the game.
  (noun)
  He *took* my brother to the game.
  (verb)
  He took my brother to the game in a big *shiny* car.
  (adjective)
- *Appositive.* A word (or words) that explains the word it follows.
  Jones, the *quarterback,* was injured on the first play.
  Jubilation, *great excitement,* filled the stadium when the home team won.

Semantic Clues

Although syntactic clues can help children get at word meaning by allowing them to limit their choices of meaning for unknown words, semantic clues provide them with more clues to word meaning. Johnson and Pearson (18) have classified the major kinds of semantic clues available to readers. A modified listing of their categories follows. Again, it is important to recognize that for semantic clues to be used efficiently, the referent for the unknown word must be in the child's experiential/conceptual background.

- *Definition or explanation.* Difficult words that children encounter in their reading are often defined within the text. Words such as *is, are,* and *means* signal explanations.

Herbivores *are animals that feed on green plants.*

- *Synonyms and antonyms.* Rather than the unknown word recurring in the text, its synonym or antonym is used.

  The *robust* rabbit loved to visit the garden. He was so *fat* he could hardly squeeze through the fence.

- *Figurative language.* Meaning of the unknown word can be obtained from metaphors and similes that are used in relation to preceding and following text.

  It was *raining cats and dogs.* Several cars stalled in the flooded streets.

- *Summary statements.* Based on connected story information, the meaning of an unknown word may become known.

  Mark used to be a *stellar* basketball player. He could make shots from anywhere on the court. The crowd always cheered when their star player was introduced.

Contextual Analysis Instruction

Throughout this chapter, emphasis has been placed on providing pupils with the opportunity to apply word identification skills in meaningful context. Such a concern for application allows pupils to continually develop an awareness for the use of context to get at word meaning. Rather than repeat these activities, a few examples of each are presented.

Bobby put the b________ in the water.
Bobby has a pet ________.
(hat, cat, bat)
We use our __ __rain (br) to think.
Clue: Used in bread __ __eat.
(wh, ch)
Mark wants to learn how to ________.
(sale, sail)
Oil comes from ________ wells.
The ________________ time I ever had was at the circus.
(great, greatest, greater)
The front window in a car is the ________.
If you can wash something then it is ________ able.
Bill has a ball and a bat. The bat and ball c________ in a set. Dad will paint Bill's n________ on the bat and ball in green paint.
Joe drank all of the water in the bottle. More water can be put in the bottle because it is ________fillable. Joe re________ the bottle with water.
A player can hit a home run in the game of ________.

Name **130**

A. Write the letter for each definition next to the vocabulary word it defines.

d	1. spectacular	a. shed an outer layer before a new growth
h	2. reputation	b. very thin or lean
a	3. molted	c. very large or great
b	4. scrawny	d. striking; sensational
e	5. sprained	e. injured by a sudden twist
g	6. despair	f. able to affect someone strongly
c	7. tremendous	g. a loss of hope
f	8. impressive	h. what others think of the character of a person

B. Use each word above to complete the sentences below.

9. The snake **molted**, leaving its old skin on the grass.
10. The child watched in **despair** as the wind carried the balloon away.
11. The display of fireworks was **spectacular**.
12. The child's talent at playing the piano was **impressive** in view of her age.
13. The **tremendous** cake was enough to feed fifty people.
14. When the puppy was finally found after a week, it looked **scrawny** from lack of food.
15. Jake fell and **sprained** his ankle.
16. The vet has a **reputation** of being kind and gentle.

Additional Activity: Write a paragraph that tries to persuade the reader to do something. Use five of the vocabulary words in the paragraph.

VOCABULARY: word identification in context
BASIC WORDS: spectacular, reputation, molted, scrawny, sprained, despair, tremendous

Level 13 "Cranes in My Corral"

An example of contextual analysis instruction.

SUMMARY

In order to become an independent reader, a child must learn to maximize the use of a variety of word identification skills. Phonics, structural analysis, contextual analysis, and basic sight vocabulary are the basic word identification skills that enable children to comprehend what they read. Competent and flexible readers do not rely heavily on any one skill but tend to use various clues in combination. In teaching word identification skills, the following principles should be kept in mind.

- Pupils' language background should form the basis for word identification instruction. Small, highly related instructional steps increase the likelihood that children will attend to the instruction and have a greater chance of success. The teacher will also be able to monitor closely each pupil's progress.
- Instruction should build on what the children know and are successful with.
- Opportunities to apply word identification skills in meaningful context should be an integral part of all word identification instruction.
- Contextual analysis should be integrated with all other word identification instruction. By combining sight word learning, phonics, and structural analysis with context, the child learns that her chances of determining meaning are maximized.
- There are an unlimited number of ways that word identification skills can be taught. Any technique that proves successful for a child is a justifiable procedure, providing that what she is taught today does not inhibit her later growth and that the instructional approach is reasonably economical in time and effort expended.
- Children should not be taught to rely heavily on any one word identification technique. Examples of an overemphasis on phonics include sounding out the same words hundreds of times and attempting to sound out words that do not lend themselves to letter-sound analysis: *once, knight, freight, some, one, eight, love, know, head, move, none, have, laugh,* and so forth.
- Children differ as to how much instruction is needed while they are learning word identification skills. Diagnosis that reveals what a child knows and does not know is essential for good instruction. In the final analysis, the *optimum* amount of word identification instruction for every child is the *minimum* that she needs to become an independent reader.

YOUR POINT OF VIEW

Discussion Questions

1. Early reading instruction inevitably causes children to develop a *set* relative to "What is reading." What reading set might children develop when no opportunities are provided to apply word identification skills in meaningful context?
2. Is it possible to teach children to rely too much on any word identification technique? Does learning to read involve the *simultaneous* application of all word identification skills? Is each a part of a unitary process called *reading?*
3. How do mature readers differ from beginning readers in their use of word identification strategies?
4. What is the optimum amount of any type of word identification instruction?
5. What role does ongoing diagnosis play in word identification instruction?

Take a Stand For or Against

1. The spelling patterns found in English writing constitute a major obstacle in learning to read English.
2. Teaching sight words, letter-sound analysis, and contextual analysis at the same time will inevitably lead to confusion.
3. Since a child must learn word identification skills before she can become an independent reader, these skills should be taught before "reading for meaning" is stressed.

BIBLIOGRAPHY

1. Adams, Marilyn J.; Anderson, Richard C.; and Durkin, Dolores. "Beginning Reading: Theory and Practice." *Language Arts* 55 (1978): 19–25.
2. Ash, Michael J.; Buckland, Pearl R.; and Rupley, William H. "The Relation Between the Discrimination of Letter-Like Forms and Word Recognition." *Reading World* 19 (1979): 113–23.
3. Caldwell, Edward G.; Roth, Sandra R.; Turner, Ralph R. "A Reconsideration of Phonic Generalizations." *Journal of Reading Behavior* 10 (Spring 1978): 91–96.
4. Carnie, Douglas W. "Phonics Versus Look-Say: Transfer to New Words." *The Reading Teacher* 30 (1977): 636–40.

5. Chall, Jeanne; Roswell, Florence G.; and Blumenthall, Susan Halm. "Auditory Blending Ability: A Factor in Success in Beginning Reading." *The Reading Teacher* 17 (1963): 113–18.
6. Clymer, Theodore. "The Utility of Phonic Generalizations in the Primary Grades." *The Reading Teacher* 16 (1963): 252–58.
7. Culyer, Richard C. "Guidelines for Skill Development: Word Attack." *The Reading Teacher* 32 (1979): 425–33.
8. Cunningham, Patricia M. "A Compare/Contrast Theory of Mediated Word Identification." *The Reading Teacher* 32 (1979): 774–78.
9. Downing, John. "Linguistic Awareness in Learning to Read." *Reading Today, International Reading Association Newsletter* (Oct.–Dec. 1979): 2.
10. Durrell, Donald D., and Murphy, Helen A. "A Prereading Phonics Inventory." *The Reading Teacher* 31 (1978): 385–90.
11. Eeds-Kneip, Maryann. "The Frenetic Frantic Phonic Backlash." *Language Arts* 56 (1979): 909–17.
12. Frenzel, Norman J. "Children Need a Multipronged Attack in Word Recognition." *The Reading Teacher* 31 (1978): 627–31.
13. Guthrie, John T. "Models of Reading and Reading Disability." *Journal of Educational Psychology* 65 (1973): 9–18.
14. Haddock, Maryann. "Teaching Blending in Beginning Reading Instruction is Important." *The Reading Teacher* 31 (1978): 654–58.
15. Hardy, Madeline; Stennent, R. G.; and Smythe, P. C. "Word Attack: How *do* they 'figure them out'?" *Elementary English* 50 (1973): 99–102.
16. Heilman, Arthur W. *Phonics in Proper Perspective.* 5th ed. Columbus, Ohio: Charles E. Merrill Publishing Co., 1985.
17. Hull, Marion A. *Phonics for the Teacher of Reading.* 4th ed. Columbus, Ohio: Charles E. Merrill Publishing Co., 1985.
18. Johnson, Dale D., and Pearson, P. David. *Teaching Reading Vocabulary.* New York: Holt, Rinehart & Winston, 1978.
19. Laberge, David, and Samuels, S. Jay. "Toward a Theory of Automatic Information Processing in Reading." *Cognitive Psychology* 6 (1974): 293–323.
20. Lesiak, Judi. "There Is a Need for Word Attack Generalizations." In *Readings on Reading Instruction,* 3rd. ed., edited by A. J. Harris and E. R. Sipay. New York: Longman, 1984.
21. Mason, Jana M. "Refining Phonics for Teaching Beginning Reading." *The Reading Teacher* 31 (1977): 179–84.
22. Muller, D. "Phonic Blending and Transfer of Letter Training to Word Reading in Children." *Journal of Reading Behavior* 5 (Summer 1973): 13–15.
23. Pollard, Rebecca S. *Pollard's Synthetic Method.* Chicago: Western Publishing House, 1889.
24. Rayner, Keith. "Developmental Changes in Word Recognition Strategies." *Journal of Educational Psychology* 68 (1976): 323–29.
25. *Reading Today, International Reading Association Newsletter* (Aug. 1977).
26. Rubeck, Patricia. "Decoding Procedure: Pupil Self-Analysis and Observed Behavior." *Reading Improvement* 14 (Fall 1977): 187–92.
27. Rupley, William H., and Blair, Timothy R. *Reading Diagnosis and Remediation: Classroom and Clinic.* 2d ed. Boston, Mass.: Houghton Mifflin Pub. Co., 1983.
28. Samuels, S. Jay. "Automatic Decoding and Reading Comprehension." *Language Arts* 53 (1976): 323–25.

29. Samuels, S. Jay. "The Method of Repeated Readings." *The Reading Teacher* 32 (1979): 403–8.
30. Samuels, S. Jay, and Schachter, Summer W. "Controversial Issues in Beginning Reading Instruction: Meaning Versus Subskill Emphasis." In *Readings on Reading Instruction,* 3rd. ed., edited by A. J. Harris and E. R. Sipay. New York: Longman, 1984.
31. Santa, Carol Minnick. "Spelling Patterns and the Development of Flexible Word Recognition Strategies." *Reading Research Quarterly* 12 (1977): 125–44.
32. Smith, Kenneth J. "Efficiency in Beginning Reading: Possible Effects on Later Comprehension." In *Language and Reading Comprehension,* edited by S. Wanat, 56–58. Arlington, Va.: Center for Applied Linguistics, 1977.
33. Taylor, Barbara M., and Nosbush, Linda. "Oral Reading for Meaning: A Technique for Improving Word Identification Skills." *The Reading Teacher* 39 (1983): 234–37.
34. Weaver, Phyllis. *Research Within Reach.* St Louis, Mo.: CEMREL, 1978.
35. Wylie, Richard E., and Durrell, Donald D. "Teaching Vowels Through Phonograms." *Elementary English* 47 (1970): 787–91.

6

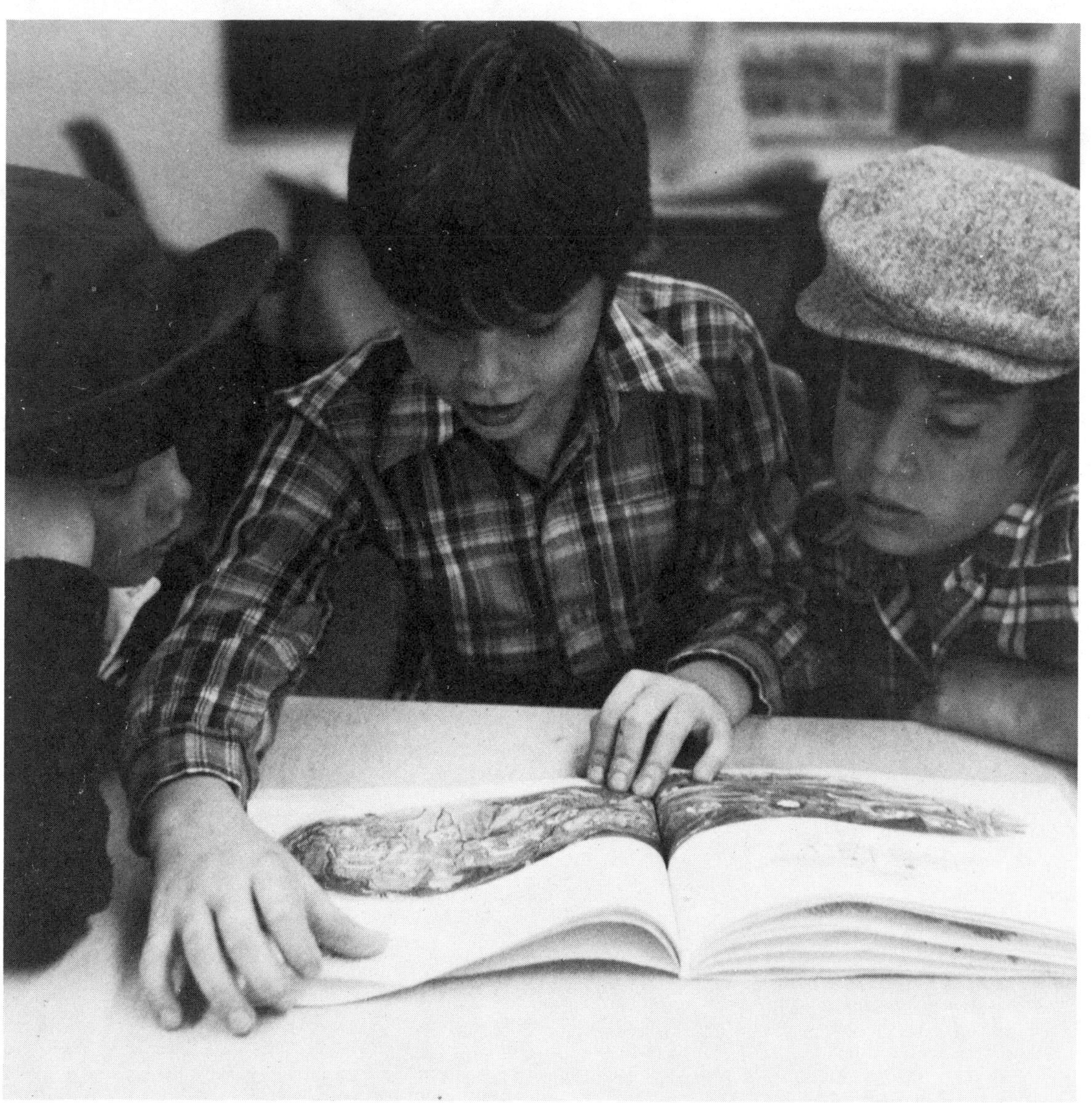

Comprehension

For the Reader

Do you sometimes read without thinking of or understanding some of the writer's message? It certainly can be done, but the end result would not be comprehension or understanding of what you read. We have all had experiences where we read material that was beyond our experiential/conceptual background, and as a result we just couldn't "make any sense of it." You can also probably recall having read something and felt that you comprehended it, but when you were asked to demonstrate your knowledge of what you read, on a test for example, your comprehension of the material was different from another person's comprehension (usually your professor's). It was not that you didn't comprehend; your purposes for reading, your perception of important information, or your level of understanding may have been different from those of the other person. The reading process is a dynamic one, requiring active, meaningful communication between the author and the reader. Reading without meaning is an unsatisfying and inconsequential exercise. As a teacher of reading, your reading program should be aimed toward furthering children's comprehension abilities. In this chapter we will examine the comprehension process and the factors affecting it and recommend teaching strategies. No other topic is of more importance in establishing a literate society.

Preview

- Read over the Key Ideas that follow.
- Read each heading and subheading.
- Read the summary.
- Read the questions and statements at the end of the chapter.
- Return to the chapter text that follows the Key Ideas and begin reading.

Key Ideas

Comprehension is a multifaceted process affected by a variety of factors:

experiential/conceptual background	language ability
word recognition capabilities	reading purposes

Reading instruction should be comprehension based.
Three levels of comprehension are literal, interpretative, and critical.

Development and enhancement of comprehension abilities require direct instruction.

Children's experiential/conceptual backgrounds for content of material read and for language functions of reading are salient factors affecting comprehension.

Effective questioning is dependent upon the concept of wait-time.

THE READING COMPREHENSION PROCESS

At the heart of understanding the comprehension process is the realization that it is an internal, mental process that cannot be observed or studied directly. Many investigators relate reading to thinking and argue that both reading and thinking are inseparable in understanding our printed language. In an often quoted study conducted in 1917 on reading comprehension, Thorndike (27) defined reading as thinking. He stated:

> The reading of a paragraph involves the same sort of organization and analysis as does thinking. It includes learning, reflection, judgment, analysis, synthesis, problem-solving behavior, selection, inference, organization, comparison of data, determination of relationships, and critical evaluation of what is read. It also includes attention, association, abstraction, generalization, comprehension, concentration and deduction.

Although direct observations of the comprehension process cannot be made, numerous research studies, theories, and models have been advanced to provide probable explanations relating to its components and development. Most of these explanations view reading comprehension as composed of a multiple number of skills and abilities that are interrelated and interdependent.

Conceptualizations of Reading

Three conceptualizations of reading comprehension, which are often referred to as models, are presently receiving considerable attention. These three models were noted briefly in chapter 1 and are the "top-down," bottom-up," and "interactive." All three models share two common features: written text and a reader. However, the role that each of these features plays is distinctly different in each model.

The top-down conceptualization gives the reader the major role in the reading comprehension process. Readers are involved in hypothesis testing as they read and bring more information to the written text than it brings to them (25). Basically, the text is sampled by readers as they use their prior knowledge (experiential/conceptual background) to predict about what they are reading. Predictions are either modified or confirmed as the readers match these with their prior knowledge.

A bottom-up view of reading comprehension places the written text in the primary role. In comparison with the top-down model, the bottom-up model is built around the idea that the print brings more information to the reader than the reader brings to the print. Readers begin reading without much prior information about the content, and they attend to the words and the word parts. They process these stimuli sequentially, and comprehension is obtained directly from such processing. Comprehension of the written text is acquired in this sequential manner as readers focus their attention on the words and word parts.

The interactive model recognizes the role that both the reader and the written text play in reading comprehension. It is neither top-down nor bottom-up. Essentially, skilled readers are simultaneously using many different areas of knowledge as they read, ranging from print features (letters, word parts, words) to interpretation of facts, to developing strategies, to modifying how they are reading (12).

The interactive view of reading considers the importance of both written text and the reader's background knowledge in comprehending print, and we feel it is most applicable to reading instruction. This view of reading comprehension reflects much of our current understanding of the process:

> A reader's background knowledge, including purposes, has an overriding influence upon the reader's development of meaning and reading comprehension involves the activation, focusing, maintaining, and refining of ideas toward developing interpretations that are plausible, interconnected, and complete. (28, p. 9)

Background knowledge can be thought of as an individual's experiential/conceptual background for (1) written text (word recognition capabilities, concept of print, understanding word order, and understanding word meanings) as well as for (2) the content of what he is reading.

Schema Theory

An important concept directly related to interactive views of the reading comprehension process has had a major impact on both reading research and instruction beginning in the mid 1970s. This concept is referred to as schema theory, which is a theory about how knowledge is represented and "how that representation facilitates the *use* of the knowledge in particular ways" (20, p. 4). A powerful feature of schema theory is that it helps to better understand how new learning is integrated with the knowledge an individual already possesses. It is a theory that attempts to explain how we learn, modify, and use information acquired through our life experiences. We have schemata (plural of schema) for places (grocery store, theater, department store, home, school, etc.), roles (father, mother, teacher, student, etc.), events (football games, television shows, weddings, etc.) and so forth (1). Our schemata are such that they can be changed as a result of new or different experiences related to existing schemata.

Strange (25) provides an example of how this may occur. A reader sees the sentence "The Indian rode off into the sunset." His schema about Indians is activated—knowledge about their dress, culture, living conditions, and so forth. His schema about transportation is cued—knowledge about riding on trains, planes, buses, horses, and so forth. However, because the reader has knowledge about Indians and transportation he would predict that this Indian was riding a horse. Such an interpretation seems probable given this sentence even though the Indian could have been riding something else. This sentence called up for the reader his Indian and transportation schemata. What if the reader sees the addition to the sentence "on a motorcycle." Strange says that the following might occur:

> Motorcycles are part of our transportation schema, but not of the Indian and transportation schemata called up by this sentence. There is nothing in our Indian schema, however, that actually prohibits riding on motorcycles, so we change our schema for this sentence, deleting horse and accepting motorcycle. Riding motorcycles is also added to our Indian schema, making this happenstance a slightly more probable interpretation the next time we read about Indians and transportation. (25, p. 394)

Relating schema theory to reading comprehension implies that readers comprehend written text in relation to their experiential/conceptual background. Readers have schemata for both concrete and abstract experiences. In reading, experiential/conceptual background knowledges exist for such things as story structure, concepts of reading, words, and language structure (17). As we read we use this knowledge of print with our knowledge of story content to make sense of the written text.

A major feature of schema theory noted by Rupley and Blair (22) is inferencing:

> Literal information serves to activate schema that lead the reader to hypothesize (infer) about story structure, words, language features, and meaning. Schema may be changed, elaborated on, or discarded as one proceeds through the text. The reader comprehends by using existing knowledge, which can change when new information is encountered. Changes in schemata can be considered new learning that may result from modifying an existing schema or from creating a new one. (p. 212)

In the interactive view of reading, the text, the reader's knowledge of the language, and the content interact to reveal meaning.

An interactive view of reading recognizes that the text, the reader's knowledge of written language features, and his knowledge of the text content interact with each other to reveal meaning. Schema theory is an interactive model that has application in classroom reading comprehension instruction. The section of this chapter dealing with comprehension instruction guidelines illustrates how features of an interactive model and schema theory could be applied in comprehension instruction.

CONSIDERING COMPREHENSION PROCESSES IN CLASSROOM READING INSTRUCTION

An interactive view of reading comprehension has direct implication for classroom reading comprehension instruction. Decoding and comprehension are both essential elements of a reading instruction program. Teaching children strategies for comprehending text and providing opportunities for them to apply these strategies to learning are major features of teaching reading. Although numerous factors must be recognized as real determinants in the comprehension process, a few that are more central to the teaching of reading comprehension have been singled out for special attention and are presented in figure 6.1.

The core of the process is the continuous development of oral and

FLASHBACK

Edward L. Thorndike has had a tremendous influence on American education. Research that he conducted in the early 1900s in reading comprehension focused on the feature of reasoning while reading, which is a major accepted feature of today's concept of reading comprehension. He also coauthored, with C. L. Barnhart, a series of public school dictionaries that are still used today.

written language ability. Affecting language development is the child's experiential/conceptual background and the development of listening abilities and speaking vocabularies through concrete and vicarious experiences (2, 10, 25).

The next layer of factors affecting the process of language comprehension is the development of abilities to react to written language with meaning and thought. The focus here is on the gradual narrowing of the gap between a child's oral language vocabulary and reading vocabulary. This gradual process is also accomplished by providing conceptual experiences with concrete objects, firsthand experiences, pictorial aids, and vicarious experiences that are represented by written language. Specific abilities in this area include the continuous development of word meanings (semantics), the ability to recognize the structure of oral and written language (topic sentence—detail, sequence, and comparison), and the ability to understand sentence structure or syntax (25). The importance of sentence structure as it relates to comprehension was highlighted in a recent study by Weaver (30). One of the major conclusions was that reading comprehension was significantly improved by giving children training in sentence organization skills.

The previously mentioned factors affecting the comprehension pro-

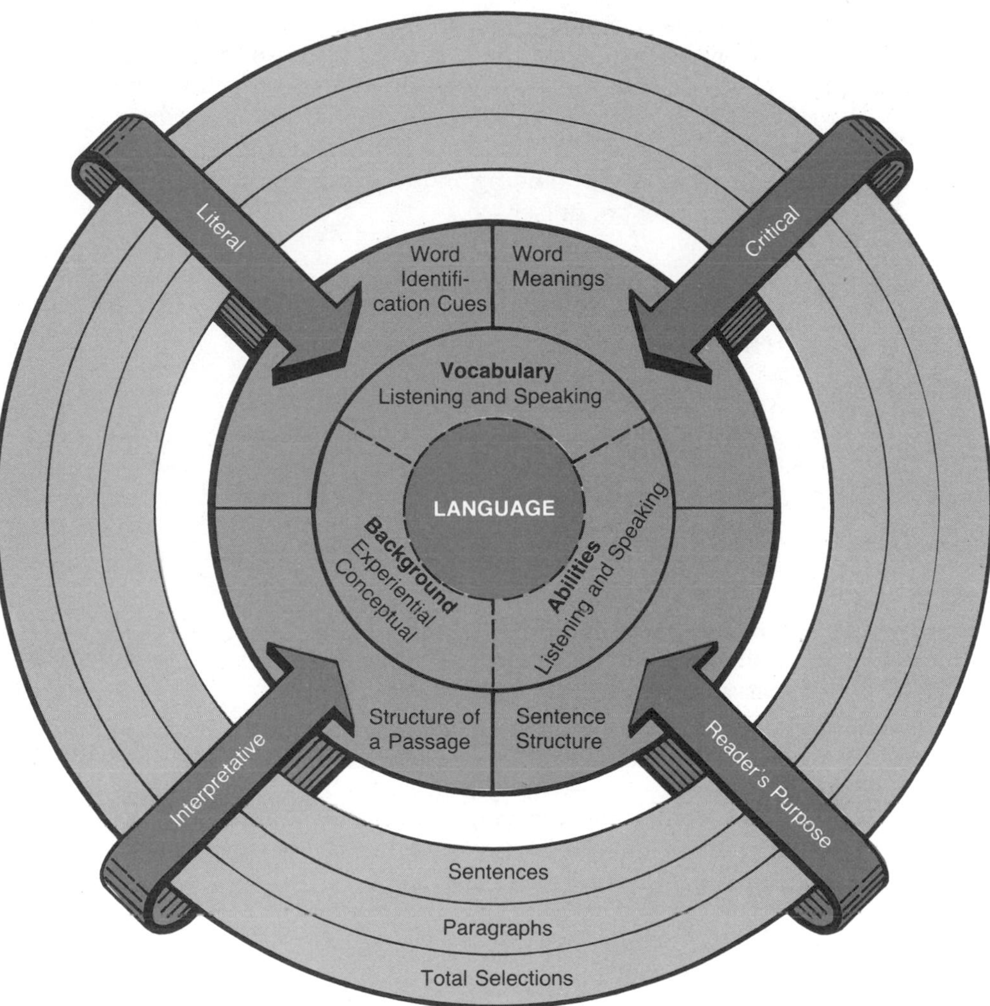

FIGURE 6.1 The comprehension process.

cess have their cumulative effect felt through what are identified as spheres of complexity of written language. Children must be able to make sense and interact with written language in the form of sentences, paragraphs, and the total selection.

The abilities in the model are developmental in nature and interact with each other. The levels of thinking (literal, interpretative, and critical) exemplify the types of dynamic reading that can be applied to written and oral language. The arrows in the model also reflect the interrelationship and interdependence of all the factors affecting the process of comprehension. Overriding the entire process is the recognition of the importance of how a reader's purpose affects the depth of understanding.

Clearly, what a reader gains from reading a sentence, paragraph, or total selection depends upon the expressed purpose for reading.

In a capsule format below, three levels of comprehension are identified. In an effort to discipline our thinking regarding the process of comprehension, a long listing of skills is not given. Only those abilities at the core of understanding and reacting to information at different levels of thinking are presented.

- *Literal Comprehension*
  Understanding the ideas and information explicitly stated in the passage.
  Abilities:
  Knowledge of word meanings.
  Recall of details directly stated or paraphrased in own words.
  Understanding of grammatical clues—subject, verb, pronouns, conjunctions, and so forth.
  Recall of main idea explicitly stated.
  Knowledge of sequence of information presented in passage.

- *Interpretative Comprehension*
  Understanding of ideas and information not explicitly stated in the passage.
  Abilities:
  Reason with information presented to understand the author's tone, purpose, and attitude.
  Infer factual information, main ideas, comparisons, cause-effect relationships not explicitly stated in the passage.
  Summarization of story content.

- *Critical Comprehension*
  Analyzing, evaluating, and personally reacting to information presented in a passage.
  Abilities:
  Personally reacting to information in a passage indicating its meaning to the reader.
  Analyzing and evaluating the quality of written information in terms of some standards.

THE ROLE OF LANGUAGE

Research about our language and the interactive stategies children adopt to arrive at meaning has greatly advanced our understanding of comprehension. Since the purpose of language is the communication of meaning, the goal of the reading process from its language base can only be viewed as communication of meaning. This obvious redundancy of terms reflects the psycholinguistic viewpoint that reading instruction be totally comprehension based from the outset. Goodman (9) echoes this position below:

> Language does not exist apart from its relationship to meaning. Now this meaning is not a property of language—the sounds or ink blotches have no intrinsic meaning. Meaning is supplied by the reader himself as he processes the symbolic system of language. As a user of the language he relates language sequences to experiences and conceptual structures. He cannot get the message unless he can process the language. But neither can he process the language unless he has the relevant experiential-conceptual background to bring to the particular task. (p. 125)

A crucial factor affecting comprehension is the importance of the reader's background of experience. One important area of a child's background of experiences is that related to language development and growth. The following factors are among those that affect the comprehension of written material:

- Oral language development related to real objects, experiences, and pictures.
- Ability to listen with understanding to stories read aloud.
- Firsthand experiences with people, objects, and places.
- Continuous development of a child's listening and speaking vocabularies.
- Oral language development of syntactic and semantic features of our language.

Development of the above abilities is best fostered through experiences that lead children from concrete experiences to abstract experiences to representation of these in written language. The development of children's listening and speaking vocabularies is dependent upon their breadth of real-life and vicarious experiences. Without experiences to relate to the concepts represented by the words you are reading, understanding is virtually impossible. Concepts, as represented by words, are not unique objects or events. Words represent a general classification scheme that shares common elements. "Language is both the storehouse and the vehicle of concepts at various levels of generality—Jonathan, apple, fruit, food" (16). An obvious example of this relationship is requiring children from a rural area to read a story about life in a city. In such a case, pupils' comprehension of the story most likely would be different from that of children who have formed concepts of city life through direct experiences.

In addition to the reader's background of experiences, there are other factors that affect comprehension of the material being read. The reader's purpose and attitude, personal experiences with a particular type of organizational format, and the ability to use various word identification strategies or cues to make sense of the message are all important to comprehension. The size of type used and the style and method of expression also play a role. Of particular importance are the reader's experiences with the three basic systems of language processing.

> Language has a grapho-phonemic system (written symbol and sound relationships); a syntactic system (grammatical relationships); and a semantic system (relationships among meanings). The grapho-phonemic system allows us to represent language with the sounds we speak or the symbols we write. The syntactic system allows us to put these sounds or written symbols together according to certain patterns familiar to all native speakers. The semantic system is used to determine the message, or meaning, which the first two systems are organized to convey. (14, p. 29)

PURPOSEFUL READING

Most reading authorities regard meaningful, purposeful reading as a major factor in promoting comprehension. The ability of the reader to establish a purpose when reading sets the limits for completing the job efficiently. A major vehicle for teachers to utilize in fostering growth in purposeful reading is the proper framing of classroom questions in relation to the desired reading comprehension outcome. Providing children with specific questions prior to reading helps engage them in learning, direct their purposes for reading, and regulate their depth and rate of reading.

Many teachers are unaware of the power they possess in influencing the level of thinking that occurs in their classrooms. Classroom observations reveal that teachers bombard students with a great number of questions every day. Shiman and Nash (23) reported a study by Sarason that indicated that while elementary teachers thought they asked between 12 and 20 questions in a thirty-minute time span, the actual number ranged from 45 to 150. The fact that these teachers underestimated the number of questions they asked suggests that little thought was given to either the kinds of questions asked or the pupils' responses. Primary level pupils and older pupils who are in the early stages of learning to read are often devoting most of their attention to word identification. As a result they are not giving their full attention to getting meaning. This is not to suggest that these children cannot comprehend, but that teachers must be certain that what children are reading is purposeful and meaningful to them. Application of word identification skills in context not only allows for meaningful practice (see chapter 5) but allows pupils to use all available cues to get to meaning.

Skills Approach

Traditionally, the concept of comprehension was best thought to be studied and taught through a listing of a great number of comprehension skills. Many basal reader programs are based upon this theory.

In an effort to control the lengthy lists of skills and to provide a framework for instructional purposes, several authors have developed taxonomies of comprehension skills. Taxonomies can be effectively used by teachers as a framework to structure comprehension questions covering a wide variety of levels and abilities.

Taxonomies can be used as guides for grouping children who exhibit a weakness with a particular area for instruction and for evaluating instructional materials (26, p. 193). However, Tatham cautions that such taxonomies be considered as classification systems only and not as learning hierarchies. She states that taxonomies are "misused whenever it is believed that they describe developmental stages in children's cognitive responses to written materials."

Further support for not using comprehension taxonomies to describe developmental levels of comprehension is offered by Rosenshine et al. (18) at the Center for Reading at the University of Illinois. He concurs that research has not revealed an ordering of comprehension skills and that, in commercial programs studied, comprehension skills were not taught in a hierarchical fashion.

Comprehension taxonomies should not be viewed as a means for specifying developmental stages of reading comprehension. However, they can assist the teacher in specifying activities aimed at certain comprehension outcomes, identifying comprehension tasks that increase pupils' chance of success, and structuring questions and activities to identify the appropriate level of structure and the degree of direct instruction (3).

A summary of Barrett's Taxonomy of Cognitive and Affective Dimensions of Reading Comprehension (4) is presented in figure 6.2. It is representative of a comprehension taxonomy that can be used when developing instructional activities, identifying questions, and specifying reading comprehension instruction. In Barrett's classification system, the following five levels of comprehension are identified: literal comprehension, reorganization, inferential comprehension, evaluation, and appreciation. Barrett's comprehension taxonomy is not based on any spe-

Literal comprehension focuses on ideas and information explicitly stated in the selection. Purposes for reading may range from simple to complex, encouraging *recognition* and *recall* of simple or detailed facts.

Reorganization requires the student to analyze, synthesize and/or organize ideas and information explicitly stated in the selection. He may utilize verbatim the author's statements or paraphrase or translate the author's statements. Reorganization tasks are: Classifying, Outlining, Summarizing, and Synthesizing.

Inferential comprehension is stimulated by purposes for reading and teacher's questions which demand thinking and imagination that goes beyond the printed page. Here the pupil uses the ideas and information explicitly stated, his intuition, and personal experiences as a basis for *conjecturing* and *hypothesizing.*

Evaluation deals with judgment and focuses on qualities of accuracy, acceptability, worth, or probability of occurrence.

Judgments of Reality or Fantasy. Could this really happen? This judgment is based on experience.

Judgments of Fact or Opinion. Does the author provide adequate support for his conclusion? Is he attempting to sway your opinion? This required *analyzation* and *evaluation* of the reader's knowledge as well as the author's and the intent of the author.

Judgments of Adequacy and Validity. Is the information in keeping with your knowledge of the subject? This requires comparing sources of information with agreement and disagreement or completeness and incompleteness.

Judgments of Appropriateness. What part of the story best describes the main character? This requires judging relative adequacy of different parts of the selection to answer the question.

Judgments of Worth, Desirability and Acceptability. Was the character right or wrong in what he did? Was his behavior good or bad? How would you have handled the situation? Such questions call for judgments of moral codes and value systems.

Appreciation involves all the previously cited cognitive dimensions, for it deals with the psychological and aesthetic impact of the selection. . . . Appreciation includes the knowledge of and emotional response to literary techniques, forms, styles, and structures.

Emotional Response to Content. The student verbalizes his feelings about the selection in terms of interest, excitement, boredom, fear, hate, amusement, etc. This is concerned with the emotional impact of the total work on the reader.

Identification with Characters and Incidents.

Reaction to the Author's Use of Language.

Imagery. The reader verbalizes his feelings in regard to the author's ability to paint word pictures which arouse sensory images.

FIGURE 6.2 Summary of Barrett's taxonomy of cognitive and affective dimensions of reading comprehension. (Adapted from Richard F. Smith and Thomas C. Barrett, Table 3.2, "A Taxonomy of Reading Comprehension," in *Teaching Reading in the Middle Grades* (Reading, Mass.: Addison-Wesley Publishing Co., 1974); table by Thomas C. Barrett originally appeared in *Reading 360, Monograph* (1972) (Lexington, Mass.: Ginn & Co.). Reprinted by permission.)

cific reading program or materials, and it could be adapted by any teacher to plan and provide for reading comprehension instruction.

COMPREHENSION INSTRUCTION

Since comprehension is the end product of the reading process, you would expect to find pupils engaged in reading comprehension instruction during a large portion of classroom reading time. At the Center for the Study of Reading, Durkin attempted to ascertain the extent to which elementary school teachers engaged pupils in reading comprehension instruction. Her conclusion was that very little instruction was provided (6). She observed teachers "mentioning," that is, providing just enough information to children in the form of workbook pages and duplicated materials. She also observed that students were asked questions at an alarming rate, with little constructive feedback. Very little instruction and practice on word meanings were given; completing worksheets and getting the right answer were more of a concern than helping youngsters become better readers. In the majority of classrooms, observations indicated that students were not given the opportunity to either learn or apply reading comprehension skills.

Features of Effective Instruction

Although knowledge of the comprehension process is still limited, we feel teachers can provide effective instruction by concentrating their efforts in the following areas:

- Design reading programs that allow for development of a meaningful vocabulary by using contextual situations based on children's experiential development.
- Concentrate on improved questioning abilities that include not only the asking of appropriate questions but also the providing of appropriate feedback to the child's response. Reward pupils' efforts and thinking rather than just correct answers.
- Provide direct instruction on comprehension abilities that is appropriate to the desired outcome (ranging from knowledge to inquiry) and pupils' grade level, SES, likelihood of success, and so forth (see chapter 3).
- Set purposes for reading comprehension that encourage pupils' attention to and active engagement in learning.
- Afford pupils the opportunity to apply their reading comprehension skills in meaningful recreational reading activities.

Teachers not only ask appropriate questions but also provide appropriate feedback to students' responses.

Direct Instruction

In order to understand and interact with written language, children need to receive direct instruction on essential comprehension abilities. This instruction need not be of great length, but worksheet after worksheet with no teacher monitoring of pupils' attention to tasks is detrimental to comprehension learnings. Taking the abilities listed under literal, interpretive, and critical comprehension as a departure point, pupils need to be shown step by step how to find the main idea, to summarize a story, and so forth. This can be accomplished by planning a series of lessons around one ability. For example, in teaching intermediate-grade children to find the main idea of a paragraph, one might design separate lessons for determining key words in a sentence, topic sentences at the beginning and end of a paragraph, topic sentences in the middle of a paragraph, and paragraphs in which the reader must infer the main idea. A comprehension workbook activity is illustrated on page 2 of the first color insert.

Whatever comprehension ability your pupils need to improve upon, you must first "teach" and monitor closely pupils' engagement in practice and application activities that optimize their chance of success. Providing direct instruction on comprehension skills requires a thoughtful, step-by-step procedure (15). The following lesson components are recommended to foster the mastery of selected goals:

1. *Past Learning.* The first step focuses on determining the existing exeperiential/conceptual backgrounds pupils possess that are needed for them to meet the purposes of reading. In a sense, the teacher is asking, "What do my pupils already know that is essential for them to relate to and understand the text?" For example, this prerequisite for reading would focus on text features (words, sentence structure, and vocabulary) and on identifying the essential understandings that pupils are to acquire from reading the text. This component is assuring that nothing new is introduced to the pupils; everything is related to and builds on their past learnings to maximize comprehension.
2. *Building Background.* After the teacher has determined what past learnings need to be activated, she focuses on how this is done in the lesson. This is the step where pupils' experiential/conceptual backgrounds are utilized. She may explain and demonstrate the lesson objective, review with concrete and written examples application of word recognition strategies, provide an immediate purpose of why it is important to learn this skill, provide and discuss information about story content relevant to desired learning outcomes, and so forth.
3. *Step-by-Step Explanation and Illustration.* This step focuses on making sure that pupils understand what they are to do and how they best can demonstrate the learning outcome. Familiar materials should be used for this purpose along with teacher modeling of appropriate strategies. For example, assume that you wanted your pupils to identify the main idea of a short paragraph. You could model the behavior that they would use by using a familiar written paragraph as an illustration and talk about how you would identify the main idea. An important point in modeling is that the teacher demonstrates and talks about the process involved and not just the steps or procedure. What she is really doing is letting the children "get inside" of her head. This component of direct instruction is the actual teaching stage or the teacher-directed instruction step.
4. *Application of Skill or Ability.* This can be either an independent assignment or group activity that is closely monitored by the teacher. This is application for the purpose of extension and reinforcement. Pupils should be encouraged to monitor their own application of the comprehension instruction they received and the transfer of this learning to other situations.
5. *Ongoing Diagnosis.* Based upon pupils' behavior in both group and independent activities, the teacher attempts to assess learning. This

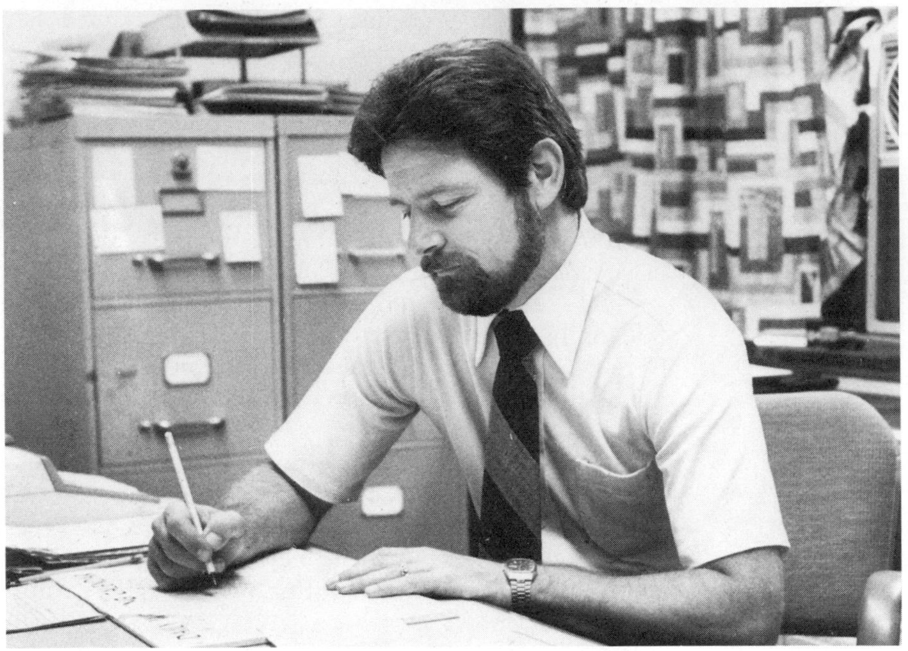

Providing direct instruction in comprehension skills requires a thoughtful step-by-step procedure.

assessment focuses on application of comprehension strategies and the learning and acquisition of information.

Each of the above components is featured in the following two examples of comprehension lessons based on a direct instruction format. Figure 6.3 deals with story grammar and Figure 6.4 focuses on vocabulary. Each of these examples is intended to help teachers understand the teacher-directed approach for teaching reading comprehension.

Classroom Questions

The importance of the quality of teacher questions on children's thinking has already been highlighted. Crucial to this end is self-awareness of teachers of the number and type of questions they ask children. Following this awareness is the ability to judiciously ask children questions on story content that elicit different levels of thinking. It is important at this point to distinguish between questions that require convergent thinking and those that require divergent thinking.

Questions that require convergent thinking are those where a right or wrong answer can be provided. This closure between the reader and

AREA OF NEEDED READING INSTRUCTION

Ability to understand story parts.

INTENDED LEARNING OUTCOME

Students will be able to match sentences from a selected passage to appropriate story parts.

PAST LEARNING

Students have an existing sight vocabulary and word identification skills for reading a simple story.

Students understand story analysis and its importance in getting meaning from print.

Students understand that story analysis is related to reading comprehension.

BUILDING BACKGROUND

Review students' past experiences with the major categories of story analysis by providing a simple story on the chalkboard, listing each sentence next to its appropriate category, and guiding children through directed discussion of each category. Explain that the major categories of analyzing a story are *setting, initiating event, internal response, attempt, consequence, reaction.* An analysis of the story *The Strange Tracks* might look like this:

Setting	Introduces character and provides background information	Once there was a man who lived on a mountain.
Initiating event	Begins the episode	One afternoon while climbing the mountain, he saw some huge, strangely shaped tracks in the snow.
Internal response	Decision	The man was curious and wanted to learn more about the tracks.
Attempt	A try at reaching a goal	He followed the tracks for two days. On the third day a heavy snow storm covered the tracks and made it impossible to search any farther.
Consequence	Outcome	The man discontinued his search and returned to his cabin on the mountain.
Reaction	Character's response	He realized that his attempt to find the source of the strange tracks was unsuccessful and that they would remain a mystery to him for a long time.

FIGURE 6.3 Direct instruction example for teaching story grammar. (From W. H. Rupley and T. R. Blair, *Reading Diagnosis and Direct Instruction: A Guide for the Classroom.* Boston: Houghton Mifflin Publishing Co., 1983, pp. 146–49. Used with permission.)

FIGURE 6.3 continued

Use guided discussion to clarify each major category of story analysis using the written example on the chalkboard to facilitate understanding of *setting, initiating event, internal response, attempt, consequence,* and *reaction.* Use the story "The Strange Tracks" as a source to specify that *setting* includes introducing the character and providing background information, that *initiating event* refers to the first episode of the story, and so forth. Be certain that students clearly understand the terminology and can associate a meaningful relationship for each component with the story.

Remind students that if they understand story analysis they will better understand story meaning. Emphasize that story analysis is directly related to reading comprehension.

TEACHER-DIRECTED INSTRUCTION

Provide each student with a copy of a simple story on a handout. Write the same story on the chalkboard to use for reference in guided discussion. "The Foggy Night" is a simple story that contains the major components *setting, initiating event, internal response, attempt, consequence* and *reaction:*

The Foggy Night

An old woman lived in a lighthouse on the edge of the ocean shore. Late one night she noticed that a deep fog had set in and would make ocean travel dangerous for several nearby ships. She decided to turn the lighthouse lamp to its brightest wattage. So she climbed to the top of the lighthouse and turned the lamp switch to high. Now the ships could tell if they were too close to the shore. The old woman knew that she had fulfilled her mission and was able to sleep soundly that night.

Instruct students to read the story silently. Guide them through discussion of each story component by examining and categorizing each sentence. Use the chalkboard to list sentences and match components accordingly:

Setting	An old woman lived in a lighthouse on the edge of the ocean shore.
Initiating event	Late one night she noticed that a deep fog had set in and would make ocean travel dangerous for several nearby ships.
Internal response	She decided to turn the lighthouse lamp to its brightest wattage.
Attempt	So she climbed to the top of the lighthouse and turned the lamp switch to high.
Consequence	Now the ships could tell if they were too close to the shore.
Reaction	The old woman knew that she had fulfilled her mission and was able to sleep soundly that night.

It is important that your students understand the meaning of the components used to analyze a story and that they can relate each component of story analysis to appropriate sentences. Again, emphasize the importance of story analysis to reading comprehension. Have the students noticed that story components such as *setting, initiating event,* and so forth, usually follow a sequential pattern? Ask students questions relating to story sequence: How would changing the sentence order of the story alter the meaning of the story? Would it make sense to list the old woman's *reaction* in the story analysis at the *beginning* of the story? Why or why not?

INDEPENDENT STUDENT PRACTICE

Distribute a second handout to complete as seat work. Instruct students to match sentences from a simple story on the handout with their appropriate story components by using the *correct letter* that precedes each sentence as is done here:

__A__ Setting
_____ Attempt
_____ Reaction
_____ Initiating Event
_____ Consequence

Jasey the Cat

(A) Once there was a cat named Jasey who lived on a farm. (B) One day Jasey was behind the barn hunting for field mice when he heard a rustling sound in a nearby bush. (C) He wanted to find out if the sound might be made by a mouse and so he decided to jump into the bush after it. (D) To his surprise and dismay the sound was coming from a skunk. (E) Jasey turned on his heels to run away but it was too late. The skunk sprayed Jasey from head to tail. (F) Jasey knew his trick didn't work and he had realized that the lingering odor on his fur would serve as a reminder never to jump into a bush unless first knowing what it holds.

Help students match the first component of the story with its appropriate sentence in order to assure their understanding of this activity. Refer children to the examples on the chalkboard to help them relate meanings of the story components with the sentences in this activity.

ONGOING DIAGNOSIS

Teacher-made tests can be used to determine strengths and weaknesses in this area. These tests should match students' capabilities and past instruction as closely as possible. Children who are having difficulty with this activity can be grouped for additional practice and further instruction in understanding story analysis.

The difficulty level of this activity can be increased by selecting a longer passage, story, or book. Children should not be expected to complete such an activity unless it is apparent that they can relate story components from shorter, less difficult passages. A less difficult activity for analyzing story components is to have students read two or more passages and identify only a specific component, such as *setting* or *initiating event,* in each passage.

Follow-up activities can include asking students to construct their own stories using story elements in an appropriate format. Use children's stories to identify major components in classroom discussion of story analysis. Share the stories with other students in the classroom and have them match the story components with appropriate sentences from these stories.

AREA OF NEEDED READING INSTRUCTION

Ability to develop and understand meaningful vocabulary.

INTENDED LEARNING OUTCOME

Students will construct a web of meaningful word associations from a word source selected by the classroom teacher.

PAST LEARNING

Students understand that words can be associated with groups of related words to construct a web of meaningful information.

Students can draw inferences and meaning from words and word associations.

BUILDING BACKGROUND

Demonstrate word associations by writing a familiar phrase on the chalkboard and asking students to help you construct a web of word associations that center around a particular theme.

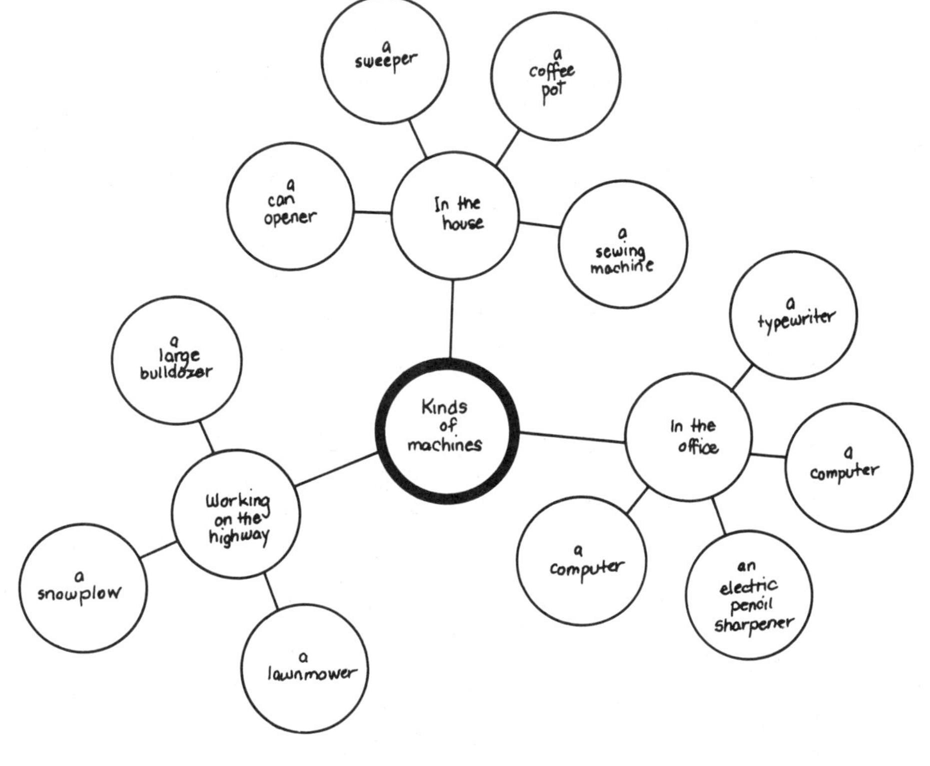

FIGURE 6.4 Direct instruction example for teaching meaningful vocabulary. (From W. H. Rupley and T. R. Blair, *Reading Diagnosis and Direct Instruction: A Guide for the Classroom.* Boston: Houghton Mifflin Publishing Co., 1983, pp. 133–36. Used with permission.)

Use the web as an example to show how we are able to associate words with other words and word meanings. Guide discussion to add more meaningful word associations to the web. Discuss with students how the web of word associations is one way to show relationships among word meanings. Remind students that they will have an opportunity to construct their own web of related word associations following this lesson.

TEACHER-DIRECTED INSTRUCTION

Provide students with a second web of word associations dealing with a familiar theme. In this instance, do not write the theme in the center of the word association web. Have students use the word associations listed in the web to infer the theme of the web.

For example, construct the following word association web and allow students to infer the theme, colors.

Stress that words in a web of word associations must relate to the word phrase in the center of the web if the web is to make sense. Remind them that in the webs drawn on the chalkboard in this lesson all the words can be directly associated with the center word.

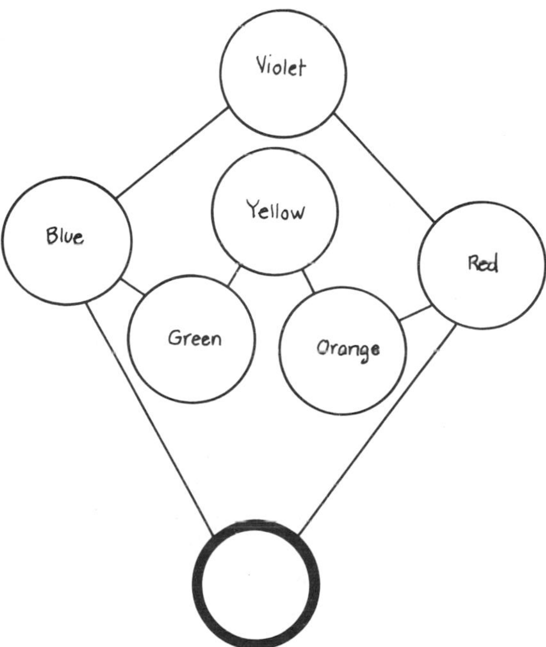

INDEPENDENT STUDENT PRACTICE

Allow pupils to construct their own web of word associations. Prepare a handout showing a word that you select at the center of the web.

Put one or two written examples on the web for them to make sure that all students understand the activity.

FIGURE 6.4 continued

ONGOING DIAGNOSIS

Teacher evaluation of students' individual word association webs.

This activity can be used as an independent instructional activity, with groups of children who have difficulty constructing webs. Hand out, for example, a web with several of the circles

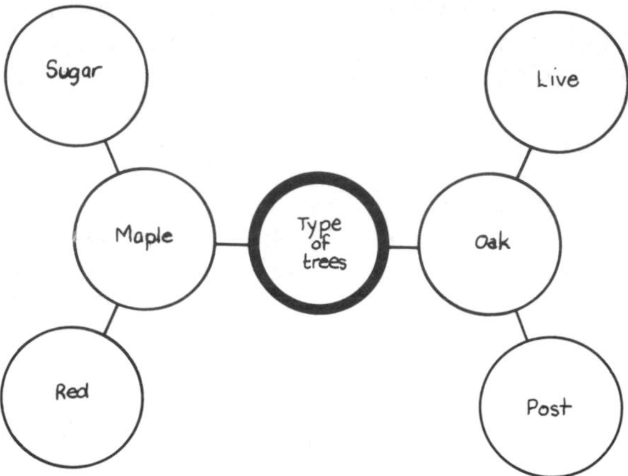

already filled in and a few blank circles for students to complete. This procedure maximizes students' chances of success. Webbing words and word phrases can be used in content-area reading as well and can encompass historical events, science terminology and activities, social studies concepts, and so forth.

the author is usually attained in all literal comprehension questions and some interpretative level questions. Questions that demand divergent thinking are those that are open ended, requiring the reader to probe, analyze, and critically react to information. There are no predetermined right answers. Divergent thinking is required of some interpretative level questions and most questions on the critical comprehension level.

Although the quality of the question is important, the teacher's response to a child's answer is equally important. In order to develop children's thinking and to improve the quality and quantity of class discussions, teachers should be aware of their own reacting behaviors to student responses. Rowe's research on *wait-time* has significant implications for teachers in this area (19). She discovered that teachers usually wait only about one second after asking a question before responding by either calling on another student or repeating the question. She

Teachers should wait at least three seconds after asking a question, with no further comment, to allow students time to respond.

found that when a teacher waits at least three seconds after asking a question with no further comment the following positive results occur:

1. The length of response increases.
2. The number of unsolicited but appropriate responses increases.
3. Failures to respond decrease.
4. Confidence, as reflected in decrease of inflected (question-like tones of voice) responses, increases.
5. Incidence of speculative responses increases.
6. Incidence of child-child comparisons of data increases.
7. Incidence of evidence-inference statements increases.
8. The frequency of student questions increases.
9. Incidence of responses from students rated by teachers as relatively slow increases.
10. The variety in type of moves made by students increases. (p. 81)

Not only should teachers wait before redirecting a question, but they should also increase the time in which they react to a student response. Rowe's wait-time research has very important implications for instruction. In order to attempt to develop abilities to sustain interaction with students, this research gives teachers something that can immediately be put in action. Increasing wait-time indicates that all students benefit (especially low-achieving students), the responsibility for the dialogue shifts to the students, and speculative and reasoning responses increase.

Coupled with the wait-time reaction of teachers, teachers should respond effectively to students' answers and comments to keep students involved with the lesson. Besides asking questions on different cognitive levels, teachers can use "probing and redirecting" questions to aid in sustaining student-teacher interaction (8). Probing involves asking clarifying questions in response to student answers. The following are examples of probing or clarifying questions:

Is this what you mean?
What happened next?
Can you give me another example?
Do you agree? Disagree?
What would you have done?
Why did the author describe it that way?
Is there another alternative?
What could the consequences of your answer be?
Can you tell me more?

To aid teachers in developing their abilities in framing appropriate questions on story content, several classroom question formats have been devised. The "Classroom Question Classification" chart presented in figure 6.5 is one that can be used for several purposes.

First, the classification scheme follows Bloom's taxonomy of goals in the cognitive domain and matches expected cognitive abilities with specific types of questions. Second, the authors list sample phrases and questions teachers can use to elicit different levels of thinking and maximize pupils' engagement in comprehension activities. Many of the sample phrases and questions can be used as purpose-setting statements prior to pupils' reading. Such purposes provide pupils with a better understanding of the task and reasons for reading and maximize their chances of successfully completing the reading. Third, the system can be used by you, the teacher, to examine your own pattern of questions or that of a colleague.

For those persons in teacher training at a preservice or inservice level, it is highly recommended that you complete one or both of the following assignments and share your results with the class.

FLASHBACK

Spelling Book. 139

bo̤o̤k, dŏve, fṳll, use, ȼan, c̃haise, ġem, thin, thou,

No. 146.—CXLVI.

THE DOG.

This dog is the mastiff. He is active, strong, and used as a watch dog. He has a large head and pendent ears. He is not very apt to bite; but he will sometimes take down a man and hold him down. Three mastiffs once had a combat with a lion; and the lion was compelled to save himself by flight.

THE STAG.

The stag is the male of the red deer. He is a mild and harmless animal, bearing a noble attire of horns, which are shed and renewed every year. His form is light and elegant, and he runs with great rapidity. The female is called a hind; and the fawn or young deer, when his horns appear, is called a pricket or brocket.

Noah Webster's Blue-backed Speller was one of the most widely used texts for primary reading instruction between 1780 and the early 1800s. The contents of the Speller included lists of spelling words, miscellaneous selections, and illustrated fables. The Blue-backed Speller made some significant contributions to the reading instructional practices of this time period. First, it helped to standardize English spelling. Second, it did not contain as much religious material for reading as the earlier primer did. Children could better relate to the reading content of the Speller because of the inclusion of content that was appealing to them. Furthermore, the language was more appropriate to their experiential/conceptual background than that found in the primer, which in most cases contained catechisms aimed at preparing children for afterlife.

- Using the classroom classification system, write three questions for each category on a basal reader story or a content reader story.
- Complete a mini-study of evaluating your own questions (tape your reading lesson) or those of a classroom teacher. Tally the questions and determine the percentage in each category. React to the results. Are you surprised? Why or why not?

Another helpful aid for teachers in structuring their reading comprehension instruction is guiding and assisting pupils to set their own purposes in reading. Pupils can be provided instruction about the basic reporter questions (who, what, where, when, why, and how) and instruction in how to use these when reading to set comprehension purposes. The reporter questions can be initially used by teachers to frame a wide range of questions on story content for the pupils. As the pupils become more competent with setting purposes in teacher-directed instruction,

FIGURE 6.5 Classroom question classification. (From Gary Manson and Ambrose A. Clegg, "Classroom Questions: Keys to Children's Thinking," *Peabody Journal of Education* 47 (1970): 305. Used with permission.)

Category Description (Part A)				Recording Form (Part B)	
Category Name	Expected Cognitive Activity	Key Concepts (terms)	Sample Phrases and Questions	Tally Column	Percent of Total Questions Asked
1. REMEMBERING (KNOWLEDGE*)	Student recalls or recognizes information, ideas, and principles in the approximate form in which they were learned.	memory; knowledge; repetition; description	1. What did the book say about . . .? 2. "Define. . . ." 3. "List the three . . ." 4. "Who invented. . . ."		
2. UNDERSTANDING (COMPREHENSION*)	Student translates, comprehends, or inteprets information based on prior learning.	explanation; comparison; illustration	1. "Explain the. . . ." 2. "What can you conclude . . .?" 3. "State in your own words . . ." 4. "What does the picture mean?" 5. "If it rains, then what . . .?" 6. "What reasons or evidence . . .?"		
3. SOLVING (APPLICATION*)	Student selects, transfers, and uses data and principles to complete a problem task with a minimum of directions.	solution; application; convergence	1. "If you know A and B, how could you determine C?" 2. "What other possible reasons . . .?" 3. "What might they do with . . .?" 4. "What do you suppose would happen if . . .?"		

4. ANALYZING (ANALYSIS*)	Student distinguishes, classifies, and relates the assumptions, hypotheses, evidence, conclusions, and structure of a statement or a question with an awareness of the thought processes he is using.	logic; induction and deduction; formal reasoning	1. "What was the author's purpose, bias, or prejudice?" 2. "What must you know for that to be true?" 3. "Does that follow?" 4. "Which are facts and which are opinions?"		
5. CREATING (SYNTHESIS*)	Student originates, integrates, and combines ideas into a product, plan or proposal that is new to him.	divergence; productive thinking; novelty	1. "If no one else knew, how could you find out?" 2. "Can you develop a new way?" 3. "Make up . . ." 4. "What would you do if . . .?"		
6. JUDGING (EVALUATION*)	Student appraises, assesses, or criticizes on a basis of specific standards and criteria (this does not include opinion unless standards are made explicit).	judgment; selection	1. "Which policy will result in the greatest good for the greatest number?" 2. "For what reason would you favor . . .?" 3. "Which of the books would you consider of greater value?" 4. "Evaluate that idea in terms of cost and community acceptance."		
				Total Questions Evaluated =	Sum = 100%

*Term used in Benjamin Bloom et al., *Taxonomy of Educational Objectives: The Classification of Educational Goals. Handbook I: The Cognitive Domain* (New York: David McKay Co., 1956).

they can be introduced slowly to set their own purposes without direct teacher guidance (5).

Setting a purpose for reading and answering specific questions are made much easier if both students and teachers realize the simple reporter questions can be phrased differently.

Who . . .? Which person . . .?	What . . .? Is the purpose . . .?
Where . . .? In what place . . .?	Why . . .? For what reason . . .?
When . . .? At what time . . .?	How . . .? In what manner . . .?

If you plan on completing the previously mentioned assignment on framing questions, another interesting exercise would be to label each one of your questions with one reporter question.

Vocabulary Instruction

Although it is popular to isolate vocabulary instruction in the reading program, emphasis upon word meanings in meaningful context throughout the school day is recommended. If children are to use their background knowledge to comprehend and words are labels for their schemata, then the broader their vocabulary the better able they are to select appropriate schemata (25). Vocabulary emphasis would include direct instruction and appropriate practice on specific skills along with the opportunity to apply these skills in meaningful, familiar reading situations.

Vocabulary instruction would be most effective by relating new words or derivations of words to the children's existing vocabulary and experiential/conceptual background. For example, if a pupil thinks that all animals are pets he would have a difficult time with such concepts as farm animals and zoo animals. Sending this pupil to a dictionary or listing words on the chalkboard would not be effective strategies for teaching him the vocabulary words associated with the different concepts of a milk cow, farm life, or lion. Imagine the possible comprehension problems a pupil might experience when encountering words such as "hedgehog," "Hereford," or "grizzly bear."

Often times context is not sufficient to help children use their prior knowledge to comprehend the meaning a word contributes to written text. Consider the following sentence: "Fennecs were crouched behind several small bushes waiting for any type of prey to come along the path to the water hole."

Are *fennecs* people or animals?

Most likely you would have to guess about what is a fennec because the sentence does not provide enough information to allow you to activate an appropriate schema. By knowing that they are animals a reader can activate his knowledge of animals. By knowing that they are wild animals the reader can use his knowledge of wild animals. Knowing that they are wild, fawn colored, and have large ears may help a reader to form a better understanding of a fennec by having more information to relate to his experiential/conceptual background. However, if the reader were told that a fennec is an African fox he could use his knowledge of a fox to make sense of the sentence. (See Figure 6.4 for an example of a vocabulary lesson.)

A strategy for teaching vocabulary that helps children to use existing knowledge, generate meanings for additional words, and which can be used in various subject areas is described by Fillmer (7). He proposes that teachers concentrate their instructional efforts on "generative" techniques for word learning. A generative reading vocabulary is "one so designed that each word pupils learn enables them to learn the meanings of several other related words" (p. 54). This feature enables pupils to add to their existing knowledge background and understand relationships between the concepts that words represent.

This approach can be followed in the learning of synonyms, antonyms, context clues, roots, prefixes, suffixes, and classification of concepts (animals, size, actions, etc.). This strategy is applicable to all school subjects. The following are a few suggested activities to help promote emphasis on meaningful word growth.

INTRODUCTORY ACTIVITY

Keep an accurate list of new words students meet and learn. Words known for special subjects, words for interest areas, words that contain the same root, prefix, or suffix, and words that possess similar concept classification properties can form the basis for expanding students' meaning vocabularies. These words can be used to teach new words by relating them (these new words) to similar words the pupils know.

Content Areas. Relate new words to known concepts in mathematics in meaningful context.

add
sum
plus
together
total
and
equal

1. 4 *plus* 4 *equals* 8.
2. 8 is the *sum* of 4 *and* 4.
3. We *add* 4 *and* 4 *together* to get a *total* of 8.

Interest Areas. Some new words for which a child interested in basketball would have a concept and which could be learned in meaningful context include:

court	shoot
score	dribbles
second	foul
scoreboard	rebound
bounce	time-out
shot	jump
rim	

Same Root, Prefixes, and Suffixes. Many of these new words can be related to other words learned for *all* new word categories. The preceding example of basketball illustrates the relationship of using same root, prefix, or suffix to learn new words.

basketball	dribbling	dribbled	rebound
baseball	jumping	jumped	retake
football	scoring	scored	remake

Mary *dribbled* the *basketball* to the side of the *court* and *scored*.

Concept Classification Similarities. Words that pupils know can be classified in terms of several similar properties and new words introduced that relate to these known properties.

Animals	*Farm Animals*	*Pets*
pig	pig	dog
cow	cat	cat
cat	sheep	
dog	dog	
sheep	goat	
goat		

Animal Sounds	*Animal Sizes*
dog—bark	little dog
—growl	tiny dog
cat—meow	small dog
—hiss	short dog
pig—oink	
cow—moo	

Write the word on the line that makes sense.

The small dog ________ at the cat.
(barks, oinks, meows, moos)

Two pigs plus one ________ equals three farm animals.
(bird, girl, goat)

Bob had a ________ that oinked on his farm.
(pig, cat, dog, fish)

PRACTICE ACTIVITY

Synonyms and Antonyms. The following examples illustrate the use of concept development to enhance pupils' meaning vocabulary.

Circle the word that means the same as the word underlined.

large	little	aid	big
help	assist	hold	huge
small	tiny	support	large

Select one word from list B that means the same as the word underlined in list A. Write the word on the line.

A		B
help the boy	______ the boy	aid
big man	______ man	little
small toy	______ toy	slick
		lake
		large

APPLICATION ACTIVITY

Meaningful application should be provided for vocabulary development. The following are representative activities that could be used with each of the vocabulary areas discussed above.

Write the word in the blank that makes sense in the sentence.

The dog was too big to go in the ______ hole.
(tiny, have, aid)

Mark liked her ______ house.
(run, help, huge)

Underline the word that means the same as the circled word.
Make sure it makes sense in the sentence.

Frank likes to (help) his mother wash the car.
(soap, assist, little)

The fish live in a (huge) lake.
(large, come, help)

COMPREHENSION INSTRUCTION GUIDELINES

We have emphasized that children need to be taught strategies that they can use to understand print. Teachers need to provide opportunities for children to learn comprehension strategies and to apply strategies in familiar and meaningful reading materials. For any instructional activity a teacher develops to teach reading comprehension, there are some important guidelines to follow. Several important considerations for teacher-directed comprehension instruction were presented earlier and include *past learning, building background, step-by-step explanations and illustrations, application,* and *ongoing diagnosis*.

Pearson (15) provides a list of guidelines that parallel those represented in the examples of teacher-directed instruction (see figures 6.3 and 6.4).

> 1. The trained skill must be instructionally relevant.
> 2. Training should proceed from simple to complex.
> 3. An analysis of training and transfer tasks should provide evidence of where breakdowns occur.
> 4. There should be direct instruction concerning when and how to use the strategies.
> 5. Feedback should be given during class discussions and for independent work.
> 6. A variety of passages (or other materials) should be used in order to facilitate transfer to new situations.
> 7. Self-checking procedures should be used as an inherent part of the training strategy. (p. 15)

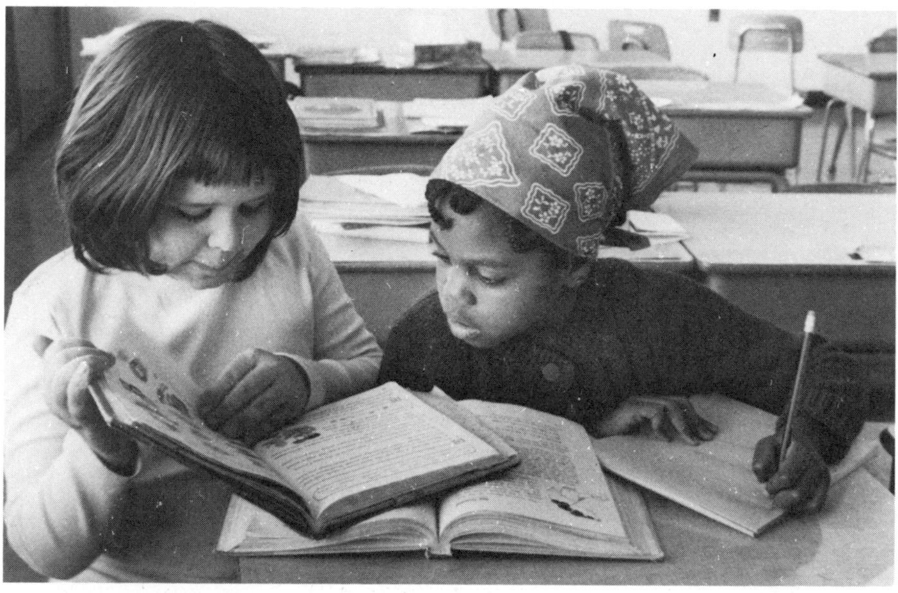

Children may use learning comprehension strategies to read familiar and meaningful materials.

Other basic guidelines that teachers might follow for teaching pupils a way to determine the central problem in a story have been recommended by Moldofsky (13):

1. *Activate pupils' schemata.* Illustrate and demonstrate for pupils the problems and solutions they know about from previous stories.
2. *Organize pupils' schemata.* Categorization of the types of problems that emerge in the story—wanting or needing, feelings, thinking differently, or thinking the wrong way. This can be done by using examples to direct pupils' thinking and can develop as they read more and expand their own ideas.
3. *Model the process for pupils.* Use examples within the pupils' experiential/conceptual background such as "The Three Pigs," "Jack and the Beanstalk," and "Little Red Riding Hood" to model how to identify the central story problem. Two strategies for modeling (25) are recall/compare (this reminds me of) and predict/justify (this will probably happen because of this). For example, the teacher could help pupils recall "The Three Little Pigs" and compare their wanting to build a house with "Little Red Riding Hood" wanting to visit her grandmother. Assisting the children to infer from other events in such familiar stories about how a story's central story develops will enable them to understand that several possibilities may exist, but these can only be credible if they fit the story is a manner that makes sense.
4. *Provide for transfer and application.* Teacher guidance and assistance are important features of this step. Help pupils evaluate their identified story problems and redirect their thinking if necessary. The teacher may have to use additional examples and illustrations within pupils' experiential/conceptual background and further modeling for those experiencing problems in independent application. As pupils become more proficient in their application, this learning can serve as a foundation for expanding the strategy.
5. *Expansion of pupils' strategy.* Moldofsky notes that there is no "level of mastery" for this strategy. The central problems of stories can be compared in numerous ways by the pupils, such as type of problem, type of solution, and multiple but related problems. Vocabulary can be taught in relation to story problems that goes beyond concepts such as good and bad. Concepts that are associated with expressive vocabulary can be used to label characters (brave, cowardly, cooperative) and build relationships between character traits and problems and solutions. Through pupils' examination of setting and its effect on story problems, teachers can continue to expand the development of comprehension strategy.

Another important area needing teacher attention in the development and teaching of reading comprehension is story schema (story structure or story grammar). Story schema is a set of expectations or rules about how stories are usually organized (10, 15). Readers have an internal organization of story knowledge that enables them to process print by retaining story information until it makes sense, storing it in memory, and adding more information as they continue to read the story. A reader's story schema also is an important feature in recalling what was read.

Story schema has been investigated by many reading researchers, and several descriptions of story grammar have been proposed. A description of simple story structure to use in classroom instruction includes setting, theme, plot, and resolution (10, 24). These features are represented in figure 6.6. All stories may not have each of the components presented in figure 6.6; however, well-written stories should contain the majority of these features. (Another example of story grammar was represented in figure 6.3.)

The story setting is made up of both major and minor settings. Major settings usually include time, place, characters, and state. For example, time may either be implied "Sally looked out her window" or it may be stated "One clear and bright summer morning." Time may also be represented by "Once upon a time" or "Long, long ago"; both of these are characteristic of fables and fairy tales. Place may also be either implied or stated directly, such as "Everyone sat down to breakfast" or "Mark went to visit Mr. Smith's farm." Major and minor characters are typically identified by name (Sue, Sally, Bob) or by occupations (bellhop, police officer, teacher) or by relationship (friends, mother, neighbor). State refers to the initial establishment of what is occurring. Examples of an ongoing state found in different stories are children attending a party and playing games; wishes and superstitions; or fishing, camping, and hiking.

Minor settings include the same features as major settings and develop the story. For example in the major setting time may be summer, minor setting time may be one day; major location may be Uncle Toby's farm, minor location may be the old barn; major character may be Frank the hired hand, minor character may be Uncle Toby; and ongoing state for the major setting may be new experiences on a farm, minor state may be new friendships.

The theme, as noted in figure 6.6, can be either the goal of the main character or the author's intended message. Billy's wanting his friends to have a good time at his birthday party or Mary working to save money for Christmas presents are examples of the goal of the main character.

Story plots are made up of five subparts that compose an episode: *starter event* is what gets the episode started and may be an action by a character or an occurrence (Billy opened his birthday gifts); *inner response* is what occurs in the character in terms of feelings, thoughts, subgoals, or plans (Billy was very disappointed when he didn't get a new

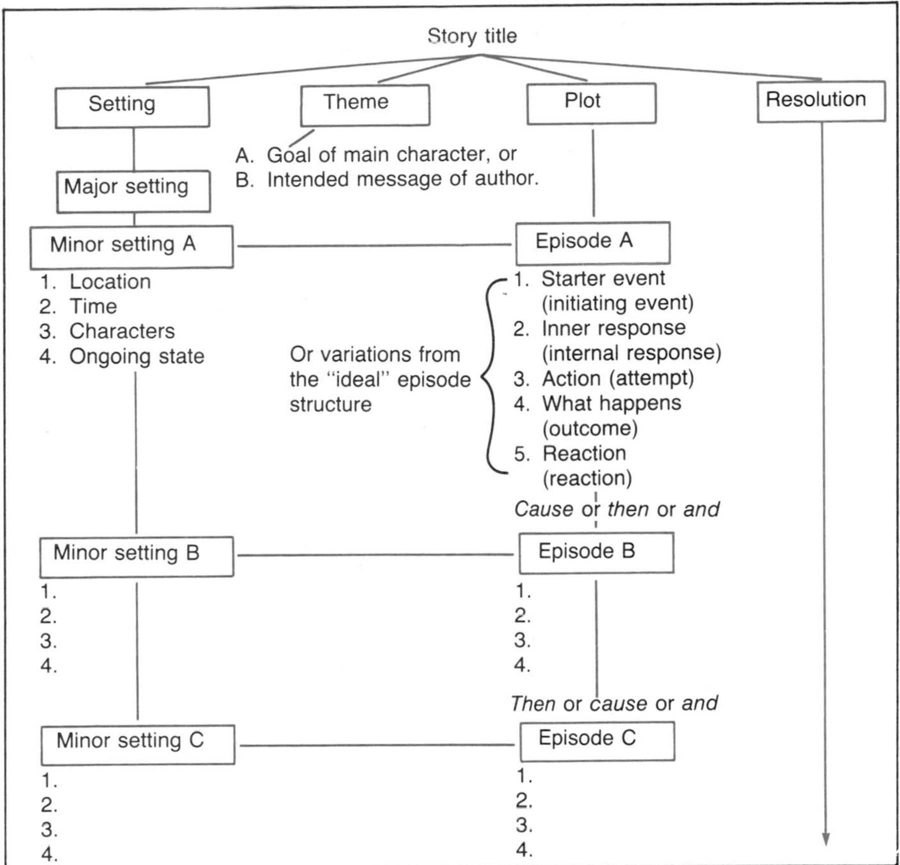

FIGURE 6.6 Schematic representation of story structure. (From C. J. Gordon and C. Braun, "Using Story Schema as an Aid to Reading and Writing," *The Reading Teacher* 37 (1983): 120. Reprinted with permission of C. J. Gordon and the International Reading Association.)

bicycle for his birthday); *action* is how the story character plans to achieve the goal or subgoal (Billy planned to work odd jobs and save his money for a bicycle); *what happens* is the outcome of the character's actions (Billy only found a few odd jobs and couldn't save enough money to buy a new bicycle); *reaction* is when there is a response to an outcome or earlier action (Billy decided to buy a used bicycle and fix it up). Episodes are tied together to each other by relationships (Billy got a used bicycle and then began to fix it up or Billy spent all his money on a used bicycle, and his parents helped him fix it up).

Resolution can be thought of as the main character's achieving his goal or the moral of a story. For the example of Billy and his bicycle, the resolution could be that he finally got a bicycle, and he was very proud of buying it himself. A possible moral could have been if a person is willing to work hard for something then he can achieve his goal.

Gordon and Braun (10) caution teachers to realize that their schematic representation of story structure is ideal and that not all main categories are found in all stories nor are all subcategories found in all episodes. They further point out that not all subparts of an episode occur in the same order. However, knowledge of story schema may help pupils to "infer content under the omitted story categories" (10, p. 118).

Some basic guidelines for teaching children story schema awareness are presented below and are adapted from Gordon and Braun's (10) recommendations:

1. *Story selection.* Well-formed stories should be used to introduce both the structure and terminology of story grammar. A diagram of the story is used, and each category is completed as responses are gotten from the children. Walking children through this initial story and several others by relating information to their experiential/conceptual background and modeling the process for them is recommended.
2. *Set and illustrate reading purposes.* It is important to activate pupils' experiential/conceptual background in relation to story content and concept of a story and guide their thinking by referring to familiar examples when needed.
3. *Use well-organized stories and focus instruction on identification of story parts before identifying all story components in one story.* Several well-organized stories should be used initially and each part of each story presented and discussed. This will enable pupils to see relationships and that structure features are not changing, just the content of the stories.
4. *Ask story-specific questions once the children can associate story content with specific story structure.* Questions should be phrased so that they match the features of story structure being addressed (Who is the main character? What does (name of main character) do?) and focus on the literal comprehension of the story. After youngsters have completed the identification of story structure with teacher direction, inferential questions can be asked.
5. *Begin to introduce less well-organized stories to assure that pupils realize that all stories do not follow the "ideal" story structure.* This supports the earlier guideline for teacher-directed instruction, recommending training proceeding from the simple to the complex.

The above guidelines for comprehension instruction are neither story specific nor content specific; they can be used for comprehension instruction in a basal reader or in a social studies text. An important point is that these guidelines are aimed at helping teachers teach children comprehension processes.

COMPREHENSION ACTIVITIES

Figure 6.7 provides activities developed by Turner and Fey (29) to help reinforce comprehension skills identified by the Florida Statewide Assessment Program. The authors emphasized the point that these activities are only supplemental in nature and that direct instruction and use of the comprehension instruction guidelines presented earlier are necessary to assure quality teaching.

Sequence of Events

A. The reading process. Each group of words is a part of a sentence: a beginning, a middle, or a last part. When you put them in the right order, they make a sentence. In each box you are to put 1 in front of the first part, 2 in front of the middle part, and 3 in front of the last part of the sentence.

Example: (1) _1_ Friday was the day
_3_ on her vacation
_2_ that Miss Spruce started

(2) ____ clear the table
____ Patty helped
____ and wash the dishes

(3) ____ and disappeared
____ the starving beast
____ leaped from the cage

(4) ____ these new books in the right order
____ on the new bookshelf"
____ Ruth said, "I'm going to put

(5) ____ so that the bee would fly out
____ the window of the bus
____ Mr. Hunter was going to raise

B. Ask students to bring in their favorite comic strips from the newspaper. Collect these for several days. Cut the comic strips into individual frames and place in envelopes. Give these to students and allow them to arrange the pieces to tell a story.

C. Prepare short stories in which the numbered sentences are out of order. Pupils are directed to rearrange the sentences so they are in proper order.

Example: (1) The strange man walked to the door and rapped.
(2) The man was invited into the house.

FIGURE 6.7 Suggested activities for reinforcing comprehension skills.
(From Edward C. Turner and T. Frederick Fey, "Improving Comprehension Skills" (Gainesville, Fla.: Florida Educational Research and Development Council, Inc.: 1977), by permission of the authors.)

FIGURE 6.7 continued

(3) The dog barked when he heard the sound.
(4) The lady of the house went to the door and opened it.

Correct answers can appear on the back of the exercise, making this potentially a self-directed activity.

Story Detail

A. Mount a detailed picture on a piece of cardboard. In an accompanying envelope, provide pupils with three-by-five cards on which individual paragraphs about the picture have been typed and numbered. Pupils are directed to find the paragraph which gives the most accurate details about the picture.

B. Provide students with a series of paragraphs in each of which a nonsensical phrase has been inserted. Pupils are directed to read each paragraph carefully and detect the absurd phrase.

C. Have students read several paragraphs each describing a different character. Have students select the character they like best and list the words found in the paragraph that describe him. Have a student read his list of words and see if classmates can identify the character.

Cause or Effect

A. Prepare or select several long paragraphs which describe several events that result in the occurrence of a final event. Ask the student to determine what happened to cause the final event.

Example: Charlie left for work late one morning because the alarm clock didn't ring. Being late caused him to hurry and he slipped on the sidewalk and twisted his ankle. At work he spilled his coffee on some very important papers and the boss was angry. Charlie was caught in the rain and his new shirt faded on his pants. When Charlie got home he kicked the cat.

Question: What happened that made Charlie kick the cat?

B. Select or prepare several short paragraphs in which there is a final act. Ask the students to explain why the final act occurred.

Example: Jack slipped out of the house and ran to his favorite climbing tree. As he neared the top, a branch broke and he fell to the ground.

Question: What happened to make Jack fall? (the branch broke)

C. Find or make up several reasoning statements for the students and have them give the answers. Discuss any that students do not agree on or have no answer for.

Example: If there are clouds in the sky it may rain;
if there are no clouds in the sky it will not rain.
It is raining;
therefore, *there are clouds in the sky.*

Inference

A. Select or prepare several sentences for each student. For each sentence provide three or four alternative answers, one of which is most likely based on the sentence.

Example: The Applegates lived near the ocean in the eastern part of the United States. They lived near the—Atlantic Ocean, Pacific Ocean, Indian Ocean?

B. Begin reading a story to the class but stop before completing it. Provide students with several possible endings and discuss which one is best and why.

C. Select or prepare several paragraphs for students. For each paragraph, provide three or four questions which are not answered directly by the facts in the paragraph. Have students prepare answers for the questions.

Example: Henry flinched as he touched his bruised, swollen eye. He was angry at himself for not being more careful yesterday in practice. The first game of the season, and Henry stepped right in front of the pitcher's first throw!

(a) What happened to Henry?

(b) What kind of practice was it?

Conclusion

A. Give each child a slip of paper on which is written a job title and the characteristics of that job. Each student describes to the class the characteristics of that job.

Example: I get up early. I wear overalls. I drive a tractor. I milk cows.

Job: A farmer

B. After students have read a story, supply them with several questions which have not been answered by the story. Have them supply answers to the questions and then discuss why they gave each answer. An example of a question might be:

In the story we noted that the pioneers always carried water with them. Why did they do this?

C. Students participate in a class activity involving riddles. In these riddles only a few facts are given and students must ask yes or no questions to obtain enough facts to provide the answer to the riddles.

Example: There is a man lying in an open field with a pack on his back. The question is, What can you determine about this situation?

Main Idea

A. Have students write short news articles and then select titles for the articles which would be appropriate for newspaper headlines.

B. Designate a story or articles in a book to which pupils have access. Provide a series of key sentences, one from each paragraph. Pupils are instructed to find the paragraph from which each key sentence was taken.

C. Cut headings from three or four short articles. Place the headings in one envelope and the articles in another. Pupils are directed to match the headings with the proper articles.

Mood

A. Provide students with large pieces of drawing paper and make crayons available but not yet distributed. Play an instrumental record for three to five minutes while students listen. Turn off the record player and allow students to choose crayons. Turn the record player back on and allow students to draw anything they feel like. At the end of an appropriate time, ask students to write how they feel on the back of their pictures. As students share their pictures with the class, the class tries to determine how the artist was feeling.

FIGURE 6.7 continued

Fact and Opinion

A. Students collect and bring to class several advertisements from magazines and newspapers. In small groups have students select advertisements to discuss with the class. Analyze the advertisements to determine their validity.

B. After discussing with students the kinds of articles found in newspapers, have them bring to class two or three of each type discussed. Have students distinguish between articles that describe actual events and those that are the writer's ideas.
Example: Report on a local bank robbery versus editorial about litterbugs.

C. Show students a short film or part of a film in which an incident takes place (an automobile accident, bank robbery, scene in a supermarket, etc.). Ask students to write about what they have seen. Discuss what they have written and then replay the film looking for things they have written about. Compare their descriptions with what actually happens in the film.

Author Purpose

A. Provide students with several types of books and articles (comics, cookbooks, science texts, fiction, history). Have them classify the books and articles as to why they were written.

B. Divide students into several small groups. Working together, each group prepares a short story to be read to the class. After hearing the story, members of the class try to determine the reason why the group wrote the story.

C. Provide students with several sets of paragraphs. In each set there are two paragraphs with the same main theme. One of the paragraphs in the set is written so as to provide the reader with factual information about the theme and the other tells a humorous story about the theme. Have the students read the paragraphs in each set and tell why each was written.
Example: The theme might be raccoons. One paragraph gives facts about the raccoon and the other tells of humorous incidents when a raccoon gets into a camper's tent.

SUMMARY

Irrespective of any commercial reading program utilized in schools, the focal point of instructional activities should be on furthering pupils' comprehension abilities. Reading comprehension was described in the chapter as an interactive process. It is a process of making sense of written text through meaningful interpretation in relation to readers' use of text and experiential/conceptual background for concepts of written language, story structure, purposes, and content of what is read. Language serves as the core of representing information, and comprehension capabilities are directly related to children's background of experience, listening ability, and listening-speaking vocabulary. Instructional implications and guidelines were given that focus on helping pupils develop processes for comprehending. These implications and guidelines can be used to develop and evaluate reading comprehension lessons that teachers intend to use for instruction. Included among these recommendations were teachers giving attention to direct instruction, story schema, author's purpose, reader's purpose, and the central theme of stories. Two fully developed lesson plans, one on story structure and the other on developing vocabulary, were provided to illustrate the importance of teaching reading comprehension as a process. Several abbreviated activities were also presented to illustrate areas of comprehension instruction for which the guidelines presented throughout the chapter could be applied. The topic of reading comprehension is finally receiving deserved attention by educational researchers. It is the fervent hope of all teachers that knowledge of this elusive area can be expanded with further practical implications for the classroom.

YOUR POINT OF VIEW

Discussion Questions

1. Many commercial reading programs delineate over a hundred comprehension skills. What are the possible positive and negative effects of this emphasis?
2. Some investigators on comprehension have reported that very little instruction was taking place in the classroom. Why do you think this is the case?

Take a Stand For or Against

1. Reading comprehension cannot be taught.
2. An emphasis on comprehension instruction should not begin before the third grade.

BIBLIOGRAPHY

1. Anderson, Richard C., and Pearson, P. David. *A Schema-Theoretic View of Basic Processes in Reading Comprehension.* Technical Report No. 306. University of Illinois at Urbana-Champaign, Center for the Study of Reading, 1984.

2. Anderson, Richard; Spiro, Rand; and Anderson, Mark. *Schemata as Scaffolding for the Representation of Information in Connected Discourse.* Technical Report No. 24. University of Illinois at Urbana-Champaign, Center for the Study of Reading, 1977.
3. Arnold, Richard D., and Wilcox, Elizabeth. "Comparing Types of Comprehension Questions Found in Fourth Grade Readers." *Reading Psychology* 1 (1982): 43–49.
4. Barrett, Thomas C. "Taxonomy of Reading Comprehension." In *Teaching Reading in the Middle Grades,* edited by Richard F. Smith and Thomas C. Barrett. Reading, Mass.: Addison-Wesley Publishing Co., 1974.
5. Cohen, Ruth. "Self-Generated Questions as an Aid to Reading Comprehension." *The Reading Teacher* 8 (1983): 770–75.
6. Durkin, Dolores. "What Classroom Observations Reveal about Reading Comprehension Instruction." *Reading Research Quarterly* 14 (1978–79): 481–533.
7. Fillmer, H. Thompson. "A Generative Vocabulary Program for Grades 4–6." *Elementary School Journal* 78 (1977): 53–58.
8. Gage, N. C., and Berliner, David C. *Educational Psychology.* Chicago: Rand McNally College Publishing Co., 1975.
9. Goodman, Kenneth S. "Comprehension Centered Reading." In *Claremont Reading Conference Thirty-Fourth Yearbook,* edited by Malcolm P. Douglas, 125–35. Claremont, Calif.: The Claremont Reading Conference, 1970.
10. Gordon, Christine J., and Braun, Carl. "Using Story Schema as an Aid to Reading and Writing." *The Reading Teacher* 2 (1984): 116–21.
11. Manson, Gary, and Clegg, Ambrose A. "Classroom Questions: Keys to Children's Thinking?" *Peabody Journal of Education* 47 (1970): 302–7.
12. Mason, Jana. "A Schema-Theoretic View of the Reading Process as Basis for Comprehension Instruction." In *Comprehension Instruction: Perspectives and Suggestions,* edited by Gerald G. Duffy, Laura R. Roehler, and Jana Mason, 26–38. New York: Longman, 1984.
13. Moldofsky, Penny Baum. "Teaching Students to Determine the Central Story Problem: A Practical Application of Schema Theory." *The Reading Teacher* 38 (1984): 377–82.
14. Page, William D., and Pinnell, Gay Sue. *Teaching Reading Comprehension.* Urbana, Ill: National Council of Teachers of English, 1979.
15. Pearson, P. David. "A Context for Instructional Research on Reading Comprehension." In *Learning to Learn From Text: A Framework for Improving Classroom Practice,* edited by James Flood, 1–15. Newark, Del.: International Reading Association, 1984.
16. Pearson, P. David, and Johnson, Dale D. *Teaching Reading Vocabulary.* New York: Holt, Rinehart & Winston, 1978.
17. Rand, Muriel K. "Story Schema: Theory, Research and Practice." *The Reading Teacher* 38 (1984): 116–21.
18. Rosenshine, Barak V.; Mason, Jana M.; and Osborn, Jean H. *A Consideration of Skill Hierarchy Approaches to the Teaching of Reading.* Technical Report No. 42. University of Illinois at Urbana-Champaign, Center for the Study of Reading, 1977.
19. Rowe, Mary Budd. "Wait-time and Rewards as Instructional Variables, Their Influence on Language, Logic and Fate Control: Part One—Wait-time." *Journal of Research in Science Teaching* 11 (1974): 81–94.

20. Rumelhart, David E. "Schemata: The Building Blocks of Cognition." In *Comprehension and Teaching: Research Reviews,* edited by John T. Guthrie, 3–26. Newark, Del.: International Reading Association, 1981.
21. Rupley, William H., and Blair, Timothy R. *Reading Diagnosis and Direct Instruction: A Guide for the Classroom.* Boston, Mass.: Houghton-Mifflin Publishing Co., 1983.
22. Rupley, William H., and Blair, Timothy R. *Reading Diagnosis and Remediation: Classroom and Clinic.* 2d ed. Boston, Mass.: Houghton-Mifflin Publishing Co., 1983.
23. Shiman, David D., and Nash, Robert J. "Questioning: Another View." *Peabody Journal of Education* 51 (1974): 246–53.
24. Stein, Nancy L., and Trabasso, Tom. *What's in a Story: An Approach to Comprehension Instruction.* Technical Report No. 200. University of Illinois at Urbana-Champaign, Center for the Study of Reading, 1981.
25. Strange, Michael. "Instructional Implications of a Conceptual Theory of Reading Comprehension." *The Reading Teacher* 33 (1980): 391–97.
26. Tatham, Susan Masland. "Comprehension Taxonomies: Their Uses and Abuses." *The Reading Teacher* 32 (1978): 190–94.
27. Thorndike, Edward L. "Reading as Reasoning: A Study of Mistakes in Paragraph Reading." *Journal of Educational Research* 8 (1917): 323–32.
28. Tierney, Robert J., and Pearson, P. David. *Learning to Learn from Text: A Framework for Improving Classroom Practice.* Reading Education Report No. 30. University of Illinois at Urbana-Champaign, Center for the Study of Reading, 1981.
29. Turner, Edward C., and Fey, T. Frederick. "Improving Comprehension Skills." Gainesville, Fla.: Florida Educational Research and Development Council, 1977.
30. Weaver, Phyllis. "Improving Reading Comprehension: Effects of Sentence Organization Instruction." *Reading Research Quarterly* 15 (1979): 129–46.
31. Weaver, Phyllis. *Research Within Reach.* St. Louis, Mo.: CEMREL, Research and Development Interpretation Service, 1978.

7

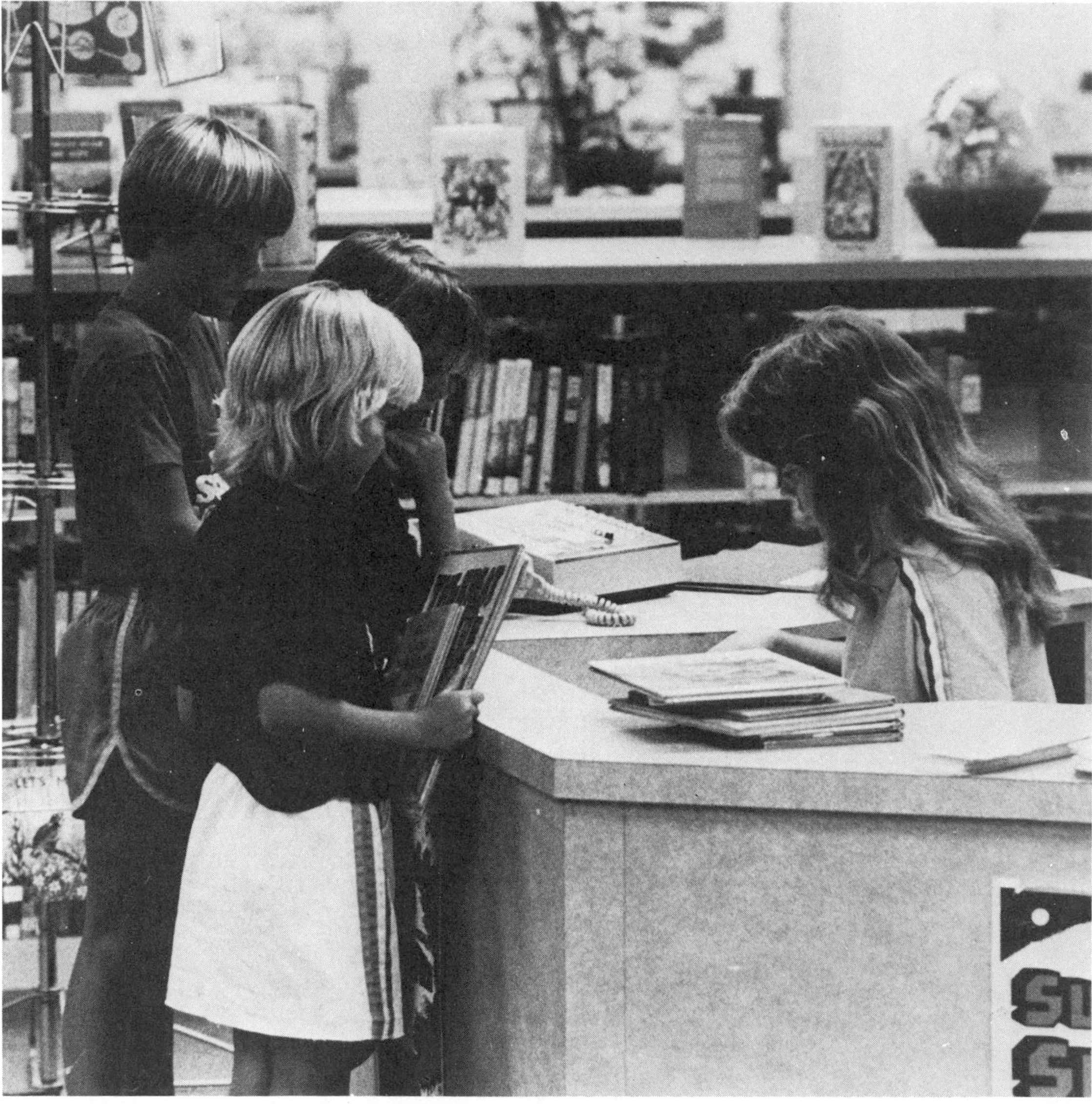

Study Skills

For the Reader

You might logically assume that concentrating on providing excellent instruction in the various word identification strategies and comprehension skills will automatically produce a mature, flexible reader. Such is not the case. Early in the reading program children are expected to read successfully in content material and to locate and synthesize information. Although you could make a case for more than one neglected area in a school's curriculum, the area of study skills is probably at the top of the list. Think of your own background for a moment and answer the following questions:

- Were you systematically taught how to study in your content subjects (math, science, social studies)?
- Were you systematically taught how to locate and synthesize information from an almanac, encyclopedia, atlas, and the dictionary?
- Were you systematically taught how to interpret various types of maps, graphs, charts, and diagrams?

Many will respond never, some may respond a little. Notice the key word *systematically* in the above statements. Many study skills are only given passing mention and attention in our schools. However, everyone needs systematic, planned instruction and practice to meet the challenges of content material and to be able to read in order to learn throughout life.

In each For the Reader section in the previous chapters, you were asked to preview the chapter before plunging into reading. We were and are attempting to change your reading habits by ensuring that you take advantage of the organization of most textbooks. By now, you have probably realized the importance of gaining an overview or preview of what you were about to read. This is but one part of the area of study skills that we recommend you systematically teach in your classes. In this chapter, the content of study skills will be presented along with recommended teaching procedures.

Preview

- Read the Key Ideas that follow.
- Read each heading and subheading.

- Read the summary.
- Read the questions and statements at the end of the chapter.
- Return to the chapter text that follows the Key Ideas and begin reading.

Key Ideas

The ability to read well in a basal reader does not ensure the ability to read well in a subject area.
Measurement of the approximate difficulty level of content material is necessary to provide effective instruction.
All readers should take advantage of organizational reader aids in textbooks.
Study skills will not be mastered by students through incidental learning but only through systematic instruction.
Teachers should strive to match their instruction to pupils' needs in content areas.

CONTENT READING ABILITY

As briefly mentioned in the For the Reader section, an adequate instructional and independent reading program does not ensure successful readers in content material. Pupils frequently experience difficulty in content materials. Possible reasons for this difficulty are the lack of systematic instruction in study skills, the difficulty level of many content materials in terms of vocabulary and concepts, and lack of transfer of skills from the basic reading program to study-type materials.[1] Underlying these possible explanations is the fact that youngsters' general reading ability does not often predict how well those same youngsters will do in various content areas (11). Although evidence of this fact is not new (18), its ramifications for instruction at all levels are still in an infancy stage. Using reading as a tool in content areas requires the use of the skills and abilities taught in a developmental program. Such reading abilities should be applied to both content materials and study skills germane to each of the content areas (5, 21, 22). In figure 7.1, Pescosolido, Schell, and Laurent (13) demonstrate how a study skill assignment requires the application of several reading skills. This example involves locating specific information about an explorer in a social studies text. Each reading skill applied in a content area needs to be taught to students in a systematic, direct fashion (see chapters 6 and 10 for illustrative direct instruction lessons on specific comprehension and study

1. John Pescosolido 1980: personal communication.

Task	General Skill	Specific Skill
Selecting appropriate texts	Locational Skill	use of title
Locate specific information	Locational Skill	use of table of contents
Locate page for specific information	Locational Skill	use of index
Obtaining general information in text	Comprehension Skill	determining author's pattern by reading center heads and paragraph heads
Reading for information	Comprehension Skill	finding main idea
Reading for information	Comprehension Skill	reading for detail
Reading for information	Comprehension Skill	differentiating important from unimportant
Reading for information	Organizing Skill	outlining
Reading for information	Organizing Skill	summarizing

FIGURE 7.1 Illustration of the Application of Reading Skills in a Study Skills Task. (From John R. Pescosolido, Leo M. Schell, and Marie-Jeanne Laurent, *Reading Approaches and Rituals* (Dubuque, Ia. Kendall/Hunt Pub. Co., 1967) p. 22, by permission of the publisher.)

skills). Teachers must not assume students know and can apply the various reading skills in content areas.

A possible explanation for students having problems in content subjects is the increased difficulty level of the materials to be read. Readability is the difficulty level of written material. The concept of readability is important for all teachers. Teachers need to "match" the difficulty level of a book with the instructional level of the student. Students need to function in challenging material that is neither too easy nor too difficult. The closer that "match," the better chance for maximum learning to occur. Of course, good teaching techniques affect how well this match is made. In addition, readability is affected by many factors relating to both characteristics of the material and of the learner, including word and sentence length, reader interest, reader background, and syntactic and semantic features of the text. In order to provide effective instruction, teachers need to be able to judge the readability level of material. Many readability formulas are available for this purpose. Fry's Readability Formula (see figure 7.2) is based on word and sentence length and is quick to use. However, it is imperative to underscore that any readability formula will only yield the approximate level, not exact level, of difficulty. Indeed, using different readability formulas on the same material can yield different results. Also, readability itself will vary within a given text. Because of the difficulties inherent in using any formula (9), teachers are encouraged to use personal knowledge of their children and of the assigned textbook in addition to using a formula to assess readability.

In contrast to providing a grade level designation for the readability level, the use of the cloze procedure on content material may indicate students' abilities to read a particular text. Results of a cloze procedure will yield information indicating if the material at hand is on a youngster's instructional, independent, or frustration reading level (see chapter 11 for a description of the cloze procedure). This procedure can be administered in a large group and can quickly indicate class and individual capabilities in reading a particular content text.

Expanded Directions for Working Readability Graph

1. Randomly select three (3) sample passages and count out exactly 100 words each, beginning with the beginning of a sentence. Do count proper nouns, initializations, and numerals.
2. Count the number of sentences in the hundred words, estimating length of the fraction of the last sentence to the nearest one-tenth.
3. Count the total number of syllables in the 100-word passage. If you don't have a hand counter available, an easy way is to simply put a mark above every syllable over one in each word, then when you get to the end of the passage, count the number of marks and add 100. Small calculators can also be used as counters by pushing numeral 1, then push the + sign for each word or syllable when counting.
4. Enter graph with *average* sentence length and *average* number of syllables; plot dot where the two lines intersect. Area where dot is plotted will give you the approximate grade level.
5. If a great deal of variability is found in syllable count or sentence count, putting more samples into the average is desirable.
6. A word is defined as a group of symbols with a space on either side; thus, *Joe, IRA, 1945,* and & are each one word.
7. A syllable is defined as a phonetic syllable. Generally, there are as many syllables as vowel sounds. For example, *stopped* is one syllable and *wanted* is two syllables. When counting syllables for

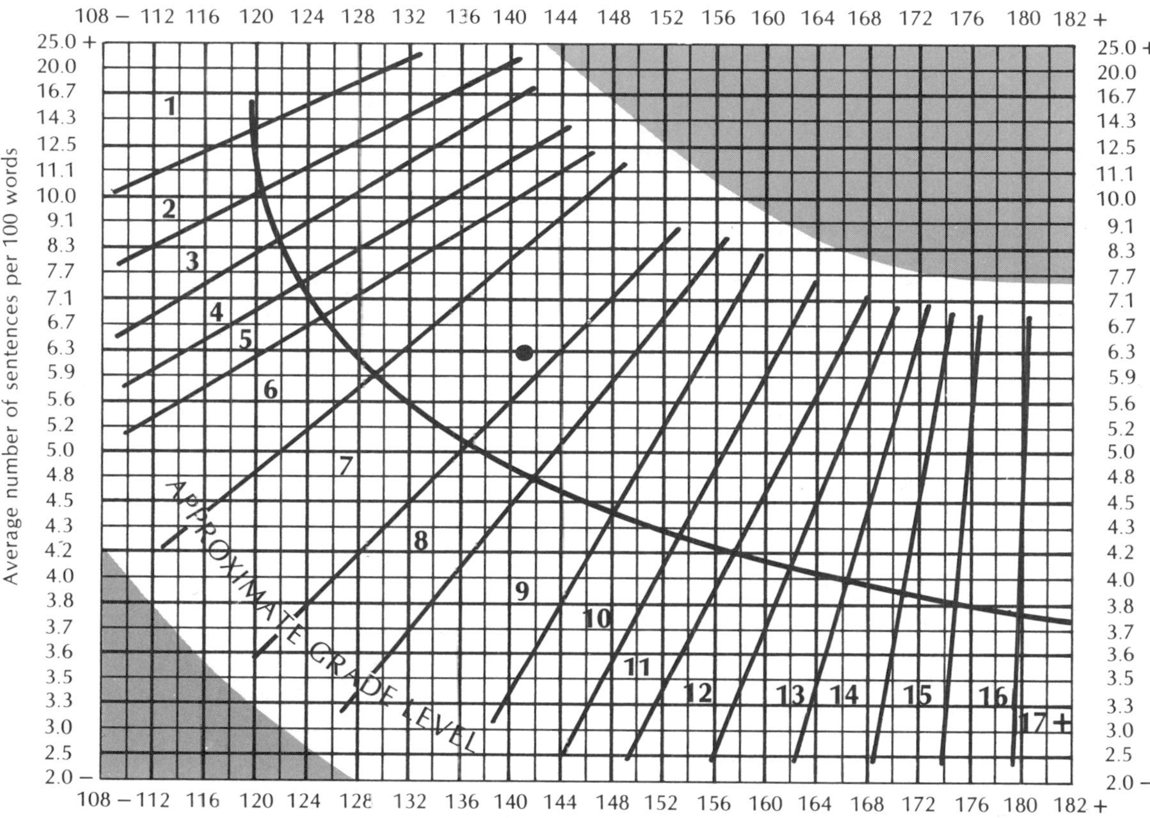

FIGURE 7–2 Graph for Estimating Readability–Extended. Note: This "extended graph" does not outmode or render the earlier (1968) version inoperative or inaccurate; it is an extension. (Source: By Edward Fry. Reprinted from *The Journal of Reading,* December 1977. Reproduction permitted. No copyright.)

FLASHBACK

GEOGRAPHY.

☞ The "Interrogative system" of teaching, has now become very general in almost every branch of school education. The introduction may be traced to the Scholar's Arithmetic, in 1801, many years before the appearance of Goldsmith and of Guy in our country. A further improvement in this system is here attempted, and instead of printing the question at length, which necessarily swells the book, a character (?) is introduced, intimating both to the Instructer, and the pupil, that a question is required, and this character is invariably placed BEFORE the word or words intended to ask the question, and to which the answer, FOUND BY READING THE SENTENCE, is to be a direct reply. For example, take the first sentence; the character is placed before the words "certain knowledge;" the question then is, Had the ancients any certain knowledge of the figure of the earth? The answer, from reading the sentence, is evident, No; or, They had not.

Where the construction of the sentence suggests no particular form in which to put the question, it may be, What is said of, &c.; as for instance, under the article "Agriculture," in Massachusetts, the character is placed before the word "agriculture;" the question then may be, What is said of the agriculture of Massachusetts?

Let the class be directed to meditate answers to the questions to be asked on those subjects or words before which the character is placed. After reading, let those questions be put by the instructer, and answered by the class in rotation. The exercise will be found both profitable and entertaining.

THE WORLD.

THE ancients had no ?certain knowledge of the figure of the earth. But later discoveries, both by astronomy and navigation, demonstrate the world we inhabit to be a large opaque globe or ball, nearly eight thousand ?miles in diameter. In proof of this it is only necessary to notice, that various navigators have actually sailed around it. Of these, the ?first was Sir Francis Drake, who in 1580 completed the circumnavigation of the globe, after an absence of two years, ten months, and twenty days, from England, his native land.

About two thirds of the ?surface of the earth are covered with water. In respect to its universal communication, the ocean may be regarded as one; but, for geographical purposes, it has been found more convenient to consider it as distributed into portions or parts. The ?largest of these

The importance of study skills and being able to read content text with a specific purpose were important in the early 1800s. The example above is from Daniel Adams, *Geography of the World,* 1830. Pupils reading the text were directed to questions the teacher would ask by the use of a superior *q*. Students were directed to ask themselves questions for each of the *q* symbols and come up with the appropriate answer.

numerals and initializations, count one syllable for each symbol. For example, *1945* is four syllables, *IRA* is three syllables, and & is one syllable.

TRANSFER AND APPLICATION

Student difficulty in content material may be due to the absence of interesting and varied practice to ensure mastery and application of a particular skill. If a specific skill is directly taught by the teacher, transfer of the skill to content materials will not be automatic on the part of students. For example, students taught how to interpret a diagram in science require additional practice in a variety of situations to ensure the transfer of this skill to their reading of science material. Following are examples of ways to effect transfer of the skill of interpreting a diagram.

- Bring in supplemental science materials containing diagrams of topics already studied. Ask pupils appropriate questions about each diagram and/or allow individual children to assume the role of the teacher and explain the diagram to the rest of the class.
- Have pupils make their own diagram on a topic of their choice. Make certain each diagram is labeled properly and ask that a series of questions be constructed concerning their diagrams.

There are numerous ways of providing meaningful practice to compel students to actually transfer a particular skill to their content reading. The essential point is that teachers are aware of this need and provide the necessary time and opportunity to ensure that this transfer happens.

Teaching Techniques

Invariably classrooms use one content textbook for each grade. This practice presents many potential problems in achieving the "correct match" due to differing student abilities. Frequently, many students will be unable to read successfully in a particular text. Understanding the concept of readability and knowing how to measure the difficulty level of a text are extremely important. Next, it is essential to know various ways to differentiate instruction for youngsters unable to read a required text. Alternative instructional approaches aimed at moving away from total reliance on a single text include providing different assignments, using multilevel content materials, providing meaningful oral reading, utilizing educational media resources, using small-group instruction, using library books of various difficulty levels about a particular topic, and incorporating the arts in instruction (2,12).

The following strategies can help youngsters be successful when using a single content text.

- *Directed Reading Activity (DRA).* This teaching strategy should be applied to all content reading, not just basal materials. The use of the elements of readiness (motivation, vocabulary, background, purpose setting), silent reading and review (comprehension check, meaningful oral reading, direct instruction lesson on a study skill, and transfer activities) will help students successfully read and learn specific content. An example of a Directed Reading Activity for science is shown on pages 4–7 of the first color insert.
- *Advanced Organizer.* This teaching technique involves providing students with a short written summary of a content chapter before the actual silent reading. This summary can highlight new vocabulary and concepts, background information, and main ideas. The use of advanced organizers fulfills the crucial functions of helping students establish a correct mind-set before reading and of aiding students in establishing purposes for reading.
- *Structured Overview.* This technique is similiar in function to an advanced organizer. A structured overview presents a chapter's key ideas and their relationships in a visual format (usually in the shape of a flowchart, hierarchy, spoke, or pie). The chapter's key vocabulary words are usually included and discussed with youngsters before and after silent reading.
- *Study Guides.* This technique provides students with a set of questions covering each section or page in a chapter to answer while reading. Study guides provide students with purposes for reading. The questions asked should be balanced among literal, interpretative, and critical comprehension levels and in terms of being vocabulary related.

Additional information on these and other techniques for content reading are available from the following sources: Cheek and Cheek (3), Forgan and Mangrum (6), Poostay (14), Readence, Bean, and Baldwin (15), Vacca (23), and Wood and Mateja (24).

INDEPENDENT LEARNING

Formal education has many goals, one of which is help the child become increasingly independent within the framework of the school setting. To achieve such independence the learner must master a number of related language tools or skills. One important cluster of skills has been designated reading-study skills or work-type reading skills. In our reading-dominated schools, these skills are of primary importance. In actual practice, they are often not given enough emphasis. Although current educational trends emphasize the basic skills and the passing of "tests" to show that a person is literate, greater emphasis should be placed upon those skills and abilities that will enable learners to acquire information on their own. In a very real sense, the quality of an educational program can be judged by the students' ability to learn on their own. A review of the literature on reading reveals general agreement about the major areas of reading-study skills. These areas include:

- Studying content material.
- Locating information.
- Evaluating material.
- Organizing and summarizing data.
- Knowing how to adjust your reading rate depending upon your purpose in reading.

Any one of these major topics would probably include numerous specific skills. For instance, *locating information* would cover:

- *Effective Use of Books*
    - Table of Contents
    - Index
        - knowledge of alphabetical order
        - use of key words
        - cross listing
        - following subtopics
        - significance of abbreviations and signals commonly used, for example, see also . . . or commas and hyphens in page listings
- *Use of Special References*
    - Encyclopedia
    - Atlas
    - Dictionary
        - extended knowledge of alphabetical order
        - selection of proper connotation of word
        - recognition of inflected and derived forms of words
        - use of diacritical marks
- *Use of Library Aids*
    - Card catalogs
    - *Reader's Guide*
    - Bound periodicals

Most skill areas are developmental in nature. Each skill area includes several specific abilities, and any given skill is taught in different ways throughout the grades. Each skill can be thought of as being on a continuum that represents both increasing difficulty of learning tasks and increasing potential usefulness to the learner. For instance, skill in using a table of contents is first taught in the first grade. With this initial experience, no child will have mastered this skill to a degree required for effective use of the table of contents in a sixth-grade geography book.

STUDYING CONTENT MATERIAL

One of the keys to successful reading is to use appropriate strategies to fulfill one's purpose. The ability to consciously monitor one's own cognitive functioning is referred to as *metacognition* (1). Applying metacognition to reading occurs when a student not only uses appropriate reading strategies but also is aware of and actually controls these strategies to fulfill a purpose.

The ability to successfully read a content chapter is dependent upon the application of many skills and strategies. The best known, systemized procedure for reading content chapters is SQ3R (16). Developed by Robinson, SQ3R stands for survey, question, read, recite, and review. Students need direct instruction and a great deal of practice on each step of the procedure. *Survey* encourages students to get an overall picture of the chapter before reading it by looking at the title, introduction, main headings, illustrations, and end-of-chapter questions. *Question* helps students read with a purpose by turning each bold heading into a question. *Read* asks students to read each chapter section to answer the purpose-setting question(s), keeping in mind the chapter organization and visual aids. *Recite* involves stopping periodically to answer the purpose-setting questions in one's own words. Students are encouraged to take written notes during silent reading. *Review* instructs students to check their memory by reviewing notes and reciting major points under each heading.

The steps we have asked you to follow so far in the text represent a modification of this procedure. We recommend the following procedure be directly taught and practiced with students to foster independent learning:

- Read the introduction.
- Survey all visual aids in the chapter and read each bold heading.
- Read the summary.
- Study the questions at the end of the chapter.
- Return to the beginning of the chapter and read.

Tadlock (20) concurs that not only should a study method such as SQ3R be taught to students, but also that students should be told why and how it will aid in their retention of content material. She states that each step in SQ3R "is designed to facilitate the processing of incoming information (print) so the reader can deal with more of it and deal with it more effectively" (p. 111).

LOCATING INFORMATION

Children who are becoming independent readers attempt to find answers through wide and varied reading. To do this they must be able to understand and use all the hints and helps available. In other words, knowing how to use the book is a prerequisite for intelligent use of supplementary reading in the subject areas and in any unit work. In the intermediate grades, the increased need for study skills stems from the nature of the materials used, the need for wide reading, and the fact that supervision is not always readily available. Although reading ability is a prerequisite for the development of study skills, this ability, in itself, does not assure that a pupil has mastered the study skills.

During the past few years, there has been a tremendous expansion in the availability of books, professional journals, and other printed matter. This advance in knowledge in the past three decades, even when compared with previous centuries, has been so dramatic that it has been labeled the era of *knowledge explosion.* Competency in any given field has taken on a new meaning, and educational methods, of necessity, will have to change radically to adapt to this new challenge.

The contents of any subject area cannot be contained within a single textbook or even a series of texts. The time lag between research, publication, and the adoption of textbooks causes even the most recent texts to be somewhat inadequate. Good teachers have always attempted to provide supplementary reading materials, but achieving this goal has not been easy. Today, providing a wide array of supplementary materials is not only desirable, it is an absolute necessity. Thus, study skills have rather abruptly increased in value to the learner while the school's respect for these skills and its ability to teach them effectively has lagged. The following discussion deals with aspects of instruction that relate to locating information.

Effective Use of Books

In teaching any of the study skills, the teacher at each grade level starts from, and builds on, what the student presently knows. To do this, the present ability level of each student must be determined. A good place to begin is with the textbook adopted for a given course. Teachers have learned from experience that many students are not particularly adept at "mining" a book, but meaningful learning situations can lead to the development of this facility (4).

It is easy to develop exercises that foster such growth. The major concern is how exercise materials and specific teachings are used in relation to the goals to be achieved. Some very important learnings deal with the mechanics of learning—*how* to use a card catalog, *where* to look in an encyclopedia, *when* an appendix or glossary might be useful, *what* is likely to be found in an appendix or glossary, and the like.

Written exercises are often provided to help pupils understand the function of an index, table of contents, or appendix. It is common to find pupils who can work out correct solutions to workbook problems consisting of sample lines from an index but who still do not know how to get help from a real index. One of the best ways to teach children how to use a book effectively is to design a learning situation around a textbook they will be using throughout the year. A social science, health, or other text would provide ample opportunities for teaching the functions of the table of contents, charts, indexes, and appendixes. The use of the text the child is using will give him something concrete to return to when he is in doubt. Skills learned in using one text should then more readily transfer to books in other areas, provided there is teacher direction and guidance.

Student deficiencies in using a table of contents, index, glossary, and appendix are frequently not detected by teachers, and often provisions may not be made for teaching these skills. Too often it is assumed these basic skills have been taught or are being taught elsewhere. For example, as an outcome of an inservice program, one group of teachers agreed to build a one-page testing-teaching exercise consisting of fifteen to twenty questions that would measure students' skill in using parts of a book. The exercise was to be specifically applicable to the textbook students were using in one of their courses. Although the books had been in use for nearly three months, few students were able to complete the exercise without error. Teachers discovered glaring deficiencies and tremendous individual differences in students' ability to use these reader aids. In one class, the time students took to do the "book-mining" exercise was noted. The range was from six to twenty-two minutes with some students unable to complete the task.

The exercise presented in figure 7.3 might be used initially with an entire class, for it can serve as a diagnostic instrument. The observant teacher will note which students have difficulty and what their problems are. Teaching small groups and individual students the skills they need should be an outgrowth of the teacher's findings. General con-

How to Use a Book

1. The region in which we live is discussed under the heading ____________________
2. The last sixteen pages in the book are called an *atlas.* Looking at these pages can you define "atlas"? ____________________
3. On what page can you find a listing of all maps, graphs, and diagrams found in the book? ____________________
4. Does the book contain a picture of Wonder Lake? ____________________ How did you go about answering this question? ____________________
5. Is there a picture of the Grand Coulee Dam in the text? ____________________
6. Under what heading must you look to find it? ____________________
7. In the index there is a main heading *Exploration.* What six subheadings are found under it? ____________________
8. The book contains a double page map called Main Air Routes in the U.S. There is no heading "Main Air Routes" in the index. How can you find this map? ____________________
9. There are two sections of the book which provide the pronunciation of difficult words, these are ____________________ and ____________________.
10. The pronunciation of the following words is provided in the ____________________. In the blank spaces show the pronunciation and page number where found:
    SHOSHONE ____________________ Page ______
    COMANCHE ____________________ Page ______
    FORT DUQUESNE ____________________ Page ______
11. A particular page contains the *definition* of difficult words used throughout the book. That page is called the ____________________ and is page number ___.

FIGURE 7.3 Example of a Study Skill Assignment and Diagnostic Test.

cepts will also be taught in the process. This particular experience was constructed for use with a sixth-grade social studies text.

The exercise teaches a number of facts about the book. Question 1 takes the readers to the table of contents and requires that they be able to associate their home state with part of a larger geographical region of the United States. Question 2 calls attention to a sixteen-page atlas; the next question focuses on a second highly specialized table of contents dealing exclusively with maps.

Questions 4 through 8 deal with ways in which the index may be helpful. The reader must locate pictures through the use of key words and be prepared to look under different headings. (Grand Coulee Dam is found under Grand Coulee Project.) Topics may be listed as subheads under a more general heading. Thus, Dutch, English, Spanish, and other explorations are all listed under Exploration. Questions 9 to 11 deal with information about pronunciation and meanings of more difficult words and call attention to the fact that these aids are divided between the index and glossary.

Profiting from Reader Aids. Students sometimes fail to realize that a number of reader aids are included in most reference books and textbooks. Unfamiliarity with or disinclination to use these aids will inhibit students from "mining" books with maximum efficiency. Although the student has a need for this skill, she does not always recognize this need since she is not aware of the value of these aids or how they might improve her learning.

For one purpose, the table of contents might be skimmed; with other goals in mind, it must be read critically. A comparison of different books would disclose that a table of contents may consist exclusively of chapter titles. This is similar to an outline composed of nothing but major topics. In some books, chapter titles are followed by a number of topics in the order in which they are discussed. Students may note that this, in essence, is a modified index containing only major headings in *chronological* order. In contrast, the index is in *alphabetical* order, dealing with smaller topics and cutting across chapters.

Every student should learn that (1) the parts of the book are deliberately designed as aids; (2) these are valuable and are used profitably by the efficient reader; (3) each of the different parts of a book has a definite purpose. The efficient reader must make instant decisions as to where to go for specific types of help; she learns what type of information is contained in each section, where the various aids are located, and how each may be used effectively. Once learned, this knowledge can be transferred and applied to any book. The following is an abbreviated treatment of what a reader might expect to gain from the aids found in most books:

"Aids" for the Reader	*Information the Reader Might Expect to Find*
Title Page	Main title and subtitle. (The latter may set forth the limitations and narrow the topic.) Name of author, where published.
Table of Contents	Chapter titles followed by major topics discussed in each chapter. Is book divided into major parts (I, II, III)? What are these? Length of chapters give hint as to thoroughness of treatment.
Preface	To whom or to what group does the author address the book? What is his stated purpose? What new features does he stress? What unique features does the author believe are found in his book?
Illustrations	Title, item, and page where found.
Index	Major topics in alphabetical order; minor topics under each heading; key phrases, cross-references, photographs, drawings, charts, tables.
Glossary	Difficult or specialized terms presented in alphabetical order with a definition.
Appendix	Organized body of facts related to subject under consideration. For example, in a geography book the appendix may give the areas of states or nations, populations, state and national capitals, extent of manufacturing, exports, imports, mineral deposits, and so forth.

Use of the Library

Effective use of library resources may well be one of the most underrated and undertaught skills in the entire school program. The library is where children read and receive guidance in both the use of books and in research techniques. Children at all grade levels need the experience of frequent contacts with a good school library.

Some teachers use the library effectively themselves but do not assume responsibility for teaching students to do so. On the other hand, there are a number of teachers who would score low on any evaluation

149

Name

Use the information listed in the newspaper index to fill in the blanks in the story below.

What's Inside

	Page		Page
Arts	16	Restaurant Guide	39
Food	38	Sports	29
Letters	40	Theater	26
News Summary	47	Weather	45

How I Subscribed to the Newspaper

I subscribed to the newspaper because of a convincing sales talk. Jeffrey delivers papers on my street and said, "You should get the newspaper. In today's paper, there is everything you need to know. Want to go out to dinner tonight? Look at the Restaurant Guide on page **39**. Want to stay home and prepare a fancy new dish instead? Page 38 tells about **food**."

"Wait a minute," I protested. "There's more to life than eating."

"OK. Is culture what you have in mind? In the **Arts** section, read about the paintings displayed at the museum. In the **Theater** section, find out about the movies and plays to see!"

"I'm a bit too busy to do all that," I mumbled.

"Well, what you need is the News Summary. Read just the most important news in short form, the highlights. That's on page **47**. And all the ball game scores are reported on page **29**."

"OK, Jeffrey. I'm sold."

Additional Activity: Write a paragraph that might appear on one of the Sports pages.

LIFE SKILLS: resources (newspaper)

Level 13 "Life Skill: Newspaper Parts"

The ability to use an index enables students to locate information quickly.

of their personal use of library facilities. To illustrate, one school librarian and principal were convinced that a substantial number of the teaching staff were somewhat derelict in their personal use of the library. Further, student use of the library for these teachers' courses seemed to be less than optimum. A one-hour library unit was incorporated into the total inservice program. Each teacher was relieved of her regularly scheduled duties for a one-hour period, and this time was spent in conference with the librarian. The librarian assumed responsibility for discussing and pointing out resources that related directly to the various subjects taught by each teacher. Pamphlets, bound volumes, pertinent books, government documents, current magazines, and the like were located, and suggestions were made as to how the librarian might help the faculty member and the students in her classes.

Records disclosed that the attitudes of a number of the teaching staff changed markedly after this experience. Some teachers visited the library more frequently, spent more time in the library, and checked out more materials. In addition, the students in these teachers' courses began to use the library much more effectively.

It is generally conceded that it is difficult to teach library usage in a classroom setting removed from the library materials themselves. However, important learning related to the library can be taught prior to a library visit.

Several teachers in one school built a model card catalog drawer using a three-by-five-inch index card box and compiled approximately one hundred author cards ranging from *A* through *Z*. This model was used in the various classrooms and was particularly useful in working with individual students who were not yet competent in the use of the card catalog.

Another useful teaching device consisted of a library checklist devised by teachers and the librarian. The list consisted of eight or ten specific tasks which the student was to perform with teacher direction. Examples included:

1. Find the book *King of the Wind* by Marguerite Henry.
2. a. Who is the author of the book *A Child's History of Art?*
   ____
   b. What is the call number of this book? ______________
   c. Fill out a library card for this book. ______________
3. Where are the bound volumes of *My Weekly Reader* located?
   ____

These items provide guided practice in using title and author cards, locating books and journals on the shelves, and the proper filling out of library cards. Other tasks cover specific learnings related to the library.

To use this checklist technique effectively, small groups or individual students go to the library at specific times. The librarian may briefly illustrate and explain how to use certain facilities in the library. Then each child may be handed a checklist of tasks. All tasks are reviewed briefly to assure that the students understand them. Such tasks should vary according to grade level and individual student needs.

Reference Materials

Using reference materials is an important study skill which, as a general rule, is not thoroughly taught in our schools. Many students reach high school or even college with only a hazy idea of how to make a systematic search of available materials. Although many children in the upper primary level are ready for limited use of reference materials, it is in the intermediate grades that teachers have a major responsibility to teach these skills.

Using the Encyclopedia. The use of encyclopedias and other reference books should be deliberately and systematically taught. If such materials are in the classroom, different groups of children can be taught their use at various times. Instruction should parallel points already covered above, for example, topics are arranged in alphabetical order, books are numbered in series, the alphabetical range covered is indicated on the cover, and cross-listings and key words will have to be used.

Teaching any given unit in any content area can provide the framework for teaching efficient use of the encyclopedia to those students who need this instruction. Assume a health class is developing the topic *The Adventure of Medicine.* Students might be directed to list all of the possible headings under which they might find information relating to the topic. The responses might range from one suggestion to "look under medicine" to a half page of suggestions, including medicine, surgery, disease, medical research, drugs, germ theory, space medicine, and public health. Other headings might include particular diseases such as cancer, tuberculosis, yellow fever, diabetes, or poliomyelitis or the names of individuals who made significant medical discoveries such as Walter Reed, Jonas Salk, or Louis Pasteur.

An encyclopedia is a book or series of books that tells a little bit about a great number of topics. One skill needed is to know what *heading* or topic to look under for particular information. Usually an encyclopedia contains hundreds of headings that tell the reader to "*see* . . . ," which is another heading under which the topic is discussed. For instance:

Baking soda; *See* Soda
Old Faithful; *See* Wyoming, Yellowstone National Park

Lennon, John; *See* Beatles
Knee jerk; *See* Reflex action
Toadstool; *See* Mushroom

PRACTICE ACTIVITY

Using the following drawing, write the number of the volume or volumes that will likely contain the information called for.

In which volume will you find these data:

1. Is more money spent on newspaper or television advertising?
   ____
2. Hitches, knots, and splices ______________
3. Timber wolves ______________
4. Is there a bird called a kite? ______________
5. What is a spelling demon? ______________
6. Data on animals that sleep through the winter ______________
7. The previous names of the city of Leningrad ______________
8. The state bird of Illinois ______________
9. Where does the sparrow hawk live? ______________
10. The habitat of the Eastern gray squirrel ______________

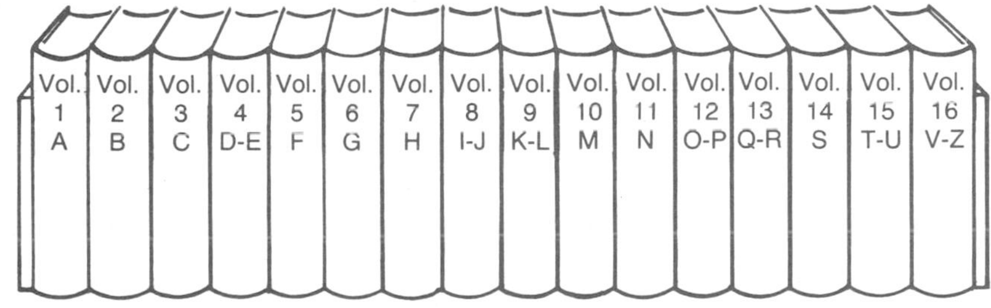

Using the Dictionary. The use of the dictionary is another important study skill associated with reading instruction at the intermediate level. The three major goals in dictionary instruction are learning to find a particular word, determine its pronunciation, and select the correct meaning of the word in the context in which it is used. Teaching dictionary skills is often neglected by teachers even when they acknowledge the value of these skills. This neglect might stem from a teacher's feeling of inadequacy about certain relatively difficult facets of dictionary use such as mastering diacritical markings or pronunciation keys. On the other hand, teaching may fall short of maximum efficiency when dictionary skills are taught as something extra rather than as an intrinsic part of the regular reading instruction. The use of the dictionary should always be seen by both teacher and pupil as a source of getting meaning, not as a form of rote drill or a penalty for making certain errors (10).

Certain prerequisite concepts are essential for successful use of the dictionary. A few of these skills or understandings include:

- The knowledge of alphabetical order.
- The understanding that a word can have many different meanings.
- The knowledge of root words and the various inflected and derived forms of root words.
- The understanding that letters and combinations of letters have different sound values in different situations and that some letters are silent.
- The knowledge that *y* on the end of most, if not all, words is changed to *i* before adding *es* for plurals.

Facility in the use of the dictionary paves the way for greater independence in reading because it:

- Unlocks the sound or pronunciation of words.
- Discloses new meanings of words that may be known in only one or a limited number of connotations.
- Confirms the spelling of a word when the reader can only approximate its correct spelling.
- Expands vocabulary through mastery of inflected and derived forms of known root words.

These skills must be refined and extended as the child moves upward through the grades. The alphabetizing ability that is adequate for successful fourth-grade work will be inadequate for junior high or high school. The success the child feels and the utility she sees in dictionary usage can be most important factors in how she reacts to the dictionary as a tool for helping her in all facets of communication. She must be shown that dictionary skills are needed throughout life; failure to master these skills can negatively influence her attitudes and learning development for many years to come.

A number of developmental tasks are associated with dictionary usage. There is general agreement among educators on what these tasks are and the order in which they should be presented.

- Recognize and differentiate between letters.
- Associate letter names with letter symbols.
- Learn the letters of the alphabet in order.

FLASHBACK

Noah Webster has been often called America's first prolific textbook writer. He is best known for *Webster's Dictionary;* however, he also wrote many books to be used in teaching children. In 1787 he published *The American Spelling Book,* which consisted of lessons in reading, spelling, elements of grammar, and morals. In 1829 a revised edition was published that focused mainly on spelling and was titled *The Elementary Spelling Book; Being An Improvement on the American Spelling Book.* This revised edition was published until the late 1800s.

By permission. From *Noah's Ark, New England Yankees and The Endless Quest,* © 1947 by Merriam-Webster Inc., publisher of the Merriam-Webster® Dictionaries.

- Arrange a number of words by alphabetical order of their initial letter.
- Extend above skill to second and third letters of words, eventually working through all letters of a word if necessary.
- Develop facility in rapid, effective use of dictionary, that is, where do *h, p, v* come in the dictionary; open dictionary as near as possible to word being studied.
- Develop the ability to use accent marks in arriving at the pronunciation of words.
- Learn to interpret phonetic spelling used in dictionary.
- Use pronunciation key given somewhere on each double page of most dictionaries.
- Work out different pronunciations and meanings of words which are spelled alike.
- Determine which is the preferred pronunciation when several are given.
- Select the meaning that fits the context.
- Profit from guide words found at the top of each page to tell at a glance if the page contains the word being sought.

- Use special sections of a dictionary intelligently; e.g., geographical terms and names, biographical data, foreign words and phrases.

Although particular skills are characteristically taught at a given grade level, what the individual child has learned or not learned should determine what it taught. Fortunately, dictionaries are available at all difficulty levels, from simple picture dictionaries to massive unabridged editions. The needs of the child and the goals of the teacher should determine how these different dictionaries will be utilized in the classroom. A child who is expected to use a dictionary that calls for skills far beyond what he has mastered will profit little from the experience. Any classroom practice that puts the child in such a position has little if any educational justification.

The ability to read maps is an important skill in our highly mobile society, and students should be provided opportunities to develop this skill in various content subject areas. Formats for teaching map reading can vary from involving the entire class, to individual pupils, pairs, or teams of pupils pursuing given learning tasks.

INTRODUCTORY ACTIVITY

Use a series of letters to represent the location of major cities. Students write the names of those cities to be identified.

Draw a line connecting two cities (San Francisco—St. Louis) and estimate the number of miles or kilometers from one to the other.

Use numbers to represent various states. Students identify and write the names of selected states.

Color or crosshatch one state. Students write the names of all adjoining states.

Identify lakes, rivers, mountain ranges, national parks, time zones, etc.

Color or crosshatch a state or region that is a major producer of oil, wheat, coal, iron ore, etc.

The following exercises are based on the use of a simple outline map of the continental United States shown on page 249.

Write the name for city A. It is a state capital and the burial place of Abraham Lincoln. ______________

The number 4 is found in the state of ______________.

The letter B locates a city identified with the "Birth of the Blues" and is the home of good Dixieland Jazz. ______________

Number 2 indicates a state formed at the outbreak of the Civil War; it is __________.

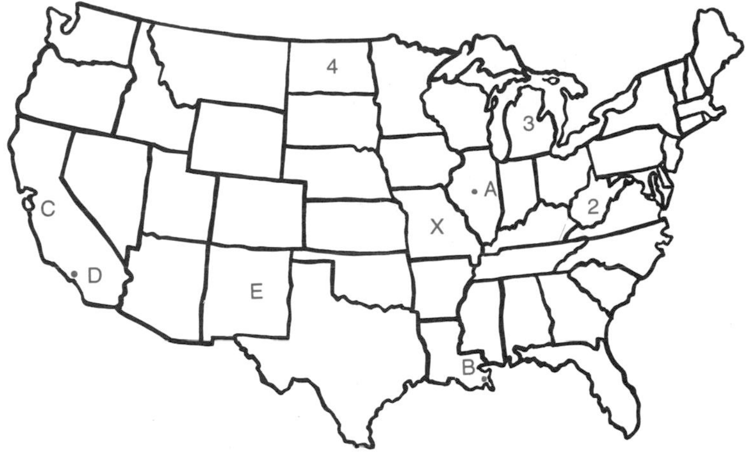

Can you locate the various states and major cities on a map of the U.S?

The state of Missouri is represented by an X. Starting at the north and moving clockwise, name the states which border on the state of Missouri.

__________ __________

__________ __________ __________

__________ __________ __________

Does Idaho border on Canada? (Answer yes or no.) __________
Write the name of the southwestern state marked with an E. __________
The inland state marked 3 has more water boundary than land boundary. It is the state of __________.
The state directly west of the state marked 4 is the state of __________.
Two cities in California are marked C and D. C represents __________; D represents __________.

APPLICATION ACTIVITY

The same type of activity can be used in map study of foreign countries and regions such as Central and South America, Europe, Africa, and Asia. An example is shown on page 3 of the first color insert. Through the use of actual road maps, a number of map-reading activities can be developed. A few activities are listed below:

Plan a trip from Lisbon, Portugal to Paris, France. Select the "fastest route" or the most scenic route.
List in order the routes on which you will travel.
Estimate the approximate distance to be traveled on each route.
Plan side trips to historical sites or parks.

Map Reading

Maps often contain guides for finding places or cities (8). Example A tells us how to locate the city of Detroit. Example B locates Austin, Texas.

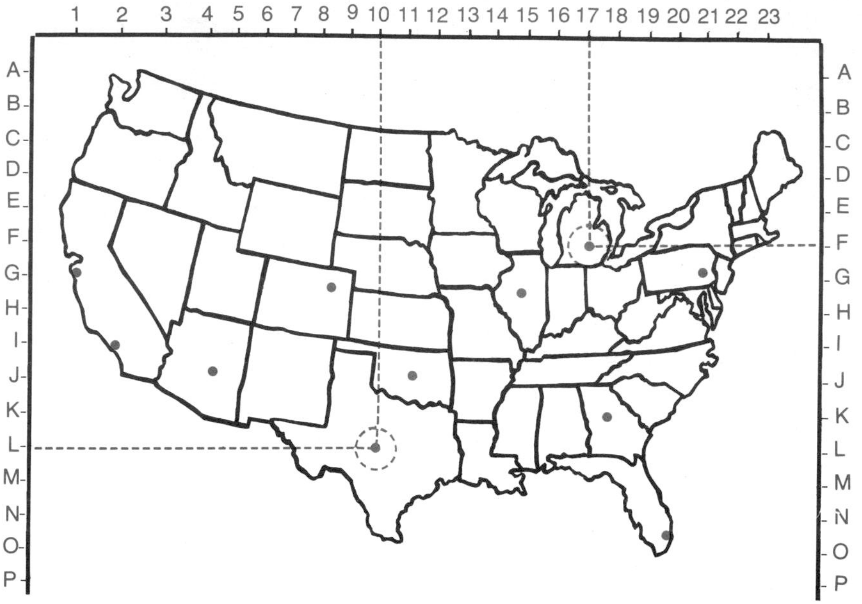

- *Example A:* Detroit, Michigan, is found by drawing a line down from 17 and a line over from F. The place where the two lines meet is the location of Detroit.
- *Example B:* Lines drawn down from 10 and over from L locate the capital city of Texas which is ____________.

PRACTICE ACTIVITY

The problems below provide clues that will guide you to the location of certain cities. You are to name these cities. Complete all the problems you can without using a map. Then use a map of the United States if needed. You need not draw lines on the map; use imaginary ones.

H–15 Capital of midwestern state; Lincoln buried there. ____________

I–1 Not a state capital, but the largest city in southern California. ____________

J–11 Capital of southwestern state (Will Rogers country). ____________

D–23 Capital of state located in northeast corner of U.S. ____________

K–17 Capital and largest industrial city of this southeastern state. ____________

C–7 Straight lines drawn from these points would intersect in the state of ______

G–21 Large city in eastern Pennsylvania (not capital). ______________
J–4 Capital of southwestern state. ______________
N–20 Altantic coastal city. ______________
G–8 The "mile-high city" and state capital. ______________

INTERPRETING AND EVALUATING MATERIAL

Locating information is an important part of the learning process, but this step is only a beginning to the goal of assimilating material. The ability to locate information will have little impact on personal or academic growth if the student is unable to read the material he has located.

Teaching students how to read critically is undoubtedly the most difficult task attempted in our schools. In fact, if the matter is pressed beyond the usual textbook definitions, asking a group of teachers to *define* critical reading is more likely to result in chaos than in unanimity. Practically all of their definitions will be abstractions, simply because critical reading involves so many variables.

Interpreting and evaluating material is probably as close a synonym for *critical reading* as can be found. Illustrations of the analytical abilities involved include:

- Knowing what the author has said.
- Grasping the validity of statements and knowing when and how to check validity with other sources.
- Differentiating between facts and opinions.
- Noting when inferences are being drawn and drawing them when they are not stated.
- Detecting author bias as well as inaccuracies that might not be traceable to bias.
- Understanding your own biases as these relate to what is being read.
- Taking into consideration an author's use of allusions, satire, humor, irony, and the like.
- Developing some criteria for judging an author's competency in the area in which he writes.

Undoubtedly this list could be extended. Each of the above abilities is developmental in nature and should be taught at all grade levels. The reading tasks found in the intermediate grades are characterized by an increasing difficulty that requires a high degree of competency if the reader is to grow increasingly perceptive. This point holds even as we move into the high school and beyond. How many adults are immune to propaganda, know both sides of controversial issues, and do not let their emotions color interpretations while reading?

The test of critical reading often applied in our schools is the students' ability to restate or write what an author has said. The inability to discern what the author is saying may well be evidence of inability to read the material critically, but paraphrasing, by itself, is not evidence of critical reading either. Restating the gist of a passage but failing to detect author bias will result in a transfer of author bias to the reader's own thought. Knowing what the author is saying without seeing that some statements are contrary to fact will inhibit critical reading, as will reciting strongly expressed opinions as if these were statements of verifiable facts.

Interpreting and evaluating calls for the application of a number of the mechanical reading skills and higher level abilities listed earlier. Students need both teacher-directed instruction and systematic practice in developing work habits and study techniques (19), a number of which are dealt with in the following discussion.

Knowledge of Propaganda

Resisting propaganda depends to a large degree on the reader's background or in her being wise to the techniques people use when they use language that does not fit the facts. The critical reader assumes responsibility for questioning what she reads. Although she respects language, she knows that some people use it to control others' behavior. The purpose here is not to explain all of various propaganda techniques that are used to obscure meaning or take the reader on a detour, but to provide examples that might help students detect these devices.

INTRODUCTORY ACTIVITY

Concept of Propaganda. List a number of popular propaganda techniques. Discuss and illustrate these with the class and then guide students to write examples. These examples should then be discussed and elaborated upon in relation to the earlier discussion.

Beg the issue or throw up a smoke screen. Here one does not discuss the real issue, but switches the discussion to other topics. For example: Candidate *A* has charged that *B* has violated the law by not filing a statement of his campaign expenses. *B* replies, "*A* has accused me of not filing a statement of expenses. Why should he care? Is he a police officer? Have I ever lied to the voters? Who voted against raising taxes last year? I'll tell you who did—I did! And I'll tell you something else—*A* voted for the tax bill. I support every worthwhile charity in this community; I was born here; I went to school here! Can *A* make this statement?"

Generalize from too few cases.

Ignore the *idea* and attack the person suggesting it.

Use a false analogy.

Appeal to authority.

Rely on guilt by association.

Use a faulty cause-and-effect relationship.

Misuse figures or statistics.

APPLICATION ACTIVITY

Step 1. Prepare a number of propositions that might be an issue in any community.

Step 2. Follow each proposition with an imaginary statement that someone included in a "Letter to the Editor." Students analyze and point out "what the writer was up to."

Proposition: "Should the city council pass an ordinance that would require fluoridation of the city water supply in an effort to decrease tooth decay among children of the community?"
Letter to the Editor: "Of course some people favor fluoridation; they spend so much time in the Roaring Twenties Bar that they probably don't drink enough water to care how it tastes."
Letter No. 2: "The real issue is that fluoride is a poison. We shouldn't poison our fine water supply." (Beware of jumping to a conclusion: Fluoride *is* a poison. What is the missing detail?)

Proposition: "Should the voters approve a proposed school bond issue?"
Letter to the Editor: "As Lincoln said, You can fool all of the people some of the time, and this is one of those times! Our schools are as good as any in the country. The people pushing this school bond proposal want to raise your taxes. I say vote this bond issue down."

Proposition: "Should we adopt a city ordinance, proposed as a safety measure, which would prohibit the sale of fireworks?"
Letter to the Editor: "The Fourth of July is one of our great holidays. This proposal is unpatriotic. It is a direct slap at free enterprise. There are a lot of American firms which make fireworks. The next thing you know somebody will try to outlaw automobiles because people get hurt in accidents."

Proposition: "Should the city construct a swimming pool in the city park?"
Letter to the Editor: "The people in this town do not want a municipal pool. It is obvious that if the people favored this harebrained idea we would have had a pool by now!"

Proposition: "Should we extend the runways at our municipal airport so that jet planes can land here?"
Letter to the Editor: "When we built the airport the planners said the present layout would be adequate for at least twenty years. That was just ten years ago. These people are experts, and we should listen to them."

Clues to Read the News

Teachers use newspapers and other mass media for both the teaching of critical analysis and the mechanical skills related to such analysis. The potential values in the use of such materials are numerous. There are also barriers to significant learning, two of which are inadequate planning and the tendency to avoid discussion of controversial issues. Children should be permitted and encouraged to interpret and analyze advertisements, political cartoons, editorials, and syndicated columns.

"Clues to the news" can be developed by teacher-directed instruction, focusing on and discussing details such as the following.

INTRODUCTORY ACTIVITY

Editorials. Compare editorials found in four or five metropolitan papers which deal with a particular current issue. Assume there are apparent differences of opinion; what might account for these differences? Political orientation of editor or publisher? Does a particular newspaper have a standing policy on certain issues (labor-management, foreign aid)?

The Political Cartoon. Gather cartoons (from different papers and drawn by different artists) that deal with the same topic. Direct students to analyze and put into words what the cartoon is attempting to say. Student interpretation of any given stimulus will vary considerably. This will facilitate discussion and help students to see the importance of "the reader's background," which includes bias, emotional attachments, and the like. Such factors always function in any interpretation of a cartoon, editorial, feature article, or news story.

Propaganda Techniques. The teacher might prepare and duplicate an editorial that by design contains biased statements, factual errors, and various propaganda techniques. Each student has a copy of the material and with teacher direction edits or rewrites the editorial. Next, have class discussion of the original material and substitutions, deletions, and corrections made by members of the group. Differences between student reactions will in many cases be marked, particularly if the topic is chosen wisely. In the discussion, students will be exposed to a variety of viewpoints different from their own.

Study a Current Issue Longitudinally.

a. Compare different newspaper and news magazine treatments of this problem.
b. Attempt to account for differences in editorial points of view.
c. Study several columnists' or news analysts' interpretations.
d. Analyze the day-to-day statements of the decision makers or those spokespersons attempting to mold public opinion. Based on the issue being studied, these might be legislative leaders, State Department officials, labor leaders, candidates for high office, the President, White House staff, etc.

Determining "Fact or Opinion"

In reading materials in the various content areas, children are frequently faced with the task of deciding whether a statement is fact or opinion. Young readers (and older ones also) develop habits that are not always helpful in this type of problem solving. One such habit is the tendency to accept "what is written" as being factual. Second, when one strongly agrees with a statement, it is frequently accepted as a fact. Third, if a position is developed logically or if something is repeated often enough, it may be accepted as factual. Thus, the statement "finding a four-leaf clover *always* brings good luck" may be doubted; the statement "finding a four-leaf clover *can* bring good luck" may seem a bit more logical.

Probably the best way to help children develop skill in differentiating fact from opinion would be planned discussion of statements as they are met in textual material. This is difficult to do when a teacher is limited to a particular textbook or certain materials. Another possibility is to collect statements of fact and opinion from various sources and plan for illustration and discussion of these. Obviously all items could pertain to one subject area such as social science, health, geography, or literature. On the other hand, exercises might deal with general statements or cut across various content areas. The following examples illustrate the latter approach.

PRACTICE ACTIVITY

Read each statement carefully. If the sentence states a fact, write "F" on the line in front of the sentence. If the sentence states an opinion, write "O."

____ Democracy is the best form of governement.
____ Wild animals will not attack if you do not run.
____ Pollution is the most serious problem in the world today.
____ Rich people do not pay a fair share of taxes.
____ Football is the roughest of all sports.

____ Different brands of aspirin are essentially the same.
____ Compact cars are not as safe as larger cars.
____ The United States spends too much money on arms and weapons during peacetime.
____ People will never be able to settle on the moon.
____ In the United States, women live longer than men.

Following Written Directions

The ability to follow written directions is a prerequisite for success in many school activities as well as real-life situations. However, in a survey of the literature, Galgoci (7) found that emphasis on teaching related to written directions is seriously lacking in the schools. Over a five-year period, only one journal entry was found in the three major reading journals surveyed.

PRACTICE ACTIVITY

Providing practice in following written directions can begin as early as first grade and continue through college. A few examples at different difficulty levels are provided here.

Read Each Statement and Follow Directions. Write the plural of each of the following words:

dog	____________	woman	____________
goose	____________	box	____________
leaf	____________	church	____________

Teaching Reading Study Skills. Cross out the word that does not belong:

coffee tea milk cup juice

Write a sentence using the following words:

repairs was the need in clock of

Circle every number that can be divided evenly by 3:

13 33 63 15 25 45

Write a homonym (same pronunciation) for each of the following words:

red	____________	cite	____________
flour	____________	wood	____________
vane	____________	paws	____________

APPLICATION ACTIVITY

Following Written Directions. Each of the numbered tasks 1–7 relates to the boxes below. Read each item carefully and follow the directions.

Row I	1 NOT	2	3	4
Row II	5	6	7 KNOT	
Row III	8	9	10	
Row IV	11	12	13	14

1. If either row II or row III contain more odd-numbered boxes than even-numbered boxes, write the word *you* in box 11.
2. If the words in boxes 1 through 7 are synonyms, circle the word in box 1.
3. If the sum of any two numbers in row I is equal to the number found in *any* box in row III, write the word *yes* in box 3.
4. If the numbers in the boxes in any row total exactly 18, write the word *very* in box 13.
5. If there are two rows of boxes which contain more odd numbers than even numbers, write the word *yes* in box 6.
6. If all of the boxes are numbered consecutively, write the word *well* in box 14.
7. If the sum of any two numbers in row II is equal to the number found in box 13, write the word *read* in box 12.

When directions are carried out correctly, the only responses called for are found in row IV.

Row IV you read very well

APPLICATION ACTIVITY

Following Written Directions. This exercise will test your ability to understand and follow written directions. Each of the items 1–10 relates to the circles below and/or to the material in Box One (p. 258). All responses are to be made in Box One.

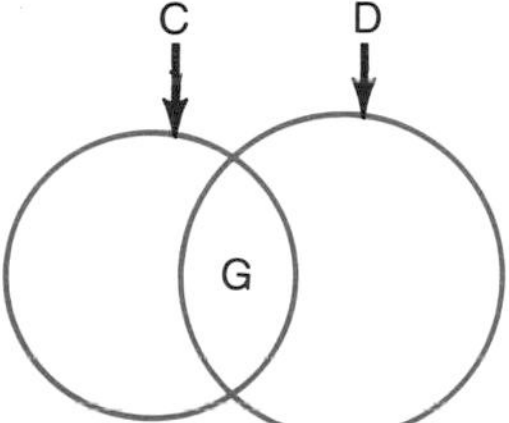

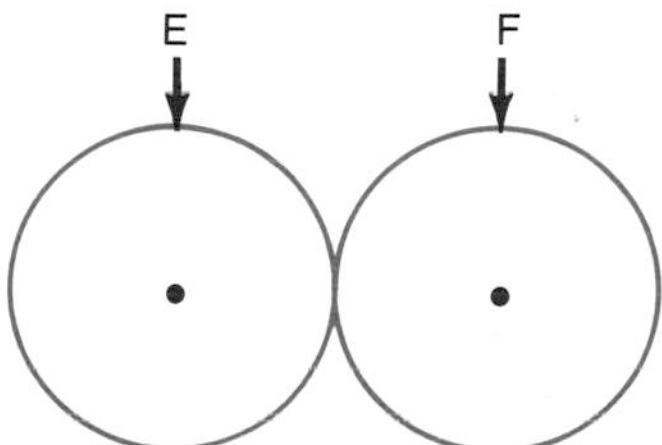

1. If the area G is common to both Circles C and D, circle the 2 in Box One.
2. If the radius of Circle E is equal to the radius of Circle F, underline the number 6.
3. If one straight line could be drawn to bisect both Circles E and F, circle the K in Box One.
4. If a vertical line could be drawn to represent the radius of Circle F, circle the M in Box One.

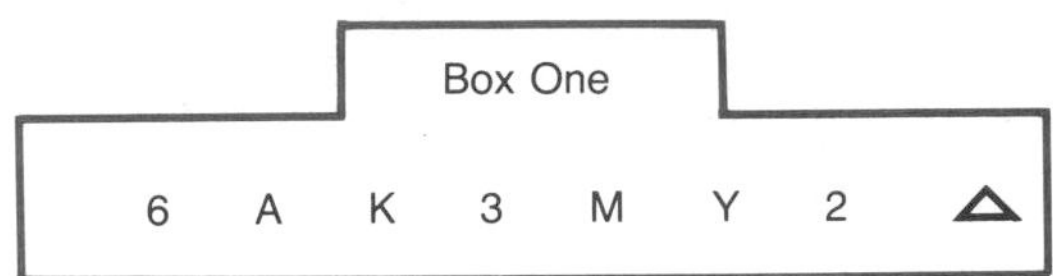

5. If the letters identifying the four circles are not in alphabetical order, circle the first digit in Box One.
6. If both a two-letter and three-letter word may be made using letters in Box One, underline the number 3.
7. If the sum of any two digits in Box One is equal to any other number in Box One, underline the letter A.
8. If the material in Box One begins with a letter and concludes with a triangle, place a dot in the triangle.
9. If circle C could fit in Circle D, draw a line under the letter Y.
10. If every number in Box One is followed by a letter, draw a straight line connecting the letters A and K.

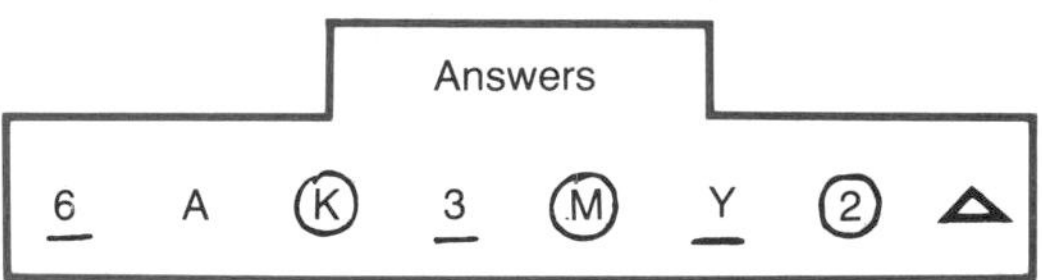

ORGANIZING AND SUMMARIZING DATA

A major task in content areas is to organize information from lectures or from several books on a particular topic, collate the information in a logical fashion, and summarize it for an oral or written presentation. Specific skills under this area include the ability to organize information in an outline format, take notes in an outline form during reading, recognize different organizational methods of writing (cause-effect, enumeration, sequence, comparison-contrast), know the logical sections of a content chapter, and identify topic sentences.

For students to become proficient in organizing and summarizing data they need (1) direct instruction in the specific skills and (2) numerous opportunities to organize and summarize data. These opportunities can be either oral or written. Examples of assignments in this area include reporting on the history of our hometown, U.S. space program, urban problems, life in India, history of our state, television programs that promote violence, how paper is made, acid rain, nuclear power, and how color affects moods.

RATE OF READING

In recent years there has been considerable emphasis on the need for improving rate of reading. The primary concern with rate undoubtedly came first at the college level, where, for the past several decades, considerable attention has been given to this problem. College reading improvement programs grew out of the conviction that many college students have the capacity to meet the demands of the college curriculum but their reading habits make them poor academic risks. Many elementary teachers are also convinced that this is also the case with many of their students.

Over the years the term *rate of reading* has been widely but not always wisely used. It has been a popular practice to speak of the rate of reading of the average high school senior, college freshman, or adult. The impression was often left that the figure quoted, such as 325 or 375 words per minute, had some real significance. The implication was that once an individual's rate of reading a given passage was established, this figure could be cited as though it were a constant for any reading situation. The emphasis on rate led some individuals to confuse the entire reading process with the number of words one could cover in a specified period of time. In an effort to lessen this tendency, it became popular to talk about *rate of comprehension,* a term emphasizing that reading is getting meaning. But this term was also subject to confusion since several factors are always at work in determining rate of comprehension (17). There are a number of variables influencing the rate at which different reading materials can be assimilated:

- The reader's experiential/conceptual background in relation to the general subject matter.
- The vocabulary load or difficulty level of words and concepts.
- The reader's familiarity with the printed language, such as sentence structure and word usages.

- The reader's degree of motivation.
- The reader's purpose for reading the material.
- The physiological state of the reader, whether fatigued, etc.
- The length of the reading period.
- Mechanical factors such as size of print and length of line.
- The readability of the material, as determined by such factors as style of writing, sentence structure, and sentence length.
- The reader's word identification skills.
- The number of figures, illustrations, cross-references, and footnotes the material contains.

Consideration of these factors reveals that no one sample of reading behavior can provide a valid base for establishing a person's rate of comprehension. Any figure arrived at would be valid only for the particular material read under the precise conditions prevailing while it was being read. Regardless of the fact that the term *rate of reading* is vague and may lead to confusion, there is little question that the rate at which pupils read curricular materials is a problem that tends to become more acute as pupils move through the grades.

Varying the Rate of Reading

A fluent reader must develop several different rates for reading different types of printed matter. The child should learn to adjust his reading behavior to the material and to the objectives for reading it. A magazine article may be read with good comprehension at several hundred words per minute while the same reader may have to spend several minutes in reading a forty-word mathematics problem. Or assume that a pupil, having read a particular passage, is attempting to recall the five largest cities in the United States. He has tentatively settled for New York, Chicago, and San Francisco, but the other two names do not come to mind. As he rereads, it would be a slow and possibly wasteful effort to read carefully every word and sentence of the entire section containing the desired information. If the pupil had mastered the technique of scanning material, he could quickly find the one or two sentences that contain the desired data; these could then be read carefully.

Developing Flexibility. The term *flexibility,* as applied to reading, refers to the ability to read different materials at different rates and for different purposes. An analogy might be made between reading and walking. Just as most individuals have settled into a particular characteristic gait in walking, they have also developed a favorite reading pace. However, all individuals can walk faster when purposes demand it. Examples would include the threat of rain, being late for an appointment, or the likelihood of missing a bus. In the absence of such purposes, the individual settles back into her characteristic gait.

It should be obvious to anyone who reads widely that there is little justification for reading all material at the same rate. Such a habit would be wasteful in many situations. The flexible reader has developed the ability to decide where more rapid reading is appropriate, and she has developed the ability to read more rapidly in such situations.

Initial training in learning to read concentrates heavily on word identification. It is obvious that the individual who is not provided the opportunity to apply such skills in meaningful context will not progress satisfactorily. The need for growth in rate of reading is an excellent example of the developmental nature of reading.

Improving Rate through Improving Reading Skills. The problem of improving rate can be oversimplified unless we keep in mind that rate is influenced by the reader's skills, habits, and attitudes toward the material being read. It would be unrealistic to attempt to improve a slow rate of reading without dealing with those factors that cause it. When slow reading is simply a habitual response stemming from a lack of practice and appreciation of basic reading skills, it can be dealt with by providing direct instruction. Inadequate word identification strategies that fail to utilize all available cues to arrive at meaning may prevent a child from reading efficiently.

Reading in phrases is a skill relating to rate of reading on two scores. Word-by-word reading is time consuming and also interferes with comprehension. A child who has not been taught to read for meaning will often have to repeat sentences and parts of sentences when he loses the thought. When word-by-word reading is habitual; that is, when it has been wrongly reinforced by many thousands of reading experiences, it is sometimes advisable to give the reader practice in reading easy phrases. Gradually the teacher can build on the child's successes, and more difficult reading material can be used. The teacher can make up exercises that use meaningful phrases to illustrate the importance of reading for meaning rather than just identifying words.

INTRODUCTORY ACTIVITY

The following passage tells something about the reading process. The material has been arranged in short phrases to provide practice in phrase reading. The ability to read in phrases is learned through practice. After reading this material several times, you should be reading it both faster and more smoothly. (Read down the columns, reading each line as a unit.)

This exercise
is arranged
in columns
of phrases
to help you
in developing
the habit of
reading phrases.
Try to read
each line
"as one unit."
That is—
do not read
each/word/
as/a/unit/.
With practice,
you will find
you can read
several words
as units.
As you read
other materials
which have not
been phrased,
let your eyes
and your mind
cooperate
in selecting
several words
which are
"logical thoughts."
This will help you
to read
more rapidly,
more smoothly,
and with good
comprehension.
Your eyes
and your mind
are capable
of dealing
with several
smaller words
or with a
very large one.
For instance—
Mississippi
Rhode Island
cheerfulness
peppermint
in olden days
cold and rainy.
The examples
cited above
are relatively
long units.
They were easy
for you to read
because they are
familiar.
You have seen
each of them
many times
and you know
their meanings.
These phrases
were not related
to each other.
Other phrases
on this page
are related.
This is a bit
more difficult
to read smoothly.
First because
the thought units
vary in length.
Secondly,
some readers
might select
different
phrasing patterns
than shown here.

APPLICATION ACTIVITY

The following phrases or short sentences are designed to give practice in reading a number of words as one thought unit. Some pupils read one word at a time; that is, they pause after each word: *up, the, mountain.* Since this is a logical thought unit, it should be read: up the mountain. Pupils should be directed to read the phrases left to right, focusing on the meaning of the phrase unit. Illustrate and explain the task to the pupils. Complete parts of each activity as a group to assure that each pupil understands the purpose and what he is to do.

In the car   down the hill   at the farm   from the house
had to leave soon   in the big house   he will be
has gone away   the white horse   eat some cake

ran to the house   the show   can see it   the pretty dress
will look good   we can see   much too much   the tiny boat
on the paper   to the fair

In the following paragraph, logical thought units have been separated. Be sure to read each phrase as a whole. There are many different ways we could read the same passage. The following is only one example.

Billy saw the car   coming down the road.
He said to himself,   I hope I can get a ride   to town.
He began to wonder   if he should   accept a ride
if he didn't know   the driver.   The car pulled up
and slowed down.   He saw a man   and two boys
about his age.
The boys shouted,   "Hi, Billy."
He recognized the twins.

Underline phrases which could be read as one unit. Remember that there may be several different ways to arrange words in thought units. Underline the way you think is best.

The twins, Roger and Sandy, had moved to town several weeks ago.
"Hop in the car," said Sandy.
"Have you met my dad?" asked Roger.
Billy shook hands with Mr. Farrell.
As they neared town, Mr. Farrell said, "Can you come and play with the boys at our house or must you go straight home?"

SUMMARY

Content reading presents many challenges to teachers. To meet the wide range of student ability, teachers should use strategies such as the DRA, advanced organizers, structured overviews, and study guides. In addition, teachers should consider various alternative approaches to using a single textbook.

Study skills, which include a study procedure, specific content reading skills, locating information, organizing and evaluating material, effective use of library resources, and adjusting reading rate to purpose and material, are a most important cluster of reading skills. Yet their importance to the learner is not always paralleled by the effectiveness with which they are taught.

Ideally, helping children develop efficient study skills should be an integral part of the *teaching* in all content areas. Ironically, in many classrooms the content itself takes precedence over the process of developing effective skills in locating, evaluating, and organizing this material.

Some important study skills do appear to deal primarily with mechanics. Examples include dictionary usage; reader aids such as a glossary, index, and appendix; and the card catalog and other library aids. However, these need not be taught mechanically. They are best learned as they are needed in actual class work as students are asked to determine definitions and pronunciations of unusual terms, decide upon the specific connotation of a word, and find related materials in a wide variety of sources. These and other opportunities for learning are ongoing—they occur daily. Thus, one need not resort to lengthy drill on dictionary or reference material skills. The study skills are developmental in nature and are best taught and learned as part of a total growth process.

Other types of study skills focus on critical reading and interpretation of a wide variety of written materials. In essence, these skills involve sorting out what is significant and relevant to one's goal, making critical judgments relative to ideas and concepts, drawing inferences, and predicting outcomes. Study skills are important tools for problem solving in all areas of the curriculum.

The classroom teacher is the key variable in helping pupils to become independent learners. It is the responsibility of each teacher to teach formally essential study skills and to provide the necessary time and meaningful activities to ensure the transfer of these skills to content materials.

YOUR POINT OF VIEW

Discussion Questions

1. Why is it possible that certain students may be proficient readers in science while at the same time be incompetent readers in social studies?
2. The statement "Every teacher should be a teacher of reading" has been proclaimed for over fifty years in the profession. Why do you think this has not become a reality in our schools?

Take a Stand For or Against

1. Reading skills pertinent to specific content areas should be exclusively taught by content teachers.
2. The organizational structure of classrooms prohibits individualizing instruction in the content areas.

BIBLIOGRAPHY

1. Babbs, Patricia J., and Moe, Alden, J. "Metacognition: A Key for Independent Learning from Text." *The Reading Teacher* 36 (1983): 422–26.
2. Blair, Timothy R., and Rupley, William H. "Incorporating the Arts into Language Arts Instruction." *Language Arts* 57 (1980): 335–39.
3. Cheek, Earl H., and Cheek, Martha Collins. *Reading Instruction Through Content Teaching.* Columbus, Oh.: Charles E. Merrill Publishing Company, 1983.
4. Dawson, Mildred A. "Learning to Use Books Effectively." *Education* (1962): 20–22.
5. Earle, Richard A. *Teaching Reading and Mathematics.* Newark, Del.: International Reading Association, 1976.
6. Forgan, Harry W., and Mangrum, Charles T. *Teaching Content Area Reading Skills.* 3rd ed. Columbus, Oh.: Charles E. Merrill Publishing Co., 1985.
7. Galgoci, Louis J. "Following Directions: Neglected in Research and Teaching." Master's paper, Pennsylvania State University, 1972.
8. Heilman, Arthur W., and Holmes, Elizabeth Ann. *Smuggling Language into the Teaching of Reading.* 2d ed. Columbus, Oh.: Charles E. Merrill Publishing Co., 1978.
9. Lake, Mary Louise. "Improve the Dictionary's Image." *Elementary English* 48 (1971): 363–65.
10. Lange, Bob. "ERIC RCS: Readability Formulas: Second Looks, Second Thoughts." *The Reading Teacher* 35 (1982): 858–61.
11. Lehr, Fran. "Content Area Reading Instruction in the Elementary School." *The Reading Teacher* 33 (1980): 888–91.
12. Miccinati, Jeannette Louise; Sanford, Judith B.; and Hepner, Gene. "Teaching Reading Through The Arts: An Annotated Bibliography." *The Reading Teacher* 36 (1983): 412–17.
13. Pescosolido, John R.; Schell, Leo M.; and Laurent, Marie-Jeanne. *Reading Approaches and Rituals.* Dubuque, Ia.: William C. Brown Co., 1967.
14. Poostay, Edward J. "Show Me Your Underlines: A Strategy To Teach Comprehension." *The Reading Teacher* 37 (1984): 828–30.
15. Readence, John E.; Bean, Thomas W.; and Baldwin, R. Scott. *Content Area Reading: An Integrated Approach.* New York: Harper & Row, 1981.
16. Robinson, Francis P. *Effective Study.* Rev. ed. New York: Harper & Row, 1961.
17. Shores, J. Harlan. "Dimensions of Reading Speed and Comprehension." *Elementary English* 45 (1968): 23–28.
18. Shores, J. "Skills Related to the Ability to Read History and Science." *Journal of Educational Research* 36 (1943): 584–94.
19. Snoddy, James E., and Shores, J. Harlan. "Teaching the Research Study Skills." In *Reading and Realism,* Proceedings, International Reading Association 13, Part I, edited by J. Allen Figurel, pp. 681–88. Newark, Del.: International Reading Association, 1969.
20. Tadlock, Dolores Fadness. "SQ3R—Why It Works, Based on an Information Processing Theory on Learning." *The Journal of Reading* 22 (1978): 110–16.

21. Thelen, Judith. *Improving Reading in Science.* Newark, Del.: International Reading Association, 1976.
22. Thomas, Ellen Lamar, and Robinson, H. Alan. *Improving Reading in Every Class.* 2d ed. Boston, Mass.: Allyn & Bacon, 1977.
23. Vacca, Richard T. *Content Area Reading.* Boston: Little, Brown & Company, 1981.
24. Wood, Karen D., and Mateja, John A. "Adapting Secondary Level Strategies For Use In Elementary Classroom." *The Reading Teacher* 36 (1983): 492–96.

UNIT 3 Reading Instruction

Chapters

Learning to read is a long-term developmental process. It consists of growing in the use of various reading and language abilities. Just as a fine orchestra studies and practices separate parts of a performance with the ultimate goal of putting the parts together in splendid fashion, the teaching of reading involves a host of understandings that must be studied and practiced, but must be combined in an efficient and effective classroom "performance." In this unit, the topics of reading approaches, primary reading, and intermediate reading are discussed. Chapter 8 will describe the two most prevalent approaches (basal reader and language experience approach) used for reading instruction in our schools. Chapter 9 will present the major functions of the teaching of reading in the primary grades (K–3); chapter 10, the intermediate grades (4–6). Each chapter will synthesize those important components of teaching reading as a whole within the total school program.

In essence, all reading programs contain two broad areas of concern: (a) the instructional program and (b) the independent program. Although emphases within these two areas will be different in the primary and the intermediate grades, the instructional program encompasses all direct instruction in the various reading abilities (word identification, comprehension, and study skills) to attain an understanding of written language. The independent program consists of the time pupils spend on their own in applying the skills taught in the instructional program and under teacher supervision. Each chapter will focus on those important components of the teaching of reading that contribute to a complete reading program.

8

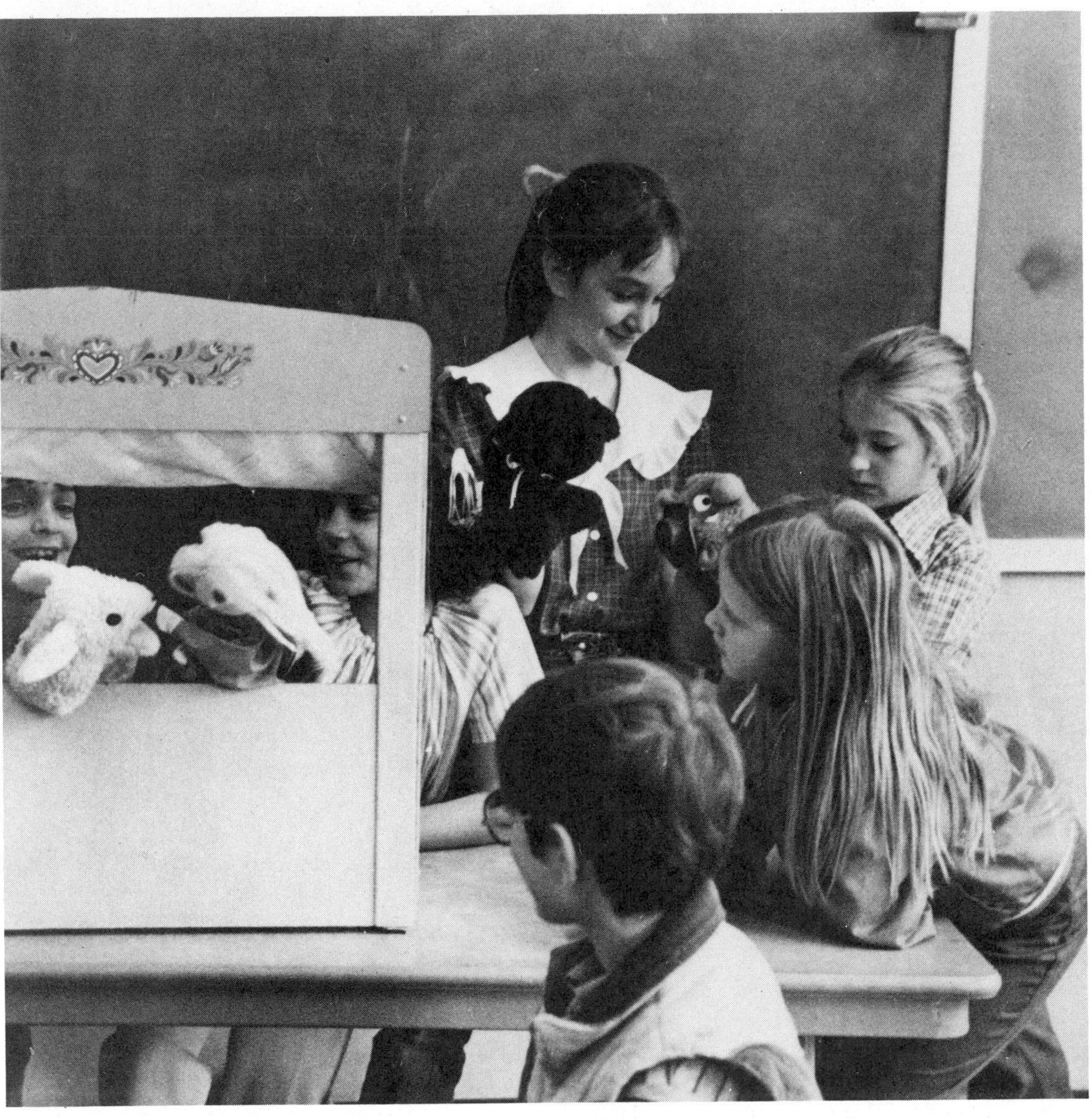

Basic Approaches to Teaching Reading

For the Reader

Imagine, if you will, an entire class of students taking a course on learning to speak and write the French language. Will everyone learn at the same rate and achieve the same success with the use of one method of instruction? Chances are that some students will do well, some average, and others may fail. These differences can be the result of several factors, among them being failure of the teacher to adapt his approach to meet students' needs. This same analogy can be applied to reading instruction. The use of a reading approach without consideration of students' needs will likely result in some children experiencing difficulty in learning how to read. In this chapter, attention is centered on how children are taught reading. The two most often used approaches for teaching developmental reading are presented. Information regarding supplemental approaches is not presented, but a listing of resources that describe these approaches is provided.

Preview

- Read over the Key Ideas that follow.
- Read each heading and subheading.
- Read the summary.
- Read the questions and statements at the end of the chapter.
- Return to the chapter text that follows the Key Ideas and begin reading.

Key Ideas

The successful implementation of a reading approach is dependent upon the classroom teacher.

Teachers need to be knowledgeable in the two basic approaches used in developmental reading instruction.

The two basic reading approaches used in elementary developmental reading instruction are the basal reader approach and the language experience approach.

Reading approaches must be modified to accommodate the needs of the students.

Effective teachers of reading can use a combination of the two basic approaches to meet learner needs.

A SHORT EXERCISE

In order that you may partially recapture the challenge of learning a symbolic process like reading, let us look at a number of familiar symbols and a number that are new. On the left of figure 8.1 are pairs of short word symbols that are very much alike. For an adult it is extremely simple to distinguish between them. On the right are the same word symbols built from a different alphabet which at this point is unknown to the reader. The new symbols represent the same words as on the left.

The unknown symbols on the right are actually easier to learn than the ones on the left, for these reasons:

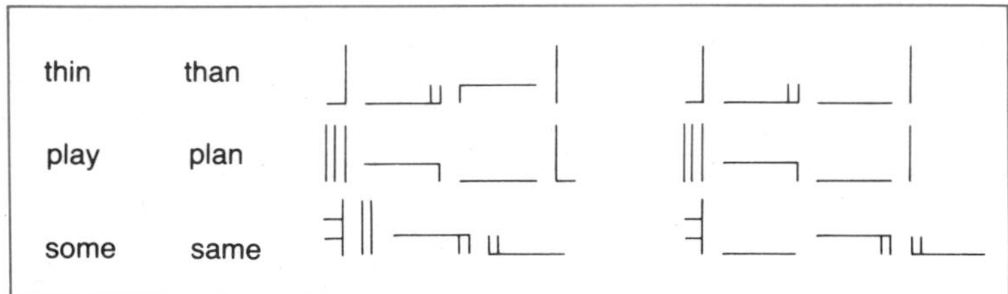

FIGURE 8.1

- All letters are composed of three or fewer straight lines.
- The lines are always horizontal or vertical (no slanting lines like *a, x, k, m;* no curved lines like *s, c, u;* no combination of straight and curved lines like *d, b, p,* etc.).
- The first thirteen letters of this alphabet are composed of long horizontal lines and short vertical lines, and the last thirteen letters are composed of long vertical and shorter horizontal lines.

This new alphabet, with its equivalent in English, is found in figure 8.2.

Most likely you had little trouble reading these simple word representations. However, the task becomes more difficult when presented with a passage. A short reading passage using this new symbol system is presented in figure 8.3. The purpose is not to present a situation analogous to beginning reading, since the reader will have to study the new alphabet in figure 8.2 prior to reading. Attempting to read the passage presented in figure 8.3 will illustrate the difficulty of mastering a symbolic task in which the symbols are unknown. In this respect, the task is similar to beginning reading.

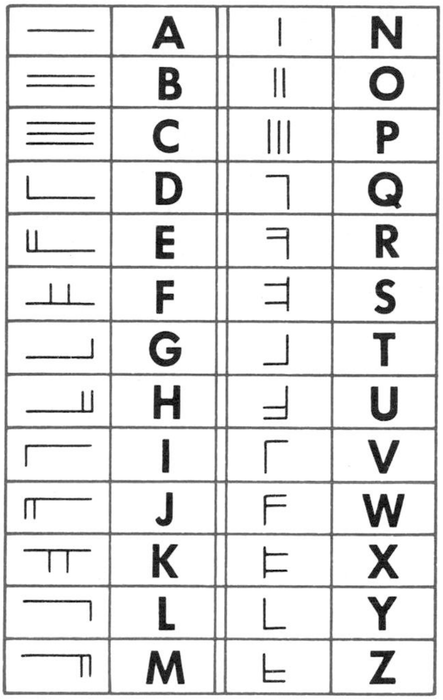

	A		N
	B		O
	C		P
	D		Q
	E		R
	F		S
	G		T
	H		U
	I		V
	J		W
	K		X
	L		Y
	M		Z

FIGURE 8.2

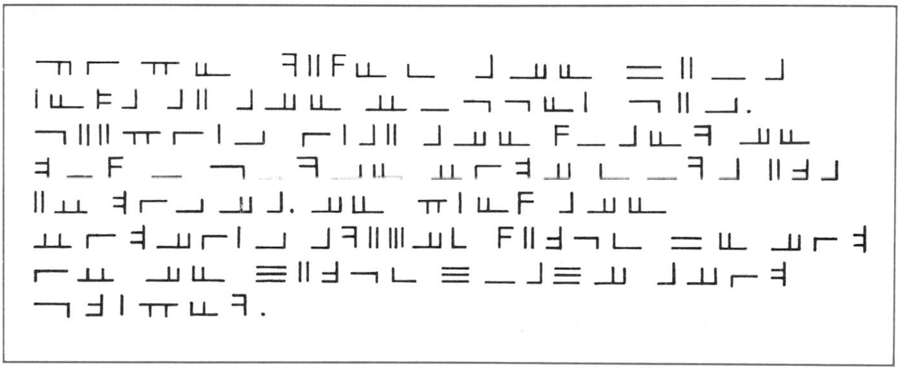

FIGURE 8.3

If you had a little trouble reading the simple passage in figure 8.3, the experiment was worth the effort.[1] Obviously, this passage is not on the first-grade level. The objective was to demonstrate that any sym-

1. Translation of passage in figure 8.3: Mike rowed the boat next to the fallen log. Looking into the water he saw a large fish dart out of sight. He knew the fishing trophy would be his if he could catch this lunker.

bolic process is potentially difficult and that when the symbols are very much alike, it becomes increasingly more difficult.

READING APPROACHES

Although an approach by itself is frequently identified with instructional materials, an approach to teaching reading is also identifiable with a recommended usage of these materials as part of a comprehensive instructional activity (4). The "how" or by what approach children are taught to read has been the object of a large number of research studies. Unfortunately, research on the comparison of reading approaches has been inconclusive. No single approach to teaching reading is successful with all children. In a sense, no reading approach is foolproof. The teacher is a major factor in determining the success of a reading approach by knowing when to modify an approach, combine approaches, or use a different approach to meet students' needs. Corder (4) speaks to this point in stating, "Failure to recognize and account for individual differences is a major failing of all the specialized approaches. . . . The combination or eclectic method, since it subsumes varied approaches, comes closest to these to providing for individual differences" (p. 107). Thus, the importance of the teacher is highlighted within the implementation of any given approach. It is the teacher who is the *key variable* in whether or not a child is successful in learning to read.

Different approaches in and materials for teaching reading are based on different philosophies regarding their interpretations of the reading process and how children learn. In this chapter the two most widely used basic approaches for teaching reading will be discussed—the basal reader approach and the language experience approach. The majority of basal readers are eclectic and include provisions for teaching word recognition, comprehension, language, study skills, and literature appreciation. The language experience approach (LEA) is based on children's own language and their experiences. We have chosen to focus on these two approaches for several reasons: (1) they are the most often used approaches for teaching reading in elementary reading programs, (2) teachers need to be knowledgeable of how to effectively teach reading with approaches that are found in most public school systems, and (3) most supplemental approaches are focused on intensive decoding, which may have detrimental effects on students' understanding that reading is a meaning-getting process. Knowing how to use and modify the basal reader approach and LEA will enable teachers to combine and use features of each that are appropriate to their pupils' needs. Furthermore, the activities recommended in chapters 5, 6, 7, 9, and 10 can be used with either approach to enhance the quality of teachers' reading instruction. An excellent source of information on more than one hundred supplementary reading approaches is *Approaches to Beginning Reading,* 2d ed., by Robert C. Aukerman.

The Basal Reader Approach

For decades, basal reader series have served as one of the chief instructional materials used in the elementary grades for teaching reading. Throughout the 1950s and early 1960s, basal series tended to be very much alike. Significant innovations were held to a minimum, and a number of criticisms were leveled against these materials. Critics alleged that the story content was boring, culturally biased, lacked literary merit, and the language used was unrealistic and repetitive, to name a few.

Some of these criticisms were justified, and authors and publishers made a number of changes in basals that most observers feel enhanced the value of these materials (2). Others criticized basal readers for the ways they were used by classroom teachers. This criticism should not have been aimed at basal materials, but rather at the ways they were misused. These particular practices were neither suggested nor condoned by any basal program. However, certain critics of basals contended that these practices were inevitable outcomes of using basals. For instance, when using basals, teachers would:

- Have a group of children read every story in a "round robin" manner. Each child would be asked to focus his attention on the same line at a given time.
- Use three groups within a classroom—these groups remained the same throughout the year.
- Make no provision for individual differences beyond this "three group" pattern.
- Hold the more capable readers to the basal material only, forcing them to move through this material at a pace far below their capacity.
- Prohibit children from selecting and reading other books in which they might be interested.

Unfortunately, these practices can be found in certain classrooms today. Recent research by Durkin (6) provides some insights about why some teachers vary their use of basals in the teaching of reading. Sixteen teachers were observed during their reading instruction to better determine how they use basal manuals. First-, third-, and fifth-grade classes were observed. Durkin's findings were not very encouraging; however,

FLASHBACK

LESSON V.

Răb Ann hăt c̶ătch sēe

ē ch s

See Rab! See Ann!
See! Rab has the hat.
Can Ann catch Rab?

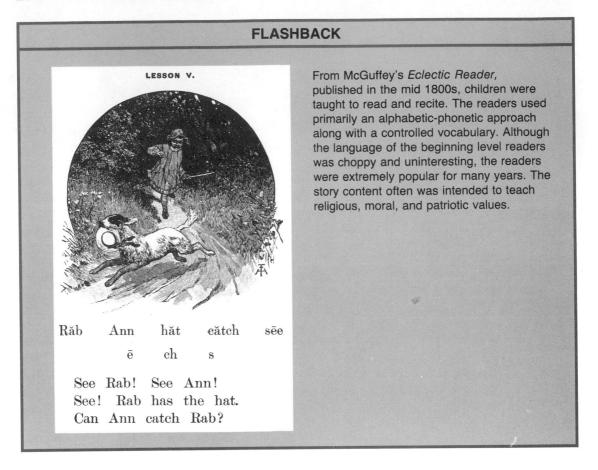

From McGuffey's *Eclectic Reader*, published in the mid 1800s, children were taught to read and recite. The readers used primarily an alphabetic-phonetic approach along with a controlled vocabulary. Although the language of the beginning level readers was choppy and uninteresting, the readers were extremely popular for many years. The story content often was intended to teach religious, moral, and patriotic values.

if teachers become aware of them it is hoped that the quality of basal reading instruction will improve. A summary of her findings is presented and discussed below.

- *Introduction and Presentation of New Vocabulary Words.* Most basal manuals suggest that new words be introduced in written context and illustrated in familiar, written sentences. Very few of the teachers followed this recommendation and rarely was any attention given to teaching and practicing new vocabulary words.
- *Discussion and Presentation of Background Information.* Basal manuals often provide background information about concepts and themes found in stories, which are intended to activate pupils' experiential/conceptual background (see chapter 6). Durkin found that none of the teachers reviewed or developed background information for their pupils.

My Friend Charlie
All about Friends

Text pages 10–19
Skillpack pages 1–4
Studybook pages 15–17
Wall Chart pages 1–3

SKILLS

VOCABULARY
- **word identification ***
- **vocabulary development (homophones) * I, P1**

COMPREHENSION: sequence * I, P1
DECODING: long words * I, P1

KEY:
- **I—Introductory Instruction**
- **P—Practice Activity**
- **R—Review Activity**
- **★—Skills to be Tested**

VOCABULARY

"My Friend Charlie"

BASIC (defined in Glossary)

owned	**follows**
reasons	**borrow(s)**

ENRICHMENT

elevator	**except**
half	**pajamas**
pitcher	**José**
President	**Charlie**
dragons	

"All about Friends"

BASIC (defined in Glossary)

person
understands
somebody

ENRICHMENT

advice	**perfect**
chorus	**sentence**
expect	**singer**
honest	

Words to Decode are listed in the back of this Teacher's Edition.

BACKGROUND

Summary "My Friend Charlie" is about a special friend who helps people and animals, and who also has a great sense of humor. In several short episodes, Charlie gets a cat down from a tree by hoisting up a basket of fish, pretends to receive a letter from the moon, and borrows his friend's dream, which he returns greatly improved. The tail tales about this special friend may spark pupils' tall tales about friendship.

"All about Friends" is a short article that gives helpful advice on making and keeping friends. Four sections define what a friend is, give advice on how to make new friends, tell how to be a good friend, and provide a few words of wisdom. The article provides a good follow-up to "My Friend Charlie" and can stimulate a discussion of friendship.

"My Friend Charlie" and "All about Friends" open a unit about friendship. The theme of the unit is exemplified by the happy tone of the narrative in "My Friend Charlie" and is demonstrated in the concern for friendship in "All about Friends."

A sample basal lesson plan and accompanying activities.

1 Preparing for Reading

INTRODUCING VOCABULARY

BASIC WORDS

borrow, follows Write *borrow* and *follows* on the chalkboard. Ask what is the same about both words. (*They both have double middle consonants and end with* ow.) Help pupils read and define both words. Read these sentences and ask volunteers to complete them.

1. Instead of buying the book, I will _____ it from the library. (*borrow*)
2. My little brother _____ me everywhere. (*follows*)

reasons, owned, person, somebody Write *reasons, owned, person,* and *somebody* on the chalkboard. Help pupils read each word, using vowel spellings as hints. Then have volunteers answer these questions:

1. Which word means "ideas" and rhymes with *seasons*? (*reasons*)
2. Which word rhymes with *loaned* and means "belonged to or in someone's possession"? (*owned*)
3. Which word means "the opposite of *nobody*"? (*somebody*)
4. Which word means "an individual" and best completes this sentence? You are a _____ I can count on. (*person*)

understands Write *understands* on the board. Ask a volunteer to read the word. Ask a volunteer to name the two word-parts. (*under, stands*) Discuss the meaning of the word by using it in a sentence and asking pupils to replace it with a synonym. For example, "He understands why I wanted to go to the baseball game." (*knows, gets the idea*)

WORDS TO DECODE/ENRICHMENT WORDS

On the chalkboard, write:

Charlie and Jose are friends.

Underline the names. Explain that these are the names of two boys who will appear in the selection. Explain that *Charlie* is a nickname. Ask if anyone knows the name from which *Charlie* comes. (*Charles*) Ask for other nicknames or names that have come from *Charles*. (*Chuck, Charley*) Explain that Jose is a Spanish name and that there are many variations of the name. (*Joseph—English; Giuseppe—Italian*)

You may wish to preview some of the Enrichment words and Words to Decode with the group. Help pupils with any definitions they do not know or have them use their dictionaries to find the meanings.

Have pupils write sentences using the following word groups in each: *Charlie, follows; José, owned; reasons, borrow; somebody, understands; person.*

You may wish pupils to keep a word book of interesting or unusual vocabulary. Word books should be divided alphabetically, and entry words listed in the appropriate alphabetical section. To begin the word book, have pupils choose three of the Basic or Enrichment words for "My Friend Charlie" and "All about Friends." Selection may be based on any criteria, including meaning, sound, spelling, interest, or shape. Have them enter the words in their new word books and write definitions or sentences for each word.

■ **Skillpack page 1**

PREPARING FOR COMPREHENSION

Write on the chalkboard: *Side by Side*. Have a volunteer read the title. Remind them that this is the title of the first unit in the book and that all the stories in this unit will be about friendship. Write the word *friendship* on the chalkboard. Ask:

> What do you think of when you see or hear the word *friendship*? What is a good friend?

Start a list of friendship words by writing pupils' ideas and thoughts on the chalkboard in a few brief words. (Examples are *shares, makes me laugh, is fun to be with, likes the same things.*)

Now explain that the first story is about two best friends and the adventures they have together, and that the second story gives advice on how to be a good friend. Point out that people who are friends give advice to help their friendship. Explain the difference between advice and rules: we can make up our own minds about whether advice is good or not and whether we want to follow it, but we must follow rules.

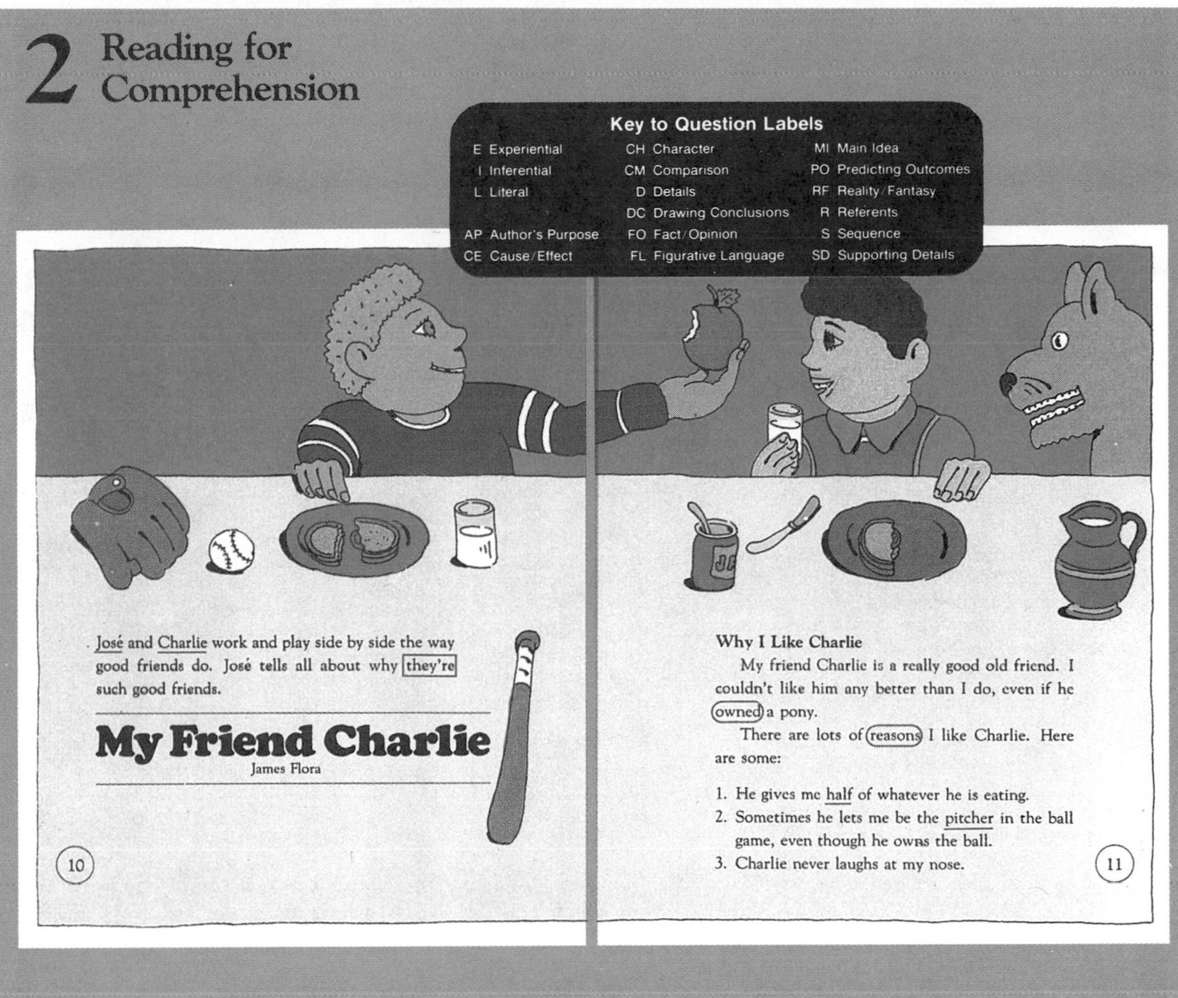

2 Reading for Comprehension

Key to Question Labels

E Experiential	CH Character	MI Main Idea
I Inferential	CM Comparison	PO Predicting Outcomes
L Literal	D Details	RF Reality/Fantasy
	DC Drawing Conclusions	R Referents
AP Author's Purpose	FO Fact/Opinion	S Sequence
CE Cause/Effect	FL Figurative Language	SD Supporting Details

José and Charlie work and play side by side the way good friends do. José tells all about why they're such good friends.

My Friend Charlie

James Flora

10

Why I Like Charlie

My friend Charlie is a really good old friend. I couldn't like him any better than I do, even if he owned a pony.

There are lots of reasons I like Charlie. Here are some:

1. He gives me half of whatever he is eating.
2. Sometimes he lets me be the pitcher in the ball game, even though he owns the ball.
3. Charlie never laughs at my nose.

11

Basic words are circled. Enrichment words are underscored. Words to Decode are boxed.

SET READING PURPOSE Ask pupils as they read to keep in mind the reasons Charlie and José are such good friends. When they read "All about Friends," ask them to think about why their own friends are such good friends.

GUIDED READING

PAGES 11–12 What does each reason tell you about the kind of friend Charlie is? (I—DC, CH; *1. and 2. Charlie shares and is generous; 3. He is kind; 4. He is courageous; 5. He is sympathetic.*)

Pages 12–13

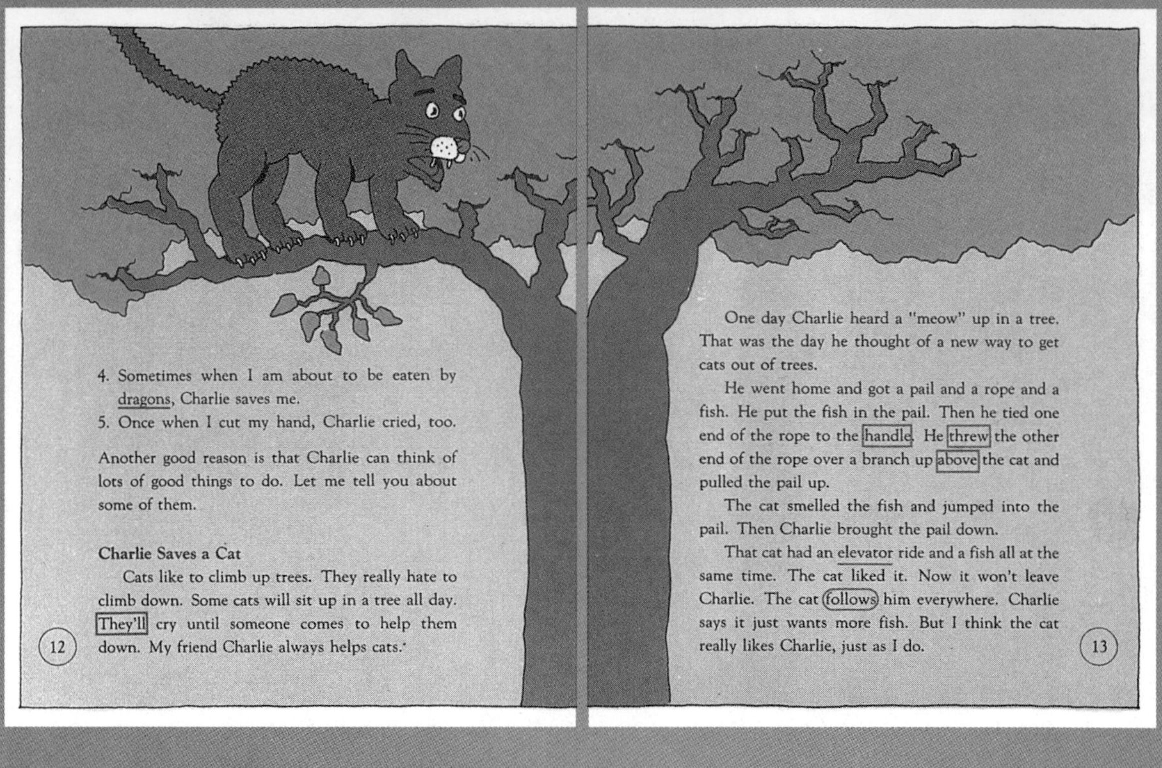

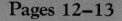

4. Sometimes when I am about to be eaten by dragons, Charlie saves me.
5. Once when I cut my hand, Charlie cried, too.

Another good reason is that Charlie can think of lots of good things to do. Let me tell you about some of them.

Charlie Saves a Cat

Cats like to climb up trees. They really hate to climb down. Some cats will sit up in a tree all day. They'll cry until someone comes to help them down. My friend Charlie always helps cats.

12

One day Charlie heard a "meow" up in a tree. That was the day he thought of a new way to get cats out of trees.

He went home and got a pail and a rope and a fish. He put the fish in the pail. Then he tied one end of the rope to the handle. He threw the other end of the rope over a branch up above the cat and pulled the pail up.

The cat smelled the fish and jumped into the pail. Then Charlie brought the pail down.

That cat had an elevator ride and a fish all at the same time. The cat liked it. Now it won't leave Charlie. The cat follows him everywhere. Charlie says it just wants more fish. But I think the cat really likes Charlie, just as I do.

13

PAGE 12 What was the sixth reason Charlie is a good friend? (L—D; *Charlie can think of lots of good things to do.*)

PAGE 13 What difficulty was the cat in? (I—MI; *It was stuck up in a tree and could not get down.*)

What three things did Charlie use to save the cat? (L—D; *a pail, a rope, and a fish*)
How did Charlie use these things to save the cat? (I—MI, S; *He put the fish in the pail and tied the rope to the handle of the pail. Charlie threw the rope over a branch and pulled the pail up. The cat was attracted by the fish and jumped into the pail. Then Charlie let it down like an elevator.*)

Pages 14–15

Charlie Gets a Letter from the Moon

"I got a letter from the moon today," Charlie said. "Do you want to know what it says?"

"Sure," I said. "I never heard from the moon in my whole life."

"It says, 'Dear Charlie: I saw you the other night when you stayed up until ten-thirty playing hide-and-seek. That is too late, and your mother was worried. I hope you won't do that again.

14

'And why do you keep telling people that I am made of green cheese when you know very well that I'm made of rocks? Please tell the truth about me.

'Thanks for sending me all the peanut butter and jelly sandwiches last week. They were very good. I don't get much good food up here except when some kind friend remembers to send me some.

'Can you come up here for a visit next week? It

15

PAGE 14 Where did Charlie say his letter was from? (L—D; *the moon*)

PAGES 14–16 What four things did the moon letter tell Charlie? (L—I; *It told him not to stay up late and not to say the moon was made of green cheese. It said thank you for the sandwiches and asked Charlie to visit.*)

Pages 16–17

would be nice to have you. Bring your pajamas, and you can bring your friend José if you like.

'Best wishes,

your friend, The Moon

'P.S. Please bring some new flashlight batteries when you come. I think mine are wearing out. I don't seem to shine as brightly as I did last year.' "

"That's goofy," I said. "How can you go to the moon? How can the moon eat peanut butter and jelly sandwiches? And you know very well it doesn't need batteries to shine. Where did you get that goofy letter, Charlie?"

16

"I made it up," said Charlie. "I always wanted a letter from the moon, but I never got one until today. I think I'll go. Do you want to go along?"

We went and had a wonderful time. Just make-believe, of course.

Charlie Borrows My Dream

"I had a good dream last night," I told Charlie. "I dreamed that I had a bike that could go anywhere. I rode it right up one side of a tree and down the other. I rode it up and down all the houses on the way to school. When I got to school, I rode all over the room and sideways across the board. Our teacher was surprised."

"Say! That's a great dream," Charlie said. "Let me borrow that dream tonight. Will you? I'll let you dream my trip-to-the-moon dream. It's a good one, too."

17

PAGE 16 Do you think the moon wrote this letter? Why or why not? (E—RF; *No, the moon cannot write or see or eat peanut butter and jelly sandwiches or invite visitors.*)

Who do you think wrote the letter? Why? (E—PO; *Probably Charlie himself, since we already know he's pretty clever.*)

PAGE 17 Why did Charlie write the moon letter? (I—D, CE; *Charlie had always wanted a letter from the moon.*)
What did José dream about? (L—D; *a bike that could go anywhere*)
What funny things could José's dream bike do? (I—D, RF; *It could go up one side of a tree and down the other, go up and down houses, go sideways across the board at school.*)

Pages 18–19

"Sure, Charlie," I said. "You can borrow it tonight."
The next day Charlie said, "I sure do like that old bike dream of yours. I'm going to keep it a few more nights and add some nice parts to it."
Charlie dreamed my dream for a whole week. When he gave it back, it was much better. It had new parts in it. I ride the bike over mountains and tugboats. I ride it under the sea and over whales and right into the White House. Then the President says to me, "You are the very best bike rider in the whole country!" He shakes my hand and gives me a prize.
18
You can always tell when somebody is your friend. A friend sometimes borrows a dream. A friend takes good care of the dream. A friend fixes up the dream and gives it back better than ever!
Focus on Comprehension
1. Charlie is a person who shares. What are some things that Charlie and José share?
2. Do you think Charlie is kind? Tell why or why not.
3. How did Charlie save the cat? What do you think of his plan?
4. Would you like Charlie for a friend? Tell your reasons.
19

PAGE 18 How did Charlie improve José's dream? (I—D, MI; *He added new parts, such as riding over mountains, tugboats, and whales, under the sea, and into the White House.*)

PAGE 19 How does Charlie say a friend treats your dreams? (I—SD; *A friend might borrow your dream, fix it up, and return it to you better than ever.*)

Pages 20–21

José told us about his friend Charlie. Here's some advice on how to make and be a good friend.

All about Friends

Jonah Kalb and David Viscott

What Is a Friend?

A friend is a person who likes some of the same things you like.

A friend is a person who trusts you and understands you. A friend likes you the way you are.

A friend is a person who shares some of the things you think are important.

A true friend already understands how you feel about things without having to be told. Friends understand how bad you feel because they hurt the same way.

Friends don't expect you to be perfect. You do the same for them.

20

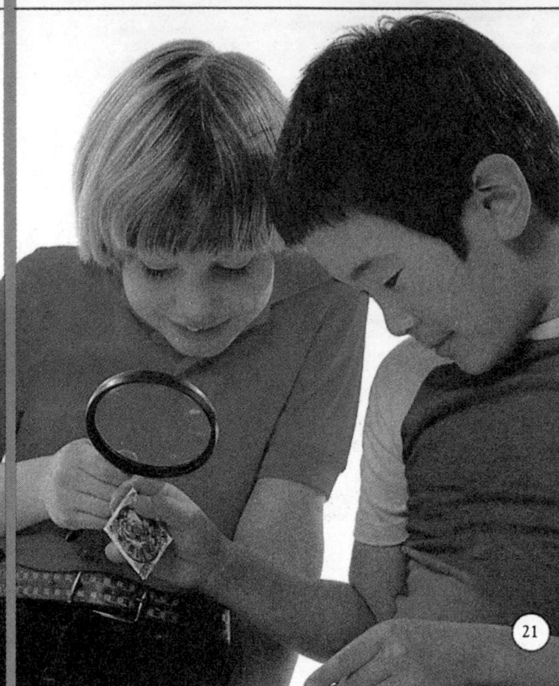

21

PAGE 20 What are some of the qualities of a friend? (L—MI; *A friend likes some of the same things you like; a friend trusts and understands you; a friend likes you the way you are; a friend shares with you; a friend doesn't expect you to be perfect.*)

Pages 22–23

How to Make Friends

1. Do things you like to do. Let's say you just moved to a new town. You don't know anyone. The best way to make friends is to do what you used to do. If you liked stamps in your old town, join a stamp club. If you liked sports in the old town, try out for some teams. If you were a singer, join a chorus. In that way, you will find people who like the things you do. You'll have a good time. It is easier to find friends when you're already having a good time.

2. Be Yourself. Being yourself is a good idea. You will make friends and keep them as well. Friends must be honest. You wouldn't want to make friends with somebody because you pretended to be someone you really weren't. You want friends to like you the way you really are. You are not perfect. Nobody is perfect.

3. Be a Friend. To make a friend, you have to be a friend. Be somebody that another person would like to have for a friend.

22

Focus on Comprehension

1. Name three things from the text that would end this sentence: A friend is somebody who. . . .
2. What are two ways to make friends in a new town?
3. Why should you be yourself when you want to find friends?

23

PAGE 22 What advice does the article give for making new friends? (I—MI; *Do what you are used to doing, act as you always do, and be a friend.*)

PAGES 22–23 Is this advice easy to follow? How could you follow it? (E—FO; *Pupils should support their opinions about whether it is easy or difficult to be a good friend with examples drawn from relationships among their own friends.*)

Putting Words Together

Match the words in both columns to form compound words.

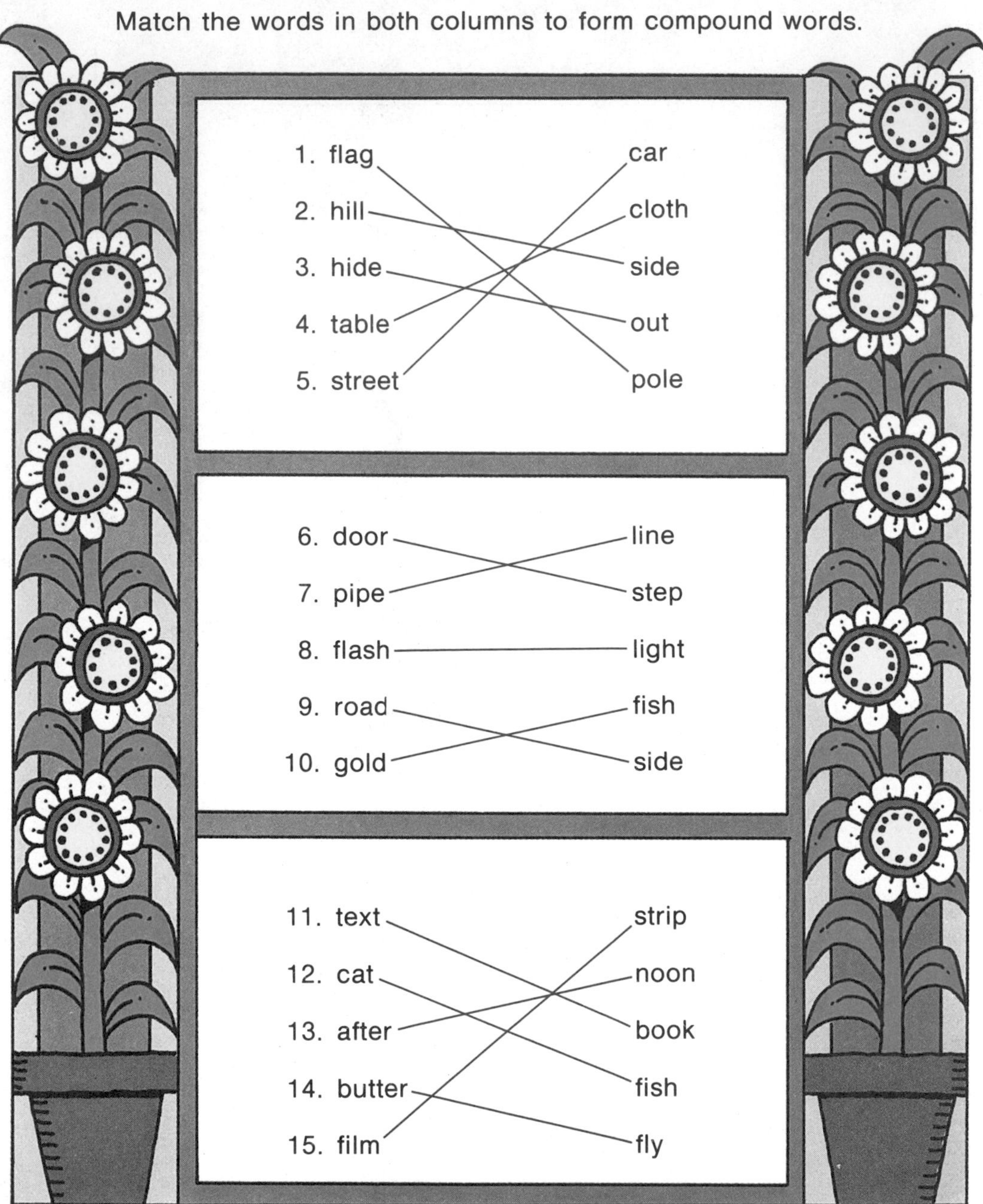

1. flag
2. hill
3. hide
4. table
5. street
car
cloth
side
out
pole
6. door
7. pipe
8. flash
9. road
10. gold
line
step
light
fish
side
11. text
12. cat
13. after
14. butter
15. film
strip
noon
book
fish
fly

A workbook page that can be used with "My Friend Charlie" and "All about Friends."

DISCUSSING THE SELECTION

DISCUSS PURPOSE Have pupils recall that when reading these stories, they were to keep in mind their ideas about friendship. Discuss why Charlie and José are friends. Encourage pupils to summarize the reasons José likes Charlie and to retell or read aloud some of the interesting things Charlie does. Ask which adventure pupils would like to have shared with Charlie. Inquire whether pupils would like to have Charlie for a friend, and why or why not.

SUMMARIZE SELECTION Ask volunteers to think about Charlie as they reread the section, "What Is a Friend," from "All about Friends." Discuss how Charlie shows that he is a good friend. Encourage pupils to read each definition of a friend and compare it with the list of five reasons that Charlie is a good friend. (For example, Charlie and José like doing the same things. They share—Charlie always gives half to José. They do not expect each other to be perfect. Charlie does not laugh at José's nose.)

APPLY IDEAS End the discussion by having pupils add to the list of friendship phrases on the chalkboard. You may wish to have them write their own personal friendship phrase lists.

FOCUS ON COMPREHENSION Focus questions may be used to summarize the selection and to check on overall comprehension. The following answers to the Focus questions in the text are provided to guide discussion. Encourage a variety of responses.

"My Friend Charlie"

1. Charlie is a person who shares. What are some things that Charlie and José share? (*They share food, Charlie's baseball, Charlie's letter to the moon, and their dreams*).

2. Do you think Charlie is kind? Tell why or why not. (*Accept all reasonable answers. For example: Yes, Charlie is kind because he shares things with José.*)

3. How did Charlie save the cat? (*He put a fish in a pail, and the cat went into the pail, then he lowered the pail.*) **What do you think of this plan?** (*Accept all reasonable answers.*)

4. Would you like Charlie for a friend? Tell your reasons. (*Accept all reasonable answers that pupils can support with details from the story.*)

"All about Friends"

1. Name three things from the text that would end this sentence: A friend is somebody who. . . . (*Any of the points made in the article will fit. After the discussion, pupils may be able to contribute ideas of their own.*)

2. What are two ways to make friends in a new town? (*You should continue doing what you like to do and join a club or chorus or try out for a team.*)

3. Why should you be yourself when you want to find friends? (*You would fail to be a friend if you pretended to like things you did not like. That would not be honest.*)

3 Developing Reading Skills

VOCABULARY

Word identification: Using new vocabulary words

You may want to review briefly the meanings of the new vocabulary words. Write these words on the chalkboard:

borrow	person
follows	somebody
reasons	understands
owned	

Ask pupils to identify the word or words that answer the questions:

1. Which word means "the opposite of *leads*"? (*follows*)
2. Which word has almost the same meaning as *someone*? (*somebody*)
3. Which word means "belonged to"? (*owned*)
4. Which word means the opposite of *lend*? (*borrow*)
5. Which word has almost the same meaning as *causes*? (*reasons*)
6. Which word means "a man, woman, or child"? (*person*)
7. Which word means "gets the meaning of"? (*understands*)

Then write these sentences on the chalkboard and have volunteers fill in the blanks:

I never have ____ a dog. (*owned*)
My friend's dog always ____ me. (*follows*)
I asked if I could ____ her dog. (*borrow*)
I had good ____ for doing that. (*reasons*)
My friend ____ my reasons very well. (*understands*)
She is ____ I trust. (*somebody*)
It's good to know such a ____. (*person*)

■ **Skillpack page 1**

If necessary, help pupils read the directions. You may want to do the first item with them. When all pupils have finished the page, have volunteers read the completed paragraphs.

▲ **Studybook page 15**

Name 1

Use the new words to finish the story. Write one word on each line.

reasons Charlie

Charlie and José are two of my best friends. We go to school together, we play together, and we even go to summer camp together. There are many reasons that Charlie and José are my friends.

person owned borrow

Charlie always lets me borrow his roller skates. He knows that if I owned a pair of skates, I would let him borrow them. Charlie is a person you know will always be your friend.

somebody understands follows José

José is somebody who is a good friend, too. When we are riding our bikes, José sometimes lets me ride in front while he follows. He understands how to be a good friend.

Additional Activity: Write a few sentences about what makes a good friend.

VOCABULARY word identification in context
BASIC WORDS owned reasons follows borrow person understands somebody

Level 9 "My Friend Charlie," "All about Friends"

VOCABULARY

Vocabulary Development: Distinguishing between homophones (Introduction, Practice 1)

RECOGNIZE To introduce the concept of homophones, write the following sentences on the chalkboard:

Jim threw his ball.
It went through the open window.

Read the sentences and ask pupils to identify the two words that sound the same. (threw *and* through) Explain that certain words may sound alike, even though they are spelled differently and have different meanings. Such words are called *homophones*. Have pupils read the words *threw* and *through*. Then ask:

Are these two words spelled the same way? (*no*)
Do they have almost the same meaning? (*no*)
Are *threw* and *through* homophones? (*yes*)
How do you know? (*They sound alike but have different spellings and meanings.*)

EXERCISE Write the following homophones on the chalkboard. Discuss the meanings of the pairs of words and have pupils use them in sentences.

red—read two—too—to knew—new
beet—beat their—they're—there

Ask pupils to think of other pairs of homophones. (*blue—blew; meet—meat*) Discuss the meanings of the homophones and have them used in sentences.

APPLY Write the following words and incomplete sentences on the chalkboard:

sea seal see
What can you ______ from your window? (*see*)
The ______ was very blue yesterday. (*sea*)

Ask a volunteer to read the three words and identify the homophones. (*see, sea*) Then have pupils complete the sentences.

Before pupils begin the page, suggest that they use dictionaries if they are uncertain about which homophone is correct.

■ **Skillpack page 2**

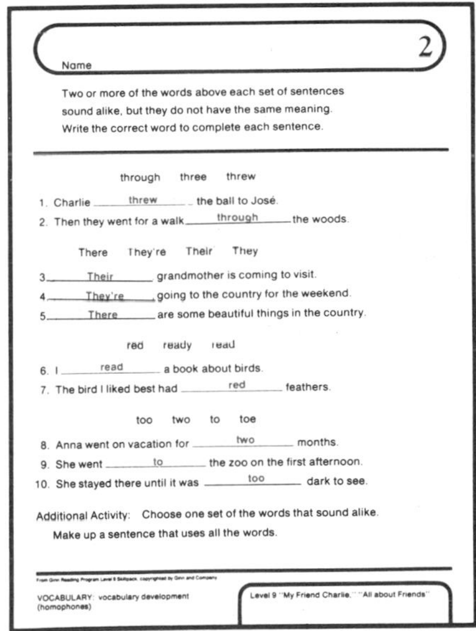
Name 2

Two or more of the words above each set of sentences sound alike, but they do not have the same meaning. Write the correct word to complete each sentence.

through three threw

1. Charlie ___threw___ the ball to José.
2. Then they went for a walk ___through___ the woods.

There They're Their They

3. ___Their___ grandmother is coming to visit.
4. ___They're___ going to the country for the weekend.
5. ___There___ are some beautiful things in the country.

red ready read

6. I ___read___ a book about birds.
7. The bird I liked best had ___red___ feathers.

too two to toe

8. Anna went on vacation for ___two___ months.
9. She went ___to___ the zoo on the first afternoon.
10. She stayed there until it was ___too___ dark to see.

Additional Activity: Choose one set of the words that sound alike. Make up a sentence that uses all the words.

From Ginn Reading Program Level 8 Skillpack, copyrighted by Ginn and Company

VOCABULARY: vocabulary development (homophones)

Level 9 "My Friend Charlie," "All about Friends"

COMPREHENSION

Sequence: Identifying the sequence of events in a story (Introduction, Practice 1)

RECOGNIZE Explain that the events in a story take place in a certain order. Being able to follow and recall the correct sequence of events will help one better understand what is being read. Write these sentences on the chalkboard:

Kerry opened the can of dog food.
Then she put the dog food into Jojo's dish.
Jojo ate the dog food.

Have pupils read the sentences. Then ask:

What happened first? (*Kerry opened the can.*)
What happened next? (*Kerry put the dog food into Jojo's dish.*)
Could Kerry feed the dog before she opened the can? Why or why not? (*No. She could not get the food out of the can.*)
What happened last? (*Jojo ate the food.*)

Underline the word *then*. Explain that such words as *then, first, next,* and *finally* are sometimes used to signal the sequence of events.

EXERCISE Direct pupils to listen carefully for the order of events as you read this paragraph:

It was Flora's birthday. She heard the doorbell ring. She went to the door, but there was no one there. Then she saw a little box. Next she looked into the box and saw a puppy. A tag around the puppy's neck said, "Happy Birthday."

Read these sentences aloud, pausing at each blank. Have pupils supply words in parentheses.

Flora heard the doorbell ring.
Flora went ______. (*to the door*)
Then Flora saw ______. (*a little box*)
She ______. (*looked into the box*)
Next she saw ______. (*a puppy*)

Make clear that each event represents something that happened in a certain order. Point out the signal words *then* and *next*.

APPLY Write these sentences on the chalkboard, omitting the correct responses given in parentheses:

> Roberto runs through the spray. (*3*)
> Ana gets out the hose. (*1*)
> Roberto turns on the water. (*2*)

Then ask pupils to listen to a story, paying close attention to signal words and the sequence of events. Read this story:

> It's a hot day. First Ana gets out the hose. Roberto turns on the water. Then Ana holds the hose so that Roberto can run throught the spray. After that, Roberto holds the hose so that Ana can run through the spray.

Have pupils identify the signal words they heard in the paragraph. Write them on the chalkboard. (*first, then, after that*) Then have volunteers read the sentences on the chalkboard and tell which sentence comes first, next, and last.

■ **Skillpack page 3**

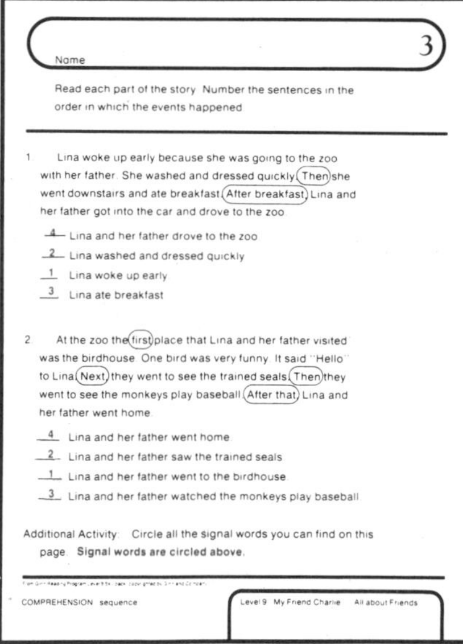

Name 3

Read each part of the story Number the sentences in the order in which the events happened

1 Lina woke up early because she was going to the zoo with her father She washed and dressed quickly Then she went downstairs and ate breakfast After breakfast Lina and her father got into the car and drove to the zoo

4 Lina and her father drove to the zoo
2 Lina washed and dressed quickly
1 Lina woke up early
3 Lina ate breakfast

2 At the zoo the first place that Lina and her father visited was the birdhouse One bird was very funny It said "Hello" to Lina Next they went to see the trained seals Then they went to see the monkeys play baseball After that Lina and her father went home

4 Lina and her father went home
2 Lina and her father saw the trained seals
1 Lina and her father went to the birdhouse
3 Lina and her father watched the monkeys play baseball

Additional Activity Circle all the signal words you can find on this page **Signal words are circled above.**

COMPREHENSION sequence

Level 9 My Friend Charlie All about Friends

DECODING

Long Words: Decoding long words (Introduction, Practice 1)

RECALL Briefly review the decoding of compound and affixed words by following these steps. Write *farm, house,* and *farmhouse* on the chalkboard. Ask pupils to read the words and then identify the word that is a compound word. (*farmhouse*) Recall that a compound is a word made up of two smaller words. Have a volunteer point to the words *farm* and *house* in *farmhouse*.

Write *playful* on the chalkboard. Remind pupils that prefixes and endings are sometimes added to such roots as *play*. Have a volunteer identify the ending. (*-ful*) Have another volunteer point to the root *play*. Below *playful* write *replay*. Have the word read, and elicit the fact that it is made up of the root *play* and the prefix *re-*. Have a volunteer point to the root and the prefix in *replay*. Establish the idea that prefixes and endings add meanings to roots. Elicit the meanings of the prefix *re-* (*again, back*) and the suffix *-ful (full of*).

RECOGNIZE Have the group read aloud the words on the chalkboard. (*farmhouse, playful, replay*) Point out that, as they are reading, they will often meet long words. Tell pupils:

> When you come across a long word in your reading, see whether it is a compound word or whether it has a prefix or an ending.

The list that follows presents three strategies for decoding long words. These will be taught over a series of practice lessons. The strategies are to be used by pupils in the order presented. If the first fails to produce a word pupils know, they should go on to the next. In addition, decoding a word may require the use of more than one strategy. You may want to write each of the three strategies on chart paper as you focus on it. Display the chart for reference by pupils.

1. Look for compound words. Find the smaller words in the compound. Say the smaller words together to read the whole word. (mailbox, toothbrush)

2. Look for prefixes and endings. Find a root and an ending or a prefix. Say the root with the ending or prefix. (walking, gladly, undo, redoing)
3. Look for the vowel and consonant spellings in the root. If you find a two-letter vowel try its most common sound first. (reason, mountain) If you find two or more consonants between the vowels, try decoding the first vowel with a short vowel sound first. (channel, chicken, banter, pitcher) If you find one consonant letter between the vowels, try decoding the first vowel with a long vowel sound first. Say the whole word. (vacant, even, tiger)

EXERCISE Write these words on the chalkboard: *careless, saucepan, unwise.* Explain to pupils that these words may be new to them; however, they should be able to use what they know about decoding longer words to read each one. Point to *careless.* Ask:

> Is this a compound word or a word with a prefix or an ending you know? (*a word with an ending:* -less) What is the root? (*care*) Who will read the whole word by saying the root with the ending?

Continue in a similar manner with the other two words, eliciting the fact that *saucepan* is a compound word and that *unwise* is made up of a root and a prefix.

APPLY Write these words on the chalkboard.

birdhouse	helpful
reread	watching

Have pupils use what they know about decoding long words to read the four words.

Then read these incomplete sentences, asking volunteers to point to and read the word that best completes each sentence. Fill in the blanks with the appropriate words.

1. There is a _____ in a tree in our yard. (*birdhouse*)
2. I was _____ TV when the telephone rang. (*watching*)
3. Jim wanted to _____the exciting part of the story. (*reread*)
4. If you want to be _____, please make your bed. (*helpful*)

■ **Skillpack page 4**

▲ **Studybook page 16**

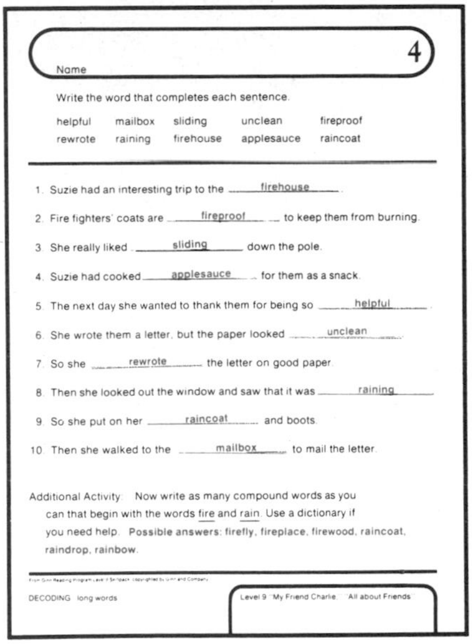
Name 4

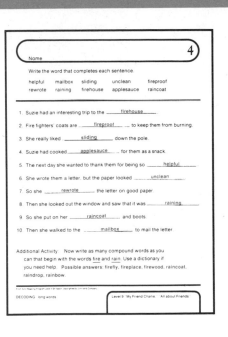

Write the word that completes each sentence.

helpful	mailbox	sliding	unclean	fireproof
rewrote	raining	firehouse	applesauce	raincoat

1. Suzie had an interesting trip to the ___firehouse___.
2. Fire fighters' coats are ___fireproof___ to keep them from burning.
3. She really liked ___sliding___ down the pole.
4. Suzie had cooked ___applesauce___ for them as a snack.
5. The next day she wanted to thank them for being so ___helpful___.
6. She wrote them a letter, but the paper looked ___unclean___.
7. So she ___rewrote___ the letter on good paper.
8. Then she looked out the window and saw that it was ___raining___
9. So she put on her ___raincoat___ and boots.
10. Then she walked to the ___mailbox___ to mail the letter.

Additional Activity: Now write as many compound words as you can that begin with the words fire and rain. Use a dictionary if you need help. Possible answers: firefly, fireplace, firewood, raincoat, raindrop, rainbow.

DECODING: long words

Level 9 "My Friend Charlie," "All about Friends"

4 Extending Reading Skills for Individual Needs

LANGUAGE

Writing: Writing an advice column

To give practice writing letters, begin by telling pupils that many newspapers have advice columns. People write letters asking for advice, and a writer for the newspaper answers them so that all can read and share the advice. Read the following sample:

> Dear Friendship Advisor:
> When my friend comes to play at my house, he plays with my favorite toys the whole time. He never lets me take a turn. What can I do? I really like him a lot, but I think he should share.
> Signed,
> George
>
> Dear George:
> Ask if you can borrow the kitchen timer. Set the timer for a certain time, such as three minutes. When the bell goes off, exchange toys.
> Signed,
> The Friendship Advisor

INDEPENDENT ACTIVITY Have pupils write letters to the Friendship Advisor. Have pupils exchange them and answer each other's letters. Read the letters and the answers. Have pupils discuss the advice. Ask if there are other ways to solve the problems. Let pupils decide which might work best.

▲ **Studybook page 17**

LITERATURE

Poetry: Listening to poetry that creates a picture

The story "My Friend Charlie" describes two friends who get along very well. The following poem describes friends enjoying a good time together. Distribute copies of the poem "Bursting" or read it aloud to the class. Point out to pupils that authors and poets create pictures in the readers' minds through their descriptive literature and poetry. Using words to suggest pictures is called *imagery*. Now read the poem several times so that pupils can form an image of what the poem is describing.

Bursting
We've laughed until my cheeks are tight.
We've laughed until my stomach's sore.
If we could only stop we might
Remember what we're laughing for.
—Dorothy Aldis

INDEPENDENT ACTIVITY Invite pupils to write about times when they have laughed so hard that their stomachs ached. Invite discussion about the pure joy of laughter. Drawings may accompany the stories

ARTS

Making posters

Explain that posters illustrate slogans or sayings, and that a piece of advice may be treated like a slogan in a poster. Point out that illustrating an idea emphasizes its meaning.

INDEPENDENT ACTIVITY Invite pupils to choose favorite pieces of advice or to write advice of their own. Have pupils create friendship posters showing the advice they like. Have them write the advice on the poster. Display posters around the room.

- *Presentation and Discussion of Prereading Questions.* Rarely did the observed teachers present and discuss questions before their pupils read a story from their basal. Most manuals present questions that can be asked of the pupils before they read a story for the first time and recommend that teachers ask such questions to guide pupils' reading.
- *Silent Reading of the Story.* Durkin reported that silent reading was uncommon in the first grade and, although third- and fifth-grade teachers used silent reading more often, they typically ignored the recommendations found in the manual. Basal manuals often recommend that teachers supervise pupils' silent reading by questioning pupils after they have read a few pages or discuss their reading immediately following silent reading of the whole story.
- *Meaningful Oral Reading or Rereading.* Basal manuals do not typically recommend oral reading or rereading of every story assigned to the pupils; however, these observed teachers spent a considerable amount of time on oral reading.
- *Instruction.* Today there is considerable emphasis being given to instructional procedures that focus on comprehension processes (see chapter 6) and meaningful supervised practice (see chapter 3). All teachers, except one fifth-grade teacher, used the manual sections on

Silent reading skills need to be developed at each grade level.

practice assignments. The focus, however, was on pupils' completing written practice assignments rather than using many of the manual's suggestions for instruction.

- *Practice Assignments.* Assignments that teachers can use are often abundant in basal manuals, but seldom is it suggested that teachers use every one of these. Fifteen of the sixteen observed teachers assigned all of the written practice activities found in the skill development portions (workbook pages and worksheets). None of these teachers used the manual when giving assignments, and there was no indication that assignments were used in terms of pupils' needs. Furthermore, these teachers failed to provide pupils with a purpose, review the format and directions, complete practice examples, or establish a relationship between the assignment and the ability to read (see chapter 3).
- *Provisions for Individual Differences.* Manuals include with most stories in the basal a section that is intended to help teachers differentiate their instruction and meet the needs of individual pupils. Durkin found that one third-grade teacher used these recommendations with the whole class, and a first-grade teacher used some of them for her whole class. The other teachers did not use the recommendations in their teaching.

Durkin's findings are limited because they deal with a small number of teachers who were observed for short amounts of time; however these findings are no different from those reported by other classroom observation studies (6). The reasons that teachers do or do not use the suggestions and recommendations in basal reader manuals center around two common explanations: (1) teachers indicated that they do not have the time to do everything the manual recommends and (2) teachers often felt that the manual recommendations were not important. It was Durkin's opinion that these two concerns should have been connected. That is, if teachers don't have the time to do all that is recommended they should give time to those recommendations that would develop and enhance pupils' reading abilities. Durkin offers the following recommendations for use of the basal manual, which have direct implications for improving the quality of reading instruction:

> Giving more time to new vocabulary, background information, prereading questions, instruction on essential topics, and better but fewer assignments, and . . . spending less time on oral reading and comprehension questions, is a possible change that is not likely to promote any more problems than were seen in the classroom. What the different allotment of time may promote, however, is better readers. (p. 744)

We will now turn our attention to many of the components found in a basal manual and the teaching of reading using a basal.

Design and Content. Basal readers are designed to bring children, through a series of books of increasing difficulty levels (a separate child's book for each level), to a high degree of reading proficiency. Each level is viewed as a prerequisite for success at the next succeeding level. Depending upon the particular basal program, each book beginning with level one (usually readiness) carefully develops reader competence in reading readiness, word identification, vocabulary, comprehension, and study skills. For example, the Ginn Reading Program 1985© basal program systematically develops reading skills through sixteen levels (3). The levels and the approximate corresponding grade(s) are given below:

Level		*Title*
Kindergarten		Animal Crackers Text, or Animal Crackers Kit
Level 1	Readiness	One Potato Two
Level 2	PP[1]	Little Dog Laughed
Level 3	PP[2]	Fish and Not Fish
Level 4	PP[3]	Inside My Hat
Level 5	P	Birds Fly, Bears Don't
Level 6	1	Across the Fence
Level 7	2	Glad to Meet You
Level 8	2	Give Me a Clue
Level 9	3	Mystery Sneaker
Level 10	3	Ten Times Round
Level 11	4	Barefoot Island
Level 12	5	Ride the Sunrise
Level 13	6	Flights of Color
Level 14	7	A Road to Travel
Level 15	8	The World Ahead

All basal programs include a tremendous number of materials. These materials are for both teachers and students. For teachers, programs may include: (1) a teacher's edition for each level, giving detailed lesson plans for each story in the child's book and a complete listing of skills to be taught at each level; (2) various instructional supplements for application of skills; (3) prepared pictures of characters and word cards for specific stories; (4) various films, filmstrips, and recordings; (5) teacher editions of student workbooks; and (6) a management system, including an informal reading inventory, criterion-referenced pre- and post-tests for each level, and various record-keeping devices. For students, basal programs may include: (1) a student book for each level, (2) a workbook for each level, (3) supplemental games and activities to practice skills being taught, and (4) high interest-low vocabulary paperback books.

Using a Basal Reader Series. Although the abundance of materials in basal programs can be overwhelming, the crucial point to remember is that materials do not guarantee an exciting and worthwhile program. It takes an effective teacher of reading to orchestrate materials based on learner needs to result in profitable instruction. Some of the advantages of using a basal series include the following:

- Basal readers have excellent photographs and artwork.
- A number of the first books used deal with the same characters, giving children a feeling of familiarity with the material and adding to their confidence in reading.
- The books are sequenced in increasing difficulty to provide systematic instruction from the prereadiness level through the upper elementary grades.
- These graded materials permit teachers a great deal of flexibility in dealing with individual differences and in working with children grouped according to attained reading skills.
- Excellent teacher guides are provided for each book or level. These provide suggestions for a step-by-step teaching program.
- If used properly, the basal reader series deals with all phases of the reading program, guarding against overemphasis on some aspects and neglect of others.
- Practice of new skills is introduced in a logical sequence.
- A great deal of review is provided in deliberate, well-thought-out procedures.
- The vocabulary is controlled to prevent frustration in beginning reading.
- Use of prepared materials saves teachers considerable time.
- Diagnostic tests provided by the series are keyed to the materials teachers will use.

Teacher's Edition. One of the greatest advantages in using a good series is the availability of teacher editions. These editions are carefully worked out by the authors with the total reading program in mind. Specific techniques are suggested, lesson plans are given in great detail, and the reasons for using certain approaches are explained. The beginning teacher would be remiss in not becoming very familiar with the rationale and concrete suggestions they contain. Experienced teachers might find the detail of these manuals a bit tedious, but they know that they can take what is offered and adapt it in light of their own experience and pupils' learning needs. However, the teacher's edition is only an advantage if teachers use it properly (3). Teachers should not be awed by these impressive volumes and follow them word for word. This is not teaching. Teachers know their students' learning needs better than any teacher's guide. Remember, a knowledgeable and flexible teacher is the key in using basal materials. Use the guide's suggestions when they meet your children's learning needs and supplement and adapt suggestions at all other times. "My Friend Charlie" and "All About Friends," a sample lesson plan from a teacher's edition of a basal reading series, was illustrated earlier in the chapter.

Use of Workbooks. As pointed out previously, workbooks constitute one of the important supplementary features of a basal reader series. The educational value of using workbooks has been debated for years. It is true that seatwork in the form of workbook exercises can deteriorate into nothing more than "busy work" if teachers permit this to occur. Yet, with proper teacher-directed instruction, the child can be guided to become actively engaged in meaningful practice. (A workbook page is shown on the last page of the color insert.)

Properly used, workbooks can have considerable educational value. Since a wide variety of skills are dealt with, it is likely that some exercises can be found that provide needed and meaningful practice in mastering essential skills. Workbooks can serve as ongoing diagnostic instruments since they will identify those children who do not understand

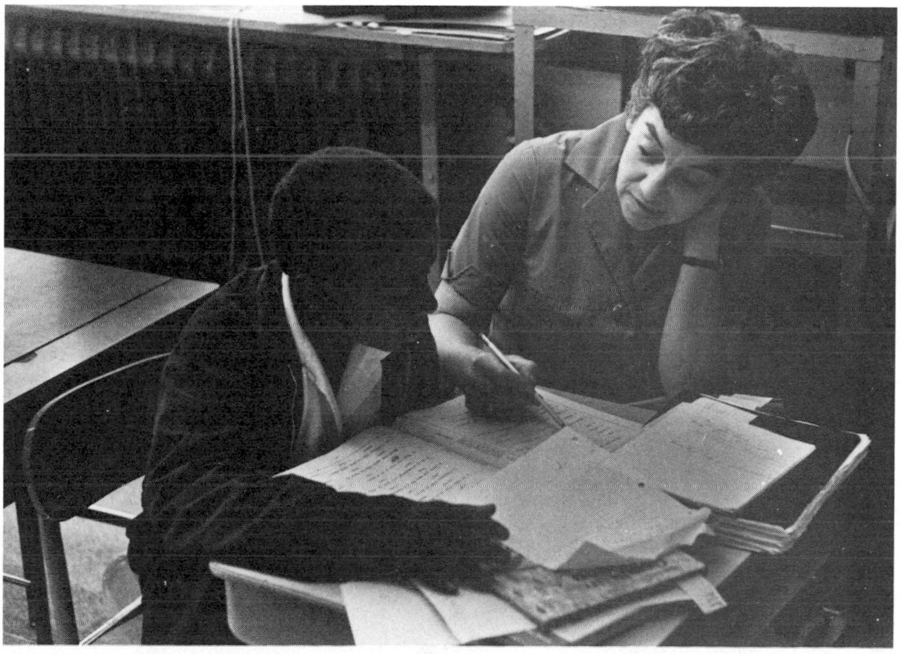

When workbooks are used properly they have considerable educational value.

a particular step in the reading process. A study of errors made by children will suggest to the alert teacher where further instruction is needed. For some children, workbook exercises have value in that they are brief—usually one page. This factor is especially appealing to the child with a short attention span.

Workbooks, like all other instructional media, are neither basically good nor bad. The ways in which workbooks are used determine whether or not they contribute to a quality reading instructional program. Important guidelines for workbook tasks have been identified by Osborn (12). These guidelines should be given careful consideration in the use of workbooks and worksheets that accompany basal reading series.

1. Workbook activities should match the instruction and learning that is taking place in the unit or lesson.
2. A part of workbook tasks should provide for systematic, cumulative, and meaningful review of what pupils have been taught.
3. Workbooks should match the most important learnings that are taking place in the reading program. Activities of lesser importance should be completed as voluntary activities.
4. Workbooks should have easily accessible provisions for relevant tasks for pupils in need of extra practice.
5. Both the vocabulary and the concept features of the workbook tasks should be within the experiential/conceptual background of the pupils and relate to the rest of the program.
6. Language features of the workbook (see chapter 2) should be consistent with those used in the instructional lesson and the rest of the workbook.
7. Instructions for completion of the workbook activity should be clear and easy to understand and follow. One or two practice examples should be completed with teacher direction to assure that pupils understand the tasks.
8. Page layout should combine both attractiveness and utility.
9. Content should be sufficient enough to assure that pupils are learning and not just being exposed to something.
10. Discrimination workbook activities should be preceded by a sufficient number of tasks that provide for practice of the components of the discriminations.
11. Content of workbook activities should be accurate and precise to assure that neither incorrect information nor rules are presented.
12. Some workbooks tasks should be fun.
13. The manner in which pupils respond should be consistent from workbook task to workbook task.
14. Response modes should match as closely as possible reading and writing.

15. Cute and nonfunctional workbook activities, which may be time consuming (busy work), should be avoided.
16. Workbook tasks should include discussions and illustrations by the teacher about its purposes and how the task relates to reading.

Economy of Time. Economy of teacher time is a major factor in the widespread use of basal series. This is closely related to the previous point of a balanced reading program. No teacher would ever have the time to match the meticulous planning that is reflected in the total program of a good basal series. When teachers have materials available for teaching and drill on every facet of reading, they will have more time to prepare supplementary exercises as needed. It will still be necessary to prepare these exercises for certain pupils since the basal program cannot meet all individual needs. However, it is easier to prepare supplementary lessons for a few than it is to build the entire program for all pupils.

Synthetic Basals. Although each basal reader program differs in its rationale, sequence of skills, story content, and supplemental materials, these differences are minimal. There are, however, a few basal reader programs that differ in the initial emphasis given to meaning and word identification skills. While most basals hold meaning to be a paramount goal from the outset, a "synthetic" basal is one that places a strong emphasis on decoding skills early in the reading process. Comprehension instruction is not forgotten, but these basals place first importance on the decoding process, under the assumption that this will lead to more successful reading. Thus, the main difference is in the rate of introduction of decoding skills. Both types of basals include a decoding emphasis, but the synthetic basal provides a greater initial emphasis. For example, the *Basic Reading Series* published by the J.B. Lippincott Company (10) is one basal program that includes an early emphasis on decoding skills. In this program, forty-four sound-symbol correspondences are taught in first grade. Coordinated within the program is a full range of word identification, comprehension, and study skills.

Linguistic Basals. Although possessing many of the same general characteristics of basal programs, such as sequential skill development and different level student texts, teacher editions, and supplementary materials, linguistic reading programs differ substantially in their philosophy and rationale. *The Merrill Linguistic Reading Program* (20) is based upon the philosophy of linguist Charles Fries (8). Reading is viewed as responding to the same language children already know in oral form.

Basal readers previously discussed have a controlled vocabulary. Words for beginning reading were primarily selected on the basis of use-

FLASHBACK

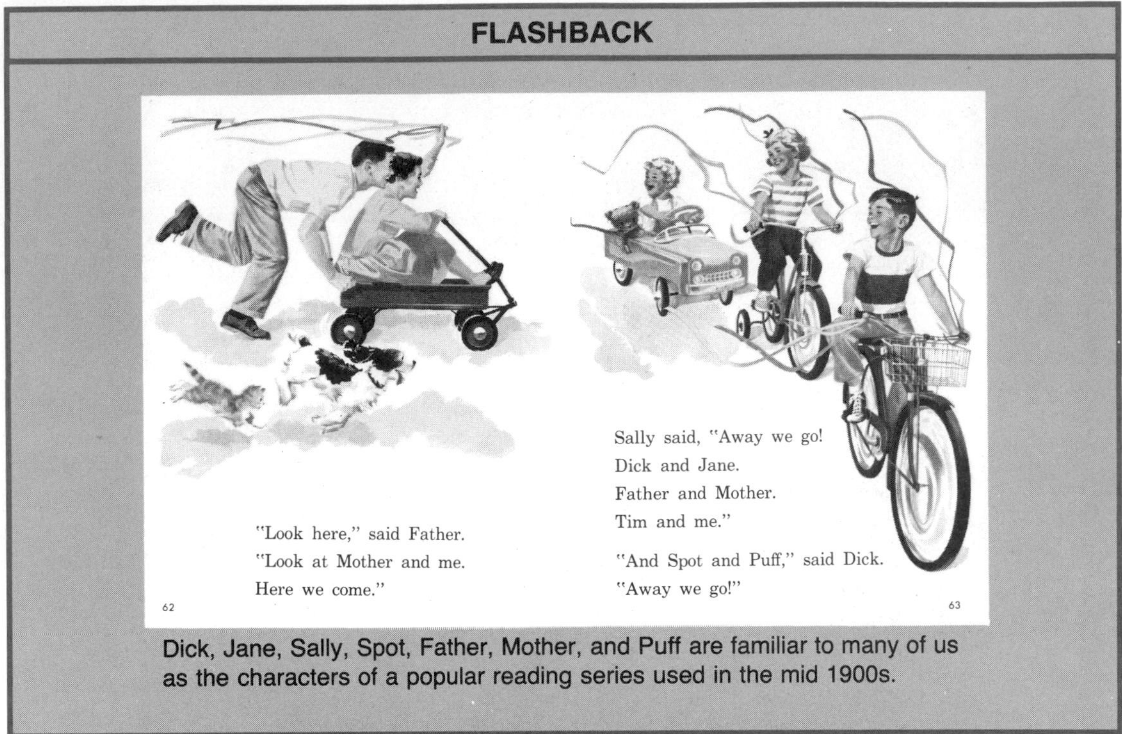

"Look here," said Father.
"Look at Mother and me.
Here we come."
62
Sally said, "Away we go!
Dick and Jane.
Father and Mother.
Tim and me."
"And Spot and Puff," said Dick.
"Away we go!"
63

Dick, Jane, Sally, Spot, Father, Mother, and Puff are familiar to many of us as the characters of a popular reading series used in the mid 1900s.

fulness (children would come across them frequently in the reader) and meaningfulness. The controlled vocabulary for linguistic readers is based upon meaningfulness and words that fit prescribed spelling patterns (CVC, VCE, CVVC).[2] New words are either first learned as sight words (irregular in nature) or taught using minimal contrasting pairs (words that reflect one of the three spelling patterns). For example, in teaching the word *hat,* the teacher would write it on the board, pronounce it, spell it, use it in a sentence, have pupils say and spell the word, and contrast the word with a word differing in only one phoneme, such as *cat.* Much practice is given in linguistic readers so children will automatically see the spelling pattern and pronounce the word.

In addition to selecting words in relation to prescribed spelling patterns and using minimal contrasting pairs to teach new words, many linguistic readers (1) provide no explicit attention to the link between individual phonemes and graphemes, (2) recommend that phonemes never be isolated from words and identified as separate entities, and (3)

2. CVC = consonant, vowel, consonant (e.g., *cat*); VCE = vowel, consonant, final *e* (e.g., *ate*); CVVC = consonant, vowel, vowel, consonant (e.g., *team*).

recommend that intonation in oral reading be stressed, as it is assumed that it relates to successful comprehension.

Directed Reading Activity. As already mentioned in the review of Durkin's article (6) on teachers' use of basal manuals and illustrated, an integral part of the basal reader teacher's edition is the systematic description of how to teach a reading lesson. It is important to understand that the ultimate purpose of each story in a basal reader is to teach children skills and abilities needed to become independent readers who can comprehend and learn from reading. Thus, each story is a vehicle that teachers can use to increase youngsters' reading abilities. This set of suggested procedures for teaching a reading lesson is commonly referred to as a directed reading activity (DRA). The DRA provides a framework to ensure systematic and sequential growth of reading and language abilities. Although every basal series has a particular description of the DRA, most contain similar components.

In an effort to provide a model for teaching an integrated reading lesson plan based upon the assumption that reading is a thinking process, Pieronek (13) lists the following steps for teaching a reading lesson:

1. Concept development
2. Vocabulary recognition
3. Setting overall goals for comprehension
4. Directed reading and thinking activity
5. Purposeful oral reading
6. Follow-up activities
7. Enrichment

There is no set way to teach a reading lesson. Information found in the manual should be viewed as recommendations, some of which may have to be modified, expanded, deleted, or reordered in relation to pupils' existing abilities. The first steps involve preparing children for reading (steps 1–3 from the preceding list).

Concept development is often referred to in the DRA as building background. Recommendations in the manual may include motivating children to read the story by using pictures, real objects, or discussion of the story's theme. Some manuals may include this step in the purpose-setting phase or in the story introduction. This step of a DRA is extremely important (6, 11) in helping pupils activate their experiential/conceptual background in relation to the story content (see chapter 6). Teachers may have to supplement or expand the recommendations found in the manual for background information. Sometimes just telling the pupils will not be as effective as using concrete examples and illustrations. Procedures that are to help pupils identify with the story may have to be modified or broken down into simpler but related parts. For example, a story set in a foreign country may require that the teacher help the children understand how events in the story are similar or different to experiences that they have had, rather than just telling them how certain events are different.

Another step in the prereading portion of a DRA is introduction of new vocabulary words. New or difficult words should be presented in written context, providing students with clues to the meaning of each word. The focus should be on the new words. Some manuals will classify the story vocabulary as new words, basic words, review words, enrichment words, and so forth. It is important that teachers evaluate whether or not their pupils know the words found in a story in relation to existing capabilities rather than how the manual has classified the words. Some words identified as review may in fact be new words for some students, and some new words may be review words for others.

Setting the stage for meaningful silent reading of the story is accomplished by providing children with purpose setting or prereading questions. Such questions can be given orally or in written form. If the teacher thinks that children may forget such questions, she can write the purpose-setting questions on the chalkboard for the children to refer to as they read. These guiding questions can be provided by the teacher or by the students themselves. Although a mix of both teacher- and student-initiated questions is desirable, encouraging student questions can lead to students' becoming more actively involved. An important consideration in identifying prereading questions is deciding whether or not those recommended in the manual are appropriate for enhancing comprehension. Manual questions may either focus too much on minor story details or be too broad and reveal too much about the story plot (6).

Following the preparatory steps in teaching a lesson, students are directed to read all or part of the story silently. The amount read silently will depend upon the story length, content, and students' ability. If the story is to be broken into two or more segments, they should be logically determined before starting the lesson. Of crucial importance to step 4 in Pieronek's model is the development of meaningful reading. In addition to the overall purpose-setting question, specific questions generated by the teacher or the student are formulated to guide the silent reading. Following the silent reading, attention to these questions is given immediately. Furthermore, comprehension questions are asked that require children to recall facts and main ideas, infer ideas, and react critically and personally to story content. A balance of such questions is paramount. (Comprehension questions are discussed in chapter 6.)

The encouragement of student-generated questions on story content throughout the DRA is advocated by Singer (17). He encourages teachers to foster "active comprehension" in students by encouraging students to ask their own questions on story content. Singer states that "the objective of teaching comprehension is to have students learn to ask their own questions and guide their own thinking so that they can become independent in the process of reading and learning from text" (17, p. 904).

Following a comprehension check of the story, an optional step in the DRA is purposeful oral reading of selected portions of the story. If oral reading (step 5) is to be included in the lesson, it must be meaningful to the students. For example, students might be asked to read the funniest part of the story, the saddest part, the answer to a particular question, or parts of the story to be acted out in class. Although some stories are meant to be read aloud, the day after day reading of every story aloud by members of the class is both a waste of time and a probable cause of difficulties. The encouragement of word-by-word silent reading and the development of a poor self-concept are two such difficulties.

The next step in a DRA involves follow-up or practice activities. Using either the story or the workbook as a vehicle, specific skills and abilities are practiced and applied, depending upon pupils' needs. Such activities may be done in a setting supervised by the teacher or independently. The guidelines presented earlier for the use of workbooks and worksheets should be used to assure that these are valuable and meaningful for the pupils and that quality reading instruction is taking place.

The final step in teaching a reading lesson is to provide enrichment activities related to the story. Although this step is important to foster independent and creative learning, it is often omitted because of the pressure to concentrate on basic skills and to cover a certain number of stories. However, this step can be capitalized upon by teachers to bring to life the joy of reading to children. Ways of providing enrichment for a particular story are endless. Ideas include panel discussions, puppet shows, choral speaking, music and art activities, dramatization, creative writing, and independent reading.

The overriding theme of an effective DRA is that the teacher is the key in selecting appropriate activities, depending upon pupil needs. No teachers' manuals can make reading a meaningful and enjoyable experience. A thinking teacher who views the lesson plans in a manual as guides and not as mandates will more likely succeed in providing effective reading instruction.

Important Considerations in Using a Basal. Basal manuals offer teachers many suggestions for teaching reading, but these suggestions should not be followed blindly nor should they be totally ignored (15). As mentioned earlier, teachers should use their knowledge of pupils' needs and entering capabilities to determine which recommendations need to be modified and which should not be used. Mason (11) has identified three important features that teachers should consider in evaluating and pre-

Teachers should use their knowledge of pupils' needs and abilities to determine what to modify and delete from the basal manual.

paring lessons in manuals. First, the organization of the lesson may have to be modified so that it focuses on the story's topic, illustrates its purpose or value, and relates to pupils' existing knowledge and to other texts. Second, activities that relate to the workbooks and worksheets should be chosen selectively; not all of them recommended in the manual need be assigned. Activities that are questionable in value, too lengthy, or do not deal with the lesson at hand could be omitted, which would allow for more teacher-directed instruction. Third, alternatives for independent pupil work and practice need to be developed by the teacher. Such independent activities as library reading, research projects, and creative writing will foster pupils' comprehension abilities. Furthermore, teachers should guard against using any basal manual recommendations that would interrupt text-related events or lesson-related events, such as assigning pupils a story to read and not discussing it following the silent reading, using a workbook or worksheet activity in the middle of a lesson, or letting worksheet exercises take the place of teacher-directed instruction focusing on enhancing pupils' comprehension abilities.

The Language Experience Approach

The process of learning to read does not depend on moving through a particular body of content. It consists of mastering a derived language process that is a long-term developmental endeavor. The child can learn needed reading skills through the use of any of a number of printed passages. Regardless of what other materials may have been adopted by schools or used by teachers, most teachers of beginning reading include teacher-written charts and stories in their reading programs. Using pupil experiences as the content for writing charts and stories is a long-standing practice. Throughout the years, modifications and extensions have resulted in renewed emphasis on this procedure. Hall (9) succinctly summarizes the rationale and philosophy of the language experience approach (LEA):

> The language experience approach for teaching reading is based on the interrelatedness of language and reading with the experience of the learner as the core from which language communication radiates. Language experience reading is viewed as a communication process closely related to communication in speaking, listening, and writing. The approach uses children's oral language and experiences for the creation of personal reading materials. This approach to reading integrates the teaching of reading with the other language arts as children listen, speak, write, and read about their personal experiences and ideas. A child's speech determines the *language patterns* of the reading materials, and his experiences determine the *content*. The language experience approach is based on the concept that reading has the most meaning to a pupil when the materials being read are expressed in his language and are rooted in his experiences. (p. 2)

Features of a Typical LEA. Although there are many variations of the language experience approach, there are some basic features of a typical LEA that would be beneficial for teachers to know when using this approach. An outline of a basic LEA is presented below and is discussed next.

- Shared experience for the students
- Shared talk about the experience
- Decisions about the written product
    - Group chart story
    - Individual student story

- Shared reading of the stories by the students
- Follow-up activities

The Experience Chart. The experience chart is a means of capturing the interest of children by tying their personal experiences to reading activities. The chart, which tells about a shared activity, is a story produced cooperatively by the teacher and the class. It is often an extension of earlier and less difficult experiences wherein the teacher wrote single words, short sentences, days of the week, names of months, the seasons, and dates of children's birthdays and holidays on the chalkboard. The experience chart provides practice and application in a number of developmental skills that are closely related to reading. For example:

- Oral language usage in group planning prior to a trip and in recounting the experience, for chart building, after a trip.
- The give-and-take of ideas as the experience is discussed.
- Sharpening sensory acuity, particularly visual and auditory, while on excursions.
- Developing and expanding print-related concepts, such as directionality (left to right), space between letters and words, punctuation, capital letters, and relationship between oral and written language.
- Expanding concepts and vocabulary.
- Experience in learning words as wholes in meaningful contexts, thus building sight vocabulary based on the child's language.
- Reading the sentence as a meaning unit.
- Reading about one's own experiences, emphasizing that reading is getting meaning from printed words.

All of the points cited above are appropriate both to readiness and to beginning reading, and the experience chart should not be thought of as belonging exclusively to one stage of development.

Preparing a Group Experience Story. The teacher plans a meaningful shared experience activity such as taking a field trip, viewing a film or filmstrip, hearing a story, reacting to a picture, observing an experiment, or participating in a class or school activity. Let us assume that the teacher has been able to make all the necessary arrangements for a trip to a nearby farm. She has organized the necessary transportation and has visited the farm to determine specifically what the children will experience. As a result of her visit, she has identified what the children need to know in order to benefit from the experience. Several days of teacher-directed instruction are devoted to preparing the children for their visit.

Following the trip to the farm, the teacher guided the children through a review of the highlights of their experiences. The review served to get all of the pupils actively involved and attending to the task

Shared experiences provide the basis for language experience stories.

that would follow—the writing of the experience story. After each student response, the teacher wrote it on the chalkboard or on large poster paper. The pupils were encouraged to respond by the teacher and to discuss their responses. The group-composed story follows:

Our Trip to the Farm

We went to Mr. Johnson's dairy farm.
We saw lots of cows.
We saw a machine that milks the cows.
The cows' heads are put in bars.
In Mr. Johnson's big barn, he milks five cows at once.

After the teacher and children read the complete story, a child was asked to point out the line that told what kind of farm they visited, the line that told the name of the owner of the farm, and so forth. In each case, the child pointed out the desired line and attempted to read it.

The same chart may be used in other ways. Each line in the chart may be duplicated on a strip of heavy paper. A child is handed a sentence and is asked to find this line on the chart. Individual words may also be printed on oaktag or cardboard and held up by the teacher while a child points out that particular word on the chart. Word cards may be prepared for each word in a particular line. These are handed to a child in mixed order, and he is to arrange them in proper order to correspond with the line on the chart. These tasks can be either seatwork or boardwork. The experience chart can be used with the class as a whole and also with various reading groups. After its main use with a unit, it may be referred to when certain words used on the chart come up in other contexts and in other activities.

Individual Experience Stories. Children enjoy talking about their experiences, particularly about incidents that involve them, their families, their pets, and the like. One of the best ways to take advantage of such motivation is to write individual experience stories. These language productions are usually brief, ranging from one to several sentences about one incident. In the early stages of reading, the stories are usually dictated by the pupils and written by the teacher. Since these brief stories relate to the child's own experiences, they encourage involvement in the reading situation. The stories are always meaningful and are written in complete sentences that parallel the child's own language usage.

Expansion/Variations of the Language Experience Approach. In addition to the features and uses of LEA that were mentioned earlier, there are a variety of ways that teachers can use this approach in reading instruction. Several ways to expand and vary the use of LEA have been suggested by Reimer (14) and are presented below:

- *Direct and Indirect Discourse.* Different colored pens can be used to record different speakers when recording a group experience story. Pupils can identify who said what by noting the color of the writing. It is important to use the same color marker for each child so children can associate that color with a particular child. Use a photograph of each child and attach a discourse balloon to help children understand who contributed what to a group story. These stories can be later rewritten with the youngsters and the color or picture replaced with the words, "Mary said," or "Billy said," to help pupils understand the function of these words in direct discourse. Indirect discourse can be taught by removing the punctuation marks and introducing the word *that*—Sue said that the horse is big.
- *Various Forms of Writing.* Group LEA can be used to introduce different forms of writing, such as the teacher demonstrating a science experiment and the group telling what happened; pupils reporting a shared experience by responding to reporter questions asked by the teacher (who, what, when, why, and where); and pupils learning about letter writing by composing a group letter to a sick classmate.
- *Shape Stories.* Children can be guided to write stories about an experience that is represented by a shape—fish, clown, car, dog, etc. As children dictate the story, the teacher writes it on the paper cut into a particular shape.
- *Written Dialogue.* This procedure works well with many youngsters at all elementary levels. Rather than talking with pupils, exchange notes. These notes may range from being extremely simple ("Good job!") to more lengthy paragraphs. Teachers should match the complexity of the note to pupils' ability to read and respond in writing. We have seen this used in several classrooms, and all of the children have been eager to participate. This variation of LEA help pupils understand the relationship between oral and written language and that written language must make sense to the reader.

A Broader View. The concept of language experience has been extended far beyond the group chart and the writing of individual stories. Today, the term *language experience* applies to practically every type of self-expression through language and every experience that involves the manipulation of language. In *Language Experience in Communication,* Allen (1) provides an excellent blueprint for expanding language experiences throughout the school curriculum.

The role of teachers has undergone considerable change also. They have assumed responsibilities far beyond those of scribes who write down stories children tell. Harnessing the child's ego by means of the personal story is still a widely used procedure. However, teachers have become more active partners in helping children expand concepts and language proficiency through the use of many other language stimuli (see figure 8.4).

Children write poetry, read poetry, and solve riddles (and make up some of their own). Language activities that focus both on learning about language and on using language as a tool for further learning are becoming major features of instruction (5). Working with homonyms and homographs, children learn that different words may be spelled the same and have different meanings and pronunciations—or spelled differently and have the same pronunciations. They learn about relationships through experiences with *analogies,* through combining sentences, and by arranging sentences into larger units. In working with language, students learn that a word may have dozens of meanings, that plurals are written in many ways, that new words are constantly being added to our language, and that over periods of time the meanings of words change.

Language experience is, thus, experiencing language. The teacher's role is to help children understand that

Writing a word is an achievement
Writing a story is a larger achievement
Combining stories into a book is quite a production.

Saying something one way is an achievement
Saying it another way and
  noting what you did the second time
  permits you to control language!

When you can control language
  you can, mold words like clay
        mix words like paints
        use words to draw pictures.

The next step is to let children try it. Let them tell or write the answer to the following question:

How many ways can a leaf fall?
"Down" you say.
Surely there's another way.
  A leaf can
  just fall—
    fall gracefully
  glide—
    glide like a glider
    glide and swerve
  sail—
    sail like a rudderless ship
    sail like it had a mind of its own

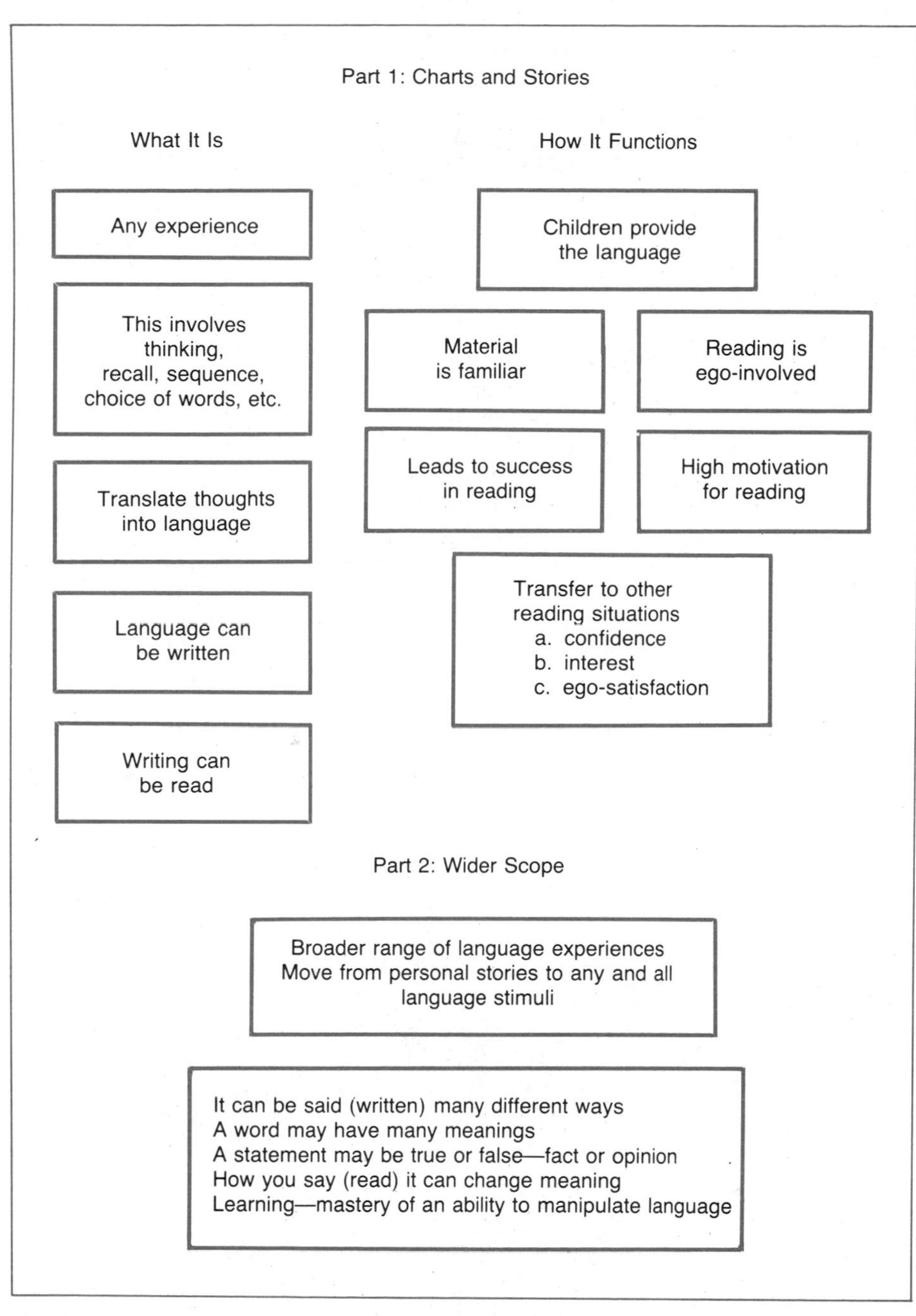

Part 1: Charts and Stories
What It Is
How It Functions
Any experience
Children provide the language
This involves thinking, recall, sequence, choice of words, etc.
Material is familiar
Reading is ego-involved
Translate thoughts into language
Leads to success in reading
High motivation for reading
Language can be written
Transfer to other reading situations
a. confidence
b. interest
c. ego-satisfaction
Writing can be read
Part 2: Wider Scope
Broader range of language experiences
Move from personal stories to any and all language stimuli
It can be said (written) many different ways
A word may have many meanings
A statement may be true or false—fact or opinion
How you say (read) it can change meaning
Learning—mastery of an ability to manipulate language

FIGURE 8.4 Basic Features of the Language Experience Approach

dip—
  dip and glide
  dip and rise and bank gracefully to a landing
dance—
  complete its solo dance
  dance with the wind
fall with no map to guide it—
  map its own course
  try many detours
  twist slowly in the wind.

How many ways can a leaf fall that we didn't write today?
"No other way," you say?
Don't you think leaves like to play?
  playfully! *(of course)*
    If in a hurry?
  plummet
    with memories of summer?
  reluctantly

The Experience Approach as a Method. Experience charts and stories can be used in any method of teaching reading or as the primary method itself. When a program limits instructional materials to this one type, the resulting instruction might be referred to as the *experience method.* Any procedure may have both merits and limitations, and this seems particularly true of the experience approach to teaching reading. The major strengths of experience stories and charts have been discussed previously; some potential weaknesses which may result from relying too heavily on teacher-written materials include:

- It is difficult to control vocabulary. Too many words may be introduced at one time.
- Basic sight words may not be repeated often enough to ensure mastery.
- When used exclusively as a method, it puts too much of a burden on the teacher, demanding much time and a high level of training.
- It is difficult to adapt this type of instruction to the needs and abilities of all children.
- It encourages memorization rather than mastery of sight words.

The strengths and weaknesses of the experience method are relative to teacher implementation and not inherent in the method itself. Under certain conditions, all of the advantages of the method might be lost through overemphasis, misuse, or lack of understanding. In other situations, the effects of certain of the cited disadvantages could be held to a minimum through a teacher's skill, experience, and clear understanding of objectives. In our opinion, the experience approach is most

The Search Begins

Once long ago in the Congo of Africa, deep in the jungle in a dark cave lived a unicorn, and a black tiger. The tiger was as black as the darkest night, and the unicorn was as white as clouds on a sunny day. The tiger was just a cub and the unicorn was just a colt, so they didn't know very much.

They loved their cozy cave home but one day their curiosity got the best of them and they started to explore parts of the cave they never saw before. The dark halls they walked through were cold and wet. The only light they had was the light of the unicorn's glowing horn and the tiger's glowing eyes, which wasn't much light.

As they walked along, they noticed it was getting bright. They turned the corner and saw a fire. The tiger was scared at first, but the unicorn liked the warm light of the fire right away but still she stayed far away from it. She thought it might be dangerous.

As they walked closer they heard a noise. From behind a rock a shadow appeared. All of a sudden a bird popped out from behind the rock. The bird was small and chubby, and she was gray as a misty morning. She was also very wise. The bird said, "Come closer."

But they just backed up. The bird said, "Come closer. Don't be scared." They came closer, slowly. The unicorn's white coat glowed as they walked closer to the fire. The tiger's black coat sparkled like the night stars.

Example of a child's creative writing, which is a variation of the language experience approach.

vulnerable when used as the total reading program. Most teachers prefer to use the experience chart as a supplement to basals and other materials. This permits certain of the weaknesses to be minimized. The basic readers provide a controlled vocabulary and systematic introduction and application of reading skills.

Language experience activities can enhance basal reading instruction and vice versa. Aspects of LEA can be used to accomplish the following:

- Provide for both individual and group reading instruction.
- Allow for practice, transfer, and application of word identification and comprehension skills in meaningful context.
- Build on and emphasize children's life and language experiences.

- Emphasize the relationship between oral and written language to help children understand that reading is the comprehension of ideas.
- Engage pupils in meaningful instruction based on their own interests.
- Encourage vocabulary development by pupils trying new words and using these new words in meaningful context.
- Develop better writers and children who will experiment with writing (16).

SUMMARY

The two major approaches to the teaching of reading have been delineated in this chapter. Attention was focused on the basal reader and language experience approaches because of their widespread use in today's elementary schools. Recommendations and guidelines for the use and adaptation of both approaches were outlined and illustrated with concrete examples. In addition to understanding the characteristics and assumptions of each of these approaches, a critical questioning attitude was recommended for their successful implementation. Since all approaches have particular strengths and weaknesses, it is imperative that teachers become thoroughly familiar with the features of an approach in relation to pupils' needs. Approaches and materials should be viewed as aids in the teaching of reading; approaches and materials do not teach reading, the teacher teaches reading. The teaching of reading at any level is a serious matter. Fitting approaches and materials to learner needs is absolutely necessary in order to give more than lip service to the importance of a successful reading instructional program.

YOUR POINT OF VIEW

Discussion Questions

1. Why are basal readers viewed as representative of the eclectic method?
2. Why would it be necessary for teachers to modify some features of a basal manual regardless of the pupils' capabilities in reading?
3. Which of the features of the basal reader lesson example (DRA) presented in this chapter would Durkin's findings suggest that teachers give the most attention?

Take a Stand For or Against

1. Someday reading researchers will find one reading approach that will work with all children.
2. All reading instruction materials that follow the structure and patterns of English usage can be said to be "linguistically sound" or to use "linguistic methods."
3. The amount of time it would take for teachers to integrate the features of a language experience approach with a basal reader approach would not be worth the effort nor would it be that beneficial to pupils.
4. Teachers who do not use the basic recommendations of a basal manual are probably better than teachers who use such recommendations.

BIBLIOGRAPHY

1. Allen, Roach V. *Language Experience Activities.* 2d ed. Boston: Houghton-Mifflin Publishing Co., 1981.
2. Auckerman, Robert C. *The Basal Reader Approach to Reading.* New York: John Wiley & Sons, 1981.
3. Clymer, Theodore, et al. *Ginn Reading Program © 1982, 1985.* Lexington, Mass.: Ginn & Co., 1985.
4. Corder, Reginald. "The Information Base for Reading: A Critical Review of the Information Base for Current Assumptions Regarding the Status of Instruction and Achievement in Reading in the United States." Washington, D.C.: National Center for Educational Research and Development, 1971.
5. Dole, Janice A. "Beginning Reading: More Than Talk Written Down." *Reading Horizons* 24 (Spring 1984): 161–66.
6. Durkin, Dolores. "Is There a Match Between What Elementary Teachers Do and What the Basal Reader Manuals Recommend?" *The Reading Teacher* 37 (1984): 734–44.
7. Feldhusen, Hazel J., Lamb, Pose; and Feldhusen, John. "Prediction of Reading Achievement Under Programmed and Traditional Instruction." *The Reading Teacher* 23 (1970): 446–54.
8. Fries, Charles C. *Linguistics and Reading.* New York: Holt, Rinehart & Winston, 1963.
9. Hall, MaryAnne, *Teaching Reading as a Language Experience.* 3d ed. Columbus, Ohio: Charles E. Merrill Publishing Co., 1981.
10. McCracken, Glen, et al. *Basic Reading Series.* Philadelphia: J. B. Lippincott Co., 1981.
11. Mason, Jana M. "An Examination of Reading Instruction in Third and Fourth Grades." *The Reading Teacher* 37 (1983): 906–13.
12. Osborn, Jean. "Workbooks That Accompany Basal Reading Programs." In *Comprehension Instruction: Perspectives and Suggestions,* edited by Ger-

ald G. Duffy, Laura R. Roehler, and Jana Mason, 163–86. New York: Longman, 1984.

13. Pieronek, Florence Terese. "Using Basal Guidebooks—The Ideal Integrated Lesson Plan." *The Reading Teacher* 33 (1979): 167–72.
14. Reimer, Becky L. "Recipes for Language Experience Stories." *The Reading Teacher* 37 (1983): 396–404.
15. Rosecky, Marion. "Are Teachers Selective When Using Basal Guidebooks." *The Reading Teacher* 31 (1978): 381–84.
16. Rupley, William H., and Blair, Timothy R. *Reading Diagnosis and Remediation: Classroom and Clinic.* 2nd ed. Boston: Houghton-Mifflin Publishing Co., 1983.
17. Singer, Harry. "Active Comprehension: From Answering to Asking Questions." *The Reading Teacher* 31 (1978): 901–8.
18. Singer, Harry; Samuels, S. Jay; and Spiroff, Jean. "The Effect of Pictures and Contextual Conditions on Learning Responses to Printed Words." *Reading Research Quarterly* 9 (1973–74): 355–67.
19. Smith, Frank. *Understanding Reading.* 2nd ed. New York: Holt, Rinehart & Winston, 1978.
20. Wilson, Rosemary G., et al. *Merrill Linguistic Reading Program.* 4th ed. Charles E. Merrill Publishing Co., 1986.

9

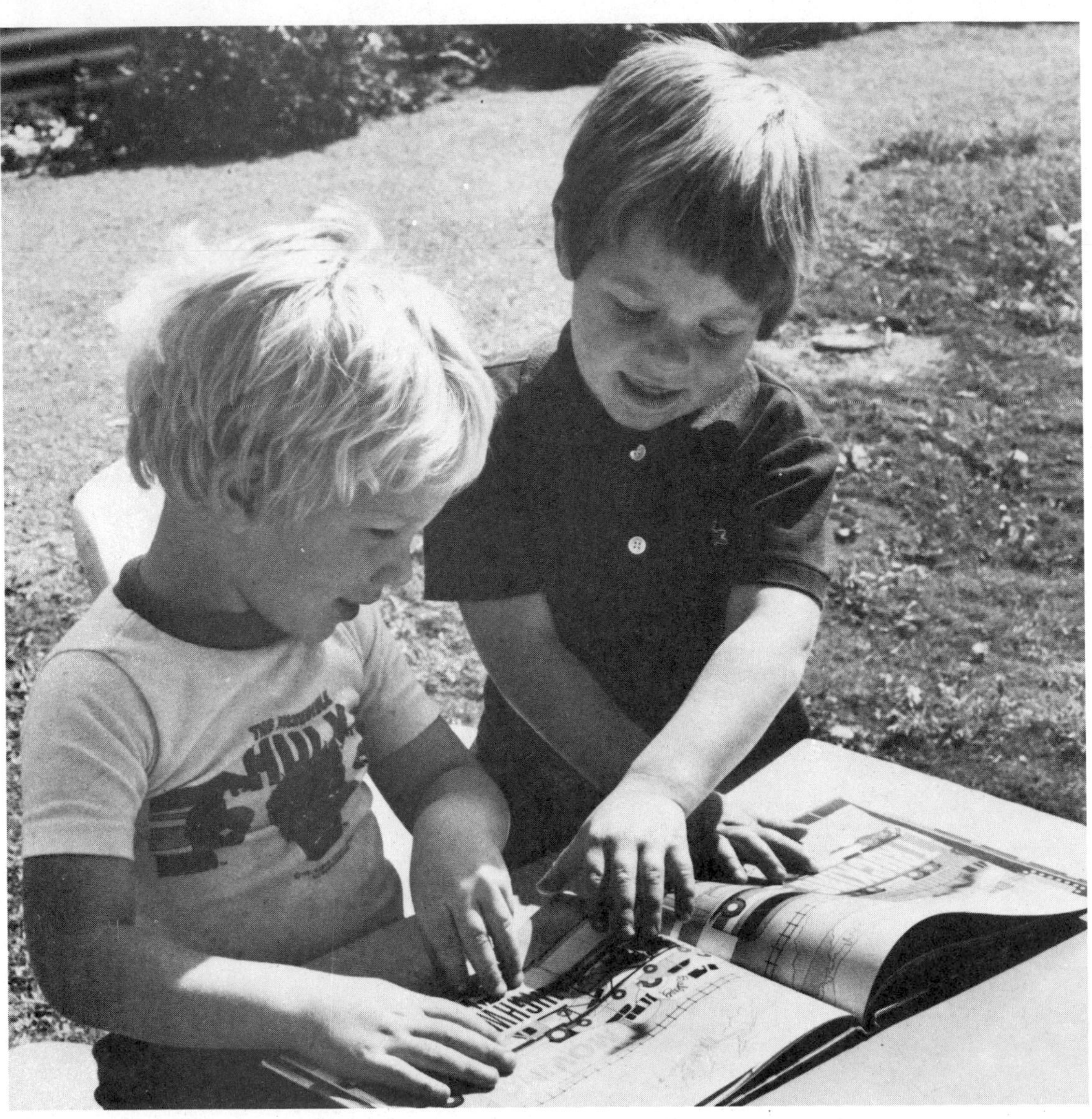

Reading: Primary Grades

For the Reader

Think back about your primary level reading experiences for a moment. Think about those things that you enjoyed. Enjoyable features of your primary grade reading were probably those that helped you understand the purposes for learning and dealt with actual reading tasks. This is not to suggest that you were not taught skills such as phonics, structural analysis, context clues, and so forth, but it was when you used these to read for meaning that they served their intended purposes. Other possible enjoyable moments may have been when:

- Your teacher read aloud to the class a good book.
- You shared an exciting part of a book with the class.
- You were introduced to the beauty of poetry.
- You wrote some original poems.
- You were taught how to apply your reading skills to get meaning from your reading.

Those features of your learning to read in the primary grades that you remember as being meaningful could most likely be classified as ones that were purposeful, completed successfully, valued by the teacher, and applied to reading for meaning. These features of effective reading instruction are extremely important in teaching primary level children to read. As we have stressed throughout the text, teaching children to read cannot be dictated by skills, grade level, or materials. The most important factor to consider when teaching reading is to meet your pupils' needs. Keep this point foremost in your mind as you read this chapter on teaching reading in the primary grades.

Preview

- Read over the Key Ideas that are presented next.
- Read each heading and subheading.
- Read the summary.
- Read the questions and statements at the end of the chapter.
- Return to the chapter text that follows the Key Ideas and begin reading.

Key Ideas

Systematic and planned primary reading instruction should be based on effective teaching strategies.

Materials and activities for instruction may include:
- basal readers
- supplementary materials (kits, newspapers, games, read-along books, predictable books, etc.)
- language experience materials
- library books
- content area textbooks
- poetry
- creative writing and dramatics
- oral and choral reading
- daily reading aloud by the teacher

Materials used for instruction should allow for extension of pupils' reading comprehension.

Reading instruction should strive to build on and to enhance pupils' conceptual, cognitive, and language development.

MEANINGFUL INSTRUCTION

Pupils' reading growth in the primary grades must be treated as developmental in nature. The accelerated pace at which new tasks are introduced makes it essential that both sound principles of teaching reading and effective instructional practices be followed. As with all reading instruction, the reading abilities that the pupil possesses are reinforced and extended.

To prevent both gaps in learning and overemphasis of particular skills, instruction must be systematic and planned. Systematic and planned primary grade reading instruction can be developed around those principles of effective teaching of reading presented in chapter 3. In review, those principles that are specific to teaching reading in the primary grades include:

Utilizing ongoing diagnosis to:
- Identify instructional activities and tasks that ensure maximum pupil success.
- Select instructional strategies appropriate to desired reading outcomes in relation to pupils' existing reading capabilities.
- Pace reading instruction by progressing in small, related steps to maximize pupils' success rate.

Employing teacher-direct instruction and structuring the classroom to:
- Direct pupils' learning with task-related comments rather than criticism.
- Vary the degree of structure in terms of the reading instructional task.
- Maximize pupils' involvement in tasks or academic activities related specifically to lesson content and desired outcomes.
- Be accessible to pupils as they work in small groups with a variety of materials.

Attending to pupils' opportunity to learn and apply skills in actual reading situations to:
- Assure that instruction focuses on desired and valued reading outcomes—comprehension of written language.
- Provide for application of reading skills in tasks that ensure maximum pupil success.
- Assure that pupils apply their reading skills for the purpose of reading enjoyment.

Maximizing pupils' attending to learning tasks to:
- Keep pupils actively engaged in their reading instruction.
- Engage pupils in reading tasks with which they will experience maximum success.
- Increase pupils' attention to and engagement in learning to read by providing feedback to them about their performance.
- Make reading meaningful by setting purposes and relating new learning to past learning by progressing in small, highly related steps.
- Help pupils understand how to apply what they have learned in meaningful reading situations.
- Reinforce specific attending behaviors by using positive reward systems that reward both pupils' thinking and efforts.

These features of effective reading instruction vary in terms of instructional focus and pupils' reading capabilities; however, attending to the four basic areas listed should enable the primary grade reading teacher to better analyze the effect of his instruction on pupils' reading growth. As specific features of primary grade reading instruction are presented in the following sections, appropriate principles of effective teaching of reading are also addressed.

Goals of Instruction

Many instructional goals for the primary reading instruction can be identified. However, as was noted in chapter 2, there are certain reading behaviors associated with children's success in reading in grades 1, 2, and 3 that must be considered by teachers of these grade levels. Several reading authorities have offered considerable insights and verification for a developmental view of reading. The important reading behaviors that were identified by Clay (5), Stanovich, Cunningham, and Freeman (24), and Chall (3) share common elements focusing on well-developed word identification strategies and understandings about the meaning features of print. A comprehensive illustration of the reading development stages for grades one, two, and three is one developed by Jeanne Chall (3). Her proposals for stages of reading development range from birth to eighteen years and above; the stages that are presented in figure 9.1 are those appropriate for the primary grades. It is important to note that there may be overlap of stages and that they are not fixed; that is, an eight year old could be in Stage 3 and a thirty year old could be in Stage 1. Characteristics associated with each stage should be viewed as representative and should serve as guidelines for planning quality reading instruction and for identifying goals of instruction.

The following list of goals of instruction for primary reading is based on developmental viewpoints of reading and cannot be thought of

1 Stage Designation	2 Grade Range (age)	3 Major Qualitative Characteristics and Masteries by End of Stage	4 How Acquired	5 Relationship of Reading to Listening
Stage 0: Prereading, "pseudo-reading"	Preschool (ages 6 months–6 years)	Child "pretends" to read, retells story when looking at pages of book previously read to him/her; names letters of alphabet; recognizes some signs; prints own name; plays with books, pencils, and paper.	Being read to by an adult (or older child) who responds to and warmly appreciates the child's interest in books and reading; being provided with books, paper, pencils, blocks, and letters.	Most can understand the children's picture books and stories read to them. They understand thousands of words they hear by age 6 but can read few if any of them.

continued

FIGURE 9.1 Stages of Reading Development for Primary Reading Instruction
(From Jeanne S. Chall, *Stages of Reading Development* [New York: McGraw-Hill Book Co., 1983], 85–86.)

Stage 1: Initial reading and decoding	Grade 1 & beginning Grade 2 (ages 6 & 7)	Child learns relation between letters and sounds and between printed and spoken words; child is able to read simple text containing high frequency words and phonically regular words; uses skill and insight to "sound out" new one-syllable words.	Direct instruction in letter-sound relations (phonics) and practice in their use. Reading of simple stories using words with phonic elements taught and words of high frequency. Being read to on a level above what child can read independently to develop more advanced language patterns, knowledge of new words, and ideas.	The level of difficulty of language read by the child is much below the language understood when heard. At the end of Stage 1, most children can understand up to 4000 or more words when heard but can read only about 600.
Stage 2: Confirmation and fluency	Grades 2 & 3 (ages 7 & 8)	Child reads simple, familiar stories and selections with increasing fluency This is done by consolidating the basic decoding elements, sight vocabulary, and meaning context in the reading of familiar stories and selections.	Direct instruction in advanced decoding skills; wide reading (with instruction and independently) of familar, interesting materials which help promote fluent reading. Being read to at levels above their own independent reading level to develop language, vocabulary, and concepts.	At the end of Stage 2, about 3000 words can be read and understood and about 9000 are known when heard. Listening is still more effective than reading.

as belonging exclusively to the primary period. Some will continue to be important throughout the intermediate, middle school, and secondary levels. The goals are intended to help children:

- Understand letter-sound relationships.
- Understand that printed words are made up of letters. These letters represent speech sounds that are blended to arrive at the identification of words that are not recognized.

- Develop the necessary visual and auditory discrimination skills that are needed for word identification strategies.
- Grasp the fact that reading is a meaning-making process.
- Expand their sight-recognition vocabulary.
- Expand language and understand that reading is working with language.
- Develop flexibility in identifying words so they can use all available cue systems to comprehend written language.
- Expand their experiential/conceptual background to broaden their knowledge of word meanings and concepts represented by print.
- Develop their ability to recognize known root words in new word forms that include prefixes or inflectional endings and understand how these influence meaning.
- Learn that some words have many different meanings and that the various meanings are "signaled" by context clues.
- Develop and expand concepts, noting that ideas are expressed through language.
- Develop continually the attitude and concept that reading is always purposeful and getting meaning is the goal of reading.

Systematic and planned primary grade reading instruction is developed around the principles of effective teaching and builds on the relationship between language and reading.

- Develop a large sight vocabulary.
- Develop the skill of reading as thought units, including phrases, sentences, and passages.
- Develop critical thinking through experiences that sharpen both critical listening ability and analysis of printed messages.

In addition to a systematic effort to build on what the pupils have learned and to extend skills previously introduced, many new developmental tasks are undertaken. A number of prefixes and suffixes are taught with an emphasis on both structural and meaning changes involved. Silent consonants (*k*nife, com*b*, i*s*land, li*gh*t) and other spelling irregularities will receive attention along with syllabication. Continued application and practice of all of these developmental tasks in meaningful context will need to be provided by the teacher.

Comprehension skills are developmental also and should be developed systematically in the primary grades. Context clues become more important as sentence structures become more complex and as new words are met more frequently. It is essential to learn new connotations for many words, and literal meanings cannot be insisted upon for figurative expressions. The reader must follow the sequence of ideas and see their relationship to each other. The ability to analyze the meaning of sentences must be extended to paragraphs and larger units so the main ideas of these larger units of materials can be grasped.

Where to Begin Instruction

Children in the primary grade reading program vary considerably in their reading capabilities. As noted in figure 9.1, some students may have reached Stage 2 or beyond in kindergarten or first grade, while others may not be at Stage 1 by the end of third grade. A concern for where to begin reading instruction is important for all primary grade teachers and is especially important for first-grade teachers because it is at this level that a strong foundation for future reading growth should be laid.

Instruction for the child who has not had a variety of experiences with written language will be different from instruction for the child who is already reading or who comes from an environment which provided him with opportunities to develop an understanding of print-related concepts. Children who have been read to; who played with books, paper, and pencils; and who can recognize signs, their names, and letters of the alphabet will require teachers to plan instruction that builds on these print-related concepts. A child who has had limited experiences with print or who perceives that reading is "sounding out words" will need instruction that helps him to understand that reading is a meaning-getting process. Placing such a child in a basal reader or jumping right into word recognition with him would be an inappropriate beginning.

Children who lack a background of reading-related experiences would benefit from initial reading instruction that is language based in its major focus. Such instruction would include many of the features noted in the "Language and Primary Reading Instruction" section and would include numerous opportunities for the children to experience print. For example, teachers could begin reading instruction with such children by using writing activities (see chapters 2 and 8), reading aloud to them daily, labeling objects in the room, using read-along books, and making many predictable books available to them. Thus, rather than placing such youngsters in the basal reader, the appropriate beginning point is to develop an environment that is "rich in print" to help the children acquire basic concepts that may not have been available to them prior to entering school.

MATERIALS AND TEACHING SCHEDULE

The prudent use of instructional materials is crucial at all levels in the teaching of reading. If meaningful instruction is to develop, materials should be looked upon as vehicles to achieve instructional goals.

Basal Materials

The relation of the basal reader series to the total reading program is much the same in first, second, and third grades. Growth in reading is developmental, and basal reader materials are designed with this fact in mind. Most facets of instruction are provided for in a logical sequence, and each receives varying degrees of emphasis. The essence of primary-level instruction is a continuous and systematic building of skills. When a child's growth does not parallel the materials found at his grade level, it is the pupil's achievement and rate of growth, not the materials, that must determine the instructional program. Basal reading materials at this level reflect a uniform eclecticism (20), emphasizing both comprehension and decoding. This balance is more likely to cultivate in the reader an attitude that demands comprehension from reading.

Pupils' purposes for reading are also broadened. Opportunities are provided to read for information, organization of data, and interpretation and appreciation of literature. Transfer and application of these reading skills to all reading situations involving subject matter and textbooks are systematically attended to by the teacher. Instructional procedures illustrating the transfer and application of such skills are discussed later in this chapter.

As children move through the primary grade levels, reading changes take place in the materials that they read. Stories become longer and include more concepts. There will be fairy tales and tales of animals who think and talk and have feelings. There will be stories of children whose experiences are similar to primary-age youngsters. There will be stories of children who live in different lands and do different things. The lives and contributions of great men and women will be studied. Teaching suggestions found in the teacher's editions of primary-level basals will often call for the readers to make interpretations. Pupils are asked to determine the mood of characters, see the relationships between events, and grasp the intended meaning of figurative or idiomatic expressions. Humor may not always be overt, and inferences may have to be drawn in the absence of absolute statements. The children may be asked to determine such things as "if grandfather was serious or just playing a joke on the boys," or "if Jerry was frightened by what he overheard," or "how the storm affected the plans for a vacation."

Primary Level Teachers' Editions. Based on your information of pupils' reading development gained from the use of ongoing diagnosis, the teaching suggestions found in teachers' editions of primary level basal series should be analyzed carefully to determine whether or not they are appropriate. Analysis of the suggested instructional procedures should focus on determining if they (1) build on pupils' past learning, (2) relate to valued learning outcomes, (3) provide for application, (4) maximize attention to and engagement in learning, and (5) possess the appropriate degree of teacher-directed instruction and structure. This analysis can result in a better match of reading instruction to your pupils' needs. How one might conduct such an analysis is presented in the following discussion.

We recommend starting your analysis by reading the pupils' text to become familiar with the reading skills required and to determine if the concepts presented are appropriate to your students' experiential/conceptual background. Also, by careful reading of the pupils' text, you can better evaluate each instructional activity to determine if it deals with skills and content presented in the story.

Following the reading of the text, shift your focus to the parts of the lesson that are for the teacher's information. Most teachers' editions contain teaching suggestions that include (1) lesson or behavioral objectives; (2) a summary or overview; (3) new vocabulary words; (4) motivation and/or purposes for reading; (5) discussion questions; (6) skill activities; and (7) supplementary, enrichment, or follow-up activities. (See chapter 6.)

As we mentioned earlier, these specific suggestions for teaching still must be carefully evaluated in terms of whether or not they fit your pupils' needs. For example, lesson objectives should be based on valued outcomes in relation to pupils' existing reading capabilities and build on past reading instruction. Objectives should also be content specific; that is, the content of the story should match the objectives. If the objectives are inappropriate for either the pupils or the story, they can be modified accordingly or replaced with ones that are more appropriate.

Text summaries or overviews are intended to familiarize the teacher with the pupils' text. However, since it is recommended that teachers read the text, they will rely less on the summaries as a means of becoming familiar with the story. A summary can serve as an overview for the students when the story is introduced to them. When it is used as an introduction, parts of it may have to be expanded or shortened in terms of the concepts that pupils need to enhance their comprehension. If the summary is used as an introduction it should be presented to the pupils just before purposes for reading are given and they begin to read. This will serve to make the purposes for reading more meaningful and increase pupils' attention to reading and engagement in instruction (14).

Other parts of the lesson in most primary level teachers' editions provide suggestions for teaching vocabulary, guiding pupils' reading, directing discussions, teaching skills, and providing for enrichment. Teachers can expand, shorten, or eliminate these suggestions, depending on the pupils' needs. Modification of each area can be addressed by the teacher by answering questions similar to those presented below.

- Are the instructional activities specific to pupils' entering abilities and do they build on what the children are already successful with?
- Do the instructional suggestions provide the appropriate degree of structure and teacher-directed instruction in relation to the desired pupil outcomes?
- Will the instructional suggestions maximize pupils' attention to learning and motivate them to become actively involved in the tasks?
- Are the suggested examples and illustrations specific enough to illustrate to the pupils what they are to do?
- Are the purposes for reading related to valued reading outcomes and do they allow for application of existing reading abilities?
- Will pupils' reading comprehension be enhanced as a result of engagement in the suggested instruction?

By using questions such as these to guide the evaluation of each lesson, you are able to decide which instructional suggestions need to be modified and how best to modify them. For example, you might determine that the purposes for reading for a given group of youngsters are too broad, and more specific purposes are written to replace them. Or the purposes for reading may not maximize pupils' attention to task and would be better if modified in relation to pupils' needs. Or the purposes may be too pupil directed and need to be replaced with ones that are more teacher directed. Decisions such as these cannot be reached unless the teacher is fully aware of pupils' reading capabilities and carefully analyzes each of the teaching suggestions.

Following the analysis and modification of the teaching suggestions there are some factors, such as time allotment, that will also have to be determined. Based on the instructional changes, the suggested time allotment may need to be either increased or decreased. It is important to have a good idea of how long it will take to complete the teaching of a lesson so that the necessary amount of instructional time can be allocated to assure that pupils are actively engaged in meaningful instruction.

The importance of careful analysis of any given primary level basal reading lesson is well summarized by Pieronek (22).

> Teachers have a great responsibility in designing lessons. Time should be spent selecting appropriate parts from manuals that accompany basals and assigning materials to accompany selections. Only well thought out plans can ensure that learners will engage successfully in the reading and thinking process. (p. 171)

Supplementary Materials

A basal reader series can provide the foundation for systematic instruction at the primary level, but these materials should not be thought of as the total reading program. Many types of materials are available for reading instruction that can be used with basal reading instruction. Many can be teacher developed. For example, the continued use of language experience stories and charts is justified at this level. Experience stories written by individual pupils, as well as charts produced by the whole class, can and should be used to supplement and complement primary reading instruction. There are also thousands of commercially published supplementary materials, such as reading kits, games, books, filmstrips, cassette tapes, and so forth, that can be used to supplement primary reading instruction. Information about published supplementary materials can be obtained from sources such as catalogs and professional reading journals and can be examined at many state, regional, and national reading conferences. As with all materials used for reading instruction, the teacher must evaluate materials carefully to make sure that they will serve the instructional needs of the pupils and possess features that reflect what is known about effective teaching of reading.

Another type of supplementary material that represents considerable potential is the graded news magazine. Examples are *News Pilot, News Ranger,* and *News Trails* for first, second and third grades, respec-

FLASHBACK

Two Poor Boys Who Made Good Are Now Running for the Highest Office in the World!

Issued weekly, from September to June, except Thanksgiving and Christmas weeks, by American Education Press, Inc., 40 South Third Street, Columbus, Ohio, and 1123 Broadway, New York, N. Y. Yearly subscription 75c a year. Special rates to schools.

A QUAKER BOY

A LITTLE boy sat in Quaker meeting. He had been there an hour. He began wiggling and wiggling, and whispered to his father, "Dost thou think meeting will be over soon?" After

church, he was punished, for Quakers were very, very strict.

That was in Iowa, about fifty years ago. The boy was Herbert Hoover. Today we are talking of making him President. Herbert was born in a small cottage. Next to it was his father's blacksmith shop.

Herbert had an older brother and a younger sister. They had lots of fun playing in the blacksmith shop. Being Quaker children, they never fought. To strike one another was a great sin.

When Herbert was six years old his father died. He did not leave much money, so Mrs. Hoover had to take in sewing. She was very religious. She even led Quaker services in the different churches. Once, while she was away, Herbert went to Oklahoma to visit his Uncle Laban. His three were the only white children in town. All the rest were Indian boys and girls.

Such fun as he had playing with the Indian boys! They taught him how to build Indian fires; how to trap rabbits and squirrels, and how to catch fish.

When Herbert was nine, his mother took a very bad cold and died. The Hoover children were orphans now.

Herbert went to live on a nearby farm with his Uncle Allan. Here he fed the pigs, hoed the garden, and helped milk the cows. He went to the country school every day. Quakers were very strict about school, too. They thought that learning was next in importance to religion.

A LITTLE NEWSBOY

FIFTY-FIVE years ago, a baby boy was born in New York City. It was on the East Side, near the river, where many very poor people lived. He was named Alfred. He, too, is running for President this year.

Many of our Presidents have been born very poor. In America, everyone has a chance to become great. It does not matter where we are born, nor what we have. It all depends on what we are.

Alfred's mother and father were born in this part of New York, too. When Alfred was born, they lived in a flat. They

You probably read Weekly Reader or a similar type of school weekly news magazine when you were in elementary school. These news magazines have been an important feature of many teachers' reading programs for several years. Such news magazines provide pupils with opportunities to apply reading skills to reading materials dealing with timely topics and current events.

tively.[1] These are weekly magazines containing news-related articles, puzzles, cartoons, humor, and illustrated stories about children from many lands. *Weekly Reader* is a graded magazine with different editions from kindergarten through advanced levels.[2] These weeklies have certain advantages over texts in that they deal with timely topics, which permit children to read and discuss controversial issues. Enjoying this flexibility, these children's magazines might score higher than certain other instructional materials when measured on the criterion of relevancy and interest. Pupils may be more motivated to actively engage in reading for a variety of purposes and have the opportunity to apply their reading skills to relevant reading materials.

Trade Books

In addition to materials designed specifically for teaching children how to read, there are a large number of "trade" or story books published every year. These materials are often referred to as "library books," but in any sound reading program such books will be present in abundance in every classroom. Today, hundreds of titles are available. Representative series include *Beginner Books, Easy to Read Books, Early I Can Read Books,* and *I Can Read Books.* Both the number of books and publishers producing such books are constantly increasing.

Trade or storybooks for beginning readers often follow the principles of controlled vocabulary and sentence repetition. Many of these books contain as few as 75 different words. At a somewhat higher difficulty level, children may participate vicariously in a space flight while reading a book containing no more than 300 different words. Sentence patterns are also carefully sequenced in many children's books, providing children with the chance to learn about language (21). In addition to story-type materials, many books are available in such areas as science, travel, biography, and exploration that are illustrated with colorful pictures and manage to deal with some fairly high-level concepts.

The extensive use of self-selected trade books is an integral part of the application phase of the reading program and is one of the basic characteristics of effective reading instruction. Today there are beginning books on a wide variety of topics ranging from fairy tales, joke books, space travel, poetry, ecology, to sports. This development has permitted primary teachers to provide their classes with the opportunities to practice and apply their reading skills in meaningful reading materials. Furthermore, the likelihood that pupils will become lifelong

---

1. Scholastic Book Services, Englewood Cliffs, N.J. and Pleasanton, Calif.
2. Xerox Education Publications, Columbus, Ohio.

FLASHBACK

The Caldecott Medal is awarded annually to the artist of the most distinguished American picture book of the year. The text also must be of a high quality and worthy of the pictures. The award is named after Randolph Caldecott, an English artist in the mid 1800s. Caldecott's picture books for children were beautifully illustrated nursery rhymes and old ballads.

readers, develop an appreciation for literature, and refine their personal values through interaction with literature is greatly enhanced (14).

Other educational advantages may accrue from the almost unlimited number of trade books now available. Black children now have a much better chance of reading *in school* about black heroes and blacks who have made substantial contributions to American culture (4). Undoubtedly of equal importance is the fact that nonblacks now also have this opportunity. One can only speculate as to what human tragedies might have been avoided and what benefits society might have gained if this "right-to-read" had been realized much earlier.

There are many sources available to primary level teachers for staying current with the large number of trade books on the market today. Both *The Reading Teacher* and *Language Arts* review and discuss children's books in each journal issue. In addition, many publishers of children's books advertise in both of these journals. New children's books are reviewed regularly by the Children's Book Council and these reviews are published in *The Calendar*.[3]

Classroom book clubs associated with commercial publishers, such as Scholastic and Xerox, are excellent sources of children's books. Children can buy books through these clubs at inexpensive prices. However, many children today may never be able to own books, even at a modest price.

Teaching Schedule

Teachers in the primary grades should have definite daily time periods scheduled for reading instruction. This does not mean that reading skills are not taught in other subject areas (math, science, social studies). It does emphasize that there must be time specifically devoted to teaching needed reading skills. Having a definite time period for reading instruction need not result in lockstep activities, and teacher-pupil contact need not be the same for all pupils every day. For instance, a number of children who are having problems may be given extra practice in word identification skills while those pupils fairly proficient in this skill read independently in a subject-area text or for recreation. At other times, the teacher may participate in the discussion of a story with a group of advanced readers while other pupils do teacher-directed activities that focus on review, reinforcement, practice, or application at their desks.

There is no one specific amount of time per day that can be said to be ideal for systematic reading instruction. Factors such as class size, pupils' achievement, the teacher's skill, and classroom organization would have to be considered in arriving at a schedule (12). In second grade, for example, an hour each morning and possibly a slightly shorter

3. Available from the Children's Book Council (67 Irving Place, New York, N.Y. 10003).

period in the afternoon would certainly be considered a minimum amount of time for scheduled instruction. Other short periods through the week should be devoted to particular reading problems as they arise in other instructional activities. Problems in word meaning, word attack, punctuation, and concept exploration involve reading instruction and should be dealt with whether or not the curricular task is in the area of reading. The key to effective scheduling is not the amount of time allocated for teaching, but the time that students are meaningfully involved in learning.

Scheduling of reading instruction in the primary grades usually involves the teacher working with a small group of pupils in teacher-directed instruction while the rest of the class is engaged in meaningful independent reading activities at their seats or in small-group settings. A typical schedule for a second grade might look like the following:

- 8:45—Teacher reads to the whole class a book appropriate to the students' background and interests. This might be a picture book where the teacher reads and shares the pictures with the class or it might be a longer book that the teacher reads sections of daily. Daily reading should be a major feature of both primary and intermediate level reading programs. Many teachers whom we have observed begin each school day by reading to their students. Some teachers schedule reading aloud at other times of the day, such as just before recess or after lunch. Reading aloud daily is an important feature of elementary reading instruction and should not be neglected because of time pressures or a perception that students would not enjoy being read to.
- 9:00—Group 1 (seven children) meets with the teacher for teacher-directed instruction. During this instruction, the other eighteen students are working on teacher-identified tasks. These tasks may include completing meaningful workbook and worksheet activities (see chapter 8), reading library books and other materials, working in cooperative tasks (two or three pupils), working on microcomputers, and so forth. As the teacher teaches the pupils in Group 1, she is also monitoring the pupils working on independent tasks. One way to do this is to meet with reading groups at the front of the room. The teacher can quickly note if the other pupils are working on the completion of their assigned work. To minimize interruptions to the reading group and to maximize the time available for independent work, here are several suggestions to consider: (1) provide practice examples and purposes for completing the independent tasks; (2) make available alternative tasks (not busy work) for those who finish or experience difficulty with the assigned tasks; and (3) familiarize pupils with the daily schedule by writing it on the chalkboard and reviewing it with pupils at the beginning of the day.
- 9:30—Group 2 (9 pupils). After the instruction has been completed

Flexible grouping recognizes students' unique needs in reading instruction.

with Group 1, the teacher sends them back to their seats with meaningful independent activities to complete and begins her instruction with Group 2. Upon her completion of this instruction, she may follow the same procedure and call for Group 3, or if she is using flexible grouping, meet with the whole class, meet with youngsters from both groups 1 and 2, or work with several youngsters from all three groups.

Many teachers typically have three groups for their classroom reading instruction. Some teachers do not change the structure of their groups during the school year and others may use flexible grouping, which allows for pupils to move in and out of groups, depending upon their needs. Flexible grouping is more advantageous than fixed grouping because it avoids the lockstep approach to teaching reading and is better for meeting the needs of individual students. The lockstep approach is where pupils are permanently "locked in" to one group during the entire school year and in many instances throughout their elementary reading program.

Some basic principles for teachers to follow in breaking away from a traditional three-group organization to flexible grouping for reading instruction have been suggested by Unsworth (26).

- No permanent groups are formed for reading instruction.
- Groups are formed and disbanded to meet pupils' needs as they arise.
- Group size varies in relation to pupils' needs and the purpose of instruction.
- Students are made aware of how groups function in terms of the overall reading program. Since flexible grouping may be a new experience for many primary youngsters they need to understand that they will be moving in and out of groups and no longer will they be placed in one group for the entire school year.
- Strategies for supervising groups should be well established.
- Tasks assigned to groups are appropriate to their needs and experiential/conceptual background.
- Provisions are made to assure that instructions for completion of tasks are clear and can be referred to if forgotten. Teachers should provide practice examples, purposes for learning, and establish procedures for how pupils can get assistance if needed (see chapters 3 and 8).
- Meaningful follow-up activities are available for pupils who complete independent tasks.
- Easily understood procedures for coding and identifying materials are used so that pupils can function independently when necessary and not disturb others. These procedures should be demonstrated by the teacher and practiced with youngsters so they understand how to behave.

As mentioned earlier, flexible grouping allows teachers to move children in and out of groups, depending upon pupils' needs. On occasion, review work may be by whole-class instruction, practice and application activities may be done independently with close teacher supervision, and introduction of new learning may use a small group, individual, or whole class approach. The key to flexible grouping is that groups are formed in relation to pupils' needs and not just their ability. Pupils' capabilities will vary in relation to the nature and context of any given learning task (26); therefore, they cannot be labeled as high, average, or low for all reading instruction.

THE INSTRUCTIONAL PROGRAM

The instructional program in the primary grades must be based on the belief that reading growth is developmental in nature. Those children who learned the skills taught in beginning reading are now equipped to make more rapid growth in the reading process. Having mastered a number of word identification skills, they can continue to build systematically on these insights. Children who can recognize several hundred words without recourse to analysis will continue to enlarge their sight vocabulary and language capabilities as a result of repeated experiences with other as yet unknown words. If children developed the *set* to demand *meaning* from their reading, they will become more proficient at profiting from context clues, and their meaning vocabularies will be expanded as a result of wider reading. The remainder of this chapter presents discussions and illustrations of teaching procedures that focus on a number of the goals of primary reading instruction. These activities are identified as either introduction, practice, or application and only the key features of instruction are specified. Teachers can use these activities in instruction by adapting them to a teacher-directed format similar to the one illustrated in figure 9.2, which is a lesson on understanding anaphor in story content. Additional examples of this teacher-directed format can be found in chapter 6.

Expanding Sight Word Vocabulary

In other contexts throughout this book, the point is stressed that all mechanical skills and reading habits are closely related to comprehension of printed material. This relationship is reaffirmed here because in the following materials particular skills are of necessity discussed separately. In the actual reading process, no skill is applied in isolation. One does not read simply to profit from punctuation, to phrase material properly, or to apply analysis skills.

A number of procedures and exercises for helping children extend sight vocabulary are found in a variety of primary level reading materials. In many instances, teachers will need to devise additional lessons that focus on application. A few typical activities follow.

INTRODUCTORY ACTIVITY

Introducing New Words. It is considered desirable to study new words that are introduced in the day's reading assignment prior to having children read the story silently. The new words are pronounced as they are printed on the chalkboard *(stump, footprints, suddenly).* Similarities to other words previously learned are pointed out, for example, the *st* in *stump,* the word *foot* in the compound word *footprints,* the root word *sudden* in *suddenly.* Not only is identification of such words stressed, but their concepts or meanings in the story are illustrated and discussed. Encouraging children to maximize the use of all available word identification cue systems should also be illustrated by writing sentences on the board that focus on how the words are used in context.

AREA OF NEEDED READING INSTRUCTION

Ability to understand the use of anaphor in story content.

INTENDED LEARNING OUTCOME

Given a teacher-made worksheet containing short sentences, students will underline the anaphor in one sentence and circle its referent in the other sentence.

PAST LEARNING

Students can read pairs of short sentences that relate to each other in content.

Students are familiar with the concept of pronouns and their uses in sentences.

Students are familiar with the terms *refer* and *referent.*

Students are able to make inferences about short sentences or passages from story content.

BUILDING BACKGROUND

Relate the definition and use of *anaphora* with students by writing examples on the chalkboard that match the children's experiential backgrounds, such as:

Mr. Thomas met his wife and daughter at the theater.
They entered the main door of the lobby.

Explain that these sentences contain an anaphor. Point out that the anaphor in this example is the word *They.* Explain that an anaphor is a way to avoid repetition and use the example above to illusrate this point. Without the anaphor *They,* the second sentence would read:

Mr. Cunningham, his wife, and daughter entered the main door of the lobby.

In this instance, the pronoun *They* is used to avoid repetition and to reduce what is being said in both sentences. Point out that the word *They* is a pronoun but that pronouns can be used as anaphoric devices.

Point out to students that some anaphors cause confusion because they do not directly refer to a specific word. Such an anaphor will only suggest or imply, as, for example:

Mary did not dance with a soldier. He is a sailor.

In this instance, the inference is that He refers not to a soldier but to the man with whom Mary danced.

continued

FIGURE 9.2 Example of teacher-directed format for adaptation of primary grade reading activities (From W. H. Rupley and T. R. Blair, *Reading Diagnosis and Direct Instruction: A Guide for the Classroom* [Boston: Houghton-Mifflin Publishing Co., 1983], 123–25. Used with permission.)

TEACHER-DIRECTED INSTRUCTION

Demonstrate anaphoric devices in written examples on the chalkboard and underline each anaphor. Ask students to read the written example and to identify the referent that is implied by the anaphor in each sentence.

Her grandparents live in a senior citizens community. They are very nice for older people.

Mother took the car downtown to buy southern fried chicken. We will have it for supper tonight.

Question pupils about the anaphors in these sentences. Ask them to identify the referent for each pair of sentences. Does the anaphor *They* have more than one possible referent? Point out to pupils that the anaphor *They* can have as referent the words *grandparents* or *senior citizens community.* Emphasize that the anaphor *They* confuses the meaning of the sentences.

Question students about the anaphor *it* in the second pair of sentences. Does this anaphor refer to the word *car* or *southern fried chicken*? Again, it is important to stress to students that anaphors can often be confusing to a reader and can sometimes hinder their understanding of a passage.

INDEPENDENT STUDENT PRACTICE

Provide pupils with a teacher-made worksheet containing short sentences in which an anaphor is used. Ask pupils to underline the anaphor and to circle its reference in the other sentence. Select pairs of sentences that clearly depict the referent of the anaphoric device used. Examples of anaphors and sentences referents include the following:

Susan and Sarah went camping together. They had a great time.

When Tim met Kay, he fell in love.

After the bread has risen, put it in the oven.

Help youngsters to underline the anaphor and circle its referent in the first example to make sure that they understand the activity.

ONGOING DIAGNOSIS

Teacher evaluation of students' written responses to determine their ability to identify and associate anaphoric devices with correct referents.

Use teacher-made tests at appropriate instructional intervals to diagnose students' strengths and weaknesses in the use of anaphoric devices in sentences and passages. Teacher-made tests should match past instruction closely. The difficulty level of this activity can be increased by asking students to identify a greater number of anaphoric devices in short sentences. As a follow-up activity have students create their own short sentences containing anaphor and identify the anaphor and referent by underlining and circling each one, respectively.

Matching Captions with Pictures. A series of pictures can be displayed and appropriate titles consisting of words, phrases, or sentences can be prepared on oak tag or cardboard. Children then match the proper written caption with each picture:

The box is empty	A jet airplane
Evergreens	Children in a school bus
A brown cow	Two boys
The tree has no leaves	A boy and a dog

PRACTICE ACTIVITY

Using Picture-Word Cards to Teach Naming Words. A picture of an object is pasted on one side of the card and the word for the picture printed on the other side. Some words you might use include *house, car, tractor, bridge, shirt, television, giraffe, piano, dress, swing, police officer, hammer.*

APPLICATION ACTIVITY

Select the Right Word. Introduce exercises that require pupils to select the proper word to fill in a space left blank in a sentence. These exercises stress both meaning and differentiating between similar words.

The kittens were asleep on the ________.
(stay, straw)

The bird built its nest in the ________.
(tree, tray)

They made a ________ for the puppy.
(bad, bed)

Mr. Brown sells ________ in his store.
(hats, hates)

A more difficult task is illustrated below where two similar words are to be placed in two blanks in a sentence.

It was their ________ to go by ________. (plane, plan)

The ________ is about a ________ from here. (mile, mill)

The dog took the ________ to the ________. (bone, barn)
The train whistle went ________ ________. (toot, toot, two, to)
We must ________ to write on the ________. (line, learn)

Combining Phrases to Form Meaningful Sentences. This exercise forces attention on both the configuration of words and their meanings. In a *finish the sentence* exercise, children draw a line from the phrase in column A to the phrase in column B that completes the meaning.

A	B
The car	is on his head.
Around the house	give us milk.
The horse	is a beautiful lawn.
A straw hat	is driven down the road.
Cows	drink milk.
Cats	has a beautiful saddle.

Developing Word Analysis Skills

Word identification includes all methods of arriving at the identification of unknown words. Gaining independence in reading implies a mastery of those techniques that permit a child to read a passage containing words that she does not recognize instantly as sight words. Instruction in the primary grades will focus on phonics, structural analysis, context, and methods in combination. These skills become increasingly important because they facilitate independent reading.

Phonic Analysis

Knowledge of letter-sound relationships is one of the three kinds of linguistic information available to readers to comprehend a written message. The child must gain insight into a large number of these relationships and be able to apply them if she is to become an independent reader (16). In some instances, pupils in the primary grades are not systematically taught skills they need because these were included in the curriculum of previous grades. In an effort to avoid teachers associating particular phonics teachings with a particular grade level, an overview of the entire program was presented in chapter 5.

In the early stages of reading it is possible for a child to learn some "sight words" without noting letter-sound relationships. When he recognizes a word configuration as a whole *(cat),* he is not forced to translate letter-to-sound and to blend the sounds to arrive at the pronunciation *cat*. However, as more and more word symbols are met, the ability to sound and blend becomes more important (9, 13). For example, the following words differ from *cat* in only one letter: *cut, cab, bat, fat, hat, can, cap, car, mat, pat, sat.* These minimal visual differences become harder to detect with the absence of phonics clues.

Formal instruction in associating printed letters with speech sounds heard in words has been preceded by years of experience with related learnings. The child can discriminate rather minute differences in spoken words *(Ted, bed, fed, led, red; sat, sad, Sam, sack).* He hears and learns these words globally, rather than perceiving that each consists of three sounds (phonemes). Nevertheless, the six year old does distinguish thousands of words on the basis of minimal phoneme differences.

The reading readiness program has extended the child's knowledge of language sounds by providing much practice in this area. Many children entering first grade have learned to make visual discriminations between some letter forms and all other letter forms; that is, they can name the letters *b, o, m, s, l, t,* and so forth whenever they see these symbols. The next step after learning to discriminate letter forms is to associate speech sounds with known letter forms. To achieve independence in reading, a child must master these letter-sound associations and be able to apply them in meaningful contextual reading situations when he meets unknown printed words.

Phonics instruction in the schools today starts in the readiness period and extends through all stages of reading instruction. The teacher works with the children to make sure that they hear the similar beginnings or endings of these words. The next step is instruction in order to understand that letter combinations correspond to the similar sounds in the beginnings or endings of words.

If the child recognizes *mine* and *many,* he is then led to perceive that *milk* and *mud* begin with the same symbol and, thus, the same sound. While he is learning sight words, he is also learning the sounds that initial letters contribute to words. If he knows the words *tell* and *sell,* he may be able to work out the word *bell,* since he also knows the words *be, by, boat,* and *boy* (13). This process of initial consonant substitution can work only in relation to other *known* words. In addition to the clues just mentioned, if the child knows all of the words in the sentence except the one new word *bell,* the context in which the new word is found will also aid him in arriving at the correct choice.

The question is sometimes asked, When should phonics instruction be introduced? The question seems to imply that this instruction is not seen as an ongoing, integral part of the total reading program, but rather as a block of skills which might be plugged in at any given point on the learning continuum. A further implication suggested by certain instructional materials is that when you decide to plug in phonics, you do it with a degree of emphasis that neglects related teachings. Evidence that balance can be achieved is provided by one teacher who describes her first phonics lesson as follows:

> I usually have a phonics lesson the first day of school. Prior to the opening of school, I print on oak tag the first name of every child assigned to my room. As the children enter, each is given his name tag. I introduce the children on a first-name basis, "Class, this is Mary. Does anyone else have a name that begins the same way as Mary?" If I get a correct response, I build on it. If not, I say, "Now I want to introduce Mike. I think Mike's name begins like Mary's. Listen, children, as I say these two names; *Mike, Mary.* I hear the same sound at the beginning of both names." I then have these two children stand at the front of the room and hold their name cards so everyone can see them. I point out that if the children look closely they will see that each name begins with the same letter and that this letter is called *M.* I then print both names on the board; we pronounce the names and look carefully at the initial letter. We then move to other names such as *Bobby, Billy;* or *Henry, Harry, Helen.*

If you observed this teacher's classroom, you would be impressed with the variety of approaches she uses to teach reading. All of these include some emphasis on word analysis. Every day she writes the day of the week, the month, and date, both numerically and spelled out. These writings often contain words which begin with the same sounds: *Today is Tuesday, the sixth of September.* In response to her questions, the children note that *Today* and *Tuesday* begin with a *T* that represents the same sound in both. They add other words which begin with the sound heard in *Today* and *Tuesday,* and the teacher writes these in a column on the chalkboard. They see the letter and say the words *t*omorrow, *t*ime, *t*ake, *t*ooth.

The teacher introduces the children to an activity that involves active engagement in language usage, listening, observation of the environment, and word analysis. "I'm thinking of something in the room. Its name begins like *dog.* What is it?" The children look around and respond *door, desk, David, dominos,* as well as *duck* and *dolphins,* which are pictured on the bulletin board. Many of these words are written on the chalkboard so pupils can associate the initial sound of a word with the letter that represents that sound. In addition to providing such opportunities to learn letter-sound relationships, this teacher also emphasizes applying phonics skills in meaningful reading. Pupils are engaged in language experience activities, recreational reading, listening to stories read by the teacher, and writing activities on a daily basis (17).

Visual and Auditory Discrimination. Although visual and auditory discrimination may be discussed separately, and lessons may be devised that emphasize one or the other, the two skills work together in the

Reading instruction provides students with many opportunities for application of skills.

reading situation. The child who learns to rely exclusively on visual clues will experience extreme difficulty as she meets hundreds of new printed words having only minor differences in letter configuration (*thumb, thump.* On the other hand, a child cannot profit from learning letter-sound relationships if she cannot visually distinguish letters.

The child cannot "sound out" such words as *big—dig, day—bay, dump—bump, bread—dread* unless she can instantly recognize the *b* and *d* configurations. Children have learned to make hundreds of minute auditory discriminations required for understanding oral language. They can build upon this previous learning only if they learn to:

- Focus on sounds (phonemes) that are blended into whole words.
- Associate these speech sounds with the proper graphic representations (letters).

Visual and Auditory Integration. A combination of visual and auditory training usually comes after children have learned to recognize letters and some words. A series of worksheets can be prepared using single letters, letter blends, or words. This type of exercise may be viewed as moving beyond readiness, since the child must be able to recognize printed words.

PRACTICE ACTIVITY

The teacher says one of the letter symbols in each group and the child circles what he hears (N–P–B–D).

(N) M R B (P) D S C (B) T B (D)

The teacher pronounces the words in each column *(a flap, the cap, a tap)* and the child underlines that word phrase.

a clap	the cap (underlined)	a map
a flap (underlined)	the clap	a top
a slap	the cat	a tap (underlined)

The child underlines the word in each column which rhymes with the stimulus word the teacher pronounces *(am, land, jump, day)*.

my hand	the lamp	Jane is	she said
a harp	the sand (underlined)	he came	I sail
a ham (underlined)	the fan	dump the (underlined)	I say (underlined)

The child is encouraged to supply one word that is similar in meaning to the "clue" words.

Clue	*Answer*
trains run on it	the __ __ack
a pretty color	is __ __een
what it costs	the __ __ice
use on teeth	a __ __ush
played with sticks	a__ __um
many people	a __ __owd
not the back	in __ __ont

Here are some blends that end with *l: bl, cl, fl, gl, pl, sl.* You always hear the sound of both letters: say *l*ed-*sl*ed; *l*ock-*cl*ock

Clue	*Answer*
could make rain	the ___ ___oud
too much rain	a ___ ___ood
it can fly	a ___ ___ane
a big fire	the ___ ___aze
wear on hand	a ___ ___ove
icy rain	some ___ ___eet

The above exercises progress in small, highly related steps that build on past learning. By providing pupils with a review of previous instruction and relating it to new learning, their chance of success is enhanced. Also, by using words in phrases, pupils can be directed to use context clues and can focus on making the phrases make sense.

INTRODUCTORY ACTIVITY

Duplicate a number of three-word series of rhyming words:

a.	I look	I cook	I took
b.	I pick	I lick	I kick
c.	My name	My game	My fame

Identify the line and pronounce one of the phrases: line a: *I cook;* line b: *I pick;* line c: *My game.* The children circle the phrase. In addition to providing practice in auditory and visual discrimination, such exercises have diagnostic value. At a glance, you can see which children are experiencing difficulty in particular letter-sound combinations.

The same type of exercise can be devised to teach and test consonant blends and digraphs as well as short and long vowel sounds.

Initial Consonant Sounds. Practice in blending initial consonant sounds with word endings is essential to successful decoding.

INTRODUCTORY ACTIVITY

There are many frequently used words which end with the same two or three letters. These common elements are referred to as phonograms, and words containing them were once referred to as "word families." Substituting initial letters in such words often helps children see and hear the letter-sound relationships. Direct pupils to focus on whether or not the words sound like ones they have heard before. Also, focus their attention on the use of the connected word to help determine which word makes sense.

Ask students to make a new word by placing a letter in the blank space in front of each word (on a worksheet). Provide pupils with letters which can be used *(b, f, h, s)* to complete the exercise to maximize their chances of success. Complete a few examples to assure that they understand what they are to do.

a __at	a __all	my __and
I __at	I __all	the __and
a __at	a __all	a __and

PRACTICE ACTIVITY

Variations can be used for practice that provide pupils with practice in short, meaningful phrases. Illustrate with a few examples how to determine if their choice makes sense.

Example: Add a *b* in front of each word and listen carefully as you pronounce the new word.

A big __and He __it it __eat the __end the

Example: Add an *s* in front of the same words and listen carefully as you pronounce the new word.

Add f	A __an	I __ail	I __ill
Add p	A __an	A __all	A __ill
Add m	A __an	The __ail	A __ill
Add h	My __and	The __ail	A __ill

Change the first letter and make a new word that names an animal.

Example: bolt the c̲olt

A boat	The __oat	A big	A __ig
I sat	A __at	The fog	A __og
My meal	A __eal	The house	A __ouse

Vowel Letter Sounds. The ability to know the various vowel sounds and to understand their importance is crucial to becoming a successful decoder. Since every syllable must have a vowel sound, children need an abundance of practice in this area of letter-sound relationships.

INTRODUCTORY ACTIVITY

See and Say (minimal contrast in vowel sounds). Many children who have no difficulty in speaking and understanding words that have only minimal phoneme differences do have difficulty when attempting to read such words. Vowel letter sounds are usually the most troublesome. Brief drill periods that focus on these minimal letter-sound contrasts can be helpful to some children. Too much drill can lead them to believe that what they are doing is reading. They should understand that they are engaging in a visual-auditory activity that can help them later in their reading.

The material on the drill cards focuses on medial vowels in CVC words (to be read across the card).

ĭ	ĕ
pin	pen
bit	bet
lid	led
sit	set
tin	ten

ŭ	ă
mud	mad
fun	fan
cup	cap
but	bat
rug	rag

ĭ	ŭ
rib	rub
fin	fun
bit	but
hit	hut
big	bug

ă	ŏ
cat	cot
map	mop
rag	dot
hat	hot
tap	top

hat	hit	hut	hot
big	beg	bag	bug
pat	pot	pet	pit
him	hum	hem	hem

sit	sat	set	sit
pin	pan	pun	pen
ten	tan	tin	ton
but	bit	bet	bat

PRACTICE ACTIVITY

Short and Long Vowel Patterns. Many children will profit from a simultaneous visual presentation of letter patterns and the speech sounds that these patterns represent in words. This provides an immediate contrast. Material such as that shown below can be developed and used for class, group, and individual study. Then such materials can be placed on the bulletin board to serve as "models" for those children who may need such reinforcement. The use of pictures assures that the child will properly identify the printed words. Although only one vowel series (e–ēa̸–ēe̸) is illustrated, picture words that can be used for the other vowel sounds are also listed below.

ă	āi̸	ā–e̸	ŏ	ō–a̸	ō + e̸
a cap	a pail	a cake	a mop	the goat	my nose
a pan	a sail	a rake	a box	the soap	my rope
a bag	a tail	a vase	a pot	the boat	my bone
a map	a nail	a gate	a top	the coat	my cone

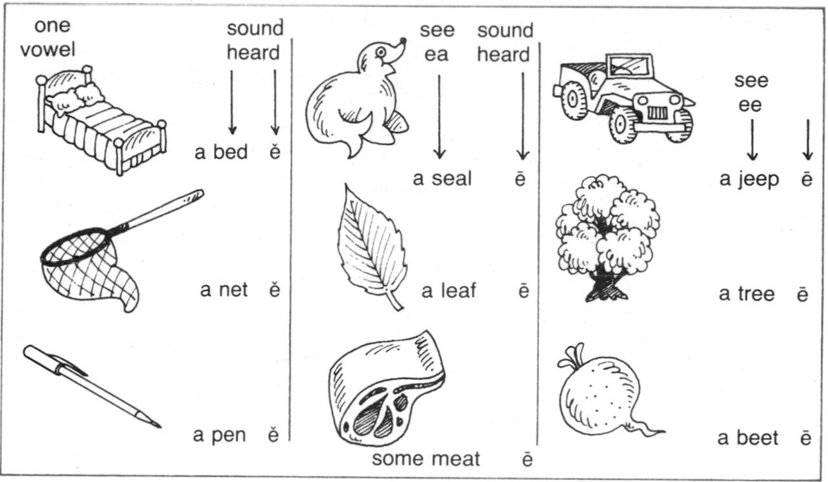

Effect of Final e. Make a new word by adding the vowel *e* to each word in column B. Pronounce the old word under column A and the new word under column B. What happens to the vowel sounds you hear? Does the new word make sense with the other words?

A	B	A	B
at	I at___	pin	pin___ tree
past	My past___	dim	a dim___
cut	cut___ dog	plan	a plan___
rid	rid___ the bike	tub	a tub___

APPLICATION ACTIVITY

Long and Short Vowel Words. Each sentence shows two blank spaces and is followed by two words which, when placed in the proper blanks, will make "sentence sense." Children read the sentence and write the correct word in each blank space.

1. Our __________ won __________ games. (ten, team)
2. John and his __________ filled the __________. (pail, pal)
3. The children put their __________ on the __________. (cot, coats)
4. They used their scissors to __________ out __________ designs. (cut, cute)
5. The boys __________ down the __________. (slide, slid)

INTRODUCTORY ACTIVITY

Homonyms (two vowel patterns). Explain and illustrate the concept that some words are pronounced the same but have different meanings and spellings. All the words in the following exercise follow regular spelling patterns and contain one of the vowel patterns *ee, ea, ai, a + e.* The purpose of the exercise is to have the child associate these visual patterns with the long vowel sound they represent. Depending on pupils' abilities, this can be done independently or with teacher direction in a group.

On each blank space write a word that sounds like the first word. The new word will have a different meaning and spelling.

week	(weak)	main	(mane)
beet	______	sail	______
steal	______	made	______
heal	______	mail	______
meat	______	pale	______
creek	______	waste	______
seem	______	plain	______
real	______	tail	______
peel	______	pane	______

APPLICATION ACTIVITY

Prepare a series of sentences, each of which contains one or more words with short vowels in which the vowel letter has been omitted. Children read the sentence, using context clues to identify the word. They then write the vowel letter that represents the sound heard in that word. Direct pupils to ask themselves if their sentences make sense.

1. The c___t drank milk from the c___p.
2. We had f___n on the b___s.
3. Two m___n wore r___d c___ps.
4. Did the p___p s___t on the r___g?
5. Billy's d___d read the m___p.

Contextual Analysis

At practically all points on the reading continuum, the one ability that sets the good readers apart from poor readers is the degree to which the context helps the reader figure out unknown words. When children do not profit from context clues, this weakness is easy to detect by observing their reading behavior. On the other hand, when a passage is read correctly, it is difficult for an observer to determine to what degree context clues contributed to the successful reading.

The good reader keeps in mind what has been read and how the sentence she is reading builds on this meaning. If context is not enough, she glances through the word to detect a prefix, the root word, or an inflectional ending. When no prefix is found, the first syllable is isolated. This may unlock the word. If not, she will work further through the word. These operations are performed so rapidly by a good reader that there may be no perceptible pause as she is reading. If the word is not solved by this attack, the reader may go on past the word for additional context clues. This step may call for rereading the sentence, but if it is successful, meaning will have been gained.

When each method of attacking unknown words is discussed and examined separately, one might conclude that in a given situation a reader uses only one method. Exclusively using one method makes for slow and inefficient reading, although some children approach reading in this manner. The more ability a reader has in profiting from structural, phonic, and context clues, the less likely it is that she can tell which one was the key in helping her solve a particular word. Early in the first grade the child learns to sound the initial letters of words. This skill, plus pictures and context clues, make it possible to eliminate many of the words that might otherwise have been plausible choices.

Mistakes in reading can be made even in situations where the reader has the ability to recognize all the words in a passage.

> Mary had a little lamp
> Its base was white as snow.

The child who knows the verse about Mary and her lamb may well be trapped into miscalling *lamb* for *lamp* and *face* for *base,* but as she reads further her mistake should become obvious.

> Mary had a little lamp
> Its base was white as snow.
> She turned it on when she came in,
> And off, when out she'd go.

Since the reader has been taught to read for meaning, the mistakes on the first two lines do not permit a good fit with the concluding two lines. The reader would likely reason somewhat as follows: "Slow down—look again; that doesn't make sense; this is not about a lamb in school."

The more difficult the level of the material, the less likely it is that the immediate context alone will be an adequate tool for analyzing unknown words. Often, however, a reader can benefit from additional clues and easily solve an unknown word. Assume that the pupil meets a sentence containing an unknown word: "Jack was sure his ____________ would let him go." This is the opening line of a story, and the author has yet to unfold the plot or background. There are many words that might complete an idea when this is all we know. Is Jack being held a prisoner? The word could be *captors.* Is he thinking of getting permission? The word might be *mother, father, friends,* or *teacher.* If the reader notes something about the unknown word, she may get a valuable clue. For instance, "Jack was sure his p(arents) would let him go." *Mother, father, teacher,* and *friends* are eliminated if the reader uses the initial sounds. Several possibilities remain such as *pal, playmates, principal,* and *parents.* The word *play* is known as a sight word. It is not found in this unknown word, so *playmates* is eliminated. With enough skill at phonic analysis to work her way through the first syllable, the reader is almost assured of arriving at the correct response. If she should try *pa rents* or *par ents,* either pronunciation will be close enough to suggest the correct word.

"It's my ______________," said Jimmy. Here a number of possibilities occur to the reader; my *idea, turn, guess, opinion* or any number of possessions. This sentence alone does not provide enough context, but rarely does such a sentence stand alone. As we take into consideration the context supplied by several previous sentences, the unknown word falls into place.

> The boys searched everywhere but they did not find the little lost puppy. "I hope Blackie doesn't get hit by a car," said Billy. Jimmy was very sad. He had been thinking all afternoon about not closing the gate when he had gone to mail the letter. The puppy must have gotten out when he left the gate open. "It's my ______________," said Jimmy. Then he told about leaving the gate open.

Structural Analysis

The teaching of structural cues should receive considerable emphasis in the primary grades. In their reading, children will meet every type of structural change in word form found in English writing. Also, the frequency with which they meet inflected forms and affixes will increase greatly. Instruction should include a review and extension of children's experiences with compounds; common word endings, including plurals and contractions; affixes, and the like.

Compound words will not be difficult for the child who forms the habit of examining unknown words and is focusing on getting meaning as he reads. The compound word he meets will be composed of shorter words that he had already learned. Basal reader series introduce a few compound words at the first-grade level and provide drill on recognition and analysis at each succeeding grade level.

INTRODUCTORY ACTIVITY

Noticing the structure of compound words helps the child develop meanings of compound words. Words that make up a compound word can be presented in two columns; children are asked to combine them to form one word. The new word is written in the next column. The pupil uses the compound word in a sentence, which the teacher writes in the last column.

after	noon	afternoon	We have recess in the afternoon.
with	out	________	I can't go outside without shoes on.
every	one	________	Everyone enjoyed the party.
club	house	________	We built a clubhouse.
air	plane	________	The airplane flew across the sky.
door	way	________	Mark is standing in the doorway.
some	time	________	He will be here sometime after lunch.

PRACTICE ACTIVITY

Building Compound Words. Combine one word from the box with a word from the list to form a compound word.

type	tooth	snap	after
any	grand	bed	light

________ache	________one
________noon	________write
________father	________shot
________house	________room

APPLICATION ACTIVITY

Recognizing Compound Words in Sentence Context. Present sentences to the pupils and illustrate that they are to select a compound word from the list of words that makes sense in the context of the sentence.

shipwreck	football	newspaper	scrapbook	afternoon
raincoat	ballpoint	sailboat	clubhouse	flashlight

Everyone went to the ________ game that ________.
John is upstairs writing in his ________ with his ________ pen.

We ran halfway to the ____________ without stopping.
Frank received a ____________, a ____________, and a ____________ for his birthday.
He read the ____________ headline, "Big fire at sawmill."
They saw the ____________ from a hilltop near the lighthouse.

INTRODUCTORY ACTIVITY

Forming Plurals by Adding es. Pupils can be introduced to the formation of plurals by activities that focus on both changes of visual patterns of words as well as the concept of *more than one.* Write sentences on the board that illustrate meaning and application in context.

Many plurals are formed by simply adding *s,* as in boys, girls, trees, farms, cats. In many words *es* is added to form plurals.

fox	foxes	inch	inches	If one fox meets another fox, then there are two foxes.
box	____	dress	____	Mother gave Mary a dress and she now has many dresses.
dish	____	lunch	____	She fixed two lunches and washed the dishes.
bus	____	match	____	Her dress matches her hat.

Forming the Plural of Words Ending in *y*. Change the *y* to *i,* then add *es*.

funny	funnies	body	bodies	
fly	____	army	____	
baby	____	party	____	
puppy	____	cherry	____	Mark and Bill each got a new puppy. They named their puppies Big and Little.
lady	____	family	____	The two ladies were standing on the corner waiting for a bus.

The structure or visual stimulus pattern of words is changed by a syllable added either at the beginning or at the end of that word. A child may know the symbol *load* as a sight word, but the first few times she sees *unload, reload,* or *unloading,* she may not see what is familiar. Instead, she may see the entire new configuration as unfamiliar. Thus, recognizing common prefixes will be an aid in learning new words where the root word is known. Children use words containing prefixes and suffixes in spoken language long before coming to school. These words are often learned as sight words before formal instruction deals with the meaning of the suffixes.

Instruction cannot deal exclusively with the structural changes resulting from the addition of prefixes and suffixes. Exercises should focus attention on both the structural change and the modification of meaning. It is as necessary to show pupils that prefixes change the meanings of words in a science, arithmetic, or social studies class as it is to discuss this point during the period devoted to reading instruction.

INTRODUCTORY ACTIVITY

Introduce prefixes and their effect on meaning by presenting sentences containing examples of prefixes. Focus pupils' attention on what happens to the meaning when prefixes are used. Once it is determined that the students understand the task, they can be directed to read the rest of the story and select the words that make sense in context. The following sentences illustrate the use of the prefix *un*.

José met a *kind* man on his trip.
The *kind* man was named Farmer John.
Farmer John had a friend who was not very friendly or kind.
José had not met anyone who was as *unkind* and *unfriendly* as Farmer John's friend.
José helped Farmer John *load* his wagon with hay.
They drove the wagon to town to sell the hay.
Farmer John's __________ friend went with them.
(unkind, kind)
José had to walk beside the wagon. He thought that it was __________ that he had
(fair, unfair)
to walk and Farmer John and his __________ friend rode in the wagon. José knew
(unkind, kind)
that Farmer John's __________ friend would not help __________ the wagon
(unkind, kind) (load, unload)
when they got to town.

APPLICATION ACTIVITY

Opportunities can be provided for pupils to practice and apply prefixes in meaningful context by using activities similar to the one just presented. These can progress from sentences to longer passages, to assure a high degree of success.

Bob *isn't able* to go to the football game with me.
Bob is __________ to go to the football game with me.
(able, unable)

The teacher said *to read the story again.*
The teacher said to __________ the story.
(reread, read)
Mary *does not agree* with your answer.
Mary ______________ with your answer.
(agrees, disagrees)
Susan gave Bill a glass of milk. Bill drank all of it and asked for more. Susan _____ (filled, refilled) his glass and said, "There is no more milk." Bill yelled, "It is __________ (fair, unfair) that Joe got three glasses of milk and I just got two." Joe said, "It is __________ (kind, unkind) of you to yell at Susan." Susan ______________ (agreed, disagreed) with Joe, "You are an _____ (kind, unkind) person, Bill."

Suffixes are word endings that give root words different shades of meaning (*er, or, ist, an, al, ure, ty, ment, ism, age, is, en, el, ive, ish, ant, ful, ly, less,* etc.). Since there are a great number of suffixes and very few have an absolutely fixed meaning, an attempt to teach definite meanings would probably produce more confusion than learning. If a child develops the habit of seeing the more common endings so that she is not prevented from recognizing known root words, the new word is not likely to cause trouble. Composing sentences and stories (similar to those just presented for prefixes) using the different forms of a word is a better method of teaching than having the child attempt to tell the precise difference between words like *joyful, joyfully, joyous; dependent, dependable, dependency.*

The English language is rich in the number of units that can be attached to any number of root words to form new words:

heat: heated, preheated, reheat, preheating, heatedly
war: postwar, warlike, warring, prewar, wartime
luck: lucky, unluckiest, luckily, unlucky
place: placing, displace, replaced, replaceable

Assume that the word *happy* is a known sight word. Identifying the word *unhappily* theoretically calls for these skills: recognizing the prefix *un* and the suffix *ly* as units, perceiving the root word *happy,* applying the rule that words ending in *y* change to *i* before adding an ending, and understanding syllabication—that is, that prefixes and suffixes usually stand as syllables and two like consonants usually divide, thus giving the pronunciation *un hap pi ly*. It is doubtful, however, that any reader goes through all of these mental steps, since the process would be most uneconomical. The reader also has the context to suggest the word, and after she has met a word on several occasions, she will probably have mastered it as a sight word and will not have to resort to analyzing it.

LANGUAGE AND PRIMARY READING INSTRUCTION

Throughout the text we have stressed that learning to read involves the interaction of many factors. Among the major factors are pupils' conceptual, cognitive, and language development. The importance of considering each of these in developing pupils' reading comprehension has focused on meaningful application in context. Drill on isolated areas of reading is meaningless if the skills are not related to the entire reading experience (2). Therefore, it is extremely important for the teacher to provide children the opportunities to apply their understandings of language to reading. The following teaching activities are representative of those that deal with the language aspect of reading and are extensions or variations of the information presented in chapter 2.

Combining Sentences

The sentence is the meaning-bearing unit of language in both speech and reading. The materials that follow emphasize this fact, while illustrating ways in which language skills and reading for meaning can be stressed.

Basic sentence comprehension is a prerequisite to understanding larger units of printed materials. Children need experience both in combining sentences for precision and economy and expanding sentences to include needed details. Riddles should be part of the reading program because they hold children's interest and motivate them to read. Riddles also represent a sophisticated use of language and involve the manipulation of language. Sentences can provide enough data from which to draw inferences. Written directions can be simple enough for beginning readers or difficult enough for high-school or college-level readers. The same is true of analogies.

These language-reading skills and dozens of others are developmental in nature. This means that if the difficulty level is controlled, working with analogies can begin in kindergarten or first grade. Relationships can be expressed orally or via pictures. At each succeeding instructional level, the difficulty level of the task can be increased by adding new types of relationships and new modes of presentation. This developmental nature of reading will be shown throughout various chapters devoted to instruction.

Beginning readers need experience with various sentence patterns. Many beginning reading materials consist primarily of short sentences, presumably because of the child's limited reading ability. Children also tend to string short sentences together in their oral language usage. One way to help children master and use more difficult syntactical patterns is to have them combine two or more short sentences into one statement (2). As an introductory activity, the teacher may involve the entire class by writing the stimulus material on the chalkboard. Later, smaller groups or individuals can work with cards (practice), each of which contain one sentence-reduction task, or with duplicated pages which contain several exercises.

PRACTICE ACTIVITY

Combine the sentences into one sentence.

Sample: Billy has a dog.
Its name is Woof.
Billy has a dog named Woof.

Mary wrote a story.
She called it "Spring is Here."

____

John likes TV.
He likes to watch cartoons.

____

Frank has a new bike.
It is blue and white.

____

Ted lost a quarter.
He lost it yesterday.
Ted felt sad.

____

Building Sentences from Scrambled Word Order

One way for children to become familiar with English syntax is to provide them with opportunities to build sentences. Children enjoy manipulating series of words into meaningful units. This practice helps them develop an awareness of the role of structure words (*the, this, that, and, when, those,* etc.) and of meaningful sequences when stringing words together (1).

INTRODUCTORY ACTIVITY

Building sentences from a series of scrambled words can be introduced to the entire class through use of the chalkboard. Words that can be arranged into a sentence are written in jumbled order. Direct pupils to follow along as the sentence is read aloud a few times. Then direct pupils' attention to determining whether or not the sentence makes sense. (This should relate to past instruction with connected words, e.g., *the dog, a bed.*)

horse hay the ate the

Call on the children to suggest how to make this into a sentence that makes sense.

The horse ate the hay.

Capital letters and punctuation are discussed and are included in the second writing. A second example might illustrate that the same words may be arranged in more than one way:

horse hay the eating was
The horse was eating hay.
Was the horse eating hay?

PRACTICE ACTIVITY

A second format could be the writing of each word separately on oak tag cards and placing the cards in an envelope.

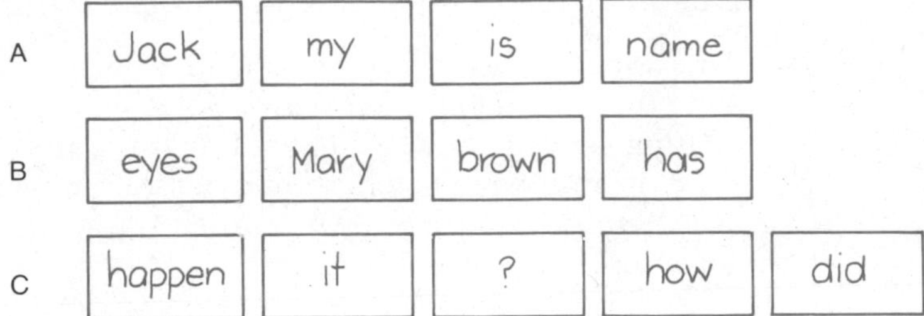

Pupils select an envelope and arrange the words into a sentence. The sentence can then be checked by the teacher, or a self-checking key can be made available.

APPLICATION ACTIVITY

A third format is to duplicate a page containing several scrambled sentences, leaving space for the students to write correct sentences.

1. won who game ball the

   ____

2. girls boys the beat the

   ____

This activity illustrates how instruction builds on pupils' past learning and progresses in highly related steps to maximize pupils' understanding and chance of success.

Expanding Kernel Sentences

Expanding sentences is a language-reading activity that pays high returns on any time invested in its use. One can start with any kernel sentence *(Birds fly, John said, "No," Frank watched TV)* written on the chalkboard. Then call on children to answer questions by supplying a word which will then be added to the sentence. They can also tell where the word is to be added and, in their own words, why it fits there. There need be no use of terms like *adjectives, modifiers, adverbs,* and so forth. In addition, as words are added, the pupils should be directed to make observations as to where and what type of punctuation would be helpful in reading the expanded sentence.

Example: Mary had a lamb.
Question: "What size?" *little* "Where do we put little?"
Mary had a little lamb.

"Describe the lamb." *woolly* "Where do we put woolly?"
Mary had a woolly little lamb.
Mary had a little woolly lamb.
"The lamb's name?" *woolly.* "Can we do this?" "How?"
Mary had a woolly little lamb named Woolly.
"What color is the lamb?" *white*
"How white?" *as snow*
"What is white as snow?" *Its fleece; its coat*
Mary had a woolly little lamb named Woolly, whose fleece (coat) was white as snow.

There are, of course, many other ways the sentence might have been developed and expanded further. This technique integrates many language-reading skills. Children experience how their language operates, how words can be strung together to convey a message, how sequence controls the stringing, how adding a word or words affects intonation.

How Many Ways?

Creating alternative ways of arranging words into meaningful units aids in children's manipulation and understanding of written language.

INTRODUCTORY ACTIVITY

This language activity demonstrates that words can be arranged in many patterns, each of which results in meaning. Select three or four words that can be arranged in different ways to produce different sentences. Write these words in jumbled order on the chalkboard. Call on pupils to arrange the words so they make a sentence that makes sense.

Example 1: friend is my Mary

Response A: Mary is my friend.

Leave this sentence on the board and ask if the words can be arranged in another way and still make a sentence (no words can be added).

Response B: My friend is Mary.
(Suggest there may be another way)

Response C: Is Mary my friend?
(and another?)

Response D: Is my friend Mary?

Example 2: say I say you what

a. You say what I say.
b. I say what you say.
c. What I say, you say.
d. What you say, I say.

PRACTICE ACTIVITY

Once the activity has been introduced and pupils understand the task and its purpose, it can be used for independent seatwork. Write the words separately on oak tag:

answer	the	no	is

These are placed in an envelope. The pupil then arranges the words into a sentence and writes it on a card. The words are arranged into another sentence that is copied on the card. This continues until no other sentences can be formed. Then the children compare their work with the answer card key that reads:

The answer is no.
No is the answer.
Is the answer no?
Is no the answer?

Using Riddles

Riddles should be used in beginning reading because they are fun, highly motivating, and can lead to valuable insights about language. Teachers have observed pupils' behavior when reading children's newspapers and other materials. When children are permitted to "self-select" what they wish to read first, they tend to choose the language games such as riddles, puzzles, and jokes. We should profit from such observations, since children are indicating they enjoy humor and the challenge of sophisticated language usage.

There are all types of riddles, ranging from the factual (which are good for beginning instruction) to those involving a ridiculous play on words. There are numerous ways that this language activity can be used in the classroom, ranging from "riddle time" to riddle banks and bulletin boards. A few types of riddles are illustrated below.

INTRODUCTORY ACTIVITY

What Am I? These factual riddles provide a good introduction to riddles and teach that "listening to the clues" is essential. Write the riddle on the chalkboard, read it to the pupils, and call on pupils for a response. Write each pupil's response on the chalkboard in a connected phrase next to the riddle. Riddles should relate to children's experiential/conceptual background to increase their understanding of the task and likelihood of success.

Factual:

What eats hay and gives milk?	cows do
What has four legs and a trunk?	an elephant
What has black and white stripes and looks like a pony?	a zebra
What turns red and green and yellow?	stoplight
What is soft and furry and rhymes with <u>mitten</u>?	kitten.

Factual with a twist:

What is bigger than a cow, has one horn, and gives milk?	milk truck
What goes up and down without moving?	staircase
What is full of holes and still holds water?	sponge
What gets wetter the more it drinks?	towel
What is it that the more you take away from it, the larger it gets?	hole

Parts of the body riddles:

What has:

legs but can't walk?	chair, table
a neck but no body?	bottle
teeth but no gums?	comb
a tongue but can't talk?	shoe
eyes but can't see? (adapt to needle, Mississippi river, etc.)	potato

Play on words:

What is the longest word in the world?	smile
When are bus drivers not people?	when they turn into a parking lot
What should you do if your left toe falls off?	call a "toe" truck
What did the dog say when it sat on the sandpaper?	"Ruff! Ruff!"

Crazies:

What is pointed, yellow, and writes?	a ball-point carrot

PRACTICE ACTIVITY

Use a "Clue Box." Duplicate a page containing five or six riddles. At the bottom of the page include a clue box which provides the answers in random or mixed order. Children use the clue box as needed. Complete a few examples to assure that they all understand the task.

Working with Fact or Opinion Statements

In the process of becoming readers, children should develop questioning attitudes toward what they read. The school, being factually oriented, is frequently interested in "what the book says." This emphasis can lead learners to believe that if information is in a book (or in print), it must be correct. The goal in analyzing statements is not to establish that a statement is a fact (or opinion), but to sharpen the process for achieving such a goal in the future.

When Paula responds that "Sunday is the best day of the week" as a fact, she may learn that it is for her, but not for Stanley. Could she and Stanley, with help from the class, rewrite the statement so that a majority of the class would agree their statement is a fact? Doug says the statement "Learning to read is fun" is not a fact, but the next day notes that "Learning to read should be fun" is a fact.

The following fact-opinion statements are only illustrative of those that can be presented on a daily basis and discussed with pupils.

Americans are friendly people.
Watching cartoons on TV helps develop your mind.

First-grade girls can run faster than first-grade boys.
Big cities are not good places to live.
School work should be done in school—not homework!
The best team always wins.
If you do the same thing every day, it gets boring.
There should not be taxes on food we eat in restaurants.
Someday, people will live on the moon.
Earth is the only planet on which there is life.

Early Analogies

Reading is often defined as a thinking process, or at least as a task involving thinking. There is no more powerful reading task than solving analogies, which are simply expressions of a relationship between two objects or word meanings. Analogies can be introduced as a listening-thinking activity by using relationships within the child's experience. They can be a highly motivating method of working with or teaching plurals, homonyms, classification, and irregularly spelled words. One of the virtues of using analogies is that the difficulty level can be controlled.

INTRODUCTORY ACTIVITY

What do we wear on our feet? (socks, shoes) When it's cold, what do we wear on our hands? (gloves) Listen carefully and tell me what word we need to finish this sentence:

Shoe is to foot as glove is to __________.
Glove is to hand as shoe is to __________.
Shoe is to foot as hat is to __________.

Other easy relationships can be used such as synonyms (big-large/tiny-small) or antonyms (hard-soft/hot-cold). After oral presentations, analogies similar to those above may be placed on the chalkboard. Children need not be able to read these perfectly as long as the teacher reads them several times. Pupils are called on to supply the missing word. A series of pictures may also be used. Children name the pictures, discover the relationship, and indicate which picture completes the analogy.

PRACTICE ACTIVITY

A page of picture analogies can be duplicated for independent work as illustrated below. A variation is to place four pictures in an envelope. The child than arranges these in sequence to express a given relationship.

In describing relationships, adult terminology (e.g., *function, classification, origin*) should not be forced upon the pupils. However, children should be encouraged to verbalize in their own words why a particular choice was made.

PRACTICE ACTIVITY

Plurals. As mentioned earlier, you can control the difficulty levels of analogies. The first several lessons of analogies involving plurals can deal only with adding *s,* the next group with adding *es,* and a third set with *changing* y *to* i *and adding* es; a fourth format can include all of these in mixed order.

boy	boys	(as)	girl ________
box	boxes	(as)	fox ________
city	cities	(as)	penny ________

PRACTICE ACTIVITY

Homonyms. Difficulty level can also be controlled by providing clue boxes that include all of the words that the child will need to complete a series of analogies. One or more foils may be included to increase difficulty. The following material could be used after some preliminary instruction on homonyms.

Directions: Use a word from the box to complete each line.

Clue Box

by too rode rap meat

1. see is to sea (as) to is to ________
2. tail is to tale (as) road is to ________
3. week is to weak (as) buy is to ________
4. sail is to sale (as) meet is to ________
5. wring is to ring (as) wrap is to ________

Changing the Meaning (Punctuation and Dialogue)

Punctuation provides clues to meaning and to intonation patterns. One of the peculiar characteristics of many beginning reading materials is the high frequency with which dialogue is used. This is one of the most difficult types of reading material. Yet, first graders are exposed to more of it then they will meet in later learning situations. Examine some early levels of basal readers and you may be surprised at the number of times you meet *he said, said Jack, she said, asked Mary, said Mom, called Jimmy, said the man.*

INTRODUCTORY ACTIVITY

In order to cope with this difficult aspect of reading, children need explanations and practice in seeing punctuation and solving its role. Place a sentence (similar to example 1 below) on the chalkboard. Read it to the class using a minimum of intonation. Hopefully, some degree of ambiguity will result. Ambiguity is a big word, and children can experience it without using the term. The fact that something is missing can be established by questions such as What does it mean? Who said what? Did it make sense to you?

Example 1:

"The teacher said the principal is your friend"

Next, punctuate the sentence as shown in example 2. Read this to the class, and then read it in unison with the class. Discuss what the punctuation does for the reader.

Example 2:

"The teacher," said the principal, "is your friend."

The punctuation can be erased from example 2 and new punctuation added, as found in example 3. Have the children read the sentence and discuss how the meaning was changed.

Example 3:

The teacher said, "The principal is your friend."

PRACTICE ACTIVITY

Obviously, many follow-up experiences will be needed by most children. In addition to the teacher-class work, materials can be designed for individual work. In these exercises, the student simply adds the punctuation called for in the directions.

Directions: Fix the sentence so that John is absent.
John said Mary is absent today.

APPLICATION ACTIVITY

A series of cards or duplicated pages can be prepared, each containing several items. In some instances, punctuation can simply be added to the material. In other situations, it may be desirable to have the pupils "rewrite the sentences" and include the needed punctuation.

	Use punctuation to show that:
1. Mike said Mary is always hungry.	Mary is talking.
2. Mike said Mary is always hungry.	Mike is talking.
3. That little boy said the teacher is smart.	The boy is smart.
4. The doctor said his friend is ill.	The doctor is sick.
5. The doctor said his friend is ill.	The doctor is speaking.

INTRODUCTORY ACTIVITY

Add a Word. The following is designed to help children understand how intonation signals the end of a sentence. Write a kernel sentence on the chalkboard. Direct children to note what the voice does at the end of the sentence.

The doctor is in.

Erase the period at the end of the sentence and add a word or two. Have children note that the signal no longer follows *in*.

The doctor is in a hurry.

(continue one more step)

The doctor is in a hurry to leave.

A series of sentences can be printed on the chalkboard (or on a worksheet), each containing two or three sentences that illustrate the above. Direct pupils to add additional words to form new sentences.

The rain fell.	Sally came in.	John is late.
The rain fell faster.	Sally came in first.	John is late again.
	Sally came in first again.	

Critical Reading

Reading skills are frequently divided into two types: *mechanical* and *critical reading.* This dichotomy is misleading because all reading skills are related to *comprehension* or *getting meaning.* For example, learning to use punctuation might appear to be totally within the framework of mechanics, yet nothing can more quickly distort meaning than the inability to profit from the clues that punctuation provides. Word-by-word reading has implications other than just in the skills area. In addition to slowing the reading rate, this habit tends to force attention on words rather than on larger units. Reading must be thought of as a unitary process that is more than the sum of its parts. When a child is asked to read a sentence or a larger unit, he must employ every skill that the situation requires, regardless of how or what these skills have been labeled.

At a given moment, a reader can comprehend at a level equal to his academic background, experience, and intellectual level (2). In the final analysis, the catalyst between writer and reader is the manner in which the latter uses his past experiences in the reading situation. As the child progresses in reading ability, the materials he reads increase in difficulty. The teacher's task becomes that of keeping children's concepts abreast of the material they are reading.

The following teaching procedures focus on developing and expanding concepts and language facility. All can be adapted to different levels of difficulty and modes of presentation. In many schools, teachers combine their efforts and jointly develop language-reading exercises.

Expansion of Meanings. Children's concept development cannot be left to chance. The school deliberately seeks to provide an environment that will lead to concept development and expansion in every area of the curriculum. The following procedures can be used in helping children develop meanings. They are not limited to a particular grade level. While many of these techniques are used in the formal reading program, they are appropriate for teaching terms and concepts in all subject areas.

APPLICATION ACTIVITY

Using Pictures. The use of pictures is an excellent method of expanding and refining concepts. A picture of an eroded hillside is much more effective in fixing the concept of *erosion* than is a word definition of the term. Early basal readers rely heavily on pictures, but it is actually in the content areas that pictures have greatest value. Pictures are more likely to fix accurate concepts of *colonial architecture,* the *iron-plated Monitor,* an *anteater,* a *Chinese junk, terrace farming,* or the *human circulatory system* than is language alone.

The same picture can be used at different levels for teaching words and meanings. For example, let us imagine a picture which would be avilable to almost any teacher—a downtown scene in a small city. We see a bus, a boy on a bicycle, various store fronts and offices, a police officer directing traffic, a fire hydrant, the city hall across from a parking lot. Without going into more detail, we might build a hierarchy of concepts. The degree of teacher direction will vary in relation to pupils' existing concepts.

"Where is the police officer standing?"
"In the street."
"Yes, he is really standing in the middle of where two streets cross—what is that called?"
"That's an intersection."
(The class level will determine whether the teacher should explain the term *intersection.*)

"How many kinds of travel or transportation do we see?"
"Some people are walking."
"A boy on a bicycle."
"There's a bus. It's a city bus."
"There are lots of cars."
"I see an airplane above the city."
"What kinds of transportation are not seen in the picture?"
"Trains."
"Don't see any boats."
"There are no big trucks—big trailers."
(Teacher points to the symbol that identifies the telephone company office.)
"What is in this building?"
"That must be the telephone office."
"What's this sign across the street?"
"City Water Company, it says."
"What do we call these types of businesses?"
(no response)
"Did you ever hear the term *utilities* or *public utilities?*"
(The teacher prints the word on the board.)
"What other *utilities* do you think this city has—what others besides the telephone company and water company?"
"Electricity."
"That's right—what other name might it have?"
"Light Company."
"Power Company."
"Do you think of any other *utility* companies? Would there be a gas company?"

Other concepts that the teacher can focus on include:

"Four stories high"
"This canvas over the sidewalk is an *awning* or a *canopy.*"
"This is a parcel post truck. Its purpose is to serve the people. How is it like the power company? How is it different?"

The picture we have attempted to visualize is a simple one that could be used at various grade levels. Through its use the teacher can stress concepts and direct pupils to attend to:

Noticing details.
Symbols standing for things (the telephone symbol on a window).
Many different *names* standing for the same things
a. power company, public service company, utility company, etc.
b. canopy, awning
The same word having different meanings according to usage (e.g., *meter:* parking meter, gas meter, electric meter; meters in cars; speedometer, gas meter, and mileage meter)

The value of pictures lies in their wealth of detail and the fact that they stay in the children's minds or can be referred to after a discussion has progressed to other things.

Synonyms

The pupils are reminded and given written illustrations that words that have the same meaning are called *synonyms.* "Give me another word that means the same as *big, work,* or *fast*" will, as a rule, elicit responses from everyone in the group.

Instructional activities of varying difficulty can be used with pupils of differing ability levels within a class. Similar exercises are applicable to expanding word meanings by teaching opposite meanings of words. The objective should always be to provide instruction that will assure that the pupils see the words, hear them pronounced, and experience their use in written sentences appropriate to their language background.

INTRODUCTORY ACTIVITY

Write a word, a synonym for it, and a sentence for each of the synonyms on the chalkboard. After it has been determined that pupils understand the concept of synonyms, ask for other words that mean the same as the words listed. Write a word from the list in the sentence blank and ask pupils to read it to determine if it retains a similar meaning.

big - huge
large
giant

small - tiny
little
wee

We got a new pet kitten. It is so ______ you can hold it in your hands. The mother cat is too ______ to hold in your hands.

APPLICATION ACTIVITY

Sentence Comprehension. The child is to read the following sets of sentences and determine if they have the same meaning. If so, he writes S in the box to indicate they have the same meaning. If not, he writes D to show that they have a different meaning. Complete one or two examples with the pupils to make sure that they all understand the task and will be successful at it.

☐ Bill took his dog *for a ride.*
Bill took his dog *in the house.*

☐ The park is *not far from* where Mary lives.
Mary's house is *near* the park.

☐ Tom has a *cat and a pony* at the farm.
Tom has a *pet goat* at the farm.

Antonyms

Review the definition of antonyms (words having opposite meanings) and provide written examples: *huge–tiny; hot–cold; legal–illegal; start–finish.* Ask children for other antonyms. There are many formats for working with antonyms; only a few will be illustrated here.

INTRODUCTORY ACTIVITY

Write the word *release* on the board. Supply children with a list of words similar to the following. They then either write or give orally a word that has a meaning nearly opposite to that of *release.* Use sentences to illustrate the different meanings. Focus on changes in meaning in relation to words substituted for *release*.

grasp	trap
relief	free
hold	capture
clutch	repeat
dismiss	catch
receive	keep
mistake	

John decided to *release* the bird.
John decided to *keep* the bird.
John decided to *free* the bird.
John decided to *capture* the bird.

APPLICATION ACTIVITY

Read each of the following. Then complete the sentences by writing an antonym for the underlined word.

Open the window and ______ the door. (close, get)
Elephants are huge, lady bugs are ______. (large, small)
The lake was shallow at one end and ______ at the other. (deep, barn)
He wiped his dirty hands on the ______ towel. (clean, clear)
Sandpaper is rough, but it can make wood ______. (smooth, hard)

Read each sentence. Then, changing the underlined word, write a sentence that has the opposite meaning.

He said, "The team <u>lost</u> the game."

____

The children were very <u>noisy</u>.

____

Did you <u>fail</u> the spelling test?

____

Be sure and go in the <u>front</u> door.

____

Homonyms

Homonyms are words that sound exactly alike but are spelled differently. They are potential sources of trouble to young readers since both sight recognition and meanings may be confusing. Many common homonyms look very much alike *(their, there; see, sea; hear, here; beat, beet; dear, deer; course, coarse).* A primary-level reader gets meaning from hearing the following sounds in these combinations, but she may not recognize all of the written symbols.

Their coats are over *there.*
The *plane* landed safely on the *plain.*
Would you please carry in some *wood?*
He felt *weak* for a *week* after he was sick.
"Oh," he said, "how much do I *owe* you?"
The boy *ate eight* pieces of candy.
See the ship on the *sea.*
No, I don't *know* where it is.

INTRODUCTORY ACTIVITY

One method of expanding both sight and usage vocabularies is to list homonyms in columns, with the word the child is most likely to be familiar with on the left. An exercise calling for the use of each word in a sentence will provide a check on the mastery of meanings.

The words in columns A and B are pronounced the same.

A	B	A	B
do	dew	sail	sale
dear	deer	hair	hare

A	B	A	B
way	weigh	made	maid
hall	haul	one	won
pair	pare	poor	pour

APPLICATION ACTIVITY

Instructional activities can use the cloze-maze technique. Children are given written sentences appropriate to their language background and asked to circle the word that makes sense in the sentence.

dew
The made the grass shine.
do

way
Mother had to the apples before she bought them.
weigh

won
The basketball team that the game is from our town.
one

Developing Different Meanings for the Same Word

The child's early language development is characterized by mastery of the concrete first and then gradually moving to more difficult levels of abstraction. She may know such words as *air, blue, mine, broadcast,* and *fence,* and she may know several meanings for each word, yet she will not be familiar with all the meanings, in terms of their use in various contexts. The child will probably have mastered a number of meanings for the word *air* such as

My daddy put *air* in the tires.
We hang clothes outside to *air* them.
We breathe *air.*

The same child may be confused by the following meanings in context.

if asked to *air* her views
that was an *air* ball
that Mrs. Jones is disliked in the neighborhood because she puts on *airs*

The child may understand what is meant by *blue* in the sentence, "The boy had a *blue* coat" but she may not be familiar with "The boy felt *blue* when his aunt left." She may understand "Grandfather rode the *horse*" but not have a concept of "The coach warned the boys not to *horse* around," or the expression "That's a *horse* of a different color," or "The mayor accused the council of beating a dead *horse*."

She may know one or two meanings of *mine* but some of the usages or concepts involving the word *mine* will undoubtedly be beyond her. The following examples point up how difficult it is to measure "size of vocabulary," for each child has several different kinds of vocabularies.

The book is *mine*.
Joe's father worked in the coal *mine*.
That corner store is a gold *mine*.
The tank was damaged by a land *mine*.
Don't under*mine* the confidence of the people.
Our break is over, let's get back to the salt *mine*.
He was stationed abroad a *mine* sweeper.

Adults' meaning vocabularies are generally larger than their speaking, writing, or reading vocabularies. The pronunciation of "kleeshay" may conjure up meaning for an individual when she hears the word used in context, yet the written symbol cliché may be meaningless if she sounds "clish." The word *cache* may be mispronounced in reading but still produce meaning in the sentence, "The bandits, under cover of darkness, returned to the mountain cache for their stolen loot." Meaning may escape the individual when the TV outlaw says, "Let's go, boys, we have to beat the posse to the kash."

INTRODUCTORY ACTIVITY

Learning meanings is a fascinating and highly motivating experience for children. The teacher can point out that most words have several different meanings according to how they are used. He might illustrate with simple words like *can, stick, run,* or *set.* As the teacher asks for different usages, he will write the children's responses on the board, at the same time attempting to fix the various meanings by using other known words.

I can spell my name. - can means able
I bought a can of beans.- can means a container
Put the garbage in the garbage can.- another type of container
My mother said "Tomorrow I will can the peaches." - can means to preserve food

The last example may not be given by any child in an early elementary grade in an urban school, but this usage may be known to many children in the same grade in a rural locality. Some other usages of the word *can* may not be known by many children at an early grade level, but would be at a higher grade level.

Can it, Mack.—an order to stop talking.
If you leave now, the boss will *can* you.—dismiss from job.
Why don't you trade in that old tin *can* and get an automobile?—a battered old car.

APPLICATION ACTIVITY

After several group exercises stressing that the objective is to supply different meanings of a word in context, not simply different sentences, the teacher can present written activities. Children are given some words for which they are to illustrate different usages. In order not to handicap the poorer spellers, the teacher should be available to spell any words the children want to use in their sentences. "Just hold up your hand and I'll come to your desk and write out the word you want to use." This exercise has considerable diagnostic value in that it yields data on spelling ability, language facility, legibility of handwriting, ability to follow directions, and ability to work independently.

Some specific findings reported by one teacher include:

Despite what appeared to be a thorough explanation and illustration of the objective, a number of pupils had difficulty and wrote different sentences using the same meaning of the word selected.

Several pupils misspelled words that they could spell correctly when the teacher pronounced or dictated these words.

The handwriting was inferior to that which the child would do on a writing test.

This exercise disclosed great differences among pupils in their ability to use expressive language as well as exposing limited concepts among some pupils.

Misconceptions were found on many students' papers. These could be corrected individually with the pupil.

Selecting Appropriate Meaning

The ability to select the appropriate meaning of a particular word in context is essential for critical reading. *Dividend* does not have the same meaning in mathematics that it does when used as an increment from investments in stocks and bonds. The literal definition of *island* as "A body of land entirely surrounded by water" is not the meaning implied by John Donne when he states, "No man is an island entire unto himself—each is a piece of the continent, a part of the whole." Nevertheless, this conventional meaning would have to be known in order to understand the author's intended meaning.

Cole (6) tells of a student in a chemistry class who asked his instructor for help in understanding the law: The volume of a gas is inversely proportional to its density. The instructor tried without success to explain the concept embodied in the law. Finally, he asked the boy to define volume, volume of a gas, density, and inversely proportional. The boy had only one concept for *volume*—a book; *gas* was what is used in a stove; *density* meant thickness; and he had no concept to go with *inversely proportional.* The boy had actually "memorized" the law. This example emphasizes the futility of such effort in the absence of understanding.

The child's need for learning new words and concepts never lessens, but sometimes the amount of material to be taught may interfere with the effective teaching of meanings. In chapters 4, 5 and 6, a number of procedures were suggested for helping children master unknown words. Use of these procedures in the primary grades must be based on their appropriateness to pupils' needs. A technique used with success by some teachers is the *word-meaning period.* Ten- to fifteen-minute periods are used in which pupils are presented words whose meanings are not known but are used in contexts that enhance the understanding of meaning.

A number of variations can be introduced to keep the period interesting and pupils actively engaged. A pupil reads the sentence containing the words he has just learned and tells its meaning in that context. Other pupils can be called on to use the word in different written contexts or supply synonyms that retain the meaning of the context.

Figurative Language and Idiomatic Expressions

Figurative language and idiomatic expressions are widely used in children's reading materials. These expressions pose virtually no problem for some readers, but can be stumbling blocks for other children in getting the meaning. This occurs because some readers have developed the habit of expecting the words they read to have literal meanings. An example of a child's literal interpretation of "it was raining cats and dogs" illustrates this point. The child said he could understand how it could rain cats because they will land on their feet. He was, however, concerned about the dogs because they could "really get hurt."

Although figurative expressions may increase the difficulty of a passage, they also add to its beauty or forcefulness. Cyrano de Bergerac, sword in hand but mortally wounded, describes the approach of death, "I stand—*clothed with marble, gloved with lead.*" Overstatements or gross exaggerations emphasize particular qualities—"He's as patient as Job," ". . . strong as Hercules," ". . . tall as a mountain." Likenesses are suggested through implied functions—"This ship *plowed* the waves"; "The arrow *parted* his hair." Sometimes, in fact, words are used in such a way as to mean just their opposite. Obviously, understanding material containing such expressions depends on the reader's realization of the intended meanings.

Some examples of expressions that will be met in the primary or elementary grades follow. The mere fact that a child can read these correctly is not an assurance that he interprets them correctly.

He is as *strong as an ox.*
The old sailor *spun a yarn* for the boys.
Don't *throw your money away* at the circus.
He returned *heavyhearted.*
The waves *pitched the boat* up and down.
It was *raining cats and dogs.*
He *made his mark* as a successful coach early in his career.
A *finger* of light moved around the airport.

Primary level reading materials usually have a limited number of exercises that attempt to give practice in interpreting figurative language. If several teachers at various grade levels cooperate, they will find that activities designed for use at one grade level are appropriate for particular children in other grades. Pooling their efforts will save time, add variety, and enhance the teaching in that school. The following activity illustrates two of the many examples designed by third- through fifth-grade teachers in one elementary school. These were then made available to all teachers.

INTRODUCTORY ACTIVITY

Present the following examples to the pupils. Direct pupils to discuss how the meaning changes as a result of using each choice. Write each choice in the space and guide pupils' discussion to arrive at a choice that makes sense.

Father said: "I was walking through the park and Mr. Brown gave me a lift.
_______ picked father up in his arms.
_______ lifted father off the ground.
_______ gave father a ride home.

The small stones in the showcase were _____.
as big as watermelons.
as strong as an ox.
as shiny as diamonds.

The following passage is filled with expressions that probably would pose no problem for adults but which might mystify a child who reads slowly or literally.

> Joe, *flying down the stairs, rested his eye* on the hawk. Grandfather *buried his nose in a book* and acted as if he were *completely in the dark.* Grandmother and Sue *put their heads together* and tried to figure out *which way the wind was blowing.* Joe *tipped his hand* by carrying the gun. On the *spur of the moment* grandmother *hit the nail on the head. Cool as a cucumber,* she called to Joe, "*Freeze in your tracks* and put that gun back upstairs!" Joe's *spirits fell* as his grandmother's words *took the wind out of his sails.* He *flew off the handle* and told about the hawk. "*That's a horse of a different color,*" said grandmother, satisfied that she had *dug up the facts.* "Let the boy alone," said grandfather. "He will *keep the wolf from the door.*" Outside, Joe thought, "I'd better *make hay while the sun shines,*" as he *drew a bead* on the hawk.

Although these expressions may not bother most children, more difficult figures of speech will constantly confront them. The children who are baffled by such expressions need more experience with them. For these pupils, the teacher should devise activities over and above those which are found in instructional materials. If the reader is *thinking while reading,* he will probably develop the flexibility necessary to deal with this type of language.

DEVELOPING LITERATURE APPRECIATION

Developing an appreciation for poetry and literature is not a function of chronological age, grade placement, or occasional contact. Appreciation evolves as a result of numerous exposures. Every teacher at every grade level should assume responsibility for introducing his pupils to good literature and poetry.

The purpose of teaching is to provide experiences that facilitate personal growth. The ability to appreciate good literature and poetry assures us of a lifetime source of pleasure. In addition, reading and understanding literature will inevitably lead to insights about ourselves and the world about us. There are few human problems, fears, or aspirations that are not treated in literature.

Basic to helping children develop appreciation for literature is the recognition that appreciation comes only from actual participation.

FLASHBACK

Nancy Larrick served as the second president of the International Reading Association (IRA) in 1956–57. As an author and editor of literature for children, she has had a tremendous effect on both the quality and the use of children's literature in reading instruction. In 1957 she initiated the Book and Author Luncheon of the annual meeting of IRA. The luncheon was enthusiastically received and has been a major highlight of each convention ever since.

Reading is, in essence, a dialogue between reader and writer. Appreciation is personal; it cannot be standardized. Thus, appreciation may not result from such tactics as

- Urging students to read good literature.
- Providing a list of acceptable authors or established literary classics.
- Prescribing an inflexible agenda of reading materials for groups of students.
- Assigning the same reading to all students in a given class.
- Assuming that all students in a given class or school year have the readiness and the skills needed to successfully read books on a traditional reading list.
- Relying on evaluation methods that imply that all students should arrive at the same interpretation of a story, analysis of a particular character, or insight into an author's purpose.

Unfortunately, the above procedures, in modified and sometimes disguised form, are often followed in actual teaching situations. These practices, of course, negate what we know about reading, readers, the

When the storm was over they explored the island. When they weren't looking, they fell into an enormous hole. They tried to get out but the owner came in (which was the Zerc)!

He was mad because he thought they wanted his food. They tried to stab the Zerc but he was to strong. Ulysses thought up a plan, but it did not work. So a man got the Zerc's attention, and Ulysses tied a rope around the Zerc's legs and he fell!

When Ulysses was climbing out of the hole, he said, "Did you have a nice trip Zerc?" He then kept on climbing.

When they got out, they started to look for a tall, straight tree. Ulysses told a man to go to the ship to get the ax. When he came back with the ax, Ulysses chopped down the tree. When he chopped down the tree, the whole crew carried it back to the ship. When they got back to the ship, they sewed a sheet on it for a sail. Then they put it over the hole where the old hollow mast was. After they got that done, they pushed the Penearo in the water.

One way of furthering children's literature appreciation is to have children create original stories based on stories they have read.

learning process, and the development of taste in reading. The schools' approach to teaching literature often fails to develop in pupils an appreciation for literature.

Enjoying Poetry

In most instances, the reading of poetry calls for a different reader set than does narrative prose. Although it is true that a poem is open to more than one interpretation, the language of a poem must take precedence in determining the reading cadence. The poet's chief concern is not with facts, but feelings.

The poem is designed to be heard. Although you can of course hear the words and the language rhythms as you read silently, there is no better introduction to poetry than to hear it read orally. If the teacher prefers, he may turn for help to expert readers who have recorded a wide array of great literature and poetry. A number of poets such as Robert

Frost, Langston Hughes, Mary McLeod Bethune, Carl Sandburg, e. e. cummings, and Arna Bontemps have recorded portions of their own works. Dozens of highly competent artists, including Julie Harris, Richard Burton, and Jose Ferrer, have recorded a number of great classics.[4]

The poet is by definition and practice a word and concept artist, using imagery, allusion, analogy, and symbolism; words are selected not for meaning alone but also for sound and rhythm. Emily Dickinson explains the process.

> "Shall I take thee?" the poet said
> To the propounded word
> Be stationed with the candidates
> Till I have further tried

Thus, to paraphrase a poem is to destroy it. This does not imply that meaning is sacrificed in order to get other effects, nor does it preclude analysis or even group discussion for arriving at meaning.

Although the reader must come to poetry prepared, she need not, as part of a planned curriculum, be continually exposed to that for which she is not prepared. Good poetry is distributed over a wide range of difficulty. The school's responsibility is to match the student's present experiential/conceptual background with the reading tasks.

Many techniques can be used for introducing children to poetry and helping them develop an appreciation of it. The use of poetry can help children realize the relationship between speaking, listening, writing, and reading. A few teaching examples are presented below; many of these relate to oral and choral reading, and dramatizing and visualizing, which are discussed later in the chapter.

INTRODUCTORY ACTIVITY

Read poems to children. Direct them to listen, with their eyes closed, to the melody of the poem and to form mental word pictures of the contents. Guide pupils to discuss both the melody of the poem and their visual images. By rereading the same poem several times with a different language melody each time, pupils can begin to appreciate and understand these important language features of poetry. For an example of illustrated poetry see the last page of the first color insert.

Poems appropriate to the children's language and experiential background can be used for both oral and choral reading. The teacher may need to read the poem to

---

[4]A wide variety of recordings may be secured from the National Council of Teachers of English. These are completely catalogued in *Resources for the Teaching of English*, NCTE, 1111 Kenyon Road, Urbana, Illinois 61801.

the children a few times to make sure they understand the importance of "how it is to be read" rather than just having them pronounce the words.

Language experience activities can focus on the composition of poems individually or in a group. An excellent poetry form for introducing such activities to primary-level children is haiku. Colorful pictorial materials, such as paintings, photographs, and drawings, can serve to stimulate pupils to form the word pictures for haiku (15).

Haiku is a seventeen-syllable pattern in three lines, with five syllables in the first and third lines and seven in the second line. A drawing of a dancing bear inspired Sally to write:

The brown dancing bear
Spinning around in his cage
Dancing on his toes

Other poetry-writing activities can be related to music, art, science, and social studies. For example, after a rhythmic music lesson third graders were guided by their teacher in the composition of the following poem:

Music floated through the air.
Music, music everywhere.
We went skipping
        sliding
        jumping
        thumping
        running
Round and round the room.

Analyzing and Dramatizing Stories

Some stories need to be analyzed and discussed. The focus should gradually lead the pupils from a discussion of specific information to an understanding of how the author is able to picture each character and show the type of person he is and how she conveys the characters' attitudes toward each other and toward themselves. Students need to be shown how the reader is led to see the difference between unkindness and thoughtlessness, how people feel after making mistakes, what they do about them, and why it is not always possible to do exactly what one wants.

Creative dramatics is an example of children acting out stories that they have read. Once children have read a story that has an identifiable plot, characters, roles, and settings this is translated into a play for dramatization. Children then act out the play for other pupils in the classroom or other classes. Stories for dramatization can come from basal readers, library books, or children's magazines. In the preparation for the play, pupils must translate from print to speech. Thus, as noted by Dole (8), the written words "Who's that tripping on my bridge?" (from Three

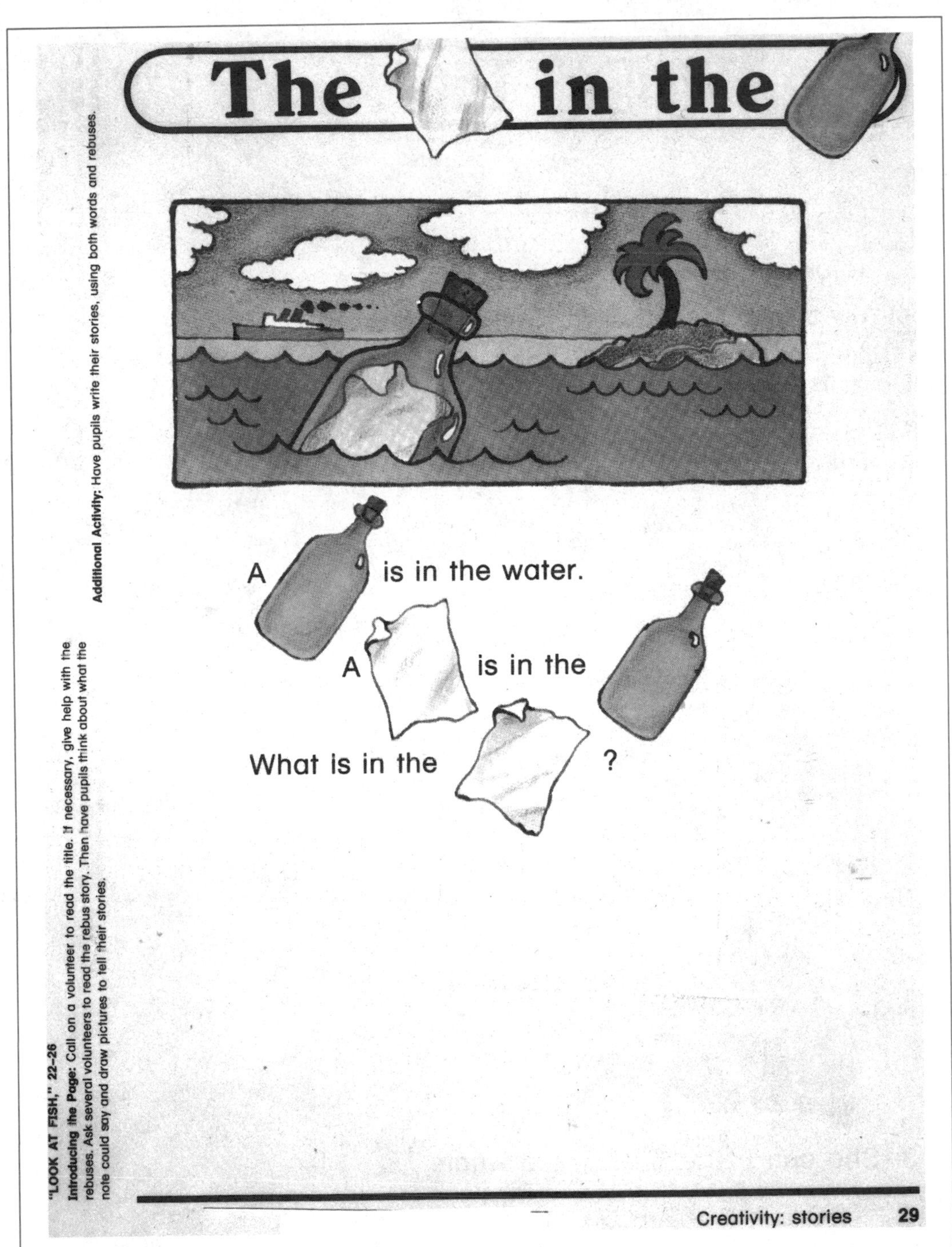

"LOOK AT FISH," 22–26

Introducing the Page: Call on a volunteer to read the title. If necessary, give help with the rebuses. Ask several volunteers to read the rebus story. Then have pupils think about what the note could say and draw pictures to tell their stories.

Additional Activity: Have pupils write their stories, using both words and rebuses.

The [note] in the [bottle]

A [bottle] is in the water.

A [note] is in the [bottle]

What is in the [note] ?

Creativity: stories 29

An activity designed to stimulate the writing of a story.

Dramatizing stories helps children develop understanding, imagination, and appreciation.

Billy Goats Gruff) now are represented as spoken words which often enables children to understand the connection between the two.

Dramatizing stories or incidents from stories helps children develop understanding, imagination, and appreciation. To dramatize a story or scene, children must read the material critically and understand the author's purpose and the feelings she wishes to convey. In the dramatization, these would find expression through tone of voice, emphasis, gesture, facial expression, and the like. In selecting material to be acted out, children will have to make correct judgments on the dramatic potential of various stories or situations. A story about a man lost on a mountain might be extremely interesting reading, but it is not well suited to a third-grade dramatic production. One major drawback is that only one character is involved.

Introducing Children to Books

There are a variety of ways that library books and teacher-made books can be used in primary-grade reading instruction. Audio tape recorders can be used to tape children's books, and commercially taped books and stories are readily available. Talking books that are taped commercially can be used to introduce youngsters to the content or to help them gain knowledge or experience literature. Books taped by the teacher should be read relatively slowly to assure that pupils can make the connection between what they hear and the print that represents the language. Once a book has been taped, pupils can listen to it and follow along in the text at a listening center. The teacher should help the children understand what they are to do and to get them started. Without proper instruction, oftentimes children will just listen to the stories, which defeats the purpose of taping the books. In addition, teacher-prepared tapes are better for developing literature appreciation than having children listen to commercially prepared tapes. Pupils can help select the books that are to be taped; this is more effective if they are given a brief overview of each book before they select the ones to be recorded. Some important features of taping books are offered by Gamby (10), who suggests that easily readable books not be taped but saved until children can read them by themselves.

Predictable books are effective in helping children begin to use strategies of prediction as they read. This frees them from being word bound or focusing on individual words as they read. A predictable book is one in which pupils can grasp easily what the author is going to say next. A basic feature of such books is much repetition of content and language structure. A technique for using predictable books would include teacher-directed instruction and would include the following steps (25).

- *Introduction.* Read the title and show cover illustration and ask children to make predictions about the story content. Direct pupils to use both the word and picture clues in making their predictions.
- *Teacher reads book aloud.* Read the book through the first set of repetitions and into the second set. Begin directing pupils to make predictions by asking them to tell you what they think will happen next.
- *Explanation of predictions.* Following the pupils' predictions ask them to explain why they made such predictions. This step is identical to the one above except instead of asking "What," the teacher is asking "Why."
- *Teacher reads the next set of repetitive patterns.* Confirmation or rejection of predictions is the focus here.
- *Reading continues and the above steps are repeated.* Close monitoring of pupils' predictions should be incorporated as they make and confirm their predictions. If pupils experience difficulty, they may lack the experiential/conceptual background for either content or language structure or both.

Once children have become proficient with teacher direction, they can begin to read predictable books on their own. Be willing to accept approximations of story language and support pupils' attempts to complete the reading of predicatable books. Opportunities should be provided to enable children to transfer their prediction strategies to other reading activities. A listing of predictable books can be found in the following:

Rhodes, Lynn K. "I Can Read! Predictable Books as Resources for Reading and Writing Instruction." *The Reading Teacher* 34 (1981): 511–25.

Tompkins, Gail E., and Webeler, MaryBeth. "What Will Happen Next? Using Predictable Books with Young Children." *The Reading Teacher* 36 (1983): 498–502.

Choral Reading

Choral reading offers many potential benefits, one of which is helping children develop good intonation in oral reading. Obviously, it is hoped that as they hear and use good models of intonation, this skill will transfer to silent reading and enhance their ability to read for meaning (18, 19).

Choral reading should not be thought of as an activity reserved for expert readers. It can and should be used at various instructional levels and for a variety of goals. The reading ability of the participants simply determines the materials which might be used successfully. For example, a teacher discovered that choral reading had extremely high motivational value for her third-grade class and increased their active engagement in instruction. She printed on chart paper poems such as "The Wind," "Watching Clouds," "Railroad Reverie," "The Owl and the Pussy Cat," "Hold Hands," and a number of limericks. Later, she prepared duplicated sheets containing several pieces of material appropriate for choral reading. She observed that choral reading often became a motivational peak of the day's activity.

Besides being an enjoyable activity, choral reading has other values, in that it

- Is a good technique for getting all children to participate.
- Can be a means of motivating children to want to read. The shy child or the poor reader is not likely to experience failure or frustration in this type of group reading experience.
- Provides an opportunity to teach good pronunciation and reading with expression.
- Permits the use of different materials for emphasizing different objectives such as phonic analysis, profiting from punctuation, and proper phrasing.

- Can be a creative experience since children can suggest different ways a poem or passage can be interpreted.
- Helps develop an appreciation for fine literature or poetry.

Reading Aloud (Oral Reading)

Instruction in reading aloud must be considered in light of the purposes for which it is used, the materials used, and how it is incorporated into the total reading program.

Opinions as to the relative value of teaching oral reading have changed considerably during the present century. At one time oral reading was widely practiced without much attention to the justification of the classroom procedures that were followed. Oral reading was equated with the school's reading program. The term *oral reading* may call to mind children in a circle reading round robin from the same book with each child in the group reading silently along with, behind, or ahead of the child performing orally. The poorer reader took her turn along with the rest and sighed, mumbled, and coughed her embarrassed way through the allotted paragraph.

The evils that resulted from a particular educational practice may be remembered long after the practice has either been discontinued or substantially modified. In some cases oral reading was overemphasized, and children spent most of their time reading aloud. As a result, they read slowly, putting all the emphasis on the mechanics of reading and little emphasis on meaning. Gray (11) tells of a boy reading a long passage orally. He read with expression and good interpretation. The teacher asked him a question about the content of what he had just read. His reply was that he could not answer because he wasn't listening.

Another abuse was that oral reading was often advanced as an end in itself rather than a means to several desirable ends. It was practiced in artificial situations, with little throught given to creating a true audience situation. As these abuses were pointed out in the literature on teaching reading, a reaction against oral reading took place. The disadvantages and potential weaknesses were stressed to the point where many teachers may have thought that the issue was oral reading versus silent reading, rather than the intelligent use of oral reading. At the moment, the most popular position is the middle ground, which embraces the idea that a proper balance should be maintained between silent and oral reading. It is difficult to argue with the logic of this latter position; nevertheless, it is almost impossible to find what constitutes a proper balance. What is adequate and desirable for one teacher with a particular class may be totally incorrect in another situation.

Teachers of beginning reading will use reading aloud for a number of purposes, and its values can be found in many natural classroom situations. The two most common situations are (1) when a child reads

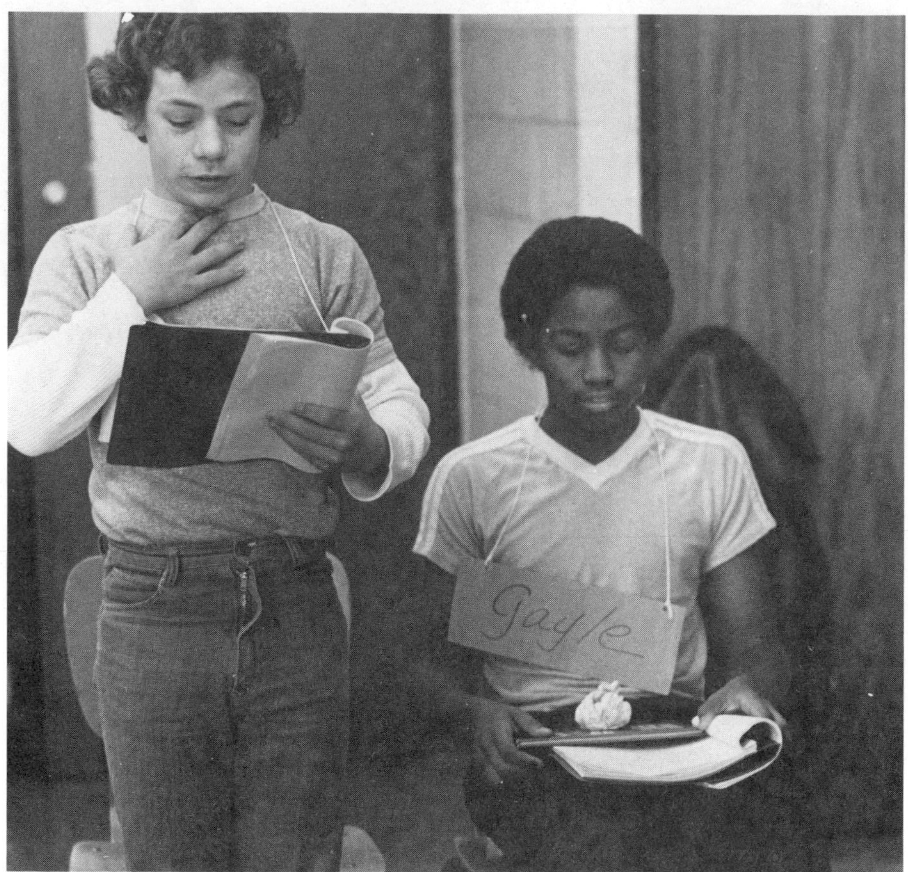

Reading aloud to an audience can be ego-building experience for students.

aloud in order to convey information or pleasure to an audience of her classmates and (2) when teachers diagnose pupils' reading. Regardless of the situation, reading aloud can be justified only when the purposes are logical, the goals educationally sound, and the preparation adequate for the occasion (27).

Reading in an audience situation can be an ego-building experience for the reader. Personal and social growth as well as self-confidence can be achieved. But the child must be able to read satisfactorily in order to elicit approval from others, and she should not be expected to read to a group unless adequately prepared. Furthermore, having one child read aloud from a book while others follow the same passage in their book minimizes the audience situation. Oral reading should, insofar as possible, make use of materials other than the basal series used for instructional purposes with the class.

Reading aloud also provides many clues about a child's reading strengths and weaknesses. A child's response after reading silently may indicate that she is having problems. If the teacher can *hear* and *observe* the child's reading, he can discover important clues as to her competence in sight vocabulary, in attacking unknown words, and in use of context, and whether she views reading as getting meaning. The teacher will not rely on only one sample of oral reading as an adequate diagnosis; each instance of reading aloud will be seen as a part of an ongoing diagnosis.

It is generally agreed that reading aloud is a more difficult task than silent reading. In reading aloud the reader must know all the words and must get the author's point and mood so that she can convey it to the listener. To do this she must focus most of her attention on articulation. Children will inevitably face situations calling for reading aloud. Since almost all purposeful oral reading takes place in a social setting, these instances will be important to the reader because her performance will place her in the position of being judged by others.

In summary, the following considerations should be observed when using reading aloud:

- The reader must have a purpose for the reading aloud. She must have interesting information that she wishes to share with others.
- The reader must be prepared. She must have mastered the mechanical skills required and have arrived at an acceptable interpretation of the author's intent.
- Children are not always well trained to *listen.* Children who make up the audience should be provided with purposes for listening.
- Instruction during the reading aloud itself will usually destroy the value of reading aloud.
- Too much oral reading can diminish its effectiveness. The stress should be on good oral reading, not on an endurance contest for either readers or listeners.
- The teacher should provide a good model of oral reading and point out with specific examples what is good oral reading when the intent is to entertain or inform.
- Reading aloud may be a considerable threat to some pupils; with these cases, the teacher should not insist that a child read orally.

SUMMARY

Reading instruction in the primary grades is a challenge to teachers, because successful readers must utilize a great number of skills concurrently. Since practically every reading skill is developmental, each must be extended at every level of instruction. The teacher will stress instant recognition of words, phonic analysis, using context clues, and application of reading skills to reveal meaning. The need for mastery of these skills is supported by a body of research findings that substantiates the developmental nature of reading. Learning the reading process involves both increased mastery and application of skills previously introduced and the adding and combining of new skills.

The motivational challenge in "decoding words" deteriorates rapidly unless this activity is accompanied by its application in meaningful context. Reading instruction should deal with teaching children language functions associated with making sense of print. They need to know how intonation influences meaning and that English abounds with figurative expressions having special meanings. Children need to have some understanding of the sentence-pattern and word-order options that English can accommodate, and they need to interact with the language of feeling as well as that of facts. Accomplishment of these skills and capabilities is best handled through a teacher-directed approach to instruction where purposes for learning are presented, past experiential/conceptual background is activated, and application is provided in meaningful reading materials.

YOUR POINT OF VIEW

Discussion Questions

1. Identify how the following should be used in primary-level reading: teacher-directed instruction; opportunities for pupils to apply their skills in meaningful reading situations.
2. Assume it is established that third-grade social studies textbooks are more difficult to read than are third-grade basal readers. What instructional considerations must a teacher attend to?

Take a Stand For or Against

1. A child made normal progress in beginning reading but is now experiencing considerable difficulty in second grade. The most logical reason for her problem is that she has failed to master letter-sound relationships.
2. The term *critical reading* implies the mastery and application of a great number of developmental skills. Therefore, a typical primary-level reader would not qualify as a critical reader.

3. One of the strengths of our schools is their success in arousing and maintaining pupil interest in recreational reading.

BIBLIOGRAPHY

1. Barnitz, John G. "Developing Sentence Comprehension in Reading." *Language Arts* 51 (1974): 902–8.
2. Burns, Paul C., & Roe, Betty D. *Teaching Reading in Today's Elementary School.* 3rd. ed. Boston: Houghton-Mifflin Publishing Co., 1984.
3. Chall, Jeanne S. *Stages of Reading Development.* New York: McGraw-Hill Book Co., 1983.
4. Chall, Jeanne S.; Radwin, Eugene; French, Valarie W.; and Hall, Cynthia R. "Blacks in the World of Children's Books." *The Reading Teacher* 32 (1979): 527–33.
5. Clay, Marie M. *The Patterning of Complex Behaviour.* Auckland, New Zealand: Heinemann Educational Books. 1979.
6. Cole, Louella. *The Improvement of Reading.* New York: Farrar & Rinehart, 1938.
7. Cunningham, Pat. "The Clip Sheet." *The Reading Teacher* 33 (1979): 214–17.
8. Dole, Janice A. "Beginning Reading: More Than Talk Written Down." *Reading Horizons* 24 (Spring 1984): 161–66.
9. Eeds-Kneip, Maryann. "The Frenetic, Frantic Phonics Backlash." *Language Arts* 56 (1979): 909–17.
10. Gamby, Gert. "Talking Books and Taped Books: Materials for Instruction." *The Reading Teacher* 36 (1983): 366–69.
11. Gray, Lillian. *Teaching Children to Read.* 3d ed. New York: The Ronald Press, 1963.
12. Gutherie, J.; Martuza, V.; and Seifert, M. *Impacts of Instructional Time in Reading.* Newark, Del.: International Reading Association, 1976.
13. Haddock, Maryann. "Teaching Blending in Beginning Reading Instruction is Important." *The Reading Teacher* 31 (1978): 654–58.
14. *Handbook for Planning an Effective Reading Program.* Sacramento: California State Department of Education, 1979.
15. Hennings, Dorothy G. *Communications in Action.* 2d. ed. Boston: Houghton-Mifflin Publishing Co., 1982.
16. Jenkins, Barbara L.; Longmaid, William H.; O'Brian, Susanne F.; and Sheldon, Cynthia N. "Children's Use of Hypothesis Testing When Decoding Words." *The Reading Teacher* 33 (1980): 664–67.
17. Johnson, Barbara, and Lehnert, Linda. "Learning Phonics Naturally." *Reading Horizons* 24 (Winter 1984): 90–98.
18. Norton, Donna E. *The Effective Teaching of Language Arts.* 2d ed. Columbus, Ohio: Charles E. Merrill Publishing Co., 1985.
19. Pearson, P. David, and Fielding, Linda. "Research Update: Listening Comprehension." *Language Arts* 59 (1982): 550–54.
20. Pearson, P. David, and Samuels, S. Jay. "Why Comprehension." *Reading Research Quarterly* 15 (1980): 181–82.

21. Pickert, Sarah M. "Repetitive Sentence Patterns in Children's Books." *Language Arts* 55 (1978): 16–18.
22. Pieronek, Florence T. "Using Basal Guidebooks—The Ideal Integrated Reading Lesson." *The Reading Teacher* 33 (1979): 167–72.
23. Rupley, William H., and Blair, Timothy R. *Reading Diagnosis and Direct Instruction: A Guide for the Classroom.* Boston: Houghton-Mifflin Publishing Co., 1983.
24. Stanovich, Keith E.; Cunningham, Anne E.; and Feeman, Dorothy J. "Intelligence, Cognitive Skills, and Early Reading Progress." *Reading Research Quarterly* 3 (Spring 1984): 278–303.
25. Tompkins, Gail E., and Weber, MaryBeth. "What Will Happen Next? Using Predictable Books With Young Children." *The Reading Teacher* 36 (1983): 498–502.
26. Unsworth, Len. "Meeting Individual Needs Through Flexible Within-Class Grouping of Pupils." *The Reading Teacher* 38 (1984): 298–304.
27. Winkeljohann, Sister Rosemary, and Gallant, Ruth. "Queries: Why Oral Reading?" *Language Arts* 56 (1979): 950–53.

10

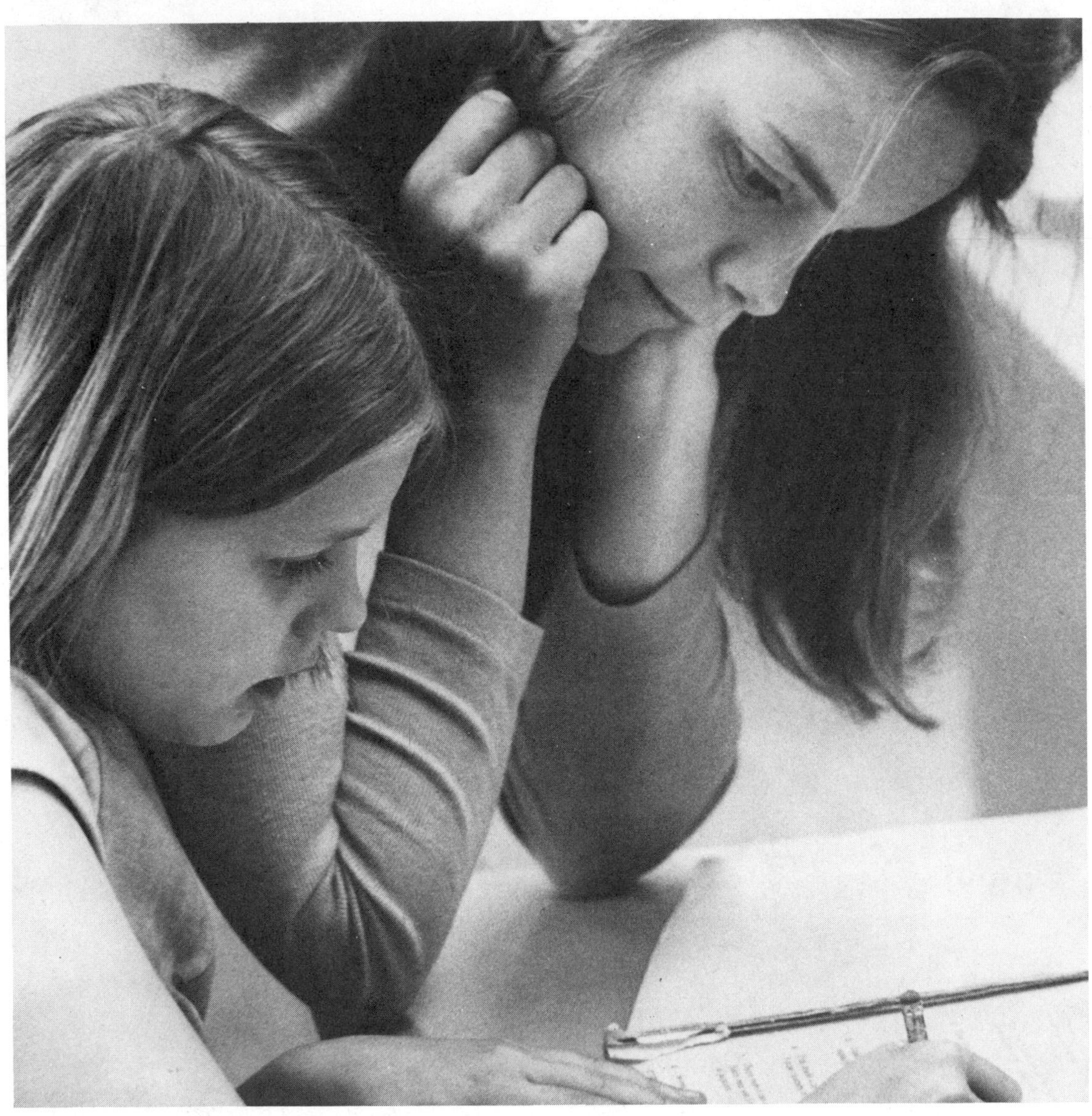

Reading: Intermediate Grades

For the Reader

Imagine a fifth-grade self-contained classroom composed of twenty-seven children with the following characteristics:

- Twelve pupils reading on grade level. Current needs: developmental reading program with emphasis on improvement in vocabulary, inference type comprehension, and basic study skills.
- Six pupils reading above grade level. Current needs: adapted program to include advanced comprehension and study skills.
- Six pupils reading below grade level (ranging from the second- through fourth-grade level). Current needs: adapted program to include instruction on basic word recognition skills.
- Three handicapped pupils to be mainstreamed for two hours each day (one emotionally disturbed pupil and two learning disabled children).

Of the twenty-seven children, ten are culturally and linguistically different.

Without a doubt, you would need a great deal more information about these children to make any sound decisions relative to their educational programs. Also, any classroom at either the primary or intermediate levels will be heterogeneous in nature. The major point to be realized in an intermediate grade is the enormous range of ability in any one classroom. Your success as an intermediate-grade teacher will depend upon your ability to deal effectively with this range of ability. This chapter will bring together your previous learning and what we currently know about effective teaching at this level to understand teaching in the intermediate grades. While there are certain competencies necessary for successful teaching at any grade level, those specific understandings relative to the intermediate level will be highlighted. Effective intermediate-grade instruction will only be achieved by an understanding of the goals and objectives of the program and specific learning needs of children.

Preview

- Read the Key Ideas that follow.
- Read each heading and subheading.
- Read the summary.

- Read the questions and statements at the end of the chapter.
- Return to the chapter text that follows the Key Ideas and begin reading.

Key Ideas

Successful reading instruction depends upon the teacher's ability to deal effectively with a wide range of ability.

SSR (Sustained Silent Reading) is a means to encourage independent reading.

Meaningful reading depends on the acquisition and continual extension of concepts.

Learning to read is a long-term, developmental process.

Instruction needs to focus on the application of reading skills in the content areas.

FEATURES OF INSTRUCTION

The intermediate grades are a crucial instructional period in a child's education. Although much of the curriculum is designed to provide advanced instruction and application of reading abilities in all subject areas, teachers must also be prepared to instruct those pupils who need additional instruction in basic word identification and comprehension abilities covered in the primary grades. Thus, intermediate-grade teachers must be ready to accommodate a wide range of student ability in their classrooms.

As in the primary grades, intermediate reading instruction should be systematic and well planned. Although many of the features of effective teaching of reading apply to all levels of instruction, their specific application to the intermediate grades is unique. The major features of effective reading instruction in need of careful teacher attention are:

- Ongoing diagnosis to determine pupils' progress in relation to the learning tasks.
- Varied teacher direction and structure to stimulate pupil interaction and discussion.
- Larger groups to allow for and guide pupils' exploration and discussion of valued topics.
- Many opportunities for application of reading abilities in a wide range of materials for a variety of purposes.
- Engagement of pupils in learning that enhances active involvement in and reinforces the development of independent reading.

INTERMEDIATE-LEVEL GOALS

The evolution of reading during the intermediate grades is best viewed from a developmental perspective. Chall's stage development theory (4) accentuates the differences between primary and intermediate grade reading (refer to chapter 9 for stages of primary grade reading instruction). Figure 10.1 highlights the characteristics of Chall's Stage 3: Reading for Learning the New, which parallels the intermediate grades and junior high school. Stage 3 is distinguished by a considerable shift to

1 Stage Designation	2 Grade Range (age)	3 Major Qualitative Characteristics and Masteries by End of Stage	4 How Acquired	5 Relationship of Reading to Listening
Stage 3: Reading for learning the new Phase A Phase B	Grades 4–8 (ages 9–13) Intermediate, 4–6 Junior high school, 7–9	Reading is used to learn new ideas, to gain new knowledge, to experience new feelings, to learn new attitudes; generally from one viewpoint.	Reading and study of textbooks, reference works, trade books, newspapers, and magazines that contain new ideas and values, unfamiliar vocabulary and syntax; systematic study of words and reacting to the text through discussion, answering questions, writing, etc. Reading of increasingly more complex fiction, biography, nonfiction, and the like.	At beginning of Stage 3, listening comprehension of the same material is still more effective than reading comprehension. By the end of Stage 3, reading and listening are about equal; for those who read very well, reading may be more efficient.

FIGURE 10.1 Stage of Reading Development for Intermediate and Junior High School Reading Instruction. (From Jeanne S. Chall, *Stages of Reading Development* [New York: McGraw-Hill Book Co., 1983], 86.)

reading to learn new information from a variety of texts. Speaking directly to the challenges presented at this level, Chall states:

> Each stage of reading development has its own tasks and crises, but the 4th grade seems to present a major hurdle. The reasons are many and the suggested solutions are varied. Evidence points to the need for more challenging instructional materials. Materials in reading textbooks (basal readers) have tended to focus on enjoyment and fun, presenting narrative fiction almost exclusively even during the middle and upper elementary grades. A developmental view of reading suggests the need for greater use of expository materials and of subject-matter textbooks and literature in the teaching of reading, particularly from Grade 4 on. (pp. 7–8)

In addition to working with the skills in the primary grades, the intermediate-level teacher must provide guidance for a large number of even more complicated reading tasks. The application of skills previously taught also becomes more complex. For instance, in getting meaning from content in beginning reading, pupils were most likely dealing with an unknown word that was in their listening or speaking vocabulary. In addition, the unknown sight word was probably only one of two or three new words on the page. In the intermediate grades, a paragraph in a social science text may contain a number of new and difficult concepts as well as several unknown words.

When perceived in a total sense of the development of independent learners, the importance of effective intermediate-grade instruction is intensified. The following objectives, while perhaps not including every facet of instruction, do provide a fairly representative picture of the breadth of the reading program in the intermediate grades.

- Individual evaluation takes place to determine the capacity of students and the present level of achievement in all facets of reading, including:
  - sight word vocabulary
  - word identification skills
  - level of silent reading
  - meaning vocabulary and concepts
  - ability to profit from listening situations, including oral directions
  - meaningful oral reading skills
  - facility in finding information, use of reference materials
  - work habits and attitudes
  - rate and purpose for which curricular materials are to be read
- Following diagnosis, the teacher devises a flexible reading program to

FLASHBACK

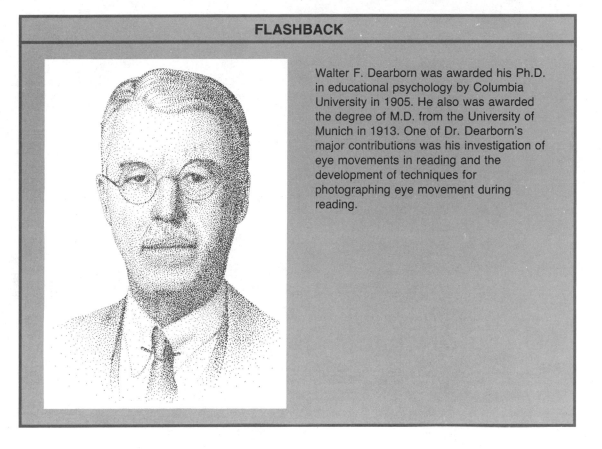

Walter F. Dearborn was awarded his Ph.D. in educational psychology by Columbia University in 1905. He also was awarded the degree of M.D. from the University of Munich in 1913. One of Dr. Dearborn's major contributions was his investigation of eye movements in reading and the development of techniques for photographing eye movement during reading.

meet individual differences and needs revealed in the initial diagnosis.

- Reading instruction is carefully planned and systematic. Severe damage to children's reading can result from the philosophy that "children learn to read in the primary grades and read to learn at the intermediate level." They must *do both* at each level.
- In addition to specific reading instruction, instruction is incorporated with the teaching of all subject matter. Children are taught to read science, mathematics, health, and social studies materials.
- Children are helped to expand their stock of concepts. This is essential in all content areas.
- Practice is provided in various types of functional reading—in newspapers, magazines, and books—to supplement basic texts in subject areas.
- Guidance is supplied in reading for recreation, pleasure, and personal growth.

- The child's reading interests are widened to build a sound foundation for lifelong personal reading activities.
- Appreciation is developed and enhanced for good literature, poetry, and drama.
- A wide selection of materials are made available in all fields—science, literature, biography, current events, social studies, and the like.
- A program is devised for guiding the growth of exceptional children, both intellectually gifted and those with learning problems.
- Children are helped to increase the rate at which they can comprehend printed word symbols in combination. This skill becomes increasingly important at this level since the curriculum materials in the various content areas make ever-widening demands on readers.
- Steps are taken to improve critical reading skills such as comprehending figurative or picturesque language, drawing inferences, classifying ideas and selecting those that are important to the reader's purpose, evaluating ideas and arriving at the author's purpose or intent, and detecting bias and differentiating between fact and opinion.
- The following reading-study skills are developed and extended: using books effectively—making maximum use of the index, table of contents, and appendix; acquiring facility in the use of a dictionary; using reference books effectively; understanding graphs, maps, charts, and tables; using library resources, card catalog, and periodical indexes; and taking notes and outlining materials for a given purpose.

Diagnosis is continuous and ongoing throughout each instructional year. An initial diagnosis serves only for initial procedures.

INDEPENDENT READING PROGRAM

As stated at the beginning of the chapter, the independent reading program consists of that time pupils spend in recreational reading. This program is critical to both primary and intermediate grades because it is paramount that students be encouraged to explore different ideas through printed material and also to practice on their own the more advanced word identification, comprehension, and study skills included in the curriculum.

A balance of direct instruction and independent reading is required to foster lifelong readers (3). The first step is to teach pupils skills that will enable them to become independent readers. The second step involves providing the necessary time and guidance to pupils so that they will use their skills in a variety of situations and develop the desire to learn on their own. Galen and Prendergast speak to this point in encouraging both competent and avid readers as goals of a complete program. They state:

> The first of these goals is generally emphasized in most classrooms. Yet in the pursuit of competence, some well-meaning teachers may drill students on various reading skills, only to deny them the opportunitics to practice these skills in a meaningful application of reading. Without sufficient practice, it is difficult for students to develop or even maintain skills taught in the classroom. To become competent readers, students must be encouraged to transfer their abilities to the ultimate goal—reading on their own. Simply put, it is difficult to become a proficient reader without lots of practice in reading. (6, p. 280)

Two important objectives of the independent program are (1) encouraging creative or "thinking" assignments that pupils can complete individually or in a small group and (2) organizing class activities for the sole purpose of promoting the enjoyment and appreciation of reading.

Creative, or thinking, assignments can be a vital means of promoting application of reading abilities. In such activities, students are encouraged to collect, organize, and criticize information on a particular topic of interest. Students additionally must classify, interpret, and react critically to information that is read. A complete listing of thinking activities for all grade levels is found in the excellent book by Raths et al. (12). Some sample topics of creative assignments, which can be done individually or as group projects, include: how we study weather, the Vietnam War, music of the 1980s, John F. Kennedy, Muhammad Ali, Martin Luther King, Babe Ruth, Albert Einstein, John Glenn, capital punishment, oil and the Middle East, China today, inflation, solar energy, third-world countries, new uses of electricity, and living in our city fifty years ago.

Organizing one's class to promote the joy of reading can be accomplished in numerous ways. The essential point is that time is allocated for students to read on their own. Some ways to promote independent reading include: book-selling sessions, class book fairs, using newspapers and magazines, using commercially prepared independent reading programs, reading aloud to students each day, creating a book corner in class, using children's literature to promote wide reading, and having free reading sessions in the classroom.

There are many ways to liven up the traditional reporting on one's reading. Criscuolo (5) describes the following ways to encourage imaginative sharing of one's reading. These have been found to be especially successful with fourth through sixth graders.

- *Lost and Found:* Write an ad for a person or object from a book—students must read various books and guess title and author of book.
- *Dress-Up Day:* Dress up as a character in a book.
- *Computerized Dating:* Set up book preferences of students and match students to books.
- *Shape It, Scrape It, or Drape It:* Students make art projects relating to books.
- *Academy Awards:* Children nominate their favorite books and the class votes.
- *Book-a-Trip:* Students read a travel book on where they would like to go and report to class with travel agency materials.
- *Quiz Shows:* Students play "Twenty Questions" on a particular book.
- *It's in the Headlines:* Make headlines on books read and encourage students to guess their title.
- *Collage Posters:* Students make posters that incorporate main ideas, characters, etc., of a book.
- *Book Friends:* Students make mobiles displaying favorite characters.
- *Reading Mobilizers:* Mobile project is expanded to include quotes, characters, and words of incidents in a book.

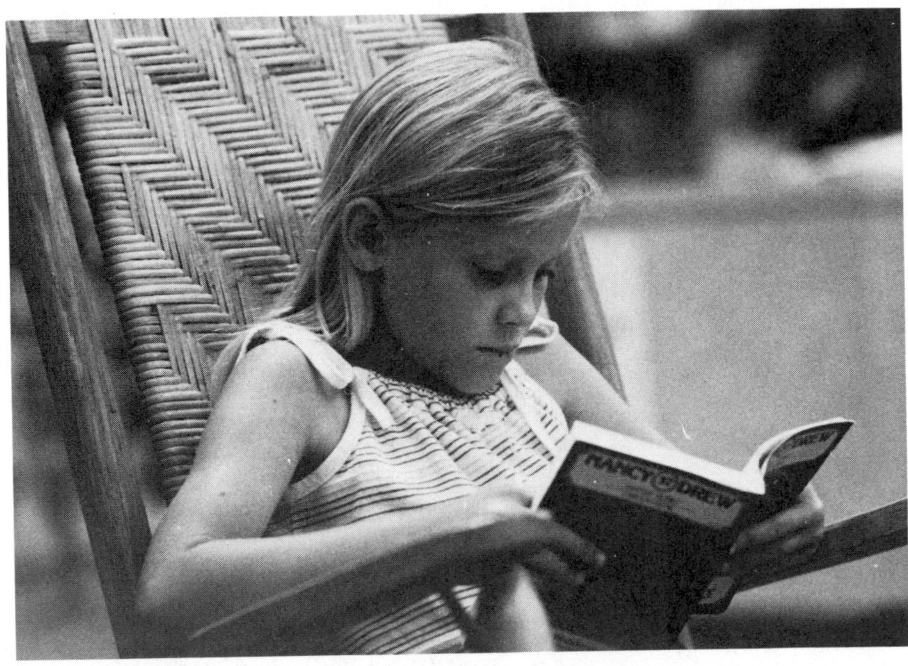

Recreational reading is integral to any reading program.

A particular time set aside each day for silent reading of self-selected materials by all students and teachers is sometimes called Sustained Silent Reading (SSR) (1, 10, 13). The object of this activity is pure enjoyment in reading material of the reader's choice; students are not held accountable for their reading in the form of written or oral reports. SSR can have a positive effect on a pupil's independent reading habits, but just allowing the necessary time is not enough. Gambrell (7) provides excellent guidelines for setting up SSR, including cooperative teacher-pupil planning in terms of responsibilities, help in locating materials, and techniques of advertising the coming of SSR through promotional displays.

INSTRUCTIONAL PROGRAM

The instructional program in the intermediate grades encompasses systematic, direct instruction in the areas of word identification, comprehension, and study skills. Although the importance of excellent primary-grade instruction is usually emphasized by educators, effective teaching at the intermediate levels is also necessary (2).

The intermediate grades present a formidable challenge to the teacher of reading. The pitfalls are as numerous and as serious as those found at any instructional level. Academic failures and loss of interest in school occur because of certain instructional practices that actually inhibit rather than enhance pupil growth. The following major barriers to good instruction are discussed in this chapter.

- A change of emphasis from *learning to read* to *reading to learn.*
- Failure to deal with variability among pupils in regard to mastery of reading skills.
- Diminished emphasis on systematic teaching of reading skills.

A Transition Period

Teachers agree that, ideally, the process of learning to read progresses smoothly without perceptible breaks through a series of grade levels. There are certain factors in the total school framework, however, that cause many teachers to feel that an abrupt transition occurs between third and fourth grades. The end of the third grade and the beginning of the fourth is often designated as the period of "independent reading." There is evidence in classroom behaviors that some teachers do succumb to the philosophy that the intermediate grades should be characterized by a shift in emphasis from "learning to read" to "reading to learn" in the various subject matter areas. The use of a number of sep-

FLASHBACK

1961

WRITTEN BY
SCOTT O'DELL
PUBLISHED BY
HOUGHTON-MIFFLIN

1927

WRITTEN BY
WILL JAMES
ILLUSTRATED BY
THE AUTHOR
PUBLISHED BY
SCRIBNER

1980

WRITTEN BY
JOAN W. BLOS
PUBLISHED BY
SCRIBNERS

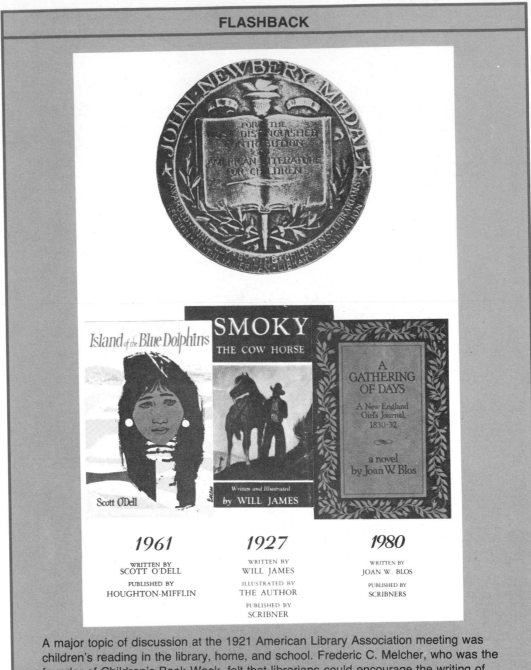

A major topic of discussion at the 1921 American Library Association meeting was children's reading in the library, home, and school. Frederic C. Melcher, who was the founder of Children's Book Week, felt that librarians could encourage the writing of quality children's books. He proposed that a medal be awarded for the most distinguished children's book written by a citizen or resident of the United States. The proposal was overwhelmingly supported. Mr. Melcher suggested the award be named the "John Newbery Medal," in honor of the bookseller who was keenly aware of children's reading interests and sought to find authors to write quality children's books.

arate textbooks in various content areas tends to substantiate the idea that this is a transitional period.

These factors form the basis for the generalization that reading skills are taught in the primary grades and applied in the intermediate and later grades. A further generalization is that since reading skills are taught in the primary grades, children who have been through these grades have mastered the skills. It is true that once pupils reach the intermediate level they are expected to do more reading, grade by grade, while less time is devoted to the actual process of learning to read. However, children need further direct instruction on various skills and continuous application to ensure their mastery. Thus, the old adage that "children learn to read in the primary grades and read to learn in the intermediate grades" is false. Youngsters need direct instruction and application in a number of reading skills included in the areas of word recognition, comprehension, and study skills.

Content Reading

Every instructional level in the school presents its own unique challenges to teachers. The emphasis on separate textbooks in the various subject areas is one of the chief sources of instructional problems. These books call for a fairly high level of independent reading ability and special facility in a number of reading-study skills, such as the ability to use the dictionary, reference materials, graphs, charts, and tables.

The idea that various facets of reading must be taught concurrently with subject matter is constantly verbalized by teachers and educators. Even in schools which are departmentalized, with one teacher responsible for social sciences, another for science, and so forth, a respect for the integration of reading and the content subjects emerges in the slogan "every teacher is a teacher of reading." The nature of the reading materials and the great difference between pupils' instructional needs make it logical and even mandatory that some reading instruction be related to the social sciences, science, literature, mathematics, and other subject areas.

Some reading skills are relevant to all subject areas; others are applied in specific ways depending upon the content materials. For example, the skills of interpreting maps, graphs, charts, and symbols are applied in different ways in the math, science, and social studies areas. On the other hand, the following skills would be used in basically the same way with every content area: adjusting rate to purpose, drawing conclusions, word attack skills, locating information, specialized vocabulary, reading for main ideas, noting and weighing details, using contextual clues, organizing ideas, and discriminating between relevant and irrelevant information.

The inability to apply these skills in any subject area would handicap the reader. For example, classification skills are needed in the reading of science material, but they are also essential in reading social sciences and mathematics. Ability to cope with precise, compact writing may be associated with mathematics, but it cannot be disassociated from the reading of history or literature. This can be illustrated with hundreds of examples, ranging from poetry to Lincoln's Second Inaugural Address to William Faulkner's acceptance speech upon receipt of the Nobel Prize for Literature. Drawing inferences cannot be thought of as belonging exclusively to one area of the curriculum. A pupil may in the course of a day be asked to draw inferences as to what happens when a decimal point is inserted between digits in two-digit numbers; what effect mountains located between the sea and the plains have on rainfall on the plains; and what happens to the circumference of an inflated balloon placed in the freezer compartment of a refrigerator.

Vocabulary and Concept Load

Curriculum materials in the intermediate grades confront the reader with an ever-increasing number of unknown and relatively difficult concepts (8). In addition, much more complex sentence structure and a variety of organizational patterns are found. It is necessary to know many new and more difficult connotations for words met previously and to understand a large number of idiomatic and figurative expressions. The amount of reading that is required is suddenly increased, and pupils must develop the ability to read and comprehend at a more rapid rate. They must also develop flexibility in their reading to be able to adjust their rate to both difficulty level and purpose. (Refer to pages 4–7 of the first color insert for an example of content area reading.)

Because of the rigid control of vocabulary in beginning reading materials, teachers frequently have the problem of arousing and maintaining interest in these materials. Difficult words and concepts are introduced in the content textbooks in such profusion that many pupils are frustrated and often lost.

Meaningful reading at the intermediate level depends on the acquisition and continual extension of concepts. Here, pupils are confronted with more difficulties per reading unit than they met in their primary reading. One of the major reading problems is coping with the gap that tends to develop between the child's store of meanings and the demands made by the curricular materials she is expected to read.

The problem of meaningful reading is complicated by the fact that in the intermediate grades, as well as at higher levels, there are found a great number of idiomatic expressions, abstract and figurative terms, and new connotations for words met earlier. In the primary grades, even

Curriculum materials in the intermediate grades confront the reader with an ever-increasing number of unfamiliar concepts.

though these occur less frequently, teachers are alerted to them through the teachers' editions accompanying the basal reader series used. Also, deliberate instruction is provided in the workbooks supplementing the reader series. With the shift to separate textbooks in the content areas, there tends to be less emphasis on helping pupils with meaning difficulties precisely at the time when help is most needed. Examples of difficult concepts from fourth- and fifth-grade geography, science, and mathematics books are cited below. Teachers found that many pupils did not understand these concepts even after the material had been assigned and covered in class.

Many years and great sums of money will be needed to *harness the river.*
It (blood) is carried through other *branching tubes* called veins.
When you are frightened, your *pupils get bigger.*
Check by doing each example again.
You bite and chew your food with the *crowns of your teeth.*
Ornithologists have examined the *crops* of many birds to find out what kind of food they eat.
Most of the *infections* and *contagious* diseases are caused by bacteria.
Birds help to keep the *balance of nature.*
We can use a *ruler* to subtract fractions.

Cloud formations make what is called a *mackerel sky.*
The native city is *backward* and ugly.
The Mediterranean became a *melting pot* for surrounding civilizations.
The people who lived in *fixed settlements* made far greater progress than the nomads.
Now, as in ancient times, the Mediterranean is a great *connecting* highway.
There is plenty of *home-grown wool.*
Business and industry were *paralyzed.*
Science has *unlocked the greatest force in nature.*
China was not entirely *sealed off* from her neighbors.
A *belt of irrigated land* stretches almost all the way along the coast.
In time, the *front of Europe* shifted from the Mediterranean Coast to the Atlantic Coast.
As the *globe* shows, Europe and Asia really form one *land mass.*
The *shrinking world* and new inventions have made this possible.
If some day the river is controlled it will be a great *life-saver* instead of a *life-destroyer.*
Gradually the continent was opened up. Another "jewel" had *been added to the British crown.*
The top of the world will have a new meaning in the future.
Almost every farmer grows some *cash crops* besides food for his family.
Britain was busy for many years in getting *stepping stones* along the seaways.

PUPIL NEEDS

Individual differences in reading ability tend to increase with reading instruction. A given group of pupils will show greater individual differences at the end of four years of schooling than they did at the end of the first year. Good teaching aims at moving children along at their maximum rate. The gifted child will move further in a given period of time than will the average child. Thus, the better the teaching, the greater will be the differences between children's achievement. Although different facets of the reading program receive varying degrees of emphasis at different grade levels, in the intermediate grades the emphasis almost has to be on what the individual child needs, regardless of what is found in the curriculum guide.

Basal materials continue to be used extensively at the intermediate level in many schools. Recent editions of these materials contain a much wider variety of content than did former editions. Nevertheless, the intelligent use of basals becomes more difficult at this level, primarily because of the wide range of pupils' needs and achievement levels. Faced with this diversity of reading ability, teachers cannot rely on a single grade-level text.

Importance of Diagnosis

Diagnosis is essential to a successful reading program at the intermediate level. Principles of teaching reading do not vary with grade level or with the materials being used. The variability of pupils in the intermediate grades makes a number of previously discussed principles particularly appropriate to this period:

1. Pupil differences must be a primary consideration.
2. Children should not be expected to deal with materials on their frustration level.
3. All children should be accommodated in the reading program rather than forced to meet the demands of the curriculum.
4. Proper reading instruction depends on the ongoing diagnosis of each child's reading strengths, weaknesses, and needs.
5. The best diagnosis is useless unless it is used as a blueprint for instruction.

An illustration of the importance of following sound principles of instruction is provided by the pupils who have failed to master phonic analysis skills. Experienced teachers know how unlikely it is that they will simply outgrow their inadequacy. The fact that children have come this far without developing insights and techniques for overcoming their problem is in itself evidence that they are not likely to do so in the absence of skillful guidance and teaching. If children have not developed the ability to hear the differences between the first syllables of words such as *dim*ple, *dem*onstrate, *dumb*found, *dom*inoes, *dam*sel or *mar*ble, *mor*tal, *mur*mur, *mer*cy, *mir*acle, it is useless to attempt to teach them a number of rules regarding short vowels, long vowels, or vowels followed by varying number of consonants. The children must be taught to make auditory discriminations, and the fact that this is ordinarily taught in first grade does not alter the fact that in this case it will have to be done now. Until the inability to discriminate between speech sounds is overcome, students can make little real progress in gaining independence in sounding. The principle of going back to where the child is applies to every learning step in phonic analysis, such as learning initial consonant sounds, learning substitution of initial sounds, recognizing blends, distinguishing between long and short vowel sounds, and understanding syllabication.

Standardized tests and teacher-made informal reading tests appropriate for all of the elementary grades will be discussed in detail in chapter 11. A commendable practice in the intermediate grades is the use of teacher-prepared comprehension questions over the various subject materials covered. Such tests can serve two purposes: from the teacher's standpoint, they are diagnostic; from the reader's point of view, they can provide excellent guidance. To devise tests serving both these purposes is difficult and time consuming. As a result, many attempts at preparing such tests tend to isolate facts and details. In this connection, it should be remembered that the pupil at the intermediate level needs practice in evaluating ideas, seeing relationships, and drawing inferences.

Grouping

The grouping of pupils for instructional purposes is essential in the intermediate grades. The great variety of reading materials available makes possible a number of grouping practices which can be used effectively. Highly structured groups become less practical in the intermediate grades, yet all the virtues of grouping can be achieved if many different tasks at varying levels of difficulty are devised.

While the teacher works with a group of pupils who need review in applying word identification skills, more advanced readers can be reading independently from supplementary sources. During some reading periods the teacher can work with the advanced group, stressing appreciation or critical analysis of a poem or story while the skills group works independently in meaningful practice and application activities. At other times the teacher may not work with any particular group but will give individual help. There will be some situations where instruction can involve the entire class: for example, when giving instruction in the use of the dictionary, in group planning of a unit, in word-meaning sessions, when reading to the group, or when giving instruction in how to find materials. These instances of whole-class instruction would undoubtedly be followed by grouping techniques based on pupils' present achievement and individual needs.

Although many pupils in a social science class may profitably use the assigned textbook, other pupils might require additional attention in order to be successful. Some of the following suggestions are appropriate to use with the entire class; other materials and tasks will be more appropriate for either accelerated or impaired readers.

- A film may be shown.
- Pictures that illustrate a particular concept appropriate to the topic can be gathered and placed on the bulletin board.
- A special vocabulary lesson can be worked out using new terms children are likely to meet in their reading.

- Children can make their own "new word list" that grows out of their reading on the topic.
- Newspaper and magazine articles may be read.
- Models, charts, or other illustrations that clarify some facet of the project may be prepared and displayed.
- Cooperative groups (heterogeneous in ability) may report to the class on material found in reference or other books relating to a particular topic.

The Intellectually Capable

The problem of arousing and maintaining interest in reading is not confined to the below-average reader. The excellent student also faces certain educational hazards in our schools. The intermediate grades can become a very critical period for gifted students, in terms of maintaining interest in reading. The challenge of the intellectually able student is present at all grade levels but becomes more pronounced at the intermediate level because the child's abilities and interests are often beyond the standard curricular materials.

It is true that there are marked differences in reading achievement and needs among pupils who are classed as intellectually gifted (9). Some of this group will need instruction in the fundamental skills of reading. Their ability to deal with concepts may be far in advance of their reading level. A larger group of the extremely capable will be advanced both in the mechanical skills and in the ability to deal with concepts. For these pupils, graded materials at their grade placement level will be mastered without as much repetition and guidance as is characteristically given to the class. The problem will not be alleviated by having these children do more work at this level, that is, by simply reading other textbooks. This solution will not extend the talented, who will acquire little additional information by spending time with other texts.

The following procedures (14) have been particularly successful in motivating the more able students:

- If the school has a central library, pupils should be allowed to visit it whenever the need arises and not be restricted to specified library periods.
- Pupils should be given systematic instruction in the use of library resources such as encyclopedias, *Reader's Guide to Periodical Literature*, bulletins, newspapers, and current magazines.
- Time should be provided for independent reading, and the reading done at such times should always be purposeful. The gifted child, or any child, should never be kept occupied with busywork.
- As gifted children develop interest in a particular topic or field, they should be kept supplied with challenging materials that will extend their growth. They should be praised for all serious effort and accomplishment.

- Children should be encouraged to make plans and carry them out independently after the intitial planning with the teacher.
- The teacher can afford to use a deeper analysis of stories or literature with the more capable pupils. This might take place on an individual or small-group basis.
- Those pupils capable of such work should be encouraged to participate in special creative activities, such as:
  a. writing biographies of famous persons from material they have gathered from many sources.
  b. describing historical events based on wide reading about these happenings.
  c. writing plays or dialogue involving historical personages.
  d. making "resource maps" in social studies.
  e. giving oral reports based on outside reading which will be a contribution to the knowledge of the group.
- Children should be provided the opportunity to gather resource materials on a topic on which the class is working. These would include pictures, articles in current magazines, bulletins, books dealing with any facet of the topic, and films. Such materials could be used in developing an "interest corner."
- Pupils should be given access to professional recordings of plays, poems, or prose. Such materials, as well as films and books, may be borrowed from libraries, curriculum centers, or the local state department of education depository.
- Children should be actively engaged in research on topics that help them see the social forces shaping their society. This type of activity will make "learning for responsible leadership" more than an empty phrase.

SYSTEMATIC READING INSTRUCTION

In order to assure that children continue to develop skills that are commensurate with the reading tasks they are asked to perform in the intermediate grades, systematic and direct instruction must be continued. Direct instruction is not only needed in basic reading abilities but also in the more advanced abilities of word identification, comprehension, and study skills. Simply put, direct instruction requires a detailed explanation of the reading skill to the children and its usefulness to their continued growth, step-by-step description with familiar material under teacher supervision, and independent practice to assure mastery. Following such direct instruction is the necessity for providing interesting and varied application throughout the curriculum.

A common oversight made by intermediate grade teachers is assuming their students possess the necessary abilities to perform well in various developmental and content reading assignments. In many instances, pupils have not been afforded direct instruction in such skills as prefixes, suffixes, fact versus opinion, use of reference materials or the ability to read a diagram, to name a few. If we expect pupils to apply certain abilities as part of the instructional and independent programs, direct instruction of those abilities must come first.

The following two sample study skills lessons illustrate the direct instruction format:

SAMPLE LESSON

Title: Previewing an Article. *Readiness.* Today we are going to discuss a word that has many meanings. The word is *preview* (write on board). Can anyone tell me what this word means? What do you see if you are at the movies when there is a double feature? (Yes, you see previews of coming attractions.) What's the purpose of this? If I had a surprise for you next week but I told you secretly a little something about it—what is this called? (Yes, it's a sneak preview of my surprise. Have two strips of oak tag with a sentence about a preview of an upcoming movie on one and a sentence previewing a certain project on the other.)

We are going to learn another use for the word *preview* which has basically the same meaning. Does anyone know what the phrase *preview an article or a chapter* means? Who can tell me why you go window shopping? What do you gain by it? (That's right, you want to size up a certain item before you buy it.) Isn't that the same purpose of previewing a movie? Can you tell me what previewing an article or a chapter means? (Right, you get acquainted with the material and its organization.) It really arouses your interest in what you are about to read. Today I am going to show you how previewing an article will aid in increased comprehension and speed.

Step-by-Step Explanation. We know the general characteristics of previewing an article or a chapter, but how do we actually do it? Well, in a preview of a movie they usually show you the highlights. How does our social studies book point out the highlights of a chapter for us? (by the headings) But even before this we must know the title. You must look at the title and study it because it tells you precisely what the article or chapter is about. What else do you usually have in a chapter besides columns of print? (pictures and maps) The second thing to do is to study these pictures because they give you a vivid picture of the people, things, and locale of the article. The third step, which has already been mentioned, is that of looking at the subheads. Why would you do this? (Right, you would get the main points of the article or chapter.) Who can tell me the three steps in previewing an article or chapter (use prepared chart).

Supervised Practice. Preview one chapter of the social studies text with the children.

Application in Context. Have children preview one chapter by themselves. Test children on their knowledge of the major points of the chapter. Finish with the question, What's so good about previewing and how does it help you out?

SAMPLE LESSON

Title: Skimming for the Main Ideas in a Chapter. *Readiness.* Today we are going to learn a new way of finding out the main ideas of a chapter in our social studies and science books. It's a method that will help you remember what you read better, and it doesn't take very long to learn. Now what's this picture about? (picture with water skiers) Who can tell me how these skiers are going over the water? (That's right, they are just flying quickly over the surface.) Are they going down deep into the water? (No, they are just touching the surface.) Another way of saying they are just touching the surface is to say they are *skimming over* the water (Write *skimming over* on board.) If I told you I liked to drink skimmed milk, what would skimmed milk be? (Right, it's the taking off the surface all the fat in the milk.) It's skimmed from the surface. Do you ever go over to the pond and pick up a flat stone and throw it across the water to make it skip? This is also called skimming a rock across the water. Now in all these examples, what is the same in each of them? (touching, surface, fast).

Today, you are going to learn another way skimming can be used. This is in skimming a chapter for the main ideas. From our previous discussion, what can you tell me about skimming a story? (Right, it has to do with the same way of just touching the surface and going at a fast pace.)

Step-by-Step Explanation. One way to skim for main ideas is to read the first two paragraphs, the first and last sentence of each paragraph in the assigned reading, and the last two paragraphs. What can you gain from reading the first two paragraphs? What can you gain from reading the last two paragraphs? Now what is so important about the first and last sentence of each paragraph? (Right, the first sentence is usually the topic sentence, and the last is usually a summary sentence.) Remember the word *usually*—sometimes this is not true. Yet if you practice reading the first and last sentence of each paragraph, the chances are good that you will be reading the main idea of the paragraph. (Put two pages of social studies text on a transparency and illustrate this to students.)

Supervised Practice. Now let's all try out this method of skimming on a chapter that you have already read in your social studies book. (Do not be concerned with the amount of time initially, but help pupils go through familiar material with this technique.) Is it easy to find the last sentence? (You are right, it isn't easy at first.) However, we will practice skimming for a few minutes each day, and you will be surprised how quickly you will improve. Remember, you are looking for main ideas and not details. The object of this technique is to skim as fast as you can just like a good water skier.

Application. Have the students skim four or five pages for main ideas and answer the three questions on the board. (List three appropriate questions on chalkboard.) Students will require much practice to perfect this technique—be sure the materials they use are interesting and varied.

DEVELOPMENTAL LEARNING

The structure of American education is embedded in, and influenced by, the grade-level system. An underlying premise of the graded system is that students finishing a given grade have mastered the language skills and concepts that will prepare them for the developmental tasks of the next grade.

The theory is sound, but in actual practice a large number of students in the intermediate grades have not mastered reading skills equal to the tasks they will be asked to perform in these grades. Another group of students may be fairly close to the expected growth level, but as months and years go by, they fail to advance in reading ability at a pace equal to the reading demands placed upon them. In recent years, the statement "reading is a developmental process" has been repeated often. However, this concept deserves more respect and attention than it has received. "Reading ability is a developmental process" means that the very complicated process of learning to read is not mastered at any particular time such as age ten or twelve. Nor can it be assumed that the ultimate ability to read critically is achieved at any particular point on the educational continuum.

Thus, an adequate reader at third-grade level may be considerably less efficient at fourth grade and have serious problems by the sixth grade. The statement implies recognition that the nature of human learning and the nature of the reading task preclude the possibility of mastering the reading process by a given chronological age or in a designated number of years of formal schooling. The developmental aspect of various reading skills is discussed next.

Illustrations of Developmental Skills

Reading is an integrated, total response that is made up of a very large number of separate skills, abilities, memory patterns, and the like. Any of the dozens of reading skills could serve as an example of how growth must take place at more advanced levels. Without attempting to determine how many separate skills go into reading, we can isolate a few and illustrate how each is developmental in nature.

Acquisition of Sight Vocabulary. The development of a sight-word vocabulary is probably one of the more obvious examples of what is implied by the term *developmental process.* Instant recognition of words is a basic skill that is a prerequisite for reading at any level. Although it

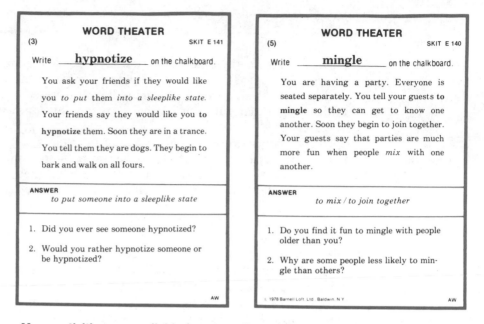

WORD THEATER

(3) SKIT E 141

Write **hypnotize** on the chalkboard.

You ask your friends if they would like you *to put* them *into a sleeplike state.* Your friends say they would like you **to hypnotize** them. Soon they are in a trance. You tell them they are dogs. They begin to bark and walk on all fours.

ANSWER
to put someone into a sleeplike state

1. Did you ever see someone hypnotized?
2. Would you rather hypnotize someone or be hypnotized?

AW

WORD THEATER

(5) SKIT E 140

Write **mingle** on the chalkboard.

You are having a party. Everyone is seated separately. You tell your guests **to mingle** so they can get to know one another. Soon they begin to join together. Your guests say that parties are much more fun when people *mix* with one another.

ANSWER
to mix / to join together

1. Do you find it fun to mingle with people older than you?
2. Why are some people less likely to mingle than others?

AW

Many activities are available for expanding pupils' vocabulary.

is true that mere recognition of words is not reading, it must be remembered that the absence of this ability precludes reading. For example, the individual who has no sight-recognition vocabulary is not a reader. A reader who fails to recognize as few as 5 percent of the words in a passage is handicapped; one who can't recognize 10 percent is a seriously impaired reader. For these people, frustration is inevitable.

Along with expanding their sight vocabulary, children will of course be using word identification skills. The point of the discussion is that normal readers are constantly learning to recognize new words instantly. They may resort to letter-sound analysis the first few times they meet a new word; however, as they meet the same word time after time, they should rely less and less on analysis. When readers fail to add words to their sight vocabulary, they are not maintaining a "normal learning pattern." The following lines of words represent visual patterns of increasing difficulty which must be mastered as children move upward through the grades:

an and hand sand band land baker barber
banker barter medal metal meddle mental medical
elegant element elephant elegance eloquence general
generous generally genesis generalize national
natural nationally naturally nationality

As an increasing number of new words are met, certain irregular spellings occur more frequently (combinations *que, ph, igh, wr, mb, ch* as *k* or *s, psy, kn,* etc.). Many words containing these patterns are learned as sight words. Children will also meet many sight words which have come to English from other languages: *debris, corps, reign, cache, rouge, yacht, sphinx, chassis, suave, chaos.*

Word Identification Skills. Applying word identification skills is developmental in nature, at least up to the point where they are utilized automatically. Experience indicates that lack of ability in phonic analysis is a major stumbling block for many pupils in the middle and upper grades. Word identification skills must be both reviewed and extended at this level. The child who has experienced little difficulty with simple compound words such as *sidewalk, anyhow, somewhere,* and *barnyard* may need drill and guidance in dealing with words like *floodgate, homespun, praiseworthy, foreshadow,* and *supernatural.*

Children who have applied letter-sound relationships in solving shorter words often experience difficulty with multisyllabic words. Some children develop the habit of "giving up" on lengthy words because they lack skill in breaking these words into syllables. They need guided practice in order to gain the confidence needed to solve words such as *overproduction, reinforcement, unworthiness, misrepresentation,* and the like.

Other Developmental Skills. The developmental nature of many other reading skills is self-evident. Examples would include locating information, using library resources, improving rate of reading, expanding meaning vocabulary, and critical reading. A final illustration consists of six sentences, each taken from a basal reader at successive levels. This material reflects the need for growth on the part of the reader in regard to sight words, sentence patterns, profiting from punctuation, using proper intonation, drawing inferences, as well as other skills.

> "I will run and bring some water."
>
> "I know where the field mouse lives down by the brook."
>
> "The next night, when his father got home, Bob said, 'I read that book about the other Bob.' "
>
> "Sir," said the duke, who was trying to recover his dignity while hopping around on one foot—not an easy thing to do, "Sir, I am minding my own business and I suggest that you do the same."
>
> The missile range was known as Station One, and when the men talked over the radio from there they would say, "This is Station One," or just, "This is One."
>
> "We can be sure that the Trojans, on hearing this, will not risk bringing her wrath down upon themselves by destroying our offering."

DIRECTED READING ACTIVITY (DRA)

Although a direct lesson on a specific reading skill can take place at any given time, the directed reading activity (DRA) provides an excellent framework for intermediate grade teachers to "teach" a needed skill. In this way, the skill being taught can immediately be practiced in the context of the story being read. The application of the DRA should also extend to the content areas of social studies and science. The same steps of preparing youngsters to read, allowing the students to read the story silently, asking appropriate comprehension questions, and providing specific instructional lessons on a needed skill should be followed in the content areas as well as the basal reader. Teaching a needed skill to youngsters as part of a total learning sequence is prudent in terms of student interest, mastery, and application.

Besides the emphasis on instructional lessons as part of the DRA, the comprehension check of the story deserves special attention by intermediate grade teachers. A crucial finding of teacher effectiveness studies (see chapter 3) at the intermediate grade levels is that high-achieving classes are characterized by teachers sustaining interaction on a particular topic or skill for an extended time. Related to the DRA, this means it is not enough to ask questions that require different levels of thinking but it is equally imperative that teachers realize what to do after the question has been asked. In order to sustain student-teacher interaction, teachers should be aware of their own reacting behaviors to student responses. Special attention should be focused on appropriate wait-time and various probing and redirecting questions to student responses (see chapter 6).

DEVELOPING AND EXPANDING CONCEPTS

Language is the tool of the school, and mastery of language serves as the basis for future learning. Children in the middle grades need experiences with reading and language that will help them expand their stock of concepts and develop the ability to make sense of what they read. Language competencies that must be taught include:

- The ability to reduce the uncertainties caused by words having the same pronunciation but different spellings and meanings.
- An understanding of how "new words" move into the language at a very fast rate.

- Mastery of words often confused. With over a half-million words in the English language, look-alike and sound-alike words must be mastered.
- A gradual mastery of words that pose problems in pronunciation and meaning. The fact that English has borrowed thousands of words from other languages has accentuated this problem.
- Acquiring the meanings of a number of root words from other languages, particularly those that are used dozens of times in different English words (*graph, logy, pseudo,* etc.)
- The ability to decode small units of language (proverbs, quotes, etc.) that pack meaning into the sentence.
- Learning different meanings for the same words, understanding figurative language, differentiating between fact and opinion.

Expanding Reading-Language Skills

The balance of the chapter presents a number of teaching exercises that can be used to help intermediate-level students expand concepts and reading skills. These are illustrative and can be modified and adapted in many ways. Each can be presented as a group or class activity. Later, as more materials are introduced, these can become activities used by individuals, pairs of students, teams, or larger groups.

Working with Homonyms. Through the study of homonyms, children expand their ability to work with language. They develop concepts and learn both the visual patterns and meanings of these word pairs. The following exercises illustrate different tasks and exercise formats. Each can be adapted to fit different difficulty levels. There are many other ways in which material could be presented; these are simply illustrative.

INTRODUCTORY ACTIVITY

Word-Meaning Study. Provide definitions of words that may present meaning difficulties or whose meanings may be confused. Introduce the word pairs by illustrating and discussing their meanings through use of written definitions. Elicit sentences from students for each word pair and write these on chalkboard. Guide a discussion of meaning of these sentences in relation to each word's meaning in context.

to raise: to elevate, cause to rise
to raze: to demolish, overthrow, completely remove

a principle: a fundamental or basic truth, law, or point
a principal: the chief officer, as head of a school

to reign: to exercise authority, to govern, "the king's reign was ten years"
a rein: a bridle to guide or control a horse

it is stationary: fixed in place, not moving
it is stationery: paper for writing

it is coarse: common, rough, inferior quality, unrefined
a course: a course of study; a path such as a racecourse, golf course, etc.

Direct pupils' attention to words written on chalkboard. Call on pupils to provide a homonym for word listed. Ask pupils to state a sentence for the homonym, and write the sentence on the board. Have pupils discuss the meaning of each sentence.

a reel	real	He is real.
a plain	plane	A plane is flying overhead.
I ate		
I made		
is pale		
a night		
I hear		
I blew		

Provide a written list of the answers if you think pupils will need them to experience success in identifying the appropriate homonym.

PRACTICE ACTIVITY

Write the homonyms that fit the definitions. Select your choices from this list:

a pain	I see
to waste	to steal
a pear	my waist
a tale	a male
a pair	some mail
a pane	the sea
a tail	some steel

Strong, heavy metal ______________________

take another's property ______________________

Large body of water ______________________

to observe visually ______________________

Breakable part of window ______________________

when something hurts ______________________

Just above the hips	to squander
______________	______________
A story or account of	dogs wag this
______________	______________
Opposite of female	delivered by mail carrier
______________	______________
Two of anything	a fruit (odd shaped)
______________	______________

Devise sentences which "sound right" but which contain the wrong word from a pair of homonyms. The child underlines each incorrect word and then writes the words that belong in the sentences.

We eight our lunch together. ______________
The old flower mill is closed down. ______________
I do not believe in whiches or goblins. ______________
The injured dear was easy pray for the wolves. ______________
Please weight for me after school. ______________

APPLICATION ACTIVITY

Select a homonym to complete each sentence below. Write your choice in the space. Sample: after a *(week)* in the hospital he felt very *(weak)*. Complete one or two examples with the pupils to assure that they understand what they are to do. This will increase their chance of success and should encourage active involvement in the practice activity.

1. The __________ (hole, whole) group worked very hard digging the huge __________ (hole, whole.)
2. It is better to diet than to just __________ (weight, wait) for your __________ (wait, weight) to go down.
3. The __________ (steel, steal) bars were so heavy that the thieves decided not to __________ (steel, steal) them.
4. Jim said, "I sort of __________ (new, knew) I would get a __________ (new, knew) football for my birthday."
5. He did have __________ (some, sum) trouble with addition, often arriving at the wrong __________ (some, sum).

The level of difficulty can be increased by providing only one of the homonyms to complete the sense of the sentence. Direct the pupils to write a pair of homonyms in the blank spaces to complete each sentence. Only one of the words needed is provided at the left. Sample:

(one) John ___won___ only ___one___ prize at the carnival.

(through) 1. The catcher ______________ the ball ______________ the infield and a runner scored.

(new) 2. Mary ______________ the ______________ coat was too expensive.

(there) 3. The twins said that ______________ house is over ____________ by the park.

(red) 4. Bill ______________ the title, "The ______________ Baron Flies Again."

(plain) 5. The pilot decided to land the ______________ on the smooth ______________ beyond the river.

(pain) 6. He felt a sudden ______________ as his arm broke the ______ of glass.

Complete the following sentences by writing a pair of homonyms in the blank spaces. If you are baffled by a sentence, go to the *clue box.* It contains *one* word that will fit in each blank. (One word in the box will not be used.)

1. It is no fun to ______________ stung by a ______________.
2. Mother said, "______________ this junk into the ______________."
3. "When ______________ these bills come ______________?" he asked.
4. Dave said, "I would have ______________ you a present, but I didn't have a ______________!"
5. The king was ______________ out after holding the ______________ for fourteen years.

Clue Box

due	be	sent	throne	house	thrown
cent	bee	haul	hall	do	

Each sentence below contains two blank spaces; complete the sentences by writing homonyms that begin with the letter shown. Be sure to ask yourself if your sentences make sense.

1. The wild b______________ in the zoo would b______________ his fangs.
2. S______________ numbers when added equal the s______________ of ten.
3. Going without food for a w______________ will make a person w______________.
4. The injury to his h______________ took several days to h______________.
5. The L______________ Ranger was in the bank getting a l______________.
6. H______________ in the park you can h______________ all kinds of birds.
7. The coach said, "Don't b______________ like a baby if you get hit by a b______________."
8. W______________ you please bring in some w______________ for the fireplace?

9. She seemed to be in a d______________ for at least three d______________ after winning the contest.
10. He took a p______________ to determine how many fishermen use a bamboo p______________.

Words of Recent Origin. English is a living language, and living things grow and change. The changes that take place in a language are determined by its users and not as a result of previously adopted rules. It is likely that more new words were added to our language in the past thirty years than in any previous century. Children should be invited to think about this phenomenon and discuss possible causes for it. An excellent way to develop insight is to prepare a list of recently coined words and then place them in categories.

The following are some newly coined words or phrases that were suggested by one class. Children had worked in small teams, relying both on their knowledge and on any and all materials available in the classroom and library.

> acid rain, AIDS, groovy, uptight, laser beam, data base, exit poll, flowchart, talking typewriter, heat shield, Xerox, dune buggy, Teflon, megaton, break dancing, Formica, rap, right on, Panasonic, smog, Nutrasweet, disk camera, skybus, astrodome, heart transplant, yuppie, lunacart, cassette, antibiotics, aerospace, polyester, Telstar, computer literacy, floppy disk, sticker shock, hacker

As a next step, the teacher directed the pupils to group words into categories. Some of the first that came to mind were *slang, computers, transportation,* and *space exploration.* In the process, they found that headings such as "science" or "technology" were too broad, since these terms cut across every other heading. There was quite a list of trade names for products: *Xerox, Formica, Nutrasweet, Teflon,* and so forth. Words such as *lunacart, yuppie,* and *Telstar* were analyzed and provided insights into the logic of coining new words. The study of slang terms proved interesting, particularly when an older *Dictionary of Slang* was studied. It became obvious that this is one of the most prolific areas for new words, but also that the mortality rate is very high.

Working on a unit devoted to new words in English leads to an understanding of how language works and how it develops. An increased respect for the power, precision, and flexibility of language is usually an outcome. Motivation is high during such study, particularly among students who have become "over drilled" on reading skills instruction. A great number of reading and writing experiences can grow out of the study of newly coined words.

Confusion of Word Meanings. Some words that look very much alike are often confused in meaning. Wide reading that ensures meeting such words in many different contexts is probably the most desirable method of expanding meanings. Teacher-made exercises can also be useful and highly motivational. As a rule, children enjoy working with word meanings, particularly if the difficulty of the exercise material is geared to their needs. Below is an example of a teaching-testing exercise.

INTRODUCTORY ACTIVITY

Words that look very much alike are often confused as to *meaning.* Present the following words in written format to the pupils. Discuss each word's meaning and have pupils provide several sentences using each word. Write selected examples of sentences on the chalkboard. Focus the discussion on the use of context as an aid to determining the word's meaning. Present sentences such as those written below and call on each student to identify the words for each blank that make sense in context. Write the pupils' selections in the spaces.

alter: to change or modify
altar: place used in worship
medal: a decoration awarded for service
meddle: to interfere
cite: to quote or use as illustration
sight: to see, act of seeing
site: location
council: a governing group
counsel: to advise
affect: to influence
effect: a result produced by a cause
carton: a box or container
cartoon: a drawing, a caricature

It might be a good idea to give a ______ to people who never ______ in others' affairs.

In over 500 years, no attempt had been made to ______ the ______.

You will find a humorous ______ on every ______ of breakfast food.

He hoped to catch ______ of the ______ where the new club was to be built.

APPLICATION ACTIVITY

The meanings of the words on the left are not given. Place the proper word in the blanks in each sentence. Use sentence context to help you in selecting the word that makes sense. Use a dictionary if you are doubtful about the meaning of any word.

miner
decent
course
minor
diary
descend
dairy
precede
cannon
proceed
canyon
coarse

1. Most states have laws which prohibit ________ from working as a ________.
2. The fairways of the golf ________ were covered with ________ grass.
3. During the day Bill worked in a ________ but each night he would write in his ________.
4. We should try to find a ________ trail if we hope to ________ the mountain before dark.
5. When an army is to p________ through a c________ surrounded by the enemy, it is the usual custom to have a barrage by c________ p________ the march.

Misconceptions. During the intermediate grades many children will encounter a number of words and concepts that will puzzle them. Many such instances will occur in subject-matter texts as well as basal readers. Children usually come to school with the "meanings" adequate for dealing with beginning reading but they are by no means familiar with the various connotations of the words with which they must cope in the primary and intermediate grades. A lack of concepts and insufficient knowledge of various word connotations are not the only problems with which the teacher must deal in expanding meaning. A related problem is that of misconceptions harbored by pupils. The school cannot be held responsible for misconceptions that children have picked up elsewhere. It may be impossible in overcrowded classrooms to prevent misconceptions from arising or going undetected. Nevertheless, the extent to which the problem exists should motivate teachers to seek ways of modifying instructional techniques, for the confusion of meanings is a barrier to reading and learning.

One of the axioms of teaching reading is that "new" words in a lesson should be mastered both as sight words and as meaning-bearing units before the child is expected to read that lesson. Often, little attention is given to mastering shades of meaning, and too much is taken for granted when the child is able to "call the word." As a result, many teachers would be shocked at the misconceptions still harbored by some children in their classes. The following responses on vocabulary tests illustrate some rather striking misconceptions, even though it is not difficult to imagine how some of these arose. The responses are given verbatim.

regard
a. like you were guarding something
b. to think of someone as a cousin
c. to redo your work

priceless
a. something that doesn't cost anything
b. you want to buy something and you think it's not worth it

brunette	a.	a kind of permanent
	b.	a girl that dances
	c.	prune
shrewd	a.	when you're not polite
	b.	being kind of cruel
	c.	guess it means rude

When asked to give the meaning of *conquer,* one boy volunteered, "It means like to *konk her* on the head." Another, when meeting the written word *mosquitoes* for the first time, concluded it was the name of a fairy—*most quiet toes.* A preschool child, hearing an older sibling make a reference to a dinosaur, immediately responded, "I like to go to the *dime* store." An eight year old listening around Christmas time to a choir on television asked, "What does *si door im* mean? His parents were at a loss until he repeated the line, "Oh come let us si door im."

Some of these examples illustrate what takes place when children are confronted with concepts beyond their present grasp. They usually change them to a more concrete meaning that is known to them. Although these examples illustrate how children deal with unknown words that they hear, they can also provide us with insight into what happens when children read unknown words.

Pronunciation and Meaning Problems. Problems can be dealt with in the context in which they are met, but there is nothing educationally unsound in reviewing or teaching a series of such words by means of either the chalkboard or a worksheet. One value of the latter procedure is that a given exercise can be used with only those pupils who reveal a need for it, several times if needed. A list of words difficult to pronounce might include: *aisle, fatigue, coyote, exit, plague, sieve, cache, posse, gauge, corps, beau, feign, nephew, antique, bouquet, isthmus, agile, chaos, ache, plateau, quay, bivouac, czar, recipe, stature, reign, viaduct, suede.* A number of practice exercises can be devised to teach the pronunciation and meaning of such words. A few are provided here.

PRACTICE ACTIVITY

In the first column the difficult words are listed, and adjoining columns contain the dictionary pronunciation and meaning:

cache	căsh	a hole in the ground, or a hiding place
feign	fān	to imagine; invent, hence, to form and relate as if true
quay	kē	a stretch of paved bank or a solid artificial landing place beside navigable water for convenience in loading and unloading vessels
bivouac	biv oo ak	an encampment for a very short sojourn, under improvised shelter or none

Use the difficult word and a synonym in the same sentence:

"As they reached the *plateau* the guide said, "It will be easier walking on this *flat, level* ground."

"Climbing mountains is hard work," said the guide. "We will rest when you feel *fatigued* so tell me when you get *tired.*"

Prepare a card for each word: one side of the card contains the difficult word and its pronunciation, the other has a paragraph using the word.

chaos (kā os)	When a tornado strikes a community, *chaos* results. Houses are blown down, fires break out, fallen trees block the streets, telephone poles and wires are down, and the fire department cannot get through the streets.

Prepare a short paragraph in which the difficult word is used in several contexts.

From the aerial photographs it was difficult for him to *gauge* whether the railroad was narrow or regular *gauge.* He recalled that the day the picture was made the fuel *gauge* registered very nearly empty. He remembered attempting to *gauge* the effect of a tail wind on his chances of returning safely.

Working with High-Frequency Root Words. English has borrowed many roots and prefixes from other languages, particularly Latin and Greek. Learning the meaning of those that appear frequently in English words can be of great benefit to children in developing language facility. Intermediate-level children will have met and will continue to meet numerous examples such as *auto, mobile, photo, graph, bio, zoo, geo, logy, crat, trans, port, sphere.* In addition, they have met many prefixes and other terms relating to the metric system: *centi, milli, kilo, meter, micro, mega.*

In the past, the teaching of roots was usually delayed until high school. One approach, that of handing out three or four pages of Greek and Latin roots and asking students to learn them, usually resulted in very little learning. This mass of material was "presented" rather than taught. The task was overwhelming and not meaningful. There are other ways to help children learn the meanings of root words.

INTRODUCTORY ACTIVITY

Demonstrate how some common words are derived from borrowed roots and how roots are often combined.

auto: (Greek for *self*)
mobile: (French for *to move*)
automobile: capable of moving under its own power
graph: (Greek for *to write*)
autograph: to write one's self, or one's name

The following illustrates how a number of other roots are combined with *graph.*

Root			
photo	(light)	+ graph	(to write): photograph (to write with light)
tele	(far)	+ graph	(to write); telegraph
phone	(sound)	+ graph	(to write): phonograph
geo	(earth)	+ graphy	(to write): geography
bio	(life)	+ graphy	(to write): biography
cardio	(heart)	+ graph	(to write): cardiograph
mono	(one)	+ graph	(to write): monograph (a writing on one topic)

Combining the root *logy* (study) with other roots:

Root

bio + *logy* = study of living things
geo + *logy* = study of the earth
theo (God) + *logy* = theology: study of God, religion
psyche (mind) + *logy* = psychology: study of the mind
zoo (animal) + *logy* = zoology: study of animals
anthrop (man) + *logy* = anthropology: study of man
Others: meteorology, pathology, audiology, phonology

Another variation is a teacher-planned period devoted to learning important word roots and to demonstrating the possibilities of word building through the addition of prefixes, suffixes, and other roots. For example, *dict* is a root meaning "to say." To *predict* is to say in advance, and implies that an event is pre*dict*able. This same root permits one to say that if one is to *dic*tate, her *dic*tion in *dic*tating should be clear and that her pronunciation should not contra*dict* the *dic*tionary. The study of word meanings can be a fascinating and rewarding experience.

Prefix		*Root*	
con	(with, together)	*tract*	(to draw): contract
re	(back)	*tract*	(to draw): retract
ex	(out of)	*tract*	(to draw): extract
im	(into)	*port*	(to carry): import
trans	(across)	*port*	(to carry): transport
re	(back)	*port*	(to carry): report

Root		*Suffix*	
port	(to carry)	*able*	(capable of): portable
dict	(to say)	*tion*	(act of): diction
grat	(thanks)	*ful*	(full of): grateful

PRACTICE ACTIVITY

When pupils express interest in word building (roots, prefixes, suffixes), the teacher can make available teacher-constructed exercises similar to the examples below. Knowledge of roots and prefixes will help a child work out the meaning of many words that at first glance may appear strange and difficult.

Build a Word. Read the definition, then add a prefix, suffix, or both to the root word shown. Make the word you build fit the definition.

depend: to rely on (clues: un, able, in, ent)

	depend	______	trustworthy, reliable
______	depend	______	not trustworthy, not dependable
______	depend	______	self-reliant
	depend	______	relies on someone else

agree: to consent, no conflict (clues: ment, dis, able)

______	agree	______	not agreeing
	agree	______	pleasing, pleasant
______	agree	______	not pleasing, unpleasant
	agree	______	a contract, or understanding

(clues: dis, ment, im, un, able)

______	content	______	not good, not helpful
______	agree	______	failure to agree
______	favor	______	not good, not helpful
______	content	______	unhappiness
______	employ	______	out of work

Working with Smaller Language Units. The teacher is the key to whether or not children experience the power and beauty of language. Crucial to this end is how children view the reading process. In a study designed to determine how children view reading, Ngandu (11) concluded that as students progress through the grades they increasingly look upon reading as a meaning process. Yet, low-achieving, intermediate-grade children tend to view reading more as a general activity or as a word identification process. Even though word identification strategies are stressed with lower grade and low-achieving older children, meaning should be continually sought after with these children. Ngandu concurs and states, "Certainly it may be argued that some prerequisite word identification skills are first needed before fluency can be attained. But, these skills should function only to enable students to search for meaning. This must be the ultimate goal of all reading programs, especially for the below average child, who tends to think of reading as something else" (pp. 274–75).

One way to encourage children to become involved with language is to design activities that have children analyze and discuss small units of printed matter. They have dialogues with the author, and they are exposed to interpretations radically different from their own. As a result, they begin to learn that language is raw material that must be shaped and molded and that using language is a creative activity.

Use of quotes. One excellent technique for developing discussion and understanding of language is to write a nonfactual sentence on the chalkboard. Children are then to determine whether the author is right or wrong. (The same result is achieved by having children indicate whether they *agree* or *disagree* with the statement.) An example that can be used at several intermediate grade levels is "Good people are more miserable than other people." Most groups divide on the issue of agreement or disagreement with the statement. Individuals then state the reasons they feel as they do. Such discussion provides valuable insights into the critical reading process: "A good person shouldn't be miserable," "she has no reason to be miserable," "Good people are made miserable when they see suffering, injustice, poverty, war," and so forth.

Many college students and adults show some hostility toward the assignment, raising such issues as "the material is taken out of context". "What does he mean by 'miserable'?" "What's the definition of a 'good person'?" As these and other questions are discussed, insights into reading are developed. It is established that the author is dead; we cannot ask him what he meant by *miserable* and *good person.* Soon the readers see that in the final analysis these words (and all words one reads) take on the meaning that each reader gives them.

INTRODUCTORY ACTIVITY

The following are a few examples of quotations that might be used as stimulus statements for discussion. When discussions begin to extend far beyond the time you think should be allotted to this activity, you can assume that children are learning much about critical reading.

It is the good reader that makes a good book.
Character is what you are when no one is watching.
Don't criticize a person until you have walked in his or her shoes for a day.
The longest journey begins with the first step.
All humankind is of one author.
You must have a good memory to be a successful liar.
You can judge a person by his or her enemies as well as by his or her friends.
The riches that are in the heart cannot be stolen.
Error of opinion may be tolerated where reason is left free to combat it.
People are lonely because they build walls instead of bridges.
Man is the only animal who can talk himself into problems that otherwise would not have existed.

Interpretation and discussion of proverbs. Working with proverbs is an excellent way to focus on smaller units of language. Proverbs are brief statements that seem to reflect great wisdom. The fact that they are brief and to the point keeps them in circulation. Their brevity also permits different interpretations, since the meaning is not spelled out in detail. People of all cultures develop and use proverbs. Since people everywhere seem to have problems, interests, and needs, the same "message" may occur frequently. It is interesting to compare the different ways one idea is expressed. For example,

> If something has to be done, do it—and get started on it right away!
> Don't put off till tomorrow what you can do today.
> A journey of a thousand miles begins with a single step.
> He who hesitates is lost.
> Procrastination is the thief of time.
> Without starting you will arrive nowhere.
> Nothing ventured, nothing gained.
> He who is not ready today, will be less so tomorrow.
> Make hay while the sun shines.

Another idea is that your choice of companions will reveal the type of person you are:

> A person is known by the company he or she keeps.
> Birds of a feather flock together.
> Better to be alone than in bad company.
> He who lies down with dogs gets up with fleas.
> If you live with the lame, you will soon learn to limp.

There are innumerable ways in which proverbs can be converted into reading-language experiences. A few illustrative examples follow.

INTRODUCTORY ACTIVITY

Prepare a number of "pairs of proverbs." Present these in a written format and ask the children to read each pair and discuss whether the two statements have *much the same meaning* or if they have *opposite meanings*. Guide pupils to discuss what each proverb is implying. Have pupils regroup the proverbs into pairs that have similar meanings and write their groupings on the chalkboard.

He who hesitates is lost.
Always look before you leap.

The road to fame is paved with pain.
The path to glory is not lined with flowers.

If at first you don't succeed, try, try again.
Everything is difficult at first.

A stitch in time saves nine.
Never put off till tomorrow what you can do today.
Beauty is in the eye of the beholder.
Tis the good reader that makes a good book.

Write on a card a pair of proverbs that appear to be contradictory. Have students explain or describe a situation in which the first of these statements is good advice. Then direct students to cite a situation in which the second proverb would be good advice.

Using library resources and children's previous experiences, make a list of proverbs from other lands or cultures. From this list, select any proverbs dealing with the same idea or topic (friendship, honesty, loyalty, courage, defeat, etc.). Direct pupils to classify the proverbs in terms of the topics and discuss why they classified them that way.

APPLICATION ACTIVITY

Directions: Sometimes we repeat a proverb without thinking about what it really means. Read each of the following statements and write in your own words what it means.

If the shoe fits wear it. ____________________
____
____

Mighty oaks from tiny acorns grow. ____________________
____
____

Too many cooks spoil the broth. ____________________
____
____

The pen is mightier than the sword. ____________________
____
____

Don't cross the bridge till you come to it. ____________________
____
____

Fact-opinion and agree-disagree statements. After several years of school and heavy reliance on textbooks, children tend to accept without question what they find in print or what is stated with authority or by an authority. Fact-oriented school tasks tend to make readers vulnerable when they meet statements that have surface validity but which may be biased or untrue. Students are constantly bombarded with advertisements, news broadcasts, politicians' statements, and conflicting scientific claims that present only one point of view. Thus, one may read that atomic energy plants are perfectly safe or definitely a hazard. Brand X aspirin is superior to all other brands. Product A contains *no* aspirin and is superior to *all* aspirin. High-cholesterol foods are/are not a threat to health and survival.

As laws are passed that attempt to make language users more responsible to the consumer, those who use language to control behavior become more sophisticated in their use of language. Thus children and adults, as consumers of print and products, must develop survival skills. Fact or opinion exercises help to develop such skills. The purpose of this type of language experience is to sharpen actual analysis of what one reads and to demonstrate how personal bias, previous experience, and background knowledge may color one's interpretation.

PRACTICE ACTIVITY

Directions: Read each sentence carefully. If the statement is a fact, write F in front of the sentence. If the statement is an opinion, write O.

____1. Air travel is safer than any other method of transportation.
____2. The American Revolution was caused by taxation without representation.
____3. The love of money is the root of all evil.
____4. It is very difficult to get a good job without a college education.
____5. All brands of aspirin are essentially the same.
____6. Before the end of this century, the United States will establish colonies on the moon.
____7. Democracy is the best form of government that has been developed by the human race.

APPLICATION ACTIVITY

One of the most successful approaches for developing and expanding concepts is a language activity called "sentence meaning." This consists of a page of numbered sentences that are unrelated to each other. Each sentence contains one or more words whose meaning should be known or learned. As the student reads each sentence she marks it *T* if it is true or *F* if it is false. Obviously, one can design exercises that deal with general concepts or with any one of the content areas. A few illustrative items follow.

Social Studies

____1. *Carnivorous* animals feed primarily on vegetation.
____2. The term *amnesty* means a loss of memory.

____3. A *glacier* is a huge mass of ice.
____4. *Monsoon* is a type of monkey widely used in medical experiments.
____5. It is not illegal to *paraphrase* a court decision.

Science

____1. An unproven scientific theory is nothing more than a *hypothesis.*
____2. Most metals *contract* when heated.
____3. *Specific* directions are very brief, with some steps omitted.
____4. Electrical current flows freely through *insulators.*
____5. *Ornithology* is the scientific study of birds.

Mathematics

____1. The radius of a circle is twice the length of its diameter.
____2. The sum of the two smallest angles in a right triangle always totals 90 degrees.
____3. The perimeter of a circle is equal to its circumference.
____4. An event that occurs biannually occurs twice a year.
____5. If the top side of square A equals the bottom side of square B, the two squares are equal.

General Vocabulary

____1. A highly skilled person with much experience is called an *apprentice.*
____2. Shoes made entirely from *synthetics* cannot have leather soles.
____3. The term *equivalent* means equal.
____4. A *travesty* is a brief written account of one's travels.
____5. The root *thermo* in thermometer means heat.

APPLICATION ACTIVITY

Agree-Disagree offers a change of pace from the above. Using this format, students write or discuss why they agree or disagree with a particular statement. Directions: Read each statement and tell why you agree or disagree with it.

1. Large cities are not desirable places to live. ____________________
____
____
2. The rich people in the United States do not pay a fair share of taxes. ________
____
____
3. The aim of advertising is to control the behavior of consumers. ____________
____
____
4. Reading ability is a major factor in determining what occupations one can enter.
____
____
5. Violence on television is a major cause of crime. ____________________
____
____

SUMMARY

The intermediate reading program was presented within the context of the developmental nature of learning to read. Providing the proper environment for pupil growth was discussed specific to the instructional and independent reading programs at this level. The major objective of the independent program is to encourage recreational reading through creative assignments and class activities that promote an enjoyment of reading. Many practical examples were provided in the chapter to promote an independent program with the plea to provide adequate time in the curriculum for this important phase of the total reading program. Without a planned independent program, youngsters may still be able to pass multiple-choice literacy tests but may never read on their own or possess the ability and the desire to be independent readers.

The instructional program was highlighted due in part to the danger of a too literal acceptance of the old dictum that "a pupil learns to read by reading" or "nothing improves one's reading like more and more reading." In order for students to progress in their reading and language abilities, direct instruction must be provided in various word identification, comprehension, and study skills. Equipping students with the necessary skills to be successful readers in the content areas is a priority of instruction in the intermediate grades. Examples of direct instruction lessons were provided to illustrate this priority.

Underlying the successful intermediate program is the attention to individual differences through appropriate diagnostic assessment and the ability to handle effectively a wide range of ability and concerns through various grouping procedures. Overriding the entire discussion of the intermediate program, as well as the primary-grade program, is the need to have children engaged in experiences in reading that illustrate the power, beauty, and precision of language. The key to this end is a knowledgeable and sensitive teacher in every classroom.

YOUR POINT OF VIEW

Discussion Questions

1. Individual differences in achievement increase as we move upward through the grades. Which one of the following factors would you prefer to defend as being most important in bringing about these differences in achievement? Why?
   a. Pupil ability
   b. School promotion policies

c. Competency of instruction
d. Factors outside of school

2. Many pupils love learning to read and school in general in the primary grades. In the intermediate grades many of these same pupils dislike reading and school. What factors could account for this situation?

Take a Stand For or Against

1. Variability among pupils in the intermediate grades could be reduced by improved teaching in earlier grades.
2. Good teaching in the intermediate grades will increase the individual differences in children's reading ability.

BIBLIOGRAPHY

1. Berglund, Roberta L., and Johnson, Jerry L. "A Primer On Uninterrupted Sustained Silent Reading." *The Reading Teacher* 36 (1983): 534–39.
2. Blair, Timothy R. "Where to Expend Your Teaching Effort (It does count!)." *The Reading Teacher* 30 (1976): 293–96.
3. Blair, Timothy R., and Turner, Edward C. "Reading to Learn: A Forgotten Objective." *The Florida Reading Quarterly* 19 (1983): 46–47.
4. Chall, Jeanne S. *Stages of Reading Development.* New York: McGraw-Hill Book Co., 1983.
5. Criscuolo, Nicholas P. "Book Reports: Twelve Creative Alternatives." *The Reading Teacher* 30 (1977): 893–95.
6. Galen, Nancy, and Prendergast, John. "Selling Reading." *Reading Horizons* 19 (Summer 1979): 280–83.
7. Gambrell, Linda B. "Getting Started with Sustained Silent Reading and Keeping it Going." *The Reading Teacher* 32 (1978): 328–31.
8. Kennedy, Larry D. "Textbook Usage in the Intermediate-Upper Grades." *The Reading Teacher* 21 (1971): 723–29.
9. Lukasevick, Ann. "Three Dozen Useful Information Souces on Reading for the Gifted." *The Reading Teacher* 36 (1983): 542–48.
10. Moore, Jesse C.; Jones, Clarence J.; and Miller, Douglas C. "What We Know After a Decade of Sustained Silent Reading." *The Reading Teacher* 33 (1980): 445–50.
11. Ngandu, Kathleen N. "Elementary Students' Definitions of Reading." *Reading Horizons* 19 (Summer 1979): 272–75.
12. Raths, Louis E.; Harmin, Merrill; and Simon, Sidney B. *Teaching for Thinking.* 2d ed. Columbus, Oh.: Charles E. Merrill Publishing Co., 1973.

13. Schaudt, Barbara A. "ERIC/RCS: Another Look at Sustained Silent Reading." *The Reading Teacher* 36 (1983): 934–36.
14. Schulte, Emerita Schroer. "Independent Reading Interests of Children in Grades Four, Five and Six." In *Reading and Realism,* edited by J. Allen Figurel, 728–32. Proceedings International Reading Association 13, Part 1. Newark, Del.: International Reading Association, 1969.

UNIT 4 Organizing and Managing Instruction

Chapters

If you were to visit a classroom of an effective teacher, you probably would be impressed with the smoothness and thoroughness of the reading program. This occurrence does not just happen; it is the result of much hard work and planning on the teacher's part. A continual focus on each individual's strengths and weaknesses is an integral ingredient of successful, quality teaching. Chapter 11 centers on areas of diagnosis for the classroom teacher of reading. Principles of diagnosis are given along with a description of various means to determine pupils' needs.

The ability of teachers to provide instruction congruent with pupils' needs in a class of twenty-five to thirty children is a demanding task. To meet this challenge, it is necessary to be skilled at organizing children to maximize their opportunities for learning. Chapter 12 will focus on effective organization and management of instruction.

The amount of core and supplementary reading instructional materials available for use in the classroom can be overwhelming. Oftentimes the claims made by the publishers of such materials suggest that the answer to effective reading instruction depends on using their materials. This is not the case. As we noted in chapter 1, materials do not teach; however, quality materials in the hands of an effective teacher lead to a quality instructional program. Recently, much attention has been given to the use of computers in the reading program. They have been advocated by some individuals as the answer to effective reading instruction. Again, their effectiveness depends on the teacher. Chapter 13 looks at the use of computers in reading instruction and management.

Providing appropriate education for culturally and language-different children, gifted, and handicapped youth in our schools is discussed in chapter 14. All teachers of reading need to be aware of current thinking and practices relating to these children.

11

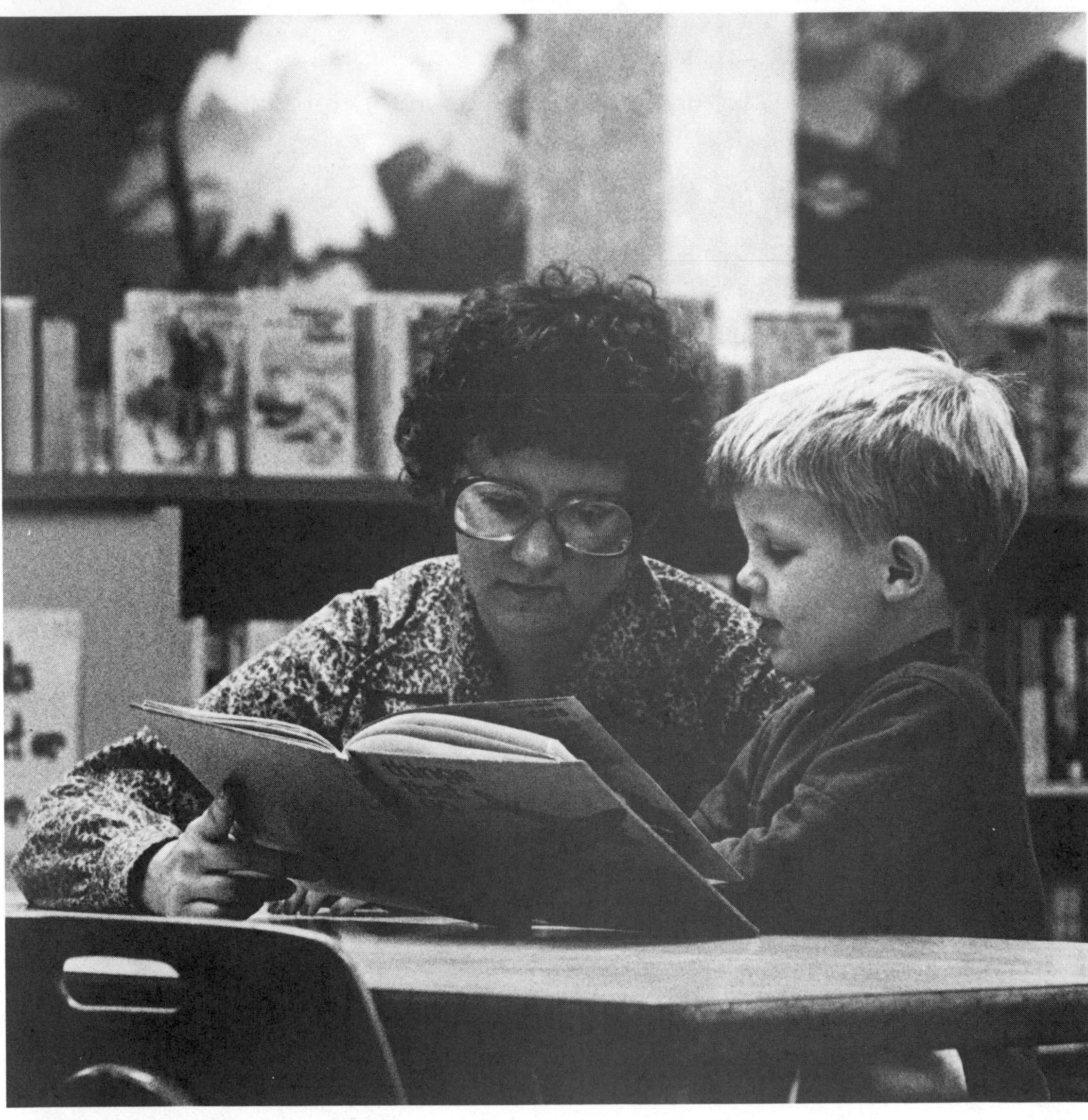

Diagnosis in the Reading Program

For the Reader

Do you remember the achievement tests you took when you were in elementary school? Each student had a test booklet and, for several days, a part of each day was spent taking the test. Such tests are still widely used today, and many new tests are appearing every year. Most of these have real merit, yet it is doubtful that reading instruction is improving as a direct result of these tests. This fact should make you consider how tests could have merit, be widely used, but not result in improved reading instruction.

The answer to this question is to be found in the way the tests are used. As pointed out in chapter 1, the only justifiable purpose for the use of reading tests is to secure data about a child's reading ability so that a reading program for him can be designed from the data secured. In actual practice, some schools and some teachers gain comfort from the use of tests because they are convinced that testing programs per se have educational value. Testing becomes an end in itself rather than a basis for instruction. In some communities a metal filing cabinet "with a folder for each pupil" is interpreted as evidence of good teaching practices. This occurrence suggests that the school has lost sight of the principle that diagnosis alone has no beneficial effect on the pupil diagnosed.

As you read this chapter, focus on learning how to diagnose pupils' reading and how to use this information in the planning and evaluation of your reading instruction.

Preview

- Read over the Key Ideas that follow.
- Read each heading and subheading.
- Read the summary.
- Read the questions and statements at the end of the chapter.
- Return to the chapter text that follows the Key Ideas and begin reading.

Key Ideas

Ongoing diagnosis of pupils' reading should be an integral part of reading instruction.

Pupils' reading can be evaluated and diagnosed through the use of:
- norm-referenced tests,
- criterion-referenced tests,
- pupil placement tests,
- Informal Reading Inventories (IRIs), and
- teacher-developed tests and procedures.

Standardized reading tests only sample pupils' reading behavior and must be supplemented with informal diagnostic procedures.

Insights into pupils' reading can be gained by employing qualitative techniques when interpreting their performance on an IRI.

Data on pupils' reading should form the basis for planning reading instruction.

MEETING INDIVIDUAL NEEDS

As highlighted in chapter 3, ongoing diagnosis of both pupils' reading development and teachers' reading instruction is a major feature of effective teaching of reading. Ongoing diagnosis in these two basic areas forms the foundation for planning reading instruction and determining its effectiveness. Diagnostic information about pupils' reading strengths and weaknesses allows the teacher to select instructional strategies and materials in relation to pupils' reading needs. The key here is not simply gathering data about pupils' reading and the effectiveness of reading instruction, but how the data are used to assure maximum reading growth for each pupil (see chap. 3).

Children at any given grade level show great differences in their reading skills and abilities. Some pupils will be reading considerably below their grade level placement, while others will be fairly advanced in their reading capabilities. Figure 11.1 illustrates the overlap between grades and the range of abilities found at the primary level.

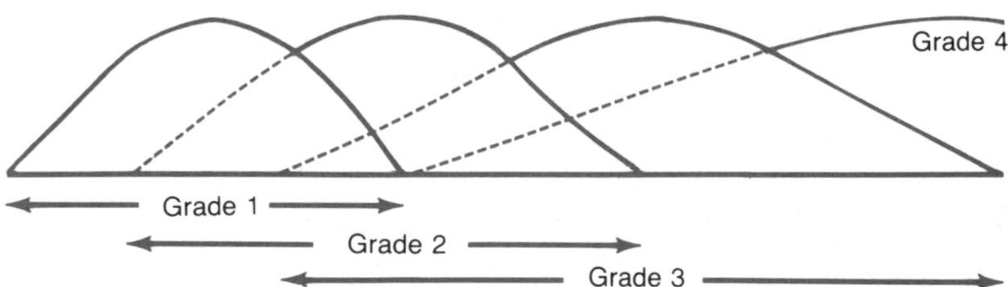

FIGURE 11.1 Graphic Representation of Reading Abilities in the Primary Grades. (Note that the range of abilities increases at each succeeding grade level.)

Effective data collection is the first step in providing appropriate instruction.

These facts, which apply to practically every classroom, emphasize the need for differentiated reading instruction. One criterion that distinguishes excellent reading programs from others is the degree to which individual needs are ascertained and met. Teachers must be alert to differences among pupils in order to follow sound principles of teaching. Only through diagnosis will the teacher be able to assess needs and plan instruction for children whose needs vary considerably. Diagnosis should be thought of as ongoing since children change rapidly. A diagnosis in September may be followed by a breakthrough on the part of the child in some vital skill or by a child's failure to master some new step in the reading process. In either case, the earlier diagnosis is obsolete.

Reading strengths and weaknesses can be assessed by standardized tests, informal tests, and teacher-developed tests and procedures. Although tests are designed for use at every grade level, no purpose would be served in a reading textbook by a separate discussion of tests each time a different instructional level is under consideration. The following discussion of tests and testing applies to the various levels of the elementary school with the exception that reading readiness tests are dealt with in chapter 4.

STANDARDIZED TESTS

Standardized tests sample pupils' reading in a controlled and systematic fashion (13). Procedures for administering, scoring, and interpreting the test have been determined under controlled experimental conditions. Commercially printed standardized tests fall into two classes: those designed for group administration and those designed to be administered individually. In both, credit is given for acceptable responses, and the child's score is determined by her correct responses, lack of errors, and rate of reading.

Essentially, two types of commercially published standardized reading tests are used in today's elementary schools: norm referenced and criterion referenced. Both types of standardized tests may possess similar types of test items, but there are basic differences in the purpose each serves and their interpretation.

Norm-Referenced Tests

Norm-referenced tests are designed to compare the performance of an individual or individuals with the performance of a norming group. The norming group is generally made up of a large sample of students who are representative of the national school population. This sample of students is administered the test, and their performance is used to establish the test's national norms. After the test is normed, a pupil's raw score (total number of correct responses) on the test can be transformed to a norm-referenced score by using the norming data.

Several types of norms are usually provided to compare an individual's relative standing in relation to a defined variable. This information is found in the administrator's manual and is based on the test's national norms. Similar norms, however, can be developed locally for a school district, school, or individual classroom. Most standardized norm-referenced tests provide for the conversion of a child's raw score to a percentile rank, stanine, and grade equivalent.

Percentile Ranks. Percentile ranks range from 1 to 99 and indicate the percentage of students in the norming group that scored at or below a given score. For example, if a pupil's raw score of 62 is equal to a percentile rank of 80, this means that she did as well, or better than, 80 percent of the individuals in the norming group. A percentile rank of 50 represents the median, or middle score, and indicates average performance.

Stanines. Stanines also indicate a pupil's relative standing in comparison to other pupils in the norming group. As the term implies, stanines range from a low of 1 to a high of 9. Stanines 1 through 3 usually indicate below average performance, 4 through 6 average performance, and 7 through 9 above average performance. Stanines represent a range of scores rather than a specific score. For example, if a raw score of 28 is at the 77th percentile and a raw score of 31 is at the 88th percentile, both scores could be equivalent to stanine 7. Stanines represent units that are approximately equal; a difference between stanines 5 and 7 is about the same as the difference represented by stanines 3 and 5. Because of this, stanines are especially useful for comparing a pupil's performance across the subtests of a test (2).

Grade-level Equivalents. Grade-level equivalents of raw scores on a norm-referenced test indicate the performance of a pupil in relation to the average score for the grade level of the norming group. Grade-level scores are reported by school grade and tenths of the school year. A grade-level equivalent of 4.0 indicates that a pupil's raw score was equivalent to the score obtained by the average fourth grader in the norming population.

A grade-level equivalent is not the same as the level at which a child should be reading (1). A fourth grader who has received a grade-level equivalent of 6.5 on a recently administered standardized test should not necessarily be given sixth-grade work. Likewise, a fourth grader who has received a grade equivalent of 2.5 probably should not be instructed at the second-grade level. In the former example, the grade equivalent provides some indication that this pupil is above average. In the latter example, the grade equivalent suggests that this pupil is possibly a low achiever for his grade.

Criterion-Referenced Tests

Criterion-referenced tests (CRT) are designed to measure pupils' levels of mastery of specific reading skills. Rather than comparing a pupil's performance to that of the norming group, CRTs are based on performance in relation to the level of mastery of one or more skills. These skills are usually stated as performance or behavioral objectives, for example, "Student will identify correctly the order of events found in short reading passages."

Several items that focus on each reading objective would be found on a CRT. A pupil's response to these items is evaluated in terms of the number of correct items appropriate to each objective. This evaluation is done typically by comparing the pupil's performance to established criteria. For example, if there are twenty items for an objective, a pupil who scores sixteen or more correct may have mastered the skill; fifteen to twelve correct answers might indicate that review is needed; less

Passage Comprehension **5** Passage Comprehension

Work until you come to a STOP sign.

Stuff was just an ordinary scarecrow. Dressed in a plaid shirt, faded overalls, and a straw hat, he stood guard day and night in the center of the cornfield. Of course, he did little good. Stuff had been there so long that the crows were no longer frightened by him. Just the same, Stuff took pride in his work. He enjoyed the prominence of his position above the corn rows.

Then one day, the farmer appeared carrying a big box. Stuff's heart pounded with excitement! He wondered what gift the farmer was bringing for him. But when the box was opened, Stuff got a lump in his throat. For inside was Flash, a modern, battery-operated scarecrow. Flash was certain to keep the crows away!

Poor Stuff! The farmer carried him back to the barn. He gently propped him against a bale of hay just outside the door. "I sure hate to do this," the farmer said. "Old Stuff's been around here so long I feel like he's part of the family. I'd like to keep him in that field forever. That new scarecrow will be expensive to maintain. But I should give him a fair chance."

From his seat by the barn, Stuff could see the field where Flash was busily scaring the crows out of the corn. Day after day he watched sadly as the crows fled in fear. One day, though, he noticed fewer crows leaving than before. In fact, as the days passed, more crows came and stayed!

They paid no attention to Flash's sudden movements anymore. Stuff realized that Flash was no more successful than he at scaring the crows. The farmer must have noticed, too. A few days later Stuff saw the farmer coming toward the barn. In his arms he carried that same big box. Stuff thought he saw the farmer wink at him as he passed.

63. Why wasn't Stuff able to scare away the crows?

① He was just an ordinary scarecrow.
② He was not battery operated.
③ The crows were no longer frightened by him.
④ The farmer had taken him out of the field.

64. Which sentence below best states the main idea of this story?

① Day after day he watched sadly as the crows fled in fear.
② Stuff realized that Flash was no more successful than he at scaring the crows.
③ Flash was certain to keep the crows away.
④ Stuff was just an ordinary scarecrow.

65. The farmer took Stuff to the barn ______.

① after he got Flash
② after the crows left
③ after Flash scared away the crows
④ after Flash was given a fair chance

66. In this story, the word prominence means ______.

① a lot of activity
② not visible; hidden
③ standing out; noticeable
④ well-known; famous

A page from a criterion-referenced test.

than twelve items correct could indicate that reteaching of the skill is necessary. Some criterion-referenced tests use only one criterion of performance to indicate mastery or lack of mastery, such as fifteen out of twenty similar items correct is mastery, fewer than fifteen correct is lack of mastery.

Standardized Diagnostic Reading Tests

In addition to standardized achievement tests that contain reading subtests, standardized diagnostic reading tests are also available for classroom use. These tests help the teacher specify specific reading strengths and weaknesses in a variety of areas. Diagnostic tests differ from achievement tests by having a larger number of subtests and test items related to specific reading behaviors. The computer-scored test in figure 11.2 is a reading diagnostic test. There are six subtests focusing specifically on reading, ranging from phonetic analysis to comprehension. The number of subtests included on diagnostic reading tests varies; however, most of them have from five to ten.

There are many standardized tests available that provide information about pupils' reading. All norm-referenced achievement batteries designed to test pupils in the elementary school contain reading subtests. A vocabulary score, a comprehension score, and a total reading score (the average of vocabulary and comprehension) are usually provided in these tests. A large number of criterion-referenced reading tests are also available with subtests focusing on specific aspects of word identification and comprehension. Since there are so many different reading tests, it is to be expected that many of them will measure virtually the same aspects of reading. Nevertheless, there are major differences among tests as to what they measure, the level of difficulty for which they are designed, the care that went into their construction, and the ease with which they can be administered. Each of these factors affects two important attributes of reading tests—the consistency with which they measure reading skills and the degree to which they actually measure the skills that they supposedly measure.

The consistency with which a test measures reading skills is referred to as *reliability.* A reliable test is one that provides a sample of pupils' reading performance that is stable. For example, if Test X was administered to a pupil in September, you would expect that administering the test two or three weeks later would result in a similar score. However, if the pupil's score was 80 on the first administration and 15 on the second administration, then it is impossible to decide which score is an accurate sampling of this pupil's reading. Such a test would be highly unreliable because it does not consistently sample pupils' reading skills.

Teacher GAIL BARNETT
School OAK STREET SCHOOL
System OURTOWN

Stanford Diagnostic Reading Test

Grade 6 Date of Testing 10/06/76
Level BROWN Form A Norms Used GRADE 5.6-6.5

Page 02 of 08 for this CLASS
Process No. 000-0000-000

THE PSYCHOLOGICAL CORPORATION Data Services

SDRT GROUP 2

INSTRUCTIONAL PLACEMENT REPORT

SUBTEST AND TOTAL SCORES

LIST SEQUENCE ALPHABETIC WITHIN GROUP / NAME, AGE (YRS/MOS) OTHER INFORMATION	PHONETIC ANALYSIS (NUMBER OF ITEMS 36) RS PR S SS GE	STRUCTURAL ANALYSIS (NUMBER OF ITEMS 78) RS PR S SS GE	AUDITORY VOCABULARY (NUMBER OF ITEMS 40) RS PR S SS GE	LITERAL COMPREHEN (NUMBER OF ITEMS 30) RS PR S SS GE	INFERENTIAL COMPREHEN (NUMBER OF ITEMS 30) RS PR S SS GE	COMPREHEN TOTAL (NUMBER OF ITEMS 60) RS PR S SS GE	READING RATE (NUMBER OF ITEMS 34) RS PR S SS GE	IA
AMES PETER J 11-09 2AN N	14 3 2.7 18 466	59 5 5.6 43 509	29 6 7.0 66 552	27 7 8.3 79 616	25 6 8.2 76 598	52 6 8.3 76 596	13 5 5.3 40 515	16
DALEY NANCY M 11-10 2AN N	4 1 K 1 312	30 2 1.9 6 373	17 3 4.0 18 435	7 2 2.4 8 406	16 5 5.2 41 501	23 4 4.0 23 455	13 5 5.3 40 515	20
SCOTT PHILIP L 12-02 2AN N	11 2 2.2 8 424	38 3 2.9 11 413	22 4 5.1 37 484	18 5 5.5 42 505	22 6 7.0 63 559	40 5 6.1 51 526	5 2 1.8 4 369	7
BRUNO JANET B 12-01 2BN N	15 3 2.9 22 476	67 6 7.3 65 560	27 5 6.4 58 532	29 8 10.2 92 692	22 6 7.0 63 559	51 6 8.0 74 588	8 3 2.8 16 435	16
MARTIN JOHN C 11-11 2BN N	10 2 2.0 5 408	64 5 6.5 55 537	13 2 3.3 6 387	11 3 3.9 20 451	4 1 K 2 353	15 2 2.9 8 393	6 2 2.1 8 393	10
NELSON ANGELA B 11-08 2BN N	7 1 1.4 1 360	46 3 4.0 19 453	19 4 4.4 25 456	10 3 3.6 17 442	13 4 4.4 31 476	23 4 4.0 23 455	9 3 3.2 20 453	20
CARTER BETTY M 12-06 2CN N	15 3 2.9 22 476	18 1 K 1 313	14 2 3.4 8 399	7 2 2.4 8 406	6 2 1.4 6 389	13 2 2.6 5 369	3 1 1.3 1 321	15
PEREZ JUAN B 13-04 2CN N	24 5 5.8 48 546	43 3 3.6 16 438	24 5 5.6 45 502	22 5 6.4 56 540	29 9 GRAD 97 730	51 6 8.0 74 588	10 4 3.7 24 470	11
QUAY NANCY R 11-01 2CN N	21 4 4.3 39 522	35 2 2.6 9 398	16 3 3.8 14 423	5 1 1.1 3 370	9 3 3.1 17 437	14 2 2.8 7 381	4 1 1.6 2 345	6

See back for aids for interpretation.

LEGEND: RS = Raw Score (Number Right) SS = Scaled Score N = National Norms
PR = Percentile Rank GE = Grade Equivalent L = Local Norms
S = Stanine IA = NUMBER OF ITEMS ATTEMPTED

SKILL DOMAIN ANALYSIS

	AUDITORY DISCRIMINATION: CONSONANT SOUNDS + −	AUDITORY DISCRIMINATION: VOWEL SOUNDS + −	PHONETIC ANALYSIS: CONSONANT SOUNDS + −	PHONETIC ANALYSIS: VOWEL SOUNDS + −	STRUCTURAL ANALYSIS: WORD DIVISION + −	STRUCTURAL ANALYSIS: BLENDING + −	READING COMPREHENSION: SENTENCE READING + −	READING COMPREHENSION: PARAGRAPH COMPREHENSION + −
Number of items			18.	18	48	30		
AMES PETER	LATER GROUP = 6		9	5	37	22		
DALEY NANCY			3	1	16	14		
SCOTT PHILIP			2	9	20	18		
BRUNO JANET	LATER GROUP = 5		6	9	40	27		
MARTIN JOHN			5	5	43	21		
NELSON ANGELA			4	3	28	18		
CARTER BETTY			6	9	15	3		
PEREZ JUAN	LATER GROUP = 5		13	11	14	29		
QUAY NANCY			9	12	17	18		
PI CUTOFF SCORE			9	9	36	18		

SKILL DOMAIN ANALYSIS BASED ON RAW SCORES

PI = Progress Indicator
+ means Raw Score at or above PI Cutoff
− means Raw Score below PI Cutoff

FIGURE 11.2 ***An Example of a Computer-Scored Diagnostic Reading Test.*** (Reproduced from the Stanford Diagnostic Reading Test. Copyright © 1974 by Harcourt Brace Jovanovich, Inc. All rights reserved. Reproduced by special permission.)

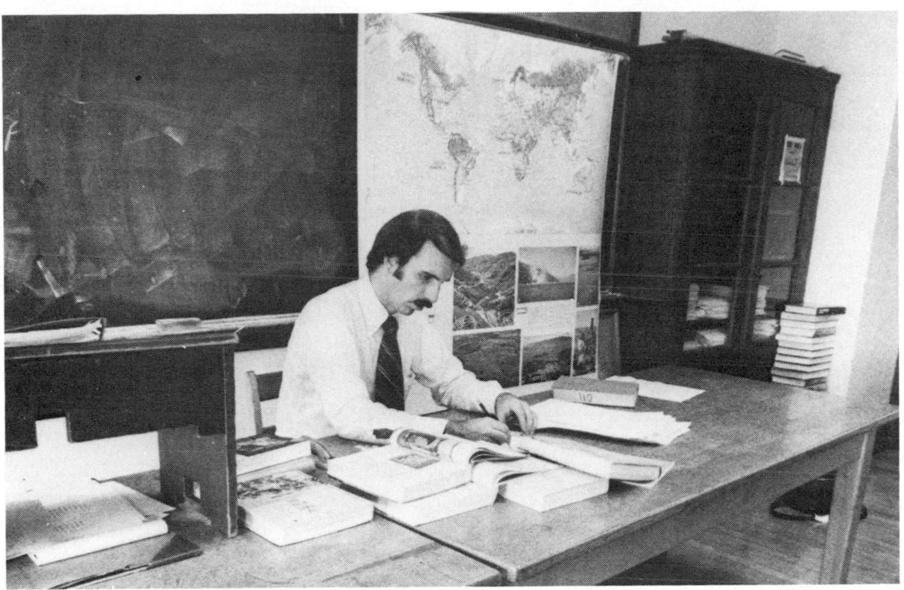

Teachers should carefully evaluate the features of any test before administering it to their students.

Reliability of a test is generally reported in the administrator's manual and is expressed as a coefficient of reliability. Tests that have reliability coefficients of .80 or above are considered to be highly reliable. Test X presented in the earlier example would have a low coefficient of reliability. Reliability is one important feature to consider when both selecting and interpreting pupils' reading performance on standardized tests. High reliability does not assure, however, that a test is also valid.

A valid test is one that measures what it reports to measure. As with reliability, the validity of a standardized test is also discussed in the administrator's manual. There are several different types of validity that are important to consider in relation to the intended use of the test results. We will discuss two of these.

Content validity means that the test items represent an accurate sampling of reading instruction content and the behavioral changes under consideration (7). A test can be titled a reading test and the test items can be easily identified as measuring reading skills, but the test may still not have content validity. Content validity means that the aspects of reading measured by the test are those which the pupils had an opportunity to learn in the instructional program (see chap. 3).

If the results from a test are going to be used to predict future reading performance or estimate current performance in a reading task (that is, mastery or lack of mastery in reading skill areas), then the test's *criterion-related validity* is extremely important. The importance of criterion-related validity is apparent in reading readiness tests that are used to predict the likelihood of success in beginning reading tasks (see chap. 4). In the readiness test's administrator's manual, criterion-related validity would be given as a coefficient of correlation between the performance on the readiness test and other standardized tests measuring beginning reading performance. The higher the validity coefficient, the more accurate the readiness test is as a predictor of later reading performance.

Important Features of Standardized Tests

Commercially published standardized tests usually provide a manual of directions for administering, scoring, and interpreting them. Information contained in the manual generally includes (1) an overview; (2) directions for administering; (3) directions for scoring; (4) a description of the types of scores; (5) procedures for using the results; and (6) information on development, national norms, reliability, validity, and other technical aspects.

The administrator's manual should be read carefully to assure that each important aspect of administering, scoring, and interpreting the test is fully understood. Failure to administer the test in the manner described in the manual can seriously jeopardize the validity of the test results and limit their use for instructional decision making. In addition to careful study of the manual, it is a good idea for teachers to take the test themselves. This allows them to become familiar with what the pupils must do when taking the test. Furthermore, by giving close attention to individual test items, a decision can be reached about how well the test "fits" the class in relation to past reading instruction. If the items do not accurately reflect past reading instruction, then the test lacks content validity and the results have little value in instructional planning.

Most standardized tests have a template or scoring key to facilitate rapid and accurate hand scoring of pupils' answer sheets. A large number of norm-referenced test publishers also provide a computer scoring service for their test users. Figure 11.2 presented earlier shows the information provided in computer-scored tests. The information presented beneath the heading "Instructional Placement Report" lists norm-referenced information for the six subtests and total number of items on each subtest. For each subtest, an individual pupil's performance is given. For example, Peter Ames's raw score in Literal Comprehension was 25, which was equivalent to the 79th percentile rank, a stanine of 7, and a grade equivalent of 8.25. The scaled score (SS) is provided to compare a pupil's performance across different levels of the Stanford Diagnostic Tests. The "Skill Domain Analysis" is to aid in content-referenced interpretation, that is, to identify pupils who are experiencing difficulty with specific reading skills (content-referenced scores *do not* indicate whether or not a pupil has mastered a skill). For example, Nancy Daley's score of 3 for consonant sounds is below the Progress Indicator Cutoff score. The interpretation of pupils' performance when a test is computer scored is detailed in the administrator's manual.

Computer scoring has the advantage of freeing the teacher from spending time scoring each pupil's test; however, there is often a period of time before the test results are returned. Thus, the teacher experiences a delay in using the test results to plan and implement reading instruction.

REPRESENTATIVE TESTS

A brief description of a limited number of both group and individual standardized tests follows. These tests are selected because they illustrate different types of reading tests and because, in most cases, they are recent publications or recent revisions. Additional information on tests can be found in the *Mental Measurement Yearbook.*[1]

Group Tests

California Achievement Test (1977–1978). Publisher: California Test Bureau/McGraw-Hill. Reading vocabulary and reading comprehension are tested. Each is covered by several subtests which yield part scores. Subtests measure vocabulary, comprehension, mathematics computation, mathematics concepts and problems, language, listening, mechanics of English, English usage and structure, and spelling. The subtests are available separately.

- *Lower Primary.* Grades 1.5–2.5.
- *Upper Primary.* Grades 2.5–4.5.
- *Elementary.* Grades 4–6.
- *Junior High.* Grades 6–9.
- *Advanced.* Grades 9–12.

[1]Oscar Buros, ed., *The Eighth Mental Measurement Yearbook* (Highland Park, N.J.: Gryphon Press, 1984).

Iowa Tests of Basic Skills (1982). Publisher: Houghton Mifflin Company (3 alternate forms). (Grades 3–9) This achievement battery yields eleven separate scores in the following major areas: vocabulary, reading comprehension, language skills, work-study skills, and arithmetic skills.

All of the subtests for each grade, 3 through 9, are included in one spiral booklet of ninety-six pages. These booklets are reusable since responses are made on separate answer sheets.

The reading comprehension test requires approximately one hour for administration at *each* grade level. It consists of a number of stories of graduated length and difficulty. Comprehension is tested by means of multiple-choice items, the reader selecting the one best answer from among the four available. As noted above, the reading comprehension test is available only as part of the entire Basic Skills Battery.

Prescriptive Reading Inventory (1977–78). Publisher: California Test Bureau/McGraw-Hill. A group-administered criterion-referenced test in four levels. Scored in terms of mastery, need of review, or nonmastery.

- *Level A.* Grades 1.5–2.5. (recognition of sounds and symbols; phonic analysis; structural analysis; translation; and literal, interpretive, and critical comprehension)
- *Level B.* Grades 2.0–3.5. (Same as Level A)
- *Level 3.* Grades 3.0–4.5. (phonic analysis; structural analysis; translation; and literal, interpretive, and critical comprehension)
- *Level 4.* Grades 4.0–6.5. (Same as Level 3)

Metropolitan Reading Instructional Tests (1979). Publisher: Harcourt Brace Jovanovich, Inc. Provides for both norm-referenced and criterion-referenced reporting of performance. Estimates of instructional reading levels (IRL) are also available, and tables are provided for matching a pupil's IRL to current basal reader series. Two forms.

- *Primer.* Grades K.5–1.4. Six subtests: visual discrimination, letter recognition, auditory discrimination, sight vocabulary, phoneme/grapheme (consonants), and reading comprehension.
- *Primary 1.* Grades 1.5–2.4. Six subtests: auditory discrimination, sight vocabulary, phoneme/grapheme (consonants), vocabulary in context, word part clues, and reading comprehension.
- *Primary 2.* Grades 2.5–3.4. Six subtests: sight vocabulary, phoneme/grapheme (consonants), phoneme/grapheme (vowels), vocabulary in context, word part clues, and comprehension.
- *Elementary.* Grades 3.5–4.9. Seven subtests: sight vocabulary, phoneme/grapheme (consonants), phoneme/grapheme (vowels), vocabulary in context, word part clues, rate of comprehension, and reading comprehension.
- *Intermediate.* Grades 5.0–6.9. Seven subtests: phoneme/grapheme

(consonants), phoneme/grapheme (vowels), vocabulary in context, word part clues, rate of comprehension, skimming and scanning, and reading comprehension.

- *Advanced 1.* Grades 7.0–9.9. Four subtests: vocabulary in context, rate of comprehension, skimming and scanning, and reading comprehension.

S.R.A. Survey of Basic Skills (1985). Publisher: Science Research Associates, Inc. These materials consist of eight levels for use at kindergarten through grade 12. There are subtests for each area of the curriculum. The following data refer only to the reading subtests.

- *Level 20, Grades K–1.* The reading test contains four subtests: decoding, auditory discrimination, letters/sounds, and listening comprehension.
- *Level 21, Grades 1–2.* The reading test consists of the subtests letters/sounds, listening comprehension, vocabulary, and comprehension.
- *Level 22, Grades 2–3.* The reading test includes the subtests letters/sounds, vocabulary, and comprehension.
- *Level 23, Grades 3–4; Level 34, Grades 4–6; Level 35, Grades 6–8; Level 36, Grades 8–10; and Level 37, Grades 9–12.* All of these levels have reading tests that consist of vocabulary and comprehension subtests.

Stanford Achievement Tests (1982). Publisher: Harcourt Brace Jovanovich, Inc. Five separate batteries cover grades 1–9. Each battery contains a number of subtests on reading.

- *Primary Battery I.* Grades 1.5–2.4 (comprehension, vocabulary, paragraph meaning, word study, listening comprehension, and spelling)
- *Primary Battery II.* Grades 2.5–3.9. (word meaning, paragraph meaning, spelling, word study skills, language)
- *Intermediate Battery I.* Grades 4–5. (same subtests as above)
- *Intermediate Battery II.* Grades 5–6. (word meaning, paragraph meaning, spelling, language)
- *Advanced Battery.* Grades 7–9. (paragraph meaning, spelling, language)

Stanford Diagnostic Reading Test (1983). Publisher: Harcourt Brace Jovanovich, Inc. Four levels are available for testing first grade through grade 13. Scores are reported as both norm and criterion referenced.

- *Red Level.* Grades 1.6–3.5. (auditory discrimination, basic phonics skills, auditory vocabulary, word recognition, and comprehension of short sentences and paragraphs)

- *Green Level.* Grades 2.6–5.5. (auditory discrimination, phonetic and structural analysis, auditory vocabulary, and literal and inferential comprehension)
- *Brown Level.* Grades 4.6–9.5. (phonetic and structural analysis, auditory vocabulary, literal and inferential comprehension, and reading rate)
- *Blue Level.* Grades 9–13. (phonetic and structural analysis, reading vocabulary, literal and inferential comprehension, reading rate, and scanning and skimming)

Individual Tests

Durrell Analysis of Reading Difficulty, New Edition (1980). Publisher: Harcourt Brace Jovanovich, Inc. (Grades 1–6). Evaluates a range of reading ability that includes oral and silent reading, listening and vocabulary comprehension, spelling, visual and auditory discrimination of letters, sound discrimination in words, sound discrimination of letters, handwriting, syntax matching, visual memory of words, phonic spelling, and phonemes. Individual record booklet includes a checklist for recording observations of difficulties, a Parent Report Form, Student Profile, and a Cumulative Record Sheet.

Gates-McKillop-Horowitz Reading Diagnostic Tests (1981). Publisher: Teachers College Press, Columbia University. (Grades 2–6). This test consists of subtests measuring oral reading, rapid recognition of whole words, untimed sight word recognition, auditory blending, spelling, recognizing word parts, and oral vocabulary (meaning). The total test yields twenty-eight scores.

Skills Monitoring System-Reading (1977). Publisher: Harcourt Brace Jovanovich, Inc. This is a diagnostic-prescriptive approach to assessing the reading objectives in grades 3–5. It is a criterion-referenced instrument that can be administered either individually or to a group. Three levels are available: the Blue Level (grade 3) has one level of word identification and three levels of reading comprehension; the Green Level (grade 4) and Purple Level (grade 5) both identify three levels of comprehension.

Woodcock Reading Mastery Test (1974). Publisher: American Guidance Service. This criterion-referenced test for kindergarten through grade 12 is available in two forms. Subtests include letter identification, word identification, word comprehension, and passage comprehension. The test yields easy reading level, reading grade score, and failure reading level for each subtest.

INFORMAL DIAGNOSIS

It was pointed out earlier that the purpose of diagnosis is to pinpoint pupils' reading strengths and weaknesses to aid in the planning of an appropriate reading program.

Standardized tests are one means to help the teacher identify pupils' reading strengths and weaknesses. However, standardized tests alone are not sufficient to accurately diagnose pupils' reading and the effectiveness of your reading instruction. As stated in chapter 3, effective teachers use ongoing diagnosis in their reading instruction. Furthermore, effective teachers utilize a variety of informal diagnostic procedures.

Informal diagnosis of pupils' reading includes placement tests, informal reading inventories, and teacher-made tests. Each of these is discussed and illustrated with examples in the following sections.

Placement Tests

A large number of published reading materials contain pupil placement tests. The main purposes of these tests are to (1) facilitate placement of pupils in the appropriate level of difficulty in the materials, (2) determine if pupils have progressed in their reading development by using the reading materials, and (3) identify *some* reading strengths and weaknesses. In comparison with norm-referenced standardized tests, pupil placement tests are not aimed at comparing pupils' performance with that of pupils at a grade level in a wide geographic area.

Many pupil placement tests provide criterion or critical scores to assist the teacher in identifying those who have or have not mastered various aspects of reading. Unlike standardized criterion-referenced tests, the criterion scores are presented only to assist the teacher in evaluating pupils' performances. Furthermore, the majority of placement tests are not diagnostic tests and thus will not identify specific areas of reading strengths and weaknesses. Figure 11.3 illustrates an example of the subtests, performance objectives, and number of items for each objective found on the *Tests for Analysis and Placement (TAP),* Level 9 of the Laidlaw Reading Program. A pupil's performance on each of the TAP subtests can be evaluated by the teacher to help her determine if the pupil is ready to move to level *10 Basic* and proceed through it at either a slow to average pace or at an average to above average pace. Criterion scores for reteaching each of the skills represented by the subtests are also provided.

Placement tests not only help you to make decisions about pupils' placement in a particular level of a basal series, but they can also be

T·A·P₉ ITEM ANALYSIS

Tests	Performance Objectives	Item Numbers
PHONEME–GRAPHEME CORRESPONDENCE (Consonant Clusters)	Each child will associate the following phoneme-grapheme correspondences: /br/*br*, /kr/*cr*, /dr/*dr*, /fl/*fl*, /fr/*fr*, /pl/*pl*, /pr/pr, /skr/*scr*, /sh/*sh*, /sk/*sk*, /sl/*sl*, /sn/*sn*, /st/*st*, /str/*str*, /sw/*sw*, /θ/*th*, /thr/*thr*, /tr/*tr*, /tw/*tw*	 18, 14, 10, 13, 16, 9, 15, 5, 12, 2, 7, 6, 17, 11, 3, 8, 4, 19, 1
PHONEME–GRAPHEME CORRESPONDENCE (Vowel Sounds)	Each child will associate the following phoneme-grapheme correspondences: /a/*o*, /u/*oo*, /ay/*i*, /e/*e*, /i/*i*, /ow/*oa*, /ə/*u*, /ey/*ea*, /ey/*ai*, /iy/*e*, /ow/*o*, /uw/*u*, /ɔ/*aw*, /uw/*oo*, /iy/*ie*, /ɔy/*oi*, /ey/*ei*, /ɔy/*oy*	 1; 2; 3, 5, 16; 4; 6; 7; 8; 9; 10; 11; 12; 13; 14; 15; 17; 18; 19; 20
STUDY SKILLS	Each child will respond to questions by locating information from a glossary, a chart, or a picture map.	1, 2, 3, 4, 5, 6, 7, 8, 9, 10, 11, 12, 13, 14, 15, 16, 17, 18, 19, 20
READING COMPREHENSION	Each child will respond to questions and complete sentences to determine literal comprehension of a paragraph that is independently read.	1, 2, 5, 6, 7, 8, 10, 11, 12, 13, 15, 16, 17, 18
READING COMPREHENSION	Each child will respond to questions and complete sentences to determine inferential comprehension of a paragraph that is independently read.	3, 4, 9, 14
LISTENING COMPREHENSION	Each child will recall details of a story.	2, 4, 6, 7, 8
LISTENING COMPREHENSION	Each child will make inferences about a story.	1, 3, 5, 9, 10

FIGURE 11.3 A Representative Example of the Subtests, Performance Objectives, and Number of Items for each Objective Found in a Basal Series Pupil Placement Test. (Courtesy of Laidlaw Brothers from *T-A-P Item Analysis* by Roger Farr and Nancy Lee Roser. Copyright 1976.)

used to evaluate pupils' progress in the materials. Placement tests are content specific; that is, they test pupils' readiness and progress in terms of the reading materials for which the tests were developed. These tests, however, should be evaluated and reviewed carefully by the teacher to determine that they closely match what is taught. Also, careful attention should be given to the number of items for each skill or ability to assure that they are enough items to adequately sample the area of reading identified (16).

Informal Reading Inventories

One of the most helpful tools one can use in the classroom to diagnose pupils' reading strengths and weaknesses is the informal reading inventory (IRI). Essentially, there are three basic types of IRIs: commercially published, those accompanying basal reader series, and teacher prepared. Regardless of the type of inventory you choose to use, its major purposes are to establish pupils' reading levels and to identify their reading strengths and weaknesses.

The typical IRI consists of graded word lists, graded reading passages, and comprehension questions.

- *Graded word lists* consist of ten to twenty word lists for each grade level represented in the IRI. Most commercially published and basal IRIs have graded word lists for preprimer through sixth grade. A child's performance on the graded word list provides you with information for placement in the graded passages, sight vocabulary strengths and weaknesses, and strategies used to identify words presented in isolation.
- *Graded reading passages* are series of passages, usually ranging in reading difficulty from preprimer or primer through eighth or ninth grade. A reader's performance on the passages gives you an indication of his reading strategies in using context, attention to meaning, identification of unknown words, and different levels of reading competence.
- *Comprehension questions* consist of five to ten questions for each graded reading passage. The questions cover several aspects of comprehension, such as vocabulary, main idea, inference, literal meaning, cause and effect, sequence, and so forth. The purposes of the questions are to identify pupils' level of reading comprehension competence and point out comprehension strengths and weaknesses.

The IRIs for most commercial and basal series have at least two equivalent forms. Either form may be administered orally, silently, or both. Pupils' performances on the oral administration of the IRI can be used to identify their independent, instructional, frustration, and listening capacity reading competence levels. The *independent level* is the competence level at which a pupil can read materials without any assistance. The *instructional level* is the teaching level where pupils can read materials successfully with teacher guidance. The *frustration level* is the level at which materials would be too difficult and, as a result,

Informal diagnostic tests are important to assess a student's strengths and weaknesses.

would be frustrating for the pupils. The *listening capacity level* is often referred to as the *potential* level and is an indication of what pupils can understand when material is read aloud to them.

Reading the passages orally and responding to comprehension questions orally results in the identification of instructional, independent, and frustration levels for both word recognition and comprehension. Silent reading of the passages identifies the same reading competence levels, but only for comprehension. The *capacity level* is identified by evaluating the reader's responses to the comprehension questions for grade-level passages that are read aloud to him.

Administering an IRI. Administering an informal reading inventory is a rather easy task. There are, however, some basic guidelines you should follow to assure that the sample of oral reading is an accurate representation of a pupil's reading capabilities. The following steps outline the procedures to follow when administering an IRI.

1. Prior to administering the IRI it is important that you are thoroughly familiar with the coding system that is used to record pupils' deviations from the text as they read passages orally. Figure 11.4 presents the coding system you can use to note such deviations. It is strongly recommended that you practice using the coding system

Type of Miscue	*How to Mark*	*Example*
Omission: Word, several words, parts of words or punctuation are omitted.	Circle (◯) the word(s), part of word, or punctuation omitted.	The large (black) dog jumped (high) into the air and grab(bed) the ball.
Substitution: Real word is substituted for text word.	Draw a line through the word substituted and write the substituted word above the text word.	huge leaped The ~~large~~ black dog ~~jumped~~ high into the bait air and grabbed the ~~ball~~.
Insertion: Word is inserted in the passage text.	Use a caret (∧) to indicate where word was inserted and write the word.	The large black dog jumped high into the big air and grabbed the ∧ ball.
Unknown or Aided Words: Word or words are pronounced for the reader.	Place a letter "P" over the word pronounced for the reader.	P The large black dog jumped high into the air and grabbed the ball.
Transposition: Order of words in the text is transposed.	Use a curved mark (∿) over and under the words transposed.	The large black dog jumped high into the air and grabbed the ball.
Repetition: Phrase or several words are repeated. Count as one miscue.	Place an "R" with lines extending in both directions over the words repeated.	The large black dog jumped high into the ——R—— air and grabbed the ball.
Mispronunciation: Word is pronounced incorrectly.	Write the phonetic spelling above the word or use diacritical markings to indicate the pronunciation.	largé jumpted The large black dog jumped high into the air and grabbed the ball.
Self-correction: Miscue is self-corrected by the reader. Important to note, but do not count as a miscue.	Place a check mark (✓) above the miscue.	✓ jumpted ✓ The large black dog jumped high into the air and grabbed the ball.

FIGURE 11.4 Marking System for Recording Oral Reading Miscues.

and, also, tape record pupils' oral reading to ensure accurate coding of miscues.

2. Select an area to administer the IRI that is free of distractions and establish a relaxed atmosphere to minimize pupil anxiety. The pupil should be told that the IRI is not a test and that he is going to read aloud some words and stories and answer some questions about each story he reads. Also, it is extremely important that he understands that the teacher will be doing some writing as he reads the story because many children become highly anxious when the teacher begins to write. Introduce the pupil to the tape recorder and let him record his name, date, and tell something about himself. Play back what is recorded to check for proper settings. (This procedure usually eliminates the novelty of the tape recorder and prevents it from becoming a distraction.)
3. Select the graded word list that is two levels below the pupil's current grade level (word lists for the pupils should be typed on separate note cards) and ask the pupil to read the list of words aloud. Encourage the pupil to read each word. If he is not sure of a word's pronunciation he should try to pronounce it as best he can. (This provides some indication of the word identification strategies pupils use.) If the pupil makes a miscue on this first word list, drop down to an easier list until there are no miscues. Continue administering more difficult word lists and noting pupil's miscues by using the coding system. Stop administering the word lists when the pupil's miscues reach the maximum number suggested in the teacher's manual. If teacher-prepared graded word lists are used, discontinue administering the lists when the pupil's miscues reach 30 percent or greater.
4. The highest graded word list on which the pupil made no miscues is the entry level for the oral reading passages. For example, if a pupil read from graded word lists 1 through 6 and made no miscues on list 4, then he would begin with the oral reading passage at level 4. Remind the pupil that he is going to be reading a story aloud and that after reading the story he will be asked some questions about it. Some published IRIs have motivation or overview statements for each passage that are to be read to the pupil just before he is to begin oral reading of the passage. As the pupil reads, record his miscues on the teacher's corresponding passage. Upon completion of reading the passage, remove it and ask the comprehension questions. Questions may be restated for the pupil if necessary. If the pupil's response to each question is correct, indicate this with a check mark beside the question. If he responds incorrectly or only partially, write his response beneath the appropriate question. He need not respond to each question as indicated on the question sheet, but he should answer correctly to get credit.

5. Continue having the pupil read subsequent passages and answer comprehension questions until a frustration level is identified for either word recognition or comprehension or both (see figure 11.5).
6. To identify the pupil's capacity or potential reading level, begin reading the level above the passage on which he reached frustration level. Again, set purposes by telling the pupil to listen carefully as the story is read aloud and that he will answer some questions after hearing the story. End the administration of passages when he answers less than 75 percent of the comprehension questions correctly. The highest level on which 75 percent of the questions were answered correctly is his capacity level.

Interpreting an Informal Reading Inventory. Interpretation of pupils' performance on IRIs should be based on both quantitative and qualitative analysis. Quantitative analysis is based primarily on the number of miscues per passage and the total number of miscues for all passages read. Counting the number of scorable miscues in each passage and the number of incorrect comprehension questions for each passage and determining reading competence levels form the basis of a quantitative analysis.

Two sets of criteria for determining reading competence levels are presented in figure 11.5. Betts' criteria (3) for independent, instructional, and frustration levels can be applied to all passages, regardless of difficulty. Powell's criteria (10,11) take into account passage level difficulty and permit more miscues below the sixth-grade level.

When both criteria are applied to a pupil's performance in both word recognition and comprehension, Betts' criteria usually place the student at lower competency levels. In chapter 3 it was pointed out that reading tasks should be at a level of difficulty that maximizes pupils' chance of success, yet not be so easy that pupils lose interest. Therefore, teachers could apply both sets of criteria to pupils' performance; if there is a noticeable difference between competency levels, it might be best to place the pupils in reading materials that have a reading difficulty between the two competency levels rather than at either extreme. This could increase the likelihood that the reading task is at an appropriate difficulty level. However, if pupils' actual reading performance suggests that the task is either too easy or too difficult, then pupils could be moved up or down to the appropriate level.

Most published IRIs have a form for summarizing pupils' performance. An example of such a summary sheet is presented in figure 11.6. The summary sheet enables the teacher to identify reading levels and tally both oral reading miscues and comprehension difficulties. Also, there is generally space provided for briefly noting reading strengths and weaknesses. Based on the information presented in the summary sheet example, this pupil should be able to read library materials at the first

Reading Competency Level	Betts' Criteria		Powell's Differentiated Criteria					
	Word Recognition	Comprehension	Word Recognition in terms of grade-level difficulty of passage being read:			Comprehension in terms of grade-level difficulty of passage being read:		
			PP–2	3–5	6+	PP–2	3–5	6+
Independent	one miscue per 100 words (99% accuracy)	90% or greater accuracy	94% + accuracy	96% + accuracy	97% + accuracy	81% + accuracy	86% + accuracy	91% + accuracy
Instructional	five miscues per 100 words (95% accuracy)	75%–89% accuracy	87–93% accuracy	92–95% accuracy	94–96% accuracy	55–80% accuracy	60–85% accuracy	65–90% accuracy
Frustration	10+ miscues per 100 words (less than 90% accuracy)	less than 50% accuracy	86% or less accuracy	91% or less accuracy	93% or less accuracy	54% or less accuracy	59% or less accuracy	64% or less accuracy
Capacity or Potential	at least 75% accuracy					at least 75% accuracy for all levels		

FIGURE 11.5 Criteria for Determining Reading Competency Levels of Pupil Performance on an IRI.

FLASHBACK

Professor Betts' contributions to the field of reading span many decades. Throughout his career his articles have been published in many professional journals. His books include *Prevention and Correction of Reading* (1936) and *Foundations of Reading Instruction* (1946).

In addition, he was a major force that led to the formation of the International Council for the Improvement of Reading Instruction, which merged with the National Association of Remedial Teachers in 1955 to form the International Reading Association. In 1971 he was presented the International Reading Association's Citation of Merit. The first sentence of the text read: "The International Reading Association salutes Emmett Albert Betts who would rather demonstrate than lecture."

grade level. It appears as if placement in instructional materials at the third-grade level would be appropriate for teacher guided instruction. In addition, John appears to have some difficulty with substitutions, long and short medial vowels, and use of context. Comprehension problems were noted for cause and effect, drawing conclusions, terminology, inference, and retelling. This quantitative information does not, however, provide any insights about whether or not these difficulties negatively affected his comprehension or what word identification strategies he employed.

Qualitative analysis of pupils' miscues means that you are not only interested in the number of miscues, but also in their quality. Not all miscues are equally destructive to getting the meaning. Teachers should note the impact of each miscue on a child's reading for meaning. Qualitative analysis enables you to determine whether or not a miscue interferes with meaning and get a better understanding of reading strategies that pupils use. An illustration of Level 4 excerpted from the Analytical

STUDENT RECORD SUMMARY SHEET

Student *John Stone* Grade *4* Sex *M* Age *9 - 10* yrs. mos.

School *Merrill Elementary* Administered by *M. L. Woods* Date *9/7/84*

Grade	Word Lists	Graded Passages			Estimated Levels
	% of words correct	WR Form *C*	Comp. Form *C*	Listen. Form *B*	
Primer	100%				
1	100%	-1 *Ind.*	-0 *Ind.*		
2	100%	-3 *Inst.*	-2 *Inst.*		Grade
3	95%	-7 *Inst.*	-3 *Inst.*	*Inst.*	Independent *1*
4	60%	-11 *Inst.*	-5 *Frust.*	*Inst.*	Instructional *2-3*
5		-18 *Frust.*	-6 *Frust.*	*Inst.*	Frustration *4*
6				*Frust.*	Listening *5*
7					
8					
9					

Check consistent oral reading difficulties:

- ___ word-by-word reading
- ___ omissions
- ✓ substitutions ← *(makes numerous word guesses)*
- ___ corrections
- ___ repetitions
- ___ reversals
- ✓ inattention to punctuation
- ___ word inserts
- ___ requests word help

Check consistent word recognition difficulties:

- ___ single consonants
- ___ consonant clusters
- ✓ long vowels } *medial*
- ✓ short vowels }
- ___ vowel digraphs
- ___ diphthongs
- ___ syllabication
- ✓ use of context *(must strengthen)*
- ___ basic sight
- ✓ grade level sight

Check consistent comprehension difficulties:

- ___ main idea
- ___ factual
- ✓ terminology
- ✓ cause and effect
- ✓ inferential
- ✓ drawing conclusions
- ✓ retelling

Description of Reading Behaviors:

John's oral reading was slow, word-by-word, and laborious. He often ignored the author's punctuation clues, gliding right into the next sentence or phrase.

Word Recognition He displayed skill in the use of initial consonants and some blends, thus allowing him to pronounce some words. I knew that John was searching for meaning as he read since sometimes he made word substitutions which were appropriate to the meaning of the text. He also self-corrected some

FIGURE 11.6 A Sample of an Informal Reading Inventory Student Record Summary Sheet. (Reprinted with permission from Charles E. Merrill Publishing Company from *Analytical Reading Inventory* by Mary Lynn Woods and Alden J. Moe. Copyright © 1985 by Bell & Howell Company.)

miscues, revealing that he was using context clues to recognize words and glean meaning from the text. I was certain that he was, in fact, using context clues since he would return to correct some words after the completion of a sentence or paragraph. Even though John's word recognition instructional level is quantitatively at Level 4, the quality of the miscues revealed more severe difficulties. Since he appears more confident at Levels 2 and 3, the actual instructional level should be stated at Level 3.

Comprehension The retellings at Levels 2 and 3 contained adequate information about the passages. Level 2 was retold in a manner which followed the author's sequence and logic more so than Level 3. The retelling at Level 4 was organized in a more random manner, never revealing the logic of the passage. After probing from the examiner, John could concisely retell the main idea of Levels 2, 3, and 4.

When he responded to comprehension questions, he consistently recalled factual information more readily than information requiring the reader to correlate portions of the text (Ce questions), or to draw inferences from the text (Inf/Con questions). At Levels 2, 3, and 4 his descriptions of some vocabulary words never adequately revealed their meanings, indicating a weak background vocabulary. When context clues at Levels 2 and 3 were available, the definitions of words became more accurate; however, at Level 4, the ability to use context clues diminished.

Based upon the nature of John's word recognition problems, the disorganization of the retelling, the lack of adequate responses to the comprehension questions, and the physical signs of tiring and stress, it appears as though Level 4 is his frustration level. A quick check done with a reading passage from the fourth grade social studies book revealed the same reading behaviors. A silent reading passage (Level 4) was also given, rendering the same comprehension patterns as found in the oral sample. The miscues at Level 5 were so numerous that comprehension was obliterated.

His listening capacity, Level 5, proved to be above both his instructional and frustration levels. The retelling at Level 4 was better organized and more logical than at Level 5; however, at Level 6, the retelling demonstrated similar organizational patterns found in the oral and silent reading samples at Level 4. This information tells us that John can adequately comprehend slightly more challenging material when he is not confronted with the task of recognizing words in a text. This information should prove useful in the selection of material which is read in class, and in determining the complexity of classroom discussions.

Summary of Instructional Level (2–3)

Word Recognition

Confident, self-correcting behavior

Use of initial consonants and some blends

Use of appropriate substitutions

Use of context clues

Comprehension

Adequate retellings following author's logic (more so at Level 2 than 3)

Main idea concisely expressed

Comprehension responses more factual than Cause and Effect or Inferential/Conclusions

Use of context clues to gain meaning of vocabulary

Inadequate descriptions of vocabulary if no context clues are available

Listening Level

Adequate retellings at Levels 4 and 5 (more organized and better use of logic at Level 4 than 5)

Reading Inventory (19) is shown in figure 11.7, and a procedure for qualitatively analyzing a pupil's miscues is presented in figure 11.8.

The miscues for all passages read are transferred from the IRI to the qualitative analysis sheet and identified by level. Text words and pupil's miscues are written in the appropriate columns. Each miscue is compared with the text to determine if it was similar in meaning, resulted in a loss of meaning, or made sense yet resulted in a different meaning; was similar in its graphic representation and sound for beginning, middle, and ending; and whether it was syntactically acceptable or unacceptable.

Following the categorization of miscues, patterns of reading behavior can be analyzed by using the following questions as guidelines (4, 5, 6).

- *Omissions, Substitutions, Insertions, Transpositions*

  Was meaning lost or changed as a result of these miscues?

  Was there a pattern evidenced for each type of miscue? For example, proper nouns omitted, inflected verbs omitted, adjectives inserted, nonsense words substituted, and so forth.

  Did these miscues interfere with responding correctly to comprehension questions?

  Did these miscues make sense in context when earlier or later miscues are taken into account? For example, in the text sentence, "He was so afraid that he ran up and down the bank wailing with fear," the pupil omitted *so,* inserted *and* between *afraid* and *that,* and omitted *that he.* It appears that the insertion of *and* may have resulted in the omission of *that he* as the pupil attempted to make sense of what he read.

  Were these miscues correct syntactically? This indicates that the reader is aware of how words are ordered and sentence structure.

- *Mispronunciations*

  Was there an attempt by the reader to use a word identification skill?

  Did the reader rely too heavily on one word identification technique? That is, did he try to sound out every word, look at only the initial letter and guess, and so forth.

  Was there a pattern to mispronunciations, such as irregular words, inflected words, proper nouns, adjectives, and so forth?

  Were mispronunciations the result of dialect differences? Dialect differences should not be scored as miscues but they should be analyzed to determine if they possibly interfered with comprehension.

Analysis of the miscues presented in figure 11.8 can provide important information not available from a quantitative analysis. Some ex-

Level 4 (144 words 13 sent.)

Examiner's Introduction (Student Booklet page 35):

If you like excitement then you will enjoy reading the *Incredible Journey* by Sheila Burnford. This story is about three pets, a cat and two dogs, whose owners leave the animals when they move to another country. The animals decide to try to find their owners but face many hardships. Please read a retelling of one of the incidents from this exciting story.

The three were growing tired from their long journey, and now they had to cross a river. It was wide and deep, so they would have to swim across.

The younger dog plunged into the icy water, barking for the others to follow him. The older dog jumped into the water. He was weak and suffering from pain, but somehow he managed to struggle to the opposite bank.

The poor cat was left all alone. He was so afraid that he ran up and down the bank wailing with fear. The younger dog swam back and forth trying to help. Finally, the cat jumped and began swimming near his friend.

At that moment something bad happened. An old beaver dam from upstream broke. The water came rushing downstream hurling a large log toward the animals. It struck the cat and swept him helplessly away.

Comprehension Questions and Possible Answers

(mi) 1. In this passage what was the difficult thing the animals had to do?
(cross a river) *swim across a river*

(f) 2. How would the animals get across the river?
(They would have to swim.) *swim*

(t) 3. What is the meaning of *plunged*?
(to jump in quickly) *to unclog like plunge a sink*

(ce) 4. Why did the younger dog bark at the other animals?
(to try to get them to follow him)

(f) 5. What is meant by the phrase "wailing with fear"?
(to be so scared that one cries out) *Don't know*

(f) 6. After the cat jumped in, what bad thing happened?
(An old beaver dam broke.) *dam broke*

(ce) 7. Why did the log come hurling downstream?
(The rushing water brought it.) *because it floated*

(con) 8. What makes you think the animals were run down and in poor health?
(Stated: They were tired; the old dog was suffering from pain.) *old dog in pain*

Miscue Count:

O 4 I 1 S 9 A 2 REP 2 REV 1

Scoring Guide	
Word Rec.	Comp.
IND 1–2	IND 0–1
INST 7–8	INST 2
FRUST 15+	FRUST 4+
19	3

FIGURE 11.7 A Marked Copy of a Pupil's Performance on an IRI. (Reprinted with permission from Charles E. Merrill Publishing Company from *Analytical Reading Inventory* by Mary Lynn Woods and Alden J. Moe. Copyright © 1985 by Bell & Howell Company.)

		Meaning			Graphic/Sound Similarities			Syntax	
Text	Pupil	Similar	Meaning Loss	Different	Beginning	Middle	Ending	Acceptable	Unacceptable
For Level 4									
growing	getting	X			X		X	X	
their	the	X			X			X	
wide and deep	deep and wide	X						X	
————	it	X							
younger	yellow	X		X	X			X	
suffering	P								
struggle	swim	X			X			X	
opposite	ŏp/pō/sitḗ		X		X				
all	————	X							
so	————	X							
that he	————	X							
————	and	X						X	
wailing	P								
younger	yellow			X	X			X	
moment	mŏm/ĕnt		X		X		X		
hurling	hurting		X		X		X	X	
helplessly	————	X							

FIGURE 11.8 Qualitative Analysis of a Pupil's IRI Performance.

amples of information about specific reading strengths and weaknesses available from this qualitative analysis are presented below.

Based on an analysis of the effect that John's miscues had on meaning it appears that eleven of the nineteen miscues used to identify a reading competency level did not change the meaning of the text. You can assume that although John did not read the passage verbatim he comprehended much of its meaning. In other words, it seems as if only eight of his miscues interfered with comprehension. This difference could indicate that the passage is at his instructional level rather than his frustration level. Furthermore, John seems to have an understanding that one must make sense from what is read. His mispronunciations of *opposite* and *moment* suggest an attempt to use phonics as a means for identifying these words. He did not, however, ask himself if these words made sense in context. It is possible that neither of these words is in his listening vocabulary in relation to how they were used in the story.

An important feature of qualitative analysis is that it focuses on the types of oral reading responses a pupil makes. If a child uses only the initial letter cues to recognize words, this could be indicated by the fact that every word beginning with *m* was pronounced *mom*. If a pupil frequently substitutes words, qualitative analysis could focus on (1) *graphic/sound similarities* (Did the substituted word have similar graphic and pronunciation features as the text word?); (2) *meaning features* (Did the substituted word have a similar or identical meaning to the text word, for example, *car* for *automobile*?); and (3) *syntactic features* (Was the substituted word the same part of speech as the text word?). Similar analysis for comprehension is frequently used by effective reading teachers (14). Pupils' responses are evaluated to determine if they could recall specific facts, make inferences, identify vocabulary words from context, evaluate critically, identify sequence of events, and so forth. Analysis of pupils' reading performance through the use of such procedures enables the teacher to identify specific reading strengths and weaknesses. The effective reading teacher evidently relies heavily on qualitative analyses to aid in the identification of pupils' reading competence.

Qualitative analysis of miscues provides you with insights into the reading strategies that pupils use in their reading. Specific reading strengths and weaknesses become more evident as miscues are qualitatively analyzed over several orally read passages. Qualitative analysis of pupils' IRI performance can be used with all three types of informal reading inventories. Some commercially published IRIs available for classroom use are listed below.

- *Advanced Reading Inventory* (1982). Jerry L. Johns. Kendall/Hunt Publishing Co.

- *Analytical Reading Inventory,* 3d ed. (1985). Mary Lynn Woods and Alden J. Moe. Charles E. Merrill Publishing Co.
- *Bader Language and Reading Inventory* (1983). Lois A. Bader. Macmillan Publishing Co.
- *Classroom Reading Inventory,* 4th ed. (1982). Nicholas J. Silvaroli. Wm. C. Brown Company Publishers.
- *Informal Reading Assessment* (1980). Paul C. Burns and Betty D. Roe. Houghton-Mifflin Publishing Co.

Teacher-Made Tests

Teachers can devise informal tests for any classroom purpose. The simplest screening test might consist of having a child read a paragraph or two from a book to determine whether she can successfully read that particular book. More thorough informal tests will yield important data about children's reading, and these tests have certain advantages for classroom use. First, they are simple to construct since the teacher has available graded reading materials from the preprimer level through the upper grades. Second, the child can be tested over longer passages of sustained reading than are characteristically found on standardized tests. Third, the use of teacher-made tests avoids the formality of the usual test situation. Informal testing is not likely to arouse the pupil tensions sometimes accompanying testing and which occasionally influence pupil performance. In this respect, the informal test more closely parallels the actual reading situations the child encounters in the classroom. Finally, the teacher-made test is inexpensive and demands no more teacher time for administration and analysis than other tests. At the same time, it yields very specific data on each child's strengths and needs, as do the individual diagnostic tests.

A checklist of reading behaviors can be devised for rapidly recording reading errors and observations of related behaviors. Figure 11.9 is an example that could be duplicated and filled out for each child in the class. The checklist can be used with any graded reading material.

In the final analysis, the act of reading is a type of global behavior that is made possible by the simultaneous application of a great number of skills. The terms *reading-related skills* and *comprehension skills,* as used in this chapter, should not lead the reader to visualize a dichotomy. The simple fact is that critical reading or *comprehending* depends on the mastery of a myriad of related skills. It is true that when we give children assignments in reading we imply that the reader is to use the global skill labeled *critical reading.* However, actual instruction in reading almost always focuses on one or a limited number of skills.

Word Identification. The following activities provide illustrative materials that can be used or adapted to determine a child's present level

Name ______________ Age ______ Grade ______ Date ______________
School ______________ Teacher ______________
Examiner ______________

I. *Word Analysis*

A. Knows names of letters — Yes No
Needs work with: ______________

B. Attacks initial sound of words — Yes No
Deficiencies noted: ______________

C. Can substitute initial letter sounds — Yes No
Further drill needed: ______________

D. Can sound out initial blends and digraphs — Yes No
Deficiencies noted: ______________

E. If root word is known, can solve words formed by adding prefixes and suffixes — Yes No

II. *Sight Words* (check if applicable)

______Knows a word one time, misses it later
______Guesses at unknown words
   ______Errors frequently do not change intended meaning
   ______Errors indicate not reading for meaning
______Frequently adds words
   ______Errors frequently do not change intended meaning
   ______Errors indicate not reading for meaning
______Omits words
   ______Errors frequently do not change intended meaning
   ______Errors indicate not reading for meaning

III. *Reading Habits Noted*

______Reads word by word
______Phrasing inadequate
______Poor intonation
______Loses place frequently
______Does not utilize punctuation
______Lacks persistence

Explain: ______________
____

IV. *Sustained Reading* (basal, textbook, trade book)
(Do quantitative and qualitative analysis using techniques presented earlier.)

	Grade Level	Approx. Number of Running Words	Number of Errors
1.			
2.			

Errors noted (example): Said *lied* for *lying; banged* for *bumped; stuck* for *start* (corrected)
Needed help with: *clown, stomach, curious, squeal.*
Read with some hesitation, not smoothly, etc.

continued

FIGURE 11.9 Reading Behavior Record.

	Excellent	Average	Below Average
V. *Comprehension*			
Recall of facts	______	______	______
Recognizes main ideas	______	______	______
Draws inferences	______	______	______
Maintains sequence of events	______	______	______
Understands humor	______	______	______
Interprets figurative expressions	______	______	______
VI. *Oral Reading Skills*			
Relates with audience	______	______	______
Enunciation	______	______	______
Adequate volume	______	______	______
Reads with intonation	______	______	______
Phrases for meaning	______	______	______
VII. *Behaviors Related to Reading*			
Attitude toward reading	______	______	______
Self-confidence	______	______	______
Background knowledge	______	______	______
Language facility	______	______	______
Originality of expression	______	______	______
Range of vocabulary	______	______	______
Stock of concepts	______	______	______
Variety of sentence patterns	______	______	______

VIII. *Other Comments:* ______________________________

____

____

____

____

____

____

____

____

____

____

FIGURE 11.9 (cont.)

of functioning in regard to a number of word identification skills. These activities focus on several aspects of word recognition, ranging from letter names to sight words, and they are intended to provide information about pupils' progress in terms of the stages of reading development presented in chapters 1, 2, 4, and 9.

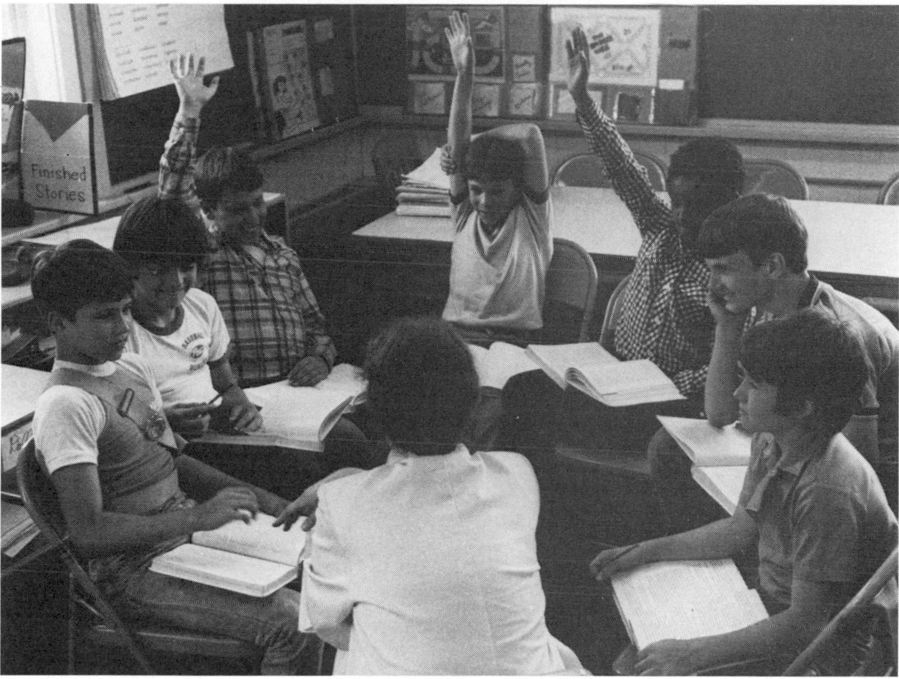

Every instructional period provides important information about both pupils' reading and the effectiveness of reading instruction.

ASSESSMENT ACTIVITY

Initial Consonants in Sentence Format. Each sentence emphasizes one initial letter sound and can provide clues as to whether a child is experiencing trouble with any particular initial letter sound.

1. Bobby brought back bunches of bananas.
2. Candy, the cat, can't come to class.
3. Dad didn't drop the dozen doughnuts on Dave's desk.
4. Father feels fine after falling four feet from the fir tree.
5. Go get a gun and a good guide if you hunt geese.
6. Henry hurt his hand with the heavy hammer.
7. Jean joined Joe in playing a joke on Jack.
8. Kate keeps the key in the kitchen.
9. The lucky lady located the lovely locket that she had lost at lunch.
10. My mother made Mike move the muddy mess.
11. Nick noticed a number of new nails in the workshop.
12. Polly put the pitcher in the pantry.
13. The rabbit ate the raw radishes, then ran rapidly down the ranch road.
14. Six surprised sailors saw Sam sneeze suddenly.

15. Ted tried to teach the tiny tot to talk.
16. On Wednesday, Wendy washed the windows.
17. Yes, your younger brother yelled in the yard yesterday.
18. Zelda saw a zebra at the zoo.

Blends and Digraphs. These words test the ability to sound most two-letter blends and digraphs in initial and final positions.

blank	church	slump	smart	skunk	speech
trump	brisk	plant	cloth	grand	champ
present	slant	which	drink	frost	chest
charm	fresh	crash	stand	crisp	swing

Auditory Discrimination. The teacher pronounces the four words in each series. The child repeats the one word that differs from the first word in the phoneme being tested.

Initial Consonants

toy	pat	did	wind	dark	farm
tall	pet	kid	went	drink	warm
hall	cot	doll	bend	dash	find
tack	put	dull	well	bark	full
ball	hard	lack	kick	march	rode
pull	yard	lock	pick	much	load
back	hunt	lamp	kill	met	right
burn	hurt	damp	kind	net	race

Endings of Words

Child repeats the one word that does not rhyme:

pig	bake	ball	wet	bug	bag
dig	make	full	bet	hug	rug
big	bark	tall	pet	did	rag
bag	wake	wall	sat	mug	sag
pot	lick	leg	cut	fell	then
not	stuck	peg	hit	fill	hen
got	stick	lap	hut	sell	thin
God	kick	keg	but	bell	pen

Initial Blends

Child repeats the word that does not begin with the blend sound.

dress	sled	blue	step	tree	plan
drop	sack	blow	sack	truck	place
draw	slip	bank	stop	train	pain
down	slap	black	steep	turn	play

Vowel Sounds

Child repeats word having short vowel sound.

mate	fame	fight	joke	cute	team
mail	fan	mile	lock	dull	tell
mad	table	fine	note	true	see
take	flame	skim	snow	tube	feed

Sight Words. Children who are progressing satisfactorily in mastering the developmental skills of reading are constantly expanding their sight vocabulary. To test sight vocabulary you could use the *Dolch Basic Sight Word Test* of 220 words. The material below consists of 100 high-frequency words taken from first-grade basal material. Any list of high-frequency words, including the one below, will show considerable overlap with the Dolch List (9).

we	horse	they	boat
with	a	jump	to
yes	an	big	walk
stop	look	come	want
like	was	go	on
help	find	think	house
very	little	and	my
all	best	could	can
this	old	boy	talk
some	try	may	girl
the	see	again	said
ball	mother	pretty	will
friend	any	which	father
went	over	then	small
did	wagon	live	blue
good	not	run	had
in	play	arm	she
me	what	up	your
hat	do	each	after
man	ran	his	clean
that	new	got	many
saw	wish	red	most
you	dog	there	around
here	under	please	open
sure	ride	name	every

Although reading words in isolation is not reading, tests can reveal whether or not the child has mastered a number of high-frequency "service words."

High-frequency words (irregular spellings)

a	I	any	are	all	too	the
been	come	do	get	head	they	his
put	good	would	have	two	very	you
give	is	use	put	done	their	what

once	of	gone	there	who	sure	does
look	some	know	said	many	was	your
one	here	only	to	could	walk	were

Comprehension. Any situation in which a child reads can provide clues to her reading strengths and instructional needs. Even the responses that children make on workbook pages can provide important diagnostic clues. Undoubtedly one of the best ways to evaluate reading is to listen to the child read a paragraph or two from a basal reader, social studies or science text, or from a trade book.

Comprehension tasks for silent reading can also focus on important facets of critical reading (15). The following list gives the different categories of comprehension tasks that could be used for constructing diagnostic tests to determine pupils' comprehension levels:

1. Tests of ability to use context clues
   a. Sentence meaning
   b. Cloze procedures, paragraph length
   c. Sentences that do not "fit"
2. Drawing inferences
3. Following directions
   a. Sentence tasks
   b. Problem solving
4. Test of word meanings (malapropisms)
5. Determining fact or opinion

The cloze procedure is an informal diagnostic procedure that can be used to identify reading levels and provide information about a reader's ability to deal with the content and structure of the information presented—syntax, word meanings, and story grammar. A cloze test is typically constructed by selecting a freestanding written passage of approximately 250 to 300 words in length and deleting every fifth word. The first sentence is left intact and the first deletion would be the fifth word in the second sentence of the passage. Every fifth word after this is deleted throughout the passage. Each deleted word is replaced with a line of uniform length, as illustrated in the following example:

> Jake saw the two horses just south of the timber ridge over by Clear Lake. He and Rusty had ______________ hunting these Mustangs for ______________ last two days. Yesterday ______________ horse ran away and ______________ gone for several hours. ______________ time that Jake lost ______________ searching for the runaway ______________ had made him think ______________ that they would not ______________ the wild horses. (The deleted text is as follows: been, the, Rusty's, was, The, while, horse, seriously, catch).

As noted in this example the words deleted from a passage may be nouns, verbs, adjectives, and so forth. The basic rule is to delete the fifth word regardless of its function in the sentence.

Administering and scoring a cloze test for determining reading levels is a simple, straightforward procedure. The pupil is instructed to read the passage and write in the blank the word that he thinks was deleted. Each of the responses is then scored as either correct or incorrect. Only the exact replacement of the deleted word is considered a correct response. The percentage of correct responses is determined by dividing the total correct replacements by the number of deleted words (30 words correctly replaced divided by 50 words deleted would be a 60 percent correct replacement). The percentage of correct word replacement can then be compared with the scale of 61 percent or more correct replacement, the independent reading level; 41 percent to 60 percent correct replacement, the instructional reading level; and less than 40 percent, the frustration level (12).

Determining the reading levels using the criterion of exact word replacement is intended to help the teacher decide if youngsters would be able to handle the content and language structure of different types of reading materials, such as science, social studies, and math texts. A better understanding of a reader's use of syntax, semantics, and reasoning can be determined by looking at incorrect word choices. If incorrect responses are syntactically correct (same part of speech), this may suggest that the pupil is using words preceding and following the deletion in an attempt to supply a meaningful response. Semantically correct word choices could indicate that the reader was getting meaning as he read but chose a word different from the author's choice. If the words are both syntactically and semantically correct, then the reader is revealing meaning and applying his knowledge of language.

Cloze testing is a useful and valuable informal diagnostic strategy that is neither time consuming nor difficult to use. Interpreting the types of responses may prove to be more valuable in securing information about a pupil's reading level than simply identifying the level. A fifth-word deletion may be too difficult for some children, and the teacher may wish to delete every eighth or tenth word. Selective deletion can also be used in the development of a cloze test. Rather than deleting every fifth or tenth word, only nouns, adjectives, or verbs can be deleted. The child's replacement of these words would have to be evaluated by looking at the type of response given rather than the exact replacement. Information about pupils' understanding of word functions, sentence structures, and how information in a reading selection develops (see chap. 6) can be gained by evaluating their responses.

A modification of the cloze procedure is the maze procedure (8). Rather than having the reader supply the deleted word, word choices are presented in vertical arrays. The cloze procedure is essentially a recall task, whereas the maze procedure is a recognition task. Typically, the cloze procedure deletes every specified numbered word; with the maze procedure, one can select any word(s) for completing a passage. This selective choice of options can enhance the use of the maze procedure both as a diagnostic and teaching device (17). Selective identification of words allows a teacher to get an idea of a pupil's attention to context as she reads and of her understanding of language.

	paddled		swimming	
The boy	swam	his boat across the large lake	searching	for a good
	leaned		moved	

fishing spot. He saw a small cove with tree limbs hanging over

	water
the	ice
	case

Obviously, any idea that is incorporated into informal testing will have to be adapted to fit the levels of the pupils involved.

Some illustrations of exercises that might be used are included in the next Assessment Activity.

A procedure for gathering information about pupils' perceptions of classroom reading activities and how their comprehension performance relates to different demands of reading instructional tasks has been developed by Wixson, Bosky, Yochum, and Alvermann (18). The Reading Comprehension Interview is intended to be used with pupils in grades 3 through 8. It takes approximately 30 minutes to administer the interview and, similar to administering an IRI, the child is told that there are no right or wrong answers and the teacher is just trying to find out what they think. During its administration the teacher uses probing questions to encourage pupil responses and to clarify responses. As with the other informal strategies noted earlier, evaluation of pupils' responses focuses on looking for patterns and attempting to gain insights into pupils' thinking.

The Reading Comprehension Interview is presented in Figure 11.10. Questions 1 through 3 focus on pupils' reading habits and interests, questions 4 through 10 deal with both the basal reader and content textbooks, and questions 11 through 15 investigate pupils' perceptions about specific comprehension worksheets. Interpretation of pupils' responses should focus on the reading comprehension factors presented in chapter 6, such as purposes for reading, concept of print, and strategies for understanding written language.

Based upon the teacher's evaluation of pupils' responses, trial lessons can be developed to correct problem areas. Once the effectiveness of certain instructional procedures has been determined, these can be used to teach the needed strategy (what, how, when, and why to use it).

Name: Date:
Classroom teacher: Reading level:
Grade:

Directions: Introduce the procedure by explaining that you are interested in finding out what children think about various reading activities. Tell the student that he or she will be asked questions about his/her reading, that there are no right or wrong answers, and that you are only interested in knowing what s/he thinks. Tell the student that if s/he does not know how to answer a question s/he should say so and you will go on to the next one.

General probes such as "Can you tell me more about that?" or "Anything else?" may be used. Keep in mind that the interview is an informal diagnostic measure and you should feel free to probe to elicit useful information.

1. What hobbies or interests do you have that you like to read about?
2. a. How often do you read in school?
   b. How often do you read at home?
3. What school subjects do you like to read about?

Introduce reading and social studies books.

Directions: For this section use the child's classroom basal reader and a content area textbook (social studies, science, etc.). Place these texts in front of the student. Ask each question twice, once with reference to the basal reader and once with reference to the content area textbook. Randomly vary the order of presentation (basal, content). As each question is asked, open the appropriate text in front of the student to help provide a point of reference for the question.

4. What is the most important reason for reading this kind of material?
   Why does your teacher want you to read this book?
5. a. Who's the best reader you know in ____________?
   b. What does he/she do that makes him/her such a good reader?
6. a. How good are *you* at reading this kind of material?
   b. How do you know?
7. What do you have to do to get a good grade in in your class ________?
8. a. If the teacher told you to remember the information in this story/chapter, what would be the best way to do this?
   b. Have you ever tried ________?
9. a. If your teacher told you to find the answers to the questions in this book what would be the best way to do this? Why?
   b. Have you ever tried ________?
10. a. What is the hardest part about answering questions like the ones in this book?
    b. Does that make you do anything differently?

continued

FIGURE 11.10 Reading Comprehension Interview (From "An Interview for Assessing Students' Perceptions of Classroom Reading Tasks," Karen K. Wixson et al., January 1984 *Reading Teacher,* the figure Reading Comprehension Interview. Reprinted with permission of Karen K. Wixson and the International Reading Association.)

Introduce at least two comprehension worksheets.

Directions: Present the worksheets to the child and ask questions 11 and 12. Ask the child to complete portions of each worksheet. Then ask questions 13 and 14. Next, show the child a worksheet designed to simulate the work of another child. Then ask question 15.

11. Why would your teacher want you to do worksheets like these (for what purpose)?
12. What would your teacher say you must do to get a good mark on worksheets like these? (What does your teacher look for?)

Ask the child to complete portions of at least two worksheets.

13. Did you do this one differently from the way you did that one? How or in what way?
14. Did you have to work harder on one of these worksheets than the other? (Does one make you think more?)

Present the simulated worksheet.

15. a. Look over this worksheet. If you were the teacher, what kind of mark would you give the worksheet? Why?
    b. If you were the teacher, what would you ask this person to do differently next time?

FIGURE 11.10 (cont.)

ASSESSMENT ACTIVITY

Use of Context Clues in Sentences. In each of the following sentences two words are omitted. Read each sentence and fill in the words that complete the meaning of the sentence.

1. It is warmer in ______________ than in ______________.
2. The bird built a ______________ in the ______________.
3. A week has seven ______________; a year has ______________ months.
4. Apples, ______________, and ______________ are kinds of fruit.
5. When you ______________ five and three the ______________ is eight.
6. Leaves fall from the ______________ in the ______________.
7. Put a ______________ on the letter and mail ______________.
8. John runs very ______________ but Bill runs even ______________.
9. A decade is ______________ years, and a century is ______________ years.
10. A baby cow is a ______________, and a baby bear is a ______________.

Cloze Procedure—Use of Context Clues in Sustained Reading. In the following passage, every sixth word is deleted. The reader writes a word in each blank space that she feels makes sense.

A helicopter is an aircraft with whirling wings. Helicopter pilots often call it ______________ whirlybird or a chopper. The ______________ blades, called rotors, go round ______________ round like a propeller on ______________ back, but they really lift ______________copter just the way a ______________ wing does.

The wonderful thing __________ rotors is that they can __________the copter almost straight up __________ the ground and bring it __________ almost straight down. They can __________ it fly backward as well __________ forward. Or they can keep __________ hovering above one spot. This __________ that a helicopter needs no __________ runway for landing or taking __________. A space just a little __________ than its rotors is usually __________.

Sentences That Do Not Belong. In each of the following paragraphs there is one sentence that does not fit. Underline that sentence and tell why it does not fit in the paragraph.

1. John visited grandfather's farm. He saw some ducks and cows. John never liked lions. He helped grandfather feed the chickens.
2. Mary loves sports. She plays tennis and basketball. This summer she earned ten dollars. Mary enjoys watching sports on television.
3. Mark Twain wrote the book *Tom Sawyer.* It is about a boy who lives on the Mississippi River. One of Tom's friends is named Huckleberry Finn. The Colorado River formed the Grand Canyon.
4. The beaver is intelligent and works very hard. He has sharp teeth and can cut down small trees. The beaver can build dams in streams. He can blow water out of his trunk. Beavers do not eat fish.
5. One of the problems troubling our country today is pollution of our air and water. Automobiles, factories, and careless individuals all contribute to the problem. Everywhere, people are pleased with the environment. It will take years and great sums of money to clean up the air and water.

Comprehension Through Drawing Inferences. Read each numbered sentence and the statements *a, b,* and *c* beneath it. Circle the statement you think is most logical.

Sample: The children went outside to build a snowman.
   a. It was May.
   b. It was August.
   (c.) It was January.

1. As we were riding along, father slammed on the brakes.
   a. It had started to rain.
   b. We were out of gas.
   c. A dog ran in front of the car.
2. The rooster crowed in the dim light.
   a. He was hungry.
   b. The sun was about to rise.
   c. He was saying, "Good night."
3. The class went to the zoo and saw:
   a. A herd of cows.
   b. Two elephants.
   c. Donald Duck.

4. When the window broke the boy ran.
   a. He had broken the window.
   b. He was late for school.
   c. The noise frightened him.
5. An elephant and a giraffe were in the barn.
   a. They had run away from the zoo.
   b. The farmer was a big-game hunter.
   c. The farmer was taking care of the animals for a circus.
6. The woman ran into the store holding a newspaper over her head.
   a. It was raining.
   b. She was going to buy the paper.
   c. She was telling everyone the news.
7. The ambulance roared down the street, sounding its siren.
   a. The ambulance was part of a parade.
   b. Traffic was very light.
   c. There had been an accident.
8. The family car was crowded with suitcases.
   a. They had been to a suitcase sale.
   b. It was vacation time.
   c. Father was going to the bank.

Following Written Directions (Sentence Tasks).

1. Put the letter l in front of each word if it will form a new word.

   ____and ____end ____make ____ate ____old ____ice ____ink

2. Write the plural form of each of the following words.

   house________ bird________ glass________
   brush________ box________ bench________

3. Add the ending ed if this will make another word.

   know____ light____ men____ park____ wish____
   talk____ ring____ visit____ jerk____ shoot____

4. Underline all compound words.

   somewhere swimming upon waterproof overnight movement
   wonderful newspaper important broadcast careless silverware

5. Rewrite the following words to make a sentence.

   the station train of rolled out the

6. Circle each word to which we could add *s* to form another word.

   fun city hurt rub came run seed tell

7. Circle each word that can mean a person or persons.

   going he Mary pretty they someone upon

8. Put the letter *s* in front of each word if this will form a new word.

____and	____car	____hot	____make	____lip	____kill
____pray	____ate	____mile	____nail	____ask	____win

9. Write the following words in alphabetical order.

elephant elm eel envelope easy

Problem Solving: Following Written Directions. Each of the directions below asks you to study Box A and Box B. Then carry out the directions found in each of the numbered sentences.

1. If the sum of two odd numbers is always an even number, place a small *x* in the middle figure in line one, Box B.
2. If the sum of the third and fourth numbers in Box A is equal to the seventh number, circle A in Box A.
3. If this is an odd-numbered sentence, circle the digit 6 in Box A.
4. If both lines 1 and 2 in Box B contain a square, put an *x* in the square on line 2.

Box A

1	2	3	4	5	6	7
A	B	C	D	E	F	

Box B

Line1	□	○	△
Line 2	○	△	□

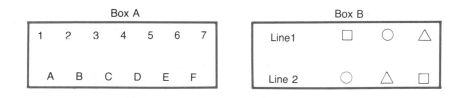

5. If the sum of the digits in Box A is greater than 28, underline D in Box A.
6. If there are the same number of digits in Box A as there are letters, place a dot (●) in the circle on line 2 of Box B.
7. If there are more odd numbers than there are even numbers in Box A, circle the E in Box A.
8. If the sum of the first two digits in Box A equals the third digit, circle the sixth letter in Box A.
9. If there are three vowels in Box A, circle one of the triangles in Box B.

Word Recognition and Meaning. People often use one word when they mean to use a different one. In each of the following sentences there is one word that does not fit. Underline this word. On the blank space following each sentence, write the word you think was intended.

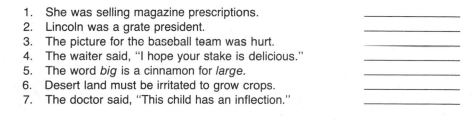

1. She was selling magazine prescriptions. ____________
2. Lincoln was a grate president. ____________
3. The picture for the baseball team was hurt. ____________
4. The waiter said, "I hope your stake is delicious." ____________
5. The word *big* is a cinnamon for *large*. ____________
6. Desert land must be irritated to grow crops. ____________
7. The doctor said, "This child has an inflection." ____________

Diagnosis is a prerequisite for tailoring reading instruction, which is essential for a reading program.

8. After a rain, the humility is quite high. ______________
9. The cliffs had become withered from the wind and rain. ______________
10. "Aisle be seeing you," he said. ______________

SUMMARY

The reading ability of children in any given classroom will cover a wide range. Diagnosis is a prerequisite for differentiation of instruction which, in turn, is an essential for a sound reading program. One of the principles stressed in chapter 1 and a basic feature of effective reading instruction presented in chapter 2 is that ongoing diagnosis provides the blueprint for instruction.

Formal testing involving the use of standardized tests is one type of diagnosis. Unfortunately, in some schools reading diagnosis is dictated by the calendar rather than by sound instructional philosophy. Diagnosis of pupils' reading should be an integral part of a reading program.

Meaningful diagnosis is ongoing and includes the use of a variety of procedures, such as standardized tests, informal reading inventories, and teacher-developed tests. It should be remembered that anytime a child reads, he provides clues to his instructional needs. Listening to a child read a paragraph or two can provide much information. The alert teacher will note whether the material was too difficult, what types of errors were made, and whether the child's sight vocabulary, word attack skills, and phrasing were adequate. The child's responses in this reading situation will suggest what other informal diagnostic approaches are now appropriate. Examples of brief testing materials have been provided throughout this chapter.

YOUR POINT OF VIEW

Discussion Questions

1. During the first week of school you suspect that Johnny cannot read the social studies text that has been adopted for class use. You wish to verify or refute the above hypothesis. What diagnostic procedures would you use? How would you interpret the diagnostic data?
2. Assume that the use of standardized reading tests in the elementary grades was prohibited for the next five years. Suggest logical hypotheses as to what would happen in reading instruction if this unlikely event occurred.
3. A new student has enrolled in your classroom and you want to plan his reading instruction. What diagnostic procedures would you use if no information is available from his former school? How would you analyze data from your diagnosis?

Take a Stand For or Against

1. In most classroom situations, critical reading is equated with supplying responses that arbitrarily have been decided upon as being correct. Creative reading that might lead to divergent interpretations is not encouraged.

2. In many schools the potential values that might be achieved from the use of standardized tests are lost because the school is more concerned with the ritual of administering tests than with "mining the test data."
3. Informal teacher-made tests can yield as much data about an individual child's reading as can standardized tests.
4. If equal amounts of expert instruction are given to all children in a class or group, those children who are lowest in reading achievement will make the smallest gain per unit of instructional time.
5. There is little basis for assuming that the school can prevent a substantial number of reading failures among pupils.

BIBLIOGRAPHY

1. Baumann, James F., and Stevenson, Jennifer A. "Understanding Standardized Reading Achievement Test Scores." *The Reading Teacher* 35 (1982): 648–54.
2. Baumann, James F., and Stevenson, Jennifer A. "Using Scores from Standardized Reading Achievement Tests." *The Reading Teacher* 35 (1982): 528–32.
3. Betts, Emmett A. *Foundations of Reading Instruction.* New York: American Book Co., 1946.
4. Goodman, Kenneth S. *Miscue Analysis: Application to Reading Instruction.* Urbana, Ill.: National Council of Teachers of English, 1973.
5. Goodman, Kenneth S. "Strategies for Comprehension." In *Findings of Research in Miscue Analysis: Classroom Implication,* edited by P. Allen and D. Watson, 94–102. Urbana, Ill.: National Council of Teachers of English, 1976.
6. Goodman, Yetta, and Burke, Carolyn. *Reading Miscue Inventory.* New York: Macmillan Publishing Co., 1972.
7. Gronlund, Norman E. *Measurement and Evaluation in Teaching.* 3d ed. New York: Macmillan Publishing Co., 1976.
8. Guthrie, John R. "Reading Comprehension and Syntactic Responses in Good and Poor Readers." *Journal of Educational Psychology* 65 (1973): 294–300.
9. Hood, Joyce. "Qualitative Analysis of Oral Reading Errors: The Inter-Judge Reliability of Scores." *Reading Research Quarterly* 11 (1975–76): 577–98.
10. Powell, William R. "Informal Reading Inventories: Points of View." Speech presented at the Annual Meeting of the College Reading Association, Miami, Florida, 1976.
11. Powell, William R. "Validity of the I. R. I. Reading Levels." *Elementary English* 48 (1971): 637–42.
12. Rankin, Earl, and Culhane, Joseph. "Comparable Cloze and Multiple Choice Comprehension Test Scores." *Journal of Reading* 13 (1969): 193–98.
13. Rupley, William H. "Effective Reading Instruction: Promising Practices."

In *Selected Articles on the Teaching of Reading,* Set C, no. 43. New York: Barnell Loft, 1978.

14. Rupley, William H., and Blair, Timothy R. *Reading Diagnosis and Remediation: Classroom and Clinic.* Boston, Mass.: Houghton-Mifflin Publishing Co., 1983.
15. Schell, Leo. "Criterion Referenced Tests: Selected Cautionary Notes." *Reading World* 19 (1979): 57–62.
16. Turner, Susan Douglass. "How to Look at the Test Components of Basal Reading Series." *The Reading Teacher* 37 (1984): 860–66.
17. Wiseman, Donna, and McKenna, Michael C. "Classroom Uses of the Maze Procedure." In *Selected Articles on the Teaching of Reading,* Set C, no. 50. New York: Barnell Loft, 1978.
18. Wixson, Karen K.; Bosky, Anita B.; Yochum, M. Nina; and Alvermann, Donna E. "An Interview for Assessing Students' Perceptions of Classroom Reading Tasks." *The Reading Teacher* 37 (1984): 346–52.
19. Woods, Mary Lynn, and Moe, Alden J. *Analytical Reading Inventory.* 3d ed. Columbus, Ohio: Charles E. Merrill Publishing Co., 1985.

12

Classroom Management and Organization

For the Reader

Do you recall your first experience with a large group of children in a classroom? If you have not as yet started to teach, do you worry about how you will handle a large group of children? In either case, we are sure you can contemplate some of the demands and constraints a classroom environment will pose for you. Your perceived notions of diagnostic teaching—pretesting, setting objectives, teaching, allowing for student practice, using a variety of materials, reinforcing abilities in a variety of situations, and posttesting—must operate in the context of a class of twenty to thirty-five children. As you know, children within any group will differ in a variety of ways. Thus, within the context of the classroom, you must strive to accommodate individual differences. Effective teachers of reading understand the organizational conditions found in their teaching situation and endeavor through various grouping procedures to maximize student learning.

This chapter will discuss the various options available to teachers in carrying out their diagnostic teaching procedures with a large group of children. As chapter 3 emphasized, current research has shown a strong relationship between classroom organization and management and student achievement. Your ability to meet the demands of the classroom setting will provide rewards for both you and your students.

Preview

- Read the Key Ideas that are presented next.
- Read each heading and subheading.
- Read the summary.
- Read the statements at the end of the chapter.
- Return to the chapter text that follows the Key Ideas and begin reading.

Key Ideas

Effective classroom management and organization are related to increased pupil achievement.

Student-engaged time relates to pupil achievement.

There are many types of groups found in the classroom:
- large groups
- small groups
  - skill
  - interest
  - research
  - ability

Cooperative learning promotes peer tutoring, encouragement, and achievement.
The ungraded school concept helps deal with student differences.
Individualized reading is based on the principles of seeking, self-selection, and self-pacing.

CLASSROOM STRUCTURE

A history of American education dealing primarily with classroom practices would be, in essence, a history of the attempts to deal with pupil differences. All of the previously discussed principles, techniques, approaches, materials, and diagnostic tools are put into action by teachers to provide instruction that pupils need. The plural *pupils* is a key word in the previous sentence because teaching reading effectively includes the ability to organize and maintain a classroom environment for twenty to thirty-five youngsters that maximizes student learning. We encourage you to review the implications for reading instruction originating from current research on teacher effectiveness (see the conclusion of chapter 3). Effective classroom management and organization are related to increased pupil achievement. In reviewing the data from the Beginning Teacher Evaluation Study, Guthrie (2) stated:

> Classroom teachers contribute to reading achievement by optimizing the scheduled time for reading and related activities, selecting materials that insure learning, minimizing the interruption of student attention, and assessing the amount of learning as a guide to assigning new materials. When these conditions are met, time in school has a handsome payoff. (p. 502)

Grouping youngsters for instruction was formerly thought to be done more for administrative convenience than anything else. However, research is now supporting the use of groups as a major contributor to increased direct instruction afforded to students by teachers. Although grouping in itself is not the answer, teachers who spend little time with their pupils negatively affect their learning. Powell (9) speaks to the heart of this issue and puts the idea of grouping into proper perspective:

> The amount of time allocated to a skill area appears to be a contributor to the amount learned. A distinction, however, needs to be

> made between allocated time and time on task (engaged time). It is time on task that is the critical factor. Engaged time has a quality of student attention. The student must be involved with active attention in the task at hand. The task at hand may be interacting either with the teacher or the learning materials. The teacher directs the process. Whether a student is in a group or doing seatwork is not the basic criterion. What is important is whether the teaching practice directs, guides, and engages the pupil. (p. 92)

TYPES OF GROUPING

Teachers must be adept at planning and organizing their classrooms by using a variety of grouping procedures. Such decisions depend upon the particular learning goals of students. There are several grouping procedures open to teachers. Basically, class grouping can be handled in one of three ways—whole groups, small groups, and individual learning. Every classroom should at various times incorporate all types of groups depending on pupils' learning needs. Different types of groups are discussed below.

Large Groups

In any classroom, large-group or whole-class instruction will be appropriate at times. When certain skills or abilities are deemed necessary for all children, it is a more efficient use of both teacher and student time to have large-group instruction. Some instances where this grouping would be appropriate are storytelling; working on art activities related to a story; teaching various study skills such as SQ3R, skimming, scanning; how to read maps, graphs, diagrams, charts, and reference books; and how to use the library effectively.

Skill Groups

This type of grouping is based upon diagnostic findings related to pupils' specific strengths and weaknesses. Such grouping brings together a small number of pupils for a specific purpose. Once the skill(s) is mastered, the group is disbanded. Examples of skill groups formed on the basis of children's needs include specific word identification instruction on a particular skill, for example, sounds represented by consonants, and specific comprehension instruction, for example, inferring character traits.

Interest Groups

Groups may be formed on the basis of a common interest in a particular topic. Group members can be on different instructional reading levels; cooperation between members is fostered and can add to increased motivation and self-satisfaction. There are many activities that lend themselves to interest grouping. Students who read books by the same author can research his life, style of writing, compare stories, or complete art work related to each of their books. Students who are interested in a particular subject can come together and read various books on their instructional level and prepare a group report. Others can listen to a recorded story and filmstrip about a particular topic together.

Research Groups

Grouping pupils together for the purpose of researching a particular topic is similar to interest grouping. Under research grouping, students are required to collect, organize, and synthesize information from a variety of sources, and produce a final product (oral report, written report, art activity, or a play). Some examples of topics include living in our community fifty years ago, how electric lights work, exploration and settlement of the West, the growth and change of the South, John F. Kennedy, the Supreme Court, Albert Einstein, hurricanes and tornadoes, how our circulatory system works, and the United Nations.

Cooperative Learning Groups

Placing youngsters into small, heterogeneous groups to foster cooperative learning has generated considerable interest. With the great range of differences found in today's classrooms, the use of cooperative groups can be effectively used to increase pupil-engaged time. The major requirement of cooperative groups is that members can only succeed if all members of the group are successful. With this arrangement, students have a vested interest in ensuring that other group members learn. Skill, interest, and research groups can be arranged to promote cooperative learning. Johnson and Johnson (4) have done a considerable amount of research on the use of cooperative groups and their implications in the mainstreaming movement. They feel that all youngsters benefit from cooperation, and this type of grouping is the only one consistent with the purpose of mainstreaming. Their extensive research comparing competitive, individualistic, and cooperative grouping structures in the regular classroom reveals the following outcomes:

> Cooperative learning experiences promote more social acceptance, liking, and friendships between handicapped and nonhandicapped students than do competitive or individualistic ones.

> Cooperative learning experiences promote higher self-esteem of all students and more basic acceptance of oneself than do competitive or individualistic learning experiences.
>
> Cooperative learning experiences promote higher achievement of all students than do competitive and individualistic ones. (pp. 7, 8)

Although there is no one set of guidelines for ensuring successful implementation of cooperative grouping, the following steps can help teachers initiate cooperative groups.

> Specify the instructional objectives.
> Select the group size most appropriate for the lesson.
> Assign students to groups (heterogeneous in nature).
> Arrange the classroom so that group members are close together and the groups are as far apart as possible.
> Provide appropriate materials.
> Explain the task and the cooperative goal structure.
> Observe the student-student interaction.
> Intervene as a consultant to help the group.
> (a) solve its problems in working together effectively,
> (b) learn the interpersonal and group skills necessary for cooperating, and
> (c) check that all its members are learning the material.
> Evaluate the group products, using a criterion-referenced evaluation system.

Using learning groups benefits all students in the regular classroom.

Ability Grouping

Grouping pupils on the basis of previous learnings and present instructional needs is a long-standing practice in our schools. Ability grouping is an accurate description when it refers to *present achievement* without reference to potential ability. However, it was (and still is) sometimes used to imply innate or intellectual capacity. When this occurred, the mere act of grouping suggested a final judgment, rather than an initial step in ongoing diagnosis.

There were certain other widespread but indefensible practices that resulted in criticism of ability grouping. It was observed that once groups were established, there was very little change in their composition. Pupil mobility between groups did not seem to be synchronized with any performance criteria. Another practice difficult to explain was that some teachers followed the same practice and procedures with the high, medium, and low groups. All read, or attempted to read, the same book(s) and attempted to *cover* the same amount of material. Since there was no differentiation of instruction, it had to be assumed the grouping was a ritual unrelated to instructional strategy.

It is realistic to assume that grouping is neither inherently good nor bad. Practices carried out under any plan of grouping may enhance pupil growth or become meaningless and even harmful educational rituals. Grouping pupils on the basis of instructional needs can provide the framework within which an alert teacher can develop meaningful, differentiated instruction. Grouping can narrow the range of differences and reading problems with which a teacher has to cope during a given instructional period. As a result, you can focus on particular short-term goals for specific pupils.

There are always practical considerations that influence grouping practices. Attempting to work with five or six groups might result in instructional time blocks that are too small to be effective. Two groups could result in too heterogeneous a collection of pupils in both groups. Such problems emphasize why grouping practices should be quite flexible. When teachers are primarily concerned with the *goals* of grouping, the mechanics tend to fall into place.

School-Wide Homogeneous Grouping

Some provision for grouping students may be handled on a school-wide basis. For instance, if a school has several classrooms for each grade level, pupils may be assigned to classes on the basis of "present reading achievement." Assume there are three second-grade classrooms. One would house the lowest third of all second-grade students, the middle achievers would be assigned to another class, and the top third, the remaining second-grade class. All grade levels would be treated in a simi-

FLASHBACK

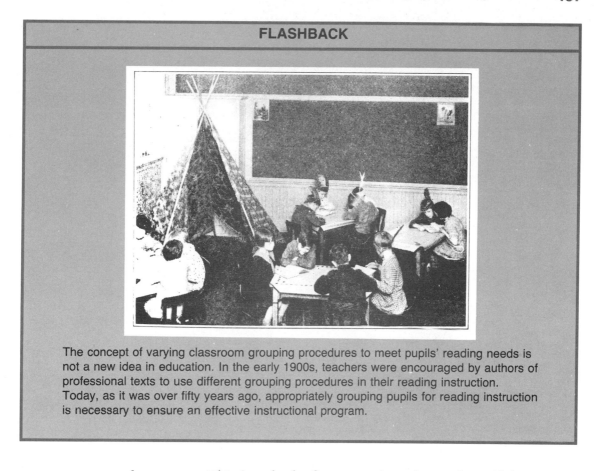

The concept of varying classroom grouping procedures to meet pupils' reading needs is not a new idea in education. In the early 1900s, teachers were encouraged by authors of professional texts to use different grouping procedures in their reading instruction. Today, as it was over fifty years ago, appropriately grouping pupils for reading instruction is necessary to ensure an effective instructional program.

lar manner. This is only the first step, since the teachers of the various classes will undoubtedly have to resort to some additional grouping practices. However, it does reduce the "range of abilities" found in each classroom.

The Psychological Impact of Grouping

Grouping is sometimes discussed as being potentially threatening to pupils. There are various points of view as to how the grouping within a classroom is to take place so as not to introduce comparisons between children. Suggestions include calling the groups group 1, group 2, group 3; giving the groups some irrelevant titles such as bluebirds, redbirds, robins; referring to the groups by the names of children in the group. The latter has the merit of being a straightforward approach. No one is being humiliated on the basis of reading ability, and it does not appear that the teacher thinks every pupil should have a certain ability to read.

Psychologically, it is inadvisable for a teacher to attempt to hide differences among beginning readers. It is impossible to fool the children about their reading, and when the poorer readers see through the bluebirds versus the blackbirds, they too start attaching a stigma to poor reading ability.

Wise teachers have different groups of children doing different things at the same time through the year, and no significance is attached to this by either the teacher or the pupils. A first-grade teacher, for example, probably did not start all children reading from level 1 on the same day. She observed the children closely and identified those who were ready to begin reading. When she started this group in a book, other groups worked on reading also. Some children worked in a readiness workbook, some worked on teacher-prepared readiness materials, and some were getting ready to make an experience chart. The teacher, in a natural way, had developed the idea that groups of pupils would be reading from different books and would be working on different workbook pages. The teacher who is successful in doing this helps pupils in many ways.

- Teachers help children build a foundation for independent work habits.
- Competition and feelings of failure are reduced, since children are not compared with each other on the same reading tasks.
- Tension and bad attitudes toward reading are held to a minimum.
- Children are permitted to progress at their own rate, and intergroup rivalry is minimized.
- Teachers are prevented from using, consciously or unconsciously, a grouping system that is too rigid.
- Teachers are granted flexibility in reducing the size of a group they work with by having some children work independently while they work intensively with others.

Organizing a Class for Instruction

Implementing reading instruction in a class requires the careful orchestration of time, materials, and instruction to meet the individualized needs of children. Based on diagnostic data, a teacher must make several decisions regarding student instructional levels, specific skill development needs of students, materials to be utilized, and types of grouping to improve learning. A visitor to a typical classroom will readily see there are many ways to organize a class for reading. Therefore, any discussion of organizing a class for reading instruction must acknowledge the fact that there is no one correct way. What should be the guiding principle in making decisions regarding the organization of reading instruction is what is the best way to meet pupils' needs in reading.

Effective teachers use different types of groups at different times to achieve desired results. Flexibility in the use of groups is a key because children are different, and needs continually change. Children need a careful blend of teacher-directed and independent activities to improve in their ability to read. Figures 12.1 and 12.2 illustrate possible ways to organize a class for reading instruction using a basal reader approach. Suggested schedules are given for two and three reading groups. Although there are many other combinations, these figures should help you visualize the decisions a teacher must make when organizing instruction. Each day's reading lesson is divided into those activities that are teacher-directed and those that are independent in nature. The schedules depict one possible way to distribute components of the Directed Reading Activity (DRA) throughout a week. The organization is such that students receive a balance of instructional and independent activities. Also, regardless of group membership, differences among pupils will always exist. Therefore, teachers need to plan time for special needs grouping. At this time, instruction can be provided to those students needing a particular skill (e.g., dictionary skills, study skills, vowel sounds). Once students in a special needs group learn the targeted skill, the group is disbanded.

In looking at the suggested time schedules, it is important to remember reading activities (both teacher-directed and student independent work) are happening simultaneously. Obviously, the teacher spends most of her time with one group (if two groups are used) or with two groups (if three groups are used). What the suggested schedules do not show are the preplanning efforts to ensure (1) the success of the teacher-directed and student independent activities and (2) the smooth transitions from one activity to another to avoid wasting instructional time. These efforts are contingent upon several considerations: (1) grouping of any type should be linked to student needs; (2) groups should be flexible in the sense that different types be used for different purposes, and students can move to other groups depending on progress; (3) groups should be task-oriented; (4) students should be working with the teacher as much as possible; and (5) students need to be productively working even while completing activities on their own. The last consideration is of critical importance. Although it may be easier to maintain a high level of academic engaged time with students in a teacher-directed activity, it isn't so easy to guarantee students will complete activities on their own. Keys to success in this area include explaining clearly what students are to do and how to do it before moving to another group, circulating around the room at times to monitor seatwork and to give feedback to students in different groups, explaining ahead of time what students are to do if they finish an assignment early, and preparing all materials ahead of time to ensure a smooth, systematic transition from working with one group to working with another (1).

<table>
<tr><th></th><th>Monday</th><th>Tuesday</th><th>Wednesday</th><th>Thursday</th><th>Friday</th></tr>
<tr><td>Group 1</td><td>Teacher Directed
DRA: Readiness; Silent Reading</td><td>Teacher Directed
DRA: Comprehension Check
Meaningful Oral Rereading
Specific Skill Lesson</td><td>Student Independent Work
Supplemental Activities
Activity: Kit and/or Worksheets</td><td>Student Independent Work
Free Reading</td><td rowspan="2">Teacher Directed
Special Needs Group
and
Student Independent Work
Supplemental Activities</td></tr>
<tr><td>Group 2</td><td>Student Independent Work
Supplemental Activities</td><td>Student Independent Work
Free Reading</td><td>Teacher Directed
DRA: Readiness; Silent Reading</td><td>Teacher Directed
DRA: Comprehension Check
Meaningful Oral Rereading
Specific Skill Lesson</td></tr>
</table>

FIGURE 12.1 Suggested Schedule for Two Reading Groups

	Monday	Tuesday	Wednesday	Thursday	Friday
Group 1	**Teacher Directed** DRA: Readiness; Silent Reading	**Teacher Directed** DRA: Comprehension Check Meaningful Oral Rereading Specific Skill Lesson **Student Independent Work** Workbook Activity	**Student Independent Work** Supplemental Activities	**Student Independent Work** Supplemental Activities Free Reading	**Teacher Directed** Special Needs Group
Group 2	**Student Independent Work** Supplemental Activities **Teacher Directed** DRA: Readiness; Silent Reading	**Student Independent Work** Free Reading **Teacher Directed** DRA: Comprehension Check	**Student Independent Work** Workbook Activities **Teacher Directed** Meaningful Oral Rereading Specific Skill Lesson	**Student Independent Work** Workbook Activities	and
Group 3	**Student Independent Work** Supplemental Activities	**Student Independent Work** Supplemental Activities	**Teacher Directed** DRA: Readiness; Silent Reading	**Teacher Directed** DRA: Comprehension Check Meaningful Oral Rereading Specific Skill Lesson	**Student Independent Work** Supplemental Activities

FIGURE 12.2 Suggested Schedule for Three Reading Groups

ALTERNATIVE MANAGEMENT APPROACHES

Organizing the classroom for instruction involves making provisions for individual differences among learners. As noted earlier, finding ways to differentiate instruction has been, and remains, a top priority in education. This is a justifiable preoccupation since success in this endeavor is the key to successful school programs. The following discussion outlines several types of classroom management that deal with individualizing instruction, promotion practices, and other factors related to instruction.

The Ungraded School

The term *ungraded* is applied to an administrative-instructional organization that deemphasizes, or suspends, the grade-level structure and emphasizes continuous pupil progress. This concept represents another approach for dealing with pupil differences. Attempts at *ungrading* have been most successful at beginning instructional levels. Thus, much of the literature focuses on the *ungraded primary school,* embracing the first three years of formal schooling.

The ungraded primary has highly structured curriculum that accommodates a wide range of student achievement. All tasks are placed within a series of "levels" arranged in order of ascending difficulty. Pupils move through the sequence at their own pace. As they master one level, they move on to the next, thus maintaining continuous progress. At the end of a year's instruction, each pupil is located somewhere on an identified continuum of skills. The next year's instruction begins at this point, meeting the student where he is in relation to skills mastered.

Although instruction in the conventional grade-level system is geared to the average, experience tells us that pupils do not cluster closely around an achievement mean. Differences in achievement are marked, and they increase with instruction. The ungraded primary starts from the premise that each child should progress at her own rate, and the instructional program centers on each child's need at the moment. This is accomplished by breaking the primary years into a number of units of accomplishment, or levels of competency. As children develop competency at one level, they are moved into work at the next level. The number of levels and the skills to be mastered at each level are worked out cooperatively by teachers in the program.

Some of the educational advantages believed to be inherent in the ungraded primary plan follow.

- It is easier to provide for the children's reading growth *early* in their reading career if you do not have to think of "grade-level norms" the first year.
- There is likely to be less failure and frustration in the reading situation if there is less emphasis on comparison and promotion.
- Teachers often stay with the same group of students two years or longer. This gives them an opportunity to know pupils better. They are less likely to push students beyond their ability during the first year, since they expect to work with them the next year.
- Students always work at the level on which they need instruction; consequently, they are not likely to miss some facet of instruction because they were absent several days.
- The slower learner will not repeat the first or second grade, but may take four years to move up from the primary level.
- The ungraded plan is flexible, allowing pupils to cover some phases of learning quite rapidly when they are capable of doing so and giving them more time when it is needed.
- Bright pupils would not "skip a grade," they would simply go through the entire primary curriculum at a faster rate.

No method of grouping will automatically solve all instructional problems. If a shift to the ungraded plan is not accompanied by an understanding of the goals to be achieved, none of the potential benefits is likely to be realized. If teachers or parents continue to think in terms of a grade-level system, the plan is doomed from the start. On the other hand, if the philosophy of the plan is believed sound and the chief reason for adopting it is to help children grow in reading, problems that do arise will not be insurmountable.

The Unit Approach

The unit approach has a long history of successful classroom use. Although it can be considered a method of instruction, it is discussed in this chapter because of its classroom management potential. The unit provides many ways for coping with individual differences, differentiating instruction, and grouping pupils for specific short- and long-term activities.

This approach provides the teacher with so many options that it has been discussed under a wide array of titles, including *resource units, teaching units, activity-centered instruction, core approach,* and *survey units.* Use of a unit approach permits the integration of reading instruction and related language skills in numerous learning activities, all focusing on a specific curricular theme.

A unit may be devised for any subject area and can cover a time span of a few days during which pupils attempt to find the answer to a particular question, or it may extend over a period of weeks and end in some class project. The end product might be a play, a school program, or a science fair with many individual and committee projects. Although the unit approach is not new, it is consistent with the aims of modern curriculum planning. Unit study can help avoid the tendency toward fragmentation of the curriculum into isolated, seemingly unrelated parts.

Units lend themselves to two types of major emphasis. The first type emphasizes *pupil experiences built around a specific topic,* such as *How We Get Our Food.* Experiences related to this topic might include visits to various types of farms, a cannery, a cold storage plant, a meat packing plant, a dairy, or a bakery. Pupils may plant and care for a garden or a window box. The second major emphasis is on *wide reading.* It is likely that emphasis on the experience approach will come at the early elementary level, shifting to reading in the subject areas in the intermediate grades. These two methods are extremely compatible, and the proper combination of the two approaches undoubtedly makes for a better total learning situation.

Advantages of the Unit Approach. The potential advantages of the unit approach are numerous. The actual benefits resulting from its use will vary with such factors as the teacher's skill, the reading ability and work habits of the pupils, and the amount of supplementary reading material available. Some of the more frequently mentioned advantages of the unit approach are summarized below.

- The unit serves as the framework within which learning experiences are shaped into larger, more meaningful wholes. The unit permits more than the superficial study of a topic and encourages application of skills in wide and varied reading.
- Units can be used in any curricular area.
- Pupils learn that reading is the key to getting information on all subjects and not just an operation performed in the basal reader and accompanying workbooks.
- The unit approach can and should include a great variety of experiences related to reading, such as excursions, field trips, and small-group participation, in working on various facets of the problem.
- Units structure the learning situation to make reading more varied, more meaningful, and more interesting.
- Units permit pupils of widely different reading abilities to work on different facets of the same project. Reading materials at many levels of difficulty can be used, and children need not be directly compared as readers.

- The unit approach gives the teacher flexibility and freedom to work with a child or a group of children engaged in some reading activity at their own level. The reader with problems and the accelerated reader can be working independently and successfully on something that is challenging.
- Units aid independent reading and help to foster independence in research reading.

Examples of Units. A unit on weather designed for a fifth-grade class may be used as an illustration. The teacher had aroused the interest of the class through an assignment of watching weather reports on television, finding interesting pictures of weather stations, and discussing stories dealing with weather in class. Out of this grew the teacher's decision to have a study unit on weather. Under the teacher's direction the pupils worked cooperatively in identifying objectives, finding questions to be answered, and working on individual projects that were within the limits of the unit. These are listed below.

- Objectives of unit on weather:
  To learn ways in which weather helps or harms people.
  To learn what causes various types of weather and changes of seasons.
  To learn the causes and effects of rainfall, temperature, fog.
  To become familiar with the instruments used in measuring or predicting weather changes.
- Questions to be answered:
  How is a thermometer constructed and how does it work?
  What is fog?
  What causes hail?
  What is lightning? Why is it followed by thunder?
  Why do we have seasons such as winter and summer?
  Why are some parts of the earth always hot and others always cold?
  Why is there very little rainfall in one part of a country and a great deal in another part?
  Why is it important for people to be able to predict the weather?
  What is a barometer? How does it work?
  What is humidity?
- Representative activities or projects, both individual and group:
  Keeping a daily record of temperature. Securing temperatures registered in cities in different parts of the country.
  Preparing charts and graphs illustrating some aspect of weather:
    Average rainfall for different states and countries.
    The relationship between rainfall and the type of crops raised in a particular area.
    The effect of rainfall on density of population.

Maps showing occurrence of tornadoes, hurricanes, or floods during past decade.

Explaining and demonstrating a thermometer and barometer.

Doing research on the work of the U.S. Weather Bureau in predicting weather—how it is done and why.

Studying the effects of weather on human dress, shelter, or diet.

Measuring rainfall during a rain.

Securing pictures illustrating any facet of weather or the effect of weather, such as floods, erosion, storms on land and sea, barren deserts, and permanent snow.

- Culminating activity:

  It was decided that at the end of the unit the class would have a Weather Fair. All individual and group projects would be displayed, including posters, graphs and charts, picture series, pupil-made instruments for measuring weather, and all written projects. Parents were invited to visit the class on a particular afternoon, and other classes in the school saw the display at certain times that day. Children explained their projects and received a great deal of satisfaction from this culminating activity.

Units Integrate Work in All Areas. This well-planned unit provided a variety of purposeful learning experiences; the teacher had structured activities so that all facets of the curriculum received attention.

- *Spelling.* Many words were learned incidentally as children printed them on their posters or charts. New words were assigned and studied as part of the unit *(weather, thermometer, mercury, rainfall, temperature, erosion, bureau).*

- *Health.* One particular topic, *How Weather Affects Our Health,* almost became a unit within a unit. The entire class participated, and all pupils were asked to write a brief account of anything they found in their reading that answered the question. The teacher had a few references for those children who needed help in finding material. What was basically a health lesson also became a lesson in communication skills as the children worked on their written assignments. Practice in oral language usage also received attention as children discussed or reported their findings to the class.

- *Mathematics.* A lack of understanding of the problems to be solved is more of a stumbling block in mathematics in the intermediate grades than is lack of computational skills. Failure to read problems critically will result in hazy concepts. In unit work the math problems that are met emerge from the immediate experiences of the learner. Problems such as finding the average rainfall, average temperature, or total foodstuffs raised are related to larger goals and become meaningful in the goal-directed activity. The need for accurate measurement becomes apparent in building a barometer or measuring a rainfall.

- *Science.* Basically this unit was a science unit. One topic that received emphasis at this particular grade level was how scientists predict and track the weather and the scientific instruments used in the process. In studying the thermometer and barometer, many scientific principles and questions evolved, such as the principles of expansion, gravity, and pressure, and the questions of whether mercury is a metal, why it is used in these instruments, and what the function of heat is in causing a thermometer to work.

- *Social Studies.* The discussion above on health led into social studies topics. A discussion of diet in relation to health led to questions and discussion on how weather affects diet or the production of foodstuffs. A discussion of the economic value of climate would logically follow. The relationship of climate to certain natural resources was discussed, for example, the relationship to forestry, deposits of coal, and petroleum. The relationships among rainfall, temperature, winds, forests, and the types of crops were discussed. Methods of cultivation and crop rotation were studied in relation to land erosion.

- *Reading.* Reading was the process that provided the vehicle for all of the curricular activities mentioned above. The unit stressed, in pupils' minds, that they were getting information for science, health, and geography. Their reading was purposeful. Neither the reading nor the teaching of it was the compulsive "let's get this workbook page finished" approach. The teacher kept in mind all the principles of teaching reading. He had to be particularly careful not to expect all children to read the same materials and to provide a variety of supplementary materials at many grade levels.

  Use of the unit method in no way restricts teachers in developing pupils' reading skills. In fact, once the preliminary planning of a unit is done, teachers will find that they have as much time and opportunity to help individual pupils or small groups as they had when working with a conventional grouping arrangement. Most unit work introduces a fairly heavy vocabulary load. It follows that much time must be spent on vocabulary development recognition. As teachers have different children read and as pupils ask for help with unknown words, teachers can prepare several word lists of new words to be studied during the course of the unit. One such list might be taken from the more difficult sources and be used exclusively with the advanced reading group. Easier words can be used in vocabulary exercises with average readers and those experiencing problems. Many new and unknown words can be used for teaching phonic analysis and for stressing the importance of context clues in solving meaning difficulties.

In developing a unit, the teacher may find that the first important task is to secure materials at various levels. The references available will vary from school to school. Basal readers at all levels could serve for such a unit as well as selected reading from subject-matter texts. *My Weekly Reader* files would provide materials on many topics, and the school or public library can be sources of books on special topics.

INDIVIDUALIZED READING

A Movement? A Method? Classroom Organization? A Philosophy of Instruction? Organizing the classroom for instruction must make provisions for dealing with students, materials, and instruction. The next format discussed in this chapter—individualized reading—meets this criterion. Granting that the term *individualized reading* has somewhat different meanings to different users, this approach has for many years enjoyed wide acceptance and use in our schools.

Paradoxically, its greatest potential strengths and weaknesses stem from the same factor. There is no concise definition of what it is and no blueprint for how to make it work. It forces freedom of choice upon teachers, and its success depends upon creative responses. However, vulnerability lies in the fact that no protection can be offered to prevent teachers from developing their own nonproductive rituals. The consensus seems to be that freedom and lack of structure cannot work equally well for all teachers.

Background and History

During the 1950s, frustration with the status quo in reading instruction reached a new high, and the climate for change seemed particularly good. A new emphasis on gearing reading instruction to individual pupils' needs and interests evolved through a movement that came to be known as *individualized reading.*

Proponents of this reform movement had great enthusiasm, which was essential if change was to be achieved. Two educational practices in particular, the use of basal readers and ability grouping, came under attack.

There is little question that certain indefensible practices were to be found in the use of basals and groupings. Some teachers relied on basal texts to the exclusion of other materials. When this occurred, reading and learning to read could easily be reduced to deadly routines. Some pupils who had the ability to move through basals fairly rapidly were kept with the group, with the result that their reading was severely limited. These students were asked to complete tasks such as workbook exercises that added nothing to their growth in reading because they could already do these things.

Children at the other end of the achievement continuum were kept reading the same primer and first grade basals for two or more years even though they did not make any progress. Relying too heavily on basals (or any other material) implies less than optimum use of other instructional techniques and materials.

The other area of concern, that of dividing a class into three groups, took on the characteristics of a mechanical ritual unrelated to caring for individual differences and meeting individual needs. In some classrooms, children did read round robin; poorer readers were not only embarrassed, but provided unacceptable models of oral reading for the remainder of the group. It was probably impossible to enjoy a story read under such adverse conditions. These practices were not inherent in the use of basals or grouping, but rather had grown as a result of teachers and school systems failing to be effective in teaching. In an effort to bring about reform, some proponents of change made sweeping charges against basal materials and grouping practices. It is generally agreed that it would have been more logical to focus on the actual *abuses* of basals and achievement grouping found in classrooms, rather than to attempt to eliminate them altogether (12). Although extreme positions have been abandoned by most advocates of individualized reading, a few examples are cited here for historical perspective.

- Individualized reading requires the complete abandonment of the basal reader and the basal reader system.
- One source of bias in many critics (of individualized reading), it should be recognized in advance, is the intellectual and emotional involvement in authorship of basal series. [Meaning that some critics may prefer individualized reading but earn their living by writing basals.]
- It is reported everywhere that children who have disliked reading change their minds. It is reported that maladjusted children change their attitudes and fit in with the group in other activities. Everywhere it is reported that all children do quantities of reading.
- Seldom are two children ready to be taught reading from the same materials at the same time.

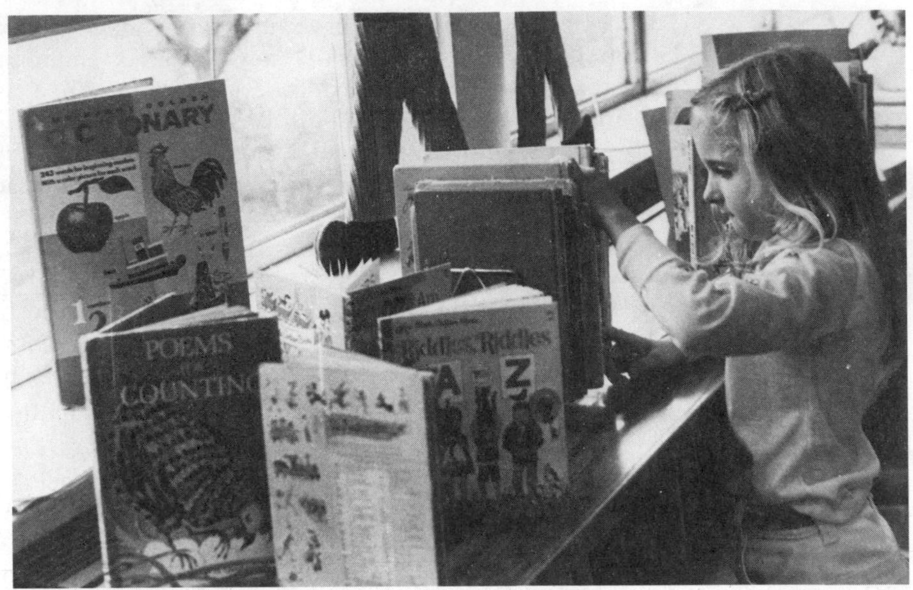

Encouraging and guiding pupils to select and read books is a basic feature of individualized reading.

Such generalizations raised more questions than they settled. Fortunately these extreme stances gradually diminished in the discussion of individualized reading. Feuds that focused on organizational mechanics separating the true believers from the suspect lost partisans. As Larrick (5) pointed out, much of what had been written about individualized reading tended to deal with "how many minutes per child (in conference), how to keep records, how to sign up for books, how to manage the class." These problems, she believed, could be solved by teachers once they viewed reading as a personal involvement of pupils and once teaching ceased to be dominated by the demand to cover a stipulated content.

Practices Associated with Individualized Reading

The philosophy of individualized reading rejects the lockstep instruction that tended to become standardized within the framework of the graded system and traditional graded materials. The success or failure of an individualized program rests almost exclusively with the teacher, which is one of the reasons why individualized reading is so difficult to define.

Over the years a number of practices have become associated with individualized reading (11). These include self-selection of materials by

FLASHBACK

Individualized reading is an approach based on the concepts of seeking, self-selection, and self-pacing. Willard C. Olson, who proposed these concepts in the early 1950s, believed youngsters, moving at their own pace, grow best when surrounded by a large selection of books from which to choose. This approach stresses that each child differs with respect to learning style, learning rate, and interests. Most reading programs today have attempted to adopt the basic tenets of individualized reading in their respective programs.

pupils, self-pacing in reading, individual pupil conferences with the teacher, and emphasis on record keeping by teacher, pupil, or both. One other notable characteristic is the absolute need for a wide variety of reading material in each classroom. This becomes mandatory if pupils are to select books that they are interested in and can read.

Self-selection and Self-pacing. Self-pacing of reading and self-selection of reading materials are basic to the individualized reading philosophy. Olson's (7,8) writing is frequently cited as the basis for the emphasis on seeking, self-selection, and self-pacing. Although these concepts are not new to education, the individualized reading movement has given them a new emphasis when focused on reading instruction.

The principle underlying the advocacy of self-selection is psychologically sound. Since there are tremendous individual differences among pupils in a given classroom, there is little justification for assuming that different pupils' needs and interests will be met equally well by one basal series or a single text.

The success of self-selection is influenced by several factors. First, children must have some interests they wish to explore further. This helps motivate children in the reading situation. Second, there must be materials available that fit their interests and that they can read independently.

The theory is that when these conditions are met, children will seek out the materials fitting their needs, interests, and present reading levels. If they select wisely, they grow. Much depends on pupil success, and some proponents of seeking, self-selection, and self-pacing appear to have assumed that success is assured by this formula.

Carried to extremes, this idea of individualized reading can minimize the role of the teacher in guiding pupils to materials to the degree that self-selection almost becomes a fetish. There is some danger in attempting to close debate by reasserting that "pupils, when permitted to do so, will select materials they can read." This may be true in a number of cases, but it is not an inevitable law of child behavior.

Self-selection on the part of pupils is to a degree often limited by the fact that teachers have previously chosen the one or two hundred books found in the classroom from among thousands available. This infringement on the principle of self-selection is not decried simply because we accept the gathering of materials as part of the teacher's role. Individualized reading and self-selection do not preclude teachers from recommending books or guiding pupils toward certain materials, but this type of guidance does call for a high level of teacher competency. They must know the children's interests, their reading abilities, and the difficulty level of materials if their suggestions are to help pupils grow.

The factor of economy in the teacher-learning situation must also be considered. If after a period of "seeking," children have not made a selection and settled down to reading, their behavior may indicate that they are not yet ready for self-selection. There is no evidence that a teacher's praising a book or offering suggestions to pupils will result in undesirable psychological side effects. On the contrary, there is evidence that pupils respect teacher judgments and tend to be favorably disposed toward materials recommended by understanding teachers. With many pupils, self-selection can safely be tempered with guidance.

Teacher-Pupil Conference. The teacher-pupil conference is one of the major identifying features of individualized reading and is potentially one of its great strengths. This potential is realized only when teachers are skillful in achieving desirable goals. The conference is a brief session in which teachers give their whole attention to one pupil so that she may express herself on a story she has selected and read prior to the conference. The primary goal of the conference is to assure children that they have an appreciative audience.

The chief value of the conference is that it involves children in the reading process. For students to share their feelings about a book with their teacher is a motivating experience. If the conference is to yield maximum pupil growth, however, teachers must be more than listeners. In addition to being an appreciative audience, teachers must also assume some responsibility for helping children develop a higher level of values and self-understanding, goals often best achieved through judicious questioning.

The teacher-pupil conference is worthy of further consideration because it also has possible therapeutic value. The conference serves as a catalyst, helping to produce teacher-pupil rapport, a factor that is highly underrated in its influence on learning. For some pupils, the teacher's positive response to their reading is a stronger motivation than the actual act of reading itself. The skillful, sympathetic teacher can provide this extrinsic reward while slowly moving the child toward accepting reading as its own reward (13).

The conference provides a means by which teachers can learn important facts about children's psychological needs and the means they have adopted for fulfilling these needs. With this knowledge, the alert teacher is in a position to become a party to sound biblio-therapeutic practices. Discussing reading with a respectful adult will help children gain insights into their own problems and afford examples of how others have met such difficulties (10).

Preparing for the conference is essential, but one should avoid a "standardized format." Veatch has listed the factors which teachers may wish to consider in setting up conferences (13).

- As a general rule, the pupils inform the teacher when they feel ready to participate in the conference.
- The teacher should be familiar with the book or story that a child plans to discuss.
- Pupils are informed when and in what order they will be scheduled for the conference.
- Provision must be made for all other pupils in the class to be engaged in some other meaningful activity. One suggestion is to have them selecting and reading books independently.
- The teacher must be prepared to stimulate pupils through the use of questions. These should be questions that stimulate thought instead of those asking only for factual information.
- The class and teacher will have worked out some system for pupils to receive help pronouncing unknown words during their independent reading.

Frequency, length, and format of conferences were the basis for many questions from teachers in the early days of the individualized reading movement. Today, it is understood that practices in these areas must vary from classroom to classroom. No single proposal relative to format, frequency, or length of conferences would be equally good for all situ-

Effective use of individualized reading demands that the teacher sometimes offer help when needed; such brief exchanges build the student's confidence.

ations. A logical schedule for a classroom of twenty-four pupils may become unworkable with a class of thirty-five. Furthermore, the length and frequency of the conference will also vary with different grade levels and different ability levels within a grade. A further complicating factor is the difference found among readers themselves. The child who has read a story consisting of only several hundred words will probably not take as much sharing time with the teacher as the pupil who read *Charlotte's Web.* In no sense is it necessary to think that all conferences will use the same procedures or last for the same amount of time.

In the case of a reader who needs little encouragement to read, a brief exchange between the teacher and pupil would be sufficient on some occasions. A word of praise, a question about whether there are still a number of books in the classroom that the pupil wishes to read, and an offer of help when needed could be considered adequate. Since the sharing-type conference is primarily a confidence-building experience, it is obvious that some children will need more attention than others. Some pupils continually avoid a conference because reading is a threat rather than a pleasure. These pupils need constant encouragement and praise for their accomplishments.

Record Keeping. Record keeping received considerable attention in the early descriptions of individualized reading. For the most part, this activity had little or nothing to do with actual diagnosis of reading needs. The purpose seemed to be to emphasize the number of books read and to offer proof that the system was working. Over the years the emphasis on this activity has diminished. In some cases this feature became dominant as children read primarily to add titles to their lists. Also, it tended to introduce the element of "comparison of achievement" which individualized reading opposes philosophically.

Problems Encountered in Individualized Reading

The thought of children reading independently, selecting what they wish to read, and reading at their own pace strikes some critics as being quite idealistic. To keep this philosophy from becoming unrealistic, a great deal of effort must be expended in classroom management. Over the years teachers have voiced a number of concerns, some of which are listed here in question form and then briefly discussed.

- What type of materials are needed?
- How does one initiate an individualized program?
- When and how is ongoing diagnosis achieved?
- How is provision made for teaching the necessary reading skills?
- When the teacher is involved in teacher-pupil conferences, what are the other students doing?
- How do these students get "instant help" on their reading problems?

How these and other issues are handled determines the success or failure of an individualized program.

Needed Materials. A reading program embracing self-selection and self-pacing and designed to meet the interests of individual pupils cannot function in a learning environment that does not include a wide selection of reading materials. This should not be thought of as a special problem related only to individualized reading. There is no justification for any classroom or school not meeting this criterion, regardless of methodological approach or program. Therefore, the need for materials is not a unique feature of individualized reading, but rather a factor which has been justifiably emphasized in this approach.

Although there is little point in attempting to settle upon a fixed number of books considered adequate, a minimum figure frequently mentioned is approximately one hundred different tradebook titles per classroom. However, these hundred books must be periodically changed throughout the year.

Factors which must be considered include grade level; range of interests and abilities of pupils; class size; whether books can be rotated with other classrooms; whether the school supports a central library; and whether the same materials are used extensively in other subject areas, such as social studies and science, in the preparation of units.

Trade books are not the only source of materials, although these would likely be the major source. Classrooms should contain magazines, newspapers, various reading kits, *My Weekly Reader, Reader's Digest* (skill-builder materials), and most other reading materials children might choose to work with. Reading materials would cover many areas such as biography, science, sports, exploration, hobbies, fairy tales, medicine, space, poetry, humor, adventure, myth, and travel.

Starting a Program. All elementary teachers are likely to be doing some things which fit logically under the heading of individualization. Any of the formal aspects of individualized reading such as self-selection or individual conferences can be started with one pupil, a small group, or the entire class. Obviously, the latter approach would present the most problems; therefore, perhaps you should start with one of the other alternatives.

Starting an individualized program by involving a small group will present fewer organizational problems than involving the entire class. The teacher begins by calling together the students selected and explaining the task of selecting their own books to read at their desks during the reading period.

Prior to this group conference, a number of books should be assembled and on a reading table. A number of "new books" should be included and you should deliberately include books that you think will appeal to the five or six students in the group.

At the end of the group conference, the teacher tells the group that, after they have selected the book they wish to read, they are to go to their desks and read their selection silently. Pupils are also told that they may keep the book at their desk until they are finished. Within a day or two the pupils meet again in the individualized group and the teacher explains that each student is to tell something about the book they just completed and also to read a part of the book that was particularly interesting. In order to do this, an individual conference is scheduled with each pupil. Pupils are to tell the teacher when they are ready for their conference.

Providing for Diagnosis. Individualized reading is an organizational-instructional approach which, by its very nature, calls for considerable diagnosis if children are to progress smoothly in reading. Some pupils may not be able to achieve in an individualized setting in the absence of ongoing diagnosis. It is doubtful that procedures such as self-selection and self-pacing were ever intended to operate independently of diagnosis and teacher guidance.

There are no diagnostic techniques associated exclusively with individualized reading, nor are there any that are unique to it. The individual teacher-pupil conference may be a major source of diagnostic information. Lipton and Kaplan (6) have provided the following list as a framework for diagnosing a child's oral reading patterns and strategies during a conference.

1. Has a cheerful/fearful approach to books.
2. Reads word-by-word.
3. Hesitates, then asks for help.
4. Sits passively when confronted by unknown words.
5. Uses graphic or configurational cues.
6. Uses phonemic cues.
7. Omits, inserts, or substitutes certain words, but does not alter the grammatical structure.
8. Omits, inserts, or substitutes certain words and alters the grammatical structure.
9. Omits, inserts, or substitutes certain words, but does not alter the meaning.
10. Omits, inserts, or substitutes certain words and alters the meaning.
11. Uses context cues to decode difficult words.
12. Uses regression to seek meaning.
13. Uses punctuation as an aid to meaning.
14. Demonstrates skills: a) main ideas, b) recall of details, c) making inferences, d) drawing conclusions, e) understanding vocabulary.

Teaching Reading Skills. The early individualized movement was in part a reaction against reading instruction that often stressed individual skills at the expense of the "total reading process." In some classrooms, all pupils received the same instruction, worked on the same skill-building exercises, and read the same materials. When these practices were prevalent, there was room for suspicion that instruction was predetermined rather than based on pupil needs and abilities. Such uniform practices inevitably resulted in some children becoming bored with reading instruction, and thus there existed a need for reform.

Unfortunately, the attack on uniform skills instruction for everyone tended to spread to the teaching of skills themselves. Actually, skills teaching was not explicitly rejected, but this facet of individualized reading instruction was neglected. In recent years the importance of skills teaching has been accepted by most proponents of individualized reading. However, the vagueness as to how and when the teaching is incorporated into the program still lingers. Questions relative to teaching skills elicited two frequently repeated responses: teach some skills in the teacher-pupil conference; and teach other skills as they are needed by the pupils.

The first answer suggests what is, on the whole, an uneconomical procedure, unless the child participating in the conference is the only one in the class who can profit from the instruction that is given. Any reading skill that can justifiably be taught to the entire class should be taught to everyone. Students who learn with the first presentation should be doing something else when subsequent presentations are made to pupils who did not learn.

The basic validity of the second response (teach skills when they are needed) cannot be faulted, but it can be argued that it is both vague and difficult to implement when each child in the class is reading a different book. Concern for providing differentiation of skills instruction need not start from the premise that no two pupils, or larger groups in a class, can profit from the same instruction. This extreme position is simply the opposite of the practice that implies that all children in a class *could* profit from the same amount of time spent with the same book. Reliance on diagnosis is the best way to identify what is appropriate instruction.

There are dozens of abilities and habits that could be listed under the heading *basic skills.* The major areas with which the elementary teacher must be constantly concerned are *word identification, the knowledge of word meanings,* and *application of reading skills in meaningful context.*

Meaningful Class Activities During the Teacher-Pupil Conference. Individualized reading calls for a high degree of planning and subtle directing by the teacher. The following brief listing is only illustrative. The tasks are not identified by grade level since many may be adapted to various levels. The listing includes class, group, and individual activities covering skill development, recreational reading, reading in curricular areas, and creative activities.

1. Self-selection of books or other reading materials. This will likely include browsing and sampling. Selection is followed by independent reading of materials.
2. Conducting library research for an individual or group report. Such an activity may relate to a unit in some other subject.
3. Planning creative writing experiences to include original stories, poems, letters to a classmate in the hospital or one who has moved away, invitations to parents to visit school, a riddle composition to be read to the class during a period set aside for such activities.
4. Preparing art work such as:
   a. Drawing or pasting pictures in a picture dictionary.
   b. Drawing a picture to accompany a pupil-dictated, teacher-written story.
   c. Preparing posters or book covers to illustrate the key point in a book or story the pupil has read.
5. Using workbook pages or teacher-prepared seatwork guides for the development of particular skills such as:
   a. A dictionary exercise that follows an introduction of a skill such as alphabetizing by initial letter, or by two or more letters; use of guide words; pronunciation guides; or syllabication.
   b. Word analysis skills (associating sounds with graphic symbols, noting compound words, abbreviations, and the like).
   c. Study skills involving effective use of parts of a book such as the index, table of contents, glossary, appendix; library card catalog; reference materials.
6. Using an appropriate filmstrip with the entire class, a smaller group, or two pupils.
7. Teaching and testing word meanings.
   a. Workbook pages or teacher-prepared seatwork may be provided.
   b. Children may work on "vocabulary building" cards or notebooks in which they write one or more common meanings for new or unknown words met in their reading.
   c. The teacher may place a list of words on the board. Pupils write as many sentences as possible, using a different connotation for the word in each sentence. Example: *Light*—light in weight, light in color, light the fire, light on his feet, her eyes lit up, lighthearted, etc.
8. Making a tape recording of a story. A group of four to six pupils may each read the part of one character. Practice reading and the actual recording may be done in the rear of the classroom or in any available space in the building.
9. Testing or diagnostic activities may be arranged. The entire class or any size group may take a standardized test (or reading subtest); tests which accompany basal series; *My Weekly Reader* tests; or

FLASHBACK

International Reading Association

CODE OF ETHICS

The members of the International Reading Association who are concerned with the teaching of reading form a group of professional persons, obligated to society and devoted to the service and welfare of individuals through teaching, clinical services, research, and publication. The members of this group are committed to values which are the foundation of a democratic society—freedom to teach, write, and study in an atmosphere conducive to the best interests of the profession. The welfare of the public, the profession, and the individuals concerned should be of primary consideration in recommending candidates for degrees, positions, advancements, the recognition of professional activity, and for certification in those areas where certification exists.

Ethical Standards in Professional Relationships:

1. It is the obligation of all members of the International Reading Association to observe the Code of Ethics of the organization and to act accordingly so as to advance the status and prestige of the Association and of the profession as a whole. Members should assist in establishing the highest professional standards for reading programs and services, and should enlist support for these through dissemination of pertinent information to the public.
2. It is the obligation of all members to maintain relationships with other professional persons, striving for harmony, avoiding personal controversy, encouraging cooperative effort, and making known the obligations and services rendered by the reading specialist.
3. It is the obligation of members to report results of research and other developments in reading.
4. Members should not claim nor advertise affiliation with the International Reading Association as evidence of their competence in reading.

Ethical Standards in Reading Services:

1. Reading specialists must possess suitable qualification (See Minimum Standards for Professional Training of Reading Specialists) for engaging in consulting, clinical, or remedial work. Unqualified persons should not engage in such activities except under the direct supervision of one who is properly qualified. Professional intent and the welfare of the person seeking the services of the reading specialist should govern all consulting or clinical activities such as counseling, administering diagnostic tests, or providing remediation. It is the duty of the reading specialist to keep relationships with clients and interested persons on a professional level.
2. Information derived from consulting and/or clinical services should be regarded as confidential. Expressed consent of persons involved should be secured before releasing information to outside agencies.
3. Reading specialists should recognize the boundaries of their competence and should not offer services which fail to meet professional standards established by other disciplines. They should be free, however, to give assistance in other areas in which they are qualified.
4. Referral should be made to specialists in allied fields as needed. When such referral is made, pertinent information should be made available to consulting specialists.
5. Reading clinics and/or reading specialists offering professional services should refrain from guaranteeing easy solutions or favorable outcomes as a result of their work, and their advertising should be consistent with that of allied professions. They should not accept for remediation any persons who are unlikely to benefit from their instruction, and they should work to accomplish the greatest possible improvement in the shortest time. Fees, if charged, should be agreed on in advance and should be charged in accordance with an established set of rates commensurate with that of other professions.

Breaches of the Code of Ethics should be reported to IRA Headquarters for referral to the Committee on Professional Standards and Ethics for an impartial investigation.

In 1958, The International Reading Association (IRA) formed a Membership Standards Committee to consider areas related to professional membership. As a result of the committee's considerations they recommended a written code of ethics for the IRA.

informal, teacher-made tests. These will be scored and studied for diagnostic information they yield.

Application of Individualized Reading in All Programs

It is important to remember that the basal reading approach, not individualized reading, is the most prevalent method of instruction in our schools. However, the basic tenets of individualized reading—self-selection and self-pacing—form part of any successful basal or other reading program as well. Every reading program should be individualized in the sense of meeting the individual needs of students. Grouping students to achieve instructional goals is a part of individualizing instruction. As discussed in chapter 3, grouping students for particular purposes is related to significant gain in achievement scores. This is the essence of individualized instruction. It is particularly satisfying to note that there are a multitude of ways to individualize instruction, depending on the teacher, the program, and the child. Effective teachers utilize diagnostic procedures and teacher-pupil conferences as previously described. The application of individual teacher-pupil conferences to every reading program is perhaps the greatest contribution of individualized reading. It is at this time that a teacher can personalize his/her teaching, diagnose student strengths and weaknesses, and teach a necessary skill and prescribe individual assignments. Teachers at every grade level in all reading programs promote independent reading habits. Also, pupil self-selection and self-pacing can be an integral part of using the basal reader book itself. In this way, teachers and students can enjoy some measure of flexibility but still retain the structure inherent in the basal system. Students can have some freedom of choice in reading particular stories. Workbook and reinforcement activities can be assigned to fit individual pupil needs. Indeed, all teachers are encouraged to embody the basic tenets of individualized reading in their own teaching, regardless of grade level taught or reading approach employed.

SUMMARY

A discussion of classroom management and organization was presented in view of the teacher effectiveness studies summarized in chapter 3. Several possible ways of grouping pupils were discussed. Options for maximizing pupil involvement include the flexible use of whole group, small group and individual learning. Small groups can be arranged according to ability, a particular skill need, interest, or a research topic. The use of cooperative learning groups was discussed as benefiting all children and as particularly relevant to successful mainstreaming practices. Alternative approaches to classroom management discussed included the ungraded school, individualized reading, and unit teaching. It was stressed that grouping in itself was not the all-important factor. The real concern is concern for individual differences and increasing the degree of pupil-engaged time on selected tasks.

YOUR POINT OF VIEW

Discussion Questions

1. A major feature of individualized reading is the pupil-teacher conference. What are some important features to consider before, during, and after a conference with a pupil?
2. What are some procedures that teachers can use to gather diagnostic information when using individualized reading?
3. What are the major advantages and disadvantages of the unit approach, the ungraded school, and individualized reading?

Take a Stand For or Against

1. Youngsters tend to look at their teachers in terms of the ability level in which they are placed.
2. Ability grouping reduces the opportunities for pupils to learn from one another.
3. The ungraded primary is, in essence, an attempt to break away from grade-level standards of achievement.
4. Most individualized reading programs have more provisions for better readers in a class than for readers having problems.
5. The unit approach relies too much on incidental learning and slights systematic instruction in reading.
6. The present structure of the classroom environment prohibits cooperative learning groups.

BIBLIOGRAPHY

1. Evertson, Carolyn M.; Emmer, Edmund T.; Clements, Barbara S.; Sandford, Julie P.; and Worsham, Murray E. *Classroom Management for Elementary Teachers.* Englewood Cliffs, N.J.: Prentice-Hall, 1984.

2. Guthrie, John T. "Time in Reading Programs." *The Reading Teacher* 33 (1980): 500–502.
3. Johnson, David W., and Johnson, Roger T. "Many Teachers Wonder . . . Will the Special Needs Child Ever Really Belong? *Instructor* (Feb. 1978): 152–154.
4. Johnson, David W., and Johnson, Roger T., eds. "Social Interdependence and Mainstreaming: A Teaching Module." In *Learning Together and Alone,* Bloomington: University of Minnesota, 1978.
5. Larrick, Nancy. "Individualizing the Teaching." In *Reading, Learning and the Curriculum,* pp. 35–38. Proceedings of the Twelfth Annual Reading Conference, Lehigh University, Bethlehem, Pa., 1963.
6. Lipton, Aaron, and Kaplan, Elaine. "The Pupil-Teacher Reading Conference." *The Reading Teacher* 31 (1978): 376–77.
7. Olson, Willard C. *Child Development.* Boston: D.C. Heath & Co., 1949.
8. Olson, Willard C. "Seeking, Self-Selection and Pacing in the Use of Books by Children." In *Individualizing Your Reading Program,* edited by Jeanette Veatch, 89–98. New York: G.P. Putnam's Sons, 1959.
9. Powell, William R. *Reading, Language Arts, and Mathematics.* Technical Report No. 3 DOE/UF Basic Skills Project, Phase III, Contract No. R5–175. Tallahassee, Fla.: Department of Education, 1979.
10. Reeves, Harriet Ramsey. "Individual Conferences—Diagnostic Tools." *The Reading Teacher* 24 (1971): 411–15.
11. Sipay, Edward R. "Individualized Reading: Theory and Practice." In *Children Can Learn to Read—But How,* pp. 82–93. Rhode Island College Reading Conference Proceedings, Providence, 1964.
12. Sucher, Floyd. "Use of Basal 'Readers' in Individualizing Reading Instruction." In *Reading and Realism,* edited by J. Allen Figurel, 136–43. Proceedings, International Reading Association 13, Part I, 1969.
13. Veatch, Jeanette. "Self-Selection and the Individual Conference in Reading Instruction." In *Improving Reading Instruction,* pp. 19–25. Joint Proceedings of Reading Conference and Summer Workshop, Vol. 1. State College, Pa.: The Pennsylvania State University, 1963.

13

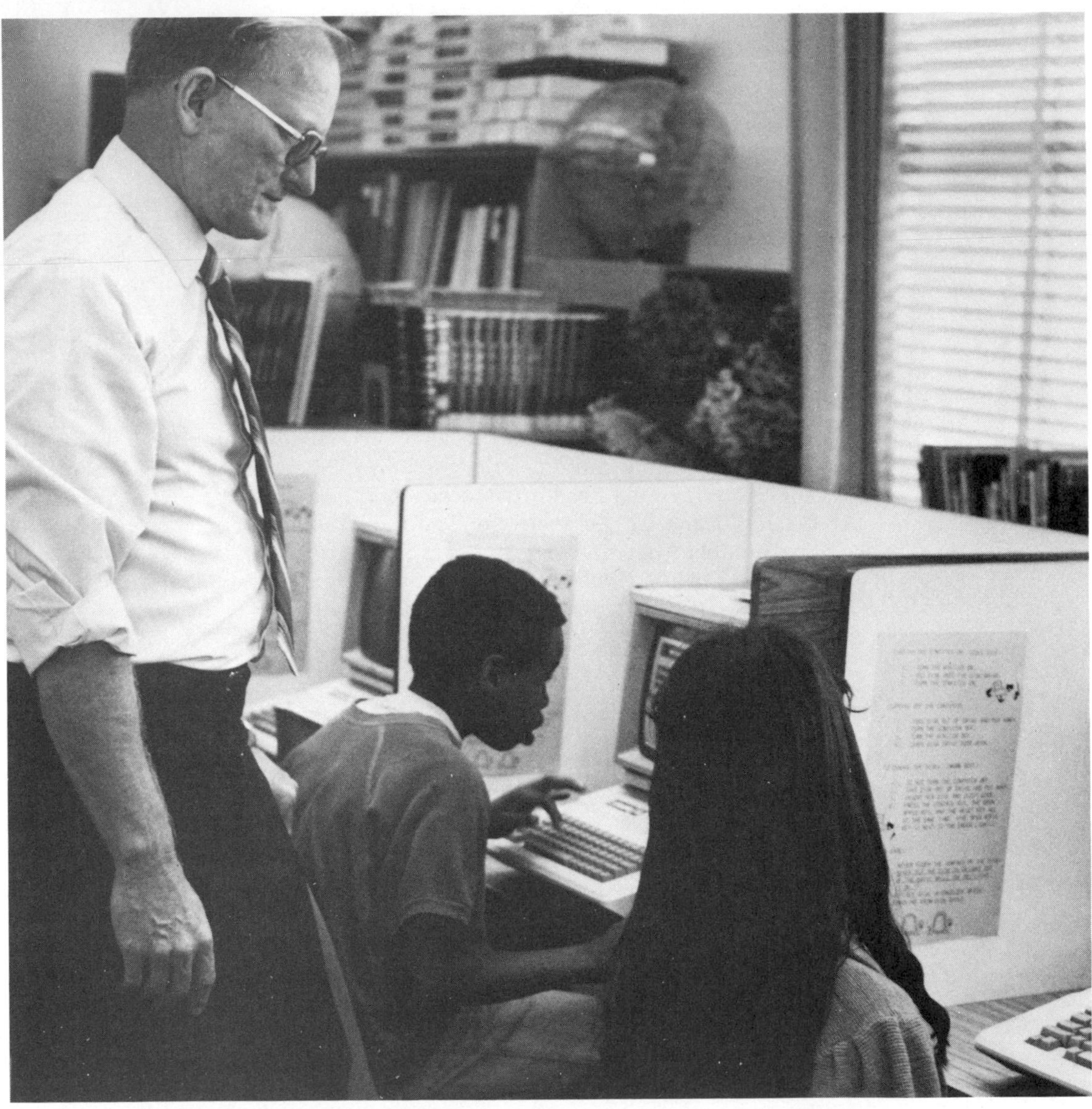

Computers and Reading

For the Reader

"Millions of students in schools across the nation have new classmates these days, and they're not the typical human kind. They're computers—or more specifically, microcomputers, those small, easily affordable alternatives to the large computers first available. From Eskimo village schools to large urban districts, the microcomputer revolution is sweeping the country, and schooling will never be the same" (16).

There is hardly a school district in our country not using microcomputers in one way or another. Furthermore, computers are becoming more and more a part of reading instruction in our classrooms. Any display of reading materials and activities today includes a myriad of microcomputer applications. Yes, our schools are using microcomputers for many reasons, including helping teachers teach reading. The key concern is how schools and teachers are using the marvelous capabilities of the computer. In this chapter, we will discuss these capabilities and how teachers can best use computers as a tool to help them in the classroom.

Preview

- Read the Key Ideas that follow.
- Read each heading and subheading.
- Read the summary.
- Read the questions and statements at the end of the chapter.
- Return to the chapter text that follows the Key Ideas and begin reading.

Key Ideas

Microcomputers should be viewed as tools to help and support the teacher to teach children to read.

The most popular form of computer-assisted instruction is drill and practice.

Teachers must carefully evaluate educational software before its actual use.

The quality of computer applications in the classroom is dependent upon the teacher.

BRIEF HISTORY

The computer revolution has swept most facets of our life, and our schools are rapidly entering the technology age. What has caused this flood of technology into our schools? Was this influx of microcomputers a natural consequence of our technological age? Interestingly, this surge of computers wasn't even predicted in Alvin Toffler's 1970 *Future Shock*. Now the uses for the computer are endless in all fields. Some of these uses include medical laboratory research, dairy farm management, library organization, entertainment and educational games, income tax preparation, mailing lists, family budget planning, bookkeeping, home monitoring, financial planning, word processing, data storage, music composition, and educational applications in all subjects at all levels.

The first electronic digital computer in the United States was built in 1946 at the University of Pennsylvania (5). ENIAC (Electronic Numerical Integrator and Calculator) was an enormous piece of hardware. It filled a large room and consisted of 18,000 vacuum tubes and 6,000 switches.

A major development of the late 1960s was the introduction of the silicon chip, which is the central processing unit of microcomputers. The tiny chip (about one centimeter square) is also called a microprocessor. It is on this microprocessor that instructions are provided that guide the microcomputer's operation. The development of the silicon chip led to the development of the microcomputer, a self-contained unit with a video display monitor, a keyboard, and a computer. Schools were first introduced to the microcomputer in 1977 (16). Today, any personal computer can outperform ENIAC. One microchip can hold the equivalent of hundreds of thousands of vacuum tubes.

COMPUTERS AND READING

The onslaught of computers has resulted in a large percentage of unaware and unprepared teachers and administrators (14). We feel the computer can be of great value to the teacher of reading. Like any other reading material, the computer and its programs are tools to help and support the teacher to teach children how to read. The challenge to all teachers is to harness the power and versatility of the computer to make it work for them (8). An unfortunate scenario finds teachers coming to school and finding ten microcomputers sitting in their classrooms. Without training and only a manual written in computerese (e.g., interface, I/O, GIGO, RAM, ROM, BOOT, input), they were then told to use the computer to help their students read better. No wonder teachers (not to mention almost everyone else) were intimidated.

FLASHBACK

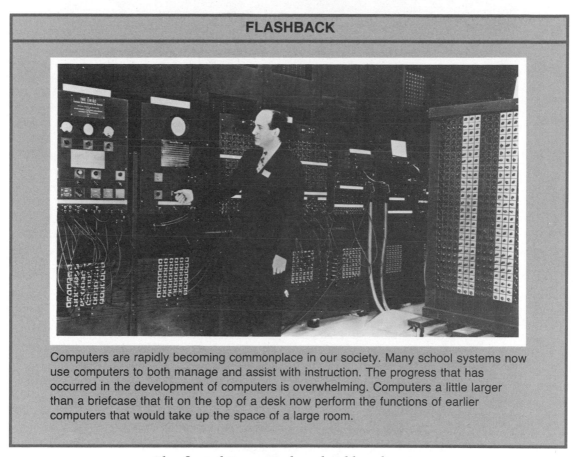

Computers are rapidly becoming commonplace in our society. Many school systems now use computers to both manage and assist with instruction. The progress that has occurred in the development of computers is overwhelming. Computers a little larger than a briefcase that fit on the top of a desk now perform the functions of earlier computers that would take up the space of a large room.

The first thing a teacher should realize is a computer cannot replace good teaching. Teachers will not have to learn a whole new set of teaching techniques and strategies to use a computer properly. The use of the computer to assist in teaching reading should be viewed in relation to the effective teaching strategies described in this book (especially chap. 3). Secondly, the microcomputer should be viewed as a tool that might or might not assist the teacher in achieving instructional goals. The indiscriminate use of the computer (or any other commerical material) in the classroom can be detrimental to learning. When used properly the computer can be very effective. Among its advantages are (1) the immediate feedback provided to students, (2) a flexible format presentation, (3) the high motivating factor due to its uniqueness and interactive capability; and (4) the capacity to provide an abundance of individually-tailored reinforcement.

The computer has the potential to expand and enhance the teaching of reading. To effectively use the computer teachers do not necessarily need to know how to program but they need to know basic computer terminology, the computer's possible applications, how to use the

See John.
See the computer.
See John run the computer.
Run, computer, run.

computer itself (hardware), the importance of evaluating the various software programs (e.g., a drill and practice lesson on long vowel sounds), and ways to incorporate the use of the computer during the reading lesson (13).

Terminology

Individuals associated with computers speak a different language just as there is a special vocabulary associated with NASA, baseball, architecture, and biology. Figure 13.1 defines many of the basic terms with which teachers should become familiar. The ability to understand and use this terminology will enable you to better select computer programs, communicate with computer salespeople, and understand computer manuals to a greater degree.

Uses of the Computer

Futurists see the classroom of the future containing a large role for the computer. Children will interact with the computer in all phases of learning to read and hold sophisticated conversations with the computer on all levels of thinking. It is true that many advanced uses of the computer have already taken place but only to a small degree (11). In reality, computers today have a limited use in the teaching of reading and its future is still unclear. Still, the present computer applications in the classroom are very powerful. We believe future applications will depend

GLOSSARY

A Teachers' Guide to Computer Terminology

byte	the computer space needed to store one character of information (a letter, symbol, number, etc.).
chip	logic unit of computer; circuitry is put on this rectangular silicon piece.
CAI	computer assisted instruction.
CMI	computer managed instruction.
debug	to correct "bugs" or errors in a computer program.
floppy disc	information storage device that resembles a 45 rpm record.
hardware	the computer components including all its nuts, bolts, cables, central processing unit (CPU), printer, disk drives, etc.
language	a code used by a programmer to organize the circuits for specific functions. Four languages are as follows: BASIC: Beginners All Purpose Symbolic Instruction Code is compact, easy to use, and popular with microcomputer users. PASCAL: An inexpensive, logically structured language, designed for more efficient programming, fewer errors and easier revision. PILOT: A dialog oriented language, quickly and easily learned, deals nicely with words and text. LOGO: Specially designed for children, LOGO includes a robot turtle that students can program.
memory	the storage area in the computer for the program and data, the RAM and ROM chips. RAM: *Random Access Memory* is used for programs and data, varies with each application, lost when power is turned off. ROM: *Read Only Memory* is a program built into the computer's memory by the manufacturer and cannot be changed.
program	sequence of instructions that a computer follows to perform a specific task.
software	the computer programs; courseware refers to programs designed specifically for the classroom.

***FIGURE 13.1* Computer Terminology.** (From *Practical Applications of Research,* Newsletter of Phi Delta Kappa's Center on Evaluation, Development and Research, Vol. 4, No. 4, June, 1982.)

"Well, today we learned to reorder segments on a random-access videodisc through the process of microcomputer interfacing."

greatly on pedagogical considerations determined by educators, not computer experts.

Computer-assisted Instruction (CAI). How are computers used in today's classrooms to assist in the teaching of reading? Most of the usage is in the form of computer-assisted instruction (CAI) (9,10). CAI involves a student being tutored by the computer in a particular skill. Teachers of reading should understand the capabilities of computer-assisted instruction as these relate to reading. The purpose here is not to explain the hardware, program writing, circuitry, and the like, but to explain the basic sequence of a computer program. When the program has been written, the system is in operation, and a child is sitting at the terminal, this instructional system has the following capabilities:

- The child views a video display screen on which can be shown anything that may appear in a workbook or any material ordinarily presented via chalkboard or overhead projector.
- A typewriter keyboard is usually a part of the microcomputer, in which case the learner types responses.
- The auditory (voice) component can provide explanations, give directions, or present supplementary data.
- The computer has the capacity to function much like an animated cartoon. A person can appear and take away a letter that is not sounded—(k)nee, (w)rap—or these letters are deleted and disappear while the audio explains that the letter is not sounded but that it will always appear when this word is met in print.

Most computer reading programs are the drill and practice type.

- If all goes well electronically, the learner can, within a second's time, receive a response to his response. This instant feedback can be visual, auditory, or both.
- Every response a learner makes can be recorded and stored. If a child is absent for a period of time, the "system" can pick him up at exactly the spot he was prior to his absence. If the child has forgotten a crucial principle, the program can ascertain this by the child's error pattern and can send the child back through a review or to easy material that fits his present needs.

The software in CAI comes in the following modes: drill and practice, tutorial dialogues, simulations, and learning games.

Drill and practice exercises are by far the most popular in the reading area. These exercises are also the most unimaginative of computer applications. In essence, many of these programs are merely electronic workbook exercises. However, this type of computer application has the potential to be successful with its primary purpose the practice and reinforcement of basic word identification and comprehension skills (3,8). Although the quality of the programs (software) themselves has been widely criticized by educators, it is hoped the quality will improve with more teacher involvement in software development. The typical sequence in a drill and practice program includes presentation of a question, student response, computer response (usually "correct," incorrect," or "let's try again"), and then the cycle begins again. Very little or no explanation of the task is given to the student. Drill and practice programs allow students to practice skills independently. Also, the programs give students the needed practice necessary for basic skills to become automatic, a necessary condition allowing more attention to comprehension (3,15). Some programs give teachers a report of student tries per item and an analysis of student performance on particular types of skills. With quality software, these programs can be most beneficial for both teachers and students in carrying out the independent practice step of the direct instruction format.

Tutorial dialogues are a bit more sophisticated than the drill and practice programs. More explanation of a skill is provided by the computer, and reteaching is provided. Instead of just giving feedback of "correct" or "incorrect," these programs will give the student a more detailed explanation. If a student response is incorrect, an explanation will appear and then the student will be given further examples similar to the one missed. This ability is sometimes called the branching quality of a software program. If the student response is correct, the computer branches to more difficult material. Very few tutorial dialogue programs are available, due in part to the complexity and expense of the programming involved. An example of a simple tutorial dialogue lesson and a flowchart outlining its steps are shown in figures 13.2 and 13.3.

Simulations are programs that allow students to role play an experience. A typical program would have the computer displaying an experiment or hypothetical situation. The student would respond with specific information. The computer runs the experiment and the student would respond with new information as needed. The computer then displays the new results. For elementary reading, few programs are available. Yet, the promise of utilizing simulation exercises as a vehicle to teach various reading skills and to practice reading in a stimulating and exciting fashion is very appealing. Balajthy (2) reports that excellent simulation programs exist in the content areas. He cites several advantages of simulation activities, including their ability to develop background schemata, improve thinking skills, illustrate the importance of following directions, and motivate children to learn in a variety of subject areas.

A variety of learning games are available in the reading area to provide interesting practice in reading skills. Many of these games (e.g., hang-man, Scrabble) reinforce vocabulary development. The instructional cycle is similiar to drill and practice programs.

Although the promise of computers in improving reading is exciting, most programs now available are the drill and practice type. The underlying assumption of CAI is based on programmed instruction the-

Targeted Skill: Multiple Meanings of Words

Step 1: Introduction of Skill
"Many times we read words that have more than one meaning. Sometimes we can figure out the meaning of these words by other words in the sentence or paragraph."

Step 2: Silent Reading
"The paragraph below has words that have more than one meaning. Read the paragraph to find out what the boys did at basketball camp."

"Tim and Bill attended the university basketball camp. The mornings were spent on passing, dribbling, and shooting. Practice games in the afternoon featured outstanding plays. The camp's activities were tiring but rewarding for the boys."

Step 3: Questions
What is the meaning of passing in the paragraph? What is the meaning of plays in the paragraph?

Step 4: Evaluation and Reteaching if Necessary
If response is correct, another exercise will appear. If response is incorrect, the word will be related to the context and the meaning will be given. Next, another practice exercise will be given to the student.

FIGURE 13.2 Sample Tutorial Dialogue Lesson

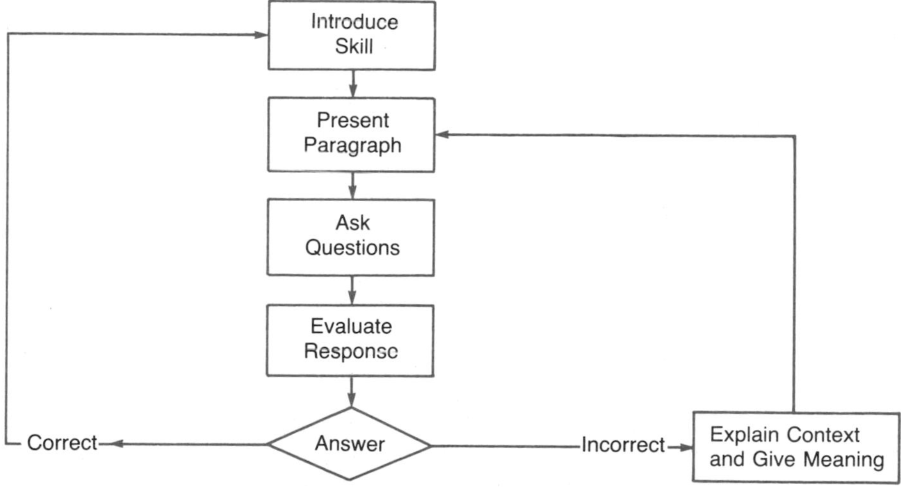

FIGURE 13.3 Flowchart of Sample Tutorial Dialogue Lesson

ory. The programs are based on operant conditioning principles and are similar in presentation to commercial programmed materials. Although research on CAI is in its infancy, initial reports indicate drill and practice programs have a positive effect on student achievement (4,8,12). These results should be viewed as positive indications but much more research has to be conducted before CAI can be hailed as having a significant impact on reading achievement.

Two successful large-scale CAI beginning reading programs have been developed at Stanford University and the University of Illinois (11,12). The PLATO Elementary Reading Curriculum (PERC) Project, a computer-based teaching system, was developed at the University of Illinois (17). The project has developed a beginning reading program used not only in first grade but also in various kindergartens, second grades, and remedial reading situations. The PERC curriculum is made up of the following components: orientation activities, visual discrimination, auditory discrimination, letter names, phonics, sight words, vocabulary building, concepts, stories, and games. The increased ability of computer-assisted reading programs such as PERC to allow the mode, content, and instructional sequence to be tailored to each child's learning needs holds significant promise for better beginning reading instruction.

Computer-managed Instruction (CMI). In addition to CAI, a growing application of the computer in the teaching of reading is using the computer to administer diagnostic tests, score the tests, record and store the results, and prescribe appropriate instruction (7,11). CMI offers excellent possibilities for executing diagnostic instruction by aiding the teacher in testing and prescribing instruction and in data storage and retrieval.

Further Applications of the Computer

New and varied uses of the computer are being continually developed and tested (11). One such application is in the area of estimating the readability levels of printed material. Another application of computers is in the area of integrating reading and writing through word processing programs. These programs allow students to type a story or any text and edit this text by inserting words, deleting words, or rearranging paragraphs and sentences. This application of computers is very popular with writers in all fields but its applications at the elementary level are only beginning to develop. One specific area is in beginning reading and the implementation of the Language Experience Approach. Teachers can type a student's story and play back the story in print and in voice. Future applications with LEA are unlimited. Programs are also available to help improve a student's reading rate by controlling the speed and difficulty level of the material. In effect, the computer operates as a con-

FLASHBACK

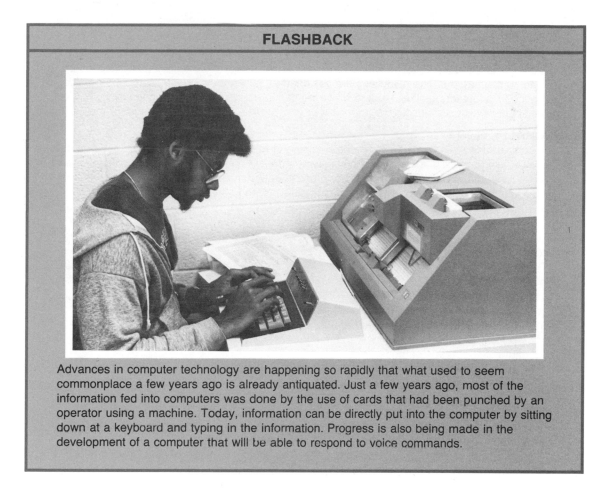

Advances in computer technology are happening so rapidly that what used to seem commonplace a few years ago is already antiquated. Just a few years ago, most of the information fed into computers was done by the use of cards that had been punched by an operator using a machine. Today, information can be directly put into the computer by sitting down at a keyboard and typing in the information. Progress is also being made in the development of a computer that will be able to respond to voice commands.

trolled reader machine showing whole lines, phrases or individual words in a left-to-right progression at a predetermined rate.

The International Reading Association (IRA) has long recognized the potential uses and misuses of computer technology. In addition to fostering scholarly inquiry on classroom use, its Computer Technology and Reading Committee issued the guidelines shown in figure 13.4 for consideration by educators.

Software Evaluation

The ultimate success or failure of CAI is dependent upon two conditions: (1) the quality of the educational software (the program containing the steps and procedures for the computer to follow) and (2) the

The Computer Technology and Reading Committee of the International Reading Association has compiled the following guidelines in an effort to encourage the effective use of technology in reading classrooms. The guidelines are designed to highlight important issues and provide guidance to educators as they work to make the best possible use of the many new technologies which are rapidly finding their way into schools and classrooms everywhere.

1. About software

Curricular needs should be primary in the selection of reading instructional software. Above all, software designed for use in the reading classroom must be consistent with what research and practice have shown to be important in the process of learning to read or of reading to learn. The IRA believes that high quality instructional software should incorporate the following elements:

- clearly stated and implemented instructional objectives.
- learning to read and reading to learn activities which are consistent with established reading theory and practice.
- lesson activities which are most effectively and efficiently done through the application of computer technology and are not merely replications of activities which could be better done with traditional means.
- prompts and screen instructions to the student which are simple, direct and easier than the learning activity to be done.
- prompts, screen instructions and reading texts which are at a readability level appropriate to the needs of the learner.
- documentation and instructions which are clear and unambiguous, assuming a minimum of prior knowledge about computers for use.
- screen displays which have clear and legible print with appropriate margins and between-line spacing.
- documentation and screen displays which are grammatically correct, factually correct, and which have been thoroughly proofed for spelling errors.
- a record keeping or information management element for the benefit of both the teacher and the learner, where appropriate.
- provisions for effective involvement and participation by the learner, coupled with rapid and extensive feedback, where appropriate.
- wherever appropriate, a learning pace which is modified by the actions of the learner or which can be adjusted by the teacher based on diagnosed needs.
- a fair, reasonable and clearly stated publisher's policy governing the replacement of defective or damaged program media such as tapes, diskettes, ROM cartridges and the like.
- a publisher's preview policy which provides pre-purchase samples or copies for review and which encourages a well-informed software acquisition process by reading educators.

2. About hardware

Hardware should be durable, capable of producing highly legible text displays, and safe for use in a classroom situation. Hardware should be chosen that conforms to established

FIGURE 13.4 Guidelines for Educators on Using Computers in the Schools. (From *The Reading Teacher* 38 [1984], 80–82. Reprinted with permission of the International Reading Association.)

classroom needs. Some characteristics to be aware of include, but are not limited to, the following:

- compatibility with classroom software appropriate to the curriculum.
- proven durability in classroom situations.
- clear, unambiguous instruction manuals appropriate for use by persons having a minimum of technical experience with computers.
- sufficient memory (RAM) capability to satisfy anticipated instructional software applications.
- availability of disk, tape, ROM cartridge or other efficient and reliable data storage devices.
- screen displays which produce legible print, minimize glare, and which have the lowest possible screen radiation levels.
- a functional keyboard and the availability of other appropriate types of input devices.
- proven, accessible and reasonably priced technical support from the manufacturer or distributor.

3. About staff development and training

Staff development programs should be available which encourage teachers to become intelligent users of technology in the reading classroom. Factors to consider include, but are not limited to, the following:

- study and practice with various applications of computer technology in the reading and language arts classroom.
- training which encourages thoughtful and informed evaluation, selection and integration of effective and appropriate teaching software into the reading and language arts classroom.

4. About equity

All persons, regardless of sex, ethnic group, socioeconomic status, or ability, must have equality of access to the challenges and benefits of computer technology. Computer technology should be integrated into all classrooms and not be limited to scientific or mathematical applications.

5. About research

Research which assesses the impact of computer technology on all aspects of learning to read and reading to learn is essential. Public and private funding should be made available in support of such research. Issues which need to be part of national and international research agendas include, but are not limited to:

- the educational efficacy of computer technology in the reading and language arts classroom.
- the affective dimensions of introducing computer technology into the schools.
- the cognitive dimensions of introducing computer technology into the reading classroom.
- the application of concepts of artificial intelligence to computer software which address issues of reading diagnosis, developmental reading, remedial reading, and instructional management.

continued

• the impact of new technology on students, reading teachers, schools, curricula, parents, and the community.

6. About networking and sharing information
Local area and national networks or information services should be established and supported which can be accessed through the use of computers. Such services should be designed to provide an information resource on reading related topics. Such services could also be used to provide linkage and information exchange among many institutions, including professional associations such as the IRA.

7. About inappropriate uses of technology
Computers should be used in meaningful and productive ways which relate clearly to instructional needs of students in the reading classroom. Educators must capitalize on the potential of this technology by insisting on its appropriate and meaningful use.

8. About legal issues
Unauthorized duplication and use of copyrighted computer software must not be allowed. Developers and publishers of educational software have a right to be protected from financial losses due to the unauthorized use of their products. Consumers of educational software have a concomitant right to expect fair prices, quality products and reasonable publisher's policies regarding licensing for multiple copies, replacement of damaged program media, network applications and the like. Without mutual trust and cooperation on this important issue both parties will suffer and, ultimately, so will the learner.

FIGURE 13.4 (cont.)

quality of computer applications in a classroom to meet instructional goals.

Software programs in elementary reading are increasing at a rapid pace. A quick glance at any magazine rack will indicate this new market is quite competitive. In fact, teachers attempting to select a few reading programs among the hundreds on the market may easily begin to feel a system overload. The question "Which program is best?" is the wrong question. The key question is "which program will best meet my students' learning needs?" Remember, the computer is a tool to aid and to support the teacher. The teacher should not feel as if he or she is in competition with the computer. Don't be overly impressed with computer graphics, color, animation, music, ability to speak, or ability of the computer to respond to student touch on the screen. Likewise, you shouldn't be overwhelmed with the color, graphics, and quality of paper commercial materials possess. Sure, the capabilities of a computer are impressive and might be helpful to the student but you must decide the educational worth of the software and its application.

Just as effective teachers select other supplemental materials in relation to student needs, so too must computer programs be selected with this same criterion in mind. Underlying this concern is determining the quality of the program itself. Do the steps in the lesson and related procedures follow the tenets of effective instruction? Furthermore, does the software allow the child to interact with the computer? Unfortunately, the verdict on a majority of software programs is that the quality reflects poor rather than good instruction. Yet, one must remember that many current programs are written by computer experts, not educators. Many of the programs today purport to teach a skill but do not fulfill this expectation. Also, although the production of software is expanding at an unbelievable rate (some experts predict the software market will jump to one billion dollars in 1987 from $93 million in 1983), it must be acknowledged that software development is still in its initial phase. Hopefully, teachers will continue to have greater influence on software development and the quality will improve.

Since the quality of the software is at the heart of effective use of the computer in the classroom, teachers should know how to evaluate it. Remember, the best hardware (the computer) is only as good as the software (the program) the teacher selects. Demand quality software for your students. The cardinal rule in software evaluation is never buy or use a program until you try it out for yourself. This will allow you to experience how "user friendly" the program is (ease of using the program without unnecessary confusion, i.e., unclear directions, difficulty in obtaining help when necessary, little control over pacing, poor exit capability). In addition, a trial run can help you to evaluate other important aspects of the program.

The guide shown in figure 13.5 should help you evaluate reading software by examining the program in the areas of ease of use, instructional design, content accuracy, and special features.

In addition to your actual running through the software program and systematically using an evaluation form, it is imperative that you have your youngsters try out the program. Their perceptions of the effectiveness of a program are most beneficial. After all, they will be required to spend their time completing the program and their judgments should be of value in the decision-making process.

Instructional Principles

In addition to quality software, CAI's effectiveness will ultimately depend on its proper implementation by teachers to improve children's reading ability. While teachers do not have to learn new teaching tech-

	Good	Adequate	Poor
Type of Program			
____drill and practice	______	______	______
____tutorial	______	______	______
____simulation	______	______	______
____learning game	______	______	______
Ease of Use/User Friendly			
clear directions	______	______	______
exit capabilities	______	______	______
control of pacing	______	______	______
provision of help	______	______	______
Instructional Design			
objective made clear to student	______	______	______
introductory explanation of skill	______	______	______
sample exercises	______	______	______
number of practice exercises	______	______	______
immediate and varied feedback	______	______	______
branching capability	______	______	______
built-in assessment of progress	______	______	______
monitoring of student responses	______	______	______
corrections made by reteaching, giving clues, or explaining skill	______	______	______
summary statement	______	______	______
length of program	______	______	______
appropriate difficulty level	______	______	______
Content Accuracy			
direct correspondence between lesson objective and lesson procedures	______	______	______
accuracy	______	______	______
procedures reflect what a reader has to do in the process of reading	______	______	______
correct sequence used in presenting skill	______	______	______
Special Features			
animation	______	______	______
speech	______	______	______
music	______	______	______
laser videodiscs	______	______	______
touch screen	______	______	______
graphics	______	______	______
audio	______	______	______
color	______	______	______

FIGURE 13.5 Reading Software Evaluation Guide

niques, they do have to apply sound educational principles to integrate CAI into the total reading program. The following principles are recommended for teachers to consider as they begin to make decisions regarding the use of microcomputers in the classroom.

- Teachers must devote considerable time in planning CAI applications in their classroom.
- CAI lessons should be designed or selected so that students have a large degree of control and interaction with the computer.
- CAI should only be used with those children who respond positively to it.
- Weekly conferences should be held with each student to review progress.
- The management of the daily use of the microcomputer should not overly disrupt normal teaching routines.
- Introduce children to the microcomputer by explaining how and why it will be used in their class.
- Always share the program's objectives with students so they will know why they are doing it.
- Be certain to use software that corresponds to your instructional goals.
- Monitor pupil involvement to ensure a high degree of time on task.
- Vary the use of CAI so students will not get bored doing the same thing each time they work with the microcomputer.
- CAI should never be viewed as being more than one part of the total reading program.
- When appropriate, teachers should assign students to work in pairs on a microcomputer.
- CAI lessons should be used in a logical sequence.
- Always revise the application of CAI after examining test results, observation data, and student evaluations.

SUMMARY

Classroom teachers and school administrators are increasingly making decisions to use microcomputers in reading. Initiating CAI in the classroom is one matter, doing it based on sound educational principles is another. Teachers should become familiar with computer terminology, hardware, educational applications, software and its evaluation, and methods of incorporating CAI into the total reading program. Of central importance is maintaining a correct relationship to CAI. Effective teachers should view the computer as a tool that might or might not help

"Gerstmeir, I don't care to interface with you anymore!"

teach what children need to know. Given this proper viewpoint, teachers should take advantage of the flexible uses and advantages of the microcomputer to motivate and to enhance reading development. As with any supplemental material, the effectiveness of CAI depends upon how teachers use it. Teachers are encouraged to systematically plan computer applications. In addition teachers should stay abreast of research investigations involving computers and reading.

YOUR POINT OF VIEW

Discussion Questions

1. How can CAI help increase pupils' academic-engaged time?
2. Why do you think children would enjoy CAI? Is it for all children?

Take a Stand For or Against

1. Computers will someday replace teachers.
2. CAI is the answer for problem readers.

BIBLIOGRAPHY

1. Auten, Anne. "ERIC/RCS: Computer Literacy, Part III: CRT Graphics" *The Reading Teacher* 35 (1982): 966–69.
2. Balajthy, Ernest. "Computer Simulations and Reading." *The Reading Teacher* 37 (1984): 590–93.
3. Balajthy, Ernest. "Reinforcement and Drill by Microcomputer." *The Reading Teacher* 37 (1984): 490–94.
4. Bath Elementary School. *Results of Computer Assisted Instruction at Bath Elementary School.* Cleveland, Ohio: Martha Holden Jennings Foundation, 1979. (ERIC Document Reproduction Service No. ED 195 245).
5. Benderson, Albert, ed. "Computer Literacy." *Focus II,* Educational Testing Service, 1983.
6. Cole, Robert W., Jr., ed. *Phi Delta Kappan* 65, no. 2 (1983).
7. Florida State Department of Education. *More Hands for Teachers. Report of the Commissioner's Advisory Committee on Instructional Computing.* Tallahassee: Florida State Department of Education, 1980. (ERIC Document Reproduction Service No. ED 190 120)
8. Geoffrion, George D., and Geoffrion, Olga P. *Computers and Reading Instruction.* Reading, Mass.: Addison-Wesley Publishing Company, 1983.
9. Grimes, Don Marston. *Computers for Learning: The Uses of Computers-Assisted-Instruction (CAI) in California Public Schools.* Sacramento: California State Department of Education, 1977. (ERIC Document Reproduction Service No. ED 161 433)
10. Kinerk, Nedra S. "Computers: Education's 'Apple Pie'." In *The Seminar* 1 (Spring 1983) Newsletter from Macmillan Publishing Co.
11. Mason, George E., Blanchard, Jay S., and Daniel, Danny B. *Computer Applications in Reading,* 2d ed. Newark, Del.: International Reading Association, 1983.
12. O'Donnell, Holly. "ERIC/RCS: Computer Literacy, Part II: Classroom Applications." *The Reading Teacher* 35 (1982): 614–17.
13. Pitts, Marcella R. *The Educator's Unauthorized Microcomputer Survival Manual.* Washington, D.C.: Council for Educational Development and Research, 1983.
14. Richardson, Judy. "The Three A's: Influencing Teachers' Awareness, Attitudes, and Anxieties about Using Computer Assisted Instruction for Reading Classes." Richmond: Virginia Commonwealth University, 1984.
15. Rupley, William H., and Chevrette, Patricia. "Computer Assisted Instruction: A Promising Tool for Enhancing Teacher Effectiveness." *Reading World* 22 (1983): 236–240.
16. Shalaway, Linda. "Students New Classmates Revolutionize Education." *Educational R+D Report* (Washington, D.C.: Council for Educational Development and Research) 3 (Spring 1980): 7–10.
17. Yeager, Bob. "Data Management and Decision Making in the PLATO Elementary Reading Project." Urbana: University of Illinois, n.d.

14

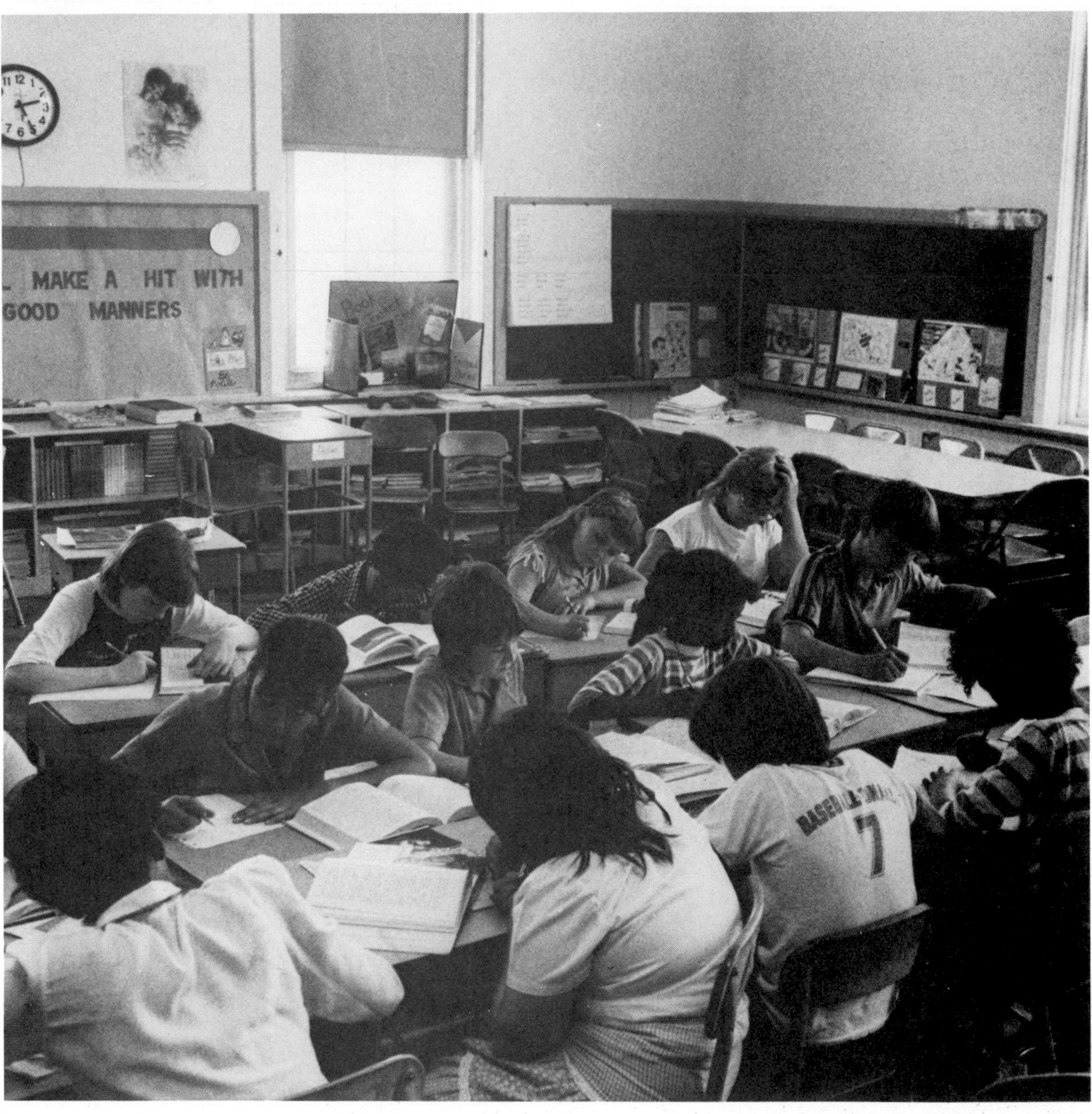

Focus on All Learners

For the Reader

Every classroom is composed of individuals who are not equal in terms of intellectual ability, social and emotional background, language ability, racial background, or physical attributes. As teachers, we all should be prepared to deal effectively with differences—it's part and parcel of the job. This chapter will focus attention on culturally and language-different, gifted, and handicapped children. Although these youngsters certainly are receiving considerable attention in professional journals, newspapers, magazines, and school programs, it is important to remember that all children are different and are in need of instruction specific to their needs. A separate chapter on this topic is offered not to encourage treatment by categorization, but to highlight important aspects of the total responsibility of teaching reading in today's schools.

Preview

- Read the Key Ideas that follow.
- Read each heading and subheading.
- Read the summary.
- Read the questions and statements at the end of the chapter.
- Return to the chapter text that follows the Key Ideas and begin reading.

Key Ideas

Principle from chapter 1: Pupil differences must be a primary consideration in reading instruction.

Teachers need to be knowledgeable of and sensitive to nonstandard dialects in their instruction.

Culturally and language-different, handicapped, and gifted children require education based on their educational needs rather than on clinical or diagnostic labels.

P.L. 94–142, the Education for All Handicapped Children Act of 1975, ensures a free and appropriate education for all handicapped children.

An Individualized Education Plan (IEP) must be developed and maintained for each handicapped child.

ACCEPTING DIFFERENCES

The acknowledgment of pupil differences carries the responsibility to provide appropriate adjustments in each child's educational program. An inescapable part of the profession is that teachers will encounter pupils who are different intellectually, psychosocially, culturally, and physically. In discussing the need to supplement the curriculum as a basic component of teaching, Raths (34) recounted a professor stating, "If a teacher wanted homogeneous groups and wanted them to stay that way, the best approach would be to arrange these homogeneous groups on the basis of weight. In practically all other ways every group of children (or men or women) is characterized by a great many differences" (p. 38).

Three important groups of children that teachers need to focus their attention on are the culturally and language-different, gifted, and handicapped youth. Knowledge of pupil backgrounds and learner characteristics is needed to provide effective instruction. It is also crucial to remember that all children are different and require educational modifications based on their needs. Additionally, the same diagnostic teaching procedures recommended throughout this book for normal children apply equally well to culturally and language-different, handicapped, and gifted children.

CULTURALLY AND LANGUAGE-DIFFERENT CHILDREN

The term *culturally and language-different* refers to children (most often economically deprived) who are not profiting from the established curriculum and who are experiencing difficulties in learning to read. The term includes speakers of dialects from all racial groups—black, white, Indian-American, Mexican-American, Puerto Rican, and so forth. Ching (14) refers to all these children as bilingual. She states, "when bilingualism is used in its broadest sense, it is considered without qualification as to the degree of difference between the two languages or systems known; it is immaterial whether the two systems are languages, dialects of the same language, or varieties of the same dialect" (p. 1).

Not all bilingual speakers are included. Many blacks, Mexican-Americans, and others do not have reading problems. The major distinguishing factor determining the reading achievement of learners from the same ethnic or racial group appears to be the socioeconomic level.

Portions of this chapter were contributed by Dr. Ruby Thompson, The Reading Center, Atlanta University.

Blacks from middle- and upper-class socioeconomic strata do not experience the difficulties that their lower-class counterparts experience; middle-class whites fare better than their counterparts from low socioeconomic backgrounds. This is to say that the cultural difference alone does not render a child a poor reader; linguistic differences coupled with economic deprivation are perhaps greater discriminators.

Reading failure has been the major educational problem of the children from these groups. Since part of the problem is that the school is alien to these children, it is felt that if teachers know and understand them, the first objective of a good reading program has been met.

The life-style of the culturally different learner who is in an economically deprived environment changes little. He lives in a culture of poverty.

- Housing is usually substandard, crowded, and in unattractive surroundings. (the ghetto, dusty rural areas, tenement shacks, dilapidated trailers)
- According to nutritional and health standards, food and clothing are often inadequate.
- Family ties are often unstable because of the restrictions imposed by the environment, poor economic conditions, and the psychological factors that these conditions manifest.
- Groups are socially alienated from middle-class society and, therefore, are not exposed to the factors that determine the criteria by which they are ultimately judged.
- Jobs are usually those on the lower end of the continuum in terms of pay, prestige, and security—if jobs are held at all.
- Educational levels of parents seldom exceed junior high school.
- Exposure to the crime, violence, and prevalence of immorality that are bred and nurtured in their environments is early and continuous.

Although teachers can do little as individuals to change these conditions, they must be more sensitive to the deficits that such an environment may have imposed on the children. These include the tendency to have a poor self-concept and low aspirational levels, to be tardy and absent frequently, to be poorly oriented to school and school tasks, to display hostility toward school and school authorities, to resist or reject values that are foreign to them and which are forced on them by teachers whom they tend to distrust.

As a potential reader, the culturally and language-different learner may come to school speaking his natural language, which is not the language upon which the curriculum is constructed. He may not have auditory discrimination for some "standard" English speech phonemes, and he will be much more limited than most middle-class children in his development of readiness skills for reading.

Martin and Castaneda (30) note that a realistic reading program for culturally different learners requires teachers who understand their pupils' linguistic and cultural needs. Teachers must view reading as a part of language development and provide children with experiences that lead to concept development. They further attest to the importance of the teacher as a "significant other." One of the most significant indicators of a child's worth is shown through behaviors that reveal teachers as adults who care. Such behaviors include showing evidence that you value children's thoughts and taking the time to encourage children in their use of language.

Myths and Facts about Language

In the late 1960s and early 1970s a number of theories were advanced regarding nonstandard English, which today are recognized as myths. These myths included:

1. Culturally different learners had very limited language facility.
2. The language they did use was haphazard and lacked a logical, systematic structure.
3. Speakers of nonstandard English could not understand spoken standard English.

These myths have long since been viewed as unfounded generalizations based on insufficient research data. Later research, such as that conducted by Nolen (32), reported that there are no significant differences between black and white children's comprehension of spoken standard English.

Labov (25) substantiates the fact that spoken standard English is understandable to culturally different learners. His subjects were able to make accurate translations from standard English into their divergent modes; that is, they could comprehend the standard model even though they did not always imitate it.

From their research, Gantt et al. (19) concluded that the effect of dialect divergency upon listening comprehension of standard English seems to be limited. Black children from two school populations (Title I and non-Title I) were tested for syntactical characteristics and listening comprehension. Children from the non-Title I population did not differ significantly in syntactical characteristics from their Title I counterparts. The non-Title I learners did perform significantly better in mean listening performance. These findings lend themselves to the theory that socioeconomic factors, not dialect divergencies, affect listening and, most possibly, reading.

Labov (25) states that linguists have long demonstrated the fallacies of the verbal deprivation theory. All linguists agree that nonstandard dialects are highly structured systems, not accumulations of errors caused by the failure of their speakers to master standard English.

Abrahams (1) points out that not only is Black English (and other nonstandard dialects by implication) a series of linguistic forms, it is an entire system of speaking behavior that contains nonverbal cues as well.

Dialect Divergencies

A young black college student was working with a large corporation during the summer break. At an orientation meeting, in which some simple technological processes were being discussed, the student was taking notes:

> The floor chart is basic to . . .
> A good floor chart must be constructed . . .
> Floor charts are keys to . . .

The notes were accurate except for one word; what the speaker was actually saying was:

> The flowchart is basic to . . .
> A good flowchart must be constructed . . .
> Flowcharts are keys to . . .

There are highly qualitative differences in the meanings of "floor charts" and "flowcharts," and this student heard and recorded a slightly different auditory signal than the speaker had intended. She transcribed what she heard and, in the process, misinterpreted much of the lecture. But she had written this key word the same way she perceived it in her dialect.

This incident points out two of the major problems in teaching the culturally and language-different learner to read—lack of experience with words and concepts and the masking of critical phonemes that cause semantic differences (the latter being a dialect factor).

Dialect, broadly conceived, is the way people speak in different parts of the country or in their specific social classes. The components of dialect are pronunciation, grammar, and vocabulary. Since many culturally different children speak a dialect, the question that has been raised by linguists and pondered by reading teachers is, Do dialect divergencies cause difficulties in learning to read standard English?

Most hypotheses relative to the question of dialect interference in learning to read have been stated in general terms. Martin and Castaneda (30) hold that children who come to school speaking a dialect other than standard American English encounter noticeable difficulty in learning to read; they experience a higher failure rate than do children who speak standard American English. But do the children fail in reading because of their dialect or because of factors such as lack of experiences that relate to reading, the quality of instruction they receive, and teacher expectations of failure? These and other factors could work together to produce a high failure rate.

After reviewing research pertaining to children speaking Black English, Weaver (39) contends that speaking a dialect does not interfere with learning to read. She feels that the most important factor affecting achievement may be teachers' attitudes and expectations of students who speak a black dialect. She recommends all teachers become familiar with standard Black English and not penalize students for oral renditions of text material due to dialect.

Although some dialects do not present crucial problems in children's learning to read, teachers of reading still need to be familiar with them (5). This knowledge is essential since they must understand the language used by the students to provide effective instruction. According to Lass (26), when teachers accept black dialect in reading situations, they understand

1. that reading is comprehending,
2. that oral reading requires productive control that is absent in most dialect speakers,
3. that black dialect is an adequate communication system, and
4. the features of the dialect.

Generally speaking, *phonological divergencies* refer to differences in speech sounds within words. A grapheme (written letter symbol) may represent different phonemes (speech sounds) in different dialects. *Grammatical* and *syntactical divergencies* refer to those differences in inflectional changes, verb forms, and verb auxiliaries, and to the ways in which words are put together in phrases and sentences. Figure 14.1 presents a contrast between Spanish and English, and figure 14.2 contrasts black dialect and English.

A potential problem relating to phonological divergencies can be teachers' misinterpretations of the significance of "errors" they detect in children's oral reading. Some errors unrelated to the child's dialect can, and possibly should, be corrected on the spot. In other instances, it may be unproductive at the moment to overemphasize errors that are perfectly logical in the child's dialect. When a child is compelled to insert phonemes that are ignored in his phonological system, he may end up with pronunciations that are unfamiliar and meaningless to him. These pronunciations may prove to be barriers to his progress in getting meaning from the printed page. Other phonological differences may involve variations in intonation (pitch, stress, and rhythm of the dialect). If the teacher insists on intonation patterns in oral reading or speaking that are unfamiliar to the reader, frustration and loss of meaning may be the result.

Vowel Sounds

In English	In Spanish
The five vowel letters *a, e, i, o,* and *u* represent at least fifteen distinctive phonemes plus blended vowel sounds in the diphthongs, *oi-oy, aw-au, ow-ou, ai-ay.*	Five vowel letters are used to represent five relatively constant sounds: *a (alto)* as heard in *father* *e (leguna)* as heard in *met* *i(e) (aqui)* as heard in *even* *o (hermosa)* as heard in *open* *u (mucho)* as heard in *moon*
English is laced with countless neutral or slurred vowel sounds: (1) *uh,* as in *up* or *cup,* (2) the *schwa* (ə) as heard in *above, melon,* and *brother.*	Spanish has no *uh* sound, nor is the *schwa* heard in the unaccented syllables of words.

Consonant Sound Substitutions

In English	In Spanish	Possible Substitutions
English has many plosive sounds which require vigorous output of air (*ch, j, zh,* etc.).	In Spanish, the air flow is low. Voiceless sounds are often substituted for the English counterparts.	chair > shair watches > washes match > mash orange > orntch
English words end in at least forty different phonemes.	Only ten main sounds are heard at the end of words, *a, e, i, o, u, l, r, n, s,* and *d.*	eyes > ice bug > buk time > tine want > wahn
th is an unvoiced continuant sound.	No unvoiced *th* sound exists.	this > dis breathless > breafless or breatless both > bof or bot
sh is a voiceless continuant.	No *sh* sound exists.	shoes > chooss fishing > fitching wish > witch
j is a plosive sound requiring high output of air.	No *j* sound exists, closest approximation is *ll* (yellow) or *y* (year)	jump > yump cage > caych
s is given the voiced *z* sound at the end of many words.	No words end in *z* sound.	freeze > freess roses > rossess pleasure > plesher

continued

FIGURE 14.1 Contrasts between the Spanish and English Sound Systems. (From Carmen A. O'Brien, *Teaching the Language-Different Child to Read,* pp. 34, 36–37. Columbus, Ohio: Charles E. Merrill Pub. Co., 1973, by permission of the publisher.)

Grammatical Structures

In English	In Spanish	Possible Substitutions
Word order pattern is *adjective, noun, verb.*	Word order pattern is *noun, adjective.*	"I ate a crisp juicy apple," becomes, "I ate an apple, crisp and juicy."
Linking verbs are used to denote tense change.	Most verbs are inflectionalized. Linking verbs not used.	She is working > She working I'm not working > I not working I will do my work later > I work later
Change of word order is made to transform a statement to a question. (He works. > Does he work?)	Question tranforms are achieved through voice inflection.	He works. > He works? This is Tuesday. This is Tuesday?

FIGURE 14.1 (cont.)

Goodman (21) points out that grammatical divergencies will be reflected in the child's reading of standard texts and in his conversation; that is, he will substitute his dialect for what is written. This substitution process must be understood by the teacher if frustration is to be kept at a minimum. The intended meaning in listening activities may be misconstrued by both teacher and pupil. This is especially true if the teacher does not realize the difference between school talk and the child's dialect, or if she is unable to accept the child's speech patterns.

APPROACHES TO READING

Several alternative approaches have been suggested for teaching reading to children who speak a different dialect from standard English or for those children whose native language is other than English. Necessary teacher prerequisites for all approaches include an awareness of the students' cultural backgrounds and the characteristics of their language.

Grammatical Patterns

Standard English	Black Dialect	The Deviation
She goes to school. He doesn't swim.	She go to school. He don't swim.	The *s* ending is not used in the verb system.
He comes to work at eight. He came at seven yesterday.	He come to work at eight. He come at seven yesterday.	Some irregular verbs have the same form for present or past tense.
She walked to school. She missed the bus yesterday.	She walk to school. She had miss the bus yesterday.	The *ed* ending is not used to form past tense.
I've been away. She's been ill.	I been away. She been ill.	The contractions *have* and *has* are often dropped.
I take Algebra. I took Algebra. I have taken Algebra.	I take Algebra. I have took Algebra. I taken Algebra.	Conjugation of verb "to take" reverses use of *have*.
I do my work. I did my work. I have done my work.	I do my work. I done my work. I have did my work.	Conjugation of verb "to do" reverses using *have.*
She is talking. She is talking.	She be talking. (at the moment) She bes talking. (habitually, she is)	Verb "to be" takes on shades of meaning.

Phonological Patterns

Black Dialect	Substitutions
The th problem:	
this > dis	voiced *th* in initial position becomes *d*.
breathe > breave	voiced *th* in final position becomes *v*.
mother > muvver	voiced *th* in medial position becomes *v* or *t*.
south > souf	unvoiced *th* in final position becomes *f*.
The r problem:	
car > cah	*r* sound is slurred or omitted (creates many homonyms).
floor > flow or flaw	
starter > stahter	
sugar > shugah	
tire > tah	

FIGURE 14.2 Contrasts between Black Dialect and Standard English. (From Carmen A. O'Brien, *Teaching the Language-Different Child to Read,* pp. 39–40. Columbus, Ohio: Charles E. Merrill Pub. Co., 1973, by permission of the publisher.)

Alternative Approaches

Instruction in reading is first provided in the native language and gradually instruction in reading is given in standard English. In the *bilingual approach,* instruction in reading in standard English is given in an environment where more than one language (in addition to English) is used in the classroom. Many bilingual programs are aided by ESL programs (English as a Second Language). Designed for the predominantly non-English-speaking student, an ESL program in some cases complements bilingual programs by providing individual or small-group tutoring in listening, speaking, reading, and writing English as a Second Language by a teacher trained in language acquisition (see sample on next page).

In the *dialect approach,* reading is taught using materials written in the language of the dialect-speaking child. However, research has not supported the use of reading materials written in black dialect (3, 38). In the standard approach, reading is taught using regular or standard materials but dialectal and cultural differences in children are taken into account. Presently, the best approach appears to be a standard one with enlightened teacher attitudes sensitive to the motivations, values, backgrounds, and aspirations of children and a knowledge of the features of nonstandard dialects.

Instructional Guidelines

It must be kept in mind that a child cannot instantly suspend the use of a dialect or language that he has used for years. Nor can he adapt completely to a different speech pattern. The learning of a new pattern must take place gradually and for a meaningful purpose clear to the children. If children do not understand why they are to speak in another way, they may resist language training in the classroom.

If training in dialect or language differences is delayed until the upper grades, the self-concept of the learner must be dealt with. Care must be taken to make him aware at this stage of the realistic values and rewards that will result from mastery of standard English.

The following principles for working with language-different children should be useful to teachers, regardless of the methodology used.

- Learning must be gradual, built on past instruction, and constantly reinforced for stability of gains.
- Children must understand why (meaningful purposes) they are introduced to a different language pattern.
- Care must be taken to remove "value" labels from the language of the learner and the language to be learned.
- The learner's language must be respected by himself and by the teacher as a complete and usable linguistic system—not a "stepchild" of standard English.

Lección 16

Evaluation and Diagnosis
Pupil's pages 34 and 35

OBJECTIVES

ORAL LANGUAGE SKILLS: Evaluating the pupils' ability to understand the concepts of tall, short, long, front, and back; evaluating the pupils' ability to follow oral directions

SPANISH READING SKILLS: Evaluating the pupils' ability to recognize the Spanish sound-symbol relationships **p** /p/, **d** /d/, **n** /n/, and **c** /k/

COMPREHENSION SKILLS: Evaluating the pupils' ability to interpret a picture story and to complete a picture story

WRITING SKILLS: Evaluating the pupils' ability to write Spanish vowel and consonant letters presented in units I–III

PROCEDURE

EVALUATION AND DIAGNOSIS

Write the numeral **34** on the chalkboard.

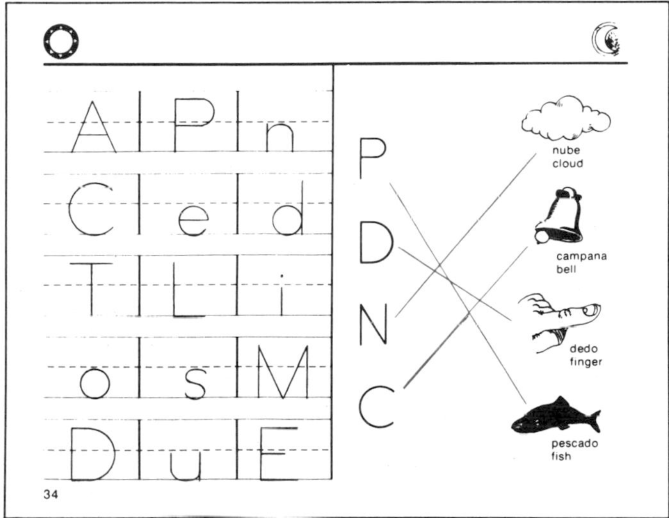

Hilera 1: Abran sus libros a la página número treinta y cuatro. En la página número treinta y cuatro van a poder mostrar que bien se acuerdan de algunas de las cosas de que hemos hablado. Al lado izquierdo de la página ven un lugar donde pueden escribir letras. Yo diré una letra y ustedes la escribirán. Vamos a empezar con la primera hilera. En el primer cuadro escriban la **A** mayúscula. En el segundo cuadro escriban la **P** mayúscula. En el tercer cuadro escriban la **n** minúscula.

Hilera 2: Miren la segunda hilera. En el primer cuadro escriban la **C** mayúscula. En el segundo cuadro escriban la **e** minúscula. En la tercer cuadro escriban la **d** minúscula.

Row 1: Turn to page 34 in your books. On page 34 you will have a chance to show how well you remember some of the things we have talked about. On the left side of the page you see a place to write letters. I will say a letter, and you write it. We will begin on the first row. In the first box write capital **A.** In the second box write capital **P.** In the third box write small **n.**

Row 2: Look at the second row. In the first box write capital **C.** In the second box write small **e.** In the third box write small **d.**

Spanish Reading Keys is a reading program for bilingual education in the primary grades. Initial instruction is provided in the pupil's native language.

- Different pupils will learn more readily from different techniques.
- Learning to read standard English should be viewed from a language arts base, with emphasis on listening and speaking vocabularies.

The teacher of beginning reading must know the different features of the learners' dialects and must be skilled in approaches for language training. She also has the task of determining which learners will benefit from language training for reading purposes and which will not.

ALTERNATIVE PRESCHOOL APPROACHES

When the culturally and language-different learner enters first grade, a major school problem is likely to be lack of school-related preparatory experiences. The school is structured to provide learning experiences that, to a large degree, are foreign to these children. There are two obvious potential solutions. We could provide the child with the experiences he needs in order to cope with the tasks he must do in school, or we may alter the curriculum to fit the learner. The practice of providing

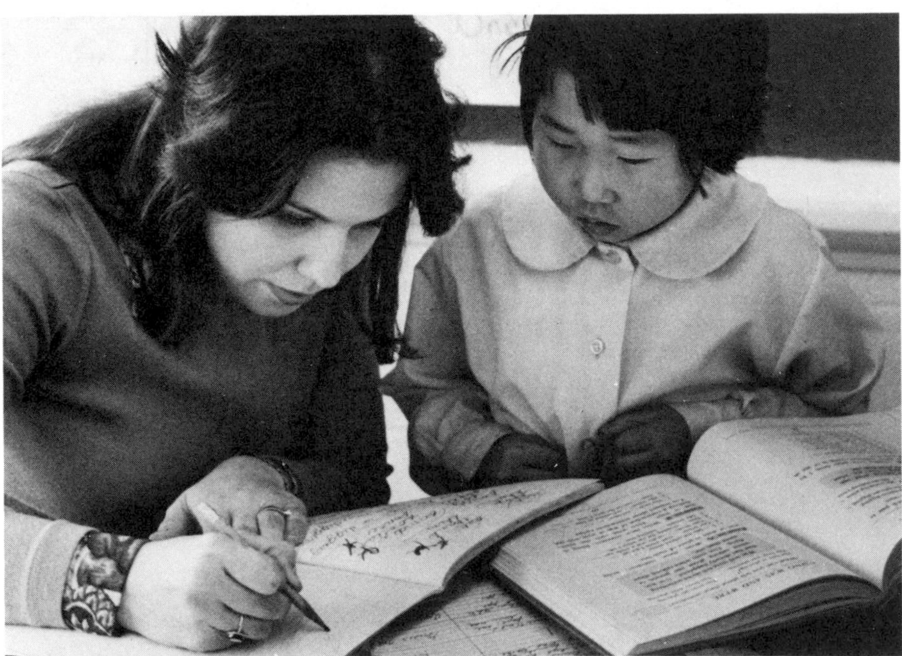

Teachers need to know about cultural differences to accurately diagnose a child's strengths and weaknesses.

readiness activities cuts across both of these alternatives. As readiness activities are varied to fit the learners' needs, the curriculum itself is altered.

In theory, readiness has for a long time been a part of most school programs. In one sense, these readiness programs represent a concession to children's nonreadiness for the schools' curricula. However, in actual practice programs for readiness have not always been well implemented. Shortly after children entered school, they received the formal reading instruction that had been planned for them. This occurred whether or not they were ready for these particular activities. Fortunately, many children had the background that enabled them to fit into the planned program. Many did not. For members of the latter group, had readiness training been realistically incorporated into their programs, many reading failures and frustrations might have been avoided.

Athough the culturally different child is on the same readiness continuum as other children, he often has experience deficits that are significant to the school. He may be so different in terms of school preparation that readiness programs, as traditionally carried out, are simply not adequate for making him a good risk for beginning reading instruction. Sometimes even a well-structured program of readiness activities may fail with this child. This failure may be attributed to the culturally different child's need for more of, or different types of, activities than those offered by the schools. For this type of learner, there must be a rethinking of readiness that will use his strengths and concentrate on eliminating his weaknesses.

The preschool approaches discussed in this section have attempted to redefine readiness in terms of the needs of the culturally different learner. They differ somewhat in philosophy and technique but share the common goal of making the culturally and language-different child ready for first-grade reading instruction. The approaches included here are intensified readiness, academic preschool intervention, enrichment programs, and the Montessori approach.

Intensified Readiness

The intensified readiness approach to preschool training is based on the philosophy that the traditional readiness program has the major components needed to prepare the culturally different child for reading instruction, but that there will be a need for reinforcement that extends for a greater duration of time.

The intensified approach is advocated by Cohen (16) who selected seven areas for emphasis with the culturally different learner: letter knowledge, visual discrimination of letters and words, auditory discrimination of sound in words, developing a love of books, interest in printed symbols, story sense, and memory for sequence. These areas were stressed by Cohen because (1) they were found to have high correlations with reading success in the first grade, (2) they are the kinds of specific activities that can be handled by the school, and (3) they are most directly related to beginning reading instruction.

The enrichment activities of the traditional preschool programs in the form of field trips, drama, and other creative activities are also included in this program. Together, these activities comprise a cluster that has been advocated for many years in the literature on readiness. This program eliminates those activities that have been alleged to have little bearing on reading success, such as identifying the sounds of animals, types of transportation, and musical instruments; matching geometric shapes; and drill in eye-hand-motor coordination activities.

Children Not Ready for Reading Readiness Activities. If, after a period of time, the learner does not respond, Cohen suggests that intensification alone may not be the answer. Many children from depressed areas have not had the experiences that prepare them for a reading readiness program. Another explanation may be that the school has not utilized the experiences these children have had to the fullest extent. The problem that must then be dealt with is "readiness for learning." Cohen lists four major goals for a "readiness for learning" program:

- *Self-control.* Teach the child self-control in working with others in the formal classroom. This goal may be achieved by the teacher ignoring misbehavior and rewarding good behavior.
- *Class Decorum.* "Schoolbreak" the child by teaching him the daily routine of the classroom, such as housekeeping, completing activities, following rules, handling of books and other school materials, and developing attention span. The direct teaching approach is perhaps the most effective procedure for teaching the daily routine; that is, the teacher openly modifies the child's behaviors with directions and stipulations. In some instances, the teacher must physically direct the pupils.
- *Perceptual Training.* Visual-motor-auditory skill development is, in essence, preparing the child in certain physiological areas. Perceptual training specifically includes eye-hand coordination, visual memory, general coordination, form perception, eye movements, and visual imagery.
- *Language and Concepts.* Teaching language and concepts necessary for beginning reading is thought by Cohen to be best met through the delineation of specific skills. The teacher provides stimuli that are designed and ordered sequentially to move the child from gross perceptions of objects to classifying objects according to

their functions. The movement from simple discrimination to classifying is illustrated:

a. Have the children *identify* an object from a large group of pictures.
b. Have the children *match* related pictures (pictures of different houses, etc.).
c. Have children *group* objects according to functions (bicycle, car, etc.).
d. Have children *construct wholes from parts* (two- to four-piece jigsaw puzzle).
e. Have children *group* then *classify* objects according to functions (e.g., those useful to people: foods, clothing, tools).

For language development, Cohen suggests the sequence of stages developed by Pasamanick as a guide for teaching the culturally different child to cope with the language of the school.

a. Stage I is based upon experiences familiar to the children and attempts to make the known more concrete. The naming of simple nouns and a few basic verbs are the focal points.
   Example: Children would name objects such as *chair, table, hat, dress* and verbs such as *running, walking, peeping, laughing.*
b. Stage II attempts to expand the child's noun and verb storehouse by having him combine two known words into a compound.
   Example: hat + box = hatbox
   shoe + shine = shoeshine
   air + plane = airplane
c. Stage III concentrates on expanding the use of language as an expressive and descriptive tool through such activities as storytelling, show and tell, role playing, and relating experiences. These activities foster the development and use of sequencing skills, descriptive language, and word connectors.
d. Stage IV encourages the child to use past language learning to categorize, catalog, and perform other reasoning tasks.

Academic Preschool Intervention

Perhaps the most radical procedures for making culturally different children ready for formal reading instruction are found in academic preschool programs. These programs concentrate on the direct teaching of specific language and reading skills. This is a teaching strategy in which the teacher presents stimuli designed to elicit specific language responses from the learner (2, 7). Figure 14.3 illustrates the use of this strategy.

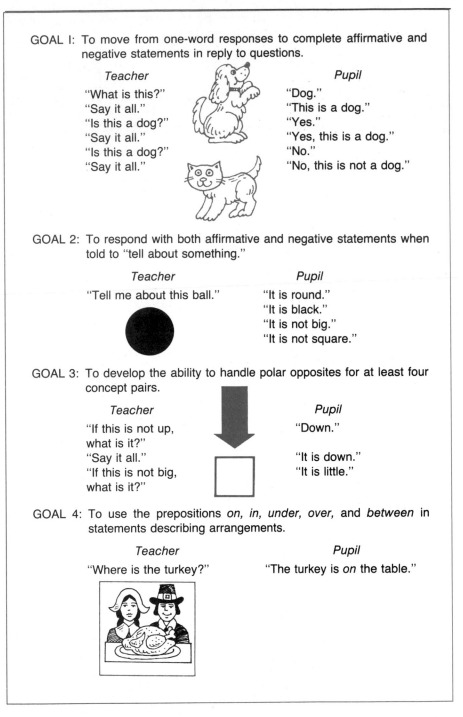

GOAL I: To move from one-word responses to complete affirmative and negative statements in reply to questions.

Teacher	*Pupil*
"What is this?"	"Dog."
"Say it all."	"This is a dog."
"Is this a dog?"	"Yes."
"Say it all."	"Yes, this is a dog."
"Is this a dog?"	"No."
"Say it all."	"No, this is not a dog."

GOAL 2: To respond with both affirmative and negative statements when told to "tell about something."

Teacher	*Pupil*
"Tell me about this ball."	"It is round."
	"It is black."
	"It is not big."
	"It is not square."

GOAL 3: To develop the ability to handle polar opposites for at least four concept pairs.

Teacher	*Pupil*
"If this is not up, what is it?"	"Down."
"Say it all."	"It is down."
"If this is not big, what is it?"	"It is little."

GOAL 4: To use the prepositions *on, in, under, over,* and *between* in statements describing arrangements.

Teacher	*Pupil*
"Where is the turkey?"	"The turkey is *on* the table."

FIGURE 14.3

"Where is the long line?"	"The long line is over the short line."
"Where is the number 2?" 1 2 3	"The number 2 is *between* the numbers 1 and 3."

GOAL 5: To name positives and negatives for at least four classes.

Teacher	*Pupil*
"Tell me something that is clothing."	"A hat is clothing." "A chair is not clothing."
"Tell me something that is food."	"An apple is food." "A pencil is not food."

GOAL 6: To perform simple "if-then" deductions.

Teacher	*Pupil*
"If the circle is big, what else do you know about it?"	"It is white."

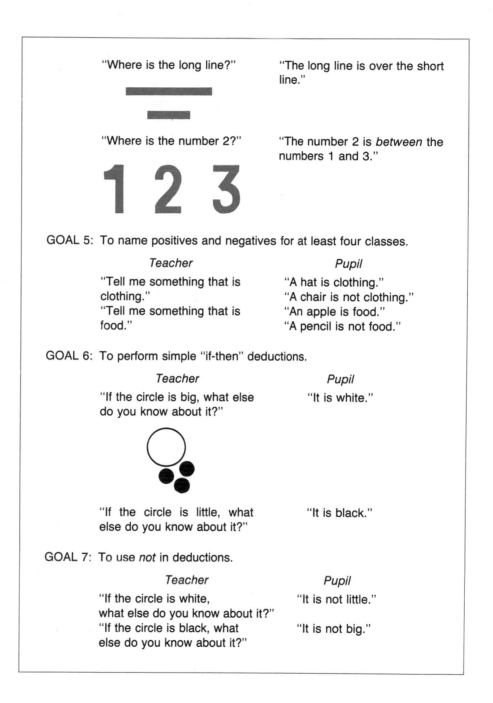

"If the circle is little, what else do you know about it?"	"It is black."

GOAL 7: To use *not* in deductions.

Teacher	*Pupil*
"If the circle is white, what else do you know about it?"	"It is not little."
"If the circle is black, what else do you know about it?"	"It is not big."

The Beginning Reading Program. The reading program is the extension of the language development program and is designed to help children become familiar with letter names, associate pictures visually with their naming words, recognize and produce rhyming words, and learn and use a limited number of sight words.

In the alphabet learning phase of the program, children familiarize themselves with the letter names of the alphabet through identity and position statements:

This is the letter A.

This is a big A.

This is a little A.

This A is standing up.

This A is lying down.

The child is taught first to spell words by letter sounds *(kuh-ah-tuh)* and is then presented clusters of words that follow the same spelling pattern *(cat, fat, hat, bat).* Word meanings are reinforced by yes-no questions of lexical terms.

Word recognition begins with the production of isolated words. A word is printed on the chalkboard and the rule "This is a word" is taught and followed by the identity statement, "This is the word *man*." The children then are encouraged to produce complete identity statements in answering questions such as, "Is this the word *dog*?" "No, that is not the word *dog*. That is the word *man*." Action words are illustrated with gestures. Children are invited to suggest other words which they wish to learn. If there are no volunteers, the teacher supplies another word.

Word placement exercises are used to teach visual discrimination of word forms and word meanings. Objects are labeled with five-by-eight-inch cards and identified by the teacher. "This card has a word on it. This is the word *toy*." Five or more words are identified in this way, and one word card is placed on the proper object by the teacher. The children are asked, "This is the word what?" (desk) "So where does it belong?" (On the desk.) Each child has a turn at naming and placing a word. These words are then identified on the chalkboard. The rule "If all the letters are the same, the words are the same" is taught. The converse rule is also presented.

Word identity exercises help the children develop a small sight vocabulary useful for developing simple sentences. The children are first taught to recognize their own names and then they receive drill on recognizing other children's names. Names of the parts of the body are also taught in this way. New sets of words *(is not, big)* are added for sentence making: "Joe is not big." Meaning is stressed in sentence reading by having children answer questions about their reading. "Is Joe big?" "No, Joe is not big." "Is Joe little?" "Yes, Joe is little." After children master the basic tasks, they are taught to read from teacher-prepared booklets.

This academic preschool program has been criticized on the basis that it is a mechanistic, conditioned response approach and that it deals only with beginning reading. This latter criticism could also be leveled against other beginning programs (programmed reading, computer-assisted instruction). Jongsma (23) raises the question of stability of gains but feels that the specific and detailed objectives of the program will be helpful to teachers.

Results of the use of this type program are impressive. Bereiter and Englemann (8) indicated that children using this approach scored from one-half to one and one-half years below average on pretests of language. By the end of the second year, their scores were approximately average for their age group. Mental age rose from about six months below average to four months above average. At the end of the second grade, their achievement averaged at the 1.5 grade level in reading.

Another experimental group (2) with whom the same techniques were used over a two-year period showed a mean reading achievement of 2.6. Although experimental data are still somewhat limited, these studies have reported statistical data to support claims of the program's effectiveness.

Enrichment Programs

The view that enrichment experiences are fundamental to overcoming the effects of economic deprivation is held by many educators. Several programs that place major emphasis on the development of readiness skills through enrichment activities have been proposed for use with the culturally different learner. The programs under Project Head Start may be looked at as prototypes of the enrichment-intervention model. The assumptions underlying these programs are

> That from birth through six years of age are important years in human development; that children of the poor generally have not had the experiences and opportunities that support maximum development during this period; that effective programs for these children must be comprehensive, including health, nutrition, social services, and education; that for their own and their children's benefit, parents should be deeply involved in the design and implementation of local programs; and that a national child development program can focus attention on the needs of preschool and elementary school children from low-income families, and, through continued review of program effectiveness, stimulate local institutions to do a better job of meeting these needs. (17)

Head Start programs will differ to meet the needs of their students and their communities.

Because of the diversity found in the numerous Head Start programs that were conducted, it is impossible to present a valid sketch of *the* program. Surveys of the curriculum emphasis found in the various programs indicated that a common feature was an attempt to influence sensorimotor development and language development. Only 50 percent of the directors responding indicated the development of preacademic or academic skills as an important goal (17).

More specifically, it was found that few classes spent more than 5 percent of the time on auditory discrimination training and that visual-perception training consumed 5 to 40 percent of class activities. Amounts of language training in the formal sense varied from 5 to 30 percent. Activities occurring with the highest frequency were motor training, informal language stimulation, and social interaction.

In reanalyzing data on the effectiveness of preschool programs of the 1960s for low-income children, the Consortium for Longitudinal Studies (4) found that those programs did have lasting, positive effects. Children who participated in preschool intervention programs were found to more likely pass minimal standards and were less likely to be placed in special education classes.

Today, Head Start programs are longer in duration with an increasing emphasis on working with mothers and young children throughout the preschool years. Furthermore, the need for a transition from the preschool program to a beginning reading program is now being met by many federally funded Follow-Through programs. An increased preschool emphasis with additional follow-up programs to reinforce or build on the child's previous learnings will hopefully prove these programs a success in the near future.

The Montessori Approach

The Montessori method cuts across many of the preschool programs previously discussed. Since it does not fit under any of the labels used thus far, and since it represents a long-established program for the culturally different child, some of the major features of this program will be reviewed.

Kohlberg (24) cites data to support the view that there is much promise in the Montessori method for stimulating the cognitive functioning that culturally different learners need for success in school.

One rationale given by Stevens (38) for using the Montessori method with culturally different children is that this approach concentrates on the development of those skills and abilities in which these children are most lacking: language facility, vocabulary expansion, an environment conducive to learning, and structured experiences for developing attention and concentration. "It has demonstrated in many cultures that it can introduce language and related reading-readiness skills to children from disadvantaged backgrounds" and "can be greatly expanded and elaborated within our current understanding of learning theory."

The Montessori Language Program (31) is somewhat analogous to a word recognition program and includes (1) exercises of silence (i.e., paying attention), (2) stress on word pronunciation, (3) recognition of printed symbols by shape, and (4) speech production through adequate manipulation of the vocal mechanisms. The language program does not deal with the language training that is felt necessary for the expression of concepts or for oral language usage.

The Montessori Reading Program (31) utilizes the "trace and say" task sequences designed to teach the child to recognize and pronounce letter sounds and to use these in word recognition. This writing-reading program stresses the sounds of the letters which is, in essence, a phonics approach. It is suggested that the time for beginning reading instruction will vary with different children, as will the pace at which they proceed. The child does not compete with the calendar or with other children. He competes only with himself.

Materials for the reading exercises consist of slips of paper or cards upon which familiar words and phrases are written. Both materials and tasks are simple: first, the child reads (sounds out) the word and places it under the object it names; second, the child reads phrases once the

FLASHBACK

Maria Montessori (1870–1952) was Italy's first woman physician. Her scientific observations of the behavior and development of young children led her to design the method of education which bears her name. Her successes at the Casa dei Bambini, a day care center in the slums of Rome, attracted international attention. From 1907 to 1952 Dr. Montessori devoted her life to traveling throughout the world, teaching, lecturing and writing. The Montessori didactic materials are sequential and concentrate on four areas of learning: everyday living, sensorial exercises, mathematics, and language (writing and reading). Her method has had worldwide influence, especially at preschool and elementary levels.

idea that "words represent thoughts" is grasped. The phrase-reading exercises are usually in the form of simple commands or directions that must be comprehended by the reader if they are to be carried out. The true reading in this program is thought of as "mental" rather than vocal. Oral reading is utilized for pronunciation, silent reading for meaning.

The total program encompasses not only major reading readiness skills but also provides for "learning readiness." It lacks completeness in the area of language training; this is the area where modifications may need to be made if it is to fully meet the needs of culturally different, dialect-speaking children.

HANDICAPPED YOUTH

Meeting individual pupil needs in reading instruction has always been an enormous task for classroom teachers of reading. The job of providing appropriate instruction for individuals within a large group has demanded many long hours of planning and hard work on the part of teachers. Today, teachers in schools are adapting their classrooms to meet individual needs and to provide appropriate education for handicapped youth. Long excluded from the regular classroom, handicapped youth are now being educated with nonhandicapped children due to a series of events, including research on segregated versus integrated environments, pressure from parent groups, and state and federal legislation. The passage of P.L. 94–142 (Education for All Handicapped Children Act of 1975) was one of the most significant developments in American education in the last fifty years. This law requires that individualization of instruction and equal opportunity of education be afforded every handicapped child. Handicapped children must be placed in the "least restrictive environment" which is being interpreted, in many cases, as the same environment as regular students. This trend to educate handicapped children in the closest possible proximity to the regular classroom in which the child can succeed is often referred to as *mainstreaming.* Caster (13) has given more detailed explanation of what is and is not mainstreaming:

> Mainstreaming is:
>
> Providing the most appropriate education for each child in the least restrictive setting.
>
> Looking at the educational needs of children instead of clinical or diagnostic labels such as mentally handicapped, learning disabled, physically handicapped, hearing impaired, or gifted.
>
> Looking for and creating alternatives that will help general educators serve children with learning or adjustment problems in the regular setting. Some approaches being used to achieve this are consulting teachers, methods and materials specialists, itinerant teachers, and resource room teachers.
>
> Uniting the skills of general education and special education so that all children may have equal educational opportunity.
>
> Mainstreaming is not:
>
> Wholesale return of all exceptional children in special classes to regular classes.
>
> Permitting children with special needs to remain in regular classrooms without the support services they need.
>
> Ignoring the need of some children for a more specialized program that can be provided in the general educational setting.
>
> Less costly than serving children in special self-contained classrooms. (p. 174)

A critical concern for a classroom teacher is, "Who is going to be placed in my classroom?" P.L. 94–142 defines the term *handicapped children* as those children being mentally retarded, hard of hearing, deaf, speech impaired, other health impaired, deaf-blind, multi-handicapped, seriously emotionally disturbed, orthopedically impaired, visually impaired, or as having specific learning disabilities, who because of those impairments need special education and related services (Sec. 121

a. 530–121 a. 534). Coupled with this information, how might a mainstreamed classroom operate? The following description is provided by Johnson (22):

> Exceptional students spend most of the day in regular classrooms, leaving occasionally to go to a resource room or resource center for educational assessments, individual tutoring, or small group instruction, or to pick up and deliver assignments prepared by the resource teacher but completed in the regular classroom. The resource teacher and the regular classroom teacher, working as a team, may schedule a student to use the resource center for a few minutes or several hours, depending on the student's learning needs. The regular classroom teacher and the resource teacher share responsibility for the learning and socialization of the exceptional students, and both take an active instructional role. The exceptional students spend more than half the day in regular classes. While the regular classroom teacher is responsible for grades and report cards, she will usually consult with the resource teacher in giving exceptional students grades. (p. 425)

The success of children placed in the least restrictive environment depends upon the cooperation of teachers, administrators, specialized personnel, and parents. However, the ability of the individual teacher to accommodate all children in the regular classroom will determine the success or failure of such efforts. Implications for teachers of reading are clear—they must capitalize upon a variety of instructional and organizational techniques to suit a wider range of student abilities and encourage the constructive interaction of handicapped students with nonhandicapped students. Mangieri and Readence (28) suggest the following emphases be considered in the instructional program:

- Further use of diagnostic-prescriptive techniques.
- Use of a variety of heterogeneous grouping plans.
- More cooperation with various teachers and support personnel.
- Use of teacher aides and volunteers.
- Emphasis on activities to build the self-concept of handicapped youth.
- Inclusion of an independent reading program incorporating bibliotherapy.

Buttery and Mason (11) reviewed characteristics of mildly mentally handicapped children (MMH) and methods of teaching them. The following is a listing of some of their conclusions:

- Generally they do not read up to their mental age levels, but come closer when instructed in regular classrooms.

FLASHBACK

General Provisions of Public Law 94–142

PART X—EDUCATION AND TRAINING OF THE HANDICAPPED

EDUCATION OF THE HANDICAPPED ACT

Part A—General Provisions
Short Title; Statement of Findings & Purpose
Definitions

Sec. 601.

(a) This title may be cited as the "Education of the Handicapped Act".

"(b) The Congress finds that—

"(1) there are more than eight million handicapped children in the United States today;

"(2) the special educational needs of such children are not being fully met;

"(3) more than half of the handicapped children in the United States do not receive appropriate educational services which would enable them to have full equality of opportunity;

"(4) one million of the handicapped children in the United States are excluded entirely from the public school system and will not go through the educational process with their peers;

"(5) there are many handicapped children throughout the United States participating in regular school programs whose handicaps prevent them from having a successful educational experience because their handicaps are undetected;

"(6) because of the lack of adequate services within the public school systems, families are often forced to find services outside the public school system, often at great distance from their residence and at their own expense;

"(7) developments in the training of teachers and in diagnostic and instructional procedures and methods have advanced to the point that, given appropriate funding, State and local educational agencies can and will provide effective special education and related services to meet the needs of handicapped children;

"(8) State and local educational agencies have a responsibility to provide education for all handicapped children, but present financial resources are inadequate to meet the special educational needs of handicapped children; and

"(9) it is in the national interest that the Federal Government assist State and local efforts to provide programs to meet the educational needs of handicapped children in order to assure equal protection of the law.

"(c) It is the purpose of this Act to assure that all handicapped children have available to them, within the time periods specified in section 612(2) (B), a free appropriate public education which emphasizes special education and related services designed to meet their unique needs, to assure that the rights of handicapped children and their parents or guardians are protected, to assist States and localities to provide for the education of all handicapped children, and to assess and assure the effectiveness of efforts to educate handicapped children".

On November 19, 1975, Congress passed Public Law 94–142. The law mandates significant changes regarding the education of children with special needs. The most significant change is the requirement that handicapped children be educated with their nonhandicapped peers as much as possible.

- Reading comprehension tends to be the most difficult skill to master. It is even more difficult than reading orally.
- When compared to normal children who are their equivalents in mental age, the MMH children are inferior in comprehension, in locating relevant facts, in recognizing main ideas, and in drawing inferences and conclusions.
- In oral reading, the MMH children are inferior to normal children who are their mental age equivalents. In word attack skills they make more vowel errors and omission of sounds. They make significantly less errors by adding sounds and by repetitions, and they require more words to be pronounced for them. They also tend to be inferior in the use of context clues.
- Research has failed to substantiate that any one method of teaching MMH children is universally superior to another.
- The teacher seems to be the most important variable in the reading success of MMH children. Superior teachers tend to find the best methods for particular children. (pp. 334–35)

One positive and immediate reaction to both of the above descriptions is that most handicapped children are not in need of "specialized" techniques, but simply good instruction. Indeed, there are more similarities among handicapped children and so-called normal children than there are differences. Labeling children (emotionally disturbed, mentally retarded, learning disabled, and so forth) tells teachers next to nothing regarding an appropriate instructional program. A positive aspect of P.L. 94–142 is the turning away from the use of labels (which are usually negative and counterproductive) and toward the consideration of youngsters' educational needs. There should be no mystique regarding the teaching of handicapped children. These children, as do all children, require the instruction that emphasizes present level of achievement, determination of pupil strengths and weaknesses, and appropriate approaches and materials. Many students carrying a fancy label have been misdiagnosed and misplaced for years in school systems. Providing effective instruction should be based on pupil needs, not labels. Schwartz (37) avoids the negative effects of labeling children by simply viewing these children as being "different." And after all, there is nothing more basic in teaching than learning how to deal with differences in individual children.

Individualized Education Plan (IEP)

The vehicle for providing the most appropriate educational program for each handicapped student is an individualized education plan (IEP). An IEP is a written plan for each handicapped child, detailing the educational program of the student. In accordance with P.L. 94–142, the IEP must include the following:

- Student's present level of achievement.
- Statement of annual goals.
- Listing of short-term instructional objectives.
- Statement detailing specific special education services to be provided to the student and the extent to which the student will participate in the regular classroom.
- Identification of person(s) (agents) responsible for teaching each objective.
- Materials to be utilized.
- Evaluation procedures.
- Project data for beginning of program services and anticipated duration of services.

The IEP is an educational program developed jointly by the schools, children, and parents (see figure 14.4). Since many handicapped children will spend part or most of the day in the regular classroom, it is mandatory that the classroom teacher be involved in developing the IEP. As shown in figure 14.4, the basic ingredients of an IEP are not new ideas, but are essentially those of a good teaching plan (pretest objectives, teaching to those objectives, and the posttest). It is important to realize that the concepts of mainstreaming or least restrictive environment should not be thought of as separate or different from the basic principles stated in chapter 1. Those principles include all aspects of an IEP and thus the process of equal education for all children. Although many problems remain unsettled regarding the implementation of P.L. 94–142, cooperative interaction among teachers, children, parents, specialized personnel, and administrators in placing every child in a setting in which he may be successful will yield benefits for all children.

GIFTED STUDENTS

A renewed thrust in the public schools is the development of programs for the gifted. U.S. Commissioner of Education Sidney Marland in 1972 defined the gifted and talented as "those identified by professionally qualified persons who by virtue of outstanding abilities are capable of high performance. These are children who require differentiated educational programs and/or services beyond those normally provided by the regular school program in order to realize their contribution to self and society" (29). The U.S. Office of Education identified six areas of gifted-

FIGURE 14.4 Individualized Education Program (Reprinted with permission of Charles E. Merrill Publishing Company from *Developing and Implementing Individualized Education Programs,* 2d ed., by Anne P. Turnbull, Bonnie B. Strickland, and John C. Brantley. Copyright © 1982 by Bell & Howell Company.)

Individual Education Plan (IEP)

Checklist

Date	Item
9-2	Referral by Mrs. Jenkins
9-8	Parents informed of rights; permission obtained for evaluation
9-21	Evaluation compiled
9-24	Parents contacted
9-26	IEP committee meeting held
9-26	IEP completed
9-26	Parent consent notification
9-27	Placement made

Committee Members

Teacher: Lew Ashley

Other LEA representative: Lois Seibler

Parents: Mrs. Betty S.

Date IEP initially approved ______

Health Information

Vision: Normal

Hearing: Normal

Physical: Normal

Other: Medication-tegratol

Yearly Class Schedule

Time	Subject	Teacher
9:00	Language Arts	Miller
10:45	Math	Miller
11:30	Social Studies	Miller
12:00	Lunch	
1:00	Science	Miller
2:00	Resource Reading	Houston

Testing Information

Test Name	Date Admin.	Interpretation
Stanford-Binet	9/13/79	low average range
Key Math	9/15/80	functioning on 1.8 level
Zaner-Bloser	9/22/80	scored "low for grade"

Identification Information

Name James S.

School C. L. Bishop

Birthdate 9/2/74 Grade 2nd

Parents' Names H. R. and Betty S.

Address 1029 Langley Avenue
Lawrence, KS 66044

Phone: Home 841-0920 Office 869-4098

Continuum of Services

	Hours Per Week	Dates
Regular class	23	9/28/80 - 6/2/81
Resource teacher in regular classroom		
Resource room	5	9/29/80 - 6/2/81
Reading specialist		
Speech/language therapist		
Counselor		
Special class		
Transition class		
Others: Counseling	2	9/30/80 - 5/29/81

Individual Education Plan (IEP)

Student's Name **James S.** Subject Area **Handwriting** Teacher **Houston/Miller**

Level of Performance **recognizes all manuscript letters; exhibits proper sitting & writing position; can write 7-10 letters per minute; makes erasures 50%-60% of time; handwriting is often illegible**

Annual Goals **Print legibly all letters of alphabet (upper and lower-case); write numerals 1-10 with no erasures; write 35 letters per minute with 10% or less erasures**

	September	October	November	December	January
Objectives	referral/evaluation, IEP development	1. Following a model, writes legibly letters: Aa, Cc, Dd, Ee, Gg, Oo 2. Following a model, writes legibly numbers 1-5 3. Following a model, writes legibly his first name 4. Writes legibly 10 letters per minute with 50% or less erasures	1. Following a model, writes legibly letters: Bb, Pp, Qq, Uu, Mm, Nn, Hh 2. Writes legibly numerals 1-5—no model 3. Writes legibly first name—no model 4. Writes legibly 13 letters per minute with 45% or less erasures	1. Following a model, writes legibly letters: Ll, Tt, Ff, Kk, Ii, Jj 2. Writes legibly numerals 6-10 with a model 3. Writes legibly last name with a model 4. Writes legibly 14 letters per minute with 40% or less erasures	1. Following a model, writes entire alphabet legibly 2. Writes legibly numerals 6-10—no model 3. Writes legibly first and last name—no model 4. Writes legibly 19 letters per minute with 35% or less erasures
Special Materials		"Beginning to Learn Fine Motor Skills" by Thurstone & Lillie →	→	→	→
Agent		1, 4-Houston 2, 3-Miller →	→	→	→
Evaluation		Informal assessment 80% accuracy of objectives 1-3 on 3 consecutive days →	→	→	→

FIGURE 14.4 (cont.)

Individual Education Plan (IEP)

Student's Name James S. Subject Area Handwriting Teacher Houston/Miller

Level of Performance recognizes all manuscript letters; exhibits proper sitting & writing position; can write 7-10 letters per minute; makes erasures 50%-60% of time; handwriting is often illegible

Annual Goals Print legibly all letters of alphabet (upper and lower-case); write numerals 1-10 with no erasures; write 35 letters per minute with 10% or less erasures

	February	March	April	May	June
Objectives	1. Following a model, writes the entire alphabet legibly 2. Writes legibly numerals 1-10 in math lesson with 4 or less erasures 3. Writes legibly first and last names on all class assignments 4. Writes legibly 23 letters per minute with 30% or less erasures	1. Writes legibly Aa, Cc, Dd, Ee, Gg, Oo, Bb, Pp from dictation 2. Writes legibly numerals 1-10 in math lessons with 2 or less erasures 3. Writes 28 words per minute with 20% or less erasures	1. Writes legibly Qq, Uu, Mm, Nn, Hh, Ll, Tt from dictation 2. Writes legibly numerals 1-10 in math lessons with 1 or less erasures 3. Writes 30 words per minute with 20% or less erasures	1. Writes entire alphabet from dictation 2. Writes legibly numerals 1-10 with no erasures 3. Writes 35 letters per minute with 10% or less erasures	
Special Materials	"Beginning to Learn Fine Motor Skills" by Thurstone & Lillie →	→	→	→	
Agent	1, 4-Houston 2, 3-Miller	1, 3-Houston 2-Miller →	→	→	
Evaluation	Informal assessment 80% accuracy of objectives 1-3 on 3 consecutive days	Informal assessment 80% accuracy of objectives 1-2 on 3 consecutive days →	→	→	

ness: general intellectual ability, specific academic aptitude, creativity, leadership ability, ability in the visual or performing arts, and psychomotor ability. A gifted child may only demonstrate a capability of exceptional performance in one or two areas.

With specific reference to reading abilities, Bond and Bond (9) defined gifted readers in the primary grades as "children who, upon entering first grade, are reading substantially above grade level or who possess the ability to make rapid progress in reading when given proper instruction." In addition, gifted readers usually possess large vocabularies, have longer attention spans, master basic skills more quickly, and can reason and can think on an abstract level beyond their classmates. Yet, gifted students' higher cognitive functioning should not be misconstrued to signify that no instruction is necessary.

Identifying gifted children and designing a curriculum to meet the learning needs of the children should be accomplished by utilizing a variety of formal and informal assessment procedures. Standardized achievement tests, intelligence tests, creativity measures, the pupil's actual performance in the reading program, peer nomination procedures, and parent and teacher observations are avenues to employ for this purpose. Also, giftedness is not reserved for any one group or class of children. Teachers should not be preoccupied with ethnicity or social characteristics when identifying the gifted and talented. Culturally diverse and handicapped gifted and talented students should be identified in each classroom.

For too long gifted children were expected to be silent and follow along with the regular curriculum designed for less able students. Many reading program administrators are realizing that gifted children have unique needs as all children do and require differentiated instructional programs to meet them. All gifted readers are not the same; each student has unique strengths and weaknesses.

As such, gifted readers need the same diagnostically based instruction afforded all learners (10, 35). Indeed, many gifted children are "disabled" readers as are children reading below grade level when performance is compared to potential. As previously discussed, we feel the labeling of students as gifted, normal, or remedial can be detrimental. Instead, educators should focus on the instructional needs of children and should provide the very best education for all children.

Two avenues available to meet the needs of the gifted reader in the classroom are reading acceleration and individualized enrichment (20). Reading acceleration involves placing students on their instructional level and providing a balanced program on that difficulty level (even if it is three, four, or five grade levels above grade placement). Enrichment entails providing students with activities that delve more deeply into material from the student's grade level textbook. Although the research literature supports reading acceleration (16, 18), many teachers do not

Gifted children require a differentiated instructional program to meet their needs.

use this approach. One underlying reason for this lack of implementation is classroom management. If each gifted child is instructed on his/her instructional level, how does the classroom teacher organize and plan for a high percentage of academically engaged time for all pupils? We recommend reading acceleration if at all possible (depending on size of class, range of ability, availability of teacher aides, and individual gifted reader needs). In most cases, a careful blend of reading acceleration and enrichment can ensure the gifted reader is receiving appropriate instruction.

Whereas the goals of the reading curriculum are the same for gifted as for all readers, Carr (12) feels the reading program should be differentiated in terms of content covered, methods taught, and pacing of instruction for gifted readers. A wide variety of literature should be used to tap the abilities and interests of gifted children. Mangieri and Isaacs (27) have compiled an excellent bibliography of interesting children's books in specified categories to use with young gifted children. The use of various types of literature can be integrated with the other language arts. In addition, a greater emphasis on thinking skills is recommended for gifted readers. An excellent source for practical classroom exercises on reading and thinking skills for gifted students can be found in *3R's for the Gifted* by Nancy Polette (33). The integration of language arts with the development of critical thinking can also be accomplished by teaching writing as a thinking process (15). Developing writing skills as a logical thinking process enables the gifted student to refine, synthesize, and elaborate upon understandings on a particular topic.

Gifted children learn material at a faster pace than other learners and thus require fewer drill exercises. Yet, the overriding concern for gifted readers is that they too need instruction in various reading skills. This provision of differentiated instruction requires a diagnosis of students' strengths and weaknesses. Alexander and Muia spoke to this very point when they stated: "What is most essential for program developers to remember, however, is that the learner and that learner's style are central to the curriculum. Therefore, maximum effectiveness of the gifted curriculum hinges on its ability to relate to the learner's abilities, needs, and interests" (3).

Further information on reading programs for the gifted can be obtained by contacting the Council for Exceptional Children and the ERIC Clearinghouse on Handicapped and Gifted Children.

SUMMARY

The ability to deal effectively with pupil differences is a crucial aspect of teaching reading. The importance of meeting the needs of culturally and language-different, handicapped, and gifted children in the regular classroom were discussed in the chapter. Although special consideration for these children is warranted in our schools, it was emphasized that all children need instruction tailored to their individual needs. The ability of teachers to handle differences effectively is translated into instructional practices that provide for each child's self-respect and lead all children in feeling secure in the classroom.

Creating opportunities for success for bilingual children requires an understanding of nonstandard dialects, characteristics of foreign languages spoken by children in your class, and children's cultural values. Although speaking a nonstandard dialect or a native language other than English presents problems in learning to read, this problem is minimized with a sensitive and knowledgeable teacher. An example given to illustrate this point is the teacher who does not penalize children for oral reading errors due to dialect. General approaches to teaching reading to those pupils who speak a nonstandard dialect include the dialect approach and the standard approach with modifications. Approaches for the non-English dominant students include the native approach and the bilingual program. Increased emphasis has been placed on preschool approaches to promote more successful skill acquisition in standard English and a more positive self-concept. Descriptions of an intensified readiness program, the academic preschool, various enrichment programs, and the Montessori approach were provided as examples of such approaches.

The trend toward educating all handicapped children in the least restrictive environment was discussed in the chapter. P.L. 94–142 presents many challenges to teachers of reading. Mainstreaming was described as providing the most appropriate education for each child in the least restrictive setting, considering the educational needs of children rather than their clinical labels. A key ingredient of the legislative mandate is the development of an IEP for each handicapped child. The importance of the regular classroom teacher being totally involved with this team process was cited as the key for the IEP's successful implementation. Although teachers of reading will need to be adept at managing student behavior and teaching various skill-building techniques, they do not need a host of specialized techniques. A handicapped child needs the same individual approach to learning that every youngster needs.

Gifted students in reading also require instruction matched to their needs. In the past, gifted students were usually not identified and their instructional needs ignored. Today's schools are recognizing the special needs of gifted students, and teachers are differentiating instruction based upon a careful diagnosis.

YOUR POINT OF VIEW

Discussion Questions

1. Research to date has not supported the use of dialect materials (books written in standard Black English) to teach reading. What are some possible explanations for these negative results?
2. Brainstorm: List ways teachers can help limited-English-speaking pupils feel more secure in the classroom environment.
3. Mainstreaming handicapped children into the regular classroom should produce a better learning environment for all pupils. However, mainstreaming can also lead to making matters worse instead of making them better. What could cause this occurrence?
4. Brainstorm: List various ways gifted students' needs can be met in the primary grades as opposed to the intermediate grades.

Take a Stand For or Against

1. Of all the factors that influence academic achievement in the school, the dialects or language habits of the culturally and language-different children are the most important.
2. An IEP should be required for all students, not just the handicapped.

3. If there are too few limited-English-speaking students to justify special grouping under a bilingual teacher, those students should not be allowed in the regular classroom.
4. Accelerating gifted students usually results in poor social adjustment.

BIBLIOGRAPHY

1. Abrahams, Roger D. "The Advantages of Black English." Jacksonville, Fla.: Southern Conference of Language Learning, 1970.
2. *Academic Preschool, Champaign, Illinois.* Washington, D.C.: U.S. Government Printing Office, 1970.
3. Alexander, Patricia A., and Muia, Joseph A. *Gifted Education: A Comprehensive Roadmap.* Rockville, Md.: Aspen Systems Corp., 1982.
4. Association for Supervision and Curriculum Development. "Investigators Find Preschool Programs Have Lasting and Positive Effects." *News Exchange* 22 (Mar. 1980).
5. Barnitz, John G. "Black English and Other Dialects: Sociolinguistic Implications for Reading Instruction." *The Reading Teacher* 33 (1980): 779–87.
6. Barthe, Charles L. "Program for Academically Talented." Paper presented at the annual meeting of the International Reading Association, St. Louis, 1980. (ERIC Document Reproduction Service No. ED 186 850)
7. Bereiter, Carl, and Englemann, Siegfried. "An Academically Oriented Preschool for Disadvantaged Children: Results from the Initial Experimental Group." In *Psychology and Early Childhood Education,* edited by Daniel Brinson and Jane Hill, 17–36. Toronto: Ontario Institute for Studies in Education, 1968.
8. Bereiter, Carl, and Englemann, Siegfried. *Teaching Disadvantaged Children in the Preschool.* Englewood Cliffs, N.J.: Prentice-Hall, 1976.
9. Bond, Charles W., and Bond, Lella T. "Reading Instruction for the Primary Grade Gifted Child." *Georgia Journal of Reading* 5 (1980): 33–36.
10. Bond, Charles W., and Bond, Lella T. "Reading and the Gifted Student." *Roeper Review* 5 (1983): 4–6.
11. Buttery, Thomas J., and Mason, George E. "Reading Improvement for Mainstreamed Children Who Are Mildly Mentally Handicapped." *Reading Improvement* 16 (Winter 1979): 334–37.
12. Carr, Kathryn S. "What Gifted Readers Need from Reading Instruction." *The Reading Teacher* 38 (1984): 144–46.
13. Caster, Jerry. "Share Our Specialty: What Is Mainstreaming?" *Exceptional Children* 42 (1975): 174.
14. Ching, Doris C. *Reading and the Bilingual Child.* Newark, Del.: International Reading Association, 1976.
15. Cioffi, Diane Harper. "A Back to Basics Model for the Gifted." *G/C/T* (1984): 13–14.
16. Cohen, S. Alan. *Teach Them All to Read.* New York: Random House, 1969.

17. Datta, Lois-Ellin. *A Report on Evaluation Studies of Project Head Start.* Washington, D.C.: Department of Health, Education, and Welfare, 1969.
18. Durr, William K. "Reading and the Gifted Student." Paper presented at the annual meeting of the Southwest Regional Conference of the International Reading Association, San Antonio, Tex., 1981. (ERIC Document Reproduction Service No. ED 197–301)
19. Gantt, Walter N.; Wilson, Robert M.; and Dayton, C. Mitchell. "An Initial Investigation of the Relationship between Syntactical Divergencies and the Listening Comprehension of Black Children." *Reading Research Quarterly* 10 (1974–75): 193–211.
20. Gaug, Mary Ann. "Reading Acceleration and Enrichment in the Elementary Grades." *The Reading Teacher* 37 (1984): 372–76.
21. Goodman, Kenneth. "Dialect Barriers to Reading Comprehension." *Elementary English* 42 (1965): 853–60.
22. Johnson, David W. *Educational Psychology.* Englewood Cliffs, N.J.: Prentice-Hall, 1979.
23. Jongsma, Eugene A. "Preschool Education and the Culturally Disadvantaged." *Viewpoints* (1970): 95–116.
24. Kohlberg, L. "Montessori with the Culturally Disadvantaged." In *Early Education: Current Theory, Research, and Action,* edited by Robert Hess and Roberta Meyer Bear. Chicago: Aldine Publishing Co., 1966.
25. Labov, William. "Language Characteristics of Specific Groups: Blacks." In *Reading for the Disadvantaged: Problems of Linguistically Different Learners,* edited by Thomas D. Horn, 155–56. New York: Harcourt Brace Jovanovich, 1970.
26. Lass, Bonnie. "Black Dialect and Reading." Master's thesis, University of Illinois, 1975.
27. Mangieri, John N., and Isaacs, Carolyn W. "Recreational Reading for Gifted Children." *Roeper Review* 5 (1983): 11–14.
28. Mangieri, John N., and Readence, John E. "Mainstreaming Implications for the Teaching of Reading." *Reading Improvement* 14 (Fall 1977): 165–67.
29. Marland, Sidney P. "Our Gifted and Talented Children: A Priceless National Resource." *Intellect* 101 (1972): 16–19.
30. Martin, Clyde, and Castaneda, Alberta M. "Nursery School and Kindergarten." In *Reading for the Disadvantaged: Problems of Linguistically Different Learners,* edited by Thomas D. Horn. New York: Harcourt Brace Jovanovich, 1980.
31. Montessori, Maria. *The Montessori Method.* New York: Schocken Books, 1964.
32. Nolen, Patricia A. "Reading Nonstandard Dialect Materials: A Study at Grades Two and Four." *Child Development* 43 (1972): 1092–97.
33. Polette, Nancy. *3R's for the Gifted.* Littleton, Colo.: Libraries Unlimited, 1982.
34. Raths, Louis E. *Teaching for Learning.* Columbus, Oh.: Charles E. Merrill Publishing Co., 1969.
35. Rupley, William H. "Reading Teacher Effectiveness: Implications for Teaching the Gifted." *Roeper Review* 7 (1984): 70–72.
36. Rupley, William H., and Robeck, Carol. "Black Dialect and Reading Achievement." *The Reading Teacher* 31 (1978): 598–601.

37. Schwartz, Lita Linzer. *The Exceptional Child: A Primer.* Belmont, Calif.: Wadsworth Publishing, 1975.
38. Stevens, George L. "Implications of Montessori for the War on Poverty." In *Montessori for the Disadvantaged,* edited by R. C. Orem, 32–48. New York: G. P. Putnam's Sons, 1967.
39. Weaver, Phyllis. *Research Within Reach.* St. Louis: CEMREL Search and Development Interpretation Service, 1978.

Index

Arthur W. Heilman served as director of the University Reading Center at The Pennsylvania State University from 1962 to 1979 and is now Professor Emeritus. He received his B.A. from Carthage College and his M.A. and Ph.D. from the University of Iowa.

Dr. Heilman has authored numerous books, including *Phonics in Proper Perspective,* fifth edition (1985) and *Improve Your Reading Ability,* fourth edition (1983). He is also the author of numerous articles in reading journals. He is active in various professional organizations, including the International Reading Association, the College Reading Association, and the National Conference on Research in English.

Timothy R. Blair is Professor in Reading and Coordinator of Field Experiences in the Department of Educational Curriculum and Instruction at Texas A&M University. He received his B.S. in Elementary Education and M.S. in Reading from Central Connecticut State University. His Ph.D. was awarded in Elementary Education with a major in Reading at the University of Illinois. He is a former elementary classroom teacher and reading teacher at the elementary, middle, and high school levels. In addition to coauthoring two college textbooks on reading diagnosis and remediation, Dr. Blair is the author of numerous articles in professional journals. He is active in various professional organizations including the College Reading Association and the International Reading Association.

William H. Rupley is Professor of Educational Curriculum and Instruction at Texas A&M University. He has been an elementary classroom teacher and a coordinator of undergraduate reading education programs. Dr. Rupley received his B.A. from Indiana University, his M.A. from St. Francis College and his Ph.D. from the University of Illinois. He coauthored two textbooks with Timothy R. Blair, *Reading Diagnosis and Remediation: Classroom and Clinic* (1983) and *Reading Diagnosis and Direct Instruction: A Guide for the Classroom* (1983) and is the author of articles in professional reading journals. He has served as an editorial advisor for several professional readiing journals and is active in several professional organizations including the International Reading Association and the College Reading Association.

YORK COLLEGE OF PENNSYLVANIA 17403
0 2003 0040319 9